Studies in Philosophy
and the
History of Philosophy

Founded in 1960 by John K. Ryan

Studies in Philosophy and the History of Philosophy

Volume 3

JOHN DUNS SCOTUS, 1265-1965

Edited by

John K. Ryan

and

Bernardine M. Bonansea

THE CATHOLIC UNIVERSITY OF AMERICA PRESS
Washington, D. C.
1965

Nihil obstat:
> John K. Ryan
> Censor Deputatus

Imprimatur:
> ✠ Patrick A. O'Boyle
> Archbishop of Washington

November 4, 1965

The *nihil obstat* and *imprimatur* are official declarations that a book or pamphlet is free of doctrinal or moral error. No implication is contained therein that those who have granted the *nihil obstat* and the *imprimatur* agree with the content, opinions, or statements expressed.

Paperback Edition Copyright © 2018
The Catholic University of America Press
All rights reserved

The paper used in this publication meets the minimum requirements of the American National Standards for Information Science – Permanence of paper for Printed Library Materials, ANSI Z39.48-1984.
∞

Cataloging-in-Publication Data available from the Library of Congress

ISBN 978-0-8132-3108-2 (pbk)

TABLE OF CONTENTS

		page
FOREWORD		vii

1. The Life and Works of John Duns Scotus
   by Charles Balić 1

2. The Originality of the Scotistic Synthesis
   by Efrem Bettoni 28

3. The Formal Distinction
   by Allan B. Wolter 45

4. A Problem for Realism: Our Multiple Concepts of Individual Things and the Solution of Duns Scotus
   by S. Y. Watson 61

5. Duns Scotus' Voluntarism
   by Bernardine M. Bonansea 83

6. Duns Scotus on the *Common Nature*
   by J. R. Cresswell 122

7. Demonstrability and Demonstration of the Existence of God
   by Felix Alluntis 133

8. Duns Scotus and the Physical Approach to God
   by Roy Effler 171

9. The Problem of the Demonstrability of Immortality
   by Geoffrey G. Bridges 191

10. Being, Univocity, and Analogy According to Duns Scotus
    by Timotheus A. Barth 210

11. Francis Suarez and the Teaching of John Duns Scotus on *Univocatio Entis*
    by Walter Hoeres 263

12. William of Vaurouillon, O.F.M., A Fifteenth-Century Scotist 291
    by Ignatius Brady

13. Duns Scotus, Nominalism, and the Council of Trent 311
    by Heiko Augustinus Oberman

14. The Contemporary Significance of Duns Scotus' Philosophy 345
    by Béraud de Saint-Maurice

15. The Nature and Value of a Critical Edition of the Complete Works of John Duns Scotus 368
    by Charles Balič

NOTES ON CONTRIBUTORS 380

INDEX 382

FOREWORD

The names of certain of the great scholastic thinkers of the middle ages—St. Anselm, Abelard, Hugh of St. Victor, St. Albert the Great, St. Thomas Aquinas, St. Bonaventure, Roger Bacon, John Duns Scotus, Henry of Ghent, and the rest—are familiar not only to students of philosophy and theology but also in varying degrees to the educated public. Abelard is known for his *Historia calamitatum* and as a figure in romantic literature, if not for his work in ethics and the theory of knowledge. Like Zeno's paradoxes and the Cartesian "cogito ergo sum," a passage in St. Anselm has become the subject of unending discussion. Certain of St. Bonaventure's books have been translated and find readers. But with the exception of St. Thomas Aquinas first-hand knowledge of the writings of the medieval masters is not a common thing.

For reasons that have varied throughout the modern era John Duns Scotus has not always received the general recognition that what he was and what he did should have brought to him. However, inadequate understanding and even hostility are being displaced by something better. Appropriately, this change is due in large measure to the research and writings of his fellow Franciscans, but the books and articles of many other scholars have aided them in their labors. As a result, the record of Scotus' life has been made fuller and clearer, what he actually taught on various subjects has been brought to light, and translations of his writings begin to appear. But the most important thing of all is the essential work of the Commissio Scotistica on the canon and the critical edition of his writings, which proceeds year by year in spite of the inherent difficulties of the task and those caused by the turmoil of our era. To all such labors the present volume, a cooperative effort of European, American, and Canadian scholars, is added as a further monument raised in honor of John Duns Scotus on the seventh centennial of his birth.

JOHN K. RYAN

The Catholic University of America
October, 1965

1

THE LIFE AND WORKS OF JOHN DUNS SCOTUS

by

CHARLES BALIĆ

LIFE AND WORKS OF JOHN DUNS SCOTUS*

It has been said that perhaps there is no other great medieval master whose life is so little known as that of John Duns Scotus.[1] In fact, some writers have claimed that he had been the disciple of Alexander of Hales, who died in 1245 when Scotus was not even born; others have maintained that he died in 1294, at a time when Scotus had not yet begun his literary activity. As far as the country of his birth is concerned, some historians were of the opinion that it was Ireland, while others maintained it to be either England or Scotland. Luke Wadding himself, the famous historian of the

---

* There is an extensive bibliography on Duns Scotus. Cf. O. Schaefer, a member of the Scotistic Commission, *Bibliographia de vita, operibus et doctrina Iohannis Duns Scoti saec. XIX-XX* (Rome: 1955), pp. xxiv + 222, with 4506 entries; U. Smeets, *Lineamenta bibliographiae scotisticae* (Rome: 1942), pp. xvi + 182; St. Simonis, "De vita et operibus B. I. Duns Scoti iuxta litteraturam ultimi decennii," *Antonianum*, 3 (1928), 451-484; E. Bettoni, *Vent'anni di studi scotisti, 1920-1940* (Milan: 1943); Béraud de Saint Maurice, *Jean Duns Scot, un docteur des temps nouveaux* (Rennes-Paris: 1953); M. Grajewski, "Scotistic Bibliography of the Last Decade (1929-1939)," *Franciscan Studies*, I (1941), n. 1, pp. 73-78; n. 2, pp. 55-72; n. 3, pp. 71-76; II (1942), 61-71; 158-73; A. Wolter (ed.), *Duns Scotus: Philosophical Writings* (Edinburgh: 1962), pp. ix-xvii; *Obras del Doctor Sutil Juan Duns Scotus*, bilingual edition, Biblioteca de autores cristianos (Madrid: 1960), pp. 105*-129*; E. Bettoni, *Duns Scotus: The Basic Principles of His Philosophy*, tr. and ed. Bernardine Bonansea, O.F.M. (Washington: 1961), pp. 201-213.

The Commission for the critical edition of Duns Scotus' works collects all available data and material on the life and works of the Subtle Doctor, but will not pass a definitive judgment on them until all the works have been critically edited. This undertaking includes the study of those works which in the past have been ascribed to Duns Scotus but now appear to be either spurious or of dubious authenticity, even though some codices list them under Scotus' name, have been compiled according to his mind (by Anthony Andreas), or go under the name of *Scotulus*. In this article we shall therefore only report those data which are already known and commonly accepted.

[1] Cf. E. Renan, *Histoire littéraire de la France*, XXV (Paris: 1869), p. 404.

Franciscan order, wrote that in regard to Duns Scotus "patria, aetas, mors, haec plus ceteris incerta,"[2] and advanced the opinion that he was born in 1274, the year in which St. Bonaventure died: "dum enim una stella cecidit," so argues Wadding, "alia in horizonte seraphico apparuit!"

Yet, despite the fact that most medieval schoolmen did not write the history of their own life and biographical notes must be construed almost entirely from occasional data in their doctrinal writings and scholastic disputations,[3] the historico-critical method that began to be applied to scholasticism in the second half of the last century has succeeded in ascertaining many facts about the life and literary activity of the great medieval masters, and of Duns Scotus perhaps more than anyone else.

As soon as the edition of St. Bonaventure's *Opera omnia* was completed in 1902, there were some who wanted to begin immediately a critical edition of Scotus' works. However, the opinion of those who claimed priority for the edition of the works of Alexander of Hales, the first master of the Franciscan order to teach at the University of Paris, prevailed. It was only after the General Chapter of the Franciscan order in 1927 that a Scotistic Commission was established at Quaracchi under the direction of Father Ephrem Longpré. In 1938 the Commission was transferred to Rome and given the official title of "Commissio omnibus operibus Ioannis Duns Scoti critice edendis."

The purpose of this article is to discuss Duns Scotus' native country, birthplace, and date of his birth, and to treat briefly of his works.

I. COUNTRY, PLACE, AND YEAR OF DUNS SCOTUS' BIRTH

In past centuries Scotus was believed to have been born either in England,[4] in Ireland,[5] or in Scotland. Today it is certain that he

---

[2] L. Wadding, *Vita R. P. F. Ioannis Duns Scoti* (Montibus: 1644), c. I, p. 3.

[3] Cf. E. Longpré, "Le B. Jean Duns Scot pour le Saint-Siège et contre le gallicanisme," *La France franciscaine*, 11 (1928), 137.

[4] Thus: Ioannes Maior, born about 1470, in *Historia Maioris Britanniae, tam Angliae quam Scotiae*, IV (Paris: 1521), c. 16, f. 74; several codices of the works of Duns Scotus compiled by John Reinbold of Zierenberg about the middle of the fifteenth century; Bartholomew of Pisa, "Liber conformitatum," *Analecta franciscana*, IV, 547. Codex 12 of the library of Todi reads: "Explicit Summa I. Duns Provinciae Anglicanae . . ."; but this can be easily explained in the sense

was born in the land that corresponds to present-day Scotland. A first argument is the undeniable fact that the Subtle Doctor, who in Britain was usually called Duns, outside of Britain was more frequently known, both in the manuscript codices of his works and among his contemporary writers,[6] as John Scotus. Some documents state explicitly that he is called Scotus because he is *de Scotia* or *nationis Scoticae filius*.[7]

What St. Isidore of Seville said in the fourteenth book of his *Etymologiae*, chaps. 65-66, namely, that Scotland was also called Ireland,[8] and therefore that the title *Scotus* given to the Subtle Doctor could also indicate—so reason some historians—his Irish nationality, cannot be held true for the fourteenth century. Many direct and indirect documents witness to the fact that Isidore's statement was true only up to the ninth century, since from that time on a clear distinction was made between Scotland and Ire-

---

that Scotus was a member of that religious Province. Cf. L. Meier, "Die Skotusausgabe des Johannes Reinbold von Zierenberg," *Scriptorium*, VII (1953), n. 1, p. 113. According to Reinbold Scotus was born in "Dunstanburgh . . . ubi collegium Mertonense habuit 'grundbesitz' ". He would have entered the Merton College and become its "socius." This hypothesis has been rejected as groundless by F. M. Powicke in his work, *The Medieval Books of Merton College* (Oxford: 1931), p. 33. Indeed, Scotus did not have the need to go to Merton College, since he could follow the same curriculum of studies in his own monastery at Oxford which was incorporated with the university.

[5] The arguments for this opinion have been collected by L. Wadding, *Vita I. Duns Scoti*, c. 3.

[6] In many codices, such as cod. 137 of the Assisi library and the Vat. lat. 876, one can read: "Expliciunt quaestiones fratris Iohannis Scoti," or "Liber Scoti," and the like.

[7] In the poem "Scotia plange," written in the early 14th century and preserved in cod. B.I. of the Canterbury library, it is said: "De Scotia genitus Iohannes." In cod. 66 of Merton College in Oxford one can likewise read: "Super I de Ordine [i.e., Ordinatione] Fr. I. Duns de Ordine Fratrum Minorum, *natione Scoti*." In cod. Patavinus, bibl. Antoniana 173: "Explicit quaestionum summa super primum Sent. edita a reverendo magistro Iohanne Dino *de Scotia*." In cod. 1461 of Rottenburg Seminary: "Explicit Tractatus primi principii parisiensis doctoris subtilis Iohannis Dinis *natione Scoti*." Anthony Andreas, Scotus' disciple, states that his master was "natione scotus." The epitaph engraved on Scotus' tomb at Cologne reads: "Scotia me genuit."

[8] S. Isidorus Hispalensis, *Etymologiarum libri XIV*, c. 6 (PL 82, 513): "Scotia eadem et Hybernia, proxima Britanniae insula, spatio terrarum angustior, sed situ fecundior; haec ab Africo in Boream porrigitur, cuius partes priores Iberiam et Cantabricum oceanum intendunt. Unde et Hybernia dicta. Scotia autem, quod a Scotorum gentibus colitur, appellata." Cf. Bartholomaeus Anglicus. *De proprietatibus rerum* (Nüremberg: 1519), 1. XV, c. 80: "Scotia a Scotorum gentibus a quibus incolitur appellatur . . . Hybernia oceani est insula . . ." Thus Scotland was larger than Ireland but smaller than the present-day land that goes under that name.

land. Thus, for example, Pope Clement III in 1188,[9] and later Pope Innocent III,[10] distinguished between the kings of Scotland and the lords of Ireland. Present-day Scotland was at that time fighting for its freedom and had its own king and independence, while the kings of England were also called "the lords of Ireland."

In the roll of the Paris archives where the names are recorded of those who in 1303 were forced to leave the University of Paris because of their refusal to side with Philip the Fair in his struggle against Pope Boniface VIII, the Scots are clearly distinguished from the Irish and the English. Indeed, in this precious document, discovered by Father Longpré, the following names are indicated: "Fr. Ioannes Scotus, Fr. Richardus Hibernensis, Fr. Odo Hibernensis, Fr. Thomas Anglicus, etc."[11] It is therefore beyond question that the Subtle Doctor was born in Scotland, and in the very same land that today goes under that name.

Just as the term *Scotus* indicates the native land of the Subtle Doctor, so the term *Duns*, which is at times found associated either with John, as Ioannes Duns,[12] or with John Scotus, as Ioannes Duns Scotus,[13] or used alone,[14] indicates both the name of the family and the name of his birthplace. In fact, the Subtle Doctor is said in many documents to be *de Duns*. Thus in codex 137 of the library of the Sacro Convento in Assisi we read: "Explicit tabula quaestionum super primum librum Sententiarum de Ordinatione unius quondam doctoris theologiae sollemnis, scilicet fratris Iohannis de Duns, Scoti, de Ordine Fratrum Minorum."[15] Moreover, in a poem composed immediately after the death of the Subtle Doctor by one of his disciples, the author deplores the premature death of his master, and then he writes: "Quid modo, Dunicae decus, artes philosophiae?"[16] Again, the *Liber Procuratorum nationis Angli-*

[9] "Clemens episcopus . . . carissimo filio Guilelmo illustri Scotorum regi. . ." *Bullarium Romanum*, VIII (Turin: 1858), 59.

[10] Cf. PL 47, 247: "Iohannes Dei gratia rex Anglorum, dominus Hyberniae." See A. Callebaut, "L'Ecosse patrie du Bx. J. Duns Scot," *Archivum franciscanum historicum* (henceforth to be quoted as *AFH*), 13 (1920), 82-84.

[11] E. Longpré, *Le Bx. J. Duns Scot, pour le Saint-Siège*, p. 155.

[12] Cod. Vat. lat. 882: "Iohannes Duns . . ."; cod. Balliolensis 208 and Vat. lat. 876: "magistri Iohannis Duns"; cod. Paris. univ. 38: "Iohannes Duns."

[13] Cod. Florent. Laurent. Plut. 20, n. 15: "frater Iohannes Duns, alias Scotus." Cod. Aschaffenburg: "Iohannes Scotus, alias de Duns."

[14] Cod. Cantuariensis A. 9, and Vat. lat. 876: "primus Duns"; Paris. univ. 38: "Iohannes Duns."

[15] Cf. cod. Valentiae 92: "fratris Iohannis de Dinis"; cod. Danzig 1968: "magistri Iohannis de Duns." In cod. Ripoll. 53: "magistri de Duns Scoti."

[16] Cf. C. Balić, *Les commentaires de Jean Duns Scot sur les quatre livres des*

canae, under the date of February 10, 1349, reports: "Dominus Thomas de Duns, Scotus . . .". When this Thomas de Duns becomes procurator of the nation, the book adds: "clericus S. Andreae dioecesis."[17] Now, in the diocese of St. Andrew, in the Scottish province of Berwick, there is a little town called Duns.

In this little Protestant town an immemorial tradition exists to the effect that John Duns Scotus was born there. Hence the Rev. Dr. Robert Bowmaker, a Protestant pastor of that town between 1769 and 1797, in a work published in 1792, argues in the following terms against those who claim that the Subtle Doctor was born in Dunstone, Northumberland:

> Nothing is more certain, than that the family, of which this extraordinary man was a branch, were heritors of the parish of Dunse and continued to be proprietors of that estate which now belongs to Mr. Christie, till after the beginning of the present century, called them in all ancient writings Duns' half of Grueldykes. These lands are adjoining to the town of Dunse.
> The father of J. Duns Scotus had been a younger brother of the family of Grueldykes, and resided in the town of **Dunse.** The site of the house where he was born is still well known, and has been in use, generation after generation, to be pointed out to the young people by their parents, as the birth place of so great and learned a man.[18]

Against this view, the opinion has been advanced and commonly accepted ever since 1931 that Duns Scotus, a son of Scot farmers, was born on an estate called Littledean, near the town of Maxton and the county of Roxburgh. He was baptized John, but became known to his people by the family name of Duns, while foreigners called him Scotus. In Blairs College, near Aberdeen in Scotland,

---

Sentences, Bibliothèque de la Revue d'histoire ecclésiastique, fasc. 1 (Louvain: 1927), p. 7.

[17] Cf. Denifle-Chatelain, *Chartularium Universitatis Parisiensis,* I (Paris: 1894), p. 130; A. Callebaut, *L'Ecosse, patrie,* pp. 86-88.

[18] *The Statistical Account of Scotland Drawn up from the Communications of the Ministers of the Different Parishes* by S. Johns Sinclair, IV, 378: "Parish of Dunse (county of Berwick) by the Rev. Dr. Robert Bowmaker," p. 390. See also R. G. Johnston, *Duns Dings A'. The Town and its Environs* (Berwick: 1953), p. 46: "John Duns [Scotus], called later the Subtle Doctor, was born in Duns, 1275. His father was the younger son of Duns of Grueldykes (originally spelt Growelldykes), adjacent of the Town on the South. The house in which John was born stood near more westerly lodge now called the Pavilion Lodge of Duns Castle. . . When Mr. Hay in 1790 made some improvements near there he caused a large stone, which then marked the site of the house, to be built into the dyke nearby, and this stone was pointed out for many generations, but has apparently been lost sight of, at least for the present. . ."

there is a *Registrum Fratrum Minorum Conventualium,* which had been transcribed by Tweedy in the sixteenth century and which Father Brockie, a Benedictine, had loaned at the beginning of the eighteenth century,[19] where the name of John Duns appears several times. The *Registrum* states that when in 1278 Father Elias Duns

[19] E. Longpré, "Nouveaux documents franciscains d'Ecosse," *AFH,* 22 (1929), 588-89. According to the account of Marian Brockie, the Franciscan archives of Scotland were kept in Haddington until the Reformation. Tweedy, a public notary of the city of Haddington, transcribed the *Registrum Ordinis* which contained several documents. In the beginning of the eighteenth century Tweedy's manuscript, which was kept in his own family archives, was given by James Tweedy to Father Brockie, O.S.B., who at the time was preparing a ten-volume history of the religious families in Scotland. His death put an end to his activity, and the ten-volume manuscript (the eighth volume is missing) which goes progressively from page 1 to page 10303 was deposited at St. Mary's College, in Blairs near Aberdeen. Cf. J. Stevenson, *The Manuscripts Preserved in the Library of the Catholic College of Blairs in Scotland. Report of the Royal Commission on Historical Manuscripts* (London: 1871), Appendix, pp. 201-203. The manuscript in question was examined by Father Longpré around the year 1928. Later I asked Father L. Meier to submit it to a further study. In February 1950 this latter reported to me that, on the authority of Father Anthony Ross, O.P., and others, the volumes by Brockie "have practically no historical value." He wrote on February 2, 1950: "Nullum diploma de familia vel patria Doctoris Subtilis a Brockie datur. Nullum simile diploma in libro Tweedy fuisse affirmatur. Nullatenus igitur quacumque certitudine historica de familia vel de loco originis Doctoris Subtilis constat." Not completely satisfied with such a report, in 1953 I went myself to St. Mary's College in Blairs and examined again the ten volumes by Father Brockie. I discovered that the author not only has a peculiar way of expressing himself but he also contradicts himself on several counts. Thus on p. 9216 Elias Duns is said to have been the son of Ninian Duns, while on p. 9248 he is called Ninian's brother, or at least the brother of a certain Ninian. On p. 2901 the supreme ruler of the order of Friars Minor is called *Magister Generalis,* while at the time of Brockie's writing the only name by which he was known was that of *Minister Generalis.* In my article, "Note di un viaggio al natio loco del beato Giovanni Duns Scoto," *Vita Minorum,* 24 (1953), 196-202, I have expounded the reasons that led me to reject the new theory claiming for Littledean the privilege of having been the birthplace of Scotus and reaffirm the traditional view that this privilege belongs to Duns. As I was studying more intensively the photostat copy of the Brockie MS which the Very Rev. Canon Stephen McGill, rector of Blairs College, had kindly sent to me, I met in Rome an earnest and talented young Scottish priest named Henry Docherty, whom I requested to make an accurate and thorough study of Brockie's *Monasticon Scotianum.* He has now completed his difficult task, and the results of his findings will soon be published in a work called *The Brockie Mss. Codex Tweedianus, and Other Forgeries.* Father Meier wrote to me at one time: "si non assumimus id [Brockie's MS] esse puram fictionem vel falsificationem, quemdam valorem historicum eius non possumus arguere." Father Docherty is now convinced that the whole thing is truly an invention and forgery by Brockie! Hence whatever Brockie says about Scotus' entrance into the order—he states wrongly that Duns Scotus was ordained priest in the monastery of Dumfries—and his studies in Haddington, has only a temporary value and will have to be checked against Father Docherty's final judgment on the matter.

went to Haddington, where he was elected Vicar General of Scotland, he brought with him from Dumfries, where he was guardian, his nephew John Duns: "Erat enim eius, a fratre Niniano Duns de Littledean, nepos." Since the Subtle Doctor is called nephew of Father Elias, it is quite probable, so argues the author of the *Registrum*, that he descended from the line of the Duns family of Littledean: "ex hac propagine Dunsiorum de Littledean prodiisse *videtur*."

The term *videtur* was transformed into an indisputable fact by Father Callebaut. This historian, who in 1920 had defended the traditional opinion that Scotus had been born on the estate of Duns, in 1931 in his article, *A propos du Bx. Jean Scot de Littledean*, proclaimed that Littledean was the birthplace of Scotus.[20] However, the *Registrum Fratrum Minorum Conventualium*, composed in the beginning of the eighteenth century, does not carry such weight as to destroy the value of the traditional view which goes back to time immemorial. In fact, while on page 9248 of the *Registrum* Ninian Duns is said to have been the brother of Elias and the father of John Duns, on page 9216 the same Ninian is called the father of Elias: "Erat autem Elias Duns filius Niniani Duns de Littledean." Further, even if Elias Duns and his father Ninian had been born in Littledean, it does not follow necessarily that John was also born there. This might explain why Brockie used the term *videtur* rather than another more definite term.

Brockie asserts that the Duns family, from which Scotus comes, derives its name from the town of Duns: "Inclyta familia Duns ab eiusdem nomine appellatur." Then he adds: "Nec ambigere licet quin antiqua familia de Duns ab eodem oppido cognomen accepit,

---

[20] A. Callebaut, "A propos du Bx. Jean Duns Scot de Littledean. Notes et recherches historiques de 1265 à 1292," *AFH*, 24 (1931), 311ff. Cf. also E. Longpré, "Nouveaux documents franciscains d'Ecosse," *AFH*, 22 (1929), 588. In the article above mentioned, pp. 311-12, Callebaut writes: "Le P. Ephrem nous apprend que le Bx. naquit dès Duns à *Maxton*, dans le comté de Roxburgh, sur la *terre* qui porte encore aujourd'hui le nom de *Littledean*, gracieusement située sur les rives du Tweed, non loin des abbayes en ruines de Melrose et de Drybourg, à 31½ milles en amont de Berwick. Aujourd'hui, la population monte, à peine, à deux cent habitants, tous protestants. De son passé catholique, Maxton ne possède plus que les ruines d'une église gothique. C'est à deux milles en aval, non loin du château de Roxburgh, que *Ninian Duns de Littledean*, père du Docteur Marial, tenait la *terre* comtale, dont il portait le nom." See likewise Béraud de Saint-Maurice, *Jean Duns Scot*, p. 64: "Jean Duns Scot naît entre le 23 décembre 1265 et le 17 mars 1266, à Maxton-on-Tweed dans le comté de Roxburgh, sur la propriété de Littledean (petit ruisseau), que possédait son père Ninian Duns..."

cum antiquitus insignia gentilitia ubique communia fuerint, prout ex iure speciali Scotorum instruimur." Hence, if we accept on the one hand the opinion of Cardinal Ehrle and Father Pelster[21] that Duns is a family name rather than a name of origin, and if we admit on the other hand that the family derived its name from the town of Duns, it is easy to understand how the family of the Subtle Doctor, once they had moved from Duns to Maxton, was called *Duns* or *de Duns* by the townspeople. But when Scotus' disciples, scattered throughout the world, began to revise the works of their master and call him John Scotus *de Duns* or *Dunicae decus,* then one cannot help but think that Scotus was so called because he had actually been born in the town of *Duns.*[22]

The date of Scotus' birth, not otherwise than his country and his birthplace, has been for centuries the subject of discussion among historians. Today it is certain that the year 1274, which was rather commonly accepted as the probable date of Scotus' birth by the Franciscans, must be discarded[23] in favor of the approximate date of 1265.[24] This date has been established on the basis of certain data concerning his entrance into the order and his ordination to the priesthood. In fact, we know that between 1278 and 1279 Father Elias Duns, the Subtle Doctor's uncle, brought his nephew

---

[21] F. Pelster, "Handschriftliches zu Skotus mit neuen Angaben über sein Leben," *Franziskanische Studien,* 10 (1923), 1, n. 1.

[22] C. Balić, "Note di un viaggio," pp. 196-202.

[23] Cf. E. Giusto, *Vita del B. Giovanni Duns Scoto, Dottore Sottile e Mariano* (Assisi: 1921), p. 11: "Opinione dei biografi, comunemente accettata, è proprio quella che determina i natali del Beato circa l'anno 1274; data che contiene tutti gli elementi costitutivi d'una certezza morale. In quell'anno medesimo San Bonaventura di Bagnorea, gloria fulgidissima dell'Ordine francescano, chiudeva i giorni della sua vita terrena nella città di Lione... Non appena sull'orizzonte delle idealità francescane tramontava un astro magnifico..., ecco che il Signore fa nascere, in un lembo della terra di Scozia, questo sole sfolgorante e limpido, che avrebbe illuminato il mondo colla luce della sua dottrina profonda." See also B. De Bottis, *Vita del sottilissimo Maestro F. Giovanni Dunsio Scoto, Dottor Mariano* (Venice: 1698), c. 2, p. 10; Ildefonsus Brizenus, *De vita et doctrina Ioannis Scoti Doctoris Subtilis* (Madrid: 1638), #1, n. 4: "apparet vero probabilius anno salutis 1275 tantum sidus orbi affulsisse, quia triginta quattuor annos vixit et a vivis excessit anno 1308."

[24] Cf. Ferguson, *Berwickshire Naturalist's Club Transactions,* XIV, 1892-1893, p. 63: "According to tradition, which in this instance has a good deal to support it, the famous schoolman, John Duns Scotus, belonged to this family, and was born in Duns about the year 1265. The site of the house where he is said to have first seen the light, is still pointed out on the south-west slope of the Lawn, a few yards from the Pavilion Lodge leading to the Castle." See also E. M. Giusto, *Vita del B. Giovanni Duns Scoto,* pp. 6-9.

to the friary of Dumfries,[25] and that John was ordained priest on March 19, 1291.[26] Since the Constitutions of the order of Friars Minor in force at that time prescribed that the canonical age of fifteen had to be observed for a candidate's admission to the order,[27] and since the Constitutions of the order of Preachers prescribed that no friar could be promoted to the priesthood before the age of twenty-five,[28] even though the canonical age for admission to the priesthood was thirty,[29] some historians conclude that Scotus' birth must be placed between December 23, 1265, and March 17, 1266.[30] This conclusion rests of course on the assumption that Scotus was exactly twenty-five years of age at the time of his ordination to the

---

[25] *Registrum*, p. 9219 (cf. Callebaut, "A propos," p. 317): "Anno 1278, frater Helias Duns, guardianus Dumfrisii, venit Hadingtoniae et in capitulo Ordinis, praesentibus aliis guardianis, officium Vicarii Generalis per regnum Scotiae suscepit, *atque* celebrem illum theologum Johannem Duns, a patria Scotum appellatum, *secum Dumfrisium adduxit* et habitu religionis donavit. Erat enim eius ex fratre Niniano Duns de Littledean nepos, et Hadingtoniae inferiores scholas frequentabat, ubi futurae doctrinae egregia specimina dedit."

[26] E. Longpré, "L'ordination sacerdotale du Bx. Jean Duns Scot," *AFH*, 22 (1929), 54-62.

[27] Cf. S. Bonaventurae, *Statuta Narbonensia*, anni 1260 (*Opera omnia*, VIII, 450): "Ut nullus recipiatur citra 18 annum nisi per robur corporis vel industriam sensus seu per excellentem aedificationem a 15 anno et supra aetas secundum prudentium iudicium suppleatur." The general statutes of the Franciscan order made in Assisi in 1316 establish: "Nullus recipiatur in Ordinem nostrum nisi 14 annum compleverit in aetate." According to the *Registrum Ordinis*, Scotus had shown to be a very talented boy from the time of his schooling at Haddington: "futurae doctrinae egregia specimina [dedit]."

[28] Cf. Reichert, *Monumenta Ordinis Praedicatorum historica*, III, 23.

[29] Cf. S. Albertus Magnus, *Sent.* IV, d. 25, a. 7, ed. Borgnet, XXX (Paris: 1894), p. 96. The canonical age for the priesthood was 30 because Christ was baptized and began his public ministry when he was thirty years old. However "in religionibus morum gravitas et disciplina supplet aetatem" (cf. Callebaut, "A propos," p. 318).

[30] A. Callebaut, "A propos," p. 319; Béraud de Saint-Maurice, *Jean Duns Scot*, p. 64: "Jean Duns Scot naît entre le 23 décembre et le 17 mars 1266." Callebaut, "A propos," p. 318: "S'il est acquis, d'une part, que notre jeune prêtre avait vingt-cinq ans révolus le 17 mars 1291 (style moderne), il est tout aussi certain qu'il entra dans sa quatorzième année avant le 17 mars 1279." Béraud de Saint-Maurice, *Jean Duns Scot*, p. 78: "Frère Jean fait régulièrement son noviciat en 1280 à l'âge de quinze ans." Whether we say that in 1291 Scotus was 25, or that in 1280 he was 15, we reach the years 1265 and 1266 as probable dates of his birth, but not before that time. However, if in 1280 he was 18, he would have been born in 1262, so that when he was ordained in 1291 he would have been 29 years of age. Although this latter opinion is not absolutely groundless, it is only slightly probable for reasons of a different order. It must therefore be said that in all likelihood Duns Scotus was born between 1262 and 1266, and that the year 1265 may be considered as the probable date of his birth.

priesthood. Yet the mere fact that he had to be at least twenty-five years old before he could be ordained does not mean necessarily that at the time of his ordination he could not have been a little older. Likewise, since he had to be at least fifteen years old in order to be received in the order, it does not follow that his reception could not have been anticipated by a special dispensation. He could also have been received after that age.[31] All things considered, we believe that the most probable date of Scotus' birth is the year 1265, somewhat closer to 1266 than to 1264, so that it is appropriate to celebrate the seventh centenary of his birth between the years 1965 and 1966.

As regards Scotus' studies in preparation for the priesthood which, in accordance with the prescriptions of the Church and the order, must have been made between 1280 and 1291, no reliable information has come down to us.[32] However, we do have some positive data concerning his academic career between 1291 and 1308. After completing his studies at the universities of Scotland and England between 1291 and 1293,[33] he was sent for further studies to the University of Paris, since the regulations of the time demanded that those students who were specially qualified *(eminentis condicionis et status)* ought to be sent to the Alma Mater of that city.[34] Scotus studied at Paris between the years 1293 and

[31] L. Oliger, "De pueris oblatis in Ordine Minorum," *AFH*, 8 (1915), 400f. The blessed John of Alvernia († 1332) was made *canonicus regularis* at the age of 10 and entered the Franciscan order when he was 13.

[32] Scotus' curriculum of studies between 1280 and 1293 has been construed by some writers in the following manner: between 1281 and 1282, student of arts; between 1283 and 1284, student of natural sciences; between 1285 and 1286, lector of arts and sciences; between 1287 and 1289, student in the *Studium sollemne* of Sacred Theology; between 1290 and 1291, Lector in some seminary of studies; between 1291 and 1292, Vice-lector in the *Studium sollemne;* between 1292 and 1293, student in the University of Paris. All these data have been established by Callebaut, "A propos," p. 323f., on the basis of what is contained in the life of William Peter di Godino, O.P., who was a contemporary of Duns Scotus. Cf. also Béraud de Saint-Maurice, *Jean Duns Scot,* pp. 80-83; *ibid.,* p. 83: "Jean Duns Scot semble avoir fréquenté le Studium de Northampton."

[33] A. Callebaut, "A propos," pp. 324-25; Béraud de Saint-Maurice, *Jean Duns Scot,* p. 83f. Duns Scotus began his university studies in Northampton. A. G. Little, in his "Chronological Notes on the Life of Duns Scotus," *English Historical Review,* 47 (1932), 6, affirms that there is no doubt that at the time of his ordination to the priesthood Scotus was studying at Oxford. Toward the end of the thirteenth century the Franciscan Custody of Scotland lost its autonomy and was placed under the jurisdiction of the Province of England. Cf. Callebaut, "A propos," p. 325.

[34] Such was the prescription of the Constitutions of the order of Preachers (cf. *AFH,* 24 (1931), 326). In the Constitutions of the order of Friars Minor

1297,[35] having as his masters Gonsalvus of Spain[36] and James of Carceto or Quarcheto,[37] among others. In England he had studied under William of Ware.[38]

Scotus commented on the *Sentences* of Peter Lombard at Cambridge between 1297 and 1300,[39] as can be shown from vestiges of his unpublished lectures in codex 12 of the library of Todi in Italy. These lectures aroused such interest that the famous Henry of Harcley wrote a sort of a commentary on them accepting to a great extent the Scotistic theses.[40] Between 1300 and 1301 Scotus lectured on the *Sentences* at Oxford.[41] Having completed all his

---

(Ehrle, *ALKG*, VI, 108), it was said: "Circa mittentes [Parisios] attendatur quod sint ad proficiendum habiles, fortes corpore, eloquentiae bonae et conversationis honestae, non contentiosi, sed mites et pacifici inter fratres."

[35] A. Callebaut, "Le Bx. Jean Duns Scot étudiant à Paris vers 1293-1296," *AFH*, 17 (1924), 7-9; Little, "Chronological Notes," pp. 571-72. As we shall see presently, Duns Scotus commented on the *Sentences* at Paris in 1302-1303. Now, according to the Statutes of the University of Paris, no one could comment on the *Sentences* in that city who had not studied there for at least nine years (cf. Denifle-Chatelain, *Chartularium Universitatis Parisiensis*, II, 699, n. 30), except the Mendicants, who were allowed to complete the last five years in the *Studium* of their own order (cf. *AFH*, 17 (1924), 7; Denifle-Chatelain, *Chartul.*, II, 144). In the Constitutions of the Seraphic order of the year 1292 (Ehrle, *ALKG*, VI, 108; Denifle-Chatelain, *Chartul.*, II, 57) it is stated: "Illi autem qui mittuntur Parisios, studeant quattuor annis ad minus, nisi adeo provecti fuerint, quod merito iudicentur idonei ad doctoris officium exercendum."

[36] A. Callebaut, "Le séjour du Bx. Jean Duns Scot à Paris," *La France franciscaine*, 12 (1929), 355.

[37] *Ibidem*, 358. Cf. also Béraud de Saint-Maurice, *Jean Duns Scot*, p. 87.

[38] Cf. E. Longpré, "Maîtres franciscains de Paris, Guillaume de Ware, o.f.m.," *La France franciscaine*, 5 (1922), 75; Bettoni, *Vent'anni di studi scotisti*, p. 11; Balić, *Les commentaires*, pp. 49-51; Simonis, "De vita et operibus B. I. Duns Scoti," *Antonianum*, 1 (1926), 45-84.

[39] Codex 66 of Merton College: "Haec de Ordinatione ven. fratris I. Duns de Ordine Fratrum Minorum, qui floruit Cant., Oxon. et Parisiis et obiit in Colonia" (cf. A. Callebaut, "Le Bx. Jean Duns Scot à Cambridge vers 1297-1300," *AFH*, 21 [1928], 611). See also Béraud de Saint-Maurice, *Jean Duns Scot*, p. 101: "Il se dépense sans compter, se rendant alternativement d'Oxford à Cambridge et de Cambridge à Oxford."

[40] Cf. C. Balić, "Henricus de Harcley et Ioannes Duns Scotus," *Mélanges offerts à E. Gilson*, Etudes de philosophie médiévale (Paris-Toronto: 1954), pp. 95-121.

[41] Little, "Chronological Notes," pp. 572-73. Scotus commented on the *Sentences* from the first to the third book. In his *Liber memorandorum* (ed. A. G. Little, *Franciscan Papers, Lists and Documents*, Manchester, 1943, p. 235), John Dalberby, bishop of Lincoln, says that on July 26, 1300, Father Hugh of Hartlepool, Minister Provincial of England, presented to him twenty-two Friars Minor from the monastery of Oxford to receive the faculty to hear confessions. Among those friars one was "Ioannes Duns." Béraud de Saint-Maurice, *Jean Duns Scot*, p. 106, states that "Jean Duns Scot revient à Paris en 1301." This is not certain.

studies and met all the necessary requirements, in the general chapter of the order held in June of 1302 he was assigned to teaching at the University of Paris upon recommendation of the Minister Provincial of England.[42] He interrupted, therefore, his lectures at Oxford after the third book of the *Sentences* and went to Paris, where toward the end of 1302 he began for the third time to comment on the first book. In 1303 he continued his lectures by commenting on the fourth book.[43]

Between June 25 and 28, 1303, because of his refusal to subscribe to a petition of Philip the Fair, king of France, against Pope Boniface VIII, Scotus was forced to leave the University of Paris and return to Oxford.[44] He remained in Oxford for one year, continuing there the lectures he had been forced to interrupt at Paris. He acted probably as the *opponens* in the *disputatio quolibetalis secunda* of Nicholas Trivet, which took place at Oxford in December, 1303.[45] As Pope Boniface VIII on April 18, 1304 revoked the decree depriving the University of Paris of the right to confer academic degrees,[46] Duns Scotus returned to that university toward the end of the same year. There, on the occasion of the conferring of the doctoral degree upon Giles of Legnaco, he acted as *re-*

[42] Little, "Chronological Notes," p. 574; Callebaut, "Le séjour," p. 365; Wadding, *Annales Minorum*, an. 1302, pp. 1ff. In 1296 England suppressed the vicariate general of Scotland and placed it under the jurisdiction of the English Province (*AFH*, 24 (1931), 325; *Registrum*, p. 9797).

[43] Cod. Vigorniensis F. 69, f. 158v: "Expliciunt quaestiones in primum Sententiarum datae a fratre [I. Duns Sco] Ordinis Fratrum Minorum Parisiis anno Domini M° trecentesimo secundo intrante tertio." It was customary in France to begin the academic year at Easter time. Although this custom was reckoned by the official documents of many chanceries, it is not easy to determine whether the *reportator* followed the French system of computation or rather the Roman system. Cf. H. Grotefend, *Taschenbuch des Zeitrechnung des deutschen Mittelalters und der Neuzeit* (Hannover: 1915), pp. 11-14; Little, "Chronological Notes," pp. 568-82.

[44] Longpré, "Le Bx. Jean Duns Scot pour le Saint-Siège," pp. 138-45; Béraud de Saint-Maurice, *Jean Duns Scot*, pp. 123-24. Some authors hold that during his exile Duns Scotus was at Cologne (A. Callebaut, "Le Bx. Jean Duns Scot, bachelier des Sentences à Paris en 1302-1303," *La France franciscaine*, 9 (1926), 312-16); others maintain that he was at Oxford where he completed his lectures on the *Sentences*. This latter view seems to be more probable. Cf. Bettoni, *Vent'anni*, p. 9; Little, "Chronological Notes," p. 580; Béraud de Saint-Maurice, *Jean Duns Scot*, p. 124: "On le retrouve réfugié à la célèbre Université d'Oxford où il passera un an, de 1303 à 1304, avec Guillaume de Ware."

[45] Little, "Chronological Notes," p. 580; Bettoni, *Vent'anni*, p. 9; B. Hechich, *De immaculata conceptione beatae Mariae Virginis secundum Thomam de Sutton O.P. et Robertum de Cowton O.F.M.* (Bibliotheca Immaculatae Conceptionis, 7), Rome: 1958, pp. 21-22.

[46] Little, "Chronological Notes," p. 101.

sponsalis or *baccalaureus formatus* during the disputation *in aula*, while Giles was the new *magister aulandus* and master Alanus the *magister aulator*. Godfrey of Fontaines was at that time either Chancellor or acting Chancellor of the university.[47] On November 18, 1304 Gonsalvus of Spain, Minister General of the Franciscan order, sent a letter to the Minister Provincial of France, in which he presented Scotus as a candidate for the doctoral degree in the following terms: "I recommend to your charity our beloved brother in Christ, Father John Scotus, whose laudable life, excellent knowledge, most subtle genius, and other remarkable qualities are fully known to me, partly because of my long association with him, and partly because of his widespread reputation."[48] In the following year Duns Scotus obtained his doctorate,[49] and between 1306 and 1307 he acted as *magister regens*.[50] Toward the end of 1307 he was transferred to Cologne,[51] where he taught as *lector principalis*,[52] and where he died on November 8, 1308.

[47] Balić, "Henricus de Harcley," p. 101.
[48] Cf. A. Callebaut, "La maîtrise du Bx. Jean Duns Scot en 1305," *AFH*, 21 (1928), 209; Little, "Chronological Notes," p. 577; Denifle-Chatelain, *Chartularium*, II, 117.
[49] Cf. Callebaut, "La maîtrise," p. 213; Little, "Chronological Notes," p. 578. This latter seems to express some doubt as to whether Duns Scotus received his doctorate during the year 1305. There is no sure information available as to what Scotus did once he obtained his *magisterium* and before he was appointed *magister regens* in 1306-1307. For this reason I used to share the view that perhaps at that time Scotus was in Oxford; but if he completed his lectures on the *Sentences* during the years 1303 and 1304, that hypothesis appears less probable.
[50] Cf. Little, "Chronological Notes," p. 581.
[51] During the general chapter of the Franciscan order held at Toulouse in 1307, Alexander of Alexandria was appointed *magister regens* at Paris, while Duns Scotus was transferred to Cologne. Cf. Callebaut, "La maîtrise," pp. 235-36; Béraud de Saint-Maurice, *Jean Duns Scot*, p. 133: "Les régents n'étaient ordinairement en charge qu'une année et l'on faisait parcourir les plus grands studia des Ordres religieux aux docteurs les plus fameux."
[52] W. Lampen, "B. Ioannes Duns Scotus, lector coloniensis," *Collectanea franciscana neerlandica*, 2 (1931), 297-300. In a document dated February 20, 130 . . ., Scotus is listed among some most respected Fathers convened for the approval of the construction of a new monastery in the city of *Ruraemunda*.
    The question as to how many times Scotus commented on the books of the *Sentences*, as well as the related question whether he commented once or several times after he was appointed *magister*, remains open for discussion. However, one must absolutely reject the traditional opinion of Scotists in the past, especially after Ferkić and Wadding, that the Subtle Doctor commented only twice on the *Sentences* of Peter Lombard. At the same time one must not forget that the medieval statutes concerning the requirements for the university students of those days should not be taken too strictly, as can be shown from various documents. Cf., for example, A. Little-F. Pelster, *Oxford Theology and Theologians*

No information has come down to us from Scotus' contemporaries on the nature of his fatal disease. In the late fourteenth and early fifteenth centuries his death was usually presented as an exemplary and peaceful transition while in a state of ecstatic rapture.[53] Later his opponents began to spread the legend of a horrifying death that would have resulted from the agonizing experience of having been buried alive, with many variations according to the whim of each reporter but with no historical foundation whatsoever.

Scotus was buried in a Franciscan church, and many eulogistic epigrams were engraved at once on his tomb.[54] His remains were transferred several times, with 1956 as the year of their latest translation.[55] Since 1870 the tomb has borne the following epitaph: "Scotia me genuit, Anglia me suscepit; Gallia me docuit, Colonia me tenet." His contemporaries awarded him the title of *Doctor Subtilis*, to which the title of *Doctor Marianus* was added later by his admirers. Scotus' name is mentioned among the blessed in the martyrology of the order of Friars Minor and he has long been the object of veneration.[56] In the cathedral church of Nola in Italy an altar has been erected in his honor. In 1904 the Sacred Congregation of Rites confirmed the process held in that city in 1710 concerning the veneration shown to the Subtle Doctor.[57]

II. THE WORKS OF JOHN DUNS SCOTUS

It is a well known fact that since the historico-critical method of investigation has been applied to the sources of scholasticism, many works previously considered as authentic have been proved to be spurious, while new works have been discovered, and new light has been shed on other works concerning their contents, historical

---

c. A. D. 1282-1302 (Oxford: 1934), p. 35; A. Little, "The Franciscan School at Oxford," *AFH*, 19 (1926), 825; M. Bihl, "Statuta generalia Ordinis," *AFH*, 34 (1941), 71-76; H. Rashadall–F. M. Powicke–A. B. Emden, *The University of Europe in the Middle Age*, I (Oxford: 1958), 491.

[53] A. Callebaut, "La leggenda del B. Duns Scoto," *Studi francescani*, 12 (1926), 6-7; G. Abate, "La tomba del Ven. G. Duns Scoto a Colonia," *Miscellanea francescana*, 45 (1945), 40-42.

[54] Cf. C. Balić, "Quelques précisions fornies par la tradition manuscrite sur la vie, les oeuvres et l'attitude doctrinale de Jean Duns Scot," *Revue d'histoire ecclésiastique*, 22 (1926), 551-66; Abate, "La tomba," p. 41.

[55] Abate, "La tomba," pp. 43-64.

[56] Wadding, *Annales Minorum*, ad an. 1308, nn. 48-50.

[57] Béraud de Saint-Maurice, *Jean Duns Scot*, p. 134.

value, and authority. It will suffice to recall the successful results that have thus far been achieved in regard to the works of such great doctors as St. Thomas Aquinas, St. Bonaventure, St. Albert the Great, and Alexander of Hales. Thus, for example, the editors at Quaracchi have placed among the spurious works more than one hundred books and treatises that a long-standing tradition had ascribed to the Seraphic Doctor, including the well-known *Speculum B. Virginis Mariae*.[58] Likewise, it has been proved that more than forty opuscules had been wrongly attributed to Aquinas.[59] Again, while new works of Alexander of Hales have been discovered, it has been shown that Roger Bacon's statement to the effect that the Friars Minor had ascribed to their esteemed master, after he entered the order, a *Summa* "quam ipse non fecit, sed alii,"[60] was not at all incorrect. Examples of this kind could be multiplied.

The Subtle Doctor has been affected by the present-day critical method of study no less than his contemporary schoolmen and his predecessors. Of the works published in the only extant edition of all his writings, the Wadding-Vivès edition, it has been proved that a good number of them are either spurious or of dubious authenticity, while others have been discovered which belong to him but are not contained in that edition. An even greater accomplishment has been the establishment of certain norms which enable us to judge about the value and importance of each individual work.

We shall now present the catalogue of Scotus' works in three separate sections. They will include in turn the authentic works that have been published, the authentic works that have never been published, and those works which Wadding-Vivès have wrongly attributed to Scotus. The list will be followed by some critical observations on those works which deserve special consideration.

---

[58] Cf. P. Glorieux, *Répertoire des maîtres en théologie de Paris au XIIIe siècle*, II, Etudes de Philosophie médiévale, 18 (Paris: 1934), 43-51.
[59] Cf. M. Grabmann, *Die Werke des hl. Thomas von Aquin* (Münster: 1931).
[60] Cf. Roger Bacon, *Opera quaedam hactenus inedita*, I, ed. Brewer (London: 1859), 328.

A.—Catalogue of Scotus' Works

I. Published Authentic Works

a) *Works Included in the Wadding-Vivès Edition:*[61]

1) Super universalia Porphyrii quaestiones (I, 51-435).
2) In librum Praedicamentorum quaestiones (I, 437-538).
3) Quaestiones in I et II librum Perihermeneias Aristotelis (I, 539-579).
4) In duos libros Perihermeneias, operis secundi, quod appellant, quaestiones (I, 581-601).
5) In libros Elenchorum quaestiones (II, 1-80).
6) Quaestiones super libros Aristotelis De anima (III, 472-642).
7) De primo rerum omnium principio (IV, 721-799).
8) Theoremata (V, 2-128).
9) Collationes Parisienses (V, 131-317).
10) Quaestiones super libros Metaphysicorum Aristotelis (VII).
11) Opus Oxoniense (VIII-XXI).
12) Reportata Parisiensia (XXII-XXIV).
13) Quodlibet (XXV-XXVI).

b) *Works not Included in the Wadding-Vivès Edition:*

1) Reportatio in I Sent. (abbreviated), Paris, 1517.
2) Reportatio in IV Sent., Paris, 1518.
3) Lectura in I Sent. (Vatican Edition, XVI-XVII).
4) Collationes Oxonienses et Parisienses.[62]

II. Unpublished Authentic Works

a) *In I Sent.:*

1) Reportatio (Parisiensis) in I Sent.[63]
2) Reportatio (Cantabrigiensis) in I Sent.[64]

---

[61] We shall place within parentheses the volume number of the Vivès edition as well as the pages of each work within the same volume, unless the entire volume is dedicated to one particular work.

[62] Cf. C. Balić, "De Collationibus Ioannis Duns Scoti, Doctoris Subtilis ac Mariani," *Bogoslovski Vestnik*, 9 (1929), 185-219.

[63] Codd.: Vindobonae, lat. 1453; Borgh. lat. 325; Ox. Balliol 205; Ox. Merton 59; Taurini K. II. 26.

[64] 3 codd.: Tuderti 12; Borgh. lat. 50; Borgh. lat. 89.

b) *In II Sent.:*
1) Lectura in II Sent.[65]
2) Additiones in II Sent.[66]

c) *In III Sent.:*
1) Lectura in III Sent.[67]
2) Reportatio (Barcinonensis) in III Sent.[68]
3) Reportatio (Valentinensis) in III Sent.[69]
4) Reportatio (Trecensis) in III Sent.[70]

III. Unauthentic Works Contained in the Wadding-Vivès Edition

1) Tractatus de modis significandi sive Grammatica speculativa (I, 1-50). Work of Thomas of Erfurt.
2) In lib. I et II Priorum Analyticorum Aristotelis quaestiones (II, 81-197).
3) In lib. I et II Posteriorum Analyticorum Aristotelis quaestiones (II, 199-347).
4) Dilucidissima expositio et quaestiones in 8 libros Physicorum Aristotelis (II, 352-677; III, 1-470).
5) Meteorologicorum libri 4 (IV, 1-263).
6) Quaestiones disputatae De rerum principio (IV, 267-717). Work of Vitalis of Furno.
7) De cognitione Dei tractatus imperfectus (V, 318-337).
8) Quaestiones miscellaneae de formalitatibus. Tractatus imperfectus (V, 338-432).
9) In XII lib. Metaphysicorum Aristotelis expositio (V, 442-725; VI, 1-600). Work of Anthony Andreas.

---

[65] Codd.: Patavii, bibl. Anton. cod. 178, ff. 1ra-83vb; Vindobonae, bibl. nat. lat. 1447, ff. 75va-120va; Romae, bibl. conv. S. Franc. ad Ripas, cod. Q.II.21, ff. 1r-139r.

[66] Codd.: Berolini, bibl. Status, lat., fol. 928; Civ. Vat., vat. lat. 876; vat. lat. 883; Cracoviae, bibl. Univ., cod. 1605; Oxonii Balliol 208; Oxonii Merton 87; Parisiis, bibl. nat., lat. 3061; Rottenburgi, bibl. Semin. 13.

[67] Codd.: Cracoviae, bibl. Univ., cod. 1408, ff. 1ra-47va; Oxonii Balliol 206, ff. 1r-141v; Oxonii Merton 62, ff. 124r-228v.

[68] Barcinone, Archiv. Cor. Arag., cod. Ripoll 53, ff. 1ra-70ra.

[69] Valentiae, bibl. cathedr., cod. 178, ff. 81ra-83rb; Pragae, bibl. cathedr., cod. 439 (C.XXI.4), ff. 3r-78v.

[70] Trecis, bibl. com., cod. 661, ff. 56ra-89vb.

10) Conclusiones utilissimae ex XII lib. Metaph. Aristot. collectae (VI, 601-667).
11) De perfectione statuum (XXVI, 501-561).[71]

B. Critical Observations

Among the Friars Minor "who excelled for learning" and "wrote on Sacred Scripture by explaining and commenting upon it, as well as by clearing up the doubts that are contained in the books of the Sentences," Bartholomew of Pisa mentions very appropriately John Duns Scotus, called "the Subtle Doctor." He says of him: "Primo in Anglia Oxoniae Sententias *legit*, deinde in studio Parisiensi, ubi doctor factus est famosissimus et fuit." Then he adds: "Hic in theologia scripsit luculenter, et praecipue super quattuor libros, quos ipse *ordinavit*; et Quodlibeta etiam *fecit*, tractatus plures *edidit*, quaestiones super libros Metaphysicae *fecit*, et super Scripturam sacram postillas *ordinavit*."[72] Thus Bartholomew of Pisa uses various terms, i.e., *scribere, ordinare, facere, edere*, which certainly do not mean the same thing in scholastic terminology. Whatever their specific meaning may be, it is a fact that he uses the terms *legit* and *scripsit* only in regard to the books of the *Sentences*. Hence we shall discuss first Scotus' questions on the *Sentences*, and

---

[71] Various other works have throughout the centuries been ascribed to Duns Scotus, which are not found among the *Opera omnia* edited by Wadding-Vivès. Cf. Glorieux, *Répertoire*, II, 210-14. Wadding stated (cf. Vivès ed., I, p. iii) that in the 12 volumes in folio he proposed to edit only those works "quae ad rem speculativam, seu dissertationes scholasticas, spectant," and promised that in a following series he would publish those works which constitute the "positive part" of Scotus' writings and contain his commentaries on Holy Scripture, namely, *Lectura in Genesim, Commentaria in Evangelia, Commentaria in epistolas S. Pauli, Sermones de Tempore, Sermones de Sanctis.* However, despite the fact that an intensive search has been conducted throughout a great number of libraries of the whole of Europe, none of these works has thus far been discovered. Many codices have been found which contain sermons attributed to "Ioannes Socci" but belong really to Conrad of Brudelshaim, O. Cist. This similarity of names may perhaps explain how in the course of time those sermons have wrongly been attributed to Duns Scotus. Cf. Wien, Nationalbibliothek, lat. 1428, f. 288*ra*: "Explicit opus de tempore fratris Ioannis Socci Ordinis S. Benedicti. . ." Cf. also L. Meier, "Nicolas de Gorham, O.P., Author of the Commentary on the Apocalypse Erroneously Attributed to John Duns Scotus," *Dominican Studies*, 3 (1950), 359-62.

[72] Bartholomaeus de Pisis, "De conformitate vitae beati Francisci ad vitam Domini Iesu," lib. I, fruct. 8, pars 2, *Analecta franciscana*, IV (Quaracchi: 1906), 337.

then his commentaries on the books of Philosophers and the disputations that he made or *fecit*.

I) *Questions on the Four Books of the Sentences of Peter Lombard.*

It has been commonly believed from the fourteenth century to the present time that Duns Scotus commented twice on the books of the *Sentences* of Peter Lombard, once at Oxford and another time at Paris. But it was only in the seventeenth century that the opinion prevailed that there are only two authentic commentaries by Scotus, the *Opus Oxoniense* and the *Opus Parisiense*. This opinion has been popularized by Wadding and Matthew Ferkić. The latter, who in the early seventeenth century devoted himself earnestly to the study of Scotus' works, held firmly to the view that Scotus *wrote* only one *Reportatio*. However, since he had in his hands two *Reportationes* under the name of Scotus, one published in 1478 and the other in 1517, he retained the former as authentic and rejected the latter as spurious.[73] Ferkić's view was shared by Wadding, who published the 1478 edition of Scotus' *Reportatio* and corrected it according to codex Vat. lat. 876.

The seventeenth century Scotists did not understand the original meaning of the terms *Reportatio* and *Ordinatio*. Thus, according to Wadding, the *Opus Parisiense* would have been called *Reportatio* because Scotus "ex Scripto Oxoniensi reportaverit, tumultaria quadam collectione, ut absolutum opus opportuno tempore continuaret";[74] whereas the *Opus Oxoniense* would have been called *Ordinatio* either because Scotus' disciples had ordered and compiled it "ex utraque lectura, Oxoniensi et Parisiensi," or because "neglectis aliis operibus, ordinarie et ex consuetudine hoc solum legebatur in scholis."[75]

On the contrary, it is absolutely certain that "reportare ab aliquo" or "reportare aliquo legente" had no other meaning in the middle ages than to report orally or in writing, the second interpre-

[73] M. Ferchius [Ferkić], *Vita B. Ioannis Dunsii Scoti* (Bologna: 1622), c. 11, n. 39; *Discussiones scoticae subtilitatis de Commentariis Metaphysicis et Reportatis Parisiensibus adscriptis Ioanni Dunsio Scoto* (Padua: 1638).
[74] L. Wadding, *Annales Minorum*, ad an. 1304, n. 31. See also A. Bertoni, *Le B. Jean Duns Scot* (Levanto: 1917), p. 429: "comme le nom 'reporter' l'indique, c'est la *répétition* des Commentaires sur les quatre livres du Maître des Sentences."
[75] Cf. *Censura Waddingi circa Commentarios Oxonienses* (ed. Vivès, VIII, 3).

tation being the more common.[76] As to the *Ordinatio*, it is now known that this term was given to the *Opus Oxoniense*, not because it had been ordered or compiled from Scotus' lectures at Oxford and Paris, and even at Cambridge, and was usually read and commented upon more than all other Scotus' works, but rather because it contains the text that Scotus himself either wrote or dictated from his various lectures and writings and ordered in such a way as to present the material in the form of a *Summa* of his entire doctrine.[77]

Briefly, the editors of Scotus' works in the past centuries did not pay attention to the fact that his commentaries on the *Sentences* have come down in three distinct forms: first, in a work that he himself either wrote or dictated and got ready for publication *(Ordinatio)*; secondly, in the writings of disciples who listened to and took down his lectures or some other public pronouncements *(Reportatio)*; and thirdly, in various works which have been published by Scotus' disciples but were either drafted or approved by their master.

From this it is evident that Scotus' commentary on the *Sentences* known as the *Ordinatio* is extremely important for a knowledge of his genuine thought, while the *Reportationes* have comparatively little value. Their value depends on the greater or lesser amount of attention with which the student followed Scotus' lectures, and on the faithfulness and ability with which he reported the words and mind of his master. Cases are well known in which the medieval masters complained about the unfaithful reports of their students *(malae reportationes)*.

Since not just one but many of Scotus' students reported the lectures of their master, and since several of these reports have come down to us, it is necessary to submit them all to a careful study. One must find out whether among them there are unfaithful reports, which of them are more trustworthy and reliable, and whether any of them have been revised or approved by Scotus himself. Matthew Ferkić and others have placed among the unfaithful *Reportationes* that which was published in Paris between 1517 and 1518. But unfortunately even the *Reportatio* published in 1478 and reproduced by Wadding does not seem to be much better. It must be admitted that among the various *Reportationes* on the

---

[76] Cf. A. Pelzer, "Le premier livre des Reportata Parisiensia de Jean Duns Scot," *Annales de l'Institut supérieur de Philosophie*, V (Louvain: 1923), 467-79.
[77] Balić, *Les commentaires*, pp. xi-xii.

first book of the *Sentences*, that which was revised and approved by Scotus and is as yet unpublished ranks first.[78]

The *Lectura Oxoniensis* is also very important. It cannot be called a *Reportatio* in the strict sense of the term, for it is a transcription of the notes that Duns Scotus used for his commentary on the *Sentences* at Oxford. The *Reportatio* revised by Scotus and the *Lectura Oxoniensis* are the basic sources used by Scotus for the compilation of his *Summa*, the *Ordinatio*.

Obviously then, Scotus did not *write* the *Reportationes*. When a text is quoted from them, one should use the term *dixit* rather than *scripsit*; on the contrary, when a text is cited from the *Ordinatio*, the proper term to be used is either *scripsit* or *dictavit*. Likewise, whenever disagreement exists between the teaching of the *Ordinatio* and the teaching of the *Reportationes*, the text of the *Ordinatio* is to be followed as that which reflects Scotus' final and definitive doctrine. The *Reportationes* and the *Lecturae* are nevertheless very useful. They help us to understand in better fashion the gradual development of Scotistic thought, and occasionally they offer us a clue to a correct interpretation of it.

II) *Commentaries on the Works of Philosophers and Various Treatises.*

As previously indicated, Bartholomew of Pisa, after stating that Duns Scotus "Tractatus plures *edidit*," adds: "Quaestiones super libros Metaphysicae *fecit*." As to the nature of such *tractatus*, he does not specify. However, he must have had in mind the treatise *De primo principio*, the treatise *De theorematibus*, and probably also the treatise or questions *De anima*, as well as several other logical works by Scotus. Of the three *Metaphysicae* ascribed to Scotus by Wadding-Vivès, namely, *Metaphysica textualis*, *Conclusiones metaphysicae*, and *Quaestiones super libros metaphysicorum*, it can be said with certainty that only the *Quaestiones* belong to Scotus, and only as far as the first nine books are concerned. The *Conclusiones metaphysicae* are the work of Gonsalvus of Spain, Scotus' master, while the *Metaphysica textualis* was written by Anthony Andreas, a disciple who testified that he followed faithfully the

[78] Cod. Vindobonensis, bibl. nat. lat. 1453, f. 125va: "Explicit Reportatio super primum Sententiarum *sub magistro Ioanne Scoto et examinata cum eodem venerando doctore*."

words and statements of Scotus.⁷⁹ Moreover, Duns Scotus did not even put the final touches to the *Quaestiones super metaphysicam.* There are in fact many texts in it which in the codices are marked "Extra," "Cancellatum," or "Additio." There seem to be also different editions or revisions of the original text. The "socius" who completed the *Quaestiones* from the tenth to the twelfth book seems to have also worked on the text of the questions that Scotus wrote but did not finish completely.⁸⁰

Although the questions *De anima* are found in approximately twenty-five codices and their authenticity rests on good grounds, it is not easy to assess the real value of the work, which is of paramount importance for the knowledge of Scotus' psychological theory. In one codex we read: "Quaestiones *Scotuli* super secundum et tertium libros De anima."⁸¹ At the present moment it is impossible to determine the parts Scotus and those *Scotulus* had in the preparation of the work.

With the exception of codex 2908 of the Bibliothèque Nationale of Bruxelles, which dates back to the fourteenth century, and codex Vat. lat. 3092, the codices in which Scotus' *Logicalia* have come down to us are generally of the fifteenth century (in one codex we read the year 1464, in another the year 1452). Codex 291 of Balliol College, Oxford, contains Scotus' teaching on the *Logica* and *Metaphysica* of Aristotle. On fol. 57r, after the words, "Explicit sententia super Praedicamenta secundum Doctorem Subtilem," the following remark is made: "Hoc qui fecit opus Duns Subtilis vocitatur—Doctor theologus logica cunctis dominatur.—Qui cupit in logica merito consultus haberi—discat dicta sua si cautus habet retineri etc." Be that as it may, Scotus' *Logicalia* did not exert a great influence upon the history of Scotism. The fact that they

---

[79] Cf. *Metaphysica textualis* (among the *Opera omnia* of John Duns Scotus, ed. Vivès, VI, 600): "Volo autem scire omnes litteram istam legentes, quod tam sententiando quam notando secutus sum doctrinam illius subtilissimi et excellentissimi Doctoris, cuius fama et memoria in benedictione est, utpote qui sua sacra et profunda doctrina totum orbem adimplevit et fecit resonare, scilicet Magistri Ioannis Duns, qui fuit natione Scotus."

[80] Berlin, bibl. publica, lat. 420, f. 29v: "Haec non dicit Ioannes, sed colliguntur ex dictis eius"; f. 40vb: "Additio usque ad quartum articulum," etc.

[81] Oxford, Magdalen College, cod. 16, ff. 59r-96r: "Expliciunt quaestiones super secundum et tertium libros *De anima, secundum Scotum,* alias *Doctorem Subtilem.*" In the Commentary *De anima* by Nicholas of Orbellis, which is preserved in Bibl. Vat. Ottob. lat. 1442, one can read the following statement on f. 151r: "Haec Iacobus de Turbio, sequax Scoti, in quaestionibus super librum De anima, quae quidem a quibusdam dicuntur omnes ipsius Scoti, quorum principium est: Utrum sensus tactus sit unus."

came down to us only in a few fourteenth-century codices seems to support this view.

A word remains to be said about two of Scotus' best known treatises, the *De primo principio* and the *De theorematibus*. No one questions the fact that Scotus is the author of the opuscule that goes under the name of *De primo principio*, nor has anyone ever raised any doubt as to its authenticity. In addition to the fact that a good number of codices, some of which go back to the fourteenth century, ascribe this opuscule to Scotus, the treatise is quoted under Scotus' name by Francis Mayron, Peter Thomas, Anthony Andreas, John of Baconthorp, John of Reading, and many others. What is even more important, Scotus himself refers to *De primo principio* in a text of the *Ordinatio* in his own handwriting. Yet it does not seem that he has been the only author of the treatise. While a great part of it is taken almost verbatim from the *Ordinatio*, the style of the two works is different.[82]

The treatise *De primo principio* leads to Scotus' other opuscule, *De theorematibus*, with which it is intimately connected. Whereas all agree in ascribing the treatise *De primo principio* to Scotus, the authenticity of the *De theorematibus* has been denied by some scholars for reasons inherent to the work itself. To be sure, no proof can be produced to the effect that Duns Scotus is the formal author of the opuscule. Upon a careful study of the four codices in which it has come down to us (Klosterneuburg, Dubrovnik, Prague, and Milan), no sure indication can be found that Scotus has either written, dictated, corrected, or even approved the opuscule. While a great discrepancy exists among the codices, the few casual statements that can be found here and there throughout the opuscule are too vague and incomplete to serve as a clue to the identification of its author.[83]

Thus, while it can be said that Duns Scotus and his "socius" have worked very closely in the preparation of the treatise *De primo principio*, it is difficult to determine which part the Subtle Doctor and which his "socius" had in the composition of the opuscule *De theorematibus*.

---

[82] Cf. C. Balić, *Ratio criticae editionis Operum omnium I. Duns Scoti*, III (Rome: 1951), 24-30.
[83] *Ibid.*, 30-32.

III) *Disputations.*

"To lecture, to dispute, and to preach," this was the program of the medieval schoolmen. Duns Scotus lectured by commenting on the *Sentences* of Peter Lombard and the works of philosophers, but he also engaged in academic debates. It is certain that at Paris he participated as a disputant "in aula" on the occasion of the promotion of Friar Giles of Legnaco and at Oxford he took part "in vesperiis" of Philip of Bridlington. He likewise had part in debates that were carried out with Hervaeus Natalis, Peter of Godino, and others.[84] Our only purpose here is to bring to the attention of the reader Scotus' excellent work, *De quolibet,* namely, *Disputatio de quolibet a quolibet proposito,* or, as some would have it, *De quolibet ad voluntatem cuiuslibet.* Of this work we do not have the first part or *impugnatio.* Hence we do not know who raised the questions, how they worded them, whether they loaded them with many or only a few arguments, and therefore who was the one who answered the questions along with the master. We have only the second part of the *Quodlibet,* the *determinatio,* in which the master reduces all different questions to some sort of a unity, makes known his own mind, and answers the objections.

Since by its nature a disputation *De quolibet* was not prepared, and many unexpected objections were raised and questions were asked without any specific order, it was extremely difficult—something that only a great mind could do—to reduce all questions to unity and answer them immediately. Whereas Richard of Middleton reduced all questions to issues of the practical and speculative orders, Godfrey of Fontaines distinguished between theological science as such and as the object of study, and St. Thomas Aquinas reduced all issues to Christ as the head of the mystical body, Duns Scotus brought the twenty-one questions of the *Quodlibet* to a logical unity by distinguishing between God and creatures and discussing them separately, as well as in their mutual relationships.

---

[84] Cf. Balić, "Henricus de Harcley," p. 100; Little, "Chronological Notes," p. 588; E. Longpré, "Philippe de Bridlington O.F.M. et le Bx. Duns Scot," *AFH*, 22 (1929), 588; F. Pelster, "Handschrifliches zu Skotus," pp. 11-16; "Eine Münchener Handschrift des beginnenden vierzehnten Jahrhunderts mit einem Verzeichnis von Quaestionen des Duns Scotus und Herveus Natalis, Cod. lat. monac. 8717," *Franziskanische Studien,* 17 (1930), 253-72.

Here is how he enunciates the plan of his work:

"*Cunctae res difficiles,*" ait Salomon, Ecc. 1. Et cur intelligat eas esse difficiles, subdit: "*Non potest eas homo explicare sermone.*" Secundum igitur distinctionem rerum potest accipi distinctio difficilium quaestionum. Res autem, prima sui divisione, dividi potest in rem creatam et increatam, sive in rem a se et in rem ab alio habentem esse, sive in rem necessariam et rem possibilem, sive in rem finitam et infinitam. Res autem increata, a se, infinita et necessaria, Deus est; res autem creata, ab alio, possibilis et finita, communi nomine dicitur creatura. De utraque re propositae sunt aliquae quaestiones.

Iterum, in divinis res accipitur essentialiter et notionaliter, iuxta illud Augustini I *De doctrina christiana,* cap. 2: "res, quibus fruendum est, sunt Pater, Filius et Spiritus Sanctus; eademque Trinitas, una quaedam summa res, communis omnibus fruentibus ea." In prima parte auctoritatis accipitur res personaliter, in secunda essentialiter. Fuerunt igitur aliqua quaesita in divinis de re essentiali, aliqua de notionali sive personali. Unicum autem quaesitum erat de ordine essentialium ad notionalia. Illud unicum primo ponitur, utpote ex cuius solutione patebit ordo procedendi circa alia quaesita.[85]

This prologue, headed by a text from Holy Scripture, shows how Scotus reaches the peak of perfection in his attempt to unify many different questions under one general theme.

Since the master was required to give a clear and distinct answer to all the questions raised during the debate, the quodlibetal literature has a very important doctrinal value, even though it does not contain a well-coordinated and complete body of doctrines of a particular master and its compilation reflects the haste with which it was prepared. This is particularly true in the case of Scotus, who in his commentaries on the *Sentences* makes a detailed analysis of all possible difficulties, often fictitious ones, and engages in interminable discussions before he manifests his mind, thus making it difficult for the reader to know exactly what is his position on the subject. It is only to be regretted that even this work, which is definitely one of Scotus' latest writings, was not carried to completion by the Subtle Doctor. In codex lat. 8717 of Munich, question 21 of the *Quodlibet* ends upon fol. 85vb with the following words: "aliquem esse bene fortunatum sicut nec ratio probabilis persuaderet. Tertium membrum." Then the codex reads: "Finis. Quodlibet repertum in suis quaternis. Quod sequitur est de Re-

---

[85] I. Duns Scotus, *Quodlibet,* Praefatio (ed. Vivès, XXI), p. 3.

portatione." Again, several codices bear witness to the fact that Scotus left his manuscript unfinished by placing on the margins certain texts which "erant signata ut ponerentur loco quorumdam cancellatorum, in quibus cancellatis voluit habere eandem conclusionem quam prius habuit in iis dispersis in marginibus, etc."

In past centuries Scotus' commentators published such works as the *Contradictiones ducentae quadraginta tres*[86] and the *Conciliationes locorum ex Quodlibetis Scoti cum aliis eiusdem Doctoris locis*.[87] Since, as was previously stated, Scotus had to give in the *Quodlibet* a clear and precise answer to the various questions presented to him, whereas in his commentaries on the *Sentences* or on Aristotle there was no such need, so that he could state his position only after a long and detailed analysis of all possible difficulties, it is easy to understand how an apparent contradiction may exist between the *Quodlibet* and some of his other works.

The foregoing catalogue of Scotus' authentic and unauthentic works has been based principally on what the critics call *criteria externa*, that is, reasons or motives that lie outside the works themselves and have no reference to their contents. Thus we have placed the *Theoremata* among Scotus' authentic works because documents and witnesses of the 14th century (the codex Claustroneoburgensis, Peter Thomas, etc.), as well as all editors of Scotus' works from the fifteenth century on explicitly ascribe it to the Subtle Doctor. On the contrary, we have placed among Scotus' spurious works the treatise *De perfectione statuum*, inasmuch as the supporting authority of the codices is of a later date, and the doctrine therein contained is such that not even Wadding dared to place the treatise among Scotus' genuine works.

The works of medieval schoolmen, including those prepared and written by themselves, cannot all be classified as authentic in exactly the same sense of the term. More specifically, one must distinguish between *authenticity* as such, by which it is meant that a particular work has come down to us from such and such an author, and the *authority* that such a work, or such and such a text, carries with it. This distinction is of paramount importance for one who

---

[86] Cf. Guidi Bartholomaei, *Opusculum de 243 contradictionibus quae in Scoti operibus apparenter videntur, quarum singulis suas adhibet solutiones* (among the *Opera omnia* I. Duns Scoti, ed. Vivès, XXVI, 403-490).

[87] Cf. *Conciliationes locorum ex Quodlibetis Scoti cum aliis eiusdem Doctoris locis, quae inter se apparenter opponi videntur, a R. P. Cavello adiunctae* (ibid., 347-401).

wants to know which of Scotus' works contain his genuine doctrine. Since not all of his works carry the same weight, a distinction must be made between those works which were *accurately* written or dictated by him with a view to their publication, and those written by his disciples as they were listening to his lectures or compiled and published under his direction. On the basis of this principle, a first and distinctive place must be assigned to the *Ordinatio*, together with the *Lectura Oxoniensis* and the *Reportatio examinata*, as well as to the *Quaestiones super metaphysicam* and the *Quodlibet*. The questions *De anima*, and especially the *Theoremata*, ought to be considered as the least reliable sources for the knowledge of Scotus' genuine thought.[88]

Athenaeum Pontificium Antonianum,
Rome

Translated from the Latin by Bernardine M. Bonansea, O.F.M.

[88] The last proofs of this article had already been corrected when Father Henry Docherty sent me his article "The Brockie Forgeries" dealing with the historical and critical value of the *Monasticon Scoticum* of Brockie (cf. above, note 19), published in *The Innes Review*, 16, 1 (1965), 79-127. He asserts that "the so-called Codex Tueedianus, to the extent that Brockie intended it to be accepted, simply did not exist; that the transcript of a Conventual Register at Haddington quite clearly belongs to that same category" (p. 94) . . . "in his anxiety to substantiate his unique thesis on the origin and early life of Duns Scotus, Brockie actually introduces the allegedly relevant clause from the Tweedie Codex and Register in no less than three different original versions, all variously corrected and two duly cancelled, and with the bold emphasis of its having been found 'his verbis', 'nominatim', and 'expressis verbis'. This is surely the high water mark of Marianus Brockie's catalogue of bogus charters, fictitious histories, imaginative hagiography, outright mendacity, and crass effrontery. On this testimony alone has rested the Maxton-Littledean theory on the birthplace of John Duns Scotus" (p. 121).

Father Docherty has accepted the theme "Duns Scotus and Brockie" for the Scholastic Congress to be held at Oxford and Edinburgh (August 29-September 3, 1966). In the meantime Scottish historians can evaluate the force of the arguments expounded so accurately by the young historian, and give judgment on a subject which interests not only the Franciscans and Duns Scotus, but the general ecclesiastical history of Scotland as well.

2
THE ORIGINALITY OF THE SCOTISTIC SYNTHESIS

by

EFREM BETTONI

The subject here considered can be approached from two distinct points of view: one historical, the other theoretical. To approach it from a historical viewpoint, one must determine on the basis of available data the aims that Duns Scotus wished to achieve in the elaboration of his system which won for him so important a place among the masters of scholasticism. To approach it from a theoretical viewpoint means to indicate and clarify the Scotistic thesis in which is found that new perspective or insight which shows Scotus' achievement of his historical objective, and is offered to us as the speculative nucleus about which the other Scotistic doctrines turn. In this study I intend to approach the subject from both points of view, beginning with the first.

For one who attempts to study a philosopher's thought, the surest way to avoid fatal mistakes and overly subjective reconstructions is that of ascertaining first of all what preoccupations and problems were facing his mind. Such ascertainment is possible only on one condition: to recall to mind with the greatest possible objectivity the picture of the speculative trends and discussions that crossed and intertwined in the schools and in the cultural environment in which the thinker grew and moved. Philosophical meditation cannot be reduced to a man's monologue with himself. To a greater or lesser extent, it always originates and explicates itself as a critical dialogue with one or more interlocutors with whom the philosopher is placed in contact by historical circumstances. It is precisely for this reason that philosophical inquiry, while always concerned with perennial problems, is reborn in every philosopher in response to movements and trends connected with a determined historical context.

Our question, then, is this: How did the situation look to the eyes of young Duns Scotus from the point of view of philosophy as he was studying and preparing himself for a teaching career? By what speculative trends was it characterized? What were the points of contact and the conflicting theses among the masters then drawing the attention of everyone at Oxford and at Paris? One needs only recall that, for reasons known to all, the fundamental problem dominating the thirteenth century was that of Aristotelianism. As scholars gradually uncovered and mastered the doctrines contained in Aristotle's works, or believed to be his, the question ever became more relevant in their minds: is it worthwhile to abandon without regret traditional doctrines derived at least in part from St. Augustine's authority and to join the school of Aristotle? In other words, does Aristotelianism really offer logical tools and philosophical categories more perfectly adapted than those of Neoplatonism to advance the theological development of revealed truths and to strengthen the rational basis indispensable to Christian thought? After a period of uncertainties and confusion, traceable to the Neoplatonic contaminations to which Aristotelianism had become subject, opinions had become noticeably clarified between 1260 and 1270 and three distinct positions had been defined.

Among the masters teaching on the faculty of Arts in Paris, the thesis of Siger of Brabant was steadily gaining greater favor. In their judgment the most logical attitude to take in regard to Aristotle was to study his thought with no further preoccupation except that of drawing out all its consequences. To approach Aristotle's works merely for the purpose of deriving from them principles and conclusions that could be useful to theological research meant to lose part of the Aristotelian lesson totally dependent on reason. That this could lead to conclusions in contrast with revealed truths should not cause worry. Is it not inevitable that human reason should show itself inferior to divine teaching?

The masters of theology were unanimous in refusing to reverse the terms of the problem in this way. Convinced that the results of rational investigation cannot be intrinsically valid when conflicting with revealed truth, they maintained that the Aristotelian doctrines were acceptable only to the extent that they could be used within the framework of theology.

But in the evaluation of the possibilities of Aristotelianism being placed in service of theological research, the theologians were divided into two different currents. While St. Thomas, continuing and perfecting the teaching of St. Albert the Great, tried to show that Aristotelian philosophy, reduced to its true principles, provides theological speculation with a set of rational, homogeneous, and coherent tools, other theologians, struck by the negative aspects of Aristotle's thought, moved from cautious optimism to a gradually increasing distrust of Aristotelianism. I refer especially to St. Bonaventure, whose opposition to Aristotelianism, kept in shadow in his *Commentary on the Sentences,* becomes conscious and explicit in his latest writings, especially the *Collationes in Hexaemeron.* "Historically," writes Fr. Veuthey, "it seems that the more St. Bonaventure comes to know Aristotle and Aristotelianism becomes dominant in the schools, the more he opposes it and defends St. Augustine and the inspiration that had hitherto prevailed in Christian philosophy and theology."[1]

It was inevitable that the conflict between these two tendencies, which had remained under cover until the death of St. Thomas and St. Bonaventure, should explode and come into open light. It was in the logic of things that at first the clash should be resolved in favor of the current that had remained more faithful to the Platonic-Augustinian tradition. This happened in 1277 when the Bishop of Paris, Stephen Tempier, promulgated the long list of theses censured by the theological faculty.

The fact that among the speculative trends censured was also the moderate Aristotelianism of St. Thomas should not surprise the historian with a knowledge of the situation. From 1270 the opposition to the Angelic Doctor's "novelties," that is, his conscious and explicit acceptance of Aristotle's metaphysical, psychological, and cosmological doctrines, had been consolidated mainly through St. Bonaventure's disciples. Dominant among them was the impetuous John Peckham, but opposition was shared more or less vigorously by the majority of masters of theology both at Paris and at Oxford.

It must not be forgotten that the philosophic-theological trend prevailing in the Roman Curia up to the end of the thirteenth century was Augustinian. The fact that until 1305 the Masters of the Sacred Palace, that is, the official theologians of the papal court, were Franciscans, and that among them were two authentic cham-

---

[1] L. Veuthey, "La philosophie augustino-franciscaine au moyen-âge," in *Scholastica ratione historico-critica instauranda, Acta Congressus Scholastici Internationalis* (Rome, 1951), p. 634.

pions of Augustinianism, John Peckham and Matthew of Acquasparta, are significant indications.

If it is correct to recognize the fact that the exaggerations of the Latin Averroists cast many shadows on the moderate Aristotelianism of St. Thomas, one must not underestimate the weight that fidelity to traditional speculative trends by the large majority of the masters had on the Bishop of Paris' decisions. Many reservations need be made, then, to the thesis of those historians who have attempted to present the condemnations of 1277 as a rash act by Stephen Tempier urged on by a small group of masters irritated by the successes of the Thomistic teaching. As certain scholars have recently proved very effectively,[2] the Bishop of Paris did not act of his own initiative, but at the solicitation of Rome, which was disturbed by the trend that things were taking.

It is possible that the bishop's intervention went further than the papal intentions. Nevertheless it is undeniable that it interpreted a sentiment and expressed a widely spread uneasiness. In fact, are not all experts on medieval studies agreed in admitting that St. Thomas' teaching marks a decisive turning-point in the line of thought followed up to then in the theological schools? Now, history uniformly teaches that novelties at first cause distrust and misunderstanding, which are all the more profound as the innovations seem to be more revolutionary.

In the light of such facts and considerations, the revival of the neo-Platonic theses in opposition to the Aristotelianism of St. Thomas, noticeable between 1270 and 1280 at Paris and Oxford, appears altogether obvious. It appears even more so if one thinks that the revival was placed under the authority of St. Augustine. Equally obvious seems the fact that the most active among the opponents of Thomism should have been direct disciples of St. Bonaventure, that is, the better known Franciscan masters of that time: John Peckham, Matthew of Acquasparta, Gonsalvus of Spain, William de la Mare, Vitalis du Four, and Walter of Bruges. To the last goes the credit of having fathered the battle-cry: *"Plus credendum est Augustino et Anselmo quam Philosopho."*

When placed in this milieu, certain stands, recalled by some historians with an air of shock, take on a precise meaning and become understandable. Such are William de la Mare's composition of the

[2] See, for instance, A. Callebaut, "Jean Pecham et l'Augustinisme," in *Archivum Franciscanum Historicum*, XVIII (1925), 441-72.

Correctorium fratris Thomae (1277-1279), the directive of the Franciscan general chapter held at Strasbourg in 1282,[3] the emotional and radical antiaristotelianism of Peter John Olivi,[4] and above all the effort to give the rather vague traditional Augustinianism a more homogeneous and precise philosophical status in order to present it as a valid alternative to Thomistic Aristotelianism.

Naturally, St. Thomas' disciples were not idle, but turned to the defense of the memory and doctrine of their great master. The Dominicans, Giles of Lessines, John Quidort, Bernard of Auvergne, Richard Clapwel, Hannibal of the Annibaldi, and others displayed remarkable activity in bringing to light in speech and writing the balance and orthodoxy of the Thomistic theses taken as targets by their opponents.

At first the masters faithful to St. Thomas' teaching restricted themselves to predominantly defensive tactics, but towards 1290 they moved to a counteroffensive with Hervaeus of Nedellec and Thomas Sutton as authors of strongly polemical writings directed first against Henry of Ghent and later against Duns Scotus. To prepare a situation favorable to a return of Thomistic Aristotelianism, Geoffrey of Fontaines and Giles of Rome had contributed in a notable way: Geoffrey by his criticism of Henry of Ghent's Augustinian psychology and by his vigorous and explicit restrictions on the propriety of the sections of the 1227 condemnations relating to St. Thomas' teaching, and Giles by returning to and developing, not without some exaggeration, the Thomistic theory of the real distinction between *essentia* and *esse*.

The authorities of the Dominican Order, too, by opportune disciplinary measures tried first to block opposition to Thomism and, later, to support that widening consent to the Thomistic theses which appeared with increasing clarity. The provincial chapter

---

[3] G. Fussenegger, "Definitiones Capituli Generalis Argentinae celebrati anno 1282," in *Archivum Franciscanum Historicum*, XXVI (1933), 127-40. My reference is to the directive which reads: "Item minister generalis imponit ministris provincialibus, quod non permittant multiplicari Summam fratris Thomae nisi apud lectores rationabiliter intelligentes; et hoc nonnisi cum declarationibus fratris Wilhelmi de Mara, non in marginibus positis, sed in quaternis et huiusmodi declarationes non scribantur per aliquem secularem."

These "declarationes" compiled by the author of the *Correctorium* are a recast of this latter work. Cf. *Declarationes Mag. Gulielmi de la Mare o.f.m. de variis sententiis S. Thomae Aquinatis*, ed. Pelster, Opuscula et Textus, 21 (Münster i.W., 1956).

[4] E. Bettoni, *Le dottrine filosofiche di Pier di Giovanni Olivi*, Pubblicazioni dell'Università Cattolica del Sacro Cuore, Nuova serie, Vol. 73 (Milan, 1960).

held in Milan in 1278 deplored opposition to the moderate Aristotelianism of St. Thomas by the Oxford Dominicans. The following year, the provincial chapter of Paris forbade masters who had little or no sympathy for the Angelic Doctor's theses to criticize them publicly. In the provincial chapter meeting in Paris in 1286 it was decided to suspend from teaching Dominicans who persisted in their opposition to the Aristotelianism of St. Thomas. By the start of the fourteenth century, Thomism was well on its way to emerging as the official doctrine of the Dominican Order. In fact both the provincial chapter of Zaragoza (1309) and that of Metz (1313) prescribed to Dominicans holding a chair to follow faithfully St. Thomas' teaching.

Thus the last three decades of the thirteenth century witness the establishment within scholasticism of two well-defined and distinct currents of thought fully armed against one another. In these years the premises and foundations were laid for the two schools, the Dominican and the Franciscan, that were to face each other through the centuries as "two different expressions of the same sense of the glory of God."[5]

At this point it is permissible to inquire: could this state of antagonism which had been developed between the masters who maintained the necessity of not deviating from the teaching of St. Augustine and those who defended the validity of the Aristotelian alternative as presented by St. Thomas but repeatedly disavowed by ecclesiastical authorities—by Stephen Tempier on March 7, 1277 and by Robert Peckham on December 29, 1294, with the tacit consent of Rome—fail to influence the spirit of the young Duns Scotus, who between 1281 and 1298 was completing his philosophical and theological studies at Oxford and Paris under the direction of the most renowned masters of the Order? He was in effect in daily contact with men assuredly venerable in his eyes who saw in the Aristotelianism of St. Thomas a dangerous deviation that must be attacked with all their powers.

Account being kept of all these circumstances, it is not likely that Duns Scotus was exposed to the temptation of espousing in full the cause of Augustinianism and of becoming rigid with extreme opposition to Aristotelianism, no matter how moderate it may be. In such a case, Duns Scotus, like other Franciscan masters, would have

[5] E. Gilson, *The Spirit of Mediaeval Philosophy*, trans. by A. H. C. Downes (New York: Charles Scribner's Sons, 1940), p. 141.

tried to deviate as little as possible from St. Bonaventure's teachings, and in philosophical doctrine he would likewise have preferred St. Augustine's guidance to that of Aristotle. Instead, Duns Scotus' writings breathe an atmosphere remarkably different from the one that prevails in the works of St. Bonaventure's disciples of the first and second generations.

If it is true that Duns Scotus criticizes many Thomistic theses, it is also true that he shuns any polemical harshness and always motivates his dissent with a critical but calm analysis of the arguments upon which St. Thomas bases his conclusions and, above all, he does so by appealing not to St. Augustine but to Aristotle. Duns Scotus has great respect for the Stagirite, whom he clearly knows in depth. I am not aware that anyone has ever accused Scotus of superficial knowledge of Aristotelian thought. Duns Scotus often disagrees with St. Thomas on the interpretation of this or that Aristotelian principle, and of this or that Aristotelian thesis. However, in every instance it can be shown that it is always possible to find support for his interpretation in the selfsame texts of Aristotle.[6] P. Raymond has gone so far as to write that "Duns Scotus is as much a disciple of Aristotle as St. Thomas is."[7] By these words, the Canadian Scotist does not mean that the Subtle Doctor is as convinced and coherent an Aristotelian as St. Thomas; he intends to underline the point that Scotus is neither more nor less familiar with Aristotle's writings than the Angelic Doctor.

A reading of Scotus' works offers clear confirmation of this. Aristotle's authority has always the first place, not only in the strictly philosophical writings (the commentaries on Aristotle's logical works and the "quaestiones" on his *Metaphysics*), but also in the many pages of his theological works where metaphysical, psychological, or cosmological problems are discussed. Aristotle's opinions are quoted and subjected to detailed analysis. In brief, Duns Scotus shows in every way that for him Aristotle is an author

---

[6] Cf. on this point the excellent study of T. Barth, "Individualität und Allgemeinheit bei J. Duns Skotus," in *Weisheit und Wissenschaft*, 16 (1953), 122-41; 191-213; 17 (1954), 112-36; 18 (1955), 192-216; 19 (1956); 117-36; 20 (1957), 106-119; 198-220. Besides, as Roger Bacon had already remarked, "Litera sua [i.e., Aristotle's] est ita meretrix (quod solebant sapientes dicere) quod exponit se cuilibet, et in omnem partem vertitur, nec est aliquis qui ea familiari intellectu potest gaudere, sed labitur a quolibet eius intentio, sicut anguilla lubrica non potest teneri manibus attrectantis." *Compendium studii philosophiae*, ed. Brewer (London, 1859), p. 468.

[7] *Dictionnaire de théologie catholique*, IV.2, col. 1940.

to whom one must turn in philosophical studies as to an incomparable master. This is significant if one keeps in mind the fact that the works of many Franciscan masters, Matthew of Acquasparta and Roger Marston, for example, are true compilations of texts from St. Augustine and display the explicit intention of substituting, even on the philosophical level, the authority of the Bishop of Hippo for that of the Stagirite.

Evidently Duns Scotus did not share such aspirations. With him Aristotle becomes once more *"il maestro di color che sanno"* and the irreplaceable guide for all who wish to dedicate themselves to a fruitful rational inquiry. Nevertheless Duns Scotus could not share St. Thomas' optimism in regard to Aristotelianism. He considers hopeless any attempt to derive from Aristotelian principles a conception of reality that would be in conformity with that of Christianity.

Gilson indicates the roots of the disagreement between St. Thomas and Duns Scotus in these terms:

> "In St. Thomas' judgment, philosophers consider natures in themselves, while theologians consider them as coming from God and on the way to return to him. Philosophy and theology are distinct sciences, with regard to their objects. For Duns Scotus, on the other hand, philosophers are those who by considering natures solely in themselves show a natural inclination to think of reality in terms of necessity to the detriment of liberty."[8]

If I have correctly understood his thought, the illustrious medievalist wishes to say this: For St. Thomas the fact that the philosopher and the theologian consider reality from different prospectives does not imply that they will inevitably derive conclusions that are opposed to one another. They can arrive rather at complementary conclusions, that is, ordained to complete one another. On the contrary, Duns Scotus thinks that the philosopher, besides drawing conclusions that are partial and imperfect from the viewpoint of theology, will inevitably arrive at intrinsically unacceptable results. This is because by focusing his reflection on natures in themselves, the philosopher shuts himself up in a purely naturalistic perspective and thus makes it impossible to include the moment of liberty within his horizon.

Perhaps Scotus' point of view may be made more understandable

---

[8] E. Gilson, *Jean Duns Scot. Introduction à ses positions fondamentales* (Paris: Vrin, 1952), p. 642.

by saying that in his judgment Aristotle, and along with him all philosophers who have not known or do not take into account Christian revelation and therefore cannot conceive God as a person or as love, find themselves in the impossibility of understanding the ultimate meaning of things and of grasping the laws that rule things in their uttermost depth. To them reality can only appear as a system of necessary and immutable relationships in which there is no place for liberty. The universe of the philosophers can only be a universe without history, totally ruled by a rigorous determinism. For this reason Duns Scotus, like St. Bonaventure, is distrustful of a pure and separate philosophy, and again like St. Bonaventure, he is always ready to denounce not only its limitations but also its inevitable errors.[9]

But Duns Scotus' position in regard to philosophy in general and Aristotelianism in particular does not coincide completely with that of the Seraphic Doctor and of the Augustinians as a whole. Scotus does not limit himself to clarifying the higher dignity of "sapientia" compared with "scientia," that is, the completeness of theological solutions compared with those elaborated by philosophers, but thinks that as a philosopher he can expose the intrinsic weakness of the rational processes through which Aristotle and his Arab commentators reach their unfortunate conclusions. In other words, he divides the critical process he directs against philosophers into two stages. After having discussed and condemned their views as a theologian, in the second stage he tries to indicate that even on the purely rational level their arguments turn out to be far from incontrovertible.

In conclusion, one can say that if Duns Scotus has in common with the other masters of his own Order a critical attitude in regard to the Aristotelianism of St. Thomas and his continuators, he nevertheless significantly modifies the line of attack. He rejects as unrealistic the plan to oppose St. Augustine to Aristotle on the purely philosophical level. Instead, he prefers to master Aristotelian thought and method so as to be able to conquer his opponents' positions from within, that is, by showing that they can be criticized even within the ambit of an Aristotelianism clearly understood and using all its resources. From this it follows that in the writings of Duns Scotus we witness an attempt to show that the

---

[9] Cf. Gilson's abundant documentation in the first part of his work, *Jean Duns Scot.*

philosophical theses of the Augustinians are not in contrast with Aristotelianism as much as opponents would have others believe. On the contrary, it is even possible to defend them in the name of Aristotelian principles.

With this it should be clear that I share the view of those students of Duns Scotus who think that despite all the Aristotelian elements contributing to it, the Scotistic synthesis remains fundamentally Augustinian. Nevertheless, it is an Augustinianism renewed and regenerated, one can say, through a more profound and unprejudiced contact and dialogue with Aristotle, made possible by an unusual familiarity with his works and an equally unusual understanding of his thought.

In a series of articles Fr. Leo Veuthey has taken a stand decidedly against this historical interpretation.[10] Some fifteen years ago, Fr. Veuthey wrote:

> "Contrary to the efforts of those who wish to make Scotus an Augustinian, we maintain that the Subtle Doctor has kept many Augustinian formulas, but the spirit of his philosophy is essentially Aristotelian, even though his system is not pure Aristotelianism and could be called Augustinian-Aristotelianism. In him the Aristotelian inspiration, abstract, conceptualistic, and indissolubly tied to the secondary causes, is predominant. Here also, the passage from one mentality to the other is characterized by abandonment of intellectual illumination for Aristotelian abstraction, which is not the same as Bonaventure's abstraction."[11]

In other words, in Veuthey's judgment Duns Scotus, starting with the intention of finding in Aristotelianism a supporting ground for the Augustinian theses, was so affected by the Aristotelian thought as to remain its prisoner. His abandonment of the illuminationist ideology would be a decisive proof of this. It is not my intention here to dispute Fr. Veuthey's opinion. For the present I am satisfied with noting that he also agrees, at least on one point, with all other Scotistic scholars. He recognizes that Duns Scotus tries to overcome the Augustinism-Aristotelism opposition and arrive at a philosophical synthesis that would reconcile whatever was respectively valid in Aristotelianism and Augustinianism. That this was the purpose sought by Scotus is confirmed by the fact that in every

---

[10] Cf. in this connection E. Bettoni, *Vent'anni di studi scotisti, 1920-1940* (Milan: Vita e Pensiero, 1943), pp. 70-75.

[11] L. Veuthey, "La philosophie augustino-franciscaine," art. cit., p. 644.

problem he opens the road to his own solution through a critical review of both the Augustinian solution and that proposed by St. Thomas.

Until not too long ago the attention of the historians of medieval philosophy was particularly drawn to Scotus' untiring criticism of the Thomistic position. Thus one had come to see in Duns Scotus the vanguard of that tumultuous and indiscriminate rebellion against Aristotelianism into which the cultural circles of Paris and Oxford in general and the Franciscan circles in particular had drifted after St. Thomas' death. The phenomenon is easily explainable if one reflects both on the importance attributed to St. Thomas' thought and on the lack of information about the personality and the teaching of the masters of post-Thomistic scholasticism.

Today, however, no medievalist is ignorant of the fact that the main target of Scotus' criticism is not St. Thomas but Henry of Ghent, that is, precisely the most authoritative and convinced defender of the Augustinian theses at the University of Paris between 1274 and 1290.[12] For many reasons, this is a historical fact of the greatest importance.

In the first place, in his method and procedure, Duns Scotus indicates that he considers as refuted certain theses dear to his contemporary Augustinians or, at least, that he holds them weak from a logical point of view and irrelevant to the arguments with which they tried to introduce them. In short, he feels as keenly as possible the need to update and rejuvenate Augustinianism by freeing it from secondary or superfluous elements and to reconsider more objectively the contribution Aristotelianism could give to Christian thought.

Secondly, this historical datum places us in a position to understand why Duns Scotus devotes so many pages of his works to the exposition and critical evaluation of the views of his contemporaries. The cliché of a Duns Scotus as primarily a critical and therefore corrosive genius, popularized by uninformed or malicious historians, still survives in some manuals of the history of philosophy. We can now know the true reason for Scotus' persistent critical preoccupation. In his search for a viewpoint that would

---

[12] E. Gilson writes in this connection: "Duns Scotus is much more willing to discuss with Henry of Ghent than with St. Thomas." This does not alter the fact that *for us* St. Thomas remains "from a theoretical point of view, the most important of his interlocutors." *Jean Duns Scot*, p. 10.

permit him to unify divergent speculative positions, it was necessary to show the opportunity and, even more, the necessity of that effort. This could only be done by bringing into relief the partiality of the respective positions through a critical review of their logical foundations.

Lastly, having ascertained that Duns Scotus aims decidedly at overcoming a speculative conflict that threatened to crystallize, provides both a valuable point of orientation for one who sets about studying his thought and a measure of the generosity of his intentions. It also brings to light the constructive and positive character of the Scotistic synthesis.

Once the emergence on the historical plane of Scotus' speculative experience has been sufficiently established, it still remains to see on which theses, on the theoretical level, hinges his attempt to mediate between Augustinianism and Aristotelinanism as represented by the masters of theology in the last decades of the thirteenth century.

I have had occasion to mention that according to Fr. Veuthey the doctrinal point in which the departure of Duns Scotus from Augustinianism is effected, is the doctrine of the intellectual illumination. Abandonment of this doctrine on the part of Duns Scotus would mark the failure of his attempt at mediation between Augustinianism and Aristotelianism that constitutes on the historical level the character of his speculative experience. Thus we should conclude that if historically the Scotistic synthesis appears to have characteristics of originality, this originality vanishes and dissolves on the theoretical level. Substantially Duns Scotus would have surrendered to Aristotle even if he continued to wear the uniform of a follower of St. Augustine.

I concede to Fr. Veuthey that the doctrine of knowledge is the observation point best fitted to verify if Scotus, while drawing closer to Aristotelianism, has remained faithful to the basic positions of Augustinianism. However, contrary to Fr. Veuthey's view, I believe that the answer to this question must be in the affirmative. Scotus' teaching on the primary object of the human intellect affords a viewpoint that permits him to correct Aristotelian empiricism and at the same time to safeguard, by simplifying it, the radical Platonism of the illumination theory.[13]

---

[13] The limits of this study do not allow me to justify my affirmation with an analytical exposition of the Scotistic doctrine here mentioned. I have to be satisfied with general statements that will be understood only by him who is familiar with my preceding writings on the subject. Cf. E. Bettoni, *Duns Scotus:*

It is an undeniable fact that Duns Scotus himself proposed his thesis on the primary object of human intellect as a middle course between the teaching of those who asserted that God is the *primum cognitum,* and the teaching of those who instead maintained that the proper object of the human intellect is the *quidditas rei materialis.* As is well known, the key to the solution suggested by Scotus must be found in the distinction between the intellect considered from a purely theoretical standpoint, that is *ex natura potentiae,* and the intellect considered in its concrete situation, that is *pro statu isto.* For Scotus teaches that the primary and proper object of the intellect *ex natura potentiae* is the totality of what is, the *ens in quantum ens*; the proper object of the intellect *pro statu isto* instead is the *quidditas rei sensibilis.*

The meaning of these expressions needs clarification. By the first expression Duns Scotus did not intend to say only that the whole reality, God and creatures, enters in some way the cognitive field of the human intellect. He also meant that by its nature the human intellect has a radical capacity to know every being, and thus also God, with an act of direct intuitive knowledge. By saying that *pro statu isto* the proper object of our intellect is the *quidditas rei sensibilis,* he meant that *in statu viae* the only mode of knowing open to man is by abstraction.

The importance of this distinction is immediately evident. Scotus, as is well known, divides the true and the false between the two currents of thought that were then contrasting each other. Theoretically, the Augustinians were right. If the human intellect were in its most suitable condition, its gaze would be fixed first of all on God, in as much as he realizes in himself the highest degree of the *ratio entis* and contains all things as in their principles and cause. In point of fact, it was the Aristotelians that were right. As things now stand, the human intellect cannot start from God but only from the things that are given in sensible experience. Instead of an ideal mode of knowledge that would gradually move from the summit of being to its lowest level, man must be satisfied with knowl-

---

The Basic Principles of His Philosophy, trans. by B. Bonansea (Washington: The Catholic University of America Press, 1961), pp. 25-46; The same, *Il problema della conoscibilità di Dio nella Scuola Francescana* (Padua: Cedam, 1950), pp. 304-355; The same, "Punti di contatto fra la dottrina bonaventuriana dell'illuminazione e la dottrina scotista dell'univocità," in *Scholastica ratione historico-critica instauranda, Acta Congressus Scholastici Internationalis* (Rome, 1951), pp. 503-516.

edge that moves laboriously from the periphery to the center, exploiting all the data that it has gathered on the way from the senses and has filtered through the intellect. In other words, man must be satisfied with a knowledge that returns to the spring from its effluents after a long and painstaking journey.

Duns Scotus was of course aware of the fact that the Augustinians of his time were far from attributing to the human intellect the capacity of grasping by an intuitive act the divine essence and in it, as in a *medium quo,* all things. Their teaching was that human knowledge, for all its being abstractive and conceptual, is nevertheless a knowing of things in God in so far as it is conditioned by some truly primordial and primitive notion of God both in its beginning and in its development. In this sense, and only in this sense, did they affirm that God is the *primum cognitum.*

But even with this qualification the ontologism of the Augustinians did not find favor in the eyes of Scotus. The reason was not only the fact that such ontologism could not be verified by psychological experience, but primarily because an intellectual knowledge of God cannot be a *primum.* In fact, every concept falls within the area of the notion of *ens,* and this alone is the true and proper *primum,* the irreducible ground of all concepts.

The moderate Aristotelians in turn, while right, according to Duns Scotus, in their claim that human knowledge grows only through the abstractive process and thus finds its origin in sense experience, were nevertheless wrong in trusting too much in Aristotle's empiricism. They traced the reason for the need of abstractive knowledge to the fact that the human intellect is the substantial form of the body. Since the metaphysical structure of the human intellect is immutable, it follows that abstractive knowledge becomes the only possible knowledge proportionate to man. Consequently, the *quidditas materialis* takes up the importance of the *obiectum primum* of our intellect not only *pro statu isto* but also *ex natura potentiae.* With this is compromised the radical capacity of man to be elevated to a direct and intuitive knowledge of God, which Christian teaching recognizes and Aristotle should acknowledge if he were to be consistent.

Duns Scotus was convinced that with his theory, based as we have seen on the distinction between the primary object of the intellect *ex natura potentiae* and the object of the intellect *pro statu isto,* he could avoid both the unacceptable consequences of the Augustinian thesis and the incoherences of the Aristotelian. In affirming that *obiectum primum et proprium in ratione motivi* of the human intellect considered in the concrete situation in which it now finds itself is the *quidditas rei sensibilis,* he squares himself with experience which clearly shows that the knowledge of God is for us a point of arrival and not one of departure. By his qualification that the *obiectum primum* of the intellect *ex natura potentiae* is *ens in quantum ens,* he satisfies the demands of the Christian concept of man and explains also how it is possible for man in his earthly existence to rise to a knowledge of God, even if only in an inferential way.

Duns Scotus fulfills the requirements of the Christian concept of man because, as he himself explains so well, by saying that the primary object of man's intellect is *ens in quantum ens,* one implies that the totality of the real is included within the field of our intellectual knowledge. With this, man's radical capacity to be raised to a direct and intuitive knowledge of the supreme Being is guaranteed. Furthermore, the possibility, and hence man's exigency, to transcend the experiential world from which human thought originates, is also justified. Indeed, if the necessity to start from sense knowledge and to progress through the abstracting process does not depend on the nature of our intellect but only on external and temporary factors, it is clear that such a situation cannot affect the cognitive field as such, but only the modality with which the intellect will fulfill its task of revealing being.

The differences between St. Thomas' position and that of Duns Scotus, in appearance so close as to seem identical, soon reveal themselves in the systematic corollaries that derive from the one and from the other. From a theoretical point of view, the most significant difference is the univocity of the concept of being, which according to the Subtle Doctor appears to be the only possible foundation for the transcendentality of being and its attributes, and therefore for the legitimacy or positive character of rational theology.

There must be a reason for the fact that the concept of being, while being grasped in sensible reality, transcends this same reality and assumes the importance of a valid foundation for all our discourse about God. While for the Augustinians this reason is to be found in the divine origin of that concept, impressed, as it were, in the human soul by God as an indestructible reflex of the Uncreated

Truth or of the *rationes aeternae,* for Scotus it is to be found in the very nature of man's intellect, that is, in the fact that the human intellect *ex natura potentiae* is open to the totality of being and it has, so to speak, a feeling for it. It is because of the dynamic presence of this natural orientation to the totality, an orientation that resolves itself into a certain awareness of wholeness, that the human intellect, though bound to start from sensible reality, will not let itself be submerged in it. It is aware, in a first moment, that material being is not the only possible being and that the *ratio entis* does not coincide with the *quidditas rei materialis.* In a second moment, it becomes aware that only an eternal reality, immutable and infinite, has all that is needed to meet the logical exigencies of the *ratio entis* and to fully appropriate its prerogatives.

Now all this implies that the *ratio entis* is of itself predicable of God, and that it carries within itself from the very first moment and apart from any further reference all the logical principles that sustain man's philosophical discourse about God. This is the reason for Scotus' assertion that ". . . teachers, when dealing with God and such things as can be known about God, use the univocity of being in their way of speaking, even though they deny it in words."[14] It is Scotus' conviction that the univocity of the concept of being is intimately connected with the doctrine of the primary object of the intellect, that is, with the belief that the totality of being, and hence also and above all God, lies within man's cognitive field. These two assertions stand or fall together. One who recognizes man's capacity to speak of God admits *ipso facto* that God is included within the field of his cognitive power and, by a logical consistency, he must also admit that the *ratio entis* and the principles implicit in it constitute its sufficient ground.

If Scotist teaching on the primary object of the intellect, of which the doctrine of univocity is but a corollary, means all this, and if with this teaching Duns Scotus succeeded in laying down the foundation for metaphysical discourse and in critically vindicating for man the possibility of arriving at a knowledge of God, even with all the restrictions imposed by the necessity of proceeding in an abstractive way, it seems to be that this teaching constitutes a notable effort to overcome the opposition between Augustinianism and Aristotelianism that emerged in his time and threatened to crystallize. By dropping the theory of divine illumination, Scotus

---

[14] *Reportata Parisiensia,* I, d. 3, q. 1, n. 7; Vivès ed., XXII, p. 95.

assimilates the substance of Aristotelian teaching and vindicates also for man that dynamic self-sufficiency which must be recognized in every finite being, and is required by the perfection itself of the creative act.

At the same time Scotus does not abandon the substance of the Augustinian positions. He corrects and completes Aristotelian abstraction by bringing to light in an unusual way and with an unusual efficacy, as well as with a new critical awareness, the importance and the function of the notion of *ens* as the expression of the all-comprehensive intentionality of human thought and as the foundation of the whole conceptual order. To this notion one can very well reduce the amount of the *a priori* that can be found in human knowledge.

It would be easy to show that it is precisely this substantial fidelity on the gnoseological level to the Augustinian spirit that permits Duns Scotus to hold fast to such doctrines of traditional Augustinianism as the cognoscibility of the individual and the pluralism of forms, the intrinsic insufficiency of pure philosophy and the trust in rational arguments in the theological field, an activistic conception of the intellect and the primacy of the will, the partial recovery of the Anselmian argument, and the preeminence of intention in the moral order. It is this fidelity that explains Scotus' Avicennian preferences and the attention he gives to the *rationes necessariae* and, in general, to St. Anselm's thought.

The limits of this study do not permit me to develop this point, but I have done this in some way in another place to which I refer the reader.[15]

Università del Sacro Cuore,
Milan

---

[15] Cf. the entry "Scoto" (*Giovanni Duns*), in *Enciclopedia filosofica italiana*, III, cols. 463-72.

Editor's note: This article was translated from the Italian by Archimedes Fornasari.

3

THE FORMAL DISTINCTION

by

ALLAN B. WOLTER

Ockham once remarked that the formal distinction was as much a mystery as the Trinity itself.[1] Though he required it to explain why the expository syllogism

  This divine essence is the Father.
  This divine essence is the Son.
  Therefore, the Father is the Son.

is invalid without having recourse to the "supernatural logic" used by some of his contemporaries, he was loath to admit it elsewhere. Much of the mystery disappears, I think, if we view the distinction in the comparatively simple context in which Scotus introduced it rather than against the more sophisticated set of distinctions employed by some of the later scholastics.

Medieval philosophers generally admitted a threefold distinction: (1) the real distinction that exists between individuals in the extramental world, (2) the purely mental distinction created by the mind, and (3) an intermediate distinction which, though defined with reference to a mind, has some kind of basis in the thing. Historically the formal distinction had its origin in the attempt to clarify the precise nature of that foundation in reality.[2]

Since the real distinction also was not always understood in the same way, we must keep in mind what it meant to Scotus. In the works of Aquinas, for example, the term seems to have two basically different meanings, only one of which corresponds to the usage of

---

[1] *Guillelmus de Occam O.F.M.: Opera plurima*, Vol. III, *In Sententiarum I* (Lugduni, 1495), d. 2, q. 1, F [no pagination].

[2] For a history of the formal distinction see B. Jansen, S.J., "Beiträge zur geschichtlichen Entwicklung der Distinctio formalis," *Zeitschrift für katholische Theologie*, LIII (1929), 317-344; 517-544; M. Grajewski, O.F.M., *The Formal Distinction of Duns Scotus* (Washington: The Catholic University of America Press, 1944), pp. 102-123.

Scotus, Ockham or Suarez.³ For the latter, the real distinction is that which exists between individuals, be they substances or some individual accident or property. It invariably implies the possibility of separating one really distinct thing from another to the extent that one of the two at least may exist apart from the other. The mental distinction on the other hand involves separability only in a thinking mind. The things to be distinguished are, so to speak, created in the very act of thinking about them. They are *entia rationis*. The need for some intermediary distinction, so the scholastics argued, stems from the fact that individuals are characterized by certain objective properties which, though inseparable in reality, are separable in concept, since neither notion includes the other. The inseparability of these properties from the individual, however, should be understood as follows. As an individual characteristic, this property cannot be separated from that individual in the way a loose stone may be removed from a particular wall, or an organ transplanted from one body to another. In this sense, there is no real distinction between the property in question and other features which inseparably accompany it in a particular individual. Nevertheless, it may be possible to discover other individuals which possess this property yet lack some of the associated features found in the first individual. A favorite example of the scholastics was the case of the human soul. As the seat not only of the higher life of reason, but also of that which man has in common with the brute animal or insensate vegetable, the soul was said to possess intellective and vegetative properties. Yet not all the scholastics regarded these as so many really distinct parts since the soul, as immortal, should be substantially simple.⁴ God might create it or destroy it as

---

³ Thomists speak of a real distinction even where the *distinguenda* are separable only in thought (e.g. the soul and its faculties, essence and existence). Contrast this with the distinction between body and soul, mind and its thoughts, matter and any given form. At the time of Scotus and Ockham, it had become customary to restrict the name real distinction to the latter type.

⁴ A common view among the scholastics during the mid-thirteenth century, especially at Oxford, seems to have been that the human soul was a composite substance consisting of really distinct parts. One of the theses condemned by the Dominican Kilwardby in 1277 was *quod vegetativa, sensitiva et intellectiva sint una forma simplex*. Though this idea of the soul as a composite unity was frequently associated with the thesis of the plurality of forms (e.g. Roger Bacon, Philip the Chancellor, John Peckham), this was not always the case. In a letter written to his confrere, Peter of Conflans, Archbishop of Corinth, Kilwardby makes the interesting statement: "Positio de unitate formarum nisi plus dicatur non satis est mihi. Scio tamen, quod unus homo habet unam formam, quae non est una simplex, sed ex multis composita, ordinem ad invicem habentibus

a unit, but even he could not alter its properties in such a way that it would become a purely animal or vegetable form such as the brute or plant possessed. Neither could he transform it into a pure intelligence such as the angel was said to be. Still the angel, so they argued, has the property of intellectivity without either sensitivity or the ability to vegetate, whereas the brute beast has a capacity for sense knowledge while lacking what is essential to the higher life of reason.

There are two ways of describing this intermediary distinction. Viewed from the vantage point of the mind which separates these properties in concept, the distinction is mental *(distinctio rationis)*. Considered in terms of the intelligible features to which these concepts refer, however, the distinction is in some sense real. Thus St. Thomas insists that the distinction arises "not merely by reason of the one conceiving it but in virtue of a property of the thing itself,"[5] whereas Scotus speaks of it in the terminology of Peter Olivi as a distinction between *rationes reales*.[6]

This distinction was adopted primarily for the epistemological purpose of saving the objectivity of concepts that express a partial insight but not the whole truth about a reality which lacks really distinct parts in the sense explained above. It should not surprise us then that there is a certain unanimity among the scholastics about its objective nature. On the other hand, they differ considerably as to whether what such distinct concepts denote can be said to be nonidentical even before we begin to think about them. On this point there seems to be a marked development of thought from the time Aquinas composed his commentary on the second distinction of Book I of the *Sentences* to the day Scotus lectured on that work of Peter Lombard.

The area of general agreement, I believe, includes the following points: (1) Some kind of isomorphism exists between thought and reality in virtue of which the former may be said to be a likeness

---

naturalem et sine quarum nulla perfectus homo esse potest, quarum ultima completiva et perfectiva totius aggregati est intellectiva." Confer A. Birkenmajer, "Der Brief Robert Kilwardby's an Peter von Conflans und die Streitschrift des Aegidius von Lessines" in *Vermischte Untersuchungen zur Geschichte der mittelalterlichen Philosophie* (Beiträge zur Geschichte der Philosophie des Mittelalters, Bd. XX, Heft 5, Münster, 1922), p. 63.

[5] St. Thomas Aquinas, *Commentum in Librum I Sententiarum*, d. 2, q. 1, a. 2, *Opera omnia* (Vivès edition), VII, p. 36.

[6] Duns Scotus, *Quaestiones subtilissimae in Metaphysicam Aristotelis*, lib. VII, q. 19, n. 10, *Opera omnia* (Vivès edition), VII, p. 470.

or picture of the latter. This "likeness" should not be construed in terms of the relatively simple way a snapshot depicts a scene; it is something more sophisticated—not unlike Wittgenstein's "logical picture," perhaps—and is based upon what "shows itself" in both the world of facts and our thoughts about that world. (2) In virtue of this community of intelligible form, we can speak of *ratio* (the same would be true of the Greek *logos* or the Avicennian *intentio*) either as in things or in the mind. (3) To the extent that this ratio is a property or characteristic of the thing, we are justified in asserting that the individual in question is a "so and so." (4) Though such *rationes* can be conceived one without the other, since their definitions differ and what is implied by one is not implied by the other, nevertheless as characteristic of extramental reality they constitute one thing. In a word they are not individuals or really distinct parts in the way the real distinction was explained above.

The main area of difference concerns the meaningfulness of saying that one *ratio* is actually not identical with the other prior to our actually thinking of one apart from its mate. Though Aquinas does not raise this question in so many words, what he writes in his commentary on the *Sentences* about the attributes of God (which are so many *rationes*) might well be interpreted as favoring such an actual nonidentity, despite Cajetan's denial that such is the mind of the saint. Thus, for example, St. Thomas tells us that when we speak of a *ratio* as a property of a thing what we mean is

> . . . that in the thing outside the mind, there is something which corresponds to the conception of the mind as the significatum corresponds to the sign . . . and this occurs in a proper sense when the conception of the intellect is a likeness of the thing.[7]

To speak of different *rationes* in God in this sense, however, does not introduce a real distinction or plurality into the divine essence. And while

> . . . we must say that wisdom, goodness and such like are in God, each of these is the divine essence itself and thus all are one thing. But because each of them in its truest sense is in God and what wisdom means is not what is meant by goodness as such, it follows that they are conceptually different not just

[7] *Op. cit.*, a. 3, p. 37.

in virtue of the one conceiving them but by reason of a property of the thing itself.[8]

And he insists further that

> ... from all eternity when creatures were non-existent, and even if they never were going to exist, it was still true to say that he [God] is wise, good and the like. Neither does one notion signify what the other does in the way that the same thing is signified by synonyms.[9]

Henry of Ghent, writing several decades later, however, takes some pains to point out that the intentional distinction, as he calls it (*intentio* being a term he uses as a synonym for Aquinas' *ratio*), is merely potential prior to the act of thought, whereas it becomes actual only in the mind when the latter conceives one intention apart from the other.[10]

Perhaps one of Scotus' more illuminating remarks is that the formal distinction does not deny the intentional distinction of Henry but merely postulates what is needed in things to account for it.[11] With reference to Henry's version he writes:

> In such notions as these, does the intellect, I ask, have as object something in the thing? If not, we have a mere fiction of the mind. If it is the same thing, then the object of both concepts should be identical unless you grant that one and the same extramental thing formally generates two objects in the intellect. But in this case, it does not seem that the thing or anything of the thing is the object of my knowledge, but that the latter is something produced by the thing. But if the intellect knows something different in each concept, then our thesis is granted, since a difference is there prior to the concept.[12]

Unless I am mistaken, the precise difference between Scotus and Henry is this. If you grant their common scholastic assumption that our concepts and reality are somehow isomorphic, then the mere possibility of conceiving one property without the other re-

---

[8] *Ibid.*, a. 2, p. 35.
[9] *Ibid.*, a. 3, p. 39.
[10] Henry of Ghent, *Summa quaestionum ordinarum*, art. 27, q. 1 (Parisiis, 1520), Tom. I, fol. 162r O; *Quodlibet* V, q. 6 in *Disputationes quodlibeticae* (Parisiis, 1518), Tom. I, fol. 161rv. See also Duns Scotus, *op. cit.*, n. 4, p. 465.
[11] Duns Scotus, *op. cit.*, n. 10, p. 470.
[12] *Ibid.*, n. 5, p. 466.

quires some actual nonidentity or distinction of properties *a parte rei* which is logically prior to, and a condition for, our thinking of one apart from the other.

Scotus' point here, I believe, is well taken. As every great philosopher from Aristotle to our own day has noted, what a thing *can be* (or in this case, *can do*) is part and parcel of *what it is*. As Ludwig Wittgenstein pointed out, a thing's "possibilities," unlike their actualization, are not something accidental to the thing. They "must be written into the thing itself," so to speak, "from the beginning."[13]

That is why the acute Aquinas insisted that this distinction cannot be reduced purely and simply to a distinction of reason; it arises in part at least *ex proprietate ipsius rei*. Scotus, with his usual subtilty, is simply spelling out what such a statement implies, viz. that such "property-differences" are based upon what a thing is or is not in actuality. Two objects are not formally identical *a parte rei*, if one can be imitated without the other or if one can be distinctly known for what it is apart from the other. Some way of expressing this nonidentity or distinction of intelligible content, or imitable perfection, is needed. To say it is purely potential does not do justice to the actual basis that makes such a conceptual distinction possible. All concede that the positive basis for the distinct concept is not created by the mind in the very act of knowing it. Neither then, Scotus argued, is the nonidentity of what is known by each of two isomorphic concepts. To argue that the precise objective correlate of each of the two is in all respects actually identical seems to commit one to the dilemma pointed out by Scotus. Either but one true concept of the thing is possible or else, if we do have two concepts, they cannot be concepts of what is actually present, but are concepts of objects produced by the thing.

Scotus ascribes various names to the objective correlate of such concepts. His usual designation for it is *realitas* or *formalitas*, though he occasionally refers to it as an *intentio* or a *ratio realis*.[14]

---

[13] L. Wittgenstein, *Tractatus Logico-Philosophicus*, 2.012-2.0121, trans. D. F. Pears and B. F. McGuinness (London: Routledge and Kegan Paul, 1961), pp. 7-9.

[14] See especially the *Ordinatio* I, d. 2, nn. 399-407, *Opera omnia* (Vatican edition) II, pp. 355-358; also Scotus' remark in *Reportata Parisiensia* II, d. 1, q. 6, n. 20, *Opera* (Vivès ed.), XXIII, p. 556: "Intelligit idem ipse Avicenna per aliam intentionem quod ego dico per aliam formalitatem." The neologism "formalitas" or "little form" invites comparison between the properties of a formality and those traditionally ascribed to the Aristotelian "form" (such as its being the principle of intelligibility and actuality, or its being equated with essence). One

The distinction or nonidentity that obtains between such correlates he prefers to call "formal" but adds that you may also speak of it as a "virtual distinction"[15] since what you find in the thing is not really two things but "one thing which is virtually or preeminently, as it were, two realities."[16] You may even call it *distinctio rationis*, he says, apparently referring to St. Bonaventure's terminology,[17] where *ratio* means not something created by the mind, but rather expresses something of what the thing is insofar as the "whatness is an object of the intellect."[18]

This raises the interesting question as to how far Scotus himself may be responsible for the usage of latter day Thomists who commonly label this intermediate distinction as "virtual"? For while we find this term in Boethius, neither he nor Aquinas apply it in this connection. Suarez, on the other hand, seems to prefer this designation and Cajetan in trying to delineate more precisely how Scotus differs from Thomas declares that where Scotus postulates in the object an "actual formal distinction," Aquinas admits only a "virtual formal distinction."[19]

---

thing is certain, by means of the formal distinction Scotus was able to simplify a doctrine that seems almost traditional among Franciscan thinkers, that of a plurality of forms in man. On the one hand, Scotus recognizes the need of a *forma corporeitatis* that is really distinct from and other than the rational soul as the highest form in man. But differing from some of the earlier thinkers of this century like Roger Bacon, Kilwardby and others (Confer T. Crowley, *Roger Bacon, The Problem of the Soul in His Philosophical Commentaries*, Louvain: Editions de l'Institut Supérieur de Philosophie—Dublin: James Duffy and Co., 1950, especially pp. 136-152 for an account of the divergent views at this time), Scotus saw no need to postulate any real composition or distinction of forms in the human soul. For him the sensitive and vegetative "parts" are only formally distinct from the rational. While the same solution might conceivably be adopted to eliminate a plurality or hierarchy of further forms within the *forma corporeitatis*, not all interpreters of Scotus hold that he postulates only one organic form for the entire organism and its various parts. Some believe that he used "form of corporeity" as a collective term for a hierarchy of subordinate forms corresponding to the different organs of the body. In this connection see B. J. Campbell, *The Problem of One or Plural Substantial Forms in Man as Found in the Works of St. Thomas Aquinas and John Duns Scotus* (Philadelphia: University of Pennsylvania, 1940); B. Baudoux, "De forma corporeitatis scotistica," *Antonianum*, XIII (1938), 429-474; B. Vogt, "The *Forma corporeitatis* of Duns Scotus and Modern Science," *Franciscan Studies*, III (1943), 47-62.

15 *Ordinatio, loc. cit.*, p. 355.
16 *Ibid.*, p. 356.
17 St. Bonaventure, *Commentaria in quatuor libros Sententiarum*, lib. I, d. 5, art. 1, q. 1, ad 1, *Opera omnia*, Tom. I (Ad Claras Aquas: Ex typographia Collegii S. Bonaventurae, 1882), p. 113; *ibid.*, d. 26, q. 1, ad 2, p. 453; *ibid.*, d. 45, art. 2, q. 1, p. 804.
18 *Ordinatio, loc. cit.*, p. 355.
19 *Commentum in Summam theologicam* I, q. 39, art. 1 in *Sti. Thomae*

More important perhaps is the fact that Scotus calls the distinction one of reason *(distinctio rationis)*. This fact alone should make it clear that he did not claim the nonidentity in question could be defined or described apart from some reference to an intellect. If no intellect could exist, there would be no formal distinction. While Scotus insists the distinction is prior to the *act* of thinking (and hence is not created by the mind), he never says it is prior to the possibility of thought. Indeed, the possibility of knowing (which is one way of describing the intellect) and the possibility of being known (which is another way of saying "formality") are correlative terms. Each entails the other. Neither is logically nor ontologically prior, but they are technically *simul natura*.

It is a historical fact that Scotus did not invent this distinction but took it over from his contemporaries. On the other hand, those who adopted it after him were not loathe to cite him as a forerunner of their own views on the subject. As Ockham himself warned, we must not attribute to the Subtle Scot all the exaggerated claims made by others for this distinction. For one thing, I think it would be a mistake to believe that he, like some of the later formalists, regarded realities or formalities as some kind of "ontological bricks" characterized by fixed dimensions. A careful reading of what he says on the subject lends no support to such an interpretation. His account of the distinction is perfectly consistent with the admission that there is something fluid about the way we think of things, and hence about the way we draw the lines that separate one intelligible aspect from another. The one essential point seems to be that however we may choose to divide the perfections of a thing, if our concepts reflect something about the latter, there must be something positive in that thing which corresponds to these concepts. This positive entity or reality is not something the thing has only because we happen to be thinking about it at the moment. Perhaps a better analogy than "ontological bricks" would be that of a stage upon which different spotlights are playing, where each illuminated area represents what we grasp in one of our concepts. It is not necessary that the spotlights remained fixed; they may move about, and the areas illumined may even intersect in part. Scotus' point, I believe, would be this. Even before you switch the

---

Aquinatis Summa theologica cum Commentariis Thomae de Vio Card. Cajetani, Tom. I (Patavii: Ex typographia Seminarii, 1698), p. 261. See also F. Suarez, *De SS. Trinitatis mysterio*, IV, c. 4, n. 15 (Borgnet edition), Vol. I, 627; *idem, Disputationes metaphysicae*, disp. 7, sec. 1, Vol. 25, pp. 250ff.

spotlights on, or, what is more, if you never turned them on or even had any lights, it would still be meaningful not only to speak of what they would reveal if you had them to turn on, but there would also be grounds for denying that one part of the stage is simply identical with the other as regards what a light will reveal. For each possibly separate area of illumination would still be just what it is and would contain what is proper to itself. And it is what each has, and not just what we reveal or think it has, that makes the one area not simply identical with the other. For some nonidentity of what exists on the part of a thing, Scotus argues, must be logically prior to and a necessary condition for our being able to think of one without the other. Though Scotus repeatedly stresses that the formal distinction is logically prior to actual thought, I can find no passage where he suggests the distinction can be defined without reference to the possibility of separating the formalities in thought. In fact the whole historical context in which the distinction was born argues to the contrary.

Though no individual thing is so simple that it does not contain more than one formality, nor are formalities so distinct that they do not form one real thing, there are different ways in which formalities may be said to be one.

Consider, for the moment, the attributes of God. Though each is infinitely perfect, one attribute is not formally the other, since their definitions differ and one asserts what the other does not. Even the mode of infinity does not fuse the formal concepts. For to say that God's knowledge, for instance, is infinite, is to say that it comprehends all that can be known. Yet this is something quite different from saying that knowledge is formally love or that the senses of their several definitions are identical. But because each of God's attributes is infinitely perfect, we have no grounds for claiming that one formality perfects another in the way that parts are mutually perfected by their forming one whole.

But, says Scotus, the same need not hold for creatures. Here we can speak of a quasi-composition, not of course in any real or proper sense as would be the case were the parts really distinct. But if, in a thing characterized by two or more formalities, their combination, as it were, turns out to be something more than we might expect of the simple sum of the two, we may say that their togetherness constitutes a *per se*, rather than a *per accidens*, unity. In man or in the human soul, where both sensitivity and intelligence are present, each adds something as it were to the perfection of the other. The creative imagination of the artist, for example, which is born of their union, is something neither the brute beast with its sensitivity nor the angel with its intellectual life as such possess. Because of this we may say that in man, or in human nature, the abstract formalities of animality and rationality, though formally distinct, are so related that together they form not a mere aggregate of intelligible items which the mind lists in catalogue fashion, but they are so ordered to one another that they constitute a single intelligible whole.[20]

Not only must the attributes of God be formally distinct, says Scotus,[21] but some formal nonidentity must be postulated between the divine essence and what is proper or peculiar to each Person, if fallacies like the one mentioned at the beginning of this essay are to be avoided. If the Father communicates his nature to the Son, and together with the latter to the Holy Spirit, his paternity is something he shares with neither. Far from depending upon the divine intellect's actual knowledge, this nonidentity is a logically prior condition for God's awareness of the same.[22] Ockham will admit the existence of a formal distinction only in this case, but not in creatures or even between the attributes of God. Scotus, on the contrary, speaks of various degrees of the distinction and admits some form of it not only in the latter case, but also between the generic perfection and that expressed by the specific difference,[23] or between the unique haecceity or individuating difference of a thing and those features it has in common with other individuals.[24] He adds that the transcendental attributes of being are formally distinct from each other as well as from being. The same holds for the soul and its powers such as intellect and will.[25]

Since Scotus denies the real distinction between essence and existence some Scotists thought he might wish to substitute a formal distinction for the same, or at least a formal modal distinction.[26]

---

[20] *Ordinatio* I, d. 8, nn. 103-107, *Opera* (Vatican ed.) IV, pp. 200-202; *ibid.* nn. 218-221, pp. 274-276.
[21] *Ibid.*, nn. 186-217, pp. 254-274.
[22] *Ibid.*, d. 2, nn. 388-410, II, pp. 349-361.
[23] *Ibid.*, d. 8, n. 219, IV, p. 275; *Quaest. in Metaphys.*, loc. cit., n. 8, p. 468.
[24] *Opus oxoniense* II, d. 3, q. 6, n. 15, *Opera* (Vivès ed.) XII, p. 144.
[25] *Ibid.*, d. 16, q. unica, n. 17, XIII, pp. 43-44.
[26] For a survey of the problem see A. J. O'Brien's unusually perceptive study "Scotus on Essence and Existence," *The New Scholasticism*, XXXVIII (1964), 61-77. In addition to those interpreters he mentions, who ascribe to Scotus a formal distinction between essence and existence are S. Day, *Intuitive Cognition:*

The latter is the type of distinction found between a formality and its intrinsic mode such as "wisdom" and "infinite" in God, or "being" and "finite" in a creature.[27] Whereas the proper concepts of two formalities may be mutually exclusive, the concept of an intrinsic mode includes somehow the notion of the formality of which it is the mode. Yet the formality, let us say, of "being" or "wisdom," is not so identical with the mode or manner in which it exists in a concrete instance that it is impossible for the mind to prescind from the mode and still say something true and objective. Thus, for instance, one could say in all truth that God possesses the formal perfection of being or wisdom and still leave open whether the perfection in question is present in a finite or infinite degree.

It does not seem sufficient, however, to characterize the formal modal distinction as nothing more than a non-mutual formal distinction such as would hold, for example, between the perfection of animality and corporeity. For animality not only includes corporeity, but adds something to the formal character of the latter, viz. what is required for sense and vegetative life. Such is not the case with an intrinsic mode. One is tempted to say that what is added to our knowledge in the latter case pertains to the order of quantity rather than quality. This is true if we do not take quality and quantity as Aristotelian categories, but in an extended or transcendental sense, viz. that one represents a reply to a question of the form: "What kind of perfection does this have?" or "What type of thing is it?" whereas the other answers a query of the form: "How great is the perfection in question?" or "To what degree is such and such a characteristic present?" (Scotus, we know, was one of the first scholastics to show how variations in quality intensity might be treated quantitatively—an insight applied by the Merton schoolmen to the problem of motion, which made Galileo's description of the free-fall of bodies possible).[28]

But in differentiating the modal from the strict formal distinc-

---

A Key to the Later Scholastics (St. Bonaventure, N.Y.: Franciscan Institute, 1947), p. 63; J. Weinberg, *A Short History of Medieval Philosophy* (Princeton, N.J.: Princeton University Press, 1964), p. 218.

[27] *Ordinatio* I, d. 8, nn. 136-150, IV, pp. 221-227.

[28] M. Clagett, *The Science of Mechanics in the Middle Ages* (Madison: University of Wisconsin Press—London: Oxford University Press, 1959), p. 206. For a concise historical account of the development of the problem of intension and remission of forms see A. Maier, *Zwei Grundprobleme der scholastischen Naturphilosophie*, 2 ed. (Roma: Edizioni di Storia e Letteratura, 1951).

tion, Scotus seems to have had more in mind than this. In speaking of the comparative simplicity of various concepts used to describe God, Scotus makes the somewhat puzzling statement that "infinite being" is a simpler concept than "good being" or "true being" since "infinite" is not a quasi-attribute of being like "good" or "true," but expresses an intrinsic mode even as a certain intensity of whiteness expresses not some formal composition but an intrinsic mode of the quality.[29] What Scotus seems to be struggling to express, if somewhat obscurely because of a lack of analytical tools, is a problem not unfamiliar to the contemporary philosopher. The ontological structure of reality is not always faithfully reflected in language or thought. Though an expression like "infinite being" bears a superficial resemblance to "true being," it has a different logical form. The reality referred to by composite terms like "infinite being" or "intense whiteness" is so simple, says Scotus, that if it were known intuitively rather than in an abstract way, the distinction between a formality and its mode would be erased. Where two formalities are known intuitively, however, they still appear as two distinct formal objects.[30] Yet infinity is not so much a part of God's goodness, wisdom, or other formal perfection that if we teach a child, for instance, that God is good, wise, loving and so on without conveying in any way the information that he is such in an infinite degree, we have deceived the child and have not told the truth. Granted the information is not complete or perfect, what we know by means of such imperfect concepts is still true.[31]

Even though Scotus' remarks on the formal modal distinction leave much to be desired as to how far he would be willing to apply it, what he does say makes it clear enough that he considered even the formal distinction inadequate to express all the intelligible differences characteristic of reality. If we pursue this point farther, I think we could say that Scotus would not reject every distinction *a parte rei* between essence and existence, even if he would not necessarily consider it to be a strictly formal, or even perhaps a formal modal, distinction.[32]

[29] *Ordinatio* I, d. 3, n. 58, III, p. 40.
[30] *Ibid.*, d. 8, n. 142, IV, p. 224.
[31] *Ibid.*, nn. 143-145, pp. 225-226.
[32] In the *Quaestiones quodlibetales*, q. 13, n. 10 (Vivès ed.), XXV, p. 522, Scotus speaks of "aliqua distinctio objecti" between what is grasped by abstractive and intuitive knowledge respectively, but goes on to add that this distinction becomes apparent only when existence is grasped abstractly. This means that a formal difference between what is known through abstract knowledge (viz. what

The proper way to distinguish essence from existence, however, would seem to be in terms of what is required *a parte rei* for intuitive versus abstractive cognition and not, primarily at least, in terms of the objective basis for different types of concepts.

Unlike some current interpretations of the thomistic position, Scotus does not hold that existence is first grasped in and through an existential judgment, but rather by a simple act of intellectual awareness called intuition. For like the generality of the scholastics, he considers every judgment—as "an act of composition and division"—to presuppose logically, if not psychologically or temporally, some prior act of simple apprehension. There are many primary contingent propositions of which we are absolutely certain (e.g. "I doubt such and such" or "I am thinking of such and such," etc.). Since this certitude cannot be explained by a knowledge of the conceptual terms of the proposition in question, we must admit some prior simple awareness of the existential situation that verifies the proposition. This cannot be mere sensory knowledge, since the existential judgment often involves conceptual or non-sensory meanings as in the examples cited above.

Some form of intellectual intuition precedes not only every existential judgment, but probably every abstract concept which the mind forms. This is certainly the case according to Ockham, who develops the scotist doctrine of intuition, but it seems to be implicit, at least, in what Scotus says on the subject.[33]

Simple apprehension, then, can be either an intuitive or an abstractive cognition. The latter is concerned with "essences" or essential features in the sense that the concepts which are the end product of such simple awareness represent answers to questions of the form *Quid est?*, that is to say, they are questions that are answerable in terms of the categories to which the features in question belong. We might note that an intrinsic mode such as infinity or finitude, or the degree of intensity of a quality like white-

---

the object is) and what is known by intuitive knowledge (viz. the object as existing and present here and now) concerns not so much the content of what is known as the way in which the object known moves the intellect, viz. in itself and by reason of existing and interacting with the mind, or (in the case of abstract knowledge) in and through a species.

[33] For a collection of texts of Scotus and Ockham on this subject see S. Day, *Intuitive Cognition: A Key to the Significance of the Later Scholastics* (St. Bonaventure, N.Y.: The Franciscan Institute, 1947); P. Boehner, *Ockham, Philosophical Writings* (Edinburgh: Thomas Nelson and Sons, 1957), pp. 18-27; idem, "The Notitia Intuitiva of Non-Existents According to William Ockham," *Traditio*, I (1943), 223-275.

ness, would seem to be an essential feature in this broad sense of the term. Intuitive cognition, on the other hand, while it may include all the data or information found in a corresponding abstractive cognition, invariably includes something more, viz. that additional knowledge or information of the fact that it exists.

The proper way of distinguishing essence from existence for Scotus then would seem to be in terms of that objective feature of any object, situation or thing that makes it possible not merely to identify what it is, but to assert that it is. At the primary level at which this datum is presented, existence is not strictly speaking "conceivable"; neither is intuitive awareness properly speaking a concept. For as we ordinarily understand this term, a concept is always the result of abstractive cognition. By reflection upon what is common to all instances of intellectual intuition, the mind can form an abstract concept of existence. And it is this concept that seems to be related to the concept of what a thing is as something formally other, or as an additional modality. But it would be a mistake, Scotus recognizes, to argue from the superficial likeness of concepts like "rational animal," "intense whiteness," and "an exising person" to the same ontological structure or distinction *a parte rei*.[34]

If our analysis of the reasoning that led Scotus to postulate the formal distinction is substantially correct, then it would seem that the strict formal distinction, the formal modal distinction and that between essence and existence have something in common and yet, for all that, differ by reason of the objective basis for the distinction.

All three arise from the desire to distinguish those characteristics of reality that make it possible to have different types of knowledge about it. The features known, however, are separable only in concept, though at the point where this becomes possible, the concepts may not represent the same level of abstraction or perhaps refer to reality in the same manner. To put the matter briefly in modern terminology, they have not the same "logical form." On the other hand, to speak of the distinction as one that is simply created by the mind does not do full justice to the fact that more is required of reality to justify one type of knowledge or concept than is needed to justify another. The meaning of "more" can be explicated as

[34] See the discussion in *Ordinatio* I, d. 3, n. 58, III, p. 40 and d. 8, n. 138ss, IV, p. 222ff; also Scotus' remarks in *Collationes seu Disputationes subtilissimae*, collatio 13, n. 5 (Vivès ed.), V, p. 202.

follows. If the information conveyed or expressed by *A* includes the information conveyed or expressed by *B*, but not vice versa, where *A* and *B* stand for two types of knowledge (e.g. intuitive versus abstractive knowledge of the same object), or for two concepts (e.g. infinite wisdom versus wisdom) or sets of concepts (e.g. rational animal versus animal), then what is denoted by *A* is not simply identical *a parte rei* with what *B* denotes, and the distinction or nonidentity in question is one of a greater or lesser degree of intelligibility.

But this way of describing the three distinctions obscures the fact that it was made possible only by conceiving the *distinguenda* abstractly, for only at the level of abstractive cognition do they appear as formally different objects of intelligibility. Two of the distinctions (the formal modal and the essence-existence distinction) evaporate as it were if the reality in question is known intuitively. Scotus made an initial attempt to indicate how the first of these differs from the formal distinction proper in terms of what he calls the relative "simplicity" of the concepts in which these objective differences are mirrored. Admittedly this mode of description may not have proved particularly enlightening to Scotus' contemporaries or immediate followers. It does seem to make a bit more sense, perhaps, in view of Russell's and Wittgenstein's early attempts to determine to what extent it is possible to express the metaphysical structure, or what they called the "logical form," of the world in thought or language.

Had Scotus been cognizant of their speculations on the subject, I think he might have pointed out that if the essence-existence distinction resembles in some respects a formal distinction, or still more the distinction between a formality and its mode, the ontological "structure" is quite different in the three cases. And, though it is far from adequate and deserves to be pursued further, it might do for a beginning at least to say that one way in which the existence of a real object differs from both a formality or an intrinsic mode like the finitude of a creature or the intensity of a color is that it is possible to grasp it primarily and perfectly only in an intuition. What a formality is, or what intrinsic mode characterizes a given object, however, is something that can be known through an abstract form of cognition with an immediacy and perfection that is not the case with the modality called existence (e.g. by infused, yet abstract, knowledge such as Scotus suggests was granted to St. Paul or the prophets).[35] In its "here and now-ness" the existence of an existing essence, quality or situation is something unique and non-universal. Only when it is grasped in some secondary and abstract form of knowledge does it appear to have a commonness or universal features, and as having such, to be related to "whatness" or quiddity as a mode to its subject.

The Catholic University of America

[35] This seems to be the whole point of Scotus' remark: "De quocumque objecto scientiae potest haberi cognitio simpliciter distinctissima abstractiva objecti citra intuitivam . . . Omnis scientia est de re non praecise, ut existens est, quod intelligo sic, quod ipsa existentia, etsi sit ratio intellecta in objecto, vel citra objectum, tamen non necessario requiritur, ut actualiter conveniens objecto, inquantum objectum est scibile" *Quaest. quodlibetales*, q. 7, n. 8; XXV, 290. An intrinsic mode like finitude in creatures or infinity in God, however, pertains to what is necessarily connected with the essence and hence what is *scibile* in the technical sense of *sciri* according to the requirements set down by Aristotle at the beginning of the *Posterior Analytics*.

4

A PROBLEM FOR REALISM: OUR MULTIPLE
CONCEPTS OF INDIVIDUAL THINGS AND
THE SOLUTION OF DUNS SCOTUS

by

S. Y. WATSON

How we can have multiple concepts of individual things presents a problem for philosophical realism. The term realism is, as everyone knows, used in a variety of more or less related senses. When authors speak of the realism of Duns Scotus, however, they are usually referring to his defense of a close correspondence of our concepts to the real and in particular of a more perfect foundation for our universal concepts as such than is generally conceded. The realism of Scotus has often been treated before, sometimes sketchily, sometimes at considerable length, sometimes with great competence, sometimes with little. In any case, the main outlines of his doctrine in this regard should by now be rather well known, so that it would serve no useful purpose merely to add another introductory account to those which already exist.[1]

What may be of use, however, is a fresh consideration, free of extensive textual analysis, of one of the important problems underlying Scotus' realism, the answers to which he was more or less consciously and deliberately seeking in the formulation of his own positions. This is what we shall attempt to do here. Our interest is

[1] The reader who is not already well acquainted with Scotus' realism and who desires a concise account of this unbroken by any lengthy consideration of the problems involved in and for themselves is recommended to consult Efrem Bettoni, O.F.M., *Duns Scotus: The Basic Principles of His Philosophy*, transl. and ed. by Bernardine Bonansea, O.F.M. (Washington, D.C., 1961), pp. 53-65; and Allan B. Wolter, O.F.M., "The Realism of Scotus," *The Journal of Philosophy*, LIX (1962), 725-36. The latter, incidentally, suggests some very stimulating comparisons on certain points between Scotus and Wittgenstein of the *Tractatus*. Moreover, in another, earlier, work, *The Transcendentals and Their Function in the Metaphysics of Duns Scotus* (St. Bonaventure, N.Y., 1946), Wolter deals (pp. 14-30; 100-11) with questions connected with Scotus' realism, and offers a particularly fine exposition of the problem of "partial" knowledge pp. 14-21).

not merely historical, but also more properly philosophical, for we believe that this problem, like the other problems referred to, is still alive and greatly needs to be discussed.[2] To be sure, it is our conviction that Scotus made a great contribution toward the solution of these problems that has led us to study them in the light of his writings.[3]

[2] The growing interest in the philosophy of Charles Sanders Peirce is one of various factors contributing to a better appreciation of the contemporaneity of some of Scotus' ideas. In this fiftieth anniversary year of Peirce's death (1914-1964) it is surely appropriate to devote some little space, if only in a note, to a consideration of the influence of Scotus' realism on this great American philosopher. Peirce himself was wont to emphasize this: "The works of Duns Scotus have strongly influenced me" (1.6). This and the following references are to *Collected Papers of Charles Sanders Peirce* [Cambridge, Mass.]. Vols. I-VI were edited by Charles Hartshorne and Paul Weiss [1931-35]; Vols. VII-VIII by Arthur W. Burks [1958]). Peirce regrets that Kant had not read Scotus (1.19). He waxes eloquent in his praise of scholasticism in general and of Scotus in particular (8.11). He gives a sketch of Scotistic realism as he understands it (8.18). He calls himself "a Scotistic realist" (4.50) and even "a Scotist" *tout court (Ibid.)*. However, he is far from agreeing with Scotus on all points. In the passage just cited he explains his stand: "In calling himself a Scotist, the writer does not mean that he is going back to the general views of 600 years back; he merely means that the point of metaphysics upon which Scotus chiefly insisted and which has since passed out of mind, is a very important point, inseparably bound up with the *most* important point to be insisted upon today." This point, to be sure, is *realism*. Peirce feels that this is especially important for science. In fact, he tells us that if the logic and metaphysics of Scotus, "not slavishly worshipped, but torn away from its medievalism, be adapted to modern culture, under continual wholesome reminders of nominalistic criticisms, I am convinced that it will go far toward supplying the philosophy which is best to harmonize with physical science" (1.6); for, as he says, "Realism is implied in modern science" (4.50). Peirce believes, however, that scholastic realism does not go far enough. "Even Duns Scotus is too nominalistic. . . ." (8.208), though, no doubt, what Peirce really means is that Scotus is not sufficiently Kantian or Hegelian! In any case, he tells us his own view "amounts to extreme scholastic realism" *(Ibid.)*.

Most full-length studies of Peirce deal with Scotus' influence on his realism. The outstanding treatment, however, is found in John F. Boler, *Charles Peirce and Scholastic Realism: A Study of Peirce's Relation to John Duns Scotus* (Seattle, 1963). Besides this excellent study one may wish to consult the brief, but densely packed essay of Charles K. McKeon, "Peirce's Scotistic Realism," in *Studies in the Philosophy of Charles Sanders Peirce*, ed. by Philip P. Wiener and Frederic H. Young (Cambridge, Mass., 1952), pp. 238-50. Allan B. Wolter (see previous note) gave a talk entitled "Some Reflections on Peirce's Scotism" at the Fifteenth Annual Meeting (March 20-21, 1964) of the Metaphysical Society of America, in Washington, D.C. It is to be hoped that this article will eventually be published in book form.

[3] We hope sometime in the near future to publish our investigations concerning two other problems of realism with which Scotus dealt. These problems may be approximately expressed in the following two questions: 1) What is the precise objective foundation for our judging that two things are imperfectly

In treating the particular question with which we are here concerned our procedure will be as follows. First, we shall briefly state the problem itself without going into all its ramifications. We shall then present and discuss at length Scotus' solution to this problem. Finally, by comparing and contrasting Scotus' solution with two other solutions we shall try to bring out what seem to be its strong points and its weak points. We shall conclude with a few remarks of more general scope.

The Problem

Paul is sentient, he is also rational. The two concepts *sentient* and *rational* refer to one and the same extramental reality. Upon reflection we find a difficulty here: How is it possible for us to have a plurality of concepts of one thing, a plurality of representations, supposing that our various concepts each truly *represents* the thing in question?[4]

Evidently no two concepts could represent the same thing perfectly, for thus they would coincide. For example, if the concept evoked by the word "sentient" were to represent everything about Paul and the concept evoked by the word "rational" were to do the same, the "two" concepts would have exactly the same content or comprehension and so, in this sense at least, would be not two, but one concept.

But if there can be only one perfect conceptual representation of a given object, there does not seem to be any reason why there should not be an indefinitely large number of imperfect representations.[5] Moreover, if imperfect representations can be thus multiplied, it is easy to see how our concepts of one and the same object can also be multiplied. However, some difficulties remain.

---

similar? and 2) What is the exact relationship between distinctness and dissimilarity? Both questions are, we believe, more fundamental than the usual questions asked about Scotus' teaching on universals.

[4] For the great scholastics of the high Middle Ages our concepts do normally *represent* objects, *i.e.*, image them in some way. See, *e.g.*, St. Thomas, *Summa Theol.*, Ia, q. 13, a. 1: "Voces sunt signa intellectuum, et intellectus sunt rerum similitudines." *Cf. De Pot.*, q. 7, a. 6: "Nam non essent verae conceptiones intellectus quas habet de re aliqua, nisi per viam similitudinis illis conceptionibus res illa responderet."

[5] Certainly, St. Thomas, for his part, saw none. See *De Pot., loc. cit.*: "Constat enim quod unius formae non potest esse nisi una similitudo secundum speciem, quae sit eiusdem rationis cum ea; possunt tamen esse diversae similitudines imperfectae, quarum quaelibet a perfecta formae representatione deficiat."

First, what precisely is an *imperfect representation*? To be sure, we may define it as an image which is like what is imaged in one or more respects, unlike it in one or more other respects. But then, what is a *respect*? Secondly, must not an imperfect representation inevitably lead to false judgments concerning what is represented? These questions must be answered before we can justly claim to have solved the problem of our many concepts of individual things.

The Solution of Scotus

Basically, Scotus' solution is in terms of *whole* and *parts*. A *respect* is for him a *part*, though not, of course, a *physical* part—but more of this shortly. Correlatively, an *imperfect* representation is an *incomplete* representation, one that does not represent all the parts of a thing. Now, clearly this offers a possible solution to our problem of the multiplication of concepts; for whatever has parts can be conceived in terms of each of these or each set of these, so that there can be as many distinct concepts of it as it has parts and combinations of parts. Thus, to conceive man as a vertebrate is, roughly speaking, to conceive him in terms of a part, that is to say, his backbone. Similarly, to conceive man as a biped is to conceive him in terms of a set of parts, namely, his two legs. Once again, if man is conceived as extended or—contingently and in particular cases—as white, the distinction of these two concepts from each other and from all other concepts may be explained, without departing from common scholastic teaching, as grounded in two distinct accidents, which are parts of the substance-accident composite, namely, quantity and whiteness.

But the parts in terms of which a whole may be conceived need not be integral parts, like a backbone or legs, nor accidents, like quantity and whiteness. Rather the word "part" must be understood in the very broadest sense so as to include any constituent whatsoever, be this material or spiritual, physical or metaphysical. The "parts" Scotus has principally in mind are most properly termed *metaphysical*.[6] These are the so-called "formalities,"[7] of which *animality*[8] and *rationality* are examples.

[6] See Philotheus Boehner, O.F.M., "Scotus' Teaching according to Ockham: II. On the *Natura Communis*," *Franciscan Studies*, VI (1946), 367. We may note here that Scotus himself uses the word "part" very broadly. For example, in *Metaph.*, IV, q. 2, n. 24; VII, 171, he speaks of the "ratio generis et differentiae

Formalities, Scotus insists, are not, properly speaking, things.[9] For things, in his acceptance of the word, can be separated, can

---

quae semper per se important partem perfectionis speciei passibilem et actualem" and states that "in creatura quaelibet perfectio contenta limitata est, et limitatior essentia continente secundum totalitatem constituta, ideo quaelibet potest dici pars perfectionis. . . ." Moreover, of the powers of the soul, which he considers to be only formally distinct from the essence, Scotus remarks: ". . . possunt etiam dici *partes*, secundum quod nulla dicit *totam* perfectionem essentiae continentis, sed quasi partialem" (*Ord.*, II, d. 16, q. unica, n. 19; II, 583). Elsewhere (*scil., Ord.*, II, d. 3, qq. 5-6, n. 16; II, 271) we are told that the nature of a thing and its haecceity "quasi sunt *primo per se partes*" of that thing.

N.B. All our references to the first 25 distinctions of Scotus' *Ordinatio* are to the Vatican edition: *Joannis Duns Scoti Opera Omnia* (Vatican City, 1950-). References to the rest of Book I and to Book II are to *Commentaria Oxoniensia*, 2 vols. (Quaracchi, 1912-14). References to Books III and IV and to all the other works of Scotus are—unless otherwise stated—to the Paris (Vivès) edition: *Joannis Duns Scoti Opera Omnia*, 26 vols. (Paris, 1891-95). For the sake of consistency we shall employ the now accepted title of *Ordinatio* throughout, even when referring to the Quaracchi and Paris (Vivès) editions, which make use of a different name. The abbreviations: "*Ord.*" and "*Metaph.*" refer respectively to Scotus' *Ordinatio* and his *Quaestiones Subtilissimae super libros Metaphysicorum Aristotelis*. The Roman and Arabic numerals following the semicolon in references to Scotus indicate respectively the volume and page of the edition in question.

[7] Scotus also terms these: "grades" of being (the so-called "metaphysical grades"). He holds them to be real—not mere logical—entities. See *Metaph.*, VII, q. 13, n. 19; VII, 420: "Cuicumque enim gradui reali entitatis, correspondet realis unitas."

[8] Animality is actually a composite formality, including *inter alia* the (presumably) irreducibly simple formality sensitivity.

[9] See *Metaph.*, IV, q. 2, n. 24; VII, 171: "Quod sicut essentia divina infinitas perfectiones continet, et omnes continet unitive sic quod non sunt aliae res, sic essentia creata potest aliquas perfectiones unitive continere. . . . In creatura quaelibet perfectio . . . potest dici pars perfectionis, non tamen realiter differens quod sit alia natura, sed alia perfectio realis, alienitate, inquam, non causata ab intellectu; nec tamen tanta quantam intelligimus, cum dicuntur diversae res. . . ." While Scotus denies that a formality is a thing (*res*), he does not hesitate to call it a reality (*realitas*), for as he tells us, ". . . Bene facio differentiam inter rem et realitatem. . . ." (*Ord.*, III, d. 22, q. unica, n. 5; XIV, 757). "Realitas" is, for Scotus, a broader term. See *Ord.*, II, d. 3, q. 6, n. 15; II, 270: "Quodlibet *commune*, et tamen *determinabile*, adhuc potest distingui, quantumcumque sit *una res*, in *plures realitates formaliter distinctas*, quarum *haec* formaliter non est *illa*. . . ." "Entitas" is also used very broadly. See, *e.g., Ord.*, II, d. 3, qq. 5-6, n. 16; II, 271, where we are told that the singular "est *per se ens*, addens aliquam entitatem entitati speciei. . . ." A formality may be termed a "ratio" if this is taken to mean "non . . . differentia formata ab intellectu, sed ut 'ratio' accipitur pro quiditate rei secundum quod quiditas est obiectum intellectus" (*Ord.*, I, d. 2, pars 2, qq. 1-4, n. 401; II, 355). Moreover, if Scotus is willing to link, if not simply identify "alia *formalitas*" and "alius *conceptus formalis*" (Wadding ed.: "alius conceptus realis") in *Ord*, II, d. 3, qq. 5-6, n. 12; II, 267, the reason, no doubt, is that he takes "*conceptus*," like "*ratio*" in the passage previously cited, in an objective sense, as *that in the object which is conceived by the intellect in a particular intellection*.

exist apart, at least through the omnipotence of God; whereas not even God can separate formalities like animality and rationality in man, since this would involve a contradiction.[10] Rationality, after all, is nothing but a determination of animality; animality is nothing but the "determinable" of rationality or its alternative irrationality. For one to exist without the other would be as unthinkable as the existence in the real order of indeterminate color (color without a determination to this or that particular color) or a determination of color without color-to-be-determined; that is, as unthinkable as having a color that would not be blue, red, or any other kind of color or as having blueness (in the sense of that which determines color to be blue) or some other such specification without color itself, which is specified.

Scotus not infrequently states that the formalities of a being, like animality and rationality in man, are not *really*, but only *formally* distinct.[11] But he is using the word "really" (*realiter*) in a technical sense, not generally employed. He means that such formalities are not distinct as *things* (*res*—which, as we have seen, he holds to be separable), but only as (inseparable) "forms." In the more common sense of the term, Scotus' formalities *are* really distinct, for, apart from any consideration of the mind, one is not the other. The mind

[10] The reason is that they are "unitive contenta" in an individual being. See *Metaph.*, VII, q. 13, n. 19; VII, 420: "Sicut . . . in aliis unitive contentis non est separatio realis, nec etiam potentialis; sic natura cui intellectus tribuit intentionem speciei, quae dicta est esse in re, est communis, sicut commune est potentiale in re, nunquam separatur ab alia perfectione unitive secum contenta, vel ab illo gradu, in quo accipitur differentia individualis. Cum etiam nunquam fiat in rerum natura nisi sub determinato gradu, nunquam est ab illo separabilis, quia ille gradus cum quo ponitur, est secum unitive contentus." Although Scotus is here primarily concerned with the inseparability of the common nature and the haecceity, the reason for this—that they are "*unitive contenta*"—is of universal application. Formalities constituting the nature itself are, of course, also *unitive contenta* and so likewise inseparable. In the question cited just above Scotus continues: "Per hoc patet ad tertium argumentum, quod contradictio includitur, quod separatur propter unitivam continentiam" (n. 20). For other passages on *continentia unitiva* and the inseparability of realities so contained see Maurice J. Grajewski, O.F.M., *The Formal Distinction of Duns Scotus: A Study in Metaphysics* (Washington, D.C., 1944), pp. 169-73. It may be good to note that *continentia unitiva* is a *per se* union and that hence the formalities so united are related to each other after the manner of potency and act, for Scotus agrees with Aristotle that of all those things "*ex quibus fit unum per se, alterum est ut potentia, alterum ut actus*" (*Super Universalia Porphyrii Quaestiones Acutissimae*, q. 28; I, 332).

[11] *E.g.*, in *Ord.*, II, d. 16, q. unica, n. 17; II, 581, speaking of "*contenta unitive*," Scotus says: ". . . sunt *unum realiter*, manent tamen *distincta formaliter*, sive . . . sunt idem identitate reali, distincta tamen formaliter."

does not make but discovers the distinction.¹² To avoid any ambiguity let us say that Scotus holds that formalities are *extramentally* distinct.¹³ In the concrete this amounts to saying 1) that

---

[12] Scotus considers as typically "formal" the distinction between the (ultimate) grounds of the generic and the differential concepts. Now, of this distinction Scotus says that "circumscripta omni operatione intellectus agentis vel possibilis, et omni *esse* in intellectu praesupposito, vel concomitante, est in re illa differentia. . . ." (*Metaph.*, VII, q. 19, n. 8; VII, 468). Scotus admits that formalities may be said to be really distinct in a broad sense of the term "really"—that they may be distinct "differentia reali minori, si vocetur differentia realis omnis non causata ab intellectu" (*Metaph.*, IV, q. 2, n. 24; VII, 171). Cf. *Metaph.*, VII, q. 19, n. 8; VII, 468, where Scotus, after telling us that the grounds of the generic and differential concepts are "aliqualiter in re realiter diversa," adds: "sed realis differentia ponitur habere gradus. Est enim maxima naturarum et suppositorum. . . . Minima diversarum perfectionum, sive rationum perfectionalium unitive contentarum in una natura." On the formal distinction and on Scotus' conception of a formality see Grajewski, *op. cit.*, esp. pp. 67-101. It should be noted that the formal distinction of Duns Scotus bears certain strong resemblances to the distinction between essence and *esse* in the philosophy of St. Thomas. In each case we have a metaphysical distinction between inseparable principles of being, which are related to each other as potency to act.

[13] This, of course, is equivalent to saying that the formalities in question are extramental, for, obviously, extramental *realities* must be extramentally distinct. A few texts may cause a doubt concerning the extramental character of a certain kind of distinction, which is "formal" at least in a broad sense of the word, namely, the distinction between a formality and its intrinsic mode, such as that between being and the mode of infinity in God. See, *e.g.*, *Ord.*, I, d. 8, pars 1, q. 3, n. 138; IV, 222: "Quando intelligitur aliqua realitas cum modo suo intrinseco, ille conceptus non est ita simpliciter simplex quin possit concipi illa realitas absque modo illo, sed tunc est conceptus imperfectus illius rei; potest etiam concipi sub illo modo, et tunc est conceptus perfectus illius rei." The all-important question is: Does the mind *make* the distinction between the reality and its mode (in which case nothing in the thing exactly corresponds to our conceptions of the reality and of the mode) or does it *find* the reality and the mode, and hence their distinction, in the thing? Can the mind abstract from the mode only because it is not altogether identical with the reality of which it is the mode? In the passage just cited Scotus distinguishes between a perfect and an imperfect concept of one and the same reality. Elsewhere (*Ord.*, I, d. 3, pars. 1, qq. 1-2, n. 67; III, 48) he distinguishes between conceiving a reality distinctly and indistinctly. But on Scotus' own principles how can we conceive a reality imperfectly or indistinctly except by leaving out of our concept something which is actually in the reality, somehow a part of it, and so somehow distinct from that in the reality which we do represent to ourselves? If Scotus were to admit in this case an abstraction that does not presuppose some extramental distinction, his entire doctrine on formalities would seem to be undermined. Though Scotus' commentators have themselves debated whether or not such a modal distinction is extramental (Scotus himself being far from clear on the matter), we believe that the Subtle Doctor's fundamental principles logically lead to the assertion here of an extramental distinction, in which, however, the interrelation of the *distincta* reaches an extreme of intimacy and necessity, in this going much beyond the ordinary formal distinction. On this matter see Wolter, *Transcendentals*, pp. 24-27. Wolter cites *Ord.*, I, d. 8, pars 1, q. 3, n.

the concepts *animality* and *rationality*, for example, each has a referent, and 2) that the referent of the one concept is *not* the referent of the other.[14]

It should be clear by now how Scotus' doctrine on the formalities enabled him to offer an answer to the problem of there being many concepts of a single thing. Each formality *as a part* (in the widest sense of the term) supplies a foundation for a concept of the whole based on it. Thus "animal" means "something having animality"; "rational" (thing understood) means "something having rationality"; and so on. These are relational concepts; nevertheless they furnish us with intrinsic knowledge, with knowledge, that is, which concerns the things in themselves, for the parts of a whole are "in" the whole.

All this is in accord with the traditional logic. Concrete words like "man," "animal," and "rational" denote a "matter" (subject) having a "form" (attribute), whereas abstract words like "humanity," "animality," and "rationality" denote "forms" without (at least explicitly) denoting any subject having these. It follows that the former can be directly predicated of a subject while the latter cannot. Paul *is* a man, *is* an animal, *is* rational, but he is *not* humanity nor animality nor rationality. In other words, the whole is not any one of its parts, nor any part the whole.[15]

Doubtless, then, Scotus through his doctrine on formalities has found a way to explain how we can have many concepts of individual things. But are these formalities, animality and rationality,

---

140; IV, 223: ". . . distinctio *in re* sicut realitatis et sui modi intrinseci. . . ." (italics ours).

[14] To be sure, the concepts *animal* and *rational* may have the same referent, for "animal" means that which has animality and "rational," that which has rationality, and one and the same thing may, and often does, have both of these. But if that from which the generic concept *animal* is derived, namely, animality, were identical with that from which the (specific) differential concept *rational* is derived, namely, rationality, then these two concepts would not differ in content and the generic concept alone would suffice for the definition of man, since the differential concept would add to it no new content. See *Ord.*, II, d. 3, qq. 5-6, n. 12; II, 267: ". . . Illa realitas a qua sumitur differentia *specifica* est *actualis* respectu illius realitatis a qua sumitur *genus* vel ratio generis, ita quod haec realitas non est formaliter illa; alioquin in definitione esset nugatio et solum genus sufficienter definiret, quia indicaret totam entitatem definiti sine *differentia.*"

[15] See *Ord.*, II, d. 16, q. unica, n. 21; II, 584: "*Animal* est de ratione quidditativa *hominis*, et tamen non sequitur quod unum abstractive praedicetur de alio; haec enim est falsa, *animalitas est humanitas*. Accipienda autem *concretive*, sic unum praedicatur de alio, ut *homo est animal.* . . ."

for example, *real* parts, that is to say, constituents of a real being, and not rather mere logical entities, parts of a concept perhaps, but nothing more? Granted that we may be under some sort of logical necessity of conceiving everything as though it were a whole compounded of such parts, is this actually the case? Is this not a merely subjective mode of thinking to be rejected by reflective judgment?

Scotus answers by appealing to the problem at issue. The data of this problem, which require the formalities as their only possible explanation, also require, so he tells us, that the formalities be extramental realities, not just fictions of the mind.[16] He was certainly not unaware that this position presents some serious difficulties. He was conscious that it seems to reduce individual things, even man himself, to what would later be caricatured as a "mosaic" of entities. But the choice appeared to him to lie between admitting the reality of the formalities or denying the proper objectivity of human knowledge, and so he did not hesitate to choose the former, while insisting, as we have seen, on the high degree of unity of the whole constituted by these distinct metaphysical realities or principles.[17]

---

[16] Scotus poses the question sharply: ". . . Videndum est, quid istis conceptibus [generis et differentiae specificae] correspondeat in re." He answers: ". . . Differentia rationis non sufficit ad distinctionem generis et differentiae. . . . Concipiendo genus, aut concipitur aliquid rei in specie, aut nihil, similiter de differentia; si nihil, isti conceptus videntur fictitii, non reales, nec dicentur *in quid* de specie; si aliquid, aut aliquid idem, et tunc erit idem conceptus; aut aliquid aliud, et tunc erit in re aliqua differentia prior differentia conceptuum" (*Metaph.*, VII, q. 19, n. 5; VII, 465). It is the specific nature of a thing which produces in us the generic and the differential concepts. These are distinct, each having, moreover, its own proper object. "Species formando duos conceptus generis et differentiae, non tantum causat duos actus in intellectu distinctos numero, sed causat duas notitias actuales vel habituales, habentes objecta propria distincta, et hoc ita distincta, sicut si illa duo objecta essent duae res extra. . . . Objecta naturaliter praecedunt actus, et distinctio objectorum, distinctionem actuum, maxime quando haec illam causat, ut hic ponitur; ergo differentia intentionis, quae est in conceptibus, concludit priorem in objectis, quae erit realis" (*Ibid.*; VII, 466).

[17] That the objectivity of human knowledge *is* a principal concern of Scotus is clear from the frequency with which he manifests it. See, *e.g., Metaph.*, VII, q. 19, n. 5; VII, 465-6, part of which was cited in the previous note. Another striking passage is contained in the previous question of the *Metaphysics*: ". . . Aliter [*i.e.*, if one rejects the opinion Scotus is here defending] in sciendo aliqua de universalibus, nihil sciremus de rebus, sed tantum de conceptibus nostris. . . ." (VII, q. 18, n. 10; VII, 459-60).

Comparisons

Comparison with St. Thomas Aquinas

It seems to us that we can best evaluate Scotus' solution of the problem of multiple concepts of individual things by comparing it with differing solutions. With two of these in particular the comparison promises to be especially fruitful. The first is the solution of St. Thomas. The Angelic Doctor deals with the problem explicitly in connection with his discussion of the various names of God.[18] Do these, he asks, signify different conceptual contents (*rationes*) and, if so, how can differing conceptual contents represent God who is simple?[19]

St. Thomas in some passages seems to come very close indeed to what Scotus will later have to say on extramentally distinct formalities,[20] but always his final solution tends to deny this. His conclu-

---

[18] See *In I Sent.*, d. 2, q. 1, a. 3; d. 22, q. 1, a. 3; *Contra Gent.*, I, c. 35; *De Pot.*, q. 7, a. 6; *Summa Theol.*, Ia, q. 13, a. 4.

[19] *In I Sent.*, d. 2, q. 1, a.3, presents the problem: "Videtur quod pluralitas rationum secundum quas attributa differunt, nullo modo sit in Deo, sed tantum in intellectu ratiocinantis." The difficulty, of course, derives from the unity and simplicity of God: "Quidquid est in Deo, Deus est. Si ergo istae rationes secundum quas attributa differunt, sunt in Deo, ipsae sunt Deus. Sed Deus est unus et simplex. Ergo istae rationes, secundum quod in Deo sunt, non sunt plures" (Mandonnet ed., pp. 63-64). In the *Summa Theol.*, *loc. cit.*, St. Thomas begins: "Videtur quod ista nomina dicta de Deo, sint nomina synonyma." Actually, this comes to the same, for if all the predicates we attribute to God signify exactly the same in God, the *pluralitas rationum* will be only in our own intellects, not in God. This, however, gives rise to a further difficulty: "Si dicatur quod ista nomina significant idem secundum rem, sed secundum rationes diversas, contra: Ratio cui non respondet aliquid in re, est vana; si ergo istae rationes sunt multae, et res est una, videtur quod rationes istae sint vanae" (obj. 2).

[20] See *In I Sent.*, d. 2, q. 1, a. 2: "Sic ergo dicendum est, quod in Deo est sapientia, bonitas et hujusmodi, quorum quodlibet est ipsa divina essentia, et ita omnia sunt unum re. Et quia unumquodque eorum est in Deo secundum sui verissimam rationem, et ratio sapientiae non est ratio bonitatis, inquantum hujusmodi, relinquitur quod sunt diversa ratione, non tantum ex parte ipsius ratiocinantis sed ex proprietate ipsius rei. . . ." And St. Thomas concludes: ". . . Ab aeterno creaturis non existentibus, . . . fuit verum dicere, quod [Deus] est sapiens, bonus et hujusmodi. Nec idem omnino significaretur per unum et per aliud, sicut idem significatur per nomina synonyma." *Cf. ibid.*, d. 22, q. 1, a. 3: ". . . Est etiam in Deo invenire distinctionem rationum, quae realiter et vere in ipso sunt, sicut ratio sapientiae et bonitatis, et hujusmodi, quae quidem omnia sunt unum re, et differunt ratione, quae salvatur in proprietate et veritate, prout dicimus Deum vere esse sapientem et bonum, et non tantum in intellectu ratiocinantis. . . ." And in his answer to the third objection St. Thomas writes: ". . . Ex hoc quod ratio sapientiae et bonitatis differt in Deo, diversificatur in creaturis bonitas et sapientia non tantum ratione, sed etiam

sion is ever the same: it is by reason of his supreme perfection that God can be imperfectly represented by many concepts.[21]

St. Thomas, unlike Scotus, does not maintain that an imperfect image of a thing is always such because it fails to represent one or more of its parts. He affirms a whole *as a whole* may be imperfectly represented, and even an utterly simple being can be represented by numerous imperfect images. Thus, of the divine nature, which St. Thomas holds to be without distinction of any kind, we can have many different concepts. None of these, in St. Thomas' view, represents any distinct formality or mode[22] in God, but each represents the divine nature as a whole, however imperfectly. Yet, though very deficient, these conceptual images need not lead us into error, for we do not, or at least should not, affirm that God is "just like" this or that image of him, but only that he is "something like," though infinitely superior to, any given conceptual representation of him. Obviously, according to St. Thomas we do not know God as he is in himself, but rather through concepts which signify him indeed, but represent him only imperfectly.[23]

Scotus was not satisfied with such a solution. It seemed to him to leave the basic problem still unanswered. For he did not see how an imperfect image of the kind described can be an *image* at all. For such an image, admittedly, does not represent the whole as it

---

re. . . ." Much, of course, depends upon how one interprets the term *"ratio"*; see above, note 9.

[21] See *In I Sent.*, d. 2, q. 1, a. 3: "Ista pluralitas rationum contingit ex hoc quod res quae Deus est, superat intellectum nostrum. Intellectus enim noster non potest una conceptione diversos modos perfectionis accipere . . . Et ideo pluralitati istarum rationum respondet aliquid in re quae Deus est: non quidem pluralitas rei, sed plena perfectio, ex qua contingit ut omnes istae conceptiones ei aptentur. . . . Est aliquid in Deo correspondens omnibus istis conceptionibus, scilicet plena et omnimoda ipsius perfectio, secundum quam contingit quod quodlibet nominum significantium istas conceptiones, de Deo vere et proprie dicitur; non autem ita quod aliqua diversitas vel multiplicitas ponatur in re, quae Deus est, ratione istorum attributorum" (Mandonnet ed., pp. 69-71). *Cf. De Pot., loc. cit.; Summa Theol.*, Ia, q. 13, a. 4, c. and ad 2um.

[22] For the sense of "mode" see above, note 13.

[23] See *Summa Theol.*, Ia, q. 13, a. 2: ". . . huiusmodi quidem nomina significant substantiam divinam, . . . sed deficiunt a repraesentatione ipsius." To be sure, what St. Thomas here terms "signification" corresponds more closely to what modern logicians usually call "reference" than to what *they* call "signification." St. Thomas, moreover, does not often make so sharp a distinction between *"significare"* and *"repraesentare."* The conceptual distinction is important, however. See J. de Finance, S.J., *Etre et agir dans la philosophie de Saint Thomas*, 2nd ed. (Rome, 1960), p. 35, with note 20; and E. Brisbois, S.J., "Qu'est-ce que l'existence?" *Revue Philosophique de Louvain*, XLVIII (1950), 214, note 12.

really is, nor a part either inasmuch as the opinion in question rejects even the least distinction in the divine nature. What, then, is there left to represent? One will repeat that each concept represents the whole, though it represents it only imperfectly. But what does this *mean*? It is easy enough to say that an imperfect image is one that represents one or more, but not all aspects of a thing, but it is then not so easy to explain what an "aspect" is if it is not a formality or mode of the Scotistic type. But cannot an image be *like* without being like *in this or that respect*? Scotus would certainly answer "No." A painting, he might point out, can be—and usually is—only a quite imperfect representation of a person, and at first we may be satisfied merely to note this fact. Still, if we reflect on the matter, we can surely indicate some details which are similar, some which are dissimilar, and, in principle, there would seem to be no limits to this process except those imposed by our lack of comprehensive knowledge of the representation and the represented.

Scotus, then, refuses to admit the possibility of imperfect images of the kind in question. To be sure, he will grant that a true image may be deficient in that it does not represent all the aspects of a thing. But the aspects it does represent must be "real aspects," that is to say, formalities (or modes); and the image must represent each formality as it is, which—if the formality be irreducibly simple (*simpliciter simplex*)—means that it must represent it perfectly.

St. Thomas does not, to our knowledge, consider with the same explicitness the problem of our multiple concepts of individual created substances. There are, however, various indications of his position here. At times he seems to solve the problem much as Scotus will do, in terms of parts. Man is that which *has* humanity, an animal that which *has* animality, and so on.[24] There are, moreover, a number of passages in which St. Thomas' language suggests even more strongly that he does in fact consider terms like "humanity" to signify a part of a whole.[25] However, he never un-

---

[24] See, e.g., *Summa Theol.*, Ia, q. 85, a. 5, ad 3um: "Non enim intellectus sic componit, ut dicat quod homo est albedo; sed dicit quod homo est albus, idest habens albedinem: idem autem est subiecto quod est homo, et quod est habens albedinem. Et simile est de compositione formae et materiae: nam animal significat id quod habet naturam sensitivam, rationale vero quod habet naturam intellectivam, homo vero quod habet utrumque. . . ."

[25] *E.g.*, in *De Ente et Essentia* (*Opusc. Phil.*, ed. Spiazzi, Turin, 1954), c. 2, nn. 14-15, St. Thomas, speaking of the specific nature and using *humanitas*

ambiguously asserts this; much that he says at least implies the contrary, and his disciples—no doubt correctly—have not thus interpreted him.[26] We must conclude that St. Thomas does not teach a doctrine of formalities.

On the other hand, "humanity" (to keep to the same example) certainly does not, for St. Thomas, signify the whole man.[27] And here we are back at an old difficulty. If "humanity" signifies neither the whole man, nor a part of him, it seems we are left with only one possible alternative: it does not signify him at all. We must add that the old dilemma now appears even more puzzling than before. For although St. Thomas might have solved the present difficulty in a way analogous to his solution of the problem of our multiple concepts of God by saying that the concepts animality and rationality refer to the whole man, but, because of the deficiency of our conceptual knowledge, represent this whole only imperfectly, actually he does not do so. On the contrary, he insists that such concepts cannot be predicated of the whole.[28]

There is, in addition, a special difficulty in regard to concepts like animality and rationality, which presumably—unlike our concepts of God—do represent things as they are in themselves. If two concepts like these have, as St. Thomas himself teaches, distinct, indeed adequately distinct, representative contents,[29] how can that which is represented by the one (animality) be identically that which is

---

by way of example, writes: ". . . se habebit per modum partis"; "pars non praedicatur de toto"; "significat . . . ut partem."

[26] J. Maritain, however, in his *The Degrees of Knowledge*, writes: "The *object* is one with the thing and differs from it only by a virtual distinction of reason. But far from exhausting the entire intelligibility of the thing, the object is only one or other of the intelligible determinations that may be distinguished within it (in other words, it is the thing as "objectifiable" under this or that aspect)" (Transl. by Gerald B. Phelan, New York, 1959, p. 392). These aspects, these "intelligible determinations," which, as described, certainly seem prior to our knowing them, are strangely reminiscent of Scotistic formalities or modes.

[27] See above, note 25.

[28] See, *e.g.*, *In VII Metaph.*, lect. 5 (Cath. n. 1378): ". . . Humanitas . . . de homine non praedicatur." A little further on the reason is made explicit: ". . . Humanitas significat ut pars" (n. 1379).

[29] According to St. Thomas the genus is not put into the definition of the difference, nor the difference into the definition of the genus (see *In III Metaph.*, lect. 8 [Cath. n. 433]). This would certainly not be the case if the concepts *animality* and *rationality* did not have adequately distinct representative contents, for the concepts *animal* and *rational*, which may have the same referent, owe their distinction entirely to the distinction between that which is "formal" in each, namely, *animality* and *rationality* respectively.

represented by the other (rationality)? Must not each represent something different about the common referent, and must not this difference be objective if our knowledge itself is to be such? To be sure, a similar difficulty presents itself in regard to certain of our concepts of God, but in this case one may, not implausibly, solve the problem by appealing to the mystery of the divine infinity.

Are, then, such concepts as animality and rationality mere mental constructs, concepts with some foundation in reality, but to which nothing in the real order precisely corresponds? Of course, one may without difficulty admit that such concepts are in fact mental constructs, but add that the important tools with which St. Thomas works are not these formal abstractions, but rather total abstractions like *animal* and *rational*. However, by this switch from formal to total abstraction the difficulty is only pushed back, not really overcome. For though the concepts *animal* and *rational* each refers to or (to use St. Thomas' own term) *signifies* a whole and may well refer to the *same* whole, the question that recurs is: What does each *represent*? For St. Thomas, like Scotus, holds that a concept not only (ordinarily) refers to or signifies something, but also is in some way a similitude of that to which it refers, in fact, refers to or signifies this *through* being a likeness of it. The question is legitimate, and must we not answer: What the concept *animal* represents about that which it refers to or signifies is, precisely, animality, that is, the sum total of the characteristics of an animal as such; and what the concept *rational* represents is rationality, namely, the sum total of the characteristics of a rational being *qua* rational. So that if the concepts *animality* and *rationality* represent nothing objective, neither, it would seem, can our concepts *animal* and *rational*. As is evident, the same would hold true of all similar cases.

One possible answer to these difficulties is that offered by Scotus' teaching on formalities. Another may lie in St. Thomas' own doctrine that in this life we have no direct knowledge of substances in themselves.[30] From this position it follows that we can know sub-

---

[30] See *De Spirit. Creat.*, a. 11, ad 3um: ". . . Formae substantiales per seipsas sunt ignotae. . . ." *Summa Theol.*, Ia, q. 77, a. 1, ad 7um: ". . . Formae substantiales . . . secundum se sunt nobis ignotae, innotescunt per accidentia. . . ." *Ibid.*, Ia, q. 87, a. 1: "Non ergo per essentiam suam, sed per actum suum se cognoscit intellectus noster." *In II Post, Anal.*, lect. 13 (Leon. ed., Vol. I, pp. 374-75, n. 7): "Sed quia formae essentiales non sunt nobis per se notae, oportet quod manifestentur per aliqua accidentia, quae sunt signa illius formae, ut patet in VIII *Metaphys*." *De Ver.*, q. 10, a. 1, ad 6um: ". . . Quia substantiales rerum differentiae sunt nobis ignotae, loco earum interdum definientes acci-

stances only as the source of such and such an activity or the term of this or that other relation. In this case our concepts, while signifying the substances themselves would *represent* not them, but some accidents produced by them and, as their effects, capable of manifesting (though not of "picturing") them. As for the formal abstractions, in accord with this theory these might well signify not the substances themselves, nor any part of them, but certain of their capacities (inferred from their actions) or various other relations of which the substances would be the inferred terms. This is approximately the second of the two solutions of which we spoke at the beginning of this section. This solution is at most only implicit in St. Thomas, for the Saint appears never to have fully realized the implications of his own strictures on conceptual knowledge.[31] His more, though never fully, explicit solution is, as we have described it, based on the notion of an imperfect image of a whole which is *not* the perfect image of a part.

Let us pass on now to a consideration of this other theory, which if found in germ in certain of St. Thomas' own statements, nevertheless, in its fully developed form, goes much beyond what St. Thomas was actually prepared to admit. It was his rejection, albeit a somewhat hesitant rejection, of a doctrine of formalities that constrained St. Thomas to tend toward the position we are about to describe. This suggests what we believe to be the case, namely, that the position in question is more directly opposed to Scotus' own. It will, therefore, provide us with a stronger contrast, which should set off even more clearly the doctrine of Scotus himself, with which, of course, we are here especially concerned.

Comparison with an "Extrinsicist" Theory of Knowledge

Scotus' solution of the problem of the plurality of concepts of individual things is, as we have observed, based on his understanding of these concepts as relational in character. Each of the various concepts is held to represent the thing in question as hav-

---

dentalibus utuntur, secundum quod ipsa designant vel notificant essentiam, ut proprii effectus notificant causam. . . ." All these and other passages are cited in William H. Kane, O.P., "The Extent of Natural Philosophy," *New Scholasticism*, XXXI (1957), 90-92, notes 5-10.

[31] See Pierre Rousselot, S.J., *The Intellectualism of St. Thomas*. Transl. by James E. O'Mahoney, O.F.M. Cap. (London, 1935), pp. 101-10.

ing a certain relation. In the typical case the relationship involved is that of the thing to one of its own parts, most commonly to one of its formalities. However, another solution based on a thing's relations is possible, one which emphasizes not relations of the thing to its *parts,* but rather its relations to *other things,* things *extrinsic* to it. Let us examine this solution in some detail. By comparison and contrast it may throw light on, and help us assess the merits of, Scotus' own position.[32]

Everything, even a perfectly simple reality, will have many relations to other things and so can be conceived in terms of each of these. The fact that a certain pen a) belongs to John, b) is on his desk, and c) is seen by him, does not necessarily and at once imply any distinct parts in the pen itself. Nevertheless, the three distinct relations expressed here provide the basis for three distinct concepts of the pen. Scotus, of course, recognizes this possibility. He is well aware that very many of our concepts are relative in this way, that is, that they are based on some relation of the thing conceived to something else.[33] This, he will grant, is a partial explanation of the plurality of our concepts. He is unwilling, however, to admit that this type of relation is the principal, much less the exclusive, source of our more important concepts. For to accept this as the

[32] Since we do not wish to extend this essay unduly by having to devote several pages to justifying the attribution of a specific theory to a particular philosopher (which would, in turn, require us to present also the individual characteristics it takes on in his particular system), we have chosen to present the "extrinsicist" theory in a highly general and to some extent "concocted" form and without historical references. There are, of course, many modern and even contemporary philosophers who hold somewhat similar theories (though these would usually speak of "phenomena," "sense data," or something else of the kind where we speak of "accidents"). But if one wished to find a medieval philosopher propounding some such theory, he could, no doubt, turn to William of Ockham. See, for example, the account of his conceptualism in Paul Vignaux, *Nominalisme au XIVe siècle,* Conférence Albert-le-Grand, 1948 (Montréal, 1948), esp. pp. 58-61. *Cf.* Philotheus Boehner, O.F.M., "The Realistic Conceptualism of William Ockham," in *Philotheus Boehner . . . Collected Articles on Ockham.* Ed. by Eligius M. Buytaert, O.F.M. (St. Bonaventure, N.Y., 1958), pp. 156-74, esp. 156-67.

[33] St Thomas too was aware that many of our concepts have this kind of relativity and that this can serve as one explanation of multiple concepts. See, *e.g., In I Sent.,* d. 2, q. 1, a. 3, ad 6um: "Tunc enim aliquid est unum re et ratione multiplex, quando una res respondet diversis conceptionibus et nominibus, ut de ea verificentur; sicut punctum, quod cum sit una res, respondet secundum veritatem diversis conceptionibus de eo factis, sive prout cogitatur in se, sive prout cogitatur centrum, sive prout cogitatur principium linearum; et hae rationes sive conceptiones sunt in intellectu sicut in subjecto, et in ipso puncto sicut in fundamento veritatis istarum conceptionum."

case would be to concede that our more important knowledge is of a merely *extrinsic* character, not knowledge of things *in themselves*, but only as terms of relations to other objects. It is evident that not *all* our knowledge can be of this sort, since we would have to know directly and in themselves some realities which may serve as *terms* of relations.

The "extrinsicist" theory denies that we have any intrinsic knowledge of substances, that is, any direct knowledge of them as they are in themselves,[34] affirming that we have such knowledge only of accidents. The implications of this doctrine are considerable. It is clear, for example, that when we know a thing as green, we are not thereby grasping the inner character of its substance. All we know is that the substance is such that, under all the given circumstances, it has (or is "informed" by) the accident *green* or, less ambiguously, *greenness*. To be sure, if one holds that color *as it appears in consciousness* is not objective, all we know is merely that the substance is such as, under the circumstances, to produce the sensation *green* in a sentient being. In no case can we ascertain from this what the "green" substance is like *in itself*, what is its *intrinsic* character or nature.[35]

It may not be at once apparent, but according to this theory the same would have to be said of such seemingly "intrinsic" concepts as *sentient* and *rational*. A sentient being is one which is capable of acts of sensation. A rational being is one which is capable of acts of understanding and reasoning. But, in this theory, what a substance must be like in itself to be able to do these things, to posit these acts—*this* escapes us. No doubt we can say that a being capable of understanding and reasoning must be of greater dignity than one which is not capable of this, must be an end in itself and not a mere means, must be spiritual (*i.e.*, not extended), a substance (*i.e.*, not "in" another), and so on. But all these are themselves relational or else negative concepts. Thus we do not grasp—so this

[34] Some who hold the general position expounded here hold also that each of us is immediately aware of his own *self*, so that this awareness gives us, by way of exception, some direct, albeit very imperfect, knowledge of at least one substance. *Cf.* what is said below, in note 36, concerning Scotus' doctrine on the intuition of substances.

[35] One might say that from its "greenness" we learn that the substance is extended. But this is merely to come to know another of its accidents. True, we know also that the substance must be such that it *can* be extended, perhaps even that it has an *exigency* for extension. Yet, what must a substance be *like* to have such a capacity or such an exigency?

position would hold—the positive intrinsic character of the sentient, rational substance.[36]

This theory seems to offer a satisfactory solution to the problem of the multiplication of concepts referring to a single thing. The solution is, as we have seen, basically in terms of extrinsic relations. However, in this view the "other things" grounding our more important concepts are as a rule the activities or effects of the thing conceived.[37] Now, these relations are obviously more significant and revealing than the types of relation we attributed above to John's pen.[38]

[36] We might have called this theory "mediate realism," namely, as regards the substantial natures of things, but the appellation would have been confusing. The terms "mediate realism" and "immediate realism" are, as we know, used in more than one sense. Mediate realism, in general, postulates some kind of medium between object and knower, whereas immediate realism rejects this. A distinction is sometimes drawn between *psychological* and *epistemological* realism. As far as intellectual knowledge is concerned, psychological mediate realism defends the necessity of some sort of *species* in the process of knowing. Scotus, for his part, holds that such a medium is necessary in abstractive knowledge, not, however, in intuitive. (See Sebastian J. Day, O.F.M., *Intuitive Cognition: A Key to the Significance of the Later Scholastics* [St. Bonaventure, N.Y., 1947], pp. 104-11.) In respect, then, to this latter type of knowledge Scotus is an immediate (psychological) realist. However, though intuitive knowledge according to his teaching grasps the existence of a particular substance—probably as here and now causing some sensation—in this life only abstractive knowledge can grasp distinctly the nature or quiddity of a thing. (See *ibid.*, pp. 122-23; *cf.* Bettoni, *op. cit.*, pp. 122-23.) Psychological mediate realism is usually presupposed in any consideration of epistemological realism. Unfortunately, however, there is no general agreement on what should be said to constitute mediate or immediate epistemological realism. If one qualifies as an immediate (epistemological) realist simply by holding that when we know particular substances we are in relation to, attend to, "intend" these substances themselves and not the psychological means (concepts) through which (at least in abstractive cognition) we know them, Scotus, like St. Thomas and indeed nearly all realists of whatever stripe, are, we would say, immediate (epistemological) realists. If, however, an immediate (epistemological) realist must deny that (at least in abstractive cognition) we know, and must know, *natura prius* our concepts in order that by means of their similitude to the object we may come to know this (much as in reading we attend to the ideas, but could not do this if we did not *natura prius* know the words on the printed page), then we should be inclined to classify Scotus, with St. Thomas and, of course, many others, as mediate (epistemological) realists. In any case, as far as mediate vs. immediate realism is concerned, Scotus seems to have differed from the theory presented here, not so much by claiming a greater immediacy for our knowledge of natures, as by assuming that our concepts in abstractive cognition are images of the object in a much fuller and more literal sense than the theory we have just presented in the text will allow.

[37] To be sure, if a substance were supposed to have no activities of any sort, we could not know it in any case.

[38] See p. 76.

Moreover, just as Scotus' solution did not by any means rule out relational concepts based on extrinsic relations, so the theory we are now considering certainly does not rule out concepts based on intrinsic relations. For apart from Scotus' formalities, all created beings are quite commonly held to consist of certain really distinct parts, principles, realities, or whatever one wishes to call them; and each of these can furnish the ground for a distinct concept. We have seen examples of such concepts above.[39] Other simple examples are *corporeal* where this is equivalent to *having a body* and *animate* where this is equivalent to *having a soul*. These concepts are in a true sense intrinsic, even though our knowledge of any substantial constituent must, in this theory, be in terms of *its* relations to other things.[40]

This theory may provide an acceptable solution to the problem of plural concepts, but this, of course, does not mean that it should forthwith be adopted, for it may be thought not to fit other data of experience. Actually, the denial of any direct knowledge of substance goes counter to the views of many scholastics. True, it is not equally clear that it is in opposition to the opinion of St. Thomas[41] or, for that matter, of Duns Scotus,[42] but if it is not, at least we

---

[39] See p. 64.

[40] If we were to stretch the term "part" to the breaking point, perhaps an immanent activity might itself be considered as a dynamic "part" of a thing.

[41] See above, [p. 74], with note 30. What we said of Scotus in the last sentence of note 36 (above), seems true also of St. Thomas as regards his general position concerning our knowledge of *created* substances, though, as we have seen, in the philosophy of the Angelic Doctor our conceptual images can be imperfect in a way not possible according to Scotistic principles.

[42] See the indications given above, in note 36. *Cf. Ord.*, I, d. 22, q. unica, nn. 4-7; V, 343-44: ". . . distinctus potest aliquid significari quam intelligi. [Scotus' distinction between "significare" and "intelligere" recalls St. Thomas' distinction between "significare" and "representare," spoken of above, [p. 71], with note 23.] Quod videtur persuaderi ex hoc, quod cum substantia non sit intelligibilis a viatore nisi in communi conceptu entis . . ., si non possit distinctius significari quam intelligi, nullum nomen impositum a viatore significaret aliquam rem de genere substantiae, sed sicut praecise concipitur ab intellectu viatoris aliqua proprietas a qua imponitur nomen . . ., ita praecise talis proprietas significaretur per nomen. . . . Concipiuntur ab aliquo multa accidentia, concurrentia in eodem, puta talis quantitas et talis qualitas,—et probatur neutrum illorum esse alterum, quia utrumque illorum manet sine altero; probatur etiam utrique illorum aliquid aliud esse subjectum commune. . . . Illud autem quod subest, non concipitur in conceptu quiditativo nisi entis, vel 'huius entis.' " A few lines down, there follows a passage found in the Quaracchi edition (I, 926), but which is really an interpolation in the *Ordinatio*. Nonetheless, it is most probably genuinely Scotistic (see Vatican edition, V, xii-xiii), and we cite it here as it makes more explicit what is stated in the lines just quoted: "Ergo

must say that neither of these philosophers seems to have realized the possibility which this theory offers of solving the problem of our multiple concepts of individual things and of answering other difficulties urged against the objectivity of human knowledge.

At present we are not concerned either to defend or attack the position which we have just sketched, but merely to compare its solution of the problem at issue with Scotus' solution of the same. However, we can at least say that considered merely as a solution to the problem in question, this theory would seem to be more satisfactory than the theory directly opposed to it, namely, the theory that we somehow intuit the essence or nature (in the sense of the intrinsic character, the "contents") of substances. This "intuitionist" view maintains that our intellectual knowledge of the substantial natures of things is direct, that by means of our concepts, not known in themselves, but used as instruments (*media quibus*), we attain to these natures in themselves. Though our knowledge of proper accidents also has an instrumental role in this theory, the nature of the substances is not known—as in the "extrinsicist" theory—by inference from the known nature of these accidents.[48] Now, if this theory be true, we are rid of the puzzle of how we can know our "images" of reality are really such—and this, surely, is no small advantage!—but the difficulty of seeing how we can have many concepts of a simple object or of a complex object as a whole is only aggravated.

Although, as far as we have been able to discover, Scotus nowhere explicitly considers in all its generality, and rejects, what we have called the "extrinsicist" theory of knowledge, that he would have rejected it if he had so considered it is clearly enough implied in his rejection of a more limited "extrinsicist" position, the position, namely, that one thing, as a whole and not by reason of any distinction of parts within it, can cause in us two concepts of itself, *scilicet* a generic and a differential concept. As in the supposition neither of these concepts would be an image of the whole nor of any part thereof, we could not, says Scotus, truly know the thing by means

---

cognoscitur aliquod tertium esse substratum, et similiter quod sit aliud a subjecto aliis; nec tamen cognosco distincte quid sit in se, nisi quod sit ens sive res, affecta talibus accidentibus; unde ulterior conceptio quam possum habere de illo, quid sit, est res aliqua habens talia accidentia et relationes . . ." (*Ord.,* V, 345, 11. 12-16).

[48] As we saw above, in note 36, Scotus, while admitting some (quite different) sort of intuition of natures, denies that, in this life, we can thus obtain a distinct knowledge of what substances are like in themselves.

of them. We would be knowing the concepts themselves, that is to say, their contents, rather than the thing itself.[44] It is true that inasmuch as these concepts would, in this theory, have been (at least partially) caused by the thing in question, they would provide the grounds for two relational concepts of it, that is, as the cause of the one and of the other. But to hold that our leading concepts are of this kind would be to concede that these are merely extrinsic and so do not reveal to us what things are like *in themselves*. Now such a concession Scotus, as we have already indicated, is not prepared to make. He does not seem to advert to the fact that since all effects bear some sort of resemblance to their cause, they may be used as a means for inferring true, if limited information concerning it. In any case, with his strongly realistic bent, he can hardly be expected to have found such an impoverishment of human knowledge acceptable.

Conclusion

Which of the solutions we have considered is the most satisfactory? We shall not venture to express an opinion. To attempt in a few pages to give a definitive solution to a problem of such enormous complexity would be rash indeed. One thing, however, we would like to point out. Scotus, as we have seen, employed his great talents in a most earnest effort to solve this intricate problem. With the extraordinary consistency of intellect which was his he arrived at a solution which appears radical only perhaps because it is pure. Now, just because it is pure and not a compromise between more or less incompatible positions, it is of special value in bringing out the ultimate option that confronts us. After Scotus it is easier for us to make our own intellectual decision in this matter—be it with or against the one he made.[45] To illuminate this

---

[44] *Cf. Metaph.*, VII, q. 19, n. 5; VII, 466: "Quaero igitur, an istis notitiis cognoscat intellectus objective aliquid in re? si nihil, fictio est; si idem, ergo objectum idem est, nisi dicas, quod una res extra facit formaliter duo objecta in intellectu, et tunc non videtur, quod res, vel aliquid rei, sit objectum, sed aliquid factum a re." N.B. We have altered the punctuation in two instances to make it accord with the sense. The Paris (Vivès) edition has: ". . . est, si idem; ergo. . . ."

[45] The logical alternative to Scotus' doctrine on formalities would appear to be some form of avowedly mediate and limited realism, perhaps even what has been termed "realistic conceptualism." Yet we do not think the option is nearly so simple as that suggested by Peirce when he wrote: "William Ockham . . . was beyond question the greatest nominalist that ever lived; while Duns Scotus . . . it is equally certain is the subtilest advocate of the opposite opinion. These

decision with his help has been one of the main purposes of the preceding pages.

Jesuit House of Studies
Mobile, Alabama

---

two men, Duns Scotus and William Ockham, are decidedly the greatest speculative minds of the middle ages, as well as two of the profoundest metaphysicians that ever lived" (1.29). Actually, St. Thomas himself may be thought of as preparing the way for the later development if Rousselot was correct when he wrote: "By insisting on the necessity of considering individual matter as an integral part of the essence while at the same time refusing reality to common matter outside of its concrete realisations thus identifying *humanitas* and *Socrateitas*, St. Thomas may be said to have introduced into the depths of things a certain nominalism" (*op. cit.*, p. 100). However, we think the use of the word "nominalism" here is unfortunate. Rousselot's point would, we think, have been better made if he had used the term we employed above: "realistic conceptualism." The doctrine so tagged is, we note, essentially different from what is commonly conceived as nominalism. On the Scotus vs. Ockham theme see a thought-provoking paragraph in Wolter, "Realism," p. 729.

5

DUNS SCOTUS' VOLUNTARISM

by

BERNARDINE M. BONANSEA

One of the principal features of Duns Scotus' philosophy is its emphasis on will, freedom, and love, in contrast to the Aristotelian-Thomistic school where intellect and knowledge occupy a privileged position. This difference of approach to man's basic tendencies and operations has given rise to what is commonly known as Scotistic voluntarism[1] and Thomistic intellectualism. While the labeling of two schools of thought from the different roles they assign to intellect and will is an oversimplification, it no doubt reflects a general trend within the schools themselves as well as some of their peculiar characteristics. Yet it can hardly be denied that many historians of philosophy in stressing the distinctive traits of each school have often succumbed to the temptation of exaggerating their differences at the expense of objective truth. Cases are also known in which school prejudices have led to a complete distortion of facts and textual evidence. Thus we have gradually been introduced to a Scotistic voluntarism that openly defies the intellectualism of St. Thomas and paves the way for the extreme voluntaristic trend that characterizes a large segment of modern philosophy from Descartes to Kant. When an eminent historian towards the end of the last century called Duns Scotus "the Kant of scholastic philosophy,"[2] he was reflecting this kind of attitude in regard to the Subtle Doctor.

[1] Although the term "voluntarism" is of recent coinage, it has been used by historians to designate Scotus' philosophy and distinguish it from the intellectualism of St. Thomas Aquinas. The term was used for the first time by Ferdinand Tönnis in his article, "Studien zur Entwickelungsgeschichte des Spinoza," *Vierteljahrschrift für wissenschlaftliche Philosophie,* 7 (1883), 169. Later the term was popularized by Friedrich Paulsen in his work, *Einleitung in die Philosophie* (Berlin, 1892) and by Wilhelm Wundt in his study, *Grundriss der Psychologie* (Leipzig, 1896).

[2] Cf. P. Zeferino González, *Historia de la filosofía* (2d ed.; Madrid: A. Jubera, 1886), II, 303. See also Cornelio Fabro's recent work, *Introduzione all'ateismo moderno* (Rome: Studium, 1964), pp. 18-19, where the author quotes approv-

Recent studies conducted in a more serene atmosphere and with a better knowledge of genuine Scotistic sources have greatly contributed to dissipate older prejudices and have opened new vistas into the thought of the great medieval master. The widely publicized contrast between Scotus and Aquinas has been reduced to its true dimensions and presented against its proper philosophical background. As a result, Scotistic voluntarism and Thomistic intellectualism are now seen less as two conflicting doctrines than as two different approaches to one and the same problem. It is the purpose of this study to show that this is the correct view. To do this we shall discuss Duns Scotus' teaching on the nature of will, the relationship between intellect and will, the superiority of will over intellect, and some of the philosophical implications involved in such a doctrine. A comparison between Scotus' teaching and the doctrine of Aquinas shall also be made on each of the foregoing issues.[3]

NATURE OF THE WILL

Man's rational nature manifests itself through intellect and will, the two highest powers of the human soul.[4] These two powers are neither identical with the soul nor really distinct from it. They cannot be identified with the soul, for they act differently, and different acts demand different principles of operation. They are not really distinct from the soul, as accidents are from substance, for to make such a distinction is not necessary and seems to break up the metaphysical unity proper to a spiritual substance. Between these two opposite views, the first held by

---

ingly Maritain's statement that "the modern *libertistic* metaphysical systems" can be traced back to Descartes insofar as he abandoned St. Thomas' intellectualism and accepted Scotus' voluntarism. Jacques Maritain, *Existence and the Existent* (Garden City, N.Y.: Doubleday, 1956), p. 14.

[3] Scotus' works used for this study are principally the *Opus Oxoniense* (Vivès ed., vols. VIII-XXI; Book I, unless otherwise stated, will be quoted from the Vatican edition under the name of *Ordinatio*), the *Reportata Parisiensia* (Vivès ed., vols. XXII-XXIV), and the *Quaestiones quodlibetales* (Vivès ed., vols. XXV-XXVI). The following abbreviations will be used: *Oxon.*, *Rep. Par.*, and *Quodl.* followed by book number and distinction (except for *Quodl.*), question (Vivès ed. only), marginal number, volume (Roman number), page and (Vivès ed.) column. E.g.: *Oxon.*, II, d. 25, q. unica, n. 22; XIII, p. 221b; *Ord.*, I, d. 2, n. 130; II, p. 205.

[4] *Oxon.*, III, d. 17, q. un., n. 2; XIV, p. 653a: "Potentiae perfectissimae naturae rationalis sunt intellectus et voluntas."

Henry of Ghent and the second by St. Thomas Aquinas, another position is possible, and this is the one that Duns Scotus defends. Intellect and will exist in the soul as two intrinsically distinct principles of operation in such a manner that the soul is neither intellect nor will nor something really distinct from them. Intellect and will are contained in the soul *unitive*, and yet they are formally distinct from it.[5]

To clarify his position Scotus compares the relationship between the soul and its faculties to that existing between being and its transcendental properties. Just as being contains within itself the reasons for its unity, truth, and goodness, and yet each one of these properties retains its specific distinction, so the soul includes within itself intellect and will, and yet these two powers are formally distinct from one another and from the soul itself.[6] Scotus' formal distinction has no counterpart in Thomistic philosophy, and it would be wrong to judge it from the Thomistic point of view.[7] If

---

[5] *Oxon.*, II, d. 16, q. un., n. 18; XIII, pp. 43b-44a: "[Intellectus et voluntas] non sunt partes essentiales animae, sed sunt unitive contenta in anima quasi passiones eius, propter quas anima est operativa; non quod sint essentia eius formaliter, sed sunt formaliter distinctae, idem tamen identice et unitive."

[6] *Ibid.*, n. 17; XIII, p. 43b: "Sicut ergo ens continet unitive rationem unius, veri et boni aliorum, sic anima continet potentias istas [intellectum et voluntatem] unitive, quanquam formaliter sint distinctae." The formal distinction between intellect and will is stated in *Ordinatio*, I, d. 3, n. 578; III, p. 342: "Non potest autem idem sub eadem ratione formali esse principium istorum duorum actuum secundorum [intellectionis et volitionis], quia isti actus secundi requirunt oppositam rationem principiandi in suis principiis: ergo oportet habere aliquam distinctionem actuum primorum, et hoc aliquam proportionaliter correspondentem distinctioni actuum secundorum." That the act of understanding and the act of willing are formally distinct is clear from *Oxon.*, III, d. 14, q. 2, n. 6; XIV, p. 500a-500b: "Possunt enim isti actus [intellectionis et volitionis] formaliter distingui, licet non habeant obiecta formaliter distincta."

[7] The nature of Scotus' formal distinction is thus explained by Efrem Bettoni: "It is not easy to grasp the meaning and value of the formal distinction met so often in the works of Duns Scotus. Formal distinction stands between real distinction and distinction of pure reason or logical distinction. There is a real distinction between two things, when the one is not contained in the other either as a fruit is contained in the germ, an effect in the cause, or something distinct is contained in something confused: one thing is perfect in itself apart from the other, so that they are two really different things. The logical distinction, on the other hand, is nothing but a distinction of concepts as regards a thing that is really and formally identical. On the contrary, two entities are formally distinct from one another when, although one is not contained in the other in any of the three ways mentioned in connection with the real distinction, i.e., potentially, virtually, or confusedly, they nevertheless lack that ultimate perfection which would make them *really different*. It is only because they are united together that they constitute a real thing. However, they are not parts or constituent principles of the thing, but only different formalities of it." *Duns*

a comparison must be made between the two approaches to the problem under discussion, Scotus seems to be primarily concerned with safeguarding the essential unity of the soul and the intimate relationship between the activities of its powers. Aquinas, on the other hand, is more preoccupied with saving the distinction between God and the human soul, as well as the metaphysical principle that act and potency must be in the same genus.[8] No matter what approach one may prefer to follow, one thing is certain: Scotus would never admit a real distinction between the soul and its faculties and between the faculties themselves, because his notion of real distinction implies separability of the beings or realities involved. Since intellect and will cannot exist apart from the soul or from one another, not even by the absolute power of God, no Scotistic real distinction is possible between them. That much must be admitted even by the Thomists.

Having clarified Scotus' position on the relationship between the soul and its faculties, we proceed now to his concept of will, which he defines as *appetitus cum ratione liber*,[9] and more simply as *appetitus rationalis*,[10] or *appetitus intellectivus*.[11] Since will is a rational appetite, it includes a double tendency, one passive, consisting in a natural inclination to will and attain the object that constitutes its own perfection, and one active, which is the act of willing as such or free volition.[12] The passive tendency is also called natural will, to distinguish it from free will proper. Natural will, strictly speaking, is no will at all, since of its nature it is a mere inclination or passive capacity to receive its own perfection.[13] The two tendencies, passive and active, exist as distinct formalities within one and the same power, not otherwise than within one

---

Scotus: The Basic Principles of His Philosophy, trans. and ed. by Bernardine Bonansea, O.F.M. (Washington, D.C.: The Catholic University of America Press, 1961), pp. 78-79.

[8] For St. Thomas' discussion of this question cf. *Sum. theol.*, I, q. 77, a. 1; for Scotus' refutation of Aquinas' arguments see *Oxon.*, II, d. 16, q. un., nn. 5-10; XIII, pp. 25b-28a.

[9] *Oxon.*, III, d. 17, q. un., n. 2; XIV, p. 653b.

[10] *Ibid.*, d. 33, q. un., n. 9; XV, p. 446b.

[11] *Rep. Par.*, II, d. 25, q. un., n. 19; XXIII, p. 127b.

[12] *Collationes*, XVI, nn. 1-2; V, pp. 208b-209a (Vivès ed.).

[13] *Oxon.*, III, d. 17, q. un., n. 3; XIV, p. 654a: "Voluntas naturalis non est voluntas, nec velle naturale est velle"; *ibid.*, n. 5; XIV, p. 655a: "Voluntas naturalis, ut sic, non est voluntas, neque potentia, sed tantum dicit inclinationem potentiae ad recipiendum perfectionem."

and the same intellect there is a natural tendency to know which is formally distinct from the actual act of knowing.[14]

The existence of two different tendencies in the will is proved by the conflict that one may experience within himself, as in the case of martyrs who choose to die by a free act of their will despite the natural fear they have for death. The *appetitus naturalis* belongs to the very nature of the will, since a nature, to be such, must tend towards its own perfection, just as a stone tends naturally towards the center of the earth. The perfection towards which the will tends by an intrinsic necessity and to the utmost degree is happiness.[15] It is not happiness in general or universal good, for this can only be known by the intellect, and the *appetitus naturalis* is prior to the act of the intellect, or else it would be a free act. It is therefore happiness in particular represented by individual goods, or such goods as are naturally agreeable to the will.[16] Among these, the infinite good, as man's ultimate end, occupies the first place, since all other goods are related to it.[17]

Although will is both a natural appetite and a free power, this latter aspect better characterizes it, for will is essentially free.[18] As

[14] *Ibid.*, p. 655b: "In una potentia est duplex tendentia, activa et passiva. . . Voluntas naturalis secundum formale, quod importat, non est potentia vel voluntas, sed inclinatio voluntatis et tendentia qua tendit in perfectionem." *Oxon.*, IV, d. 49, q. 10, n. 2; XXI, p. 318b: "Sicut se habet appetitus naturalis intellectus ad actum suum, sic appetitus voluntatis ad actum suum; sed appetitus naturalis intellectus non est actus elicitus ab eo; ergo sic erit de voluntate."

[15] *Ibid.*, n. 3; XXI, pp. 318b-319a: "De illo appetitu naturali patet quod voluntas necessario et perpetuo et summe appetit beatitudinem, et hoc in particulari. Quod de necessitate, patet, quia natura non potest remanere natura quin inclinetur ad suam perfectionem, quia si tollas illam inclinationem, tollis naturam; sed appetitus naturalis non est nisi inclinatio talis; ergo ut sic necessario appetit beatitudinem, quia illa est maxima perfectio."

[16] *Ibid.*, p. 319a: "Illud appetere non est actus sequens cognitionem, quia tunc esset liber; universale autem non est nisi obiectum intellectus, vel consequens actum intellectus; ergo ille appetitus non erit nisi beatitudinis in particulari." *Oxon.*, III, d. 17, q. un., n. 3; XIV, p. 654b: "Dicitur voluntas naturalis, ut elicit actum conformem inclinationi naturali; quae semper est ad commodum."

[17] *Ord.*, I, d. 2, n. 130; II, p. 205: "Videtur quod . . . inclinatio [voluntatis nostrae] est naturalis ad summe amandum bonum infinitum, nam inde arguitur inclinatio naturalis ad aliquid in voluntate, quia ex se, sine habitu, prompte et delectabiliter vult illud voluntas libera; ita videtur quod experimur actu amandi bonum infinitum, immo non videtur voluntas in alio perfecte quietari." *Oxon.*, III, d. 15, q. un., n. 22; XIV, p. 598a: "Voluntas nihil vult naturaliter primo et propter se nisi finem ultimum, et per consequens omne aliud vult non primo, sed in ordine ad ipsum . . . [Hoc] patet ex rectitudine inclinationis naturalis, quae non est recta si esset maxime et principaliter ad minus bonum et non ad ultimatum."

[18] *Oxon.*, II, d. 25, q. un., n. 16; XIII, p. 210a: "Ratio autem formalior volun-

a self-determining power, will has complete control over its acts.[19] Indeed, in St. Augustine's words, which Scotus quotes approvingly, "nothing is so much in our power as the will itself."[20] To conceive the will as being forced to act is an evident contradiction.[21] Freedom of the will includes not only the power to act or not to act in any particular case (freedom of exercise or of contradiction), but also the power to decide between two opposing acts concerning one and the same object, such as to will or not to will (freedom of contrariety), and the power to choose between acts and objects specifically different among themselves (freedom of specification).[22] Will can even suspend its own decision concerning a particular act to be done, or change its decision during a course of action and will the opposite of what it had willed previously. This is because of the contingent nature of the relationship that obtains between will, its acts, and its effects. Just as there is no effect that must be necessarily produced by will, so there is no act that will must necessarily perform.[23]

Yet the will cannot will and not will something at one and the same time, since this involves a contradiction; nor can it refrain

---

tatis est magis libera quam ratio appetitus, quare est ratio recipiendi inquantum libera, sicut ratio libertatis est magis ratio constituendi"; *ibid*, I, d. 17, q. 3, n. 5; X, p. 56b (Vivès ed.): "[Voluntas] est libera per essentiam."

[19] *Quodl.*, q. 16, n. 15; XXVI, p. 199a: "Ipsamet [voluntas] est tale activum, quod seipsam determinat in agendo"; *Oxon.*, III, d. 17, q. un., n. 4; XIV, p. 654b: "Omnis voluntas est domina sui actus"; *Rep. Par.*, III, d. 17, q. 2, n. 4; XXIII, p. 376a: "Non potest esse voluntas, nisi sit domina sui actus, et ita est domina voluntas sui actus."

[20] *Oxon.*, II, d. 25, q. un., n. 2; XIII, p. 198a: "Augustinus *primo lib. Retract, cap. 22* . . . dicit quod *nihil est tam in potestate nostra quam ipsa voluntas;* igitur ex hoc potest haberi, quod nulla actio in nobis est ita a nobis, sicut volitio voluntatis."

[21] *Oxon.*, IV, d. 29, q. un., n. 6; XIX, p. 218a: "Contradictio est voluntatem simpliciter cogi ad actum volendi."

[22] *Quodl.*, q. 18, n. 9; XXVI, p. 241b: "Voluntas autem sola habet indifferentiam ad contradictoria, et talem, quod ipsa est sui determinativa ad alterum eorum"; *Oxon.*, II, d. 25, q. un., n. 6; XIII, p. 201a: "In potestate voluntatis nostrae est habere nolle et velle, quae sunt contraria respectu unius obiecti"; *Ord.*, I, d. 1, n. 149 II, p. 100: "In potestate voluntatis est non tantum sic et sic velle, sed etiam velle et non velle, quia libertas eius est ad agendum vel non agendum."

[23] *Oxon.*, IV, d. 49, q. 10, n. 10; XXI, p. 333b: "A quolibet actu in particulari potest [voluntas] se suspendere hoc vel illo"; *Ord.*, I, d. 39, Appendix A; VI, p. 418: "Voluntati enim ut actus primus, etiam quando producit hoc velle, non repugnat oppositum velle: tum quia causa contingens est, respectu effectus, et ideo non repugnat sibi oppositum in ratione effectus: tum quia ut subiectum est, contingenter se habet ad istum actum ut informat, quia subiecto non repugnat oppositum sui 'accidentis per accidens'."

entirely from all act of willing, for even such a suspension seems to be possible only in terms of a voluntary act.[24] Likewise, it does not seem possible for the will to seek evil as evil or to hate the good as such, since by its very nature the will tends towards the good.[25] But the will can seek a certain evil for its own satisfaction, in such a manner that the evil sought becomes for will an apparent good. This is possible because will as a free power can choose any being as the object of its desire and make it an ultimate end, were it not for any other reason than its own pleasure in abusing freedom and performing an evil act.[26] Thus a rational creature, with full knowledge of what it is doing, can hate God and find satisfaction in such a hatred, not because God is hateful or because the hatred of God is not something evil, but because of the pleasure that even such a hatred can bring to a rational creature in the form of an apparent good.[27] However, a formal hatred of God seems impossible, since it would amount to willing evil as such. Accordingly, even the fallen angels cannot formally hate God. All they can do is to hate the pains and sufferings decreed for them by divine justice.[28]

---

[24] *Ibid.*, p. 419: "Voluntas volens *a*, potest non velle *a*. Haec . . . [propositio] in sensu compositionis falsa est, ut significetur possibilitas huius compositionis 'voluntas volens *a*, non vult *a*'; vera est in sensu divisionis, ut significetur possibilitas ad opposita successive, quia voluntas volens pro *a* potest non velle pro *b*"; *Oxon.*, II, d. 7, q. un., n. 24; XII, p. 405b: "Non videtur quod [voluntas] possit se suspendere ab omni actu sine volitione." See also *Ord.*, I, d. 1, n. 150; II, p. 102.

[25] *Oxon.*, IV, d. 49, q. 10, n. 9; XXI, pp. 332b-333a: "A voluntate excluditur actus volitionis respectu miseriae, et actus nolitionis respectu beatitudinis, quia miseria non est nata esse obiectum actus volitionis, nec beatitudo obiectum actus nolitionis, sicut actus videndi disgregando excluditur a visu respectu nigredinis, quia non est nata esse obiectum talis actus; sic in proposito, voluntas non est capax talis actus respectu talis obiecti." The same thought is expressed in *Quodl.*, q. 16, n. 5; XXVI, pp. 188b-189a. However, there are passages in Scotus' works which seem to indicate the possibility for the will to seek evil as evil. See, for example, *Ord.*, I, d. 1, n. 151; II, p. 103; *Collationes*, XVII, n. 11; V, pp. 216b-217a; and the specific question, "Utrum voluntas creata possit peccare ex malitia, volendo aliquid non ostensum sibi sub ratione boni veri, id est, boni simpliciter, vel boni apparentis et secundum quid?", *Oxon.*, II, d. 43, q. 2, n. 1; XIII, pp. 490b-494a.

[26] *Ord.*, I, d. 1, nn. 16-17; II, pp. 10-11; *Oxon.*, II, d. 43, q. 2, n. 2; XIII, pp. 493b-494a.

[27] *Ibid.*, n. 1; XIII, p. 491ab.

[28] *Rep. Par.*, II, d. 43, q. un., n. 5; XXIII, p. 229b: "Non potest Deus odiri ab aliqua voluntate"; *ibid.*: "Quia formaliter [Deus] non potest odiri." See *Oxon.*, II, d. 6, q. 2, n. 13; XII, p. 359b, for Scotus' teaching on the nature of the hatred of God by the fallen angels. The question of the possibility or impossibility of a formal hatred of God is closely related to the question of whether or not the will can seek evil as evil, which Scotus solves in the negative but not without

Scotus is quite consistent in carrying to its logical conclusions his notion of will as an essentially free power. In so doing, he must face St. Thomas' position that will, as an appetitive faculty, cannot be conceived apart from its natural object of desire and final end, which is happiness or the good in general. Will, says Aquinas, tends by its nature towards good in general, so that it is not free not to desire it. This is not something imposed upon it from without, but a necessity of nature proceeding from will itself which has no choice but to seek happiness as its ultimate end.[29] Thus for Aquinas no specific distinction obtains between natural appetite and deliberate volition, since the latter is for him merely an application to a particular good of the original movement of will towards good in general.[30]

Scotus discusses St. Thomas' position very carefully, and with his usual subtlety answers all his arguments, along with the arguments advanced by Henry of Ghent, who follows Aquinas on this score.[31] Here is the general line of his reasoning. Starting with St. Augustine's saying that nothing is so much in the will's power as the will itself, he argues that this has no meaning except insofar as it refers to the elicited acts of will, or those acts which are performed by will as a free power. Now if the will has the power to tend or not to tend towards happiness through the acts of another faculty, as in the case of all elicited acts, it must also have the power, and even more so, to tend or not to tend towards happiness immediately, i.e., by its very nature. To deny this is to admit the contradiction that, for the attainment of its ends, the will necessarily depends on something over which it has a complete control. But will has the power to tend or not to tend towards happiness or good in general through the acts of intellect, since it can divert intellect from the consideration of that good and thus avoid tending towards something which it does not know. Hence the will has also the power to will or not to will happiness immediately.[32] In more

---

raising some doubts as to the probability of the opposite view. See n. 25 above and the texts therein referred to, especially *Ord.*, I, d. 1, n. 151; II, p. 103.

[29] For Aquinas' teaching on this point cf. *Sum. theol.*, I, q. 82, a. 1 and 2; I-II, q. 5, a. 8; q. 10, a. 1 and 2; *III Sent.*, d. 27, q. 1, a. 2; *De veritate*, q. 22, a. 5; *De malo*, q. 6.

[30] Cf. Robert E. Brennan, O.P., *Thomistic Psychology* (New York: Macmillan, 1941), pp. 232-35.

[31] Cf. *Ord.*, d. 1, nn. 77-158; II, pp. 59-108; *Oxon.*, IV, d. 49, q. 10; XXI, pp. 317-83; *Quodl.*, q. 16; XXVI, pp. 180-201.

[32] *Ord.*, I, d. 1, nn. 91-92; II, pp. 66-67.

simple terms, Scotus says that since the will is free in directing the intellect towards its final end, or happiness in general, it is also free in its tendency towards happiness as such.

To support his thesis, Scotus uses another argument. Every agent that is bound by nature to act and is not otherwise impeded, removes necessarily and as best he can every obstacle to his action. Thus a heavy body will of necessity fall downward until it meets a resistance superior to its own weight. If the resistance can be overcome, the heavy body will necessarily overcome it and continue in its descent, since it is of its nature to do so. Likewise, if will is forced by its nature to tend towards its final end and, as we know, is not otherwise impeded to do so, it will also remove by an intrinsic necessity and to the extent of its power all obstacle to its volition. An obstacle to volition is the nonconsideration of the end, for nothing can be willed that is not previously known. Since this obstacle can be easily removed by forcing the intellect's attention to the end, the will will necessarily do this if by its nature it tends towards happiness as its final end.[33] In other words, if will tends of necessity towards happiness as its final end, and it is within its power to apply intellect to the consideration of that end, it will do so at all times and necessarily. But this, as Scotus' reasoning implies, is not the case, since it is against our everyday experience. Hence the will is free in tending towards its final end.

A third argument is that every agent acting by a necessity of nature must act to the full extent of its power, since the intensity of action is no more in its power than action itself. This means that the agent has no choice as to the intensity of his action. Hence if will tends of necessity towards happiness, it will have no choice but to seek it necessarily and to the full extent of its power. This again is contrary to our everyday experience.[34]

St. Thomas argues that natural necessity of the end is not repugnant to will, since according to Aristotle (*Physics,* II, 9; 200a 21) the end is in practical matters what a principle is in speculative matters. Just as intellect of necessity adheres to first principles, so will must of necessity adhere to the last end, which is happiness.[35] In

---

[33] *Ibid.,* n. 93; II, pp. 67-68.
[34] *Oxon.,* I, d. 1, q. 4, n. 9; VIII, p. 359a (Vivès ed.). According to the critical edition of the *Opus Oxoniense,* the argument was later dropped by Scotus with the remark: "Conceditur conclusio quando est aequalis apprehensio et nihil retrahens." Cf. *Ord.,* I, d. 1, n. 133; II, pp. 88-89, note.
[35] *Sum theol.,* I, q. 82, a. 1 c. Quoted in *Ord.,* I, d. 1, n. 83; II, pp. 62-63.

answering this argument, Scotus objects to the comparison between the intellect's assent to first principles and the will's assent to the last end. Intellect is a mere natural faculty which cannot but accept the evidence of its object once it is presented to it. Will, on the contrary, is essentially a free power, and as such it always tends freely towards its object, no matter what degree of goodness it may contain. Accordingly, not even the last end or happiness in general can force the will's consent.[36]

It is further argued by St. Thomas that since the formal object of will is the good, and happiness as such contains only good and no evil, will tends of necessity towards it, just as any other faculty tends of necessity towards its formal object.[37] Scotus disagrees once more with this line of reasoning. While accepting the premises that the good is the formal object of will and that this latter has a natural inclination towards it, since it is precisely by attaining the good that will perfects itself, he questions the conclusion that the good or happiness in general has such an appeal to will as to necessarily draw its assent to it. He argues that when our will is confronted with happiness or good in general, we can think of three possibilities: the will can will it *(velle)*, reject it *(nolle)*, or simply refuse to make any decision *(non velle, non nolle)*. While it would be wrong to say that will can reject happiness or good as such and choose misery as its end (see however our previous observation in this regard), it is not at all inconceivable that will, in virtue of its radical freedom, may refuse to act. Not to will to be happy, Scotus acutely remarks, is not the same as to will to be unhappy, just as not to will to be miserable is not equivalent to willing to be happy. Between these two opposing acts of the will—for both to will and not to will are positive acts—there is a middle course which consists in not willing at all. This, Scotus concludes, is what absolutely speaking will can do even when it is confronted with its final end or happiness in general.[38]

---

[36] *Ord.*, I, d. 1, n. 147; II, pp. 97-98. See also *Oxon.*, II, d. 7, n. 27; XII, pp. 407b-408a; *Quodl*, q. 16, n. 6; XXVI, p. 189ab.
[37] Cf. St. Thomas, *Sum theol.*, I-II, q. 10, arts. 1 and 2.
[38] *Oxon.*, IV, d. 49, q. 10, n. 8; XXI, p. 332b: "Respondeo, non sequitur, non volo beatitudinem; ergo nolo eam, sive non volo esse miserum; ergo de necessitate nolo esse miserum, quia *nolle* est actus positivus nolentis, sicut est *velle*, et ita liberum unum sicut aliud, quia neutrum elicio necessario circa quodcumque obiectum, et ideo possum non elicere *nolle* circa malum, sicut *velle* circa bonum. Tamen sicut circa malum ostensum non possum elicere actum voluntatis nisi *nolle*, sic circa bonum oblatum non possum elicere actum voluntatis nisi *velle*,

To sum up the whole discussion, will is completely free in determining itself as to the attainment of its end, regardless of whether this is happiness in particular or happiness in general.[39] The simple apprehension of its formal object cannot be the determining reason for the will's adherence to it, nor does the will act necessarily in its attainment of the object or the continuation of its act of willing it.[40] To think otherwise is to reject the notion of will as a self-determining power.

Scotus' insistence upon the will's radical freedom in pursuing its objective is no doubt disconcerting to those who are accustomed to think of will and freedom in purely Aristotelian-Thomistic terms. However, if we look at his doctrine from the perspective of the Augustinian-Franciscan school, as must be done in order to understand Scotus' philosophy, we need not be concerned as to the orthodoxy and consistency of his teaching. St. Augustine's conception of will as a fundamentally free power is well known, and the Subtle Doctor never tires of repeating the Augustinian saying that nothing is so much under the will's power as the will itself. Primarily, of course, St. Augustine speaks of freedom of choice, as a type of freedom that belongs to will, but he subordinates it to freedom proper, which consists in the radical dominion that will has over its own acts and belongs, although in different degrees, to God, angels, and man. St. Anselm, following in the steps of his great predecessor, defines freedom as *potestas servandi rectitudinem voluntatis propter ipsam rectitudinem*,[41] or the power of maintaining righteousness of the will for its sake. The meaning is that the real nature of freedom is to do what is right, and to do it knowingly and with complete control over one's own acts.

The Anselmian definition of freedom is accepted by both St.

---

et ideo debet sic argui: Non possum velle esse miserum; ergo non possum odire beatitudinem; sed ex hoc non sequitur, ergo necessario volo beatitudinem, quia nullum *velle* necessario elicitur a voluntate."

[39] *Ibid.*, n. 5; XXI, p. 331a: "Etsi voluntas libera velit ut in pluribus beatitudinem apprehensam in universali vel particulari, quando intellectus non dubitat in illo particulari esse beatitudinem, non tamen necessario vult nec in universali nec in particulari"; *ibid.*, n. 6; XXI, p. 331b: "Dico ergo quod [voluntas] contingenter vult finem, tam in universali quam in particulari, quamvis ut in pluribus velit utrumque."

[40] *Quodl.*, q. 16, n. 5; XXVI, p. 188a: "Voluntas viatoris simpliciter contingenter tendit in illud [obiectum in quo est ratio omnis boni] etiam quando est in universali apprehensum, quia illa apprehensio non est ratio determinandi voluntatem ad necessario volendum illud; nec ipsa voluntas necessario se determinat illo posito, sicut nec necessario continuat [velle] illud positum."

[41] St. Anselm, *De libero arbitrio*, c. 3; PL vol. 158, col. 494.

Bonaventure and Duns Scotus who make it their own and develop it further.[42] The characteristic of this definition consists in stressing the fact that freedom is essentially a power of self-determination in regard to the good known by the intellect. It is a simple perfection of intelligent beings which, in Scotus' words, can obtain even when there is no possibility of choice on the part of the will.[43] Actually, freedom of choice is an imperfection of the human will, and God alone, who loves himself by an absolute necessity, is absolutely free.[44] In this sense Scotus can maintain that the blessed in heaven enjoy a greater degree of freedom than does *homo viator,* or man in his earthly existence, even though the blessed cannot possibly turn away from the supreme good because of a positive decree of the divine will.[45] Essentially, the will of the blessed re-

---

[42] Cf. St. Bonaventure, *II Sent.,* d. 25, pars 1, dub. 2; Duns Scotus, *Ord.,* I, d. 8, n. 72; IV, pp. 185-86; *Oxon.,* II, d. 7, q. un., n. 25; XII, p. 406b; *ibid.,* n. 26; XII, p. 407a; *ibid.,* d. 44, q. un., n. 2; XIII, pp. 497b-498a.

[43] *Oxon.,* II, d. 44, n. 2; XIII, p. 497b: "Libertas absolute est perfectio simpliciter"; *Rep. Par.,* I, d. 10, q. 3, n. 3; XXII, p. 183b: "Necessitas agendi stat cum libertate voluntatis"; *Quodl.,* q. 16, n. 9; XXVI, p. 195a: "Possible est aliquod liberum, stante libertate, necessario agere."

[44] *Ord.,* I, d. 39, Appendix A; VI, p. 417: "Prima libertas [voluntatis ad oppositos actus] habet necessario aliquam imperfectionem annexam, quia potentialitatem passivam voluntatis et mutabilitatem"; *ibid.,* p. 425: "Voluntas divina non est indifferens ad diversos actus volendi et nolendi, quia hoc in voluntate nostra non erat sine imperfectione voluntatis"; *Quodl.,* q. 16, n. 8; XXVI, p. 194a: "Voluntas divina necessario vult bonitatem suam, et tamen in volendo eam est libera." To illustrate his point that in God freedom of the will is not incompatible with the absolute necessity of his nature, Scotus uses the example of a man who hurls himself from a high place, and while falling necessarily by the law of gravitation, he continues to will to fall by a free act of his will. *Ibid.,* n. 18; XXVI, p. 201ab. It should be noted, however, that in God the freedom of the will does not extend to the intrinsic constitution of the divine nature, which precedes, as it were, the act of the will. God is not God because he wills to be so, but because of an intrinsic necessity. Scotus makes this point very clear when he speaks of the relationship between intellect and will in God: "Intellectus divinus ex necessitate naturae est speculativus, et non est ad hoc formaliter libertas, licet non sit sine voluntate complacente; Deus enim necessario est sciens, non autem voluntate est sciens proprie, sicut necessitate—non voluntate—est Deus . . . libertas eius non est ad intrinseca (quae quasi praecedunt actum eius)." *Ord.,* I, d. 38, n. 9; VI, p. 306. The divine essence enjoys absolute priority over all relationships in God: "Recte ergo in divinis in comparatione ad essentiam, tanquam ad entitatem, simpliciter primam et absolutam, consideratur omnis ordo cuiuscumque, sive quorumcumque, quae in divinis sunt." *Quodl.,* q. 1, n. 3; XXV, p. 7a. For a more detailed analysis of Scotus' conception of the divine will and its misrepresentation by many theologians, both Protestant and Catholic, the reader is referred to Parthenius Minges, O.F.M., *Der Gottesbegriff des Duns Scotus auf seinen angeblich excessiven Indeterminismus geprüft* (Vienna: Mayr, 1907).

[45] *Oxon.,* IV, d. 49, q. 6, n. 4; XXI, pp. 232b-233a.

mains the same as the will of the *homo viator*, for the attainment of the end does not change the nature of the faculty attaining it but only increases the degree of intensity of its acts.[46] Thus the act by which the blessed love God remains a contingent act and not a necessary one, just as God does not necessarily have to reveal himself to them.[47] Yet the blessed in heaven feel such an attraction towards God clearly seen in the beatific vision that they love him by what may be called moral necessity or necessity *secundum quid*. This becomes for them like a second nature and is similar to the natural tendency by which stones and metals tend to the center of the earth.[48]

As to the question why stones and metals tend to the earth by an intrinsic necessity and will tends to its end freely, Scotus answers that they are different types of beings and have therefore different natures. Beyond this, he adds, we can say nothing.[49] Likewise, there is no real answer to the question as to the way in which freedom and necessity can be reconciled for, as Aristotle says, no reason should be asked of those things which admit of no reason, just as a demonstration of a principle is no demonstration. Hence the divine will wills of necessity divine goodness, because it is such a will and such is divine goodness; the divine will wills contingently the goodness of other things, because such is the nature of the divine will and such is the nature of the goodness of other things. All we can say is that the infinite will necessarily loves an infinite object because this is a perfection, but it cannot love neces-

---

[46] *Ord.*, I, d. 1, n. 136; II, p. 91: "Voluntas autem habens eandem caritatem quam modo habet [per visionem Dei], prius contingenter eliciebat actum fruendi, ergo modo non necessario elicit actum illum, cum nulla sit facta mutatio ex parte eius"; *ibid.*, n. 138; II, p. 93: "Diversa approximatio passi ad agens non causat necessitatem sed tantum intensiorem actionem."

[47] *Oxon.*, IV, d. 49, q. 6, n. 9; XXI, pp. 187b-188a: "Illa necessitas videndi [Deum clare visum] est simpliciter necessitas, sed tantummodo necessitas si obiectum praesens moveat; et istud est sic mere contingens, quia obiectum istud voluntarie et contingenter movet quemcumque intellectum creatum; sed etiam voluntas contingenter fruitur illo viso contingenter." In this sense Scotus can say that absolutely speaking the blessed in heaven, as well as the angels, still retain the capacity to sin. This is merely a physical and remote capacity which they will never use, since they are made impeccable by the preserving action of God, a free gift like beatitude itself. *Ibid.*, n. 15; XXI, pp. 233b-234a. In traditional scholastic terms, Scotus says that the blessed in heaven cannot sin *in sensu composito* but could sin *in sensu diviso*, i.e., if the grace of God would not prevent them—which of course will never be the case. *Ibid.*, n. 11; XXI, p. 229a.

[48] *Ibid.*, n. 9; XXI, p. 188ab.

[49] *Quodl.*, q. 16, n. 16; XXVI, p. 199a.

sarily an object that is not infinite because this is an imperfection.[50]

From the foregoing discussion it should be clear that the Scotistic notion of freedom is quite different from the Thomistic concept of it. While both Thomas and Scotus hold that freedom is a simple perfection, at least as far as the power of choosing the good is concerned, Thomas maintains that freedom is essentially freedom of choice or contradiction;[51] Scotus, on the other hand, asserts that choice is not of the essence of freedom but rather a mark of imperfection. Thus, according to Aquinas, when no choice is possible between acting or not acting, acting one way or another, freedom ceases to exist, since for him freedom and necessity are two contradictory terms. On this premise it is of course meaningless to speak of freedom of will as regards happiness or good in general, since everyone wants to be happy. This is even more true in regard to the blessed in heaven who have no choice but to love God. Furthermore, it would be outrageous to attribute such a freedom to God's love of himself, since God's self-love is just as necessary as his own essence.

While Scotus agrees with Thomas on this last score, since he never thinks for a moment of denying the intrinsic necessity of God's self-love, he still maintains that God is absolutely and essentially free even in regard to his operations *ad intra*, for in his understanding of the terms, freedom and necessity are not contradictory of one another. The contradiction obtains rather between a *natural* principle and a *free* principle, since the former is necessarily determined, while the latter is self-determining. This self-determination may be either by an intrinsic necessity or contingently. In the first case we have essential freedom or freedom of dominion; in the second case we have freedom of contingence, inasmuch as there is a possibility of choice between acting or nonacting, acting one way or another. As can be readily seen, this latter coincides with the only type of freedom admitted by the Thomistic school.[52] To state it in more simple terms, freedom is for Scotus like a genus containing two distinct species, essential freedom and freedom of contingence. For St. Thomas

[50] *Ibid.*, n. 9; XXVI, p. 195b.

[51] St. Thomas, *Sum. theol.*, I, q. 83, a. 4 c: "Voluntas et liberum arbitrium non sunt duae potentiae, sed una"; *ibid.*, a. 3 c: "Proprium liberi arbitrii est electio: ex hoc enim liberi arbitrii esse dicimur, quod possumus unum recipere, alio recusato, quod est eligere."

[52] *Oxon.*, III, d. 17, q. un., n. 3; XIV, p. 654ab; *Rep. Par.*, IV, d. 43, q. 4, n. 2; XXIV, pp. 520b-521a; *Quodl.*, q. 16, n. 15; XXVI, pp. 198b-199ab.

there is no such thing as essential freedom, for freedom does not belong to the essence of will and means simply freedom of choice or of contradiction. It becomes clear then that to judge the Scotistic doctrine on freedom from purely Thomistic premises, as is often done by ill-informed historians and manualists, is just as wrong and unfair as to evaluate St. Thomas' teaching from the exclusive viewpoint of Scotistic principles. The two schoolmen speak different languages and each one must be interpreted according to the principles of his own teaching.

INTELLECT AND WILL

Scotus' teaching on the nature of the will has a definite bearing on the issue of the relationship between intellect and will. When Peter Lombard defined *liberum arbitrium* as a faculty of reason and will,[53] his medieval commentators began to speculate on the specific role that reason and will play in man's free act. While they all agree in saying that the term *arbitrium* suggests a judgment of reason and the qualification of *liberum* refers to a decision of the will, they are not of one opinion as to the intrinsic relationship between the two faculties in the performance of a free act. This question concerns the very root or proximate cause of freedom, which for the intellectualists is to be placed in reason, while for the voluntarists it resides in the will. If freedom is essentially freedom of choice and powers are distinguished chiefly by their acts and objects, as the intellectualists maintain, it is only logical to admit that the root of freedom lies in the nature of the objects known and in the activity of the intellect. Thus the objective indifference of the judgment of the mind in regard to particular goods becomes, both in the psychological and the ontological orders, the proximate cause and the root of freedom.[54] But if freedom is not merely freedom of choice and faculties are distinguished through their specifically different entities, as the voluntarists and Duns Scotus in particular contend, then the root of freedom must be placed in the will. In this latter case the will,

---

[53] *IV Sent.*, 1. 2, d. 24, n. 5; PL vol. 192, col. 702: "Liberum . . . arbitrium est facultas rationis et voluntatis."

[54] St. Thomas expresses this doctrine in *Sum. theol.*, I-II, q. 17, a. 1, ad. 2, where he states: "Radix libertatis est voluntas sicut subiectum; sed sicut causa, est ratio."

as a self-determining power, remains essentially free even in regard to the last practical judgment of the intellect. The exact nature of the relationship between intellect and will is therefore to be investigated in the light of Duns Scotus' principles. This will give us a further insight into his notion of freedom as a specific characteristic of human acts.

Scotus is well aware of the difficulty inherent to the problem under consideration. As a rational appetite, the will cannot simply follow the dictate of intellect. This would be the destruction of human freedom, since by its nature the intellect is not free. On the other hand, the will must be intellectually aware of its decisions, and this awareness is only possible through an act of the intellect. Knowledge on the intellectual level is in effect an exclusive act of the intellect. To hold, as many scholastic manualists do, that will is a blind faculty and the last practical judgment of the intellect is sufficient to safeguard the rational nature of its decisions as well as its freedom, is no solution to the problem. In such a case, it is the intellect that is responsible for the will's decisions, not the will. Nor is it enough, in order to preserve the freedom of human acts, to say that the will has the power to direct the intellect to the consideration of any particular object, including that of the last practical judgment. Apart from the fact that this seems to involve a vicious circle, inasmuch as intellect determines will, and will in turn determines intellect, we can further ask, How is the will going to direct the intellect except by another practical judgment determining it to do so? This would lead to an infinite regress, and we would never escape some sort of determinism. This is precisely what Scotus wants to avoid. Besides, it must be frankly admitted that the will as a blind faculty is a pure abstraction of our mind; in practice the will never acts blindly. To harmonize the rational nature and essential freedom of the will is the task Scotus imposes upon himself.

For Scotus, it is worth recalling, intellect and will are not really distinct powers, nor are they really distinct from the soul. They are rather virtual parts of the soul from which they are only formally distinct. The essential identity of the soul and its powers helps us to understand why intellect and will are so closely related to one another that they are mutually dependent in their activity.[55] It also explains why their acts are received

---

[55] *Rep. Par.*, IV, d. 45, q. 2, n. 9; XXIV, p. 560b: "Fundantur enim

immediately into the essence of the soul, although by nature the act of intellect precedes the act of will.[56] The entitative order existing between the two higher powers of the soul makes it impossible for will to act without a preceding act of intellect.[57] Thus the old scholastic maxim, *nihil volitum quin praecognitum*, is fully endorsed by the Subtle Doctor.[58]

Knowledge is not only a necessary requirement for the act of will, but the object known carries a certain weight in the will's decisions by inclining it either towards or against it.[59] The good, as previously stated, has a natural appeal to the will in proportion to its entity. This is also true of the intelligible, the good of the intellect, which has therefore a natural tendency to draw the will's assent to it, especially when this takes the form of a last practical judgment or the last dictate of practical reason. This, Scotus affirms, the will can abandon but not without difficulty.[60]

Clearly Scotus is neither an irrationalist nor an indeterminist. The charges that in his system the will makes purely arbitrary decisions without any reference to the judgments of intellect are absolutely groundless. His critics fail to consider the many texts in which Scotus shows the will's natural dependence on intellect, and misinterpret his statements on the will as a self-determining power. Self-determination, it is worth emphasizing, is not the same as arbitrary determination, and much less as lack of determination. Self-determination means simply that the will is free in its deci-

---

[potentiae] in eodem *esse* animae ut partes virtuales, et ideo ad operationem perfectam alicuius potentiae concurrunt coagendo circa idem obiectum, quia quaelibet nata est intendere actum alterius propter concomitantiam earum naturalem."

[56] *Oxon.*, II, d. 16, q. un., n. 8; XIII, p. 17b: "Immediate intelligere et velle in eodem susceptivo recipiuntur, scilicet in essentia animae"; *ibid.*, d. 25, q. un., n. 19; XIII, p. 212b: "Volitio est effectus posterior intellectione naturaliter."

[57] *Ibid.*: "Propter illum ordinem necessarium [inter intellectionem et volitionem] non potest causari volitio a voluntate, nisi prius causetur ab intellectu intellectio."

[58] *Oxon.*, II, d. 1, q. 1, n. 23; XI, p. 44b. See also *ibid.*, d. 42, q. 2, n. 3; XIII, p. 451a: "Omnis volitio requirit necessario intellectionem naturaliter priorem, licet simul duratione."

[59] *Collationes*, XVI, n. 3; V, p. 209b: "Impressio facta ab obiecto in voluntate est pondus et inclinatio."

[60] *Oxon.*, II, d. 6, q. 2, n. 8; XII, p. 354a: "Voluntas . . . inquantum est mere appetitus intellectivus, summe inclinaretur actualiter ad optimum intelligibile, sicut est de optimo visibili; tamen inquantum libera est, potest se refraenare in eliciendo actum, ne sequatur istam inclinationem"; *Rep. Par.*, II, d. 39, q. 2, n. 5; XXIII, p. 205a: "Difficile est voluntatem non inclinari ad id quod est dictatum a ratione practica ultimatim, non tamen est impossibile."

sions, since freedom is part of its nature. Far from doing away with knowledge or motivation, it presupposes it.[61] The precise role played by knowledge, and hence intellect, in the act of the will, is what remains to be seen.

Scotus devotes an entire question of his commentary on the *Sentences* to the problem of whether something other than will is the effective cause of volition. There he mentions the opinion of a "modern doctor" (Godfrey of Fontaines) according to whom the effective cause determining the act of the will is the phantasm. The principal reason given is that the mover and the moved must be located in two distinct subjects. Since will is an intellective appetite, the cause that sets it in motion must be found outside the intellective soul, and this can only be the object present in the phantasm. Another opinion, which Scotus attributes to an "older doctor" (St. Thomas Aquinas), is that the moving cause of the will is the object known by the intellect, just as in sensation it is the appetible object that moves the sensitive appetite. These two opinions have this in common, that they both hold the will to be moved by an extrinsic agent, although they do not agree on the specific nature of this agent. Scotus rejects both opinions and contends that the object, whether present in the phantasm or in the intellect, cannot be the efficient cause of volition.[62]

---

[61] For a defense of Duns Scotus from the charges that have just been mentioned cf. Parthenius Minges, O.F.M., *Ist Duns Scotus Indeterminist?* (Münster in W.: Aschendorffsche Verlagsbuchhandlung, 1905). See also Ephrem Longpré, *La philosophie du B. Duns Scot* (Paris: Société et Librairie St. François d'Assise, 1924), pp. 194-227.

[62] *Oxon.*, II, d. 25, q. un.; XIII, pp. 196ff: "Utrum aliquid aliud a voluntate causet effective actum volendi in voluntate?" See also *Rep. Par.*, II, d. 25, q. un.; XXIII, pp. 117ff: "Utrum aliud a voluntate causat actum eius effective?" In his *Scholia* preceding Scotus' text of the *Opus Oxoniense*, as well as in the marginal notes, Cavellus identifies the *doctor modernus* with Godfrey of Fontaines, a contemporary of Duns Scotus, and the *doctor antiquior* with Henry of Ghent and refers to some specific questions of their *Quodlibeta*. Parthenius Minges follows Cavellus on this score but gives no references to the *Quodlibeta* or any other work of the two doctors (Cf. *Ioannis Duns Scoti doctrina philosophica et theologica*, Quaracchi: Collegium S. Bonaventurae, 1930, I, 343-44). After careful reading of the pertinent questions referred to by Cavellus, the present writer has been unable to find in the *Quodlibeta* of Godfrey of Fontaines any specific text to the effect that the phantasm as such is the moving cause of the act of the will. Godfrey always speaks of the object as the efficient cause of the act of the will. He writes: "Non videtur ergo esse negandum quin voluntas vere ab obiecto moveatur quantum ad actus volitionis." *Quodlibetum sextum*, q. 7, in *Les philosophes belges*, ed. by M. De Wulf and J. Hoffmans (Louvain: Institut Supérieur de Philosophie de l'Université, 1914), III, 159. Also: "Sed illud magis est ad nostrum propositum, scilicet ad ostendendum quod voluntas non

A natural agent, Scotus argues, cannot by itself be the cause of contrary acts in one and the same subject, for by its nature it is determined to produce one effect only. But our will has the power to produce contrary acts as regards the one and the same object; it can either accept it or reject it. Hence the object, as a natural agent, cannot be the cause of volition.[63] The major premise of this argument can be illustrated by the following example hinted at by Scotus and his commentators. If a natural cause could produce two opposite effects, such as heat and cold, it would produce none at all or it would produce both at one and the same time. There is no reason, in fact, why it should produce only one effect and not the other, since it would be equally determined to both of them.

---

moveat se, sed quod moveatur ab obiecto apprehenso, quia bonum secundum quod apprehensum movet voluntatem vel ad actum volitionis ut hoc dicitur secundum rationem causae efficientis, licet secundum quod est in se ipso moveat in ratione finis." *Ibid.*, p. 164. Again: "Unaquaeque potentia determinatur ad actum suum per se et directe solum ab obiecto, quod scilicet determinat actum cui dat forman et speciem. Et sic universaliter actus intellectus per se determinatur ab obiecto intelligibili et actus appetitus ab obiecto appetibili secundum rationem causae moventis et agentis." *Ibid.*, p. 221. However, Godfrey makes it clear that although the act of the intellect precedes by nature the act of the will, the object moves both intellect and will *at one and the same time*, since the two faculties are rooted in the same soul. "Est dicendum quod voluntas proprie et per se non movet intellectum nec e converso, sed obiectum quod intellectum movet ad actum intellectionis movet etiam voluntatem ad actum volitionis. Unde, pro tanto intellectus movet voluntatem in quantum voluntas non fit in actu a suo obiecto nisi natura saltem prius intellectus factus sit in actu ab eodem obiecto. Unde unum et idem obiectum secundum rem efficit duplicem actionem ordine naturae, tamen prius unam quam alteram, sed simul tempore in eodem subiecto, id est in anima ratione dictarum eius potentiarum, scilicet intellectus et voluntatis." *Ibid.*, p. 170. Hence Scotus' presentation of Godfrey's view can be said to be substantially correct, since it is only through the phantasm that the object can move intellect and will. For an analysis of Godfrey's teaching on the role that the object plays in the act of the will cf. D. O. Lottin, "Le libre arbitre chez Godefroid de Fontaines," *Revue néoscolastique de philosophie*, 40 (1937), 213-41.

As to Henry of Ghent, he denies explicitly that the intellect is the moving cause of the will. The intellect is only a necessary condition for the act of the will. He writes: "Voluntas quantumcumque inclinetur ab intellectu, libere potest huiusmodi inclinationi contraire et non moveri in id ad quod intellectus inclinat: immo si movetur et fertur in illud volendo, hoc libere facit et sua propria virtute . . . quia voluntas respectu suiipsius habet vim motivam per se, et movet se per se: mota autem a se non ab alio, movet alia a se: *intellectum autem praesupponit voluntas sicut causam sine qua non tantummodo"* (italics ours). Henricus Gandavensis, *Quodlibeta* (Paris, 1518), quodl. XI, q. 6, fo. 455 BC. The *doctor antiquior* to which Scotus refers is most likely St. Thomas Aquinas, who is known to have held the view that the intellect is the moving cause of the will.

[63] *Oxon.*, II, d. 25, q. un., n. 6; XIII, p. 201a.

But since contrary effects, such as heat and cold, cannot exist together without contradiction, so a natural agent cannot produce two opposite effects but only that to which it is determined by nature.

A second argument against the aforesaid opinions is this. Whenever an act is received only passively, it must be attributed to the agent rather than to the recipient. Hence, if the object is the effective cause of volition, the latter will not be under the will's control, nor will be any other act commanded by the will. Thus all distinction between good and evil acts disappears.[64]

These arguments, it is hardly necessary to remark, rest on the assumption that for the upholders of the two preceding views the object is the total cause of volition, a psychological determinism to which neither Godfrey nor Aquinas would subscribe. Yet it must be admitted that some of their expressions tend to overemphasize the role that the object plays in volition at the expense of the act of the will proper. Thus, to mention only St. Thomas, he states that "the appetitive power is a passive power, which is naturally moved by the thing apprehended."[65] Moreover, he quotes Aristotle's *De anima* and *Metaphysica* to the effect that "the apprehended appetible is a mover which is not moved, while the appetite is a moved mover."[66] It is statements of this kind that provoked the criticism of the Subtle Doctor, who is more concerned about the consequences they might lead to than the actual intention of their authors.

Answering more directly the reason underlying the view of the "modern doctor," Scotus says that the principle that the mover and the moved must be distinct as to their subjects cannot be applied to spiritual substances. Indeed, he adds, even "another doctor"—he refers here to St. Thomas Aquinas—admits that the will can be moved by the object apprehended by the intellect, despite the fact that both intellect and will are powers of one and the same soul. Moreover—and here Scotus goes beyond St. Thomas—the mover and the moved not only need not be distinct as to their subjects, but one and the same thing can at the same time move and be

---

[64] *Ibid.*

[65] *Sum. theol.*, I, q. 80, a. 2, Resp.

[66] *Ibid.* Cf. Aristotle's *De anima*, III, 10 (433a 13-26); *Metaph.*, XII, 7 (1072a 26).

moved. It can be in virtual act with regard to a certain perfection and in potency to the formal act of this same perfection.[67]

As to the comparison between the motion of the appetible object in sensation and the motion of the object known by the intellect in volition, which is used by the "older doctor" to support his opinion, Scotus retorts that the analogy, far from supporting that view, is a further proof of his own theory. In fact, the appetible object can move the sensitive appetite precisely because the latter is not free. The intellective appetite, on the contrary, is free, and hence it cannot be moved by the object as by its effective cause. In the words of St. John Damascene, *sensitivus ducitur et non ducit, sed intellectivus ducit et non ducitur*.[68]

Scotus concludes his long discussion, of which only the major points have been highlighted in this study, with the following statement: *Dico ergo ad quaestionem quod nihil aliud a voluntate est causa totalis volitionis in voluntate*.[69] This passage, which we have quoted in its original Latin text because of its importance, is somewhat ambiguous. It may mean that nothing but the will is the total cause of volition, and it may also mean that nothing that is extraneous to the will is the total cause of volition.[70] The first interpretation is the most widely accepted and seems to be more in keeping with recent findings, as we shall see presently; however, the second interpretation is not without some textual evidence. Scotus' statement comes as a conclusion to his arguments against those who, in his opinion, contend that will is merely a passive power and must be moved by an extrinsic agent in order to act. In such a case the object present in the phantasm or in the intellect becomes the determining cause—Scotus calls it the total cause—of the act of

---

[67] *Oxon.*, II, d. 25, q. un., nn. 12-15; XIII, pp. 207b-209b. For a further explanation of Scotus' teaching on this point cf. Roy R. Effler, O.F.M., *John Duns Scotus and the Principle "Omne quod movetur ad alio movetur"* (St. Bonaventure, N.Y.: The Franciscan Institute, 1962), pp. 52-97.

[68] *Oxon.*, II, d. 25, q. un., n. 21; XIII, p. 220b. St. John Damascene's text is contained substantially but not literally in his *De fide orthodoxa*, Book 2, chaps. 22 and 23.

[69] *Oxon.*, II, d. 25, q. un., n. 22; XIII, p. 221b. See also *Rep. Par.*, II, d. 25, q. un, n. 20; XXIII, p. 127b: "Dico igitur ad quaestionem, quod nihil creatum aliud a voluntate est causa totalis actus volendi in voluntate."

[70] The first interpretation has been followed, among others, by Étienne Gilson in his *Jean Duns Scot. Introduction à ses positions fondamentales* (Paris: Vrin, 1952), p. 590, n. 2. Ephrem Longpré follows the second interpretation. Cf. his work, *La philosophie du B. Duns Scot*, p. 221.

the will.[71] This is the view that Scotus wants to condemn. In so doing, he does not necessarily imply that the object has no part in volition. In fact, he adds in the same context, that if one wishes to maintain that the object moves the will effectively but not as a total cause, then he would go along with such a view and even claim Aristotle's authority to its support.[72] Moreover, Lychetus' commentary on the foregoing texts makes it clear that Scotus' teaching does not rule out the possibility for the object known to be called partial cause of volition, even though the Subtle Doctor does not state this explicitly.[73] What Scotus does say, is that the object is either a *causa sine qua non* of the act of the will or a cause that moves the will effectively but only *per accidens,* inasmuch as its presence is a necessary condition for the will to act but has no direct bearing on the will as a free power.[74]

Thus, throughout the entire question it appears that Scotus is chiefly concerned with saving the will from any interference that might jeopardize its freedom. In this sense one may say that the

---

[71] When arguing against the *doctor modernus,* Scotus prefaces his answer with these words: "Contra primam opinionem arguitur specialiter: Si phantasma est causa totalis et aequivoca intellectionis et volitionis etc." *Rep. Par.,* II, d. 25, q. un., n. 9; XXIII, p. 121a.

[72] *Oxon.,* II, d. 25, q. un., n. 24; XIII, p. 223a: "Qui diceret quod obiectum movet voluntatem effective, non tamen ut totalis causa, sed ut aliquid ibi faciens, tunc non esset glossanda auctoritas, quod movet, scilicet metaphorice, et tunc auctoritas esset pro me." And even more clearly in *Rep. Par.,* II, d. 25, q. un., n. 21; XXIII, p. 128b: ". . . sustinendo quod obiectum movet effective voluntatem, non tamen est causa totalis, tunc auctoritas Aristotelis est pro me." See also *Rep. Par.,* IV, d. 49, q. 2, n. 14; XXIV, p. 626b, where it is stated that the intellect is a partial cause of volition: "Est igitur [intellectus] causa partialis [volitionis]."

[73] *Oxon.,* II, d. 25, q. un., Commentarius, n. 20; XIII, p. 225b: *"Dico ergo ad quaestionem etc.* Hic Doctor vult expresse quod nihil aliud a voluntate sit causa totalis ipsius volitionis, sed non negat expresse quin aliquid aliud possit esse causa partialis, et probat quod voluntas est causa volitionis saltem partialis"; *ibid.,* n. 22, p. 226a: *"Ad primum principale etc.* Nunc Doctor respondet ad argumentum, primo dicit sustinendo quod obiectum cognitum sit causa partialis volitionis, quod auctoritas Aristotelis sic debet intelligi, quod appetibile extra tantum movet partialiter, id est, est causa partialis volitionis, quod est rationabilius."

[74] *Oxon.,* II, d. 25, q. un., n. 21; XIII, p. 220ab: "Si sustineatur quod obiectum movet potentiam obiective, licet non sit causa totalis, potest tunc sustineri quod . . . intra movet ut efficiens et extra ut finis. Sustinendo tamen quod sit tantum causa sine qua non, et nullo modo movens effective, tunc oportet glossare quod non movet effective per se, sed per accidens." See also *ibid.,* n. 19; XIII, p. 212b; "Unde est quod phantasiatio vel obiectum apprehensum requiratur ad hoc quod sit volitio, non tamen requiritur nisi sicut causa sine qua non."

will is totally responsible for its own acts.[75] However, since a rational appetite cannot act blindly, the object known plays a definite and necessary role in the act of the will considered in its totality, or in its entire complexity as a rational decision.[76] In this latter sense the object may be called *causa sine qua non* or *causa per accidens,* and even a partial cause of volition. Followers of the first interpretation of the Latin text above mentioned would disagree with this last connotation.

We have expounded at considerable length the content of distinction 25 of the second book of Scotus' commentary on the *Sentences* because it is there that the Subtle Doctor specifically takes up the question of the relationship between intellect and will in the act of volition. The conclusion reached at the end of the study of all the pertinent texts does not seem to be completely satisfactory and is likely to raise many questions in view of apparently conflicting passages in the *Opus Oxoniense* itself and in other of Scotus' works. Does such a conclusion, unsatisfactory as it may be, represent Scotus' final word on the subject? If one considers that the *Opus Oxoniense* is his definitive work, he may be inclined to believe so. However, this is not the case.

The eminent scholar, Father Charles Balić, has proved that distinction 25 of the second book of the *Ordinatio* does not contain Scotus' teaching at Oxford but rather his lectures at Paris. Distinction 25, along with eleven others in the same book, i.e., d. 12 and dd. 15-24, was introduced later into the *Ordinatio* from the *Additiones magnae* of William of Alnwick, a Scotus disciple, in order to fill the gap left by the master who had omitted it entirely. The *Additiones magnae* are for the most part reports of Scotus' lectures at Paris, although they also contain sections from the *Lectura*

---

[75] This seems to be the meaning of Lychetus' pertinent observation: "[Doctor] quaerit istam libertatem voluntatis salvare, quod si obiectum cognitum esset causa partialis illius, non posset ita salvari sua libertas." *Oxon.,* II, d. 25, q. un., Commentarius, n. 18; XIII, p. 221a. This statement should not be construed as meaning that the object known can in no way be called a partial cause of volition taken in its totality, i.e., as an all-embracing rational decision, and not merely in its formal aspect as a free act. Otherwise Lychetus' previous statements quoted above in n. 73 would be meaningless and even contradictory.

[76] Scotus alludes to the act of the will taken in this sense when, speaking of the will as an indeterminate cause, he writes: "Alia est causa indeterminata, quae est causa completa potens se determinare ad unum istorum, *et ita est rationalis complexa, ut voluntas cum intellectu,* et hoc necesse est dicere, si aliquid sit contingens" (italics ours). *Rep. Par.,* II, d. 25, q. un., n. 23; XXIII, p. 129b.

Oxoniensis. They are very valuable, not only because of the close relationship between their author and the Subtle Doctor, but also because of the helpful remarks which accompany the text.[77] Thus, as far as our question is concerned, namely, whether something other than the will is the effective cause of volition, William of Alnwick reports in the *Additiones magnae* first Scotus' teaching from the *Lectura Parisiensis* that the will is the *total cause* of volition and the object known is only a *causa sine qua non,* then he remarks that Scotus refuted this opinion in many ways at Oxford and gives his master's arguments to this effect.[78]

In concluding the arguments and shortly before resuming the report from the *Lectura Parisiensis,* he makes the further observation that Scotus taught differently at Oxford than he had at Paris.[79] The content of a pertinent question from the *Secundae additiones,* which has been published for the first time by Father Balić and is attributed by him to Duns Scotus, seems to support William of Alnwick's statement. In fact, Scotus takes there the same position

[77] For a more detailed information on the findings of Father Balić, especially in regard to the topic of our discussion, see the following studies by the eminent scholar: *Les commentaires de Jean Duns Scot sur les quatres livres des Sentences* (Louvain: Bureaux de la Revue, 1927), pp. 92-134; 264-301; "Circa positiones fundamentales I. Duns Scoti," *Antonianum,* 28 (1953), 286-90; "Iubilaeum Commissionis Scotisticae: Commemorativus sermo P. Caroli Balić," *Acta Ordinis Fratrum Minorum,* 83 (May-June, 1964), 315-23.

[78] Balić, *Les commentaires,* pp. 276-77: "Notandum quod secundum hanc opinionem, quae ponit voluntatem esse totam causam activam volitionis et obiectum non esse causam eius nec cognitio obiecti, sed quod obiectum requiritur ut causa sine qua non, cognitio vero per amotionem sive solutionem impedimenti, quia cognitio unius obiecti impedit ne aliud non cognitum possit appeti et ideo voluntas removet impedimentum imperando [intellectui] ad cognoscendum sive considerandum aliud obiectum, *hanc—inquam—opinionem* [Scotus] *multipliciter Oxoniae improbavit* . . ." This statement of William of Alnwick has been checked against Balić's more recent presentation of it in *Acta Ordinis Fratrum Minorum,* art. cit., p. 318.

[79] Balić, *Les commentaires,* p. 282: *"Ideo et aliter dixit Oxonie ad quaestionem."* Concerning the structure of the question, "Utrum aliquid aliud a voluntate causet effective actum volendi in voluntate," as reported in the *Additiones magnae* of William of Alnwick and published for the first time in *Les commentaires,* pp. 264-301, Father Balić has this to say: "Itaque tres quaestiones de eadem materia a Guilelmo de Alnwick, ex *Lectura Parisiensi* et *Oxoniensi* extractae afferuntur: prima, ut videtur Parisiis habita, quae ponitur pagina 265-276; deinde venit extractum ex *Lectura Oxoniensi* (pp. 277-286); tertia, indicata tamquam alia questio Parisiensis (pp. 286-301). Dubium ponitur utrum quae in secunda quaestione ponuntur de modo concurrendi obiecti et voluntatis (pp. 282-285) sint fideliter ab Alnwick reproducta ex *Lectura Oxoniensi* an modo proprio exposita: nam in commentario inedito in *II Sententiarum,* in quo praelectiones *Oxoniensis* inveniuntur, eaedem expressiones non leguntur." *Antonianum,* art. cit., p. 287, n. 2.

in regard to the relationship between intellect and will that William ascribes to him as a lecturer at Oxford.[80] There is, therefore, good ground for believing that Scotus' approach to the problem under discussion underwent a certain evolution which reached its final stage during his teaching at Oxford but never took concrete shape in the *Ordinatio* because his untimely death prevented him from carrying out his project.[81]

Having seen the first phase of Scotus' approach to the problem as represented by the *Lectura Parisiensis*, we shall now investigate his teaching at Oxford by making use of the *Additiones magnae*, the *Secundae additiones*, and some scattered passages from the *Opus Oxoniense* other than those contained in distinction 25 of the second book which, as stated above, does not really belong there. The section of question III of William of Alnwick's *Additiones magnae*, where Scotus' teaching at Oxford is reported, is to some extent the reverse of the preceding section taken from the *Lectura Parisiensis*.[82] Indeed, in section two Scotus refutes one by one all the arguments favoring the doctrine that the will is the total cause of volition and the object known is only its *causa sine qua non*, a doctrine that he himself had apparently embraced at one time. We shall follow him in his reasoning.

When agent and recipient are in close contact and no obstacle is in their way, action follows necessarily in the case of natural principles, and can follow at all times if the agent is free. Hence if the will were the total active cause of volition, just as it is its total re-

[80] Cf. P. Ch. Balić, "Une question inédite de J. Duns Scot sur la volonté," *Recherches de théologie ancienne et médiévale*, 3 (1931), 191-208.

[81] That Scotus intended to include distinction 25 in his second book of the *Ordinatio* and defend what seems to be his new approach to the problem of the relationship between intellect and will, is evident from his statement in *Opus Oxoniense*, II, d. 7, q. un., n. 15; XII, p. 392a: "Voluntas quidem respectu rectae volitionis *est principium activum partiale*, sicut tactum fuit distinctione 17 primi, et tangetur infra distinctione 25" (italics ours).

[82] The different teaching in the two sections had already been noticed by a reader of the codex *Veronensis* (210) who inserted the following note on the margin of question 25: "Nota quod ista quaestio, scilicet 'Notandum' etc., non debet esse in isto libro, sed fuit addita a cancellario vel ab aliis; et verum est quod est in alia *Lectura* [i.e., *Oxoniensi*], et fuit extracta; et tenebat oppositum istius quod tenet hic." This reader, observes Father Balić, did not know that both the "Notandum" and the preceding question had been extracted from the *Additiones magnae* of William of Alnwick who had taken the question from the *Reportatio Parisiensis* of the codex Patavinus and inserted it, along with the "Notandum," in the *Additiones magnae* immediately before the report from the *Lectura Oxoniensis*. Cf. Balić, "Iubilaeum Commissionis Scotisticae," *Acta Ordinis Fratrum Minorum*, p. 319.

ceptive cause, one must say that, as long as it is not impeded, it can always act, even if no object is present. This, Scotus asserts, is certainly not the case.[83] To the objection that when no object is present the will is by that very fact prevented from acting, so that the object known is a necessary condition for the will's activity rather than its effective cause, Scotus retorts that this line of reasoning is faulty for it rests on a false assumption. In fact, one could equally well say that a wood is the total cause of its own calefaction, and that every natural recipient is the total cause of the act it receives, for in these cases the relationship between agent and recipient is the same as that between the object known and will in the act of volition. But since this is evidently wrong, so it is also wrong to affirm that the object known is merely the *causa sine qua non* of volition.[84]

It is commonly admitted, Scotus argues further, that the four metaphysical causes are sufficient for the production of all effects. If a fifth cause is introduced, such as the *causa sine qua non*, then one must choose between these two alternatives: either the doctrine of the four causes is wrong, or the so-called fifth cause must be reduced to one of the four causes. Since the first alternative is unacceptable, one must say that the *causa sine qua non* is not a cause in its own right but is reducible to one of the four causes. Besides, Scotus adds, nowhere in the world is there such a thing as a *causa sine qua non* which is absolutely necessary for the action of an agent and at the same time has no causal relationship to it.[85]

Again, if the object is merely a *causa sine qua non* of volition, then the act of the will does no more receive its formal specification from the object and all volitions are of the same kind, for they would proceed from one and the same total cause. This no one can accept. Nor can it be rebutted that the will is a universally active cause which of itself is capable of specifically different acts, just as the sun can by its own power produce specifically different effects. To hold this is tantamount to saying that the will has an infinite power. Indeed, since there is no limit to the power of God in producing new species, it takes an infinite power to perform as many acts of volition as new species are, or can be brought, in existence.[86]

In conclusion, since a free agent can only act on something that

---

[83] Balić, *Les commentaires*, p. 277.
[84] *Ibid.*
[85] *Ibid.*, p. 278. See also *Ord.*, d. 3, n. 415; III, p. 252.
[86] Balić, *Les commentaires*, pp. 279-80.

is previously known, knowledge is not merely an accidental requirement for the act of the will, but it exerts on it a real causality.[87] Hence volition is *per se* from the will as an active cause and from the object known as its partial cause, in such wise that the total cause of volition includes intellect in its first and second act, will in its first act, and the object.[88]

The same teaching can be gathered from the pertinent question of the *Secundae additiones* which is conducted in a slightly different manner from the preceding one but reflects also Scotus' position at Oxford. The question asks, whether the act of the will is caused in the will by the object moving it or by the will moving itself.[89] Taking a stand between two extreme positions, one maintaining that the only effective cause of volition is the object (Godfrey of Fontaines), and the other that such an effective cause is the will (Henry of Ghent), Scotus asserts that both object and will concur in the volitional act. Volition is thus from both of them as from its effective cause.[90]

Having made clear his position on the question concerning the effective cause of volition, Scotus pursues his inquiry further and takes up the problem of the specific contribution that each of the partial causes brings to the act of the will considered in its totality. Skillful analyst that he is, he paves the way for his solution by distinguishing three ways in which partial causes may concur in the production of an effect. They may concur on an equal basis and independently of one another, like two men pulling the same

[87] *Ibid.*, pp. 281-82: ". . . non agit aliquid libere per se nisi circa per se cognitum, igitur cognoscere non est per accidens requisitum ad velle; habebit ergo aliquam causalitatem per se in eliciendo actum." It is precisely at this place that William of Alnwick makes the remark, "*Ideo et aliter dixit Oxonie ad quaestionem.*"

[88] *Ibid.*, p. 282: ". . . volitio est per se a voluntate, ut a causa activa, et ab obiecto intellecto ut ab alia causa partiali, ita quod totalis causa volitionis includit intellectum in actu primo et secundo, voluntatem in actu primo [other codices read "in actu secundo"] et obiectum."

[89] Balić, *Une question inédite*, p. 192: "Circa libertatem voluntatis quaero, an actus voluntatis causetur in voluntate ab obiecto movente ipsam vel a voluntate movente seipsam."

[90] *Ibid.*, p. 202: "Respondeo igitur ad quaestionem, quod causa effectiva actus volendi non est tantum obiectum, ut phantasma, quia hoc nullo modo salvat libertatem, prout ponit prima opinio, nec etiam causa effectiva actus volendi est tantum voluntas, quemadmodum ponit secunda extrema, quia tunc non possunt salvari omnes conditiones quae consequuntur actum volendi, ut ostensum est. Ideo teneo viam mediam, quod tam voluntas quam obiectum concurrat ad causandum actum volendi, ita quod *actus volendi est a voluntate et ab obiecto cognito ut a causa effectiva*" (italics ours).

boat. Such causes are only accidentally related to one another and their concurrence can be eliminated by increasing the efficiency of one of them. A very strong man can pull a boat that takes the combined effort of two ordinary men. Partial causes may also concur in such a way that one cause depends on the other for its causation, so that between them there is an essential relationship as between inferior and superior causes. Thus the cue moves the ball only to the extent that it is moved by the hand, since the cue cannot of itself be the cause of motion in another body. There is a third way in which partial causes may concur in the production of an effect, and that is when each cause is a cause in its own right and yet one is the principal agent and the other, although equally necessary and indispensable, is somehow subordinated to it. A typical example is the process of generation, where father and mother concur as partial causes in the production of offspring, each one bringing his own distinct but necessary contribution in such wise that while the father may be called the principal agent, both father and mother preserve their relative independence.[91]

Applying these principles to the case under study, Scotus says that in volition collaboration between the object known and the will must be placed in this third type of concurrence. Both object and will are essentially related to one another, inasmuch as neither of them can act without the other, and yet each one is in itself a perfect cause and relatively independent as to the specific nature of its causality. The total causation of the act of the will is thus from the intellect, the object known, and the will as partial causes. But since the act is posited freely, and freedom belongs to will as the power that can act or not act, as well as dispose of the other causes for the production of the effect, will must be called the principal cause (*causa principalior*) of volition.[92] This teaching is fur-

[91] Balić, *Les commentaires*, p. 282; The same, *Une question inédite*, pp. 202-203; *Ord.*, I, d. 3, n. 496; III, pp. 293-94.

[92] Balić, *Les commentaires*, pp. 282-83; The same, *Une question inédite*, p. 203: "Voluntas unius causae habet rationem, sc. causae particularis respectu actus volendi, et anima actum cognoscendi obiectum ratione alterius causae partialis, et utrumque est simul causa totalis respectu actus volendi, voluntas tamen est causa principalior et natura cognoscens minus principalis, quia voluntas libere movet"; *ibid.*, p. 204: "Voluntas igitur cum potentia rationali concurrit ut una causa et una sine altera est tantum causa remota, unde potentia rationalis cum voluntate determinante est causa per se actus communiter volendi." Scotus explains the meaning of *causa principalior* in *Ord.*, I, d. 3, n. 560; III, p. 333: "Illa est principalior causa, qua agente, alia causa coagit, et non e converso."

ther confirmed in the *Opus Oxoniense* where intellect is also called, although somewhat hypothetically, the partial cause of volition, while will is said to be its principal agent.[93] In other works, such as the *Quodlibetum* and the *Collationes,* Scotus stresses the independent role of will as a free agent without taking any specific stand on the part played by intellect in the volitional act.[94] He sets however a limit to the power of the will. This consists in its inability to suspend *all* acts of intellect, for any attempt to do so is only possible in terms of an act of the intellect itself.[95] The will is likewise unable, Scotus tells us in the *Oxoniense,* to prevent the first thought of the mind or the simple and, as it were, spontaneous apprehension of an object prior to any reflection on it.[96]

In an attempt to assess the results of our inquiry about Scotus' teaching on the relationship between intellect and will in volition, the following points can be established.

First, neither the intellect nor the object known can be the determining factor in the act of volition, which belongs principally to the will as a self-determining power.

Second, the will is totally responsible for the act of volition as

---

[93] Here are some of Scotus' statements concerning the role of the intellect in volition: *Oxon.,* IV, d. 49, q. ex latere, n. 16; XXI, p. 151b: "Respondeo, nec actus intellectus est totalis causa actus voluntatis, sed partialis causa, si est aliqua"; *ibid.;* "Intellectus autem, si est causa volitionis, est causa subserviens voluntati, tanquam habens actionem primam in ordine generationis"; *ibid.,* n. 18; XXI, p. 155a.: "Posset dici quod intellectus dependet a volitione, ut a causa partiali, sed superiori; e converso autem voluntas ab intellectione, ut a causa partiali, sed subserviente"; *ibid.,* II, d. 26, q. un., n. 5; XIII, p. 237b: "Intellectio per se si sit causa partialis respectu volitionis, ut dicunt aliqui, etc."

The role of the will as a principal cause of volition is pointed out in the following texts: *Oxon.,* II, d. 7, q. un., n. 6; XII, p. 377a: "Cum voluntas sit causa principalis sui actus, quodcumque ponatur in voluntate respectu actus eius, vel non erit causa actus sic eliciendi, vel si sit causa, est secunda causa respectu voluntatis, et non causa principalis"; *ibid.,* IV, d. 49, q. ex latere, n. 17; XXI, p. 152a: "Ut salvetur libertas in homine, oportet dicere, posita intellectione, [hanc] non habere causam totalem volitionis, sed principaliorem respectu eius esse voluntatem quae sola libera est."

[94] *Quodl.,* q. 18, n. 9; XXVI, p. 241b; *Collationes,* III; V, pp. 149ff.

[95] *Quodl.,* q. 16, n. 4; XXVI, p. 185a.

[96] *Ord.,* I, d. 6, q. un., n. 13; IV, p. 93: "In intellectu nostro habente naturaliter primam intellectionem—quae non est in potestate nostra—potest voluntas nostra complacere in illa intellectione iam posita, sed proprie loquendo non elicimus illam actionem volentes sed eam elicitam volumus esse"; *Oxon.,* II, d. 42, q. 4, n. 9; XIII, p. 457a: "Illa simplex intellectio obiecti, ad quam debet intellectus discurrere, non est in potestate voluntatis."

a distinct formality that makes it a free act and proceeds from a principle that is formally distinct from the intellect.[97]

Third, the act of volition, considered not as a distinct formality but rather in its complexity as a rational decision, can only result from the joint cooperation of intellect and will in such wise that the will is its principal cause and the intellect is its secondary but nonetheless important cause, and not merely a necessary condition, as Scotus seems to have taught at one time.[98]

Thus it appears once more that Scotus' voluntarism is a well-balanced doctrine in which intellect and will are each one assigned their specific role in accordance with his own notion of them. Such a voluntarism, while far removed from the extreme voluntaristic trends of some modern and contemporary philosophies, comes close to the intellectualism of St. Thomas, who in his later writings had already moved a step forward towards the position of the Franciscan school by crediting the will with a more active role in volition.[99]

[97] Balić, *Les commentaires*, p. 299: "Nihil aliud a voluntate potest esse totalis causa volitionis in voluntate secundum quod voluntas determinat se libere ad actum volendi causandum." Although this text is taken from a section of the *Additiones magnae* which reports Scotus' teaching at Paris, it contains nevertheless a point of doctrine that is in complete agreement with his notion of the will as an essentially free power formally distinct from the intellect. Cf. *Ord.*, I, d. 3, n. 578; III, pp. 341-42. To the best of our knowledge, Scotus has never rejected such a doctrine.

[98] Our position differs from that of Gilson, *Jean Duns Scot, op. cit.*, pp. 590-93, inasmuch as he fails to see a change in Scotus' approach to the problem of the relationship between intellect and will, as stated by William of Alnwick and evidenced by the *Additiones magnae* and the *Secundae additiones*; it differs also from the position of Walter Hoeres, who in his recent work, *Der Wille als reine Vollkommenheit nach Duns Scotus* (Munich: Pustet, 1962), does not take into consideration the two sets of the *Additiones* and presents Scotus as inclining towards the view that the act of the intellect is only a *causa sine qua non* of the act of the will: "Daher neigt Scotus der Auffassung zu, dass der Erkenntnisakt nichts anderes als *causa sine qua non* für den Vollzug des Willensaktes sei." *Ibid.*, p. 208. However, we wholeheartedly agree with Gilson's observation that in the study under discussion we must distinguish between two problems, one concerning the act of the will as such, and the other concerning the act of the will in its totality, i.e., as including the act of choice. *Op. cit.*, p. 590. The only difficulty is to know in each case which text refers to the act of the will taken in the first sense and which refers to the act of the will taken in the second sense.

[99] St. Thomas' change of approach to the problem of will and freedom is described by Odon Lottin, O.S.B., in his work, *Psychologie et morale aux XIIe et XIIIe siècles* (Louvain: Abbaye du Mont César—Gembloux: Duculot, 1942), I, 226-43; 252-62. The same author summarizes the results of his findings in *Principes de morale* (Louvain: Éditions de l'Abbaye du Mont César, 1946), II, 16-19. He concludes: "On le voit, sans renier la thèse du *De veritate*, q. 24, l'exposé du *De malo*, q. 6, souligne beaucoup plus l'aspect actif de la volonté;

The main difference that distinguishes Scotus' system from that of St. Thomas consists in his emphasis on will as a self-determining power and the preeminence he assigns to it in regard to the intellect. This last point is the subject matter of the following section.

PRIMACY OF THE WILL

If Scotus' attitude towards the problem of the intellect and will relationship has gradually shifted in the direction of a better understanding of the intellect's role in volition, there is one point of doctrine in which his teaching has remained unchanged, and that is the superiority of the will over the intellect. This doctrine, which takes its concrete form in the affirmation that love is above knowledge and has many practical applications in the theological and ascetical fields, is so characteristic of the Scotistic school that it has come to be known as one of its principal features. This is not to say that the doctrine originates with Scotus, for in the words of his Irish commentator, Anthony Hickey, "it is the opinion most commonly held before and after St. Thomas."[100] However, Scotus gave it a great impetus and helped to establish it on more solid grounds. It is mainly because of its intrinsic value and natural appeal that the doctrine has won the admiration and often the outright acceptance of thinkers even outside the Scotistic school who have seen in it an important achievement of philosophical speculation and theological insight. The doctrine will be considered briefly along the general lines of Scotus' treatment.

Scotus discusses the question whether intellect or will is the nobler faculty in a theological context, inasmuch as the question follows immediately the treatment of the related issue whether beatitude consists essentially in the act of the intellect or in the act of the will.[101] He examines first the arguments of the opposite view

---

la raison n'exerce plus qu'une causalité formelle, laquelle se réduira bientôt, dans la Ia-IIae, qq. 9-10, à une simple présentation de l'objet par la raison. Par ces nouvelles formules, saint Thomas se rapprochait sensiblement des énoncés franciscains et séparait ostensiblement sa position de la position déterministe des averroïstes des environs de 1270." *Ibid.*, p. 19.

[100] Commentary on *Oxon.*, I, d. 49, q. ex latere; XXI, p. 125b: "Haec [Scoti] est sententia communissima antiquorum ante et post D. Thomam."

[101] The discussion on the essence of beatitude is found in q. 4 of dist. 49 of the fourth book on the *Sentences;* the related issue, "Utra potentia sit nobilior, intellectus an voluntas," is a *quaestio ex latere, Oxon.*, IV, d. 49, nn. 10-21; XXI, pp. 123-64.

represented by St. Thomas and his followers, next answers them one by one, and then presents his own viewpoint, which usually takes the form of a counter-argument.[102]

A first argument used by Aquinas to prove the superiority of the intellect over the will is derived from the nature of their objects. The true is closer to intellect, and therefore more perfect, than is the good to will, for intellect understands inasmuch as it becomes the object known, whereas will tends to the object as it is in itself. Scotus answers that one could just as well argue that will is higher than intellect because its object is the good in itself, whereas truth is only a good by participation. Similarly, universal good is higher than a particular good, such as the true, the good of the intellect. However, he observes, this kind of reasoning is based on the false premise that the true and the good are really distinct from one another, which is not the case; consequently, they cannot serve as a criterion for judging about the lesser or greater degree of perfection of their respective faculties. Furthermore, if it is questionable whether the good as such can be called the object of will, it is certainly wrong to call the true the object of intellect. The truth of the matter is that the object of both intellect and will is being under the aspect of truth and goodness.[103]

A second argument aiming to prove the primacy of intellect over will is based on the habits predisposing the two faculties to act, for an act is as good and noble as the habit from which it proceeds. Now a habit of the intellect is nobler than any habit of the will, for according to Aristotle wisdom is the noblest of all habits. Thus intellect is superior to will. Here the Subtle Doctor engages on a long discussion the substance of which is an attempt to prove that love, a habit of the will, is the greatest of all habits, not wisdom, a habit of the intellect. He quotes to this effect both St. Paul and St. Augustine. Since the discussion is mostly theological in character, it suffices to have mentioned it.[104]

The third proof is strictly philosophical and argues from the nature of the acts of the two faculties. An efficient equivocal cause, so reason the intellectualists, is more perfect than its effects. But intellect is the efficient cause of the acts of will, for nothing can be willed that is not previously known. Hence the intellect is more

---

[102] For St. Thomas' view cf. *Sum. theol.*, I, q. 82, a. 3; *De veritate*, q. 22, a. 11.
[103] *Oxon.*, IV, d. 49, q. ex lat., nn. 10-12; XXI, pp. 123-24.
[104] *Ibid.*, nn. 13-15, pp. 140-41.

perfect than the will. Scotus grants the major of the syllogism but uses it to his own advantage and arrives at a conclusion that is directly opposite to that of his opponents. If it is true, he writes, that the will depends on the intellect for the knowledge of its object, it is equally true, and perhaps even more so, that the will can command the intellect by directing its attention to one particular object rather than to another. Hence the will can rightly be called the efficient equivocal cause of the acts of the intellect. Yet, Scotus continues, the truth is that neither the intellect is the total cause of volition, nor the will is the total cause of intellection, since each faculty is primarily responsible for its own acts and exerts only a partial influence on the acts of the other faculty. The argument from the nature of an equivocal cause is therefore out of the question, since it applies only to a total cause. If an argument is to be built on a partial cause, it can only be in favor of the will, for it is the will that commands the intellect, not vice versa. The intellect is at most a subservient cause in that it presents to the will the object on which the latter will act.[105]

Granting that the will can command the intellect, the intellectualists rebut, it is nevertheless an incontestable fact that the intellect has an activity of its own, independently of the will. The same cannot be said of the will, which depends necessarily on the intellect for its volitive act. Since dependence is a mark of imperfection, it remains true that the intellect is more perfect than, and therefore superior to, the will. To this Scotus replies that dependence is not always a sign of imperfection. As Aristotle says, a being that is generated can be more perfect than the beings which are the cause of its generation. Similarly, the end depends on the means and form on matter, and yet the end is more perfect than the means and form is superior to matter. The dependence of will on intellect is analogous to this kind of dependence: volition depends on knowledge but only as end depends on the means and form on matter. Intellect, on the other hand, depends on will as on a partial but superior cause of its acts.[106]

The dialectical contest goes on. This time the intellectualists come back with a new kind of weapon, an argument that is based on a pure hypothesis but serves nevertheless to point out, so they say, the superiority of knowledge over volition. If it were at all

[105] *Ibid.*, n. 16, p. 151.
[106] *Ibid.*, n. 18, p. 155.

possible, they argue, to isolate intellection from volition, intellection would still be a perfect act of an intellectual nature, but not volition, which is merely an inclination comparable to the law of gravitation in a heavy body. Thus intellection is of a higher order than volition. Scotus' answer is as follows: that must be held as more perfect the opposite of which is a greater evil. But to hate God—in the hypothesis that hatred can exist without knowledge—is a much greater evil than not to know him, even if this means a positive act of ignorance. Love is therefore superior to knowledge.

The same principle holds true in regard to contradictory acts of the two powers in question. Thus, when one is conscious of his obligation to love God, not to love him is sinful, but merely not to think of him is not sinful. Again, to think of something evil is not necessarily a sin; but to think approvingly of something evil is a sin. Finally, and this is Scotus' direct answer to the argument of his opponents, even if love alone remained, this would not be merely like the natural inclination of a heavy body towards its gravitational center. It would still be an act of an intellectual nature, for that is precisely what distinguishes will as a free power from the tendencies of a physical body and other inferior beings. The fact that love in its concrete reality is always accompanied by an act of the intellect does not mean that love derives its activity from the intellect, since love has a formality of its own. It simply means that love acts in conjunction with the intellect.[107] More specifically, the human will is by definition a rational appetite, and to make it dependent on the intellect for its element of rationality is to downgrade it and falsify its true nature. Scotus' concern with the will's essential characteristic of rationality is in accordance with his notion of freedom as a perfection that goes hand in hand with rationality. To deprive the will of its rationality is to jeopardize the freedom of its acts.

The intellectualists resort to a final attack which takes the form of a twofold objection. The intellect, they assert, is superior to the will because its act is not vitiated, as it were, by the object as the act of the will is. Thus one can know evil without any loss of moral integrity, but he cannot desire evil, for any such desire is wrong. Moreover, it is a mark of imperfection to have to tend towards something that is outside of oneself. But such is the nature of will in regard to its object. Intellect, on the contrary, draws things to-

---

[107] *Ibid.*, n. 17, pp. 152-55.

wards itself, so that, in the words of Aristotle, truth and falsity are in the soul, good and evil are in the things outside (*Met.*, VI, 4; 1027b 25-29). To the first objection Scotus answers that the better and the more perfect a thing is the worse is its corruption. But such is the will for, as the objectors are ready to concede, the very act of willing evil is wrong, while there is nothing reproachable in the mere knowledge of evil.

As to the second objection, the argument on which it rests can also be retorted against its proponents. By their own admission, when the will is directed towards a good that is superior to itself, its act is nobler than the act of the intellect. Now since the will can perform acts which are more perfect than the corresponding acts of the intellect, and since on the other hand it is permissible to judge of the nature of a specific category of acts from any individual act of that category, the will must be considered as a higher faculty than the intellect. Furthermore, an act is all the more perfect insofar as it leads to a real union of the faculty with its object. But this can only be an act of the will, for it is through it that the will attains the object as it is in itself; in intellection, on the contrary, there is only a union between intellect and the object as it is in the soul, not as it is in itself. Hence again the superiority of will over intellect is manifest.

As to Aristotle's text that truth and falsity are in the soul, whereas good and evil are in the things outside, the following observation is in order. While it is true that intuitive knowledge and the ensuing love tend to the object as it is in itself, abstractive knowledge and the love thereby generated tend to the object as it is in the mind alone. In this respect no difference is seen between intellect and will, for both powers can direct their acts to the object as it is in itself or as it is found in the intellect. However, Aristotle speaks solely of abstractive knowledge and of the act by which the will desires something to be attained in the future. Since this object is not present to the will as yet, the will cannot tend towards it as it is in itself but only as it is understood by the intellect.[108] Briefly, Aristotle's text does not affect the principle that a greater union exists between the will and its object in concrete reality than between the intellect and its object since this is solely obtained by the process of abstraction, the only kind of object that in Aristotelian-Thomistic philosophy is possible to the intellect in this life. Thus one

[108] *Ibid.*, nn. 19-20, pp. 162-63.

of the most common arguments used by the intellectualists to support their theory of the primacy of intellect turns out, in Scotistic dialectic, to prove the opposite view, namely, the superiority of will over intellect.

The Scotistic doctrine of the primacy of will has a direct bearing on the question concerning the essence of beatitude, a much debated issue among scholastics. All scholastics agree in saying that man's supreme beatitude consists in the attainment of his final end and infinite good, God. Likewise, they all agree with very few exceptions that God can only be attained—whether naturally or supernaturally is not our concern here—by man's highest powers of intellect and will, and that the operation of both faculties is needed for his complete happiness. This is what scholastic terminology calls "extensive beatitude." The controversy arises as to whether the act of one of the two faculties could so attain the supreme good as to constitute man's formal and essential happiness, or what scholastics call "intensive beatitude." Otherwise stated, the question comes down to this: Do knowledge and love play an equal role in beatitude or does one excel the other? If one excels the other, which of the two is predominant, knowledge or love?

St. Albert the Great, St. Bonaventure, Richard of Mediavilla, and Francis Suarez, to mention only a few leading figures, maintain that the operation of both intellect and will is required for man's essential beatitude, so that knowledge and love contribute to it on an equal basis. On the other hand, St. Thomas and Scotus hold that beatitude consists essentially in the act of one faculty alone, which for Aquinas is the intellect, for Scotus the will. Since the arguments used to support these two latter theories, the only ones which interest us in this study, are chiefly those used by their proponents to uphold their stands on the question of which of the two faculties enjoys a primacy over the other, it can be said that, successfully or not, Scotus has already made his case quite clear in the preceding dispute. However, because certain additional arguments have been advanced which concern directly the essence of beatitude, it is necessary to state Scotus' position on the subject and see how he justifies his view that beatitude consists essentially in love.[109]

[109] Scotus discusses the problem in *Oxon.*, IV, d. 49, q. 4; XXI, pp. 93-100; *ibid.*, q. 5, pp. 170-77; *Rep. Par.*, IV, d. 49, q. 2; XXIV, pp. 620-31; *ibid.*, q. 3, pp. 631-35; *ibid*, q. 4, pp. 635-40. See also pertinent material in *Ord.*, I, d. 1, nn. 1-158; II, pp. 1-108; *Rep. Par.*, I, d. 1, qq. 1-3; XXII, pp. 54-61, as well as in qq. 1-3 of d. 49 of the fourth book of the *Sentences* in the *Opus Oxoniense* and the corresponding q. 1 in the *Reportata Parisiensia*.

Beatitude, writes Scotus, is man's supreme perfection which he achieves by attaining the final end to which he has been destined.[110] It consists, properly speaking, in the operation of his most perfect faculty, for only such a faculty can attain the ultimate end in the most perfect way.[111] This faculty cannot be the intellect, for man's final end is also his supreme good, and the good is the object of will, not of intellect. Moreover, the natural order existing between the act of intellect and the act of will clearly indicates the superiority of the latter. One does not will in order to know; he knows in order to will.[112] It is true that will cannot attain its object without first knowing it, so that the act of intellect precedes the act of will, but this is merely a priority of nature, not one of perfection. Formal and essential beatitude is the attainment of the end by a priority of perfection, which consists in the full and perfect attainment of the object as it is in itself and not merely as it is in the mind.[113]

Scotus has yet to meet the main objection to his position, which even today is the one most widely used by his opponents. The objection, as formulated by St. Thomas, runs somewhat like this. Beatitude is the attainment of the ultimate end. This cannot be done by an act of will as such, for will can only tend towards an end by desiring it, or enjoy the end once this has been attained. In neither case can it be said that will attains the end properly speaking, for desire is of something that is absent, and joy comes after the end has already been achieved. Hence the ultimate end can be attained solely by an act whereby the end is actually present to man, and that is the act of the intellect.[114]

Scotus takes notice of the objection and, as usual, has his answer ready for it. He concedes that the attainment of an end cannot be merely by an act of desire; understandably enough, the very notion of desire excludes the actual possession of the object so desired. He

---

[110] *Oxon.*, IV, d. 49, q. 4, n. 9; XXI, p. 100b: "Beatitudo est assecutio [finis] prima primitate perfectionis"; *ibid.*, q. 6, n. 24; XXI, p. 269a: "Accipimus beatitudinem pro summa perfectione beatificabilis naturae, ipsam summe suo obiecto perfectissimo coniungente."
[111] *Rep. Par.*, IV, d. 49, q. 1 n. 2; XXIV, p. 614b; "Cum beatitudo sit finis et finis potentis operari est operatio sua, igitur beatitudo consistit in operatione"; *Oxon.*, IV, d. 49, q. 3, n. 7; XXI, p. 81ab: "Planum est quod non consistit beatitudo nisi in unica operatione, quia non nisi unica potentia in natura perfectissime attingit obiectum."
[112] *Ibid.*, q. 4, n. 4; XXI, p. 97b.
[113] *Ibid.*, n. 5; XXI, p. 98a, n. 9; XXI, p. 100b. See also *ibid.*, nn. 108 and 110.
[114] *Sum. theol.*, I-II, q. 3, a. 4 c.

concedes further that joy, or the complacency consequent upon the attainment of the end, is not what constitutes the essence of beatitude as such; rather, it presupposes it. Besides, joy is a passion, whereas beatitude is a most perfect act and operation. Having granted this much, he strongly objects to having the acts of will reduced to desire and joy. What of the act whereby the will does actually attain the object and does not merely desire or enjoy it? Before the will can draw any satisfaction from the possession of an object, it must first attain it, and that attainment is precisely what constitutes the essence of beatitude in the strict sense of the term. Beatitude is therefore the act by which the will comes in contact with the object presented to it by the intellect and loves it, thus fully satisfying its natural desire for it. To ignore such an act, Scotus affirms in rather strong terms, is completely to disregard the principles of logic and reason. Indeed, if will can act in regard to an object that is absent and only imperfectly known to intellect, it must also be able, and much more so, to act in regard to an object that is perfectly present to it because it actually sees it through the intellect. Thus, in Scotus' reasoning, the principal argument of his opponents is faulty because it fails to consider one of the most important acts of the will.[115]

It is beyond the scope of this study to discuss the nature of this act which Scotus calls *fruitio* and distinguishes from the ensuing *delectatio*. It will suffice to point out that fruition, in which the essence of beatitude consists, is the perfect love of God for God's sake (*amor amicitiae*), and is thus distinct from the love of God for one's own sake (*amor concupiscentiae*). The latter, although not evil in itself, is nevertheless less perfect than the former and must be moderated.[116]

If we compare Scotus' teaching on the essence of beatitude with the teaching of other scholastics, we may say that he holds a somewhat middle position between those who, like St. Albert the Great and St. Bonaventure, place essential beatitude in intellect and will,

---

[115] *Oxon.*, IV, d. 49, q. 4, nn. 5-9, XXI, pp. 98-100. The following passage is particularly important: "Si enim accipiatur quietatio pro consequente operationem perfectam, concedo quod illam quietationem praecedit perfecta consecutio finis; si autem accipiatur quietatio pro actu quietativo in fine, dico quod actus amandi, qui naturaliter praecedit delectationem, quietat illo modo, quia potentia operativa non quietatur in obiecto, nisi per operationem perfectam, per quam attingit obiectum." *Ibid.*, p. 99b.

[116] For a complete discussion of Scotus' notion of *fruitio* cf. *Oxon.*, IV, d. 49, q. 5; XXI, pp. 170-77; *Rep. Par.*, d. 49, q. 4; XXIV, pp. 635-40.

and those who with St. Thomas place it in intellect alone. For Scotus the essence of beatitude resides formally in the act of the will, but since the will cannot act independently of the intellect, the latter contributes to it in the same way as it contributes to all acts of volition.[117] This seems to be the mind of Scotus himself who, in the very question where he discusses the nature of fruition, speaks of the act of the intellect as a partial and *per se* cause of volition.[118]

To sum up his thought, if beatitude is considered in its strict sense as the attainment of the supreme good, then it consists formally and ultimately in the act of the will. If beatitude is considered in a broader sense so as to include in its concept the part that intellect plays in volition, then beatitude consists in the act of the will as its principal cause and in the act of the intellect as its secondary but nonetheless important and necessary cause.[119] Thus Scotus' teaching on the essence of beatitude is but a reflection of his doctrine on the relationship between intellect and will, and the primacy he assigns to love over knowledge is in accord with the Platonic-Augustinian tradition which he helped in many ways to bring closer to the Aristotelian-Thomistic school.[120]

The Catholic University of America

[117] Cf. *Oxon.*, d. 49, q. 4; XXI, pp. 115 and 123, where Scotus' commentator, Anthony Hickey, presents the doctrine of the Subtle Doctor as a middle position between the two other views.

[118] *Ibid.*, q. 5, n. 5; XXI, p. 176ab: "Si enim ponatur quod intellectio est causa, licet partialis ipsius volitionis, et intellectio viatoris et visio beati differunt specie; ergo et effectus qui necessario requirunt istas causas diversas"; *Rep. Par.,* IV, d. 49, q. 4, n. 9; XXIV, p. 639a: "Intellectio est aliqua causa voluntatis per se ad eliciendum actum suum."

[119] *Ibid.*, IV, d. 49, q. 2, n. 20; XXIV, p. 630a: "Dico igitur ad quaestionem, quod beatitudo simpliciter est essentialiter et formaliter in actu voluntatis, quo simpliciter et solum attingitur bonum optimum quo fruatur"; *ibid.*, q. 3, n. 7; XXIV, p. 634a: "Si autem ambae potentiae concurrunt ad beatitudinem, sic illa, quae est principalior potentia, habet principaliter beatitudinem, et sic voluntas magis quam intellectus. Si autem accipias secundum aliam ultimationem, sic tantum voluntas ultimate beatificatur."

[120] Scotus' attempts in this direction are well described in Bettoni's work, *Duns Scotus: The Basic Principles of His Philosophy*, which purports to prove "that Scotus' philosophy is an Augustinianism that aims to meet Thomistic Aristotelianism, and to fuse it into a more complete and therefore more vital and modern synthesis." *Ibid.*, p. 21.

6

DUNS SCOTUS ON THE *COMMON NATURE*

by

J. R. Cresswell

Does the universe contain only particulars? Plato answered "No!" and asserted the existence of real universals existing apart from particulars. He himself was aware of the serious objections to this position but apparently found himself unable wholly to reject it. In order to find an answer to the question, I propose to examine a solution peculiar to Duns Scotus as it is set forth principally in his *Opus Oxoniense* II, dist. 3, question 1.[1] I have judged that a continuous presentation of what appears a consistent view is preferable to considering the interpretations of various commentators and the consequent controversy. This accounts for the absence of many footnotes.[2]

Scotus raises the question "Is a material substance singular and individual in its own right?" An answer that leaps to the eye of common sense is "Yes." But he does not admit this, because if things are singular in virtue of their own nature, our intellect conceives them in a way contrary to their own nature when it conceives them as universals. It is evident that when I say of a certain object "This is a stone," I am asserting it to be a member of a class (species). Scotus says that it is sufficient for discriminating this *specific* unity that it be a "less than numerical unity." He holds the position that between the unity of the singular, which is a numerical unity, and the pure universal, there is place for a unity "less than numerical" which is nonetheless real. By "numerical unity" he means that the material substance, for example a stone, is one existing thing distinct from other material substances; it is the *infima species* of material substance in general and, in this sense,

[1] The text used is the *Commentaria Oxoniensia, In Lib. Sententiarum*, Tom. II. Edited by Marianus Fernandez Garcia, O.F.M. Ad Claras Aquas, 1914.

[2] I must also state that without the aid of my able and ingenious colleague Professor K. Lambert, this article would never have attained any degree of clarity.

the final end to a series of classes from the most extensive to the least extensive. It is impossible to divide the singular substance any further either logically or even physically; for if I "divide" a stone into several others, none of these will be the stone I divided, but a collection of other individuals. Scotus' view is an attempt to find some basis in the material thing that explains how the stone can be an individual and, at the same time, a member of a class (species) such that the intellect can form a concept of it. Before proceeding further we must come to an understanding of the term "unity" which Duns Scotus uses so frequently. A consideration of the contexts in which the term appears leads me to believe that by the term "unity" he seems to mean a basis for singling out what we are referring to. Thus, the object before me can be "singled out" as an individual or as the kind of thing, (a species) we call a "stone." Hence, the numerical unity of an object is that which shows it to be a single individual, while a "unity less than numerical" will turn out to be the characterization of the common nature. The further clarification of the idea of a common nature must wait until the end of this article is approached. In this connection, I am less concerned with a philological exegesis than with a philosophical interpretation of Scotus' words that will render the discussion intelligible and reasonably consistent.

Scotus starts with criticism of the position that the nature of an object is a singular only, and hence that there is no need to seek a reason beyond the singular itself. To say that there *is* a need to seek a reason beyond the singular itself would be to speak as though the nature in question were temporally prior to the object or as though the nature were first of all an independent nature before it became a singular (n.1.). But this is a form of Platonism that Scotus wants to avoid. Suppose we hold the first position that the nature of an object is a singular only. If this were the case, we would have to argue thus: if there were, therefore, no unity less than numerical present, for example, in a stone (n.2.), and if all other forms of unity were only unities imposed by reason, then there would be no ontological (real) basis (unity) by means of which we could classify stones. I believe Scotus means to say the following: If the concrete, existing unity of any object consists only in its singularity, then it is impossible to see how, for example, one stone can stand in relation to many stones. That is to say, if "stone" is a word referring only to a single thing (a numerical unity), then it is impossible for that word to refer to any one of a multitude of things each of which is called a stone. But this is false. Therefore, the word "stone" must refer to something in things which he calls a unity less than numerical.

After this preliminary skirmish, as Gilson expressively calls it, Scotus will offer seven ways of "proving" that a material substance has a unity less than numerical.

The first way is this. According to Aristotle in *Metaphysics* x, (n.3), in every genus there is one primary thing which is the "measure" of everything in that genus. The individual cannot be this measure or starting point for forming the genus. One cannot, for example, use a particular stone for selecting other classes in the genus material substance. The species are ordered to the genus as classes included in a larger class. But the individual members of a species are not so ordered. That is, the individual is not itself a class included in a larger class. Moreover, it is not appropriate to posit the idea of a larger class (the genus) through participation in which all the species are what they are. Thus, to give an account of the species "triangle," one need not say that it "participates" in a genus of Euclidean plane figures; that is to say, the species triangle is not the measure of all in the genus plane figure. I might add that this mode of explanation by placing members in a class and that class in another could go on indefinitely, an explanation that Scotus would no doubt reject. To account for the order from genus to species to individual, Scotus continues, we must regard the individual thing as possessing some unity less than numerical by means of which a species can be formed which in turn can be a class within the genus. That is, the individual stone must have a nature that identifies it as belonging to the species of stone, and makes the species a class within the genus.

The second argument seems to run as follows: One can compare the individual members (*atoma*) of a species because they all possess one nature. But the classes within a genus cannot be compared in this way because the genus does not have this kind of unity. But since the concept of a genus is as much a unity (*una*) in the intellect as the concept of a species is, the unity of a species is in fact not one imposed by reason. If this were not the case, no concept could be predicated of many species and hence no concept would be a genus. At this point the argument of Scotus becomes extremely obscure and I can explicate it only by the following conjecture. Let us suppose that the term "unity" refers to the grounds for identifying the kinds of unity discussed. Although the concepts of the genus and of the species are both present in the intellect, the ground for identifying the species is quite different from that for identifying the genus; in the former case the ground is the common nature really possessed by the members, in the latter case it is a unity imposed by reason. If the grounds were the same in both cases, the distinction between genus and species would be obliterated. The Aristotelian tradition regards genus and species as belonging to different strata or levels. Take away this difference and one could predicate a species of a species. For some reason, perhaps because of the paradox involved in self-referential classes, Scotus regards this as undesirable. Hence the genus formulated by reason and the species based on members having a common nature must represent a valid distinction. Therefore, the specific unity is not the abstract unity of the genus, but a different kind of unity which Scotus calls a less than numerical unity.

In the two preceding arguments, Scotus has made it clear that the ordering of genus to species to individual depends in part on the presence of a common nature in two or more individuals. In order that two or more individuals may belong to the same species, they must possess some nature in common; in order that two or more species belong to a genus, a conceptual unity must be apprehended. The nature common to Socrates and Plato taken as members of the species "man" is a unity of a kind more intimate than that by virtue of which we call the species of man and monkey mammals. The ground for determining membership in a species is less than a numerical unity.

The third proof (n.4) runs thus: The relations of identity, similarity and equality are based on a unity in the thing of such a nature that, although likeness has as a real basis in something in the genus "quality," yet the relation is not real unless it has a real foundation in a thing. The unity required is, therefore, real but is not a numerical unity.

Two comments on these three proofs can be made. Scotus is first of all confining his discourse to class terms, such as the common nouns, dog, stone, in the search for a common nature which is to be the objective basis for the universal, for the reason that many such class terms obviously refer to existing things. The question on what we could ground the use of the words "or," "if," and "all," or "some" does not enter the discussion. These are logical constants or "syncategoremtatic" terms as the medieval logicians called them. They are terms necessary for discourse but do not have objects signified by them. There is a second interesting feature of the discussion so far. The third "proof" makes it clear that a term such as "stone" does not refer to a combination of qualities *a, b, c, d,* resembling instances of which occur. He is seeking for some ground of resemblance itself, some non-verbal ground prior to it and independent of our conceptualization of it, and having a unity less than numerical. It is as though the nature of being as such carried within itself a metaphysical element that is manifested to the human senses as resemblance and to the intellect as the concept of the universal. His view is an attempt to account for the fact that the universe at large contains things and persons that are metaphysically composed of something that makes them have family resemblances and something that makes them distinct individuals.

The fourth proof: There are only two extremes of a real opposition; contrariety is a relation of opposition, and this is evident because the one extreme denies and destroys the other. Now either of the primary extremes of such real opposition is one through some real unity, but not through a numerical unity, because then precisely *this* white would be the primary contrary to *this* black, and precisely *this other white* would also be the primary contrary to this black, and so on. But this is absurd because then there would be as many primary relations of contrariety as there were individual contraries. Hence, the primary contraries must have a unity less than numerical. That is, there is a nature common to this, that, and the other white things.

This argument shows once more that the common nature is not reducible to a relation of similarity between, say, numerically distinct whites or blacks. For if it were so reducible, *this* black would simultaneously have not only *this* numerically and really distinct white as its contrary but also *that* white and other whites as contraries. Hence, every contrary would have several extremes contrary to it. But this is absurd. Therefore, the contraries cannot each be numerically one. The argument reveals that only when the contrary is taken as having less than a numerical unity can the law of non-contradiction be applied to things.

The fifth proof considers what is cognized in an act of sensing. Every act of sensing has one kind of object proper to it and having a certain kind of unity; but this unity is not numerical. Therefore, it is a real unity but other than numerical. Thus, for example, the act of seeing has color as its proper object. What kind of unity is present in such an object? Scotus intends to show that the unity must be other than a numerical unity. For example, should divine power create two "patches" (*quanta*) exactly similar in whiteness, the sense of sight by itself could not distinguish them as *two* whites; what is seen is just "whiteness" and not patches of white. Hence the unity of the sense quality is not a numerical unity. Again, if all the common *sensibilia*, even difference in location, are included in a sensing of an object, no act of any sense distinguishes this ray of the sun even though they may be different because of the sun's motion.

Scotus seems to be saying that the senses alone are incapable of distinguishing between separate patches of the same white taken as directly apprehended sense data. Scotus insists, in other connections, that, of course, everything outside the mind is really singular and one in number. But sense does not have the faculty for counting objects as separate units. Hence the proper object of any act of sensing gives one a clue to a different type of unity possessed by that object.

Before proceeding to the sixth argument, Scotus writes thus: One might claim (n.5) that the primary object of sense has in itself a certain kind of real unity. Just as the act of sensing precedes intellectual apprehension, so its kind of unity precedes every act of the intellect. But this is not as conclusive an argument as the argument in the two preceding paragraphs. For one might assert that the first adequate object of a faculty is something common abstracted from all particulars, and hence has only a unity of commonness with respect to the several particular objects. But it seems impossible to deny that the object of a single act of sensing necessarily has a real unity that is less than numerical. That is to say, an argument of this sort would show merely that object of a power is a unity founded only on some property, whether abstracted by sense or by intellect, a unity which takes the form of a property common to the particulars. Since presumably the abstract property is obtained by the examination of countable particulars, this mode of argument does not yield a unity less than numerical. The fifth argument and the addition enable the reader to infer that the common nature of which we are in quest is not obtained directly by sense nor by abstraction from particulars, an important conclusion.

The sixth proof: If all real unity is numerical, then all real difference is numerical. But the consequence is false, because then all diversity would be the same and each thing would be equally (and only numerically) distinct from everything else. It would then follow that the intellect could no more abstract something common from Socrates and Plato than from Socrates and a line (n.6). A universal of this sort would be purely fictitious. If each object were numerically one and the same in its own right, then Scotus can assert that we might as well group together any collection of objects whatever and thus there would be no real basis for universal concepts.

The seventh proof is evidently intended as a way of verifying the reality of the common or specific nature, and is stated thus. If no intellect existed, fire would still cause fire and "destroy" water. Thus there would still be a real unity of the generating cause and the result generated. For this reason such generation is univocal, that is, the term fire is applied univocally to the fire and to its result. The intellect which contemplates this situation does not *make* it univocal but *knows* it to be univocal. Hence the material thing is not a singular in its own right but exists as a real unity that is less than a numerical unity.

If these arguments are accepted, then Scotus can give a straight answer to the original question "Is a material substance singular and individual in its own right?" The answer is, of course, "No." Material substance is a peculiar combination of the common nature and that which makes the individual a "this," that is, an individual. In the Question I, under consideration in the present discussion, Scotus is not yet occupied with what it is that makes a substance an individual, but only with what it is that enables us to group things in classes. The seven arguments purported to show that, apart from all operations of the intellect (n.7), there is a real unity in things that is less than numerical.

In the latter part of Question 1, Scotus states the peculiarities of the common nature. First, things exist in reality as singulars, in the intellect as universals. Yet the common nature is neither singular nor universal. It is "contractible" to a singular in real things, though there is nothing in a nature as such by which it could be "contracted" or determined to this or that one individual; no nature however inferior or contracted enables us to say "This is this" (no.8). Second, it is false to say that it is the intellect which causes universality by simply abstracting a quiddity from the sense data *(phantasmata)*. The common nature is, therefore, not a universal and intrinsic characteristic. It is the counterpart of the universal and indifferent to it, for the universal is a logical concept, a second intention, whereas the common nature is a metaphysical concept. One may conclude then that the common nature is indifferent to universality and to singularity.

In connection with this matter of abstracting the quiddity, Scotus might have drawn attention to a difficulty. To hold that the universal is founded on a quiddity abstracted by the intellect from particulars is at least very dubious, especially if the quiddity is to represent something similar in all the particulars. A simple case, in which similarity between particulars does not obtain, and well known to medieval philosophers is the one mentioned in several places by Aristotle. The adjective "healthy" is applied to, say, a healthy body, a healthy complexion, and healthy exercise. The quality of being healthy in these different circumstances does not designate anything common to them all. Exercise is productive of healthy bodies, the complexion results from a healthy body, and so on. This and other samples arouse in me a "Scotistic" and "healthy" suspicion of the common scholastic view.

Let us return for a moment to the expression "less than a numerical unity." As stated in paragraph 2 of this exposition, the numerical unity of a single object consists in being one existing thing identical with itself and distinct from a multitude of other things. It is one, as distinct from a countable many. Again, two classes may be called numerically identical if there are the same members in each. However, the property used to place an object in the first class need not be the same as the property used to place an object in the second class. For example, though the class of things possessing a heart is identical with the class of things possessing a liver, the property of possessing a heart and that of possessing a liver are not identical. Let these remarks serve as an explanation of "numerical unity" when applied to a single thing or to the identity of classes. But this will not suffice to explain what it is in things that enables us to place them in classes. As we have already seen, Duns Scotus does not identify the common nature with similar properties of the things, nor with an abstracted quiddity or form.

Perhaps one way to arrive at the notion of this strange "less than numerical unity" is to suggest an account of how we cognize it. Scotus has already told us that the common nature is not sensed and is not abstracted by the intellect. A brief illustration may make his position clearer. Is the universal concept of humanity a partial one only, since it contains only the shared characteristic of Plato and Socrates and ignores difference? If so, the universal would not yield a true account of what exists. Socrates and Plato may be said to "share" in humanity, but only insofar as the humanity of Socrates is a Socratic humanity and the humanity of Plato is a Platonic humanity. It seems to me that there is only one recourse for our obtaining knowledge of the common nature. Consider the seven arguments given above in their totality. I can see, I think, a view present in them something like this. We know the common nature through discursive reasoning by showing the need for it whenever we group individuals in classes. This view is tacitly present in arguments 1, 2, and 3. In argument 4, only if there is a distinct common nature in things, can we claim that there are real contraries. The common nature is not sensed, so runs part of argument 5. Argument 6 provides a reason for denying that there can be a "real" class consisting of Socrates, Plato and a line. Argument 7 claims that even if no intellect were present, fire would still cause fire; there would be, in general, no rational connection between that which generates and that which is generated without a common nature. In conclusion, one may say that the common nature present in things is necessary for distinctions made, explanations offered and, in general, our reasonings whenever we try to understand the world around us.

The position is not unlike Kant's system of *a priori* concepts insofar as he treats them as presuppositions of our understanding an objective world. But although Kant and Duns Scotus both appear to be concerned with the same issue, there is a great and fundamental difference. The aim of Kant's transcendental deduction of the categories is to show that these "pure concepts of the understanding" when applied to the manifold of sense are necessary conditions for experiencing "objects." Duns Scotus seems to be saying that the presence of the common nature in things is a necessary condition not merely for understanding objects but is a really existing component of things even if no intellect were present. Duns Scotus' arguments are primarily concerned to show the necessity for this ultimate metaphysical component. Kant's view is "subjective," that of Scotus "realistic."

Now that the ground for the community of things has been found in the very nature of the thing taken in its proper entity and unity, it is necessary to seek for the principle of individuation. Question II of the same section (*Distinctio III*) contains Scotus' discussion of this. First he excludes views that manifestly cannot serve as principles of individuation. Some philosophers have asserted that privation or negation is such a principle. The singular is individual, that is, not divided; being and being one are inseparable so that to be and to be one are the same thing. This view, says Scotus, is insufficient, for a mere absence of division does not account for the fact that an individual is not divisible. The fact that a certain stone is not, at the moment, "divided" is hardly a sufficient reason for speaking of it as a distinct individual. It is even easier for Scotus to dismiss quantity as the foundation for individuation. A stone may be divided into smaller stones, but the smaller stone is not the same as the larger stone, yet both are single, individual stones. What remains as an account of individuation? For Scotus there is only one answer. The individual possesses an intrinsic uniqueness, it is a "this." Though Scotus used the term only some three or four times, *haecceitas* was adopted by the later Scotistic school as the word to designate this component in the thing. The two components, the common nature and the haecceity, constitute the individual. Scotus has already shown that the common nature is indifferent to universality and singularity, but is yet the real basis for the intellect's forming of universals. In a parallel fashion, the haecceity is the objective element making a thing a singular individual. The thing is an inseparable conjunction of the common nature and haecceity, these aspects being analytically distinguishable; they are formally distinct but in actuality one. A descriptive account of the haecceity would always be misleading and even false, for a description would use general terms and thus never touch the distinctness and uniqueness of the individual thing. Hence, the singularity of the individual can be seen but never defined. We can proceed from the genus including its proper entities to the species with its proper entities; but the individual is the irreducible "last." The world is a world of unique individuals.

Scotus has made it plain that for him the individual is a compound of two distinguishable aspects, the common nature and the haecceity. But what are we to say of the connection between the two aspects? He has already shown that the common nature as such is indifferent to universality and singularity and that the aspect of haecceity adds nothing essential to the existing thing. Yet everywhere in the created world we find the two aspects always conjoined in such a way that every individual is distinct from every other.

Through the real conjunction of the common nature and the individual difference, natures in this or that individual are really different, although neither the common nature nor the haecceity possesses the active distinguishing principle in itself. Scotus provides a clue in at least one statement:

> De intentione naturale dico quod intentio naturae in specie sistit .... tamquam in perfectiori quam sit genus, et sistit in individuo tamquam in entitate perfectiori et realiori quam sit speciei (*Rep. Par.* I, d. 36, q. 4, n. 25).[3]

There is a persistent tendency (*intentio*) of nature towards the species, so much more perfect than the genus, and towards the individual so much more perfect and real in being than the being of the species. This ontological principle once more affirms the extreme importance of the individual. The whole aim of being itself is directed towards the existence of individuals.

I must confess that, especially in the last two paragraphs, I have gone somewhat beyond the exact words of Scotus in order to suggest an ontology not common in the thirteenth and fourteenth centuries. Two things afford me with a warrant for doing so. One, Scotus treats each particular problem as it arises with a peculiar exhaustiveness; witness his examination of an argument for God in *De Primo Principio*, his discussion of the will, and his exposition of evidence. This manner of treatment involves his throwing out notions and suggestions that stimulate the mind. Two, I cannot think that I have gone too far afield, since all readers of his works recognize not merely the penetration but also the flexibility of the mind of the man rightly called the Subtle Doctor.

West Virginia University.

[3] I have taken this important quotation from *Sein und Person nach J. Duns Scotus*, by Heribert Mühlen, (Werl/Westfalen, 1954), p. 34.

7

DEMONSTRABILITY AND DEMONSTRATION OF THE EXISTENCE OF GOD

by

FELIX ALLUNTIS

It has been rightly said that no other scholastic philosopher worked with such concentration and perseverance as Scotus in constructing a truly valid and complete proof of the existence of God. He outlines it in *Quaestiones subtilissimae super libros metaphysicorum Aristotelis,* and develops it, with new details and improvements, in *Lectura I, Reportata Parisiensia, Ordinatio,* and *De primo principio.*[1] In *Lectura I* Scotus expounds the proof in a twofold way, that is, starting from both a factual premise, "something is effected," and a possible premise, "something can be effected." In later works he develops the proof exclusively in the possible or quidditative order, but always noting that the contingent way is manifest. The reason why he considers the proof for God's existence based on contingent premises as conclusive is that *ex contingenti sequitur necessarium:*[2] contingent facts and beings call for a necessary being. However, Scotus prefers to start from the quidditative order, or from the level of possibility, because he wants to give a strict demonstration. According to Aristotle, such demonstration must be from evident and necessary premises,[3] and the premises based on possible being are necessary. Even if, for example, no man should exist, his existence is always possible, and the proposi-

---

[1] For the first seven distinctions of *Lectura I* and the first book of *Ordinatio* we shall use the Vatican edition: *I. Duns Scoti Opera omnia,* studio et cura Commissionis Scotisticae ad fidem codicum edita (Civitas Vaticana: Typis polyglottis Vaticanis, 1950-). Seven volumes, the first six and the sixteenth, have been published. For the *De primo principio* we shall use the BAC edition: *Obras del Doctor Sutil Juan Duns Escoto.* Latin text and Spanish translation, vol. I: *Dios Uno y Trino* (Madrid: Biblioteca de Autores Cristianos, 1960), pp. 595-711. For the last three books of the *Ordinatio* and the other works of Scotus we shall use the Vivès edition: *I. Duns Scoti Opera omnia.* Editio nova iuxta editionem Waddingi. 26 vols. (Paris: Vivès, 1891-1895).
[2] *Lectura I,* d. 2, n. 56; XVI, p. 131.
[3] Aristotle, *Posterior Analytics* I, ch. 4, 73a20-25.

tion, "some man can exist," is a necessary proposition. Scotus justifies the premises based on possible being by the facts of experience according to the principle, *Ab esse ad posse valet illatio*:[4] what is true of the facts is true of their possibility, not vice versa. Therefore, it should not be overlooked that although the facts of experience do not enter the formal structure of the Scotistic demonstration of the existence of God, its first premise is founded on and justified by them.

Again, Scotus wants to give a complete proof, that is to say, a proof of the existence of God, or of the infinite being which, according to him, is the most perfect concept we can have of God. He is not satisfied with proving the existence of a first efficient cause, an ultimate end, or a supreme nature. In the process of the proof he demonstrates the existence of a first being in the threefold order of efficiency, finality, and eminence, but he is most careful not to call such a being God, a precaution some of his interpreters at times forget. Scotus is fully conscious of the possible objection against a proof that would not go further than a being with the triple primacy, an objection which has been and is still being made against the Thomistic ways.[5] The answer to the objection is, of course, that St. Thomas, in subsequent articles and questions, proves that the first efficient cause, as well as the subject of the conclusions of some of the other ways, is and must be *a se*, necessary, and omniperfect, viz., God. But this answer implies that three or four of the ways, considered in themselves independently of further development, are not complete proofs of the existence of God. For this reason Scotus will not consider his proof to be complete until he has proved the existence of an infinite being. We could add that by always establishing the unicity of the infinite being immediately after the demonstration of his existence, he seems to consider the demonstration of unicity as a complement of the proof. After all, a God who is not unique will not be God. Polytheism and pantheism, it has been rightly said, are really forms of atheism. Hence Fernand van Steenberghen, for example, writes that demonstration of the existence of God must include proof of his unicity.[6]

---

[4] *De primo principio*, l. c., p. 623: "Sed malo de possibili proponere conclusiones et praemissas. Illis quippe de actu concessis, istae de possibili conceduntur; non e converso."

[5] Fernand van Steenberghen, *Dieu caché, comment savons-nous que Dieu existe?* (Louvain: Publications Universitaires, 1961), p. 182.

[6] *L.c.*, pp. 183-184.

In his commentaries on the *Books of Sentences* (*Lectura I, Reportata, Ordinatio*) Scotus proves the existence of God in the second distinction of the first book before the discussion of the cognoscibility of God in the third distinction. This procedure is common to scholastic authors and is due to the order Peter Lombard follows in his *Books of Sentences*. It is clear, however, that the demonstration of the existence of God presupposes an affirmative solution of the problem of God's cognoscibility. The gnoseological problem of the value of the concepts by which we conceive God is prior to the metaphysical problem of demonstrating his existence and must be solved first. The difficulty of the criteriological problem involved in this case is obvious for it is not limited to the problem of universals or the problem of the value of our abstract concepts as applied to creatures from which they were abstracted. It includes the much more difficult question of the value of such abstract concepts as applied to God, who in his individual existence is not the natural object of our cognitive faculties and cannot, therefore, be the starting point of our abstractive activity. Hence, not only positivists or nominalists but even philosophers who can be classified as realists profess skepticism or agnosticism when faced with the problem of God's cognoscibility.

In the light of the preceding observations, this article will be divided into five sections: I) nature and origin of our concepts of God; II) the non-self-evidence of God's existence; III) demonstrability of God's existence; IV) demonstration of God's existence; V) final remarks and evaluation.

I

NATURE AND ORIGIN OF OUR CONCEPTS OF GOD

Scotus rejects ontologism in all its forms. Our intellect is incapable of a natural intuition of God; by its natural powers *(viribus naturalibus)* it cannot know directly and immediately the divine essence in its actual presence. The reason is that the divine essence does not naturally move our intellect. Hence, if some creatures do in fact have an intuition of God—and theology tells us that the blessed enjoy this intuition—it is due to the free motion of God's will, not to the natural motion of his essence.⁷ Let us examine this further.

According to Scotus, our intellectual knowledge is the effect of two partial efficient causes: the object and the intellect.⁸ Unless the object can naturally move our intellect, knowledge of it, if there is any, is not natural. Our intellect can be considered either in its present state or in its nature *(ex natura sua)*. The object that naturally moves our intellect in its present state of union with the body is sensible quiddity, or rather, everything included in sensible quiddity.⁹ Sensible quiddity not only includes the concrete phenomena of experience but every intelligible note which can be abstracted from them, such as the concepts of being, its transcendental properties, and the simple perfections, which we use in our imperfect knowledge of God.¹⁰ As will be seen later, every object, either by itself or through its intelligible species, can generate in our mind knowledge of everything essentially or virtually contained in it. Let us keep in mind this important point: our intellect abstracts naturally from sensible quiddity the concept of being as such, which is the object of metaphysics.¹¹

The "adequate" object which naturally moves our intellect considered in itself *(ex natura sua)* is every limited or finite being, whether material or spiritual. "In any state [therefore even under the best conditions] the adequate object of the created intellect as

---

⁷ *Ord.* I, d. 3, n. 57; III, p. 39; *Quodl.* 14, n. 10; XXVI, p. 39.
⁸ *Ord.* I, d. 3, n. 494; III, p. 292ff.
⁹ *Ibidem*, n. 186; III, p. 113; *Quodl.* 14, n. 12; XXVI, p. 46.
¹⁰ *Quodl.* 14, n. 12; XXVI, p. 406; *Ord.* Prologus, n. 33; I, p. 20; *Ibidem*, d. 3, n. 123; III, p. 76: "Concordant hic Aristoteles et 'articulus', quod quiditas rei sensibilis est nunc objectum adaequatum, intelligendo 'sensibilis' proprie, vel inclusi essentialiter vel virtualiter in sensibili. Aliter, intelligendo quiditas 'specifica' (vel remota vel virtualiter inclusa, in idem redit utrumque). Non igitur nunc est adaequatum objectum eius quod supremae sensitivae, quia intelligit omne inclusum in sensibili essentialiter, usque ad ens, sub qua indifferentia nullo modo sensus cognoscit—et etiam inclusum virtualiter, ut relationes, quod non sensus. Nec oportet hic distinguere quod solum sensible est objectum motivum: ens terminativum—quia inclusum in sensibili sic vel sic—non tantum terminat sed movet, saltem intelligentiam per propriam speciem in memoria, sive a se genitam sive ab alio." Cf. Carolus Balić, "Circa positiones fundamentales I. Duns Scoti," *Antonianum*, XXVIII (1953), pp. 268ff.

¹¹ The transcendental concept of being, abstracted from sensible things, is for Scotus the first and adequate object of our intellect by *reason of its primacy of community and virtuality (ratione primatiae communitatis et virtualitatis)*, since, Scotus tells us, "Whatever is of itself intelligible either includes essentially the notion of being or is contained virtually or essentially in something else which does include being essentially." *Ord.* I, d. 3, n. 137; III, p. 85.

such is limited being, because this being as such can be known by virtue of a cause which naturally moves the intellect."[12] The main reason Scotus gives in different works to prove this doctrine of the adequate object of the intellect *ex natura sua* is theological, namely, that by its nature our intellect is not essentially inferior to the angelic intellect,[13] and in the state of separation from the body it will intuit its own substance and also other created beings, both spiritual and material, by its natural forces without infused species.[14]

The divine essence, however, although it is the "first and natural" object of the intellect's inclination (*inclinationis, tendentiae*), does not naturally move our intellect. Every being, including the divine essence, is the object of inclination of our intellect.[15] This means that our mind has the capacity to receive the intuitive knowledge of the divine essence if such knowledge is given to it. This receptive capacity of the intellect, Scotus adds, is natural. It is not the result of a previous transmutation of the intellect by a habit or accidental quality such as the *lumen gloriae*. A habit or quality of this kind never gives the basic capacity to realize a specific action; it merely perfects a pre-existing capacity.[16] Besides, the soul is not beatified by an accident. God is seen by the intellect, which for Scotus is not really distinct from the soul; he is not seen by something added to

---

[12] *Quodl.* 14, n. 11; XXVI, p. 40: "Pro quocumque statu, cuiuscumque intellectus creati praecise, ens limitatum est objectum adaequatum, quia praecise illud potest attingi virtute causae naturaliter motivae intellectus."

[13] *Ord.* II, d. 1, q. 5; XI, p. 192; *Quodl.* 14, n. 12; XXVI, p. 46: "Objectum adaequatum intellectui nostro ex natura potentiae non est aliquid specialius objecto intellectus angelici."

[14] *Ord.* IV, d. 45, q. 2.

[15] *Quodl.* 14, n. 11; XXVI, p. 40; *Ord.* Prologus, n. 57; I, p. 57. The Scotistic doctrine concerning the different objects of our intellect can be summarized as follows: The "first and natural" object of inclination is every being, including the divine essence as an object of intuition. The object which naturally moves our intellect in its present state is the sensible quiddity or rather everything essentially or virtually contained in the sensible quiddity, including the transcendental concepts. The "adequate" object which naturally moves the intellect *ex natura sua* is every *finite* being, whether spiritual or material. The "first and adequate" object of our intellect by reason of its primacy of community and virtuality is the abstract concept of being, which is abstracted naturally from the sensible quiddity. In our opinion the confusion existing among Scotus' interpreters as regards the object of our intellect is due to their failure in making the necessary distinctions. Question XIV of the *Quodlibetales* is of capital importance for the interpretations of other Scotistic texts and for the solution of the problem.

[16] *Ord.* I, d. 3, nn. 113-114; III, pp. 70-71; *Quodl.* 14, n. 12; XXVI, p. 46.

the intellect. It cannot be said that the soul is intrinsically changed in the sense that it receives a new nature, for such a change would amount to its destruction—what is simple cannot be intrinsically changed.[17] Hence it follows that our soul possesses the intrinsic potency to receive knowledge of the divine essence. This, of course, does not mean that our intellect can naturally intuit the essence of God. Even though the intellect is naturally inclined to an object, still if the latter does not naturally move it, the knowledge of such an object is not natural,[18] and the divine essence does not naturally move our intellect in any of its possible states.

Scotus proves the thesis that the divine essence does not naturally move our intellect by describing the order of divine movements or motions in the broad and improper sense of the term. The absolutely first motion is the motion of the divine intellect by its object, namely, by the divine essence. Next comes the natural motion of the divine intellect by the divine essence to the knowledge of all simple intelligibles as opposed to propositions.[19] The order of natural or necessary movements is followed by the contingent movements, whose principle is not the divine essence but the divine will. First, there is the contingent movement *ad intra,* by which the divine will determines itself to will that something be, and the intellect, seeing this infallible determination of the will, knows that the object will exist in the future.[20] This explains why the divine essence does not naturally move the divine intellect to the distinct knowledge of the truth of every proposition, for then it would know necessarily one of the two possible alternatives regarding the future contingent events. This implies either that the divine intellect could err or that the opposite alternative could not happen, and what is said to be contingent would not be contingent but necessary.[21]

The contingent movement *ad intra* is followed by the movement *ad extra* which is wholly contingent and derives immediately from the will. Hence the divine essence as such and insofar as it is naturally a motive does not move any created intellect. If, there-

---

[17] *Ord.* I, d. 3, n. 114; III, p. 71.
[18] *Ibidem* Prologus, n. 57; I, p. 35.
[19] *Quodl.* 14, n. 14; XXVI, p. 52. Cf. E. Gilson, *The Spirit of Mediaeval Philosophy,* trans. A. H. C. Downes (New York: Charles Scribner's Sons, 1940), pp. 248-269.
[20] *Quodl.* 14, n. 15; XXVI, p. 52.
[21] *Ibidem,* nn. 15-16; XXVI, p. 53.

fore, a created intellect sees the divine essence—and the blessed do see it—the immediate cause of such vision is God's free will.[22]

Our intellect not only cannot have a natural intuition of the divine essence, but it also cannot naturally have an immediate abstract concept of the divine essence. The reason for this impossibility is again that God is not naturally present to our intellect and does not naturally move it. An immediate abstractive concept or representation of God could only be caused by God himself. Hence if God could be known by an immediate representation, such a representation would be caused by his free will.[23] Further, our intellect is not naturally capable of reaching a perfect mediate concept of God. In other words, we cannot know God distinctly through the knowledge of an intermediary object.[24] No being can be known distinctly and perfectly by means of a concept abstracted from another being or object unless it is contained essentially or virtually and perfectly, i.e., in all its knowability, in this intermediate object. But no other object contains essentially or virtually or perfectly the divine essence.[25] Therefore, our intellect cannot perfectly know God with mediate abstractive knowledge.

By its natural capacity our intellect can only form imperfect concepts of God.[26] From the perception of a singular being, good, truth, our intellect can abstract the concepts of being, truth, and good by which it knows God in a confused way. By further elaboration our intellect can and does form the concepts of essential and supreme being, good, truth, and so on, which concepts are in a sense proper to God.[27] To put it in a slightly different way, every concept that transcends the creature can be understood in its indifference. By such a concept we conceive God confusedly, as when by conceiving "animal" we conceive man. This is possible because from a less universal concept our intellect can ascend to a more

[22] *Ibidem*, n. 16; XXVI, p. 54.
[23] *Ibidem*, n. 10; XXVI, p. 39. It is obvious that an immediate representation of God cannot be caused in our intellect by any other object. *Ibidem*.
[24] *Ibidem*, n. 21; XXVI, p. 97; ". . . dico, quod anima ex naturalibus in quocumque statu . . . non potest cognoscere essentiam divinam sub ratione propria mediate, sic intelligendo, quod per obiectum cognitum medium, vel in obiecto cognito medio cognoscatur ratio eius, quia nihil potest per se distincte intelligi hoc modo mediate, nisi in illo medio contineatur essentialiter vel virtualiter, et hoc perfecte, scilicet secundum totam rationem cognoscibilitatis suae; essentia divina in nullo alio sic continetur; igitur, etc."
[25] *Ibidem*.
[26] *Ibidem*. n. 3; XXVI, p. 5; *Ord*. I, d. 3, n. 61; III, p. 42.
[27] *Quodl*. 14, n. 4; XXVI, p. 6; *Ord*. I, d. 3, n. 61; III, p. 42.

universal one. If to common transcendental concepts we add the notes of supreme, first, or infinite, we obtain concepts which are proper to God and apply exclusively to God.[28]

Such concepts are quidditative.[29] They express something of the essence of God. In fact, Scotus says, it is impossible to know the existence of a being without somehow knowing the essence of the being.[30] This does not mean that we can decide *a priori* whether or not the different notes of the complex concepts, supreme being, infinite being, and others similar to them, can be united in reality. True, our intellect does not see any contradiction in them, but, Scotus repeatedly tells us, from the logical non-repugnance or possibility of such notes we cannot deduce with certainty the existence of the reality signified by them. The possibility of actually unifying the concepts of "being" and "infinite" can only be demonstrated *a posteriori*. The transcendental concepts of being, good, and truth, as well as the concepts of simple perfections, abstracted from crea-

---

[28] *Quodl.* XIV, n. 3; XXVI, pp. 5-6: "Dico quod anima ex perfectione naturali . . . potest . . . ex cognitione huius entis abstrahendo, cognoscere ens secundum se, et sic de bono. . . Consimiliter per hoc verum potest intelligi ipsum verum. . . Breviter dico, quod quodcumque transcendens per abstractionem a creatura cognita, potest in sua indifferentia intelligi, et tunc concipitur Deus quasi confuse, sicut animali intellecto, homo intelligitur. Sed si tale transcendens in communi intelligitur sub ratione alicujus specialioris perfectionis, puta summum, vel primum, vel infinitum, jam habetur conceptus sic Deo proprius, quod nulli alii convenit." *Ord.* I. d. 3; III, p. 42: "Dico quod ista quae cognoscuntur de Deo, cognoscuntur per species creaturarum, quia sive universalius et minus universale cognoscantur per eamdem speciem minus universalis sive utrumque habeat speciem sui intelligibilem sibi propriam, saltem illud quod potest imprimere speciem minus universalis in intellectu, potest etiam causare speciem cuiuscumque universalioris: et ita creaturae, quae imprimunt proprias species in intellectu, possunt etiam imprimere species transcedentium quae communiter conveniunt eis et Deo—et tunc intellectus propria virtute potest uti multis speciebus simul ad concipiendum illa simul quorum sunt istae species, puta specie boni et specie summi et specie actus ad concipiendum aliquid 'summum bonum et actualissimum'; quod apparet per locum a minori: imaginativa enim potest uti speciebus diversorum sensibilium ad imaginandum compositum ex illis diversis, sicut apparet imaginando 'montem aureum'". Briefly, according to Scotus, we abstract the transcendental concept of being and other transcendental concepts from sensible things. Therefore, the "virtual innatism" of Scotus' transcendental concept of being Bettoni speaks about is not backed, but excluded, by Scotus' texts. Cf. E. Bettoni, *Il problema della cognoscibilità di Dio nella scuola francescana* (Padua: Cedam, 1950), pp. 348-355; *L'ascesa a Dio in Duns Scoto*, pp. 11-103. See in this connection Timotheus Barth, "De univocationis entis Scotisticae intentione principali necnon valore critico," *Antonianum*, XXVIII (1953) 72-110.

[29] *Ord.* I, d. 3, n. 25; III, p. 16.

[30] *Ibidem*, n. 25; III, p. 17.

tures, can be applied to God because they are univocal.[81] Whether Scotus held all along the univocity of such concepts or adopted it in his later works after having denied it in his early work, *Quaestiones subtilissimae super libros metaphysicorum Aristotelis,* there is no doubt that the univocity of the transcendental concepts and the concepts of simple perfections is for him the basic and *sine qua non* condition of the possibility of our knowledge of God.[82] However, it should be noted that Scotus explicitly frees his demonstration of God's existence from the thesis of univocity.[83] Those who think that God can be reached by means of analogous concepts, he tells us, could use his demonstration prescinding from univocity.

It has been noted that Scotus' theses of univocity and the adequate object of our intellect are intimately connected, and his proof of the existence of God depends on his thesis of the adequate object of the intellect.[84] This is true as regards the adequate object of our intellect by reason of its primacy of community and virtuality—the abstract concept of being as such.[85] It is not true, if by the object of our intellect we understand the object of inclination, which

[81] *Ibidem,* nn. 26ff; III, pp. 18ff.

[82] Scotus speaks of metaphysical univocity, not merely of a logical univocity. The text "*ad quaestionem, concedo quod ens non dicatur univoce de omnibus entibus*" (*Quaestiones subtilissimae* ... IV, q. 1, n. 12; VII, p. 153) apparently is authentic. Cf. Carolus Balić, *l.c.,* pp. 279ff. According to A. B. Wolter, in this text Scotus speaks of the *term* "being." Cf. A. B. Wolter, *The Transcendentals and their Function in the Metaphysics of Duns Scotus* (Washington, D.C.: The Catholic University of America Press, 1946), pp. 46-48. A simpler explanation would be that Scotus changed his mind and that after having denied the doctrine of univocity in his earlier work, *Metaphysics,* he embraced it in subsequent works.

[83] *Ord.* I, d. 2, n. 29; II, p. 141a: "*Adnotatio Duns Scoti*: Haec minor ponitur ex opinione de univocatione conceptus communis Deo et creaturae, qua opinione mutata minor sumetur haec: 'multi conceptus in quibus concipimus Deum non sunt simpliciter simplices,' et concluditur conclusio particularis, non universalis sicut per duas primas rationes. Aliter potest sumi minor sic: 'nullus conceptus noster proprius Deo et quem percipimus esse proprium Deo est simpliciter simplex,' quia licet conceptus entis factus per creaturam sit simpliciter simplex et proprius Deo secundum aliam opinionem, tamen non est perceptus proprius, quia secundum Henricum videtur quod in illo conceptu propter similitudinem et simplicitatem non distinguimus Deum ab aliis,—intellige: non distinguimus perceptibiliter, quia licet conceptus sit distinctus, non tamen percipitur a nobis ut distinctus conceptus."

[84] E. Bettoni, *L'ascesa a Dio in Duns Scoto* (Milano: Vita e Pensiero, 1943), pp. 91ff; E. Gilson, "Les seize premiers Theoremata et la pensée de Duns Scot," *Archives d'histoire doctrinale et littéraire du Moyen Age,* XII-XIII (1937-1938), pp. 5-86, particularly pp. 54-80.

[85] In *Ordinatio* I, d. 3, n. 57; III, p. 39, Scotus writes: "Univocatio enim non est nisi in generalibus rationibus."

is every being, or the adequate object which naturally moves our intellect *ex natura sua*, which is every *finite* being, whether material or spiritual. The conclusion some interpreters have drawn from Scotus' connection between the object of the intellect and the demonstration of the existence of God—namely, that since the thesis of the adequate object of our intellect *ex natura sua* is theological, the Scotistic proof of the existence of God based on it is also theological[36]—is unwarranted. Such a conclusion derives from a confusion of the different objects of our intellect Scotus distinguishes according to the different aspects under which the problem can be considered and the different states in which our intellect can live and act.[37]

The most perfect concept by which we know God in a descriptive sort of way is obtained by conceiving all pure perfections and each in the highest degree. But among the individual concepts proper to God, that of infinite being is more perfect and simpler than the others. It is more perfect because it virtually includes more than any other concept we can conceive. As being virtually includes the good and the true, so infinite being includes the infinitely good, the infinitely true, and all pure perfections under the aspect of infinity. It is more simple, since infinity is not a quasi attribute or property of "being" or of that of which it is predicated. Rather it signifies an intrinsic mode of that entity, so that the concept of "infinite being" is not composed accidentally, as it were, of a subject and its attribute; it is a concept of what is essentially one, namely, of a subject with a certain grade of perfection, which is infinity.[38] According to Scotus, the idea of an infinite being not only can be formed naturally by the human intellect,[39] but it was actually reached by pagan philosophers independently of revelation. Even if historically the concept of infinite being had derived from theology, it would not thereby be a theological notion. Every concept obtainable by natural reason is in itself philosophical, and the rational demonstrations and conclusions in which it intervenes are philosophical.[40]

---

[36] E. Gilson, *l.c.*, p. 66, etc.

[37] The thesis concerning the adequate object of the inclination of our intellect is theological and possibly the doctrine of the adequate object of any created intellect *ex natura sua* is also theological. Cf. *Ord.* Prologus, n. 33; I, p. 19; II, p. I, q. 5; XI, p. 192; *Quodl.* 14, n. 12; XXVI, p. 46.

[38] *Ord.* I, d. 3, nn. 58-59; III, pp. 40-41.

[39] *Ord.* I, d. 2, n. 132; II, pp. 206-207.

[40] Cf. E. Bettoni, *l. c.*, pp. 114ff; cf. C. Balić, *l. c.*

II

THE EXISTENCE OF GOD IS NOT SELF-EVIDENT

The existence of an infinite being is not self-evident. Or, as Scotus prefers to state it, the proposition, "The infinite being exists," is not self-evident or *per se nota*.[41] According to him, a proposition is self-evident if it is evident from the conception of its terms as such.[42] In other words, a proposition is self-evident if the relationship between its subject and predicate is evident from the conception of the extremes as such. If in order to see this relationship it is necessary to define the subject or the predicate, or both of them, the proposition is not self-evident. For the concept suggested by the term as such is different from the concept obtained by the definition. "Since the clear concept of the quiddity expressed by the definition and the confused concept of the same quiddity expressed by the name are distinct, it follows that a proposition which is not known unless the quiddity is distinctly conceived by the definition is not *per se nota* by the quiddity confusedly known."[43]

In the contrary hypothesis every proposition which is necessary and *per se* in the first mode,[44] such as the proposition, "Man is an animal," or "He is a substance," would be self-evident, for if both extremes of these propositions are distinctly conceived, the inclusion of one extreme in the other is manifest. Again, if a proposi-

---

[41] *Ord.* I, d 2, n. 26; II, p. 138-139. Cf. Hans Louis Fäh, "Joannes Duns Scotus: Ist Gottes Dasein durch sich bekannt? *Ordinatio* I, d. 2, q. 2, übersetzt und erklärt," *Franziskanische Studien*, XLIII (1961), 348-373.

[42] *Ibidem*, n. 21; II, p. 135: "Est igitur omnis et sola illa propositio per se nota quae ex terminis sic conceptis, ut sunt eius termini, habet vel nata est habere evidentem veritatem complexionis." Cf. also n. 15, p. 131.

[43] *Ibidem*, n. 18; II, p. 133: "Cum propositio sit per se nota, quae ex propriis terminis habet evidentem veritatem, et alii termini sunt conceptus quidditatis distincte, ut importantur per definitionem, et conceptus quidditatis confuse, ut importantur per nomen, sequitur quod propositio non erit per se nota de quidditate confuse accepta, quae non est nota nisi per definitionem eadem distincte concipiatur." According to Scotus, the property of being known *per se* or self-evident pertains to the proposition in itself independently of the knower. Hence he rejects the distinctions between *per se* known and *per se* knowable propositions, between propositions that are self-evident in themselves and those that are self-evident for us. Again, he does not admit propositions which are self-evident for the wise but not for the ignorant. According to St. Thomas a proposition is *per se nota* if the predicate is contained in the subject. Hence he admits with Boethius *per se* known propositions which are *per se* known only to the wise. *S. Theol.* I, q. 2, a. 1, corp.

[44] Cf. Aristotle, *Posterior Analytics*, I, c. 4, 73a34-37.

tion in which one or both extremes have to be defined could be *per se nota*, every proposition of special sciences which the metaphysician knows distinctly through the definition of its terms would be self-evident. But this inference cannot be accepted; the geometrician, for example, only considers as self-evident those propositions which are evident by the terms confusedly conceived, such as, "The line is longitude without latitude." He does not consider other propositions which the metaphysician can conceive, such as, "The line is quantitative," as self-evident.[45]

If the only self-evident propositions are those which are or can be evidently true through the conception of their terms as such, a proposition of complex terms will not be self-evident unless the possible or actual union of the different notes of the complex term or terms is known. In quidditative propositions it will be necessary to know the possible union of the notes, and in existential propositions their actual union. Otherwise there always exists the possibility that the notes of the complex concept will be mutually repugnant, in which case the resultant proposition, far from being evidently true, will also be false. Scotus illustrates this with examples. In the quidditative predication the proposition, "The irrational man is an animal," is false for it contains contradictory concepts. In the existential order the proposition, "The white man exists," will only be self-evident if it is known that a man exists and that such man is white; if no white man should exist in reality, the proposition would be false and its contradictory, "Nothing is a white man," or the converse of this, "No white man exists," would be true.[46]

Applying these principles to our case, the proposition, "The infinite being exists," or "The necessary being exists," is not self-evident. "To the question of whether existence pertains to any concept which we conceive of God so that the proposition in which existence is asserted of such a concept is self-evident... I say no for three reasons."[47] In the first place, the proposition, "The infinite

---

[45] *Ord.* I, d. 2, n. 19; II, pp. 134.

[46] *Ibidem*, n. 30; II, pp. 141-142.

[47] *Ibidem*, n. 26, pp. 138-139: "Sed si quaeratur an esse insit alicui conceptui quem nos concipimus de Deo, ita quod talis propositio sit per se nota in qua enuntiatur esse de tali conceptu, puta ut de propositione cuius extrema possunt a nobis concipi, puta, potest in intellectu nostro esse aliquis conceptus dictus de Deo, tamen non communis sibi et creaturae, puta necessario esse vel ens infinitum vel summum bonum, et de tali concepto possumus praedicare esse eo modo quo a nobis concipitur—dico quod nulla talis est per se nota, propter tria."

being exists," is demonstrable and considered in itself is demonstrable by a *propter quid* demonstration (although, as will be shown later, we can demonstrate it only by a *quia* demonstration.) Proof: it can be demonstrated *propter quid* that whatever primarily and immediately pertains to a being pertains to everything contained in it. But existence pertains to *this* divine essence *(haec divina essentia)* as the blessed intuit it. Therefore, by using the divine essence as the middle term, the existence of everything that can be conceived of it either as its superior, in the logical sense, or as its attribute can be demonstrated *propter quid*, just as by the proposition, "The triangle has three angles," it can be demonstrated that some figure has three angles, and so on. Therefore, the proposition, "The infinite being exists," or the proposition, "The necessary being or the supreme good exists," is not self-evident by its terms; if it were, it could not be demonstrated.[48]

Secondly, a self-evident proposition is evident to every intellect that conceives its terms. But the proposition, "The infinite being exists," is not evident by its terms; we accept it by faith or by demonstration.[49] Thirdly, none of our proper concepts of God is simply simple. They are composite, such as "necessary being," "supreme being," and "infinite being." But, as previously noted, no proposition with a complex subject is self-evident unless the union of the different notes of the subject is self-evident. In the existential proposition, "The infinite being exists," the actual union of the realities expressed by the complex subject must be self-evident; and such a union, as the preceding reasons prove, is not self-evident, but must be demonstrated.[50]

III

THE EXISTENCE OF GOD CAN BE DEMONSTRATED
WITH A *QUIA* DEMONSTRATION

Scotus does not deal *ex professo* with demonstration in any of his

[48] *Ibidem*, n. 27, pp. 139-140.
[49] *Ibidem*, n. 28, p. 140.
[50] *Ibidem*, n. 29, pp. 140-141. After having explained positively his notion of a self-evident proposition and proved that the proposition "The infinite being exists" is not self-evident, Scotus answers several objections. The most important of them is the one based on St. Anselm's argument. We discuss it in the V section of this article.

authentic works.[51] However, his ideas on the notion and division of demonstration appear sufficiently clear from his references to it in different places and contexts. The most complete and fully satisfactory text is found in the *Quaestiones quodlibetales:*

> The first distinction is known from the *Posterior Analytics.* It is the distinction of demonstration into *propter quid,* or by the cause, and *quia,* or by the effect. This distinction is proved by reason: every necessarily true proposition which is not evident from its terms but has a necessary connection with another proposition which is necessarily evident from its terms can be demonstrated by the latter. But some true and necessary proposition which is not evident from its terms has a necessary connection with another true proposition concerning the effect —for not only truths regarding causes are impossible without some truths regarding effects, but the contrary is also true [truths concerning effects are impossible without some truths concerning causes]. Therefore, some true propositions can be demonstrated by another true and evident proposition based either on the cause, in which case the demonstration is *propter quid,* or on the effect, in which case the demonstration is *quia* . . . How a truth based on the effect can be evident while a truth based on the cause is not evident appears clear if we consider the mode of acquiring science which is experience. By experience, through many singular cases perceived by the senses we often know that the effect is before knowing why it is, for the knowledge of the cause is not obtained through the senses but by further investigation.[52]

In this text Scotus gives the definition and division of demonstration. Demonstration consists in inferring a necessary truth not immediately known by its terms from another evident truth with which it is necessarily and evidently connected. This necessary and evident relation or connection can exist not only when the premises express the ontological cause of the inclusion of the conclusion's predicate in the subject, but also when the premises express an effect of the cause stated in the conclusion. The reason is that there are no truths concerning the causes without some truths concerning the effects, and vice versa.

Hence, there are two kinds of demonstration. When the premise is a necessary and evident truth based on the cause, the demonstration is *propter quid;* when the premise is a necessary and evident

---

[51] The *Commentary on the Posterior Analytics* is not regarded as a genuine Scotistic work.
[52] *Quaestiones quodlibetales,* 7, n. 3; XXV, pp. 283-284.

truth based on the effect, the demonstration is *quia*.⁵³ The demonstration *propter quid* or by the cause is *a priori*. Apparently, according to Scotus, the demonstration *quia* is always *a posteriori* or from the effect, although perhaps he identifies them because they usually coincide. Following Aristotle, scholastics subdivide the demonstration *quia* into *a posteriori*, or from the effect, and *a priori*, or from a remote cause (the *propter quid* demonstration would proceed exclusively from a proximate cause). Let us keep in mind that the demonstration *a priori* is from the cause and the demonstration from the effect is *a posteriori*.⁵⁴

According to Scotus, therefore, not only the *propter quid* demonstration but also the *quia* demonstration concludes necessarily and evidently. After having firmly established this point and as if answering a possible objection, he explains how a proposition based on the effect can be evident while a proposition based on the cause is not. As Aristotle says, experience is a way of acquiring science, and we often know with evidence from experience the existence of an effect without knowing its cause since the causes are not perceived by the senses. In other places Scotus amply explains the degrees, structures, and value of this experiential way of acquiring science.⁵⁵

Scotus has in mind both kinds of demonstration when, following

---

⁵³ Cf. Aristotle, *Posterior Analytics* I, ch. 13, 78a22-78b34. For Aristotle, of course, the *propter quid* demonstration is much more perfect than the *quia* demonstration. But this does not mean that the latter does not deduce a certain and evident conclusion. *Ibidem*. St. Thomas in his commentary on this whole passage of Aristotle, after writing that only the *propter quid* demonstration is demonstration *simpliciter*, adds: "Nihil ... prohibet duorum aeque praedicantium, id est convertibilium, quorum unum sit causa, et aliud effectus, notius esse aliquando non causam, sed magis effectum. Nam effectus aliquando est notior causa quoad nos et secundum sensum, licet causa sit semper notior simpliciter, et secundum naturam. Et ita per effectum notiorem causa potest fieri demonstratio non faciens scire propter quid, sed tantum quia." *In Anal. post.* I, lect. 23, nn. 1ff. For St. Thomas, therefore, to say that the *quia* demonstration is not a demonstration *simpliciter* does not mean that its conclusion cannot be evident.

⁵⁴ The demonstration from the effect starts from the existential or quidditative reality of the effect, not from its *concept*, and it is based on the principle of causality, not merely on the principle of non-contradiction although the latter is always involved in the former. Again, the demonstration from the effect is always *a posteriori* and, as Scotus says, it is ultimately founded on experience. However, even if the demonstrative syllogism should prescind from contingent facts of experience and start from a possible being, the demonstration would be *a posteriori*, not *a priori*, for the causable is always posterior, at least in nature, to its cause.

⁵⁵ Cf. P. Raymond, "La théorie de l'induction, Duns Scot précurseur de Bacon," *Études Franciscaines*, XXI (1909), pp. 113-123; 270-279.

Aristotle, he also defines demonstration as *syllogismus faciens scire*,[56] that is, a syllogism that draws a scientific conclusion. Hence he speaks of *scientia quia* and *scientia propter quid*.[57] Both realize the conditions he requires for science or a scientific proposition or conclusion, namely, that it be a certain, not only probable, knowledge of a necessary truth which receives its evidence from a previous evident truth or principle through a syllogistic reasoning.[58] In both kinds of demonstration the premises are causes of the evidence of the conclusion and of our perception of this evidence. Of course, in the *propter quid* demonstration the premises also contain the ontological cause of the conclusion.

By which of these two kinds of demonstration can the existence of God be proved according to Scotus? Considered in itself, he says, the existence of God can be demonstrated with a *propter quid* demonstration, by using the divine essence as the middle term.[59] We cannot demonstrate the existence of God in such a way because we do not know the divine essence in itself. However, we can demonstrate the existence of an infinite being and its unicity with a *quia* demonstration, from the effects or from the creatures. The texts of Scotus are numerous and perfectly clear.

> The existence of God is proved here [in metaphysics].[60] As far as we are concerned, the proposition (The Infinite Being exists) is *demonstrable* with a *quia* demonstration from the creatures.[61] To the second objection . . ., which says that the proof starts from contingent premises and is not therefore a *demonstration*, I answer that it could be argued as follows: some nature is effected . . ., and then the first premise would be contingent although manifest. However, it could be argued in this other way . . . some nature can be effected . . ., starting from *necessary* premises.[62] I do not think that the reasons for proving it [God's unicity] are lacking. [The conclusion that there is only one God] is demonstrated.[63]

There is no reason to deny or doubt that in these texts Scotus

---

[56] *Super universalia Porphirii quaestiones*, q. 1, n. 2; I, p. 51. Cf. Aristotle, *Posterior Analytics*, I, ch. 2, 71b17.
[57] Cf. *Metaphysica* I, q. 1, the whole question; VII, pp. 11-40.
[58] *Rep. par.* Prologus, q. 1, n. 4; XXII, pp. 7-8; etc.
[59] *Ord.* I, d. 2, n. 27; II, p. 139.
[60] *Metaphysica* VI, q. 4, n. 1; VI, p. 348.
[61] *Ord.* I, d. 2, n. 39; II, p. 148; *Rep. par.* I, d. 2, q. 11, n. 2.
[62] *Ord.* I, d. 2, n. 56; II, p. 162; *De primo principio*, ch. 3, pp. 623ff.
[63] *De primo principio*, p. 707; *Rep. par.* I, d. 2, q. 4, n. 3; XXII, p. 75; *Ord.* I, d. 2, n. 165; II, p. 226.

is using the term "demonstration" in its proper sense, namely, as reasoning from necessary and evident premises to a necessary and evident conclusion. The structure of the proofs themselves clearly shows that Scotus starts from necessary premises which he proves evidently. He carefully distinguishes, even in his so-called theological works, between demonstrable truths, such as the existence of an infinite being and his unicity, and truths which cannot be demonstrated but at most persuaded as, for example, God's immediate omnipotence. Again, in establishing the demonstrable theses themselves he carefully distinguishes between really apodictic and merely probable reasons. There cannot be, therefore, any reasonable doubt that, according to the authentic works of Scotus, God's existence can be demonstrated with a true and proper *quia* demonstration.

However, as regards this problem of the rational demonstrability of the existence of God, there remains the problem posed by the fifteenth and sixteenth theorems of the *Theoremata*. While the *Quaestiones subtilissimae super libros metaphysicorum*, the *Reportata Parisiensia*, the *Ordinatio*, and *De primo principio* affirm the demonstrability of the existence of God, the *Theoremata* denies it.

> In essentially ordered beings there is a principle which is unique and coexistent with the coordination. In every genus of cause there is an essential order. Let us assume these two propositions *(petantur)*; the first contains three parts; the second is simple; although both are probable, it would be difficult and perhaps impossible for us to prove them with a simply necessary and purely natural reason.[64]

This text denies that in essentially ordered causes the existence of a first cause coexistent with the series can be demonstrated, something Scotus categorically affirms in other books, including the *Ordinatio* and *De primo principio*. Gilson, in a notable article written some years ago, attempts to prove that there is no contradiction between the *Theoremata* and the so-called theological works of Scotus.[65] According to Gilson, in the *Theoremata* Scotus speaks as a pure philosopher, while in the other works he speaks as a theologian and does not say anything different. The main reasons by which he tries to prove his interpretation are the following. 1) The

[64] *Theoremata*, XV, 1-2; V, p. 51. We do not think that any special significance should be attached to the fact that the text speaks of "*simply* necessary and *purely* natural reason."
[65] E. Gilson, *l.c.*, pp. 60-67.

quia demonstration is not a true demonstration or a necessary and evident conclusion from necessary and evident principles. 2) The so-called demonstrations of Scotus in his theological works are necessary proofs but not evident and necessary, for in the last analysis, they are based on a theological thesis, on the doctrine of the adequate object of our intellect. From the purely philosophical point of view such "demonstrations" are merely probable arguments. 3) Metaphysics, according to Scotus, is the science of being, not of God; the science that has God as its object is theology. Hence metaphysics does not deal directly with God, and by implication the metaphysical proofs of God's existence are at best probable.[66]

The first reason cannot be accepted from either the philosophical or the historical point of view. A *quia* demonstration from necessary and evident premises is in itself certainly possible; and, as we have already seen, by a *quia* demonstration Scotus means precisely reasoning which concludes from necessary and evident premises. The second reason adduced by Gilson is groundless. The assertion that in the texts in which Scotus affirms the demonstrability of the existence of God by demonstration he means necessary proofs, but not evident and necessary proofs, is arbitrary. The attempted justification of this interpretation, namely, that the Scotistic demonstration of the existence of God is based on the doctrine of the object of the intellect, which is a theological thesis, derives from a confusion of the different objects of the intellect. The adequate object of our intellect presupposed by the proof is not the *objectum inclinationis* nor the object which naturally moves our intellect *ex natura sua* but the object by reason of its primacy of community and virtuality, that is, being as being; and according to Scotus this thesis is purely philosophical. Without the help of any revelation we naturally abstract from sensible things the concept of being as being and the other concepts by which we conceive God. Gilson's third reason is based on a misinterpretation. Of course, according to Scotus metaphysics cannot demonstrate *propter quid* the existence of God. But it can and does demonstrate it by a *quia* demonstration. The fact that metaphysics is the science of being, far from being an obstacle to the demonstration of God's existence, makes such a demonstration possible. Or, as Scotus puts it, metaphysics is a science of being because, among other things, it demon-

[66] E. Gilson, *l.c.,* pp. 54-80.

strates the existence of God,⁶⁷ and also something of his essence, including his infinite perfection.⁶⁸ In later years, it seems, Gilson has abandoned to a great degree his interpretation of Scotus' doctrine on the demonstration of the existence of God.⁶⁹

Between theorems XV and XVI and the other authentic works of Scotus there is, therefore, a real contradiction. How could it be explained? Assuming that the literary genus of the *Theoremata* has been determined and that its author positively expounds his own thought, assuming also that the *Theoremata* as a whole is an authentic work of Scotus, it would be necessary to prove that theorems XV and XVI (or the tract *De creditis*) are also authentic, and this has not been done. The fact that Scotus in *De primo principio* promises a *Tract on Things Believed* does not prove that he ful-

---

⁶⁷ *Metaphysica* VI, q. 4, n. 1; VII, 348: "Primo, quia Deum esse probatur hic."
⁶⁸ *Ibidem*, I, q. 1, n. 41; p. 32: "concluditur tam esse quam quid est." *Ibidem*, n. 39; p. 31: "Similiter potest esse [Deus] subjectum primo modo in scientia *quia*. Supposito enim quid dicitur per nomen, si tale est causa talis effectus, ex effectu potest concludi tale et esse ex esse, et hoc ex hoc tam quantum ad essentialia quam quantum ad proprietates, et hoc demonstratione quia." *Ibidem*, VI, q. 4, n. 1; VII, pp. 348-349: "Item perfectior conceptus de Deo possibilis Physico est primum movens, possibilis autem Metaphysico est primum ens. Secundus est perfectior, tum quia absolutus, tum quia requirit perfectionem infinitam, nam primum perfectissimum. . ." Cf. also *Ord.* I, d. 3, n. 25; III, p. 16. On all this discussion see A. B. Wolter, "The 'Theologism' of Duns Scotus," *Franciscan Studies*, VII (1947), pp. 367ff.

⁶⁹ Cf. E. Gilson, "L'objet de la métaphysique selon Duns Scot," *Mediaeval Studies* X (1948), p. 72: "Ainsi, *simplement théologiques* parce qu'elles portent sur l'objet de la théologie, toutes les connaissances sur Dieu que nous prouvons à partir de ses effets sont *relativemente métaphysiques*, parce qu'elles empruntent à la métaphysique son mode de demonstration." In note (64) he adds: "Sur l'ensemble de ce problème, voir le travail de R. P. J. Owens, C.SS.R., publié plus loin, notamment les pages où cette question complexe nous semble discutée avec une remarquable précision. . ." J. Owens, in the article Gilson refers to, writes among other things:
"c) Being which is the subject of metaphysics, includes God as first being, necessary being and the like. These notions are proper to God. They are obtained by adding more special concepts to the general concept of being.
"d) The *metaphysician* argues from finite being to infinite being. The demonstration of the being of God on the basis of finitude and infinity takes place in *metaphysics*. These statements are explicit in the text.
"e) The concept of infinite being is natural in origin, even in the present state. It is formed by taking the general concept of being and joining with it the more particular concept of 'infinite.' Both these concepts are taken from sensible things. The combined concept is limited in extension to God, but has no more comprehension than the content of the two original simple notions. This concept was known to pagan philosophers." J. Owens, "Up to What Point is God Included in the Metaphysics of Duns Scotus?," *Mediaeval Studies* X (1948), pp. 172-173. Cf. also E. Gilson, *Jean Duns Scot. Introduction à ses positions fondamentales* (Paris: J. Vrin, 1952), pp. 116-215.

filled his promise and that these two theorems are the promised work. In the hypothesis that they were written after the *De primo principio*, they could have been written by someone else.[70] If the *Theoremata* were written before the *De primo principio* the premise would refer to another treatise *De creditis*, which was never written either by Scotus or by any of his disciples. There are those who are of the opinion that the *Theoremata* is one of the first works of Scotus, anterior even to his *Metaphysics* where they see allusions to the earlier work.[71] In this hypothesis the contradiction could be explained by a change or evolution in Scotus' thought.

As long as these points are not settled, we cannot reject or misinterpret a doctrine which is so clearly and repeatedly stated by Scotus in his certainly authentic works, even in such later works as the *Ordinatio* and *De primo principio*.

IV

DEMONSTRATION OF THE EXISTENCE OF GOD

We will follow the exposition of the proof as developed in *De primo principio*, where it is more fully elaborated. To interpret and clarify certain points we will also use the expositions found in *Lectura I*, *Reportata parisiensia*, and *Ordinatio*. The demonstration can be divided into four parts: A) there exists a first efficient cause, an ultimate final cause, and a supreme nature; B) the triple primacy of efficiency, finality, and perfection pertains to one nature; C) the first nature is infinite; D) it is unique.

A.   There exists a first efficient cause, an ultimate final cause, and an eminent nature.

Scotus demonstrates the existence of a first efficient cause, an ultimate end, and a supreme nature by proving in a similar fashion that each of them is possible, uncausable, and therefore existent.

---

[70] As regards the authenticity of the Theoremata, cf. Carolus Balić, *Theologiae marianae elementa* (Sibenik: Kacic, 1933), pp. CXXI-CXLV; "La questione scotista," *Rivista di filosofia neo-scolastica*, XXI (1938), 235-245; "De critica textuali Scholasticorum scriptis accommodata" *Antonianum*, XX (1945), 293ff; E. Bettoni, *L'ascesa a Dio* . . ., pp. 104-121; A. B. Wolter, "The 'Theologism' of Duns Scotus," *l.c.*, 367-398; Gedeon Gál, "De J. Duns Scoti 'Theorematum' authenticitate ex ultima parte operis confirmata," *Collectanea Franciscana*, XX (1950), 5-51.

[71] Cf. Gedeon Gál, *l.c.*

1. *A first efficient cause exists.*

Some nature can be effected; therefore, some efficient cause is possible.[72] The premise of the enthymeme is proved because, as experience shows, some nature is contingent or capable of being after not being. The conclusion rightly follows from the premise because no being can be its own cause or derive from nothing. An efficient cause is therefore possible. Now this possible efficient cause is either the first or depends on another efficient cause. If it depends on another, this other cause is either the first or depends on another, and so on. In this way we have either a possible first efficient cause or a circle of causes or an infinite regress wherein each cause would be secondary or dependent on a previous cause. However, a circle of causes is impossible for they would be their own causes. An infinite regress is no explanation either for such a regress is impossible in essentially ordered causes; it is possible only in accidentally ordered causes if the infinite regress is based on the essential order. If the essential order is denied, no infinite regress in any kind of causes is possible. Therefore, we must conclude to the possibility of a first efficient cause.[73]

[72] Strictly speaking Scotus does not express himself in this way. He writes: "*aliqua natura est effectibilis, ergo aliqua natura est effectiva.*" In the premise the possibility refers to the subject, *aliqua natura*. In the conclusion, if we take it literally, the possibility refers to the causality, not to the existence of the subject. It is clear, however, that the proposition, "*aliqua natura est effectiva*," cannot be translated as "there exists some nature that can cause." Scotus prescinds from the existence of the subject. Otherwise, no meaning could be attached to the words, "*et tunc probatio primae conclusionis est de esse quidditativo sive de esse possibili, non autem de existentia actuali. Sed de quo nunc ostenditur possibilitas, ultra ostendetur actualis existentia.*" Ord. I, d. 2, n. 56; II, p. 162; cf. also *De primo principio*, pp. 623-624.

[73] *De primo principio*, p. 624; Ord. I, d. 2, n. 43; II, p. 151. Experience, therefore, does not enter the formal structure of the demonstration. The first premise does not express an empirical fact. However, it is ultimately justified by experience and is based on the principle of causality. The contention of L. Puech that Scotus' proof starts from the *notion* of effect independently of experience and is based on the principle of non-contradiction, not on the principle of causality, cannot be accepted. L. Puech, "Une preuve oubliée de l'existence de Dieu," *Nos cahiers*, IV (1939), pp. 225-271. See a detailed refutation of this interpretation in Bettoni, *l.c.*, pp. 60ff. On the other hand, Pietro Migliore's new terminology has no foundation either. According to him, Scotus' proof is *quia*, but *a priori*, not *a posteriori*, because it starts from a necessary and metaphysical premise. Cf. Pietro Migliore, "Apriorismo nella dimostrazione scotistica dell' esistenza di Dio," *Miscellanea Franciscana*, LII (1952), pp. 336-378. Although the first premise is not contingent, it is justified by experience. Besides, a proof that concludes from effectibility to effectivity is *a posteriori*; effectibility is posterior to effectivity, just as the effect is posterior, at least in nature, to its cause.

The last minor, or the impossibility of an infinite regress both in essentially ordered causes and in accidentally ordered causes, unless they are based on the essential order, is proved by Scotus with exceptional thoroughness. Causes are essentially ordered, when the posterior depends on the prior for the exercise of its causality, the causality of the prior cause is of a different type and order, for the superior is always more perfect, and all causes must coexist at the time the effect is produced. Accidentally ordered causes, on the contrary, are those in which the posterior depends on the prior for its being or something else but not for the actual exercise of its causality, the causality of the different causes is univocal, and their coexistence is not required for the production of the effect.[74]

The impossibility of an infinite regress in accidentally ordered causes, independent of an essential order, is proved as follows: the succession can only be perpetuated by virtue of something permanent which is foreign to the succession, essentially anterior to it, and of a different order from it. Even supposing that accidentally ordered causes could exist and act independently of the action of an intrinsic cause, an infinite regress in accidentally ordered causes cannot be explained without an uncaused extrinsic cause. This cause would be coexistent with the series, it could not cease to exist after having exercised its own causality. As Scotus will prove in one of the subsequent conclusions, an uncaused cause is intrinsically necessary and cannot cease to exist.

The impossibility of an infinite regress in essentially ordered causes is proved by five arguments. Whether or not Scotus attaches the same value to all five proofs, there is no doubt that he con-

---

[74] *De primo principio*, pp. 625ff; *Ord.* I, d. 2, nn. 49-52; II, pp. 154-155. It has been objected that the Scotistic description of essentially ordered causes is not applicable to all such causes; that there are cases in which the second cause does not wholly depend upon the first for its action, as the intellect and the object in the intellection, that in such cases it would be difficult to decide which one is more perfect, and that the necessity of simultaneity in the action of all essentially ordered causes is not proved. Cf. William of Ockham, "Ordinatio I, d. 2, q. 10, K," *Franciscan Studies*, VIII (1948), 186; Ignatius Brady, "Comment on Dr. Wolter's paper," *Proceedings of the American Catholic Philosophical Association*, XXVIII (1954), 127-130; Reinhold Messner, *Schauendes und begrifliches Erkennen nach Duns Skotus* (Freiburg: Herder, 1942), p. 8. A possible answer to the first two parts of the objection: in the case of more or less autonomous causes, they would essentially depend on other causes which would be higher and more perfect. Answer to the third part of the objection: the causes which do not have to act simultaneously in the production of an effect are not essentially but accidentally ordered, and the principles concerning the latter should be applied to them.

siders the first and the fourth as really conclusive. The totality of
essentially ordered causes, the first proof says, is caused; and it must
be produced by some cause which does not pertain to the totality.
The whole totality of dependents is dependent, but it cannot depend upon any of its members; otherwise it would be its own
cause. This reason should not be understood in the sense that an
infinite series of essentially ordered causes is possible provided that
the existence of an extrinsic cause is admitted. Such an interpretation would imply a contradiction, for the series of essentially ordered causes is vertical, and to admit a cause beyond the series
would be *ipso facto* to deny its infinity. Scotus does not allow this
contradiction. He admits the possibility of an infinite regress in
accidentally ordered causes if it is based on the essential order, but
he simply says that an infinite regress is impossible for essentially
ordered causes. It is impossible because, since each cause and the
whole series is caused, they have to be caused by an extrinsic cause,
which necessarily imposes a limit to the series. The fourth argument against the possibility of an infinite series of essentially
ordered causes is based on the equivocal character of such causes:
the higher cause is more perfect in causing. Consequently the infinitely higher cause—which would be infinitely more perfect—
would be of infinite perfection in causing, and hence would not
cause in virtue of another.

The third proposition, namely, that if the essential order is denied no infinite regress in causes is possible, is obvious from what
has been already said. For it has been proved that an infinity of
accidentally ordered causes is only possible if it is based on the
essential order, or at least, on an uncaused cause which is extrinsic
to the series.[75] The only explanation of the effectibility of some
nature is, therefore, the possibility of a first efficient cause.

Now the first efficient cause would be uncausable. Obviously,
being first, it could not be effected or have an efficient cause. It

---

[75] *De primo principio*, pp. 626ff; *Ord.* I, d. 2, n. 53; II, pp. 157-159. The other three proofs are the following: a) infinite causes essentially ordered would be simultaneous in act, a consequent no philosopher posits. b) The prior is nearer the beginning; consequently, where there is no beginning, there is nothing essentially prior. c) Efficient causality does not necessarily imply imperfection. But if it is in none without dependence upon a prior, it is in none without imperfection. Therefore independent efficient causality can belong to some nature and that nature would be simply first. Consequently an efficient causality simply first is possible. This suffices because later it will be concluded from this that it exists in reality.

could not be ordered to an end or have a final cause either for final causality implies efficient causality; the end can only exercise its own causality by metaphorically moving the efficient cause to produce that which is ordered to the end. It could not have a material cause nor a formal cause for matter and form cannot be united except by the action of an efficient cause which acts for an end.[76]

From the preceding two conclusions demonstrated *a posteriori*, namely, that the first efficient cause is possible and that it is uncausable, it follows that the first efficient cause actually exists. Otherwise, it would not be possible; only what is virtually contained in its causes is possible without being actual; what is uncausable can only be possible by being actual.[77]

2. *An ultimate final cause exists.*

It is possible that something can be ordained to an end, therefore, some final cause is possible. The premise is proved because the effectibility of a being implies its ordainability to an end; every effect is actualized insofar as the end to which it is ordained moves metaphorically the efficient cause to produce it. An infinity of ends is impossible for the same reason given to prove the impossibility of an infinity in efficient causes. Hence we conclude that an ultimate final cause is possible. This ultimate end would be uncausable. It could not have a final cause for it is the last end. It could not have an efficient cause because every agent *per se* acts for an end. It could not be constituted by material and formal causes because matter is actualized and form is induced into matter by an efficient cause. Therefore the ultimate final cause actually exists; otherwise it would not be possible, for every effect is caused in view of an end, and the last end could not be effected in view of a further end.[78]

3. *An eminent nature exists.*

It is possible that some nature be exceeded, therefore some eminent nature or some nature that is first in perfection is possible. As has been stated, some nature can be ordered to an end.

[76] *De primo principio*, pp. 629-630; *Ord.* I, d. 2, n. 57; III, p. 39.

[77] *De primo principio*, pp. 630-631; *Ord.* I, d. 2, n. 58; II, p. 162. Scotus adds a confirmation: the first possible efficient nature not only would be prior to all other efficient causes but to think of something prior would imply contradiction; therefore it exists. This conclusion is proved as the previous one, because the first efficient nature is uncausable. A similar confirmation is added to the proofs of the existence of an ultimate end and a supreme nature.

[78] *De primo principio*, pp. 636-637; *Ord.* I, d. 2, nn. 60-63; II, pp. 165-167.

But the end which insofar as it is loved moves the efficient cause to produce that which is ordered to the end cannot be either less than or equal to the latter but has to be greater than it, and no infinite series of natures is possible. Therefore, an eminent nature or a first nature in perfection is possible. That the end cannot be equal to, or *a fortiori* less than that which is ordered to it, is proved because otherwise the latter would be as lovable as the end and could be its own final cause; this is impossible since nothing can be essentially ordered to itself. The first possible nature would be uncausable. It could not be ordered to an end for what is ordered to an end is exceeded, is not supreme. It could not be effected for only what has an end can be effected. It could not be constituted by matter and form for matter is actualized and form is induced into matter by an efficient cause. Therefore, the supreme nature actually exists; otherwise, it would not be possible for it is uncausable.[79]

B. The Threefold Primacy of Efficiency, Finality, and Perfection Pertains to One Nature.

Scotus speaks here of a unity of nature, not of individual unity or unicity in the strict sense of the term. Undoubtedly what induces him to introduce this conclusion as a part of his demonstration of the existence of God is to prevent the admission of the existence of different natures which would be first, not in all three orders, but in the orders of efficiency and finality, or at least in the order of efficiency. According to some of his interpreters, Aristotle himself thought of intelligences in this way.[80] Scotus proves this conclusion concerning the unity of the first nature by establishing, first, that the nature which is first in any of the three orders is intrinsically necessary, and, second, that no two intrinsically necessary natures can exist.

A being that is first with any of the three primacies and is uncausable is intrinsically necessary. Proof: If it did not exist necessarily, it would be due to the existence of another nature which,

[79] *De primo principio*, pp. 637-638; *Ord.* I, d. 2, nn. 64-66; II, p. 167. In *Ordinatio*, before proving that the triple primacy pertains to one nature, Scotus establishes the mutual implication of all three primacies. *Ibidem*, nn. 68-69.
[80] *De primo principio*, p. 644ff; Cf. A. B. Wolter, "Duns Scotus and the Existence and Nature of God," *Proceedings of the American Catholic Philosophical Association*, XXVIII (1954), p. 111.

being incompatible with the former, would impede or obstruct its existence. But a being which is either positively or privatively incompatible with an uncaused being is impossible. Therefore the nature that is first with any of the three primacies of efficiency, finality, and perfection, is intrinsically necessary. Proof of the minor: A being positively or privatively incompatible with an uncaused being would be either uncaused or caused. In the first case there would exist two incompatible beings or rather neither would exist for one would destroy the other. In the second case the caused being which would impede the existence of the uncaused being would have to be endowed with a more perfect or more intense existence; this is impossible for a caused and dependent being cannot have a more perfect existence than an uncaused and independent being.[81]

No two intrinsically necessary natures are possible. Proof: If two intrinsically necessary natures existed, they would be distinct from each other by some proper entity. This entity would be formally necessary or not. If it were formally necessary, each nature would possess two formal reasons of its necessity: its proper and distinctive entity and the entity common to both. This would imply the absurdity that each nature would be necessary by virtue of an entity, the elimination of which would not affect its intrinsic necessity, for it would continue existing necessarily by virtue of the other entity. If the distinctive entity were not necessary and therefore, not the formal reason of the necessity of nature, it would not be an essential part of the nature; but a necessary being cannot include any contingent element.

Final conclusion: Since the nature which is first with any of the three primacies is intrinsically necessary, and no two intrinsically necessary natures are possible, it follows that the nature which contains one primacy also contains the others.[82]

---

[81] *De primo principio*, pp. 632-635; 639; *Ord.* I, d. 2, nn. 70-73; II, pp. 169-174.
[82] *De primo principio, l.c., Ord.* I, d. 2, nn. 70-73; II, pp. 169-174. This conclusion, Scotus says, is the principal conclusion of the third chapter of *De primo principio*. It includes six partial conclusions, three as regards the unity of the nature to which each primacy pertains and three as regards the identity of the nature to which one of the primacies pertains with the nature which contains the other primacies. All these conclusions have been proved in the preceding general conclusion by the intrinsic necessity of the being which is first in the triple order and the impossibility of two intrinsically necessary natures. However, Scotus, after establishing that in the same genus of causality there is only one total cause of the same effect and that a being can depend totally on only one first being, proves in particular the six partial conclusions. He adds another proof of the

C. The Nature Which Is First in the Triple Order Is Infinite.

Scotus proves in the first place certain conclusions which, along with theses already stated, are the bases of his demonstration of the infinity of the first nature. These conclusions are: the first being is simple with essential simplicity, contains all simple perfections, is endowed with intellect and will which are identical with his essence, and knows and loves simultaneously all intelligible objects.[83] Having established these conclusions, Scotus demonstrates the infinity of the first being in seven ways: the first three are based on his intelligence and knowledge, the fourth on his essential simplicity, the fifth on his eminent perfection, the sixth on the finality of his will, and the seventh on his infinite power. Not all have the same demonstrative value.[84]

The first way is based on the infinity of objects the first intelligence knows: when plurality implies greater perfection, numerical infinity implies infinite perfection. The capacity to know simultaneously and distinctly two objects implies greater perfection than the capacity to know only one. Therefore, the capacity to know an infinite number of objects implies an infinite capacity. The argument could also be formulated in another way: to understand an object is a perfection and to understand another object is another perfection. Hence the knowledge of two objects by one simple act cannot be as distinct as its knowledge by two acts unless the single act includes the perfections of both. The same is true as regards three or more acts of understanding. Since the intellection by which the first nature knows an infinite number of objects is simultaneous and distinct, it implies infinite perfection. The possible objection that many acts of intellection only conclude to a greater

---

same thesis of the triple identity of the nature to which pertains the triple primacy: the first efficient cause is most actual, the ultimate end is most lovable, and the supreme nature is most perfect. But the most actual, the best and the most perfect being can only be found in one nature. Therefore . . . Finally, he answers the possible objection that there might exist different natures which are first, if not in all three primacies, at least in two or one of them. *Ibidem*, pp. 644-647.

[83] *De primo principio*, pp. 648-651. After having proved the infinity of the first nature, Scotus adds other proofs of the essential simplicity of the Infinite Being. *Ibidem*, pp. 696-703. He thinks that the absolute simplicity of the first being which would also exclude contingently inhering accidents cannot be demonstrated by reason. *Ibidem*, p. 702.

[84] In *Ordinatio* Scotus gives four proofs of the infinity of the first nature: from efficiency, intellect, finality, and eminence. The confirmation of the proof from the intellect appears as an independent proof in *De primo principio*.

perfection when they possess formal and distinct perfections, and only the intellections of species that are not infinite contain such perfections, is baseless. The individuals as such, which are infinite, possess proper and positive entities or perfections, and their intellection implies perfection.[85]

The second way is based on the efficient objective causality involved in knowledge. If the first cause alone can produce much more perfectly an effect which can be caused simultaneously by it and a secondary cause, it does not receive any perfection from the secondary cause and is infinite; for every finite cause is perfected by any additional element or agent. But the supreme nature, without the co-causality of any other object, is the medium in which the first intellect knows, and knows perfectly, every object. Therefore, it is infinite in cognoscibility and consequently in entity for there is a direct proportion between the knowability of an object and its entity.[86]

The third way is based on the accidental character of all finite intellection. No finite intellection is substantial or identical to the substance of the knower; being essentially a quality, it is accidental. But, as has already been proved, the first being's intellection is identical with his substance. Therefore, it is infinite.[87]

The fourth way follows the same line, but it is ultimately based on the essential simplicity of the first being. Every finite substance pertains to a genus for it agrees with other substances in the common concept of substance and is formally distinct from them. The common element does not include the distinctive element with perfect identity; both elements constitute the substance as genus and difference. But the first nature is simple and does not pertain to any genus. Therefore it is not finite but infinite.[88]

After these four ways Scotus writes: "It seems that by these four ways the infinity of the first being can be concluded."[89] There is no doubt that he considers them truly demonstrative. The phrase "It seems" (*videtur*) is the modest way in which he constantly expresses his own thought. He adds three more ways, from eminence, finality, and infinite power, to which he does not attach the same

[85] *De primo principio*, pp. 671-675; *Ord.* I, d. 2, nn. 125-128; II, pp. 201-205.
[86] *De primo principio*, pp. 675-676; *Ord.* I, d. 2, nn. 128-130; II, pp. 204-206.
[87] *De primo principio*, pp. 681-683.
[88] *Ibidem*, pp. 683-684.
[89] *Ibidem*, p. 684; "His viis quatuor videtur infinitas posse concludi de Deo: tribus ex mediis sumptis de intellectu, quarto ex simplicitate in essentia, quae superius est ostensa."

demonstrative value although he thinks that the way from power can be transformed, with a few touches, into a real demonstration.

The way from eminence, or fifth way, says: It is incompatible with the notion of an eminent being that there be a more perfect being. But it is not incompatible with a finite being that there be a more perfect being. Therefore the most eminent being is infinite. The minor is proved because infinity is not repugnant to being, and an infinite being is greater than every finite being. Scotus also formulates this proof in another way: If that to which intensive infinity is not repugnant is not infinite it is not the most perfect being, it can be exceeded. But infinity is not repugnant to being. Therefore the most perfect being is infinite.

The value of this way from eminence depends on the proposition, "Infinity is not repugnant to being," which in the first formula is the proof of the minor and in the second is the minor. Can it be demonstrated *a priori*, as the way purports? The positive compatibility or agreement of the notions of being and infinite, Scotus says, cannot be seen through a conceptual analysis. Such an analysis is impossible because, on the one hand, the concept of being is the most simple and prior to every other concept and, on the other hand, the concept of infinite is known by us through the notion of finite.[90]

The reasons in favor of the proposition, "Infinity is not repugnant to being," are persuasive but not demonstrative. They are the following. Just as everything whose impossibility is not manifest should be declared possible, so also everything whose incompossibility is not manifest should be declared compossible. But no incompossibility is apparent between being and infinity for finitude is not contained in the concept of being nor is it a convertible property of being. Again, as the infinity which consists in receiving parts after parts is not repugnant to quantity, so the infinity which consists in being simultaneously perfect is not repugnant to being. Again, the intellect whose object is being, far from detecting any repugnance in understanding the infinite being, rests in the highest degree in such a concept. It would be surprising indeed that, if "being" and "infinite" were mutually repugnant, no intellect should detect such a repugnance in its proper object. Therefore, infinity is not repugnant to being.[91]

[90] *De primo principio*, pp. 684-685; *Ord.* I, d. 2, nn. 131-133; II, pp. 206-207.
[91] *De primo principio*, pp. 685-687; *Ord.* I, d. 2, nn. 133-137; II, pp. 207-209. Scotus discusses the value of St. Anselm's argument in connection with this

The sixth way is based on the finality of the first being's will, and is also a probable argument. Our will, says the proof, can love something greater than any finite being, just as the intellect can know it. In fact, our will seems to be naturally inclined to love in the highest degree the infinite good. (The existence of a natural inclination in the will is argued from the fact that of itself without a habit the will promptly and delectably wills it, and our will seems to will in such a way the infinite good and is not satisfied in any other good.) "How would it [the will] not naturally hate the infinite if it were opposed to its object, just as it naturally hates non-being?"[92]

The seventh and last way is based on the infinite power of the first mover, as found in Aristotle's *Physics*[93] and *Metaphysics*.[94] The first mover cannot be finite because it causes motion through an infinite time, and no finite mover has an infinite power.[95] In its original Aristotelian form the argument is not conclusive. In the first place, it is based on the assumption that neither motion nor time has had a beginning, which contradicts Christian belief in temporal creation. Besides, the argument would only prove the merely extensive infinity of the agent, not its intensive infinity for in a given moment a finite amount of energy would suffice to explain the motion. If some agent has the power to lift a finite weight of, say, ten grams and lifts ten-gram weights successively throughout an infinite period of time we cannot conclude thereby that it has the power to lift an infinite weight. It would be necessary to prove either that in a given moment the agent has the power to produce simultaneously infinite effects, which is not proved, for it is not demonstrated that secondary causes are not necessary for causing imperfect effects; or that the first agent possesses simultaneously and eminently, but not formally, all the causality of secondary causes, including their proper causality, as regards infinite effects, even though these effects are produced successively, and this has been proved. Accordingly, the proof of the infinity of the first being based on its power can be stated as follows. If the first being possesses formally and simultaneously all causality,

---

proof of the infinity of the first nature, based on the concept of the most eminent being. See section V of this article.

[92] *De primo principio*, p. 688; *Ord.* I, d. 2, n. 130; II, p. 205.
[93] *Physics*, VIII, ch. 10; 256a12-256b2.
[94] *Metaphysics*, XII, ch. 7; 1071b2-22.
[95] *Metaphysics*, XII ch. 7; 1073a6-7.

even if the causables cannot be produced, it is infinite, for of itself it could cause simultaneously infinite effects, and the power to produce simultaneously many effects concludes to a greater intensive perfection. But the first being possesses all secondary power more eminently than if it had it formally. Therefore, it possesses an intensively infinite power.[96] There is no doubt that Scotus considers this argument conclusive, since he immediately adds: "Even though I have deferred omnipotence properly so-called . . . to the *Tract on Things Believed*, nevertheless, . . . an infinite power is proved . . ."[97]

D. Unicity of the First Nature

Scotus' method of demonstrating the unicity of the first being consists in proving the unicity of the infinite intellect, the infinite will, the infinite power, the necessary being, and the infinite goodness. From each of these conclusions the unicity of the first nature as such is deduced.

The infinite intellect is unique because it knows everything knowable and knows it perfectly, and because its knowledge is independent of the causality of any other being. It would lack some of these properties, should there be more than one infinite intellect. The infinite will is unique; otherwise, it would not supremely love what is supremely lovable, namely, the other infinite will for it would love itself more; besides, it would be supremely happy in something, namely, the other will, whose destruction would not affect its happiness in the least. The infinite power is unique; otherwise, the same beings would wholly depend on two first beings,

---

[96] *De primo principio*, pp. 688-693; *Ord.* I, d. 2, nn. 117-121; 189-200.

[97] *De primo principio*, p. 693: "Licet igitur omnipotentiam proprie dictam, secundum intellectum Catholicorum, usque ad Tractatum de Creditis distulerim, tamen illa non probata, infinita potentia probatur quae simul ex se habet eminenter omnem causalitatem, quae simul, quantum est de se, si esset formaliter, posset in infinita, si essent simul factibilia." See also *Ord.* I, d. 2, n. 119. Scotus rejects two other arguments that were used at his time and are still used today to prove the infinity of the first being: 1) Creation implies an infinite distance between its extremes; therefore, it presupposes an infinite creator; 2) The first being is not a form which should naturally be united to a matter; therefore, it is infinite. Scotus answers the first of these two arguments by saying that there is no infinite distance between the extremes of creation, because the distance is no greater than the higher or positive extreme, which is finite. To the second argument he replies that no finite form is limited by matter, that it is limited in itself as a determinate nature, before being limited by matter. *Ibidem*, pp. 694-696; *Ord.* I, d. 2, nn. 121-125; II, pp. 198-202.

which is impossible. A necessary being is unique; since a multiplicable species is of itself infinitely multiplicable, if a necessary being could be multiplied, an infinite number of necessary beings could exist or rather would exist; for a necessary being, unless it be, cannot be. The infinite goodness is unique; by definition an infinite good fully satisfies the will; but if there were more than one infinite good, the will could rightly wish both and would not be completely satisfied in only one of them.

Therefore, the first being, in which intellect, will, power, and goodness are infinite, and which is intrinsically necessary, is and must be unique.[98]

V

FINAL REMARKS AND EVALUATION

In the preceding Scotistic demonstration of the existence of God there are two points that should be correctly interpreted, namely, the notion of quidditative or possible being and the transition from the possibility of the first efficient cause, or the ultimate final cause, or the supreme nature, to its actual existence. As regards the first point the following observations are in order. Quidditative or possible being is not a possible being in the strict sense of the term, that is to say, a being which has neither existed nor does exist, but can exist. According to Scotus, the possibles as divine ideas have only a purely mental or intentional being, which he also calls *esse diminutum* or *secundum quid*.[99] Neither does quidditative being mean the actual common nature *(natura communis)*, considered independently of the individual entity from which it is formally distinct. Otherwise it would be difficult or impossible to understand Scotus' words: "*et tunc probatio primae conclusionis procedit vel concludit de esse quidditative, sive de esse possibili, non autem de existentia actuali.*[100] Quidditative or possible being means the essential being abstracted from existing things. Such a being is real for our abstract concepts have a real content.[101]

What precedes is the key for the solution of the second point

[98] *De primo principio*, pp. 707-710; *Ord.* I, d. 2, nn. 157ff; II, pp. 222-236.
[99] *Ord.* I, d. 36, q. un.; VI, pp. 271-299.
[100] *Ord.* I, d. 2, n. 56; II, p. 162. If the *"esse quidditativum"* were the actual *natura communis*, Scotus could hardly speak of possible being.
[101] Cf. E. Bettoni, *L'ascesa a Dio in Duns Scoto*, pp. 73-74.

concerning the transition from the possibility of the first efficient cause to its actual existence: if it is possible, the proof concludes, it exists. This conclusion should not be understood as a transition from logical possibility to actuality. Scotus rejected such a transition as false in general and as inconclusive in the very special case of an infinite being.[102] How should then the inference of actuality from possibility be understood? Scotus has proved by an *a posteriori* demonstration, starting from the possibility of effects (which is ultimately based on their actual existence), the necessary possibility of a first efficient cause. In other words, he has not proved the mere logical possibility of such a being. This positive possibility of the first efficient cause necessarily implies its existence; if it did not exist, it would not be possible for it is first and uncausable. In other words, the demonstration of the possibility of a first efficient cause proves also its existence; it is possible by existing.

The preceding discussion leads us to the problem of the relationship between Scotus' proof and St. Anselm's argument.[103] Scotus considers the Anselmian *ratio* in two different contexts: in discussing whether the existence of God is self-evident and in proving the infinity of the first being in the triple order of efficiency, finality, and eminence. One of the objections which purports to prove that the existence of God is self-evident is that the proposition "the being the greater than which cannot be conceived exists" is self-evident,[104] because the opposite of the predicate is repugnant to the subject.[105] Scotus replies that Anselm does not consider the proposition as self-evident for the obvious reason that what is self-evident is not demonstrated and Anselm's proof is a deduction which implies two syllogisms: first, being is greater than non-being; but nothing is greater than the supreme being; therefore, the supreme being is not non-being. Second, what is not non-being is being; but the supreme being is not non-being; therefore it is being. To the reason given, namely, that the opposite of the predicate is repugnant to the subject, Scotus answers: it is not self-evident because the actual union of the different notes of the subject, which is composite, is not self-evident.[106]

---

[102] *De primo principio*, pp. 685. See also other places, previously quoted, in which Scotus denies that the existence of God can be derived *a priori* from the concepts of "infinite being," "perfect being," and other similar concepts.
[103] *Proslogium*, ch. 5; PL 158, 229.
[104] *Ord.* I, d. 2, nn. 11, 35-36; II, pp. 129; 145-146.
[105] *Ibidem*, nn. 35-36.
[106] *Ibidem*, nn. 137-140; II, pp. 208-211; *De primo principio*, pp. 687-688.

Scotus discusses the value of the Anselmian argument in connection with the proof of the infinity of the first being based on the concept of the most eminent being. Hence some commentators have asserted that Scotus does not consider or evaluate St. Anselm's argument in relation to the existence of God but only in relation to his infinity.[107] This is a misinterpretation. The proof from eminence in favor of the infinity of the first nature affords Scotus the occasion to discuss the value of St. Anselm's *ratio*, which refers to the existence of God.[108] Besides, Scotus never proves the infinity of God, but the infinity of the first nature; according to him, we cannot speak of God until the existence of an infinite being has been demonstrated.

What is Scotus' conclusion as regards the value of St. Anselm's proof? Some say that he rejects it; others are of the opinion that fundamentally he accepts it.[109] We believe that he considers it, once it has been properly understood and "colored," as a probable argument.[110] After having expounded the proof of the infinity of the first being from the notion of the most eminent being, Scotus writes:

> By it (per illud) Anselm's argument in the *Proslogium* about the highest conceivable being can be "colored" or touched up. His description must be understood in this way. God is a being conceived without contradiction, who is so great that no greater being can be conceived without contradiction. For that in the thought of which there is included a contradiction is said to be not thinkable, and it is truly so. For there are then two thinkables opposed, in no way making one thinkable because neither determines the other. It follows that there exists in reality such a highest thinkable as mentioned through which God is described. This is shown first with regard to quidditative being because in such a highest thinkable the intellect reposes in the highest degree. Therefore, there is in it the character of the first object of the intellect, namely, of being, and in the highest degree.
> Furthermore, this is shown with regard to existential being. The highest thinkable is not merely in the thinking intellect;

---

[107] Séraphin Belmond, *Dieu. Existence et cognoscibilité* (Paris: Beauchesne, 1913), p. 21, n. 1; Zacharias van Woestyne, *Cursus philosophicus*, II (Malines: Typographia S. Francisci, 1925), p. 712, n. 2: "Unde ratio S. Anselmi coloratur tantum in ordine ad ostendendam Dei infinitatem."

[108] *Ord*. I, d. 2, nn. 137-140; II, pp. 208-211.

[109] See authors who hold these different opinons in E. Bettoni, *op. cit.*, pp. 19-31.

[110] *Ibidem, l.c.,* pp. 19-31.

because then it could be, because it is repugnant to its meaning for it to be from another . . . therefore, that which is in reality is a greater thinkable than that which is in the intellect only. It is not meant by this that the same thing, if it be thought of, is a greater thinkable on the condition that it exists, but that any thinkable which exists is greater than everything which is in the intellect only.[111]

By "coloring" the argument, which consists in adding twice the words "without contradiction," Scotus invalidates Gaunilon's criticism, who objected that, if Anselm's argument was conclusive, then "an island the greater than which cannot be conceived" should also exist. The concept of such an island implies contradiction. An island means necessarily an imperfect being, and it is always possible to think without contradiction of a being greater than the greatest island. St. Anselm's argument, after having been touched up or "colored" by the double addition of the words "without contradiction," would argue, says Scotus, that the supremely thinkable is real with quidditative being since, far from seeing any contradiction in it, our intellect reposes completely in it, and that it is also real with existential being, for otherwise it would be both possible, for it is thinkable, and impossible, for it cannot be by another. In other words, it would not be thinkable without contradiction.

Thus Scotus assimilates St. Anselm's argument to the proof of the infinity of the first being from the concept of the most eminent or infinite being. To prove that the being the greater than which cannot be conceived exists he uses the same *a priori* reasons which seem to prove that the most eminent, perfect, or infinite being must actually exist. What are these reasons? That our intellect does not see any repugnance in such concepts, that it rests in them, that they seem to realize perfectly the proper object of the intellect, and that everything whose incompatibility is not apparent should be considered compatible. Scotus does not consider these reasons demonstrative but merely probable.[112] Therefore, for him Anselm's argument, which is *a priori*, is merely probable. The possibility and existence of an infinite being, Scotus says, cannot be demonstrated *a priori*, but only *a posteriori*, and the same is true of the possibility and existence of the highest thinkable being. St. Anselm's argument would become a real demonstration, if the possibility of the being the greater than which cannot be conceived were first

---

[111] *De primo principio*, pp. 687-688; *Ord.* I, d. 2, nn. 137ff; II, pp. 208ff.
[112] *De primo principio*, pp. 684-687; *Ord.* I, d. 2, nn. 131-137.

established *a posteriori*. But then it would not be St. Anselm's, but Scotus' argument.[113]

As regards the Scotistic demonstration of God, we could ask whether or not St. Thomas Aquinas would have accepted it. E. Bettoni, it seems, would have answered negatively for he believes that the gnoseological and metaphysical differences which separate Scotus from St. Thomas intrinsically affect Scotus' demonstration.[114] He refers chiefly to the theses of univocity, the adequate object of our intellect, and the cognoscibility of God's essence. J. Owens answers the question negatively. According to Scotus, he says, the perfection of the infinite being implies his existence while, according to St. Thomas, quidditative perfection, no matter how high it may be, cannot include the least existential act.[115] E. Gilson doubts that St. Thomas would have approved the Scotistic demonstration because he would not have abandoned his starting point or the empirical existence of things, which allows him to affirm the existence of their cause, in order to adopt the univocal concept of being and establish the reality of the first cause by the intrinsic possibility of its essence.[116] A. B. Wolter thinks that St. Thomas would not have objected to Scotus' proof.[117]

We agree with this last opinion. The reasons offered by those who deny or doubt that St. Thomas would have accepted Scotus' demonstration of the existence of God are the Scotistic theses concerning the object of our intellect, the univocity of being, the quidditative knowledge of God, and the legitimacy of the transition from the possibility of the first cause to its actual existence. However, the adequate object of our intellect involved in our knowledge

---

[113] *De primo principio*, pp. 684-687; *Ord.* I, d. 2, n. 139. Cf. Bettoni, *l.c.*, pp. 19-31. Scotus also "colors" or touches up St. Anselm's *ratio* in another way. What exists is a greater thinkable, that is, perfectly thinkable, because it is visible. What does not exist either in itself or in a more noble being to which it adds nothing is not visible. But what is visible is more perfectly knowable than what is not visible and can only be known in an abstract way. Therefore, what is perfectly knowable exists. *Ibidem*, p. 687. However, in order to affirm that God is a greater thinkable in this sense, it will be necessary first to prove that He exists. Only the existent can be intuited or "seen."

[114] E. Bettoni, *l.c.*, pp. 80ff.

[115] J. Owens, "The Special Characteristic of the Scotistic Proof that God Exists," *Analecta Gregoriana*, LXVII (1945), p. 326.

[116] E. Gilson, Jean Duns Scot. *Introduction à ses positions fondamentales* (Paris: J. Vrin, 1952), pp. 139-140.

[117] A. B. Wolter, "Duns Scotus and the Existence and Nature of God," *Proceedings of the American Catholic Philosophical Association*, XXVIII (1954), p. 120 and note 46.

of God, as repeatedly noted, is the adequate object by reason of its primacy of community and virtuality, which is being as being, abstracted from sensible things. It is true that St. Thomas makes the material quiddity the formal and proper object of our intellect, but it should not be forgotten that, according to him, the common formal object of our intellect is being as such.[118] As regards the doctrine of univocity, we have seen how Scotus explicitly frees his proof of the existence of God from it. As to Bettoni's contention that, according to Scotus, we somehow know God's essence while, according to St. Thomas, we only can know *an Deus sit* (God's existence), it should be noted that St. Thomas also admits some knowledge of the divine essence.[119]

In our opinion, therefore, the only point that could offer difficulty is the transition from the possibility of the first cause to its actual existence. We have previously explained the meaning of this transition. It is not *a priori* deduction of existence from the logical possibility or the apparent nonrepugnance of the concepts "first cause" and "existence." Scotus denies the legitimacy of such a deduction. The conclusion, "if possible, it exists," means that the positive possibility concerning the extramental existence, which is proved *a posteriori*, necessarily implies actual existence. In the exceptional case of the first being the demonstration of its possibility also proves its existence. The negation of the predicate, "exists," is repugnant to the subject, "possible first cause," whose possibility has been demonstrated *a posteriori*. Would St. Thomas have rejected the value of such an explicitation? We do not think so. Such a refusal would amount to denying the value of the deduction of a possible first efficient cause from the possibility of effects, based on the experience of existing things which begin and cease to exist and are subject to numerous changes.

The chief merit of the Scotistic demonstration is its completeness. It is not the proof of a first efficient cause, an ultimate final cause, or an eminent being, but the proof of the existence of an infinite being or God. No one can deny that the infinite being is God. Hence the proof is impervious to one of the most common objections against the Thomistic ways. From the point of view of its

---

[118] Cf. *In De An.* III, lect. 13, nn. 787ff; *C. Gent.* II, ch. 83 and 98; *In Met.* IV, lect, 6; *S. Theol.* I, q. 79, a. 7; a. 2; q. 12, a. 4, ad 3; q. 78, a. 1; q. 79, a. 9, ad 3; q. 82, a. 4, ad 1; q. 105, a. 4; I-II, q. 94, a. 2; *In III Sent.* d. 14, a. 1.

[119] Cf. *S. Theol.* I, q. 13, a. 2, ad 3; a. 3, etc.

persuasiveness, however, the nonspecialists find the proof too complicated, and many specialists object to the final conclusion from possibility to actuality. Hence the proof would perhaps be more effective in practice with the following modifications. Instead of starting from the possible premise, "something can be made," we could start with the contingent premise, "something is made." Scotus develops the proof on this existential level in the *Lectura prima,* and in all his subsequent expositions of the proof from the quidditative point of view he always notes that the existential way is a manifest or valid way. Another modification could be the suppression of the section concerning the unity of nature to which the triple primacy of efficiency, finality, and eminence pertains. With these changes the structure of the demonstration would include the following elements: (1) There is a first being in the triple order of efficiency, finality, and perfection. (2) Such being is infinite. (3) It is unique. Therefore God exists.

The Catholic University of America

8

DUNS SCOTUS AND THE PHYSICAL APPROACH TO GOD

by

Roy Effler

In the history of philosophy we witness a persistent effort to come to a natural knowledge of God by a scientific study of nature. In this effort, the positive sciences are called upon to play a major role. Of course, it is recognized that the sciences of and by themselves alone cannot aspire to such an exalted goal, since their method precludes conclusions which are not in some way capable of empirical verification.

The question is: Can the findings of the positive sciences provide premises which, together with premises from metaphysics, support solid argumentation for the existence of God? Or in other words, can a philosophy of nature, which is a combination of science and metaphysics, provide a natural access to God. This question continues to engage the interest of some contemporary philosophers.

For a scholastic living in the thirteenth century, an age of special admiration of Aristotle, an affirmative answer to the question before us might seem altogether normal and proper. As is well known, Aristotle reasons to the existence of a prime mover, or prime movers, in his *Physics*.[1] The Aristotelian argumentation, moreover, finds a staunch defender in Averroes. In fact, with the Commentator the Aristotelian physical approach to God takes on a singular importance. It is the task of physics to prove the existence of God and of pure spirits, for they are the very subject matter of metaphysics.[2] Metaphysics thereby becomes systematically subordinate to physics. This view of Averroes continues on in some form among certain

[1] *Physic.* VII c. 1 241b-243a; VIII c. 4-5 254b-259a.
[2] *Physic.* VII com. 1-3, *editio Iuntina* of Aristotle (Venetiis, 1550-52) IV 139-41; VIII com. 27-33, IV 165-9; I com. 83, IV 22.

modern-day Thomists who present it as the authentic doctrine of St. Thomas.[3]

What is the position of Duns Scotus on this matter? First of all— this will be the main part of our study—does Duns Scotus accept the motion proof for the existence of a prime mover, the famous way of Aristotle's physics, which was so well known to the great scholastics?

The answer to this question is a very definite negative. This negative answer rests on his rejection of the premise, the principle of motion: everything which is in motion is moved by another. Scotus rejects this principle, whether it is restricted to the sphere of bodily motion or construed more broadly to include the sphere of spiritual activity.[4]

What is the meaning of the motion principle that the Subtle Doctor rejects? Quite obviously, it is the principle that denies self-motion, that things can move and change themselves. It means that one and the same thing cannot be both the efficient cause of some perfection and at the same time the recipient principle of that same perfection. If the motion principle is applied to the will, it means that the will cannot be the active efficient cause of an act of willing and at the same time be the recipient principle of that same act of volition.[5] Another way of stating the meaning of the principle is the following: one and the same thing cannot contain some perfection in virtual actuality and at the same time be in potency to the formal actuality of that same perfection.[6]

It is to be noted that the motion principle which Scotus rejects asserts that the recipient principle of some perfection can to no degree whatsoever be the efficient cause of the same perfection. The recipient principle cannot be accorded even a minimal partial efficient causality, although inadequate, in reference to the received perfection. Thus Duns Scotus believes that the motion principle is falsified if he can show that a receptive principle is to any extent,

---

[3] See, for example, Vincent Edward Smith, "The Prime Mover: Physical and Metaphysical Considerations," *Proceedings of the American Catholic Philosophical Association*, XXVIII (1954) 80-90.

[4] *Metaphy.* IX q. 14, VII 582-606; *Ord.* I d. 3 p. 3 q. 2, III 245-330; *Op. Oxon.*, II d. 2 q. 10, XI 523-46; *ibid.* d. 25 q.u., XIII, 196-224; *Additiones magnae secundi libri* d. 25 q. 1, (ed. Carl Balić) in *Les Commentaires de Jean Duns Scot sur les Quatre Livres des Sentences* (Louvain: Bureaux de la Revue, 1927), 264-301; *Quodl.* q. 15, XXVI 118-79.

[5] *Metaphy.* loc. cit., 584-6; *Ord.* loc. cit., 307; *Op. Oxon.* II d. 25 q.u., XII 199-208.

[6] *Metaphy.* loc. cit., 597-601; *Ord.* loc. cit., 304.

no matter how small this may be, the efficient cause of the perfection it receives as a passive principle.

It is a fact that some neoscholastics do not understand the principle in this way, as excluding even a minimal amount of self-motion. Such thinkers propose the motion principle simply in an assertive sense. Thus the principle comes to mean that everything which is in motion is moved either by another alone or by itself and another. Historically, it is significant that such an assertive acceptance of the principle is unknown to Duns Scotus. In fact, as Pedro Descoqs makes clear, this acceptance of the principle has been elaborated precisely to withstand the Scotist critique of the principle.[7] The compatibility of the assertive construction of the principle with Scotist teaching will be scrutinized later.

It must be emphasized here that the motion principle is not just another variant formulation of the metaphysical principle of causality. In his commentary on the *Metaphysics*, Scotus explicitly distinguishes the two principles, and while he affirms the one, he denies the other.[8] The principle of causality asserts that a being which begins to exist requires a cause, that nothing causes itself. The principle does not assert that a being which begins to exist or a contingent being, such as an act of willing, is always and necessarily caused by a being other than the principle, such as the will, which receives the new or contingent being. The motion principle, on the contrary, makes this assertion, and according to some of its proponents, it makes this assertion even in reference to spiritual activities.[9]

It is true that a thinker may distinguish the motion principle from the causal principle but still argue that the latter implies the former. On this basis, the motion principle could be viewed as an application of the metaphysical principle. Later we will counter-argue this implication and application.

Duns Scotus denies the motion principle in the sphere of spiritual activity, such as intellection and volition, as well as in the sphere of bodily motion, such as local motion, qualitative and quantitative

---

[7] *Praelectiones Theologiae Naturalis* (Paris: Gabriel Beauchesne, 1932), I 290-2.
[8] *Metaph. loc. cit.*, 586.
[9] This is the clear teaching of Godfrey of Fontaines. See *Le Huitième Quodlibet de Godefroid de Fontaines*, ed. J. Hoffmans, quodl. IX q. 19 in *Les Philosophes Belges* (Louvain: Institut Supérieur de Philosophie, 1924), IV 275-6; ibid. quodl. VIII q. 2, IV 23; quodl. X q. 14, IV 379; *Les Quodlibets Cinq, Six et Sept de Godefroid de Fontaines*, ed. M. De Wulf and J. Hoffmans (Louvain: Institut Supérieur de Philosophie, 1914), VI q. 7, III 170-2.

change. Thinkers before him, viz. William of Ware[10] and Henry of Ghent,[11] denied the principle in the sphere of spiritual activity. The Subtle Doctor, however, appears to be the first to attack the principle in practically all its significant applications in the sphere of bodily change.

The philosophy of Scotus is sometimes pejoratively referred to as essentialist. This categorization we believe to be in many ways misleading. For one thing, it obscures the pronounced empirical tendency of his thought. In the present topic of investigation, this tendency comes strongly to the fore and is decisive. According to many indications of experience, at least some things move themselves. These facts of experience conclusively disprove the motion principle, which is a universal statement. According to Scotus' view of the matter, the defenders of the principle overwork the method of *a priori* analysis of concepts and do not sufficiently look to the facts.[12] The *a priori* arguments of adversaries, of course, are not given short shrift, and hence Scotus himself engages in extended conceptual analyses, but primarily to show that strict self-motion is not the impossibility it is asserted to be. In this way, Scotus would show that the self-motion testified to in experience does not always and necessarily break down into mover and moved.

We will now survey Duns Scotus' empirical defense of self-motion. This will be followed by a presentation of his defense of the possibility of self-motion from an analysis of the concepts of potency and act.

In his *Physics,* Aristotle singles out four kinds of change or motion undergone by bodies: substantial, qualitative, quantitative, and local.[13] But motion can also be taken broadly enough to include acts of thinking and willing. Sometimes the relation between an essence and its essential property is spoken of as a motion, a motion of causality. The essence causes the essential property, as for example, the essence of man causes the essential property of risibility. For Scotus, this causality seems to be motion in an analogical sense.[14]

[10] Augustinus Daniels, *Beitraege zur Geschichte der Philosophie des Mittelalters,* VIII: *Quellenbeitraege und Untersuchungen zur Geschichte der Gottesbeweise in Dreizehnten Jahrhundert* (Muenster: Aschendorff, 1909), 91.
[11] Roy R. Effler, *John Duns Scotus and the Principle "Omne Quod Movetur ab Alio Movetur"* (St. Bonaventure, N.Y.: Franciscan Institute, 1962), 15.
[12] *Metaphy. loc. cit.,* 600-1; *Ord.* I d. 3 q. 2, III 306.
[13] III c. 1 201a 4-9.
[14] In Scotus, the causality of an essence in reference to its essential properties

In all these spheres of motion or change, Scotus finds instances of self-motion except in that of substantial change or generation and corruption. Consideration of the motion principle in these various spheres shows the wide application of the principle in Aristotelian philosophy and the role it plays in different philosophic and scientific problems. Thus one need not be surprised that Scotus' most extended considerations of the principle are not made in those questions where he attempts to demonstrate the existence of God. This fact, we believe, has led one expositor astray.[15]

A scientific problem in which the motion principle figures for not a few medieval thinkers is the local motion of light and heavy things. Light things, air and fire, go upward; heavy things, earth and water, naturally move downward. What is the cause of this upward and downward motion? St. Albert, St. Thomas, and Godfrey of Fontaines invoke an agent of generation, which has the virtue of being really distinct from the light or heavy object in motion.[16]

For Scotus, this theory is inadmissible, since the generating agent may no longer be in existence when a particular heavy body falls downward. After reviewing various other theories, such as that concerning the center of the earth attracting a heavy body or some

---

passes as a kind of self-motion. For the essence is both the cause and the recipient principle of the property. See *Metaphy. loc. cit.*, 587-8.

[15] It is a fact that Scotus does not assert the invalidity of the motion argument in those sections of his works where he presents his proof for the existence of an infinite being. In the *Lectura in Librum Primum Sententiarum* (I d. 2 p. 1 q. 1-2, XVI 125-6), where Scotus presents his proof, a reference is made to the motion argument. Here he emphatically asserts his preference for the metaphysical approach over a physical approach. But again he does not say that the motion argument simply does not hold. We encounter the same situation in Scotus' treatment of the subject of metaphysics (*Metaph.* VI q. 4, VII 348-9). There is the further fact that Scotus does not generally disagree with Aristotle expressly and verbally, but rather labors to *interpret* the Philosopher according to his own positions. These facts may suggest that Scotus does not reject the motion argument but simply has a strong preference for the metaphysical approach to God. But to the contrary and along with other scholars, we are convinced that Scotus forthrightly rejects the motion principle. The problem involved here, however, we have considered at length in another work: *John Duns Scotus and the Principle "Omne Quod Movetur Ab Alio Movetur"* (St. Bonaventure, N.Y.: Franciscan Institute, 1962). In ascertaining the real position of Duns Scotus, we believe that it is paramount to keep in mind the sophisticated medieval practice of "interpreting" authorities. Practically all the other issues treated in this essay are studied at much greater length in the above cited work.

[16] Anneliese Maier, *An der Grenze von Scholastik und Naturwissenschaft* (2d ed.; Roma: Edizioni di Storia della Letteratura, 1952), 158-9; James A. Weisheipl, "The Concept of Nature," *The New Scholasticism*, XXVIII No. 4 (October, 1954), 400-4.

medium moving it, Scotus maintains that the body moves itself.[17] In the absence of any obvious external mover, he refuses to invoke one that he cannot point to in experience.

Surely, from a modern viewpoint, Scotus' empiricism here is naive. Nevertheless, his theory of gravity does give us a clear insight into the fundamental self-motion that he is willing to admit. When a heavy body moves downward in its free fall, it does not move itself in virtue of some efficient mover entity lodging in and really distinct from the rest of the body which is passive and the moved. On the contrary, the heavy body simply moves itself downward. It pertains to its nature to move in this way.[18]

The local motion of animals also appears to be at odds with the principle of motion. The examples of a bird flying in the air, a fish swimming in water, a dog running to meet its master appear to be genuine instances of self-motion. Here a defender of the motion principle can object that this self-motion necessarily breaks down into a mover and the moved, such as the soul in reference to the body.

In reference to the local motion of animals, Scotus generously allows that one part of an organism might well be a mover in reference to another part which is moved, and the latter in turn might be a mover in reference to some third moved part.[19] The soul itself might well move the body through a system of organic parts. But to originate such organic movement, a qualitative change is postulated in the soul or some animated part of the body. There is no reason why this qualitative change cannot be an instance of self-motion.[20]

As a Christian theologian, Scotus faces the question whether an angel can move itself locally. Or is an angel perhaps forced to remain fixed in one place until it is transferred to another place by some other being? This question constitutes no serious problem for Duns Scotus, for as he argues, if lower beings have the power to move themselves, then surely an angel has this power.[21]

Scotus defends strict self-motion in the sphere of alteration or qualitative change. His example of self-motion in this sphere is water making itself cold.[22] St. Thomas has an opposing view, and

---

[17] *Metaph. loc. cit.*, 589-90; *Op. Oxon.* II d. 2 q. 10, XI 524-8.
[18] *Ibid.*, 527.
[19] *Op. Oxon.* IV d. 49 q. 14, XXI 476-8; *Metaph. loc. cit.*, 590.
[20] *Ibid.*
[21] *Op. Oxon.* II d. 2 q. 10, XI 524.
[22] *Metaph. loc. cit*, 592; *Op. Oxon.* II d. 25 q.u., XIII 209.

to illustrate the necessary distinction between the mover and the moved, he gives the example of fire making potentially hot wood actually hot.[23]

It seems that neither of the two medieval masters has an adequate understanding of the physical process involved when a hot body becomes cold or a cold body becomes hot. Today the process is described in terms of temperature balance. But even according to the modern understanding of this matter, it would hardly be correct to say that bodies are completely passive in many of their qualitative changes, although of course they would be notably worked upon by the surrounding medium.

In the sphere of qualitative change, Scotus accords a seed the power of self-motion. A seed has the power to effect certain minor changes in itself which lead up to the act of generation. The seed, however, is not the efficient cause of the very act of generation and the new being generated.[24]

In the sphere of quantitative change, nutrition and growth are proposed as instances of self-motion. The active principle of these processes is the animated composite. According to the indications of sense experience, the growth of an organism is not effected by an extrinsic agent or agents. Nor is the food the active cause of nutrition and growth. Rather it is the material which the animated composite uses in nourishing itself in providing for its own growth.[25]

Certainly the nutrition and growth of a living organism appears to be self-motion, an activity proceeding from within and terminating in the organism. But perhaps that which appears to be self-motion on the level of ordinary experience breaks down into two parts, a movent part and a moved part, which escape ordinary sense detection. This objection is urged by Godfrey of Fontaines, who holds that the motion principle is a metaphysical verity of absolute necessity and universality.[26]

In answer to this objection, Scotus has recourse to the imperfect biological knowledge of his day. His explanation is quite extended, but in the end he maintains that the small homogeneous parts of

[23] *Summa Theologica* Ia q. 2 a. 3 (Paris: L. Vivés, 1871), I 18.
[24] *Metaph.* VII q. 12, VII 399; *Op. Oxon.* III d. 4 q.u., XIV 191; *Op. Oxon.* II d. 18 q.u., XIII 94.
[25] *Metaph.* IX q. 14, VIII 591.
[26] *Les Quodlibets Cinq, Six et Sept de Godefroid de Fontaines*, ed. M. De Wulf and J. Hoffmans (Louvain: Institut Supérieur de Philosophie, 1914), VI q. 7, III 167.

the body, in which the nourishment of the body takes place, are active causes. These small animated parts convert the food, which has been prepared for conversion, into living flesh and give it the form of the body.[27]

Even today, no physiologist would assert that a cell is completely passive in taking in food from the blood stream. The nourishment and growth of cells, mysterious as they may be, do not take place simply by some new, juxtaposed material being pressed upon it by some extrinsic agent. The growth of a cell is different from the case of a crystal increasing in size. The cell truly appears to be very active in nourishing itself and promoting its own growth.

In the sphere of thought and volition, Scotus is once again a defender of self-motion. His defense of the intellect and will as active causes of their proper acts is extensive. But in maintaining the self-active character of these two powers, he does not go as far as Henry of Ghent. In reference to intellectual knowledge, both the intellect and an objective factor (an object known intuitively, the phantasm or species) function as partial co-causes. As essentially ordered causes, they form one total cause in producing intellection.[28] In a similar way, acts of volition are caused both by the will and the intellect knowing an object.[29]

The application of the motion principle to the sphere of human volition Scotus sees as a denial of human freedom. For if the will is exclusively passive and to no degree whatsoever an active, efficient cause of its acts of volition, then clearly the will is not a free power.[30] It is no wonder then that the application of the motion principle to the human will gives rise to a condemned proposition in the condemnation of 1277:

> Quod anima nihil vult, nisi mota ab alio. Unde illud est falsum: anima seipsam vult. Error, si intelligatur mota ab alio scilicet ab appetibili vel obiecto, ita quod appetibile vel obiectum sit tota ratio motus ipsius voluntatis.[31]

[27] *Op. Oxon.* IV d. 44 q. 1, XX 163-92; *Op. Oxon.* III d. 16 q. 2, XIV 631-2. For a lengthier explanation, see Roy R. Effler, *John Duns Scotus and the Principle "Omne Quod Movetur Ab Alio Movetur"* (St. Bonaventure, N.Y.: The Franciscan Institute, 1962), 133-9.

[28] Ord. I d. 3 q. 2, III 289-99.

[29] In *Op. Oxon.* II d. 25 q.u., XIII 221 and *Rep. Par.* II d. 25 q.u., XXIII 127, Scotus holds the will to be the sole secondary cause of volition. But he modifies this position in *Additiones magnae* d. 25 q. 1 (ed. Carl Balić) in Les Commentaires de Jean Duns Scot sur les quatre livres de sentences (Louvain: Bureaux de la Revue, 1927), 265-66.

[30] *Op. Oxon.* loc cit., 200; *Addit. Mag. loc. cit.*, 268.

Christian theologians are bound to oppose the error formulated in this proposition, as they will always have to oppose denials of human freedom. It is therefore no wonder that St. Thomas is also clear on this point. In the *Summa Theologica*, the Angelic Doctor writes:

> Free choice is the cause of its own movement, because by his free choice man moves himself to act.[32]

Aquinas proceeds to point out that the power of free choice is not the primary cause of a free act. Scotus would agree with this assertion, but systematically the assertion presupposes the existence of God as already proved.

The real adversary of Duns Scotus here is Godfrey of Fontaines. On the basis of the motion principle, Godfrey holds the will to be absolutely passive in reference to its proper acts.[33] This teaching of the Belgian philosopher is also opposed by Henry of Ghent.[34]

The Augustianian tendency of Duns Scotus is to the fore in his defense of the will as a self-moving power. This same tendency is clear in his stress on the activity of the intellect in knowing. In the *Ordinatio*, Scotus marshals various arguments to defend the intellect as a self-moving power, i.e., a power which is a partial efficient cause of its own acts.[35]

Some of these arguments, one of them expressly, indicate a pervasive characteristic, one might almost say a prejudice, revealing something of the personal psychology of the Subtle Doctor. This characteristic is his concern to maintain the dignity of nature, particularly of human nature. Accordingly, he argues that to deny the intellect active causality in reference to its proper acts vilifies the nature of the soul. For intellection as a proper activity of man is more perfect than a phantasm. If intellection were efficiently caused only by the phantasm, then an effect would exceed its cause in perfection. But this cannot be the case, especially in the sphere of equivocal causality.[36]

---

[31] *Propositions Condamnées 1277*, ed. Pierre Mandonnet, prop. 151, in *Siger de Brabant et L'Averroisme Latin au XIIIme Siècle*, p. II, *Textes Inédits* (2d ed. rev.; Louvain: Institut Supérieur de Philosophie, 1908) VII 187.
[32] I q. 82 a. 1 rep. 3, ed. Anton C. Pegis (N.Y.: Random House, 1945), I 787.
[33] *Les Quodlibets Cinq, Six et Sept de Godefroid de Fontaines*, loc. cit., 170; *Le Huitième Quodlibet de Godefroid de Fontaines*, loc. cit. VIII q. 2, IV 21-2 25-6.
[34] Maurice De Wulf, *History of Medieval Philosophy*, tr. Ernest C. Messenger (3d Eng. ed. rev.; N.Y.: Longmans, Green & Co., 1938) II 261.
[35] I d. 3 p. 3 q. 2, III 260-71.
[36] *Ibid.*, 261-2. See also *Metaph.* IX q. 14, VII 592-3.

The view that accords active causality to the phantasm alone in the production of intellectual knowledge seems to involve other difficulties. First, the intellect would seem to be deprived of all intellectual habits, which would be formed by its activities as an active power. Secondly, there is the theological difficulty of explaining how an angel could acquire new knowledge. Could an angel, bereft of all organic powers and acting as a secondary cause, produce any actual knowledge in itself, even if its habitual knowledge covered regions of untold immensity? These difficulties the Subtle Doctor ponders.[37]

Six other arguments in favor of the intellect as at least a partial efficient cause of intellection are presented. Five of these arguments, however, Scotus finds to be inconclusive. The fifth one purports to show the intellect as the active cause of logical intentions, logical relations, and the act of comparison required for the latter. But this argument too he proposes as something to be pondered.[38]

Unquestionably, Duns Scotus labors painfully in defending his position concerning the active role of the intellect in knowledge. Outside of an Aristotelian framework, many a contemporary thinker would experience considerably less difficulty in ascribing an active and even a highly constructive character to the mind in various spheres of its knowledge, such as logic and mathematics.

But one thing is clear: Scotus is convinced that Godfrey's denial of the self-moving character of the intellect is not supported by conclusive argumentation. For the chief support of Godfrey's position is the motion principle, which he defends on the basis of the incompatibility of potency and act.[39] This *a priori* argument against the very possibility of self-motion now merits our consideration.

The argument against self-motion from the incompatibility of potency and act is rehearsed in several places of the works of Scotus.[40] But for our study here we may just as well reflect on it as it is presented by Aquinas in the *Summa Theologica*.[41]

A being in motion is in potency. It is in potency to act or "to

---

[37] *Ord. loc. cit.*, 262-4.
[38] *Ibid.*, 264-71.
[39] *Ibid.*, 303-8.
[40] *Op. Oxon.* II d. 2 q. 10, XI 523; *Op. Oxon.* II d. 25 q.u., XIII 199; *Ord. loc. cit.*, 257; *Metaph.* IX q 14, VII 583; *Rep. Par.* Pro. q. 1, XXII 13.
[41] I q. 2 a. 3, ed. Anton C. Pegis (N.Y.: Random House, 1945), I 22.

that towards which it is moved." But the being which actively causes the motion, the mover, is in act. For nothing can be reduced from potency to act except by a being in act. Therefore, the moved is in potency, but the mover is in act. But the same thing cannot simultaneously be in potency and act according to the same respect. Therefore the moved and the mover must always be two distinct things, and consequently self-motion is impossible, and everything which is in motion is moved by another.

In presenting Scotus' critique of this argument, it will serve clarity to indicate various elements in this argument which he accepts. First, Duns Scotus accepts the statement that nothing can be reduced from potency to act (from non-existence to existence) except it be reduced from potency to act by a being in act. Thus an act of willing cannot go from potency to act except it be reduced from potency to act by a being in act. The being in act which effects this reduction, at least as a partial efficient cause, is the will. Definitely, the act of willing does not produce itself.

The transition from the non-existence of an act of willing to its existence is a transition from objective potency to act. Let us now consider a transition from subjective potency to act. Here again the human will and an act of willing may provide us with a clarifying example. The human will as a power of the soul is in act or actually exists. But presently it does not have a particular act of willing, although it is about to have it. In its present state, it is in a state of potency in reference to this particular act of willing. In other words, it is in a state in which it does not actually have this act of willing but can have it. Now according to Scotus, it is not *a priori* impossible that the will itself as a partial efficient cause reduces itself from this subjective potency to actuality. In other words, the will itself actively brings it about that it goes from a state in which it does not have the act of willing to a state in which it actually has this act of willing.

Upon reflection it will be seen that this situation does not entail the coming into existence of a new being without any cause whatsoever. The new being is the act of willing, and it is produced by the will as a partial efficient cause. The will itself is not producing itself, because it already existed.

If the aforementioned statement (nothing can be reduced from potency to act) is interpreted to mean that nothing can reduce itself from *subjective* potency to act, then the aforementioned statement is rejected by Scotus. For he definitely teaches that one and the same thing can be both the efficient, active cause and also the recipient principle of one and the same perfection.[42] In the case of the will, this power of the soul can both be the partial, efficient cause of an act of willing and at the same time be the recipient principle of this same act of willing.[43]

But another statement in the motion argument accepted by Scotus is: the same thing cannot simultaneously be in potency and act according to the same respect.[44] This statement is the principle of the incompatibility of potency and act. But the terms 'potency' and 'act' in this principle are to be taken as modes of being (potential being or being in potentiality and actual being or being in actuality) and not as principles.[45] Crucial for Duns Scotus is this distinction between potency as a mode and potency as a principle.[46] As a mode, potency refers to a being which does not actually exist but which can exist. Potential being is thus incompatible with its corresponding actual being. Thus when an act of willing is in potentiality, it is not in actuality; when it is in actuality, it is not in potentiality. As a principle, potency is either an efficient cause or receptive principle (material cause).[47] The intellect and will are potencies or powers of the soul. They are also potencies insofar as they are receptive principles of acts of thinking and volition.

Self-motion, according to Scotus, does not entail a violation of the principle of the incompatibility of potency and act. For in instances of self-motion, the same thing is not in potency and act *according to the same respect*. The reason for this is that self-motion is not produced by a univocal cause, but only and exclusively by an equivocal cause. If a self-movent cause were univocal, then the principle of the incompatibility of potency and act would be violated. For a univocal cause produces an effect the same in nature as itself. Thus a self-movent, univocal cause would possess some perfection in its formal actuality and at the same time be in potency to this same perfection. The cause would be in potency

---

[42] *Metaph. loc. cit.*, 584-6; *Ord. loc. cit.*, 307.
[43] *Op. Oxon. loc. cit.*, 209; *Addit. mag. loc. cit.*, 289-91.
[44] *Metaph.* IX q. 1, VII 532; *ibid.* q. 14, 596; *Op. Oxon. loc. cit.*, 208; *Op. Oxon.* II d. 2 q. 10, XI 540; *Op. Oxon.* II d. 3 q. 8, XII 200; *Rep. Par.* II d. 25 q.u., XXIII 122; *Addit. mag. loc. cit.*, 289.
[45] *Metaph.* IX q. 1, VII 531; *Addit. mag. loc. cit.*, 291-2.
[46] *Metaph. loc. cit.*, 530.
[47] *Metaph.* IX q. 4, VII 545; *Op. Oxon.* II d. 25 q.u., XIII 208.

and act according to the same respect, according to the same perfection. But since a self-movent cause is always equivocal, no violation of the potency and act principle is involved. For the equivocal agent is not simultaneously in potency and act according to the same formal perfection. Prior to its causal activity, the equivocal agent does not possess the perfection to be caused in its formal actuality, but virtually. Hence at this time, it can be in potency to the formal actuality of this perfection.[48] The doctrine here can be further tested by reflecting once again on the concrete case of the will and a particular act of volition.

Prior to the act of willing, the volitional act is in modal potency. When the act is actually being caused by the will, it is in modal act or actuality. Prior to the volitional act, the will is in modal actuality as a power, and of course, it continues to be modally actual when it elicits the volitional act. Prior to the volitional act, the will is in subjective modal potentiality to the volitional act. Once it is eliciting the volitional act, the modal subjective potentiality is replaced by a modal actuality.[49] In other words, the will is no longer in a state in which it does not have this particular volitional act, but in a state in which it actually has it.

While the will is actually eliciting a particular volitional act, it continues to be a potency in the sense of an active, efficient principle or cause. It is also a potency in the sense of being a receptive principle of the volitional act it causes.

Before the will actually produces a particular volitional act, it would seem that it does not have the act. But then an objector can say: *Nemo dat quod non habet.* Every effect must be contained in its cause. How then can the will produce the act? The answer is that prior to the production of the volitional act, the will does not have the volitional act in its formal actuality, but it does have the volitional act in its virtual actuality. This is no more than to say that the will, prior to the actual production of the volitional act, has the actual *virtus* or power to produce the act.

Here it cannot be emphasized too much that in producing a volitional act, the will functions as an *equivocal,* efficient cause. The latter kind of efficient cause produces an effect different in nature from itself. One difference in nature between the will and a volitional act is seen in this, that the former is a human power

[48] *Ord. loc. cit.,* 303-4; *Op. Oxon. loc. cit.*
[49] *Metaph.* IX q. 2, VII 537-8.

really identical with the substance of the soul, while the latter is an accidental entity of the soul.

It is a characteristic of every equivocal cause not to precontain its effect in its formal actuality but in virtual actuality. To demand more than this virtual precontainment is to deny equivocal causality. Scholastic philosophy finds no difficulty in ascribing equivocal causality to God. For example, God is the equivocal cause of a stone. For the perfection of a stone is not contained in God formally but virtually. It is also generally admitted in scholasticism that creatures can function as equivocal causes, and for Duns Scotus, this is the only kind of cause capable of self-motion and self-change. Since an equivocal cause does not and cannot precontain the perfection of its effect in its formal actuality, Scotus holds that one and the same thing can contain some perfection in virtual actuality and at the same time be in potency to the formal actuality of this same perfection. Try as hard as he may, Duns Scotus can see no contradiction in this latter statement. But a denial of this statement (one and the same thing can contain some perfection in its virtual actuality and at the same time be in potency to the formal actuality of this same perfection) is what the motion principle really gets to mean.[50]

We have reached a crucial point in the Scotist analysis, which has been a stumbling block for others. It is said that Scotus misses the real problem, the problem of new being or increase in being. Such is the view of Owens:

> Neither the one nor the other (Aristotle nor Scotus) seems to feel any need to explain the new act of existing that actuates a formal act which before was found only virtually in its cause. Both proceeded as though there were in this regard no problem that called for a metaphysical explanation. From the viewpoint of formal causality alone the equivocal agent may be capable of accounting fully for the different effect. But what accounts for the effect as existentially different. No answer is forthcoming; no treatment even is given; no problem seems to be felt.[51]

To us it seems that Owens misses Duns Scotus' explanation, which is really embodied in his teaching concerning the virtual precontainment of an equivocal effect in its equivocal cause. To return

---

[50] *Metaph.* IX q. 14, VII 600-1; *Ord. loc. cit.*, 304-307; *Addit. mag. loc. cit.*, 290.
[51] Joseph Owens, "The Conclusion of the Prima Via," *The Modern Schoolman*, XXX No. 3 (March, 1953) 210-1.

to our example of the will and a volitional act, the will as a secondary, partial, efficient, equivocal cause gives being or actual existence to a particular volition. The will does not only produce some kind of an essence of a volitional act, its finiteness, contingency, accidentality, and other such features, but the all-important and the very positive element of being itself in the mode of actual existence. On the day of judgment, we will hardly be able to tell God that our wills did not cause the actual existence of our sinful volitions but only certain formal elements or specifications of these acts.

Perhaps Scotus' explanation of new being tends to be missed, because it is a kind of creativity explanation, and creativity has an aura of mystery about it. Be that as it may, the Subtle Doctor's thought definitely allows that creatures can produce new beings and precisely the existence or *esse* of a new being.[52] This creative power is particularly clear in reference to the intellect and will. Because of its highly active character, the intellect itself is a cause of the new being of knowledge.[53] As a free faculty, the will can and must originate something. Other creatures, likewise, participate in this creative power. Thus it seems that Scotus' thought is open and capable of enrichment along the lines of modern creativity philosophy.

But it must be acknowledged that to ascribe creativity to creatures is not to use Scotus' own terminology. On the contrary, he expressly distinguishes two meanings of creation and denies creative power to creatures in these two senses.

First a creature cannot create in the sense that it can produce something independently of the primary cause which is God. Secondly a creature cannot create in the sense of producing something without the co-causality of a material cause. Creatures, therefore, cannot create spiritual or material substances, material accidents, and also, it would seem, spiritual accidents. The reason why the production of spiritual accidents would not be an instance of creation in this second sense is that they also require a material cause in the sense of a receptive principle.[54]

[52] *Op. Oxon.* IV d. 1 q. 1, XVI 17: quia a quocumque efficiente generatur compositum, ab eodem effective est esse compositi; sed aliquod compositum generatur a causa aliqua creata, nisi tollatur omnis actio creaturae.
[53] *Ord. loc. cit.*, 289.
[54] *Rep. Par.* IV d. 1 q. 1, XXIII 539-42; *Op. Oxon. loc. cit.*, 85-90. Our last two statements in this paragraph we intend as a correction of what we have written in *John Duns Scotus and the Principle "Omne Quod Movetur Ab Alio*

Already in the last century E. Pluzanski had discovered a dynamistic tendency in Duns Scotus, precisely on the basis of his rejection of the motion principle. But as Pluzanski adds, this tendency remains undeveloped.[55] This latter observation no doubt is true. As a matter of fact, there are explicit limitations to the dynamistic tendency in Scotus. For while he rejects the motion principle in its universality, he firmly asserts that some things are moved by another. Indeed, there is much causal interaction of beings in the Scotist universe.

Hence Scotus would not go along with the later conception of Leibniz. For while Leibnizian dynamism might not imply an intrinsic contradiction, still this doctrine would be in conflict with experience or the more reasonable interpretation of facts of experience. The empiricist tendency in Scotist thought is too strong to be at home with the great proponent of pre-established harmony. Nevertheless, it still remains true that Scotist philosophy is open to dynamistic views supported by science and experience.

Since Scotus' teaching generously allows for both self-motion and movement by another, it might be asked if he would admit the motion principle in the assertive sense. This acceptation of the motion principle, previously referred to, is defended by not a few neoscholastics.

According to the assertive sense, everything in motion is moved by another alone or by itself and another. In other words, nothing moves itself by itself alone. For nothing can change itself and be the total adequate cause of some new perfection acquired by the change.

Understood in this way, the motion principle comes to express divine concursus, the concursus of God the primary cause in the

---

Movetur" (St. Bonaventure, N.Y.: The Franciscan Institute, 1962), 88. In the *Rep. Par. loc. cit.*, 539, Scotus says that it is difficult to deny a creature the power to create accidental forms such as faith, hope, intellection, and willing. Subsequently, in the text he does not expressly argue for such a denial, although he does make the general statement that to create is repugnant to any creature (p. 543). However, the issue is treated more clearly in *Op. Oxon. loc. cit.*, 89. Here it is said that an angel cannot create an accident, because no creature can create an accident. The reason for this is that an accident, at least naturally speaking, always requires a subject. Thus the very definition of creation in the second sense excludes the creation of accidents by creatures. This situation, we believe, should not prevent one from seeing in creatures a creative power in a lesser sense, especially if one holds with Scotus that a creature can produce the very *esse* of a new being.

[55] *Essai sur la Philosophie de Duns Scot* (Paris: E. Thorin, 1888), 141-2.

activities of all creatures and secondary causes.⁵⁶ So interpreted, the motion statement would be altogether acceptable to Scotus and fit into his metaphysics. But here it must be pointed out that divine concursus is a conclusion of metaphysics. Hence a statement formulating it could not be used as a premise to prove the existence of God. Quite evidently, the assertive acceptation is no longer the historical motion principle.

But perhaps one could understand the assertive acceptation of the motion principle in another way. While a particular thing can cause some new perfection in itself, still the production of this perfection would always and necessarily require some other secondary cause. Understood in this way, the motion principle would allow for self-motion but would also in some way express the interaction among things of our restless universe.

This view might be given abundant empirical justification, but still the absolute necessity of the principle so understood could still be doubted, and one might appeal to radioactivity as an exception to it. Currently at least, science teaches that radioactive substances disintegrate entirely from within. Then for Duns Scotus, the only secondary efficient cause of the free fall of a heavy body is the body itself, and the only secondary efficient cause for bodily growth and nutrition are the small homogeneous parts of the body. In the case of intellectual knowledge and volition, however, Duns Scotus expressly invokes more than one secondary cause, the faculty and some object-factor. The faculty and the object are partial causes, essentially ordered in the production of the effect. As Scotus sees it, the secondary causes form a unit and one cause, and no other secondary cause is required here and now for the production of the effect.⁵⁷

Now one might wish to push the inquiry further and ask about the two causes making up this causal unit. Thus one might ask whether the object-cause in knowledge was caused. In answer to this question, an appeal might be made to some known agent which brought the object into existence. But as far as the construction of a proof for the existence of God is concerned, care would have to be taken lest the impossibility of an infinite regress in a series of accidentally ordered causes be assumed. From some such an as-

---

⁵⁶ Ioseph Hellin, *Theologia Naturalis* (Madrid: La Editorial Catolica, 1950), 209.

⁵⁷ *Ord. loc. cit.*, 292.

sumption there would result an efficient causality argument, the validity of which would be denied by many Christian thinkers, St. Thomas included.

One might also examine the object cause and find it characterized by potentiality, dependence, transiency, or some other significant metaphysical aspects. For Duns Scotus, as for other Christian thinkers, an adequate explanation of these aspects would demand the existence of some first being which is pure act, altogether independent, and absolutely permanent. But this is a significantly different argument. It does not precisely assert that one secondary efficient cause cannot produce an effect except in causal conjunction with another secondary efficient cause. As a matter of fact, experience might present us with cases in which one secondary cause A is dependent in causing on another secondary cause B or requires another secondary cause B to exercise its own (A's) causality. One might go further and point out that this situation shows A to be dependent and imperfect and then argue to some absolutely perfect being. This is one thing. But it is quite another and different thing to say that a secondary efficient cause necessarily and essentially requires another secondary efficient cause to produce an effect.

It now behooves us to return to the issue raised at the beginning of this chapter: does Duns Scotus accord philosophy of nature the competency to reach God? Clearly, he finds the Aristotelian physical approach seriously defective. The motion principle on which it stands is false. But Aristotle's argument suffers from another defect. For even if the argument were valid, in the end it really does not reach God. It only reaches a prime mover, which is not moved as a body or a power in a body is moved, or which is not moved as the soul is moved *per accidens,* when the latter's body is moved. As Scotus sees it, therefore, the prime mover might well be some inferior being or creature.[58]

At this juncture, the following objection might be urged. In arguing to the existence of God (infinite being), Duns Scotus himself proceeds by way of a long series of well ordered steps. In this protracted process, he too argues to three different primacies; a first efficient cause, a first final cause, and a first eminent being.[59] Clearly Scotus realizes that a unique infinite being is not reached by simply arguing to a primacy, as for example, a first efficient cause. If this

[58] *Ord.* I d. 8 p. 2 q.u., IV 281.
[59] *Ord.* I d. 2 p. 1 q. 1, II 149-69.

is the case, why is the Subtle Doctor so unfavorable to the prime mover? Could not the prime mover be viewed as a primacy which could serve as a base for additional arugmentation towards an infinite being?

Scotus' answer here is that the prime mover cannot serve as such a base, because this primacy does not have the necessary implications:

> ... primum movens tantum respectum dicit, et non necessario ex formali ratione sui requirit infinitatem nec sequitur: primum movens, ergo primum ens...[60] Nunc autem ex primitate inferioris non sequitur primitas superioris nisi illud inferius sit nobilissimum (unde non sequitur, est asinus nobilissimus, igitur est animal nobilissimum).[61]

But perhaps one might wish to save the prime mover by some argument such as the following. The prime mover is either potential or pure act, changeable or absolutely unchangeable, caused or absolutely uncaused. If it is potential, changeable, and caused, then some other being must be admitted which is pure act, unchangeable, and uncaused. If it is pure act, unchangeable and uncaused, then the prime mover can be shown to imply infinity. In either case, the prime mover leads us to an infinite being.

But the fact is that one can argue in this fashion about any being whatsoever. There is no need to make use of a prime mover. It would be far simpler to appeal to some being of experience, and this, we believe, is at least part of Scotus' point. In constructing an argument for the existence of God, the better and more efficacious point of departure in experience is always some metaphysical aspect or property (such as caused being, potential being, transient being) and not a physical property.[62]

Anyone acquainted with Scotus' extended proof for the existence of one infinite being will agree that the metaphysician's road to God is long and arduous. Surely, every solid effort at simplification in this matter is to be applauded. In the Scotist effort, the prime mover of Aristotle appears to be unnecessary baggage, to say the least. This evaluation is part of Duns Scotus' view that meta-

[60] *Metaph.* q. 4, VIII 348.
[61] *Lec. Pri.* d. 2 p. 1 q. 1, XVI 125-6.
[62] *Metaph. loc. cit.*: Contra Averroem ex quolibet effectu ostenditur, causam esse, quia impossibile est effectum esse nisi a causa tali, sive nisi talis causa sit; hujusmodi sunt multae passiones Metaphysicae, *prius* et *posterius, unum* et *multa, actus* et *potentia;* quomodo enim haec causatis insunt, nisi sit aliquod unum primum?

physics and metaphysics alone can reach the unique infinite being. This task metaphysics is to accomplish as an autonomous science, built on experience but independent of a philosophy of nature. As Scotus puts it in the *Lectura Prima,*

> Et ideo male dixit Averroes in fine I Physicorum—contra Avicennam—quod solum ad physicum pertinet ostendere Deum esse quia hoc solum potest ostendi per motum et non alio medio, ac si metaphysica inciperet a conclusione probata a physica et indigeret ea, quasi non exsistens certa in se (falsum enim dixit ibi in fine I Physicorum); immo verius et multiplicius potest ostendi per passiones metaphysicas, quae consequuntur ens.[63]

Whatever value is to be accorded this clear and definite view of Scotus, a final remark seems to be in place. The Scotist preference for the metaphysical approach should be understood in relation to the goal which is envisioned, namely, the philosophical attainment of the unique infinite being. Now if an individual thinker chooses to adopt a less demanding goal, and if he chooses to work out secondary and less rigorous arguments, arguments perhaps which lead only to some higher, albeit powerful and awe-inspiring being, then perhaps a philosophy of nature could be of real value in such an effort. We believe that Scotus' thought is at least open to such a view. He himself frequently uses secondary and so called persuasive arguments in establishing his positions. He also suggests expositions for remedying the defects of the Aristotelian motion argument.[64] The important thing is that the efforts carried on in a philosophy of nature to reach God be properly assessed. However subjectively appealing and spectacular in scope they may be, they will ever remain inferior to the metaphysical approach from the standpoint of goal and rigor.

Yet within the framework of Scotist philosophy there remains the open possibility that a new philosophy of nature, availing itself of the new science of the future, may realize a measure of success in this matter. Along with this possibility, there remains the fact that the argumentation for a prime mover in Aristotle's *Physics,* so well known in the medieval world, is seriously defective for Duns Scotus.

Duns Scotus College, Southfield, Michigan

[63] *Lec. Pri. loc. cit.*
[64] See our dissertation, *John Duns Scotus and the Principle "Omne Quod Movetur Ab Alio Movetur"* (St. Bonaventure, N.Y.: The Franciscan Institute, 1962), 120-4.

9
THE PROBLEM OF THE DEMONSTRABILITY OF IMMORTALITY

by

GEOFFREY G. BRIDGES

The question of life after death is one of those problems which will never die. Some may say it is because man instinctively knows that he is meant for more than the severe limits of the present life. And some may say that man is incorrigibly optimistic, always hoping for a better world here below and a best world hereafter. Whatever may be the reason, and certainly ultimately the reason will be found in man's nature viewed in all its dimensions, the re-investigation of the question always arises from the ashes of "irrefutable" proofs that the hope is vain.

The fact of immortality was not a problem for the medieval scholastics. Faith in immortality was the starting point of discussion for all the great and most of the lesser philosopher-theologians. The spirit is that of St. Anselm: *fides quaerens intellectum*; that of Scotus who opens his treatise on God: "May the First Principle of things grant me to believe, understand, and make known those things which may please his Majesty and elevate our minds to contemplation of him."[1] Believing, the scholastics sought to establish the extent of rational understanding.

The crux of the problem in this and many other questions for Scotus is: granted that we know by faith, can we understand by reason? Are we capable of arriving at more than persuasive indication? Specifically, are we able to establish our conclusion with the highest level of human understanding, according to medieval standards, the demonstration?

To comprehend with some accuracy the position of Scotus on immortality, but more important, the reason for his position, it is necessary to know the historical setting of intellectual endeavor in his day. In this framework his position can be analyzed. And as a

[1] *De Primo Principio*, tr. by Evan Roche (St. Bonaventure, N.Y., 1949), p. 3.

conclusion we might attempt some estimate of the modern relevance of Scotus' position and outlook.

I

The atmosphere in the University of Paris after the condemnations of Bishop Tempier in 1277 was notably different from the quieter days when St. Bonaventure and St. Thomas were companions on the faculty. The tension between the faculty of the arts and the faculty of theology, it is true, had existed from the first introduction of Aristotle. Suspicion of philosophy, a remnant of the anti-dialecticism of the eleventh and twelfth centuries, lingered in the minds of certain masters of theology. Hence the complaints to the Holy See and subsequent prohibitions on the use of Aristotle's texts in the lecture room. By the time of Bonaventure and Thomas, however, Alexander of Hales, Roger Bacon, and St. Albert had gained a fairer hearing for the Philosopher.

The middle of the century witnessed a glorious period of scholastic endeavor to extend the understanding of the deposit of the faith by means of Aristotelian and Augustinian philosophy. It was a period of disciplined probing of the limits of human reason with regard to a wide variety of subjects. The discipline was that of Aristotelian logic. But even with such a discipline, at times enthusiasm outstripped rigor, giving rise to exaggerated claims of validity and certitude.[2]

More immediately the cause of the change in atmosphere is to be found in the faculty of the arts. Opposition often drives to extremes. Masters in this faculty, reacting to the opposition of lesser minds in the faculty of theology, concentrated on an effort to arrive at a pure Aristotelianism. This attempt by the radical Aristotelians or Latin Averroists to follow philosophy alone without theology even as a negative norm soon led them to conclusions opposed to revealed truths. Both St. Bonaventure and St. Thomas vigorously opposed these philosophers.[3] When they died the movement was persisting in its boldness.

[2] Henry of Ghent, for example, held the philosophical demonstrability of the Trinity. Cf. Scotus' refutation: *Oxon.*, prol., q. 1, n. 15; Vivès VIII, 35a.

[3] St. Bonaventure delivered his *Collationes in Hexaemeron* in part as a refutation of "some 'artists' (who) have opposed His teaching by their erroneous propositions." *Hexaem.*, coll. 1, n. 9, V, 330. St. Thomas, *De unitate intellectus contra Averroistas*, 1270.

Bishop Tempier's precipitous condemnation of 1277, which landed a few blows on St. Thomas through the strong influence of Thomas' opponents, increased the breach between the faculty of arts and the faculty of theology.

The question raised by certain masters in theology who retained a strong respect for philosophy now was, what are the limits of reason? Granted that reason can aid to a fuller understanding of theology, what are its limitations? With Scotus there was a further defensive motive. If too great claim to certitude is made where such does not exist, the moderates are open to refutation and ridicule. Better to be modest in one's claims than foolishly bold. A case can be made for the fact that Scotus, far from wishing to undermine the balance between philosophy and theology, actually was seeking to protect it.[4]

Both by temperament and background Scotus was disposed to such an attitude. Whereas the preparatory intellectual training of the young cleric at Paris was mostly logical, at Oxford it was also strongly mathematical. Scotus therefore brought to Aristotelian logic a desire for greater rigor, a desire derived from his studies in mathematics. Hence his tendency was to seek the rigorous demonstration when possible and to root premises in immediately evident principles.[5]

When Scotus arrived in Paris there was no predominant school. Thomism was on the defensive against the "Augustinians"; Giles of Rome was a prominent teacher, as also Henry of Ghent. As for the Franciscan school, Scotus had been trained at Oxford in a tradition of mixed Augustinian and Aristotelian doctrine which made him akin to his Parisian brethren and yet independent of loyalties to Alexander and Bonaventure. He could choose to follow sentiment and espouse the cause of his Paris confreres, or follow one of the other systems, or launch out on his own ignoring all other systems, or develop his own system building on others. He chose this last way. To his mind the work of assimilating Aristotle was not yet successfully completed. His attempt created another medieval synthesis.[6]

[4] Cf. P. Boehner, *The History of the Franciscan School* (St. Bonaventure, N.Y., 1954), III, 24-25.

[5] Cf. P. Vignaux, *Philosophy in the Middle Ages: An Introduction* (New York, 1959), 151. D. Knowles, *The Evolution of Medieval Thought* (Baltimore, Md., 1962), p. 304.

[6] Boehner, *op. cit.*, p. 15; E. Bettoni, *Duns Scotus: The Basic Principles of His Philosophy*, tr. by B. Bonansea, (Washington, D.C., 1961), p. 18-21.

The false image of Scotus as a harping critic, stumbling over his own subtleties, proposing no system of thought worthy of serious attention, has often enough in recent times been rectified.[7] Each man has his genius. Clarity and order were preeminent in St. Thomas. Scotus, admittedly no stylist, had the gift of dialectical rigor. He is the refutation of the modern contention that the systematists of the middle ages were monolithic and uncritical. It is in such a spirit that he attacks the problem of the immortality of the soul.

There is, however, more that must be understood about the condition which contributed to Scotus' viewpoint. It would seem that the necessitarianism in Avicenna's view of creation was one of the main reasons for Scotus' preoccupation with the notion of contingency.[8] God the omnipotent creator did not necessarily create; this would entail a world contradictorily opposed to the one we actually live in. He freely decided what he would create and freely brought it into existence. This is a governing viewpoint in the system of Scotus as in that of Ockham. Scotus draws the inexorable conclusions. There are in the universe no absolutely necessary essences, no absolutely necessary causes. Essences are necessary; they are rooted in the divine ideas; but they could not have been, and could have been otherwise; at any moment all created instances could not be. The necessity of possibles and essences is not a perfection of things in themselves but is rooted in the divine intellect.[9] The absolute dominion of a free and omnipotent God was always present in Scotus' view of the world. Natural causes act necessarily; but this is contingent on the non-intervention of the freely creating, freely conserving cause. At root all essences and all laws of nature are contingent.[10] This viewpoint plays an important role in Scotus' analysis of the soul.

[7] F. Copleston, *History of Philosophy* (Westminster, Maryland, 1950), II, 481-486; Vignaux, *op. cit.*, pp. 146-147.

[8] *Ordinatio*, I, d. 8, pars 2, q. un.; Vat. IV, 294f.

[9] Cf. A. Wolter, "Ockham and the Textbooks: On the Origin of Possibility," *Franziskanichen Studien,* xxxii (1950), 76.

[10] *Rep. Par.*, IV, d. 46, q. 4, n. 10; Vivès XXIV, 585b: "Potest enim Deus secundum justitiam suam juste agere, quod terra sit sursum et ignis deorsum, et potest facere secundum oppositum actum, faciendo ignem frigidum, etc." Cf. Bettoni, *op. cit., 159;* E. Gilson, *Jean Duns Scot* (Paris, 1952), 323-329. N. B. The fact that one of the key questions on contingency, *Ordinatio*, I, q. 39, has been relegated to an appendix by the Scotus Commission will not cause any revision of thought on Scotus' doctrine. The question is considered by the editors to be a compilation by one of the first redactors; it reflects the same doctrine ex-

The Averroistic doctrine of one agent intellect for all men proposed by the men in the school of arts at Paris accounts for two of the most controverted questions in the last third of the 13th century. Scotus entered the field late in the battle. The process of intellection was the primary area of controversy. It was necessary for St. Thomas to write a special tract on the subject. He defended the traditional doctrine of the division of the human intellect into an agent and passive faculty. Though he took the radical step of proposing for the human intellect the power of reaching truth and certitude without any special divine illumination, he was in basic agreement with the trend in philosophy in his century of locating the active and passive powers in the individual human intellect.

St. Thomas and St. Bonaventure resisted the Averroistic doctrine, not only because it was a less defensible explanation of the human process of intellection, but also because of the implications with regard to the ultimate end of the soul. This was the second area of controversy. The doctrine of one agent intellect for all men entails the Averroistic (and Aristotelian?) conclusion that no individual immortality is possible. This the radical Aristotelians were asserting; though they professed at the same time to hold on faith that there is personal immortality. When pressed for an explanation of the seeming contradiction they took refuge in their science, maintaining that pure philosophy leads to no other conclusion than Averroes', and they could not deny their reason; yet they did not deny their faith either. While this profession saved them from heterodox theological doctrine, St. Thomas and St. Bonaventure had no doubt about the dangers inherent in such an attempted distinction. Some indication about the urgency still felt in Scotus' time to offset these dangers is evidenced by his vehemence in referring to Averroes as "accursed."[11]

The result was that those holding the orthodox position launched into treatises on the nature of the soul and arguments for personal immortality. Scotus came late into the dispute and with an outsider's viewpoint, so that he could look at the problem objectively and critically. His treatment of the nature of the soul and its destiny is part of his critical appraisal of the situation.

---

pounded in authentic texts. Cf. *J. D. Scoti Opera Omnia* (Vatican, 1963), VI, 26*-30*.

[11] *Oxon.*, IV, d. xliii, q. 2; cf. A. Wolter, *Duns Scotus: Philosophical Writings*, p. 138. (References and quotes in English of this Question subsequently will be from Wolter's translation.)

Historically the tradition in the Franciscan School into which the Oxford scholar came firmly held the necessity of immortality. Jean de la Rochelle, author of the first *Summa de anima* in the thirteenth century, followed Dominicus Gundisalinus in proposing extrinsic arguments *(rationes communes)* and intrinsic arguments *(rationes propriae)* for the immortality of the soul. In the first type, from God's justice, wisdom, goodness, he argues to the necessity of immortality. The intrinsic arguments are based on the soul itself; its incorruptibility, its inexhaustible power, its desire for happiness which is not satisfied in this life and cannot be frustrated lead to the conclusion that the soul is necessarily immortal. Eudes de Rigaud, St. Bonaventure, Peter Olivi draw upon Jean and conclude likewise that external and internal reasons necessarily demand the immortality of the soul.[12]

Scotus, however, coming to the question of the immortality of the soul in the frame of mind we have attempted to describe, managed to keep aloof from " school" loyalties and to take a new look at the old arguments.

II

Scotus approaches the problem of immortality in a typically scholastic question: Can it be understood by reason [what we hold by faith, namely,] that there will be a general resurrection of mankind?[13] To answer this, he says it is necessary to demonstrate (a) that the intellective soul is the form of man; (b) this intellective soul is incorruptible;[14] (c) the specific form of man will not remain forever outside the composite. Scotus concedes that from the fact that man formally and properly as man understands, has immaterial knowledge and is capable of free self-determination, it can be demonstrated that the intellective soul is the specific form of man. He denies that the third proposition can be proven from reason. In addressing himself to the second proposition he enunciates his position on the power of human reason to arrive at the ultimate destiny of the human soul.

---

[12] Cf. Boehner, *op. cit.* II, 19-20. For a complete history of the doctrine on immortality in the Franciscan School see S. Vanni Rovighi, *L'Immortalita' dell'Anima nei Maestri Francescani del Secolo XIII* (Milano, 1939).

[13] *Oxon.*, IV, d. xliii, q. 2; *Writings*, p. 134f.

[14] The correct term here would be "immortal," the term which Scotus uses throughout his discussion of the second proposition.

If the Latin Averroists took their stand on texts from Aristotle, the opponents would naturally seek to place the Philosopher solidly on their own side. Scotus, therefore, enters immediately upon a critique of the Aristotelian texts. His general remark at the outset expresses the situation faced even today by commentators on Aristotle on many a question:

> "First of all, it is doubtful what the Philosopher really held on this point, for he speaks differently in different places and has different principles, from some of which one thing seems to follow whereas from others the very opposite can be inferred."[15]

A prime reason for difficulty in the Aristotelian texts is the distinction he makes between the soul as form and the soul as intellective. Aristotle can deny that the soul (i.e. the form of the body) is imperishable and maintain at the same time that the soul (the intellective soul) is imperishable. Scotus is inconsistent in responding to Aristotle because he does not bear this in mind. In commenting on the third of the seven classical texts he introduces in this question, he correctly distinguishes with Aristotle. But in commenting on the first text he does not. Aristotle is arguing from the ability of the intellective soul to operate without the body to its independence of the body and consequent ability to survive the body. Scotus in responding against this position quotes Aristotle on the fate of the passive intellect which, as is well known, Aristotle considered to be a power of the soul as form, a power which ceases upon the dissolution of the body.[16] Boehner attributes Scotus' difficulty to the defective Latin translations he had to work with, which did not use a consistent set of terms for the two souls.[17]

However, Scotus finds real difficulties in Aristotle's argument for the survival of the intellective soul. Aristotle held that the intellective soul is not the form of the body but "enters from the outside," consequently it need not cease to exist when the composite is corrupted.[18] Scotus asks, what is the origin of the intellective soul and of its coming to the body? If the Prime Mover does not create, and if on the other hand there is no pre-existent state as in Plato, what can be said with any certainty of the origin of the intellective soul in the doctrine of Aristotle? Not much. Aristotle did not hold

---
[15] *Writings*, p. 148.
[16] *Ibid.*, p. 150, [to III]; p. 149-150, [to I].
[17] Boehner, *op. cit.*, III, 113.
[18] *De generatione animalium*, Bk. II, c. iii, 736b, 28.

a theory of creation. Is the intellective soul the effect of natural causes? Besides the fact that he nowhere indicates such an origin, there is the fact that no form that is the effect of a natural agent is imperishable in an unqualified sense. Rather, Aristotle seems to presuppose the imperishability of the soul when he speaks of its coming to the body.[19] Hence, while Aristotle is convinced that the soul is imperishable, he leaves himself no adequate way to demonstrate it. This may be the import, Scotus suggests, of Aristotle's remark: "For it is *perhaps* impossible that all the parts of the soul are imperishable." He was convinced of this not from demonstrable reasons but simply from probable ones.[20]

Scotus thus shows that in each of the seven arguments adduced from texts of Aristotle that no valid argument can be drawn from the text, or at least that no demonstrative argument is possible. In effect Scotus draws Aristotle into his own position:

> "Therefore, [Aristotle] agreed to things sometimes because of probable persuasive reasons, at other times because [he] had asserted as principles propositions which were not necessary truths. And this reply would suffice for all the testimonies cited above."[21]

Of more current interest is the response given by Scotus to the argument of St. Thomas from the incorruptibility of the soul.[22] This, together with the argument from natural desire, which Scotus examines in responding to Aristotle, are the old standbys of even current treatises on immortality.

The philosopher who wishes to know the nature of the human soul must begin with the soul as it is found in the composite and reason to its nature in itself. St. Thomas and Scotus proceeding thus arrive at somewhat different views of the soul and its relation to the body.

For St. Thomas the soul, because it is capable of immaterial acts and of operating without bodily organs, is spiritual. Notwithstanding this it is also the form of the body. As the sole substantial form it brings to the body its own being *(esse)*: by communicating its being to the body, the body has being. The being of the soul is

---

[19] *Writings*, p. 151.
[20] *Ibid.*, p. 150.
[21] *Ibid.*, p. 149.
[22] *S.T.*, I, q. lxxv, a. vi.

the same as the being of the composite.²³ Consequently, there is no problem for the soul to exist separately from the body.

As Scotus sees it, the body has its preliminary or disposing being *(esse)* from the form of the body. The soul communicates to the body its constitutive being and the body communicates to the soul its constitutive being; the two contribute to the being of the whole, which is other than the being of the soul and the being of the body. The whole is different than either of its constituent parts in themselves. Reason tells us that the soul is ordered to the body, and the body to the soul. That the soul has a proper being whereby it is capable of existence apart from the body is not known from reason.²⁴

There is here a basic disagreement as to the nature of the soul in itself. If one's reason should lead one to accept the view of St. Thomas, then one can continue on with him and argue thus to the immortality of the soul. A thing can be corrupted either through the dissolution of the parts that compose it (corruption *per se*), or through the loss of the necessary support of its being (corruption *per accidens*). The human soul, because it is a spirit having its proper being, can be corrupted in neither way. Being simple it cannot be corrupted *per se*, as is evident. Being independent of the body in its operations, it must be independent in its being. Since the being of the soul in separation is the same as the being of the composite, except that in the composite it is communicating its being to the body, there is no difficulty in holding that the soul can exist in separation. Since this is the nature of the soul *per se*, it is incorruptible *per se*, that is, it is immortal.²⁵

If reason leads one to view the soul as Scotus sees it, then the foregoing is incorrect. The being of the soul and the being of the composite cannot be the same. Otherwise the part would be the same as the whole. Furthermore, it would not be true that the soul in separation is in a less perfect state than in union, as is commonly held. Man, the composite, is the result of the union of the being of the soul *(esse animae)* and the being of the body *(esse corporis)*; the being of the whole *(esse totius)* is the result of the union of these two.²⁶ The soul, however, is different from other forms in that

---

²³ *Ibid.*, q. 75, a. 6.
²⁴ *Quod.*, IX, n. 15, Vivès XV, 389b.
²⁵ *S.T.*, I, q. 75, a. 6.
²⁶ *Quod.*, IX, n. 15.

while it is ordered to union with the body it is not totally absorbed by it. The reasoning here is the same as in St. Thomas. "It possesses operations and energies that are proper to itself, independently of the body."[27] The soul while ordered to the composite is not totally dependent upon the composite for its existence and operations. Nevertheless, as far as reason can tell us it is by nature the form of the body. That this form, even though capable of operating without bodily organs, is able to exist without the body is not demonstrable by reason.[28]

There would appear to be an inconsistency in Scotus' thought. He is convinced that the soul is in itself as a spiritual, intellective principle incorruptible *per se* and *per accidens,* as St. Thomas teaches.[29] Yet he will not take what seems the obvious step of concluding to the immortality of the soul. Scotus apparently reasons: the soul as intellective is clearly a simple, incorruptible reality. But the soul is also the form of the body, and it is beyond reason to prove that as such it is capable of separate existence. As long as the compatibility of these two views of the soul is not demonstrable, the demonstrability of the immortality of the soul is not possible.[30] St. Thomas has attempted to solve the problem by identifying the being of the whole and the being of the soul. Scotus rejects the solution as involving contradictions, as indicated above. He is convinced that reason leads us into this impasse: if the soul has *per se* existence (subsistence), it cannot communicate it to another; if it does not have *per se* existence, it cannot exist without the body.[31]

Sofia Vanni Rovighi points out perceptively when analyzing Scotus' doctrine on immortality that underlying St. Thomas' doctrine is his uniform hylomorphism, just as pluriform hylomorphism underlies Scotus' doctrine. But she does Scotus an injustice in suggesting that he somehow does not deal fairly with St. Thomas by opposing his pluriformism against the latter's uniform theory.[32] Actually Scotus has already in Distinction 11 of this fourth book of the *Ordinatio* refuted to his own satisfaction the uniform hylomorphism of St. Thomas, which St. Thomas proposes in these same terms of one being *(esse)* for the soul and the composite, therefore

---

[27] *Ibid.,* n. 8.
[28] *Writings,* p. 154.
[29] *Quod.,* IX, n. 16, Vivès XXV, 390a.
[30] Cf. Commentary of Hickey, *Rep. Par.,* IV, d. 43, n. 17, Vivès XXIV, 497b.
[31] *Writings,* 153-154.
[32] S. Vanni Rovighi, *op. cit.,* p. 222.

only one form.³³ It would be useless repetition for him to reargue the issue here.

Certainly in the discussion of the respective positions on immortality of these two men it would be wise to start from this preliminary question of uniform or pluriform hylomorphism. Otherwise, arguments against Scotus' position are *non sequiturs* based on presuppositions which Scotus rejects. The same can be said of arguments of Scotists against the position of St. Thomas. The question basically today is, can the uniform hylomorphism of Thomism be maintained in the face of modern scientific knowledge? Can even the modified pluriformism of Scotus be held? Can any theory of hylomorphism not essentially different from the Aristotelian and Scholastic type be held? Further historical questions can be posed: did St. Thomas let faith draw him into a leap unjustified by reason, the constant psychological danger confronting any Christian philosopher? Did Scotus let the role of the soul as form of the composite blind him to the possibility of understanding by reason that the soul is capable of independent existence naturally and not by any miracle?

The above mentioned author, who on the whole has given a penetrating and objective analysis of Scotus' position, seems to miss Scotus' intent on one other matter. She suggests that Scotus actually does not refute the central point in St. Thomas' argument by attacking the unity of the being of the soul and of the composite. The central point is the demonstration of the subsistence of the soul through its *per se* operations.³⁴ However, Scotus in a quodlibetal question clearly considers St. Thomas' argument for subsistence to be founded ultimately on his doctrine of the identity of the being of the soul with the being of the composite. Scotus shows that, even though the *per se* operations of the soul would seem to indicate the possibility of separate existence, the mind cannot necessarily and evidently proceed to the soul's immortality, especially not through the doctrine on the being of the soul proposed by St. Thomas.³⁵

Even if Scotus could have accepted St. Thomas' view of the proper being of the soul, he would not have been able to accept the immortality as following necessarily from it. Granted that the soul is

---

³³ *Oxon.*, IV, d. 11, q. 2, n. 46; Vivès XVII, 429a.
³⁴ *Op. Cit.*, p. 211.
³⁵ *Quod.*, IX, n. 13-19, Vivès XXV, 388-391.

immaterial; granted that it is simple and hence incorruptible *per se,* it would not follow of necessity that the soul is immortal. For it is a creature subject to the continuous, free conservation by God. Since this is a free action the opposite may occur at any moment. God could annihilate it. That he will not annihilate it we know from faith alone. On this point Scotus writes:

> "I concede that apart from God, no being is formally necessary, but simply contingent; nevertheless something created is said to have incorruptible being, insofar as it either has no contrary, or cannot be destroyed by anything else created, but can only be annihilated by God's not conserving it in being; in this manner beatitude can be said to be incorruptible; but such a thing is not of itself perpetual, but only possibly perpetual, due to the fact that just as it possesses being contingently, through God's conservation, so also does it possess perpetuity."[36]

The step from incorruptibility to immortality appears necessary and immediate to those who concentrate their attention on the plan of the ordered will of God, i.e., on the plan freely established by God. God established this order, and in this order it must be. But to one who, like Scotus, cannot forget the absolute power of God, the power to do all that is possible, the possibility remains that what God has freely ordained he can freely rescind. Granted that he will not, we do not know enough from reason about the nature of God to demonstrate that this order of nature must be so. On the contrary, we can demonstrate this is a contingent order.[37] Faith tells us that God has freely decided to grant unending existence to human beings; that this existence shall consist in perfect enjoyment of the vision of God (heaven) or everlasting deprivation of this vision (hell). Reason tells us, as the modern existentialist is acutely aware, that human existence is precarious; at any moment we could not be. In such a contingent universe it can never be demonstrated that the human soul will exist forever.

It can be argued, the good God would never annihilate the human soul; it would be contrary to his goodness and mercy. These are persuasions; and Scotus admits such persuasions. The point is that no demonstration can be constructed along such lines.

At the stage in the history of the question of immortality when Scotus put his mind to it, this is the specific question at issue: is

---

[36] *Oxon.,* IV, d. 49, q. 6, n. 6, Vivès XXI, 185b.
[37] *Ordinatio,* I, d. 44, q. un., Vat. VI, 363f. Cf. Bettoni, *op. cit.,* p. 90.

the immortality of the soul demonstrable? Can we know with absolute certitude by reason alone that the soul is immortal? Scotus answers unequivocally: "It can be stated that although there are probable reasons for this second proposition (that the soul is immortal), these are not demonstrative, nor for that matter are they even necessary reasons."[38]

"Demonstration" is a word used loosely these days. In most neo-scholastic textbooks any proof is called a demonstration. Traditionally, however, a clear distinction was made between the ideal scientific proof proposed by Aristotle in his *Posterior Analytics* and a probable or dialectical proof. For the scholastic, whose project philosophically often was to seek the extent of rational understanding of what he firmly believed, the demonstration was the apex of human intellectual endeavor.

Here Scotus is probing the limits of human understanding with regard to a conclusion which he held in faith. He finds in this case that it is not possible to satisfy the conditions for a true demonstration. Demonstrative knowledge, he has declared elsewhere, requires the simultaneous verification of four conditions. First, it must be knowledge of truth which is certain; second, it must be knowledge of necessary truth, that is, of something which cannot be other than it is; third, it must be caused by a reason which is evident to the intellect, that is by principles which have prior evidence in themselves and are the proper causes of the conclusion; finally, the connection between the principles and conclusion must be established by syllogistic inference.[39] According to the Aristotelian formula, to which Scotus frequently alludes, the premises must be "true, primary, immediate, better known than and prior to the conclusion."[40] Scotus sums it up: "Thus through necessary and proper premises one proceeds to necessary conclusions."[41] Of these requirements, the first three, i.e., true, primary, and immediate, are ultimately reducible to one: the premises must be indemonstrable because they are immediately evident. All demonstrations must be ultimately reducible to some self-evident truth for if it were necessary to demonstrate everything, nothing could be demonstrated; instead one would be involved in an infinite regress of proof.[42]

[38] *Writings*, p 148.
[39] Cf. *Rep. Par.*, prol. q. 1, n. 4, Vivès XXII, 7b.
[40] *Post. Anal.* I, c. 2, 71b, 19-22.
[41] *Univ. Porph.* q. 1, n. 2, Vivès I, 52a.
[42] *Oxon.*, II, d. 1, q. 2, n. 9, Vivès XI, 165a.

Over and above self-evidence, the demonstration requires that its premises be "better known than, and prior to the conclusion, which is further related to them as effect to cause." As Aristotle points out in his discussion of these requirements, the phrases are open to dual interpretation. The priority and causal relation can exist either with respect to our knowledge of the premises, or with respect to reality itself, independent of our knowledge. In the first case, there is present a chronological and relative priority; and a given premise, better known to us because of its relation to sensible phenomena, is the cause of our knowing a conclusion, i.e., a *causa cognoscendi*. In the second case, there is absolute and ontological priority, in which the given premise contains the true cause of the being of the thing, and therefore the reason for the conclusion, i.e., the *causa essendi*. In the first case, we argue from effect to cause; in the second from cause to effect.[43] Upon this dual relationship Scotus bases the distinction of demonstrations into the principal kinds.

A necessary truth, not immediately evident, but having a necessary connection with, and evidence in, another truth which is evident, can be demonstrated by means of the latter. Now there are two ways in which such a necessary connection can be present, the first in a cause, the second in an effect. There is a kind of necessity in both cases, for just as there cannot be truths about causes without truths about effects, so there cannot be truths about effects without something being true about a cause. Therefore, Scotus concludes, we can demonstrate a truth about a cause, and this is called a demonstration of the reasoned fact *(demonstratio propter quid)*; and we can demonstrate a truth from an effect, and this is a demonstration of the simple fact *(demonstratio quia)*.[44] The former gives the reason why the predicate is contained in the subject; the latter establishes a necessary relation between subject and predicate, but it does not give the reason or cause of the connection. Because the latter establishes a necessary relationship it is productive of scientific knowledge, but in a secondary sense of the term "science."[45]

It is the demonstration of the reasoned fact that is relevant to the

---

[43] *Post. Anal.*, I, c. 2, 71b, 29-72a, 5.
[44] *Quod.*, VII, n. 3, Vivès XXV, 283b.
[45] *Rep. Par.*, III, d. 23, q. un., Vivès XXIII, 435. Scotus' proof for the existence of God demonstrates the simple fact that a self-explanatory being is the necessary condition for the existence of the non-self-explanatory beings of our experience; a demonstration of the reason of God's existence is, of course, impossible.

question of immortality. Such a demonstration expresses the ontological cause or reason why an attribute necessarily and proximately inheres in a subject. Scotus does not deny the validity of the proof for the incorruptibility of the soul, based on its intrinsic independence of matter. But he does deny that immortality follows with intrinsic necessity from the incorruptibility of the soul. Since the reason for perpetuity of being lies in God and not in the being itself, in this case the soul, the argument based on incorruptibility is not intrinsic. There is nothing in the soul as far as the soul is known to us at present, which is the proper, proximate, and specific ground for the necessary inherence of this property. A demonstration of the reasoned fact is thus excluded.

Furthermore, it is not a self-evident truth that "God will actually conserve in perpetuity whatever he has made capable of conservation in perpetuity." If such a proposition were evident, then a valid demonstration of the reasoned fact based on the proper extrinsic efficient cause could be formed. But the mind of God is not *naturally* known to us and the principle is not immediately evident.[46]

Scotus, as noted above, rules out both a demonstration of immortality and a proof from necessary reasons. The premises in a demonstration must be both necessary and evident. Premises known by faith are not evident naturally, but they may be necessary. For example, "God is just" would be considered a necessary proposition, because it is based on the immutable nature of God. Such necessary but not evident propositions Scotus calls "necessary reasons." A proposition such as "God will actually conserve in perpetuity whatever he has made capable of conservation in perpetuity" is not a necessary reason. It states a contingent fact, a free decision on the part of God. Lacking both necessity and evidence such a proposition cannot contribute to a demonstration of immortality.[47]

There remains to be considered the argument greatly favored in the Augustinian tradition but also rooted in Aristotle, that from natural desire. A natural desire, Aristotle says, cannot be in vain.[48] Man, however, has a natural desire to live forever; therefore. This is the argument based on the final cause, that is, the tendency of the soul toward happiness in the possession of the good as its ex-

[46] Cf. O. Lynch, *The Concept of Demonstration in the Philosophy of John Duns Scotus*, Washington, D.C., ms., 1943, 19-23.
[47] *Writings*, p. 186, fn. 14.
[48] *Nich. Ethics*, I, c. 2, 1094a, 20-21.

trinsic final end. Success in constructing this argument into a demonstration has a double importance: it proves that immortality is demonstrable; but it also gives a demonstrated starting point for a natural ethics. If, on the other hand, it is not demonstrable, if its certitude is rather from faith than reason, then not only is immortality not demonstrable, but a natural ethics based on man's final end has a probable starting point. In which case it may be preferable to admit that the end of man is not known with sufficient certitude for a demonstrative science, and having admitted that, construct what conclusions on moral conduct one can, as Maritain suggests.[49]

Scotus sees an inevitable circularity in the attempt to prove immortality from natural desire. He writes:

> "If the argument is based on the notion of natural desire taken in an exact and proper sense, and a natural desire in this sense is not an elicited act but merely an inclination of nature towards something, then it is clear that the existence of such a natural desire for anything can be proved only if we prove first that the nature in question is able to have such a thing. To argue the other way round, therefore, is begging the question. Or if the natural desire is taken in a less proper sense, viz. as an act elicited in conformity with the natural inclination, we are still unable to prove that any elicited desire is natural in this sense without first proving the existence of a natural desire in the proper sense of the term."[50]

The natural desire in the proper sense Scotus speaks of here is not a conscious, elicited act; it is an ontological relation between the perfectible and its perfection.[51] Obviously, to assert such a desire of man is presupposing that he is immortal by nature, which is the point to be demonstrated. Even taking the natural desire in the sense of an elicited act, however, it is not possible to construct a demonstration. For it would have to be proven that such a desire is rooted in a natural desire in the proper sense.

There appears to be an inconsistency in this latter conclusion. Scotus subscribes to the Aristotelian method in psychology of proceeding from act back to power or faculty to nature. If there is an elicited desire for unending life it must proceed from a nature which is fitted and destined for such an end; therefore. So it would seem the argument should easily and certainly proceed. Scotus has

---

[49] J. Maritain, *Science and Wisdom* (New York, 1954), 117-119, 165-166.
[50] *Writings*, p. 158.
[51] *Rep. Par.*, IV, d. 49, q. 9, nn. 3-5, Vivès XXIV, 659-660.

no argument with the process. He calls in question the possibility of proceeding demonstratively along this line. If we grant that men as a general rule more or less frequently elicit the desire for unending life, we must ask, is this desire according to man's nature, or is he erroneously conceiving this as a possibility for his nature? (He could be influenced by myths of the tribe.) If this desire is in accord with his nature then it is a desire according to right reason. How do you prove that it is in accord with man's nature? By proving that man has the capacity for unending life. But this brings the argument back to the first proposition and ultimately to the non-demonstrative proofs of Aristotle and St. Thomas.

Maritain expresses the belief that "there is in man a natural, an instinctive knowledge of his immortality."[52] Perhaps someone would be inclined to argue that an explicit knowledge of one's end is not necessary to root a desire for immortality; rather that if such a connatural knowledge as Maritain speaks of were the basis of man's elicited desire, then it would necessarily follow that man is by nature capable of immortality. This knowledge Maritain goes on to elaborate, is not inscribed in man's intelligence; it is not rooted in the principles of reasoning, but in our substance. (Scotus, I am sure, would call it a natural desire in the proper sense.) This instinctive belief is not conceptual or philosophical knowledge, but a lived and practiced one. It is the reason why man acts as if there were life after death, and why he continues to raise the philosophical question of immortality. But precisely because it is instinctive and non-conceptual knowledge it falls outside rational and elaborated knowledge which can achieve demonstrated certitude. It is not possible to demonstrate that it exists in man, nor is it possible for such knowledge to enter into a demonstration of the immortality of man. Scotus concludes:

> "To put it briefly, then, every argument based on natural desire seems to be inconclusive, for to construct an efficacious argument, it would be necessary to show either that nature possesses a natural potency for eternal life, or that the knowledge which immediately gives rise to this desire, where the latter is an elicited act, is not erroneous but in accord with right reason. Now the first of these alternatives is the same as the conclusion to be established. The second is more difficult to prove and is even less evident than the conclusion."[53]

[52] J. Maritain, "The Immortality of Man," *Review of Politics*, III (1941), 413.
[53] *Writings*, p. 159.

Scotus is not rejecting outright either the proof from incorruptibility of the soul or that from natural desire. These are dialectical proofs, strong persuasions. As he said, these are probable reasons; they are not demonstrative. This, as we have seen, is the point he wished to establish against those who in his day too readily claimed to have attained the heights of demonstration. And so he draws the moral:

> "From all this it is apparent how much thanks must be given to our Creator, who through faith has made us most certain of those things which pertain to our end and to eternal life—things about which the most learned and ingenious men can know almost nothing."[54]

III

What relevance does Scotus' doctrine on the immortality of the soul have for contemporary thought? For one thing, any systematic philosophy needs a timely reminder that it is well not to claim more validity for its proofs than can be justified, lest the whole be discredited. On this present point, reason can give strong indications as to the future destiny of the soul. Such indications presented for what they are worth may possibly be a predisposition, practically speaking, for the leap of faith (*a praeambulum fidei*); whereas an overstated case invites outright rejection.

The theme of contingency underlying Scotus' reasoning has obvious relevance. This is an insight variously conceived, more or less perfectly expressed, by contemporary existentialists. Scotus' thought, stripped of its scholastic terminology, can be developed into a solidly grounded view of man's finiteness and contingency. Man's existence *is* precarious; he is up against the nothingness of his own limits and the unknown moment of the end of his earthly existence. Such a view rooted in Scotus' doctrine on the goodness of God who holds the strings leads to a humble, tentative, yet optimistic undertaking of the task of daily living.

The emphasis on the rigor of the Aristotelian demonstration will hardly be considered by most philosophers today as relevant. The modern symbolic logician espouses a different system of logic and seeks not certitude but validity for validity's sake. Within neo-scholasticism,

[54] *Ibid.*, p. 162.

as already noted, most philosophers seem content to settle for a looser understanding of demonstration. Nevertheless, the Aristotelian method of demonstration is a valid though rigorous one for investigating the mind's ability to understand the necessary conditions and consequences of reality. A distinction must be kept in mind as regards purpose. A Christian philosopher can approach a problem as a believer seeking the extent of natural understanding, or as an apologist seeking to move to assent those whom he addresses. If the latter is his purpose, he will accommodate himself to the intellectual milieu of those he addresses. Like a St. Bonaventure he may seek to sweep all along to a conclusion more by the multiplicity and diversity of arguments than by his logical rigor. If the former is the purpose, then like Scotus he will settle on a rigorous norm and see if human reason can in this case meet the norm. There is still relevance to the scholastic question: what conclusions with what degree of certitude can be reached by man using the divine gift of reason? Provided that the premium is not set only on demonstrated conclusions to the exclusion of others, that is the majority of conclusions, a Christian philosopher may legitimately probe the limits of human understanding. For he is not only an apologist; he is a Christian engaged in his profession of philosophy.

To concentrate on this method to the exclusion of more recent phenomenological and existential analyses of the human condition would merit the contempt which in some quarters is being shown toward the scholastic method in general. On the other hand, it would be a great loss to philosophy if with inordinate and imprudent haste the methods and insights of scholasticism were jettisoned as antiquated and irrelevant. The human mind needs the discipline of logic; granting at the same time that logic should not exert a tyranny that dims intuition.

San Luis Rey College, California

10

BEING, UNIVOCITY, AND ANALOGY ACCORDING TO DUNS SCOTUS

by

TIMOTHEUS A. BARTH

To understand the specific nature of the Scotistic concept of being as well as the doctrine of univocity and analogy based on it, it is necessary to show the metaphysical-theological background against which this important and still debated question must be discussed. We can best do so by following the so-called *Ordinatio* of Duns Scotus' commentary on the *Sentences*, which is regarded as the most complete and relatively most reliable text we have on the subject. Other writings are either a preparation *(Quaestiones super Metaphysicam Aristotelis, De anima, Theoremata)* or a complement *(Collationes, Quodlibetum)*[1] of the *Ordinatio*. Our problem is discussed mainly in two places in the *Ordinatio*, viz., I, d. 3, p. 1, q. 1-3, and I, d. 8, p. 1, q. 3. We turn to the first part of the third distinction, where the general theme is the natural knowability of God in our present life. The question is treated from a threefold point of view: (1) whether God can be naturally known by the human intellect in this life; (2) whether in the present state God can be naturally known as the first object of our intellect; (3) whether God can be naturally known as the first and adequate object of our cognition here on earth.

The chief concern is therefore the way and method of our natural knowledge of God. The question concerning being and its univocation is not specifically mentioned. If it is touched on, it is in relation to the natural knowability of God, and it serves logically as a

---

[1] Since we have a critical edition of the *Ordinatio* and the *Lectura in Sententias*, we shall use the *editio Vaticana* (Rome: 1950 ff.), cited as *ed. Vat.*, according to volume and page. The other texts will be taken from the Wadding-Vivès edition (Paris: 1891-95), cited as *ed. Viv.* according to vol. and page.

means of solving a metaphysical-theological problem. Each of the three questions is intended to be a solution of one part of the problem. The first question, which deals with the natural knowability of God by the human intellect in this life, proposes five theses: (1) We do not know merely God's attributes but also something of his essence *(conceptus quiditativus de Deo)*. (2) We do not have mere analogous concepts of him but also certain, i.e., minimal univocal, concepts of him *(in conceptu aliquo univoco)*. (3) God is not naturally cognized by our intellect here on earth in a way adequate to his concrete, i.e., individual, essence *(sub ratione huius essentiae ut haec est in se);* we cannot go beyond certain general structures. (4) The most perfect concept of God possible to us here below is that of *ens. infinitum*. (5) God is now cognized by us through the *species* of creatures; creatures provide conceptual constructs of a transcendental type *(species transcendentium)* which are common to them and God. The second of these five theses is especially important for us. From it we can see that univocation is closely bound up with being and the *perfectiones simplices* and that it serves as a means for a possible cognition of God and is intended to support the analogy of being.

The second and third questions continue the subject and particularize its several problems. Hence we ask whether God can be cognized by us in this life as the first, i.e., as the first and adequate, object of our cognition. In answer to this question Scotus distinguishes a threefold order of possible intelligible objects, viz., an *ordo originis secundum generationem,* an *ordo perfectionis,* and an *ordo adaequationis sive causalitatis praecisae.* The three orders, which we shall study in the following pages, complement one another, and we shall emphasize the essential aspects of Scotus' doctrine of being, its knowability, and its internal structure.

The eighth distinction has in its first part a metaphysical-theological background: the *simplicitas Dei.* In the third question Scotus speaks again of being and univocation and makes important additions, which in the main pertain to the reality and the transcendentality of being. In what follows we shall have occasion to deal with two main problems: first, how being manifests itself in the *triplex ordo intelligibilium,* and what is the fundamental structure of its content; second—this is based on the first—what Scotus means in the last analysis by *univocatio entis transcendentis,* and how this is related to the traditional *analogia entis.*

PART I

BEING IN THE THREEFOLD ORDER OF INTELLIGIBILITY

1. The Threefold Order of Intelligibility

Human cognition may be considered in a threefold respect or order: first, in respect to its actual genesis *(ordo originis secundum generationem)*; second, in respect to its perfection *(ordo perfectionis)*; third, in respect to its assimilation *(ordo adaequationis)*. This respect or order is not a mere impersonal and general principle, but behind its reality stands a personal and absolute director, God, who plans everything wisely and then acts according to his wise plan. So here we find ultimate metaphysical and theological reasons in the background, which is not surprising since Duns Scotus is both a theistic metaphysican and a Christian theologian.[2]

The *ordo originis* considers human cognition, and primarily our intellectual cognition, as it actually originates and progresses. Human cognition is here subject to the law of temporal succession from what is initially undetermined to what is fully determined. The difference is very significant and will have weighty consequences for the approach to being and its determination.

The *ordo perfectionis* goes an important step further, proceeding from being to perfection. Here it will become manifest that being is open to an essential differentiation and capable of receiving it; through its intrinsic modes and primary differences, being can become concrete in a relatively or absolutely perfect entity. Thus at the same time the horizon and scope of our intellectual cognition come into view.

The final possibilities and limits of philosophical intellections manifest themselves. On the one hand, they are determined by their dependence on our senses, especially those of sight, hearing, and touch, and on the other hand, they are arrested at certain general structures when we refer to cognition of the most perfect being, God.

The *ordo adaequationis* completes the other two orders, especially the *ordo originis,* fastening on its results to draw further conclusions from it. The conceptual analysis *(resolutio)* has already in

---

[2] *Ord.* II (ed. Viv. XIII, 353): . . . Eius (sc. Dei) actus . . . ordinatissimus. Cf. E. Longpré, *La philosophie du B. J. Duns Scot* (Paris: 1924), pp. 54-66.

the *ordo originis* come upon something ultimate and altogether simple that is basic for everything conceivable—it has come upon being. This discovery is made fruitful for the entire intellectual cognition in the *ordo adaequationis*, and in particular is applied to the different kinds of necessary judgments *(praedicationes per se primo, resp. per se secundo modo)*. In other words, being proves itself to be the foundation of our intellectual cognition *(primum objectum adaequatum)* and unites the different related terms in a judgment as subject and predicate. Being itself is essentially included in the essential structures of finite being and in the infinite being. The assimilating and combining function is here not to be taken in a quantitative sense, as a quantitative increase or diminution of being, but in the sense of a relationship. Things originally different *(primo diversa)* can come (on the basis of an *aequalitas proportionis*) from an ultimate foundation of equality (as *ratio subjecti*) to concretization and enter into a relationship with one another.[3]

2. Being and Actual or Habitual Process of Cognition

a. Being and Confused Cognition

The *ordo originis* first considers the actual process of our intellectual cognition as it develops from a state of indeterminateness to a state of determinateness. It will be of interest to see if being will show itself in the very beginning of our intellectual cognition, or only make its appearance later. Both scholasticism in general and Scotus call the initial but still confused intellectual cognition *simplex intelligentia,* because it is only a simple perception or acceptance of something *(simplex intelligentia, conceptus simplex).* Genuine conception *(distincte concipere)* and judgment *(componere)* appear only in a later phase of our cognition.[4]

In the initial but still confused intellectual cognition we meet the following distinct problems: first, the intimate relation between sense cognition and intellectual cognition and the problem of distance; second, the cooperation of the intelligible object and the faculty of intellection in natural or necessary causality; and third,

[3] *Ord.* I (ed. Vat. III, 48-123, 48): Triplex ordo intelligibilium . . . ordo originis . . . ordo perfectionis . . . ordo adaequationis; *Quodl.* (ed. Vivès XXV, 227b): . . . Adaequatio secundum proportionem.
[4] *Ord.* I (ed. Vat. III, 49); Conceptus simplex . . . actus simplicis intelligentiae; cf. *Metaph.* I (VII, 53a).

the relation between our human intellect and its sensory expression in language.[5]

The most important consequence in our context is this, that being, in its transcendental function, is not yet attained through the confused intellectual perception. Our intellect, as *potentia transcendens,* transcends the phenomenal domain of sensibility *(totum genus sensationis)* and turns in its first step toward essential intelligibility. However, this encounter *(occursus)* is only the first contact with essential intelligibility; it does not yet penetrate into the depth of the thing, nor apprehend its inner structure; hence it perceives something of the concrete essence of things in a manner still very external and inarticulate. The result of this encounter is an initial or simple concept of the concrete essentiality of things, as we find them in our unreflecting everyday experience. We can express this encounter in the words of human speech, which by means of information and question is an important instrument of communication. Our terminology still leaves us epistemologically in the dark with regard to the essential components of things (e.g., form and matter) and the difference between species and individuality; it restricts itself to the common contours of the lowest species *(species specialissimae).*

Hence we can say that our first intellectual cognition, however undetermined it may still be, nevertheless takes an important step beyond the world of sense phenomena and so effects a first abstraction. It neglects individual phenomena and turns to the essence of concrete things which show themselves to us as *species specialissimae.* Such lowest species are still conceived in an undifferentiated fashion, since the texture of the individual constructs remains in a global indeterminateness. However, the first indeterminate or confused cognition is already more than nescience and less than definite or distinct knowing. Therefore it takes a mediating position between not-knowing and distinct-knowing, and determinate intellectual cognition takes its departure and works forward from it. Inasmuch as the confused cognition terminates with the *species specialissima* and does not penetrate it in its structural composition, it follows that being also remains unknown and hidden to our intellectual cognition.

b. Being and Distinct Cognition

Our intellect does not stand still at this confused cognition of

[5] Cf. *Lect.* I (ed. Vat. XVI, 251-52); *Ord.* I (ed. Vat. III, 50-54).

the *species specialissima*, but strives rather to overcome the indeterminate and undifferentiated *species specialissima* and to make the already existent ontological structure also distinct for our cognition. This task is undertaken, in place of the more psychological abstraction, which likewise appears at times, by the more acute logical procedure of *resolutio* and *divisio*.

The *resolutio* is an ascending and analytical process of thought. It aims at apprehending the altogether simple structures of the object *(simpliciter simplicia)* which it encounters in the concrete but composite objects *(entia composita)*. The resulting thought consists in very simple concepts *(conceptus simpliciter simplices)* which cannot be reduced to anything else. What the *resolutio* initiated is continued by the *divisio* in a descending and more synthetic manner. In doing so it takes its departure from very simple conceptual elements and returns to concrete essences by means of other conceptual elements which are also simple but originally diverse. Through this logical descent the object becomes transparent in its structure and is cognized distinctly. The division ends with the definition.[6]

Let us now see what in particular the *resolutio* does for our cognition. The result may be expressed in a twofold respect: first, the *resolutio* as a conceptual cognition seeks to retain what is contained in the essential structure of an object *(in ratione essentiali)*; second, it puts our cognition on a solid foundation since it exposes the principles on which our cognition of singular things is based, and so renders them accessible and indubitable to our intellect.[7]

Thus the *resolutio*, in an analytical process, prepares the conceptual penetration of the essential structure of an object. The first proof for the distinct intellectual cognition brings us further details in this matter. Such a conceptual clarification succeeds only when we come upon the *simpliciter simplicia* which cannot be resolved any further. Such very simple elements can be arrested and grasped by means of very simple concepts. Two groups of very simple structures appear here. The one group signifies the ultimate common *quid* which is included in all inferior and not absolutely

[6] Cf. *Lect.* I (ed. Vat. XVI, 252-54); *Ord.* I (ed. Vat. III, 54-60); *Ord.* I (ed. Vat. III, 62): Abstrahibile ... resolvendo; *Ord.* I (ed. Vat. III, 82): Resolutio entium compositorum stat ultimo ad simpliciter simplicia; *Ord.* I (ed. Vat. III, 56): Reditio per viam divisionis ad inquirendum quiditates terminorum in scientiis specialibus.

[7] *Ord.* I (ed. Vat. III, 54): Concipiuntur omnia, quae sunt in ratione eius essentiali; *Ord.* I (ed. Vat. III, 55): Certificare principia aliarum scientiarum.

simple essential constructs. The other group contains the differential *quale* and manifests itself in the various differences (of the individual, specific, and transcendental type), in the attributes and properties of being (of the coextensive or disjunctive type), and finally in the so-called *perfectiones simplices* (e.g., intelligence, will, justice, goodness).[8]

We restrict ourselves primarily to the first group, since it is basic for the *ratio essentialis* and for the *cognitio distincta*. The basic and absolutely simple structural element is being *(ens)*. We arrive at it in its absolute simplicity through analysis *(resolutio)*. Being can be distinctly cognized or conceived without its concrete essential constructs. That is to say: purely essential being is apprehended and prescinded *(praecisio)* through analysis while the concrete essential structures are not considered *(non considerando)* and epistemologically recede into the background.

This calls for an additional remark. Being as a mere "something" is the foundation of our distinct cognition. There is still another moment of being that unites itself with pure quiddity *(Wassein)*, namely, existence *(Dasein)*, more exactly possible existence. For Scotus they are both inseparably united and can only be distinguished by our intellect *(ratione)*. On the occasion of his dealing with the divine ideas, Scotus also speaks of an *existentia secundum quid*. What he wants to say in final analysis is that every essence involves at least a possible existence *(Dasein)*. The "so-being" *(Sosein)* has therefore a conceptual priority over the *Dasein*, since it is conceptually apprehensible as a moment of content. This is not so with existence *(Dasein)*, since existence is without content; one can only have immediate experience of it, posit it in thought, or cognize it mediately. Nevertheless *Dasein* is always joined with *Sosein*, even if in distinct cognition it yields precedence to *Sosein*. Besides, being is not only absolutely simple *(simpliciter simplex)*, but also the ultimate common element of all concrete structures. Being has a communicative character, and this character gives being a preeminence over all other structures, whether simple or composite. In this sense the axiom holds: what is near to being is prior, and what is farther away from being is posterior.[9]

---

[8] *Ord.* I (ed. Vat. III, 82, 84, 91, 93); *Quodl.* (ed. Viv. XXV, 108). Cf. A. B. Wolter, *The Transcendentals and Their Function in the Metaphysics of Duns Scotus* (Washington, D.C.: 1946).

[9] *Ord.* I (ed. Vat. III, 49): Praecisionem; (ed. Vat. III, 44): Non considerando;

As regards the concrete essential structures this must be said: for the concrete essences (genera, species, and individuals) to be distinctly cognized, they have to have being that is essentially contained in them. Without being, the inferior essential structures cannot be distinctly cognized. They remain in an indefinite obscurity and appear to us as a *confusum* whose constructs are not yet articulated.

The *resolutio,* through its analytical process, discloses the internal structures of the concrete objects and penetrates to being. In doing so, it also renders an eminently epistemological-metaphysical service: it secures the foundation of our knowledge and with it the foundation of the special sciences which are based on it. The Subtle Doctor speaks of this in connection with the distinct intellectual cognition and takes a classical thought from the metaphysics of Avicenna, who holds that it is the task of metaphysics to secure the foundations and principles of the other sciences.

This means that the special sciences, such as physics, mathematics, and geometry, always deal with a special object, an *ens speciale.* Geometry, e.g., investigates lines and figures. The lines are determined insofar as the *cognitio confusa* permits it, namely, the line is a length. With this still indefinite intellection we do not yet know whether the line has the being of a substance or of a quantity. To arrive at a decision we must go beyond geometry as a science and turn to geometry as philosophy or metaphysics. It is for metaphysics to determine the common fundamental concepts and the principles that flow from them, and so give them a solid basis. The common fundamental concepts are discovered only when their ultimate simple structures are grasped by our intellect. The significance for our conceptual apprehension is this: such absolute simplicities are either totally apprehended or they are not apprehended at all. When we apprehend them totally, we have certain cognition; when we do not apprehend them, we have no knowledge of them and are still in a state of nescience.

The thought of giving a solid basis for our fundamental concepts, among which, in the first place, being belongs, will play an important part when Scotus develops the first argument for his *univocatio entis.* The first thing we cognize in an object is that it is an *ens,* i.e., that it has quiddity and can exist. Only then does

---

(ed. Vat. III, 54): Communissimum; (ed. Vat. III, 160): Existentiam ... secundum quid.

our intellect proceed to investigate the further structure of a being, e.g., whether it is finite or infinite, created or uncreated, existent in itself or in another.[10]

Through the *resolutio quiditativa* we have reached quidditative being as the ultimate structural element. This pure quidditative being can indeed be conceived and apprehended by itself, but it never occurs by itself alone but only and always together with and in concrete being. *Entia concreta* contain it essentially in themselves and are therefore for our intellect what is first cognizable— the *prima intelligibilia*.

How can the intellect have clear and evident cognition of the transition or the relation of being as being and its inferiors? This is brought about by the logical process of the descending and ultimate synthetic division. Scotus formulates it briefly: *Divisio artificialis statum habet ad speciem specialissimam*. The descending division unites being with the simple differences and so arrives at a contraction or concretion of being. The first division of being takes place through the contracting differences of infiniteness and finiteness and so reaches the *ens infinitum* and *finitum*. Finiteness and infiniteness are here the first differences or determinations of being, they determine being from within as *modi intrinseci entis*. In the domain of finiteness division has a wide field of activity and descends from the highest genera, through the intermediate genera and species to individuals. Thus the ontological structure of reality is grasped by our intellect and is made clear and distinct to it. The division terminates in a definition-concept which comprises all structural elements, from being through all genera and differences to the ultimate species. Hence man, for instance, is first of all a being, then a substance which is corporeal, living, sensitive, and spiritual. With that, distinct cognition has reached its goal: distinct cognition attains its completion in a definition-concept.[11]

Distinct comprehension in the definition permits a continuation in judgment. It pertains to a judgment to attribute to a given subject everything that belongs to its entity. We shall speak of this specifically in connection with the so-called *ordo adaequationis*,

---

[10] *Ord.* I (ed. Vat. III, 18-21, 86, 91; IV, 178-84).
[11] *Ord.* II (ed. Viv. XII, 146b): Divisio artificialis statum habet ad speciem specialissimam; *Ord.* I (ed. Vat. III, 119): Descendendo; *Lect.* I (ed. Vat. XVI, 272): Descendit per differentias (sc. determinantes); *Ord.* I (ed. Vat. IV, 221): Isti conceptus contrahentes dicunt modum intrinsecum ipsius contracti; *Ord.* I (ed. Vat. III, 55): Cognoscere distincte habetur per definitionem.

which passes from what is purely conceptual to a judgment and so expresses in a formal statement whatever is contained in a subject.[12]

c. Being and Habitual-virtual Cognition

Habitual and virtual cognition is intimately connected with actual intellection. Both types of cognition influence but do not coincide with each other. Let us look closer and see how our habitual and virtual cognition may be determined, and what role it plays in the process of our cognition.

Habitual cognition is reducible to one or more cognitional acts which were actually posited before, and so it gives a definite direction to our intellectual faculty. Through the *habitus* our intellectual faculty achieves a facility to operate with a certain joy, ease, rapidity, and inclination. Aristotle knew this and in the sixth book of his *Nicomachean Ethics* he distinguishes between theoretical and practical conditions or fundamental attitudes *(habitus)*. Among the theoretical attitudes he places especially wisdom, intelligence, and science. Science has to do with special being: thus, arithmetic with numbers, geometry with figures, physics with animate and inanimate bodies. It employs concepts that derive their orientation from sense experience and still possess an indeterminate character *(conceptus confusus)*. Wisdom has to do with the highest and noblest causes, with God and pure spirits. Intelligence has to do with the most common concepts and the principles derived from them. Human cognition can be operative in all three dimensions and impart to one of them a certain priority; in this way our cognition achieves a definite orientation.

Intelligence here taken in a definite sense, namely, as a *habitus*, is of importance in our context, since it fixes and establishes in our faculty of cognition whatever is known as metaphysical cognition. Through the *habitus metaphysicus* human intelligence acquires a definite attitude and basic direction, which consists in the fact that we make evident the foundations of our cognition and acquire the ensuing principles in definite concepts and propositions.[13]

The fundamental concepts are of particular importance since they expose the basis for the intelligibility of things. The ground

[12] *De an.* (ed. Viv. III, 613a): Adaequatio secundum virtutem . . . adaequatio secundum praedicationem; *Ord.* I (ed. Vat. III, 81 sqq.).
[13] Aristotle, *Eth. Nic.* VI, 3 (1139b 16-36); *Ord.* I (ed. Vat. IV, 142): Operari delectabiliter, faciliter, expedite et prompte; *R.P.I. Prol.* (ed. Viv. XXII, 46a): Habitus metaphysicae . . .; cf. A. Wolter, *Duns Scotus, Philosophical Writings* (Edinburgh: 1962) 9-12, 169.

of intelligibility is connected with the being of essence, which is capable of manifesting itself. We obtain a habitual cognition when the object, on the ground of its intelligibility, is so present to the intellect that the intellect can at once elicit a cognitional act *(actus elicitus)*. Emphasis is here on the words "can at once," since an object's ground of intelligibility need not always be expressly cognized if the *habitus* of metaphysical intelligence has been established.

Virtual cognition supplements habitual cognition as to content, which is determined by the *aliquid*. In the *aliquid* of a concrete object there are several structures which are apprehended in a first, although confused cognition. When, for instance, we cognize "being human" as the lowest species *(species specialissima)*, we also apprehend along with it "being animate." Of course the "being animate" is cognized only virtually or cognized together with "being human," since it is really not what we cognize first. What is first cognized is rather the "being human" as a confused concept.

For habitual and virtual cognition a general thesis is now established: in the case of habitual and virtual cognition, in so far as the origin of our cognition *(via generationis)* is concerned, the more common structures are always cognized virtually before or together with the object known. The reason for this lies in a certain correspondence between the order of being and human cognition. Different forms perfect the same object in a definite order; some do it mediately or after; others do it immediately or before. The same is true when one and the same form contains virtually in itself the perfection of several forms in a certain order. In such a case the total form perfects the respective object in a definite order through the partial forms of the object. Thus the matter of a concrete object is determined first by substantiality and then by corporeity, animation, sensitivity, and the like.

This order of being returns in our conceptual cognition. Here the more common but less perfect concepts perfect or determine our cognition before the less common but more perfect do so. This also happens when a superior total concept virtually contains in itself the other partial concepts. In this case, too, the more common conceptual constructs have precedence over the less common.

Even if in the case of the habitual virtual intellectual cognition nothing is as yet expressly said about the cognition of being, we are nevertheless in closest proximity to it. The reason for this is easy to understand: where there are *conceptus communiores* and *conceptus minus communes,* they have a *conceptus communissimus* underlying them which is the ultimate measure for them. The *primus conceptus communissimus* is being, which our actual distinct intellectual cognition discovers through the resolution, and through the division unfolds into the distinct *species specialissima* definitively apprehended.

What Scotus really wished to say by his habitual-virtual cognition we can describe a little more exactly and clearly. Being is apprehended at a relatively early time by our intellect, although still in an indistinct or unformed manner as an indefinite horizon of our cognition. This shows itself in all unreflected questions and spontaneous answers. They refer for the most part to the *quid est* and the *si est* of an object and attempt a first answer to them. Underlying them is a simple and still undifferentiated concept of being, which enables us first of all to form a judgment and above all to have a subject of judgment *(ratio subjecti).* This simple and still undifferentiated concept of being could mean what Scotus in the final analysis wanted to express by his habitual-virtual intellectual cognition. In its tendency to what is originally common it is already a vague anticipation of being. It is a preparation for what leads *in cognitione actuali* to the first distinct object of our intellectual cognition: to being as *conceptus simpliciter simplex et communissimus.* Next, the *ordo adequationis* ties in with this and continues the thought from conceptual cognition to a judicial proposition. It is precisely judgment which will show what a leading role falls to the *ens communissimum.*[14]

3. Being, Perfection and Cognition

a. *Ordo originis* and *perfectio*

The *ordo originis* showed something of the process of our intellection, which developed from a confused to a distinct intellectual cognition. The confused intellectual cognition stopped at the still unarticulated *species specialissima.* The articulation was left for the subsequent distinct cognition to undertake.

Distinct intellectual cognition had primarily a material-logical

---

[14] *Ord.* I (ed. Vat. III, 60-61, 266 sqq.); *Lect.* I (ed. Vat. XVI, 255); cf. Z. van de Woestyne, *Cursus philosophicus,* II (Mechliniae, 1925), p. 382 sq.; E. Bettoni, *Il problema della conoscibilità di Dio nella scuola francescana* (Padova: 1950), p. 308 sqq.; E. Coreth, *Metaphysik* (Innsbruck: 1961), pp. 133-158.

objective, with which a more formal epistemological objective was connected. The material-logical objective was the penetration of a structure of being still unarticulated or confused. To make this structure distinct or evident, being had to be discovered as well as its genera, differences, and species. Thus the still confused *species specialissima* was converted into a distinct concept of essence. The leading role here fell to being, since as a pure *quid* it became the point of departure for our distinct intellectual cognition. The formal-epistemological objective was the positing of our intellectual cognition on the ontological foundation of being. The first thing we cognize for certain about an object is that it is a being, i.e., an essence capable of existence.

In this very abstract discussion we have repeatedly come upon the opposition of perfection and imperfection, which is connected with the unfolding and concretion of being. In dealing with confused intellection, which made a first contact with the concrete object, we learned that the content of our cognition is a completely perfect effect *(effectus perfectissimus)*, and that it coincides with the species which does not allow further specification, the *species specialissima*. Since the conceptually apprehensible structures are not as yet disclosed, it follows that this kind of cognition is still imperfect or confused, although it is already more than mere nescience and therefore already an initial cognition. In dealing with the habitual-virtual cognition something else came into view, namely, that the *conceptus communiores* are cognizable prior to the *conceptus particulares*, but the *conceptus communiores* are more imperfect. This led to the distinct cognition, which took its departure from the commonest concept, namely, that of being. However, the pure concept of being, since it is altogether simple and still undifferentiated, is also altogether imperfect. With the aid of the differences and determinations being was able to develop from a void and indeterminateness to the fullness and determinateness of the concrete and perfect being. Being and perfection, therefore, have an internal mutual relation and cannot be separated from each other. What being begins and makes possible is completed and realized by perfection.[15]

---

[15] *Ord.* I (ed. Vat. III, 52): . . . Effectus perfectissimus . . . species specialissima; (ed. Vat. III, 57): Ab imperfecto ad perfectum . . .; (Vat. III, 61): Imperfectior semper prior; cf. Z. van de Woestyne, *Cursus philosophicus* (Mechliniae: 1933²), II, 290.

b. *Ordo perfectionis* and *primum perfectum*

In the domain of intelligible objects there is also an order of grades of perfection. This order can be considered in a twofold respect: first, in respect to the absolute perfection of the object to be cognized; and then in respect to the perfection of the cognitional act, which in our case is the human act.

With regard to the absolute perfection of being, God is the *perfectissimum cognoscibile*. For he is the absolute measure and fulfillment of being, and all other beings in the world receive from him their place in the order of perfection of being. Accordingly, in the world about us the *species specialissima perfectior* occupies the highest rank in perfection, then comes that species which is next to it, and so on to the ultimate species. After all the *species specialissimae* comes the *genus proximum*, which can be abstracted from the *species perfectissima*. This process may be carried further through analysis, and it finally arrives at the ultimate structural elements. Because of their absolute simplicity and indeterminateness, these last are utterly imperfect and need to be supplemented and determined by other structural elements.

The order of perfection in being, as we have it here, can be adequately comprehended only by an absolutely perfect intellect, namely, that of God. With human cognition the result is quite different. Since our intellect depends on the senses and their objects, the *sensibilia*, it is limited in the perfection of its cognition. The more perfect objects of sense, those of sight, hearing, and touch, determine our senses more effectively than those of other sense areas. This has also an effect on our intellectual cognition. The *sensibilia perfectiora* bear a more immediate and a more perfect relation, or proportion, to our intellect than the *objecta insensibilia et immaterialia*. Our intellect attains more data in cognizing the lower objects than in cognizing the higher. But the case is different in cognizing immaterial being, to which also God belongs. Here human intellection is still very imperfect, since it must halt at the common structures of being and cannot know the special constructs adequately. But we may here recall what Aristotle has declared in *De partibus animalium:* even if our knowledge of immaterial things is imperfect and minimal, it is nevertheless more important and more desirable than the knowledge we obtain of material things and can therefore be comparatively more extensive.

The horizon and the scope of intelligibility show themselves in the order of perfection. Its lowest limits are the *entia materialia;* intermediate are the organic life of plants and the inferior consciousness of the animals; the end is represented by the *entia immaterialia* in the essential order of men, angels and God. The degree of perfection in cognition is lowest with human beings, since their knowledge is greater and more perfect in the domain of material things than in the domain of immaterial things.[16]

c. Perfection and Internal Modes of Being

Weighty ontological questions arise in connection with the treatment of perfection. In our context they pertain primarily to the relation between being and its first intrinsic modifications, and to the relation between the concrete subject and the pure or simple perfections of being. While being as an utterly simple concept is absolutely empty and undifferentiated and therefore imperfect, it receives its first determination and perfection through the modes of infiniteness and finiteness. Finiteness and infiniteness are the first determinations of being and are more intimately related to it than the other differences. Because of this pre-eminence Scotus calls them internal modes of contracted being or internal grades of perfection, since they determine being from within and so conduct it to perfection.[17]

This is especially apparent with the mode of infiniteness. Infiniteness here does not mean quantitative but qualitative or intensive infiniteness, which is proper to God and constitutes his being from within. As such it signifies not only the highest perfection, but also that perfection which is absolute and unsurpassable by anything else. It must be added that infiniteness transcends being as essence and comprises existence. The infinite being is not only an absolutely supreme being, but also such a one as to exist of itself, i.e., because of its real nature. The reason is this: intensive infinity is of itself the inner mode of the divine essence, and eternity is the inner mode of the divine existence. But since the existence of God has its ultimate reason in the divine essence and therefore originates *ex natura rei,* one can also say with equal right that infiniteness and eternity are, ultimately, connected with the

---

[16] Cf. *Ord.* I (ed. Vat. III, 62 sq.); *Lect.* I (ed. Vat. XVI, 265 sq.); Aristotle, *De part. anim.* I, c. 5 (644b 31-33).

[17] *Ord.* I (ed. Vat. IV, 206): Enti, ut indifferens . . .; (ed. Vat. IV, 222): Conceptus imperfectus; (ed. Vat. IV, 221): Modi intrinseci ipsius contracti; (ed. Vat. II, 212): Gradus intrinseci perfectionis; cf. W. Hoeres, *Der Wille als reine Vollkommenheit nach Duns Scotus* (München: 1962), 25-45, spec. 34.

divine essence. What is infinite in its essence has everything of itself and nothing from anything else. Hence the divine essence has its existence of itself. Its existence is thus the ultimate effluence or the ultimate completion of the divine being.[18]

The thought of the infinite perfection which conceives of existence as the ultimate consequence of the divine essence may also be formulated with the aid of other modalities, especially with the aid of possibility and necessity. Scotus can here refer to long-recognized insights, already to be found in Aristotle. Thus we read in *Physics* II, 4, that in things eternal, possible (ἐνδέχεσθαι) and real existence (ἐίναι) constitute no difference. Besides, everything eternal is also necessary, and conversely everything necessary is also eternal. On the strength of these propositions Scotus formulates a proof, more exactly, a *demonstratio quia,* that a first being exists, since it is possible and necessary. What serves him here is the minimum of an *a posteriori* basis: that some being is effectible and therefore in need of a cause which can be self-existing and is consequently necessary. In the case of the mode of finiteness the relation to being, "so-being" *(Sosein)* and "being-existent" *(Dasein),* is different. Finiteness confers upon being and its moments a determination also, but of a limiting nature. The limitation manifests itself not only with regard to the essence, which is finite, but also with regard to existence. A finite being does not exist of itself, but primarily has only a mental reality as an idea of God. Inasmuch as God thinks all finite ideas from eternity, it follows that they already have a being which, however, is not yet full-blown nor possessed of essence and real existence. As beings thought by God the ideas are distinct from the really existent essence of God and have the diminished being of an *esse* or *existere secundum quid,* which indeed is capable of existence but does not yet really exist.[19]

Finite being obtains real existence only through the creative act of God. God creates the entire being of the finite being which is distinct from him. He confers upon it *Sosein* and *Dasein* in an inseparable unity, so that *Sosein* and *Dasein,* also in a finite real being, are not distinct from each other in reality but only *ratione.*

---

[18] *Ord. I* (ed. Vat. IV, 211): Non potest excedi in perfectione; (ed. Vat. III, 41): Ens absolute summum; *Quodl.* (ed. XXV, 251a): Existentia ex natura rei.

[19] Aristotle, *Phys.* II, 4 (203b 30), cf. Scotus, *Ord.* II (ed. Viv. XI, 74); Aristotle, *De gen. et corr.* II, 11 (337b 35-338a 2), cf. Scotus *Ord. I* (ed. Vat. IV, 288); cf. P. Borgmann, *Seiender oder werdender Gott, in Theologische Gegenwartsfragen* (Regensburg: 1940), 70 sqq.; *Ord.* II (ed. Viv. XI, 63b): . . . Esse intelligibile . . . esse secundum quid.

Hence real existence, also in finite real being, is the terminating mode which brings finite being to its perfection. However, as far as this final perfection is concerned, it is always God's creative power that is the true and only sufficient cause, since finite being can give itself neither ideal nor real being.[20]

d. Pure Perfection and Concrete Subject

A further and no less weighty problem concerns pure perfections and their relation to definite concrete subjects which through these perfections acquire a special priority over other beings. These definite concrete subjects all belong to the spiritual domain and are divided into human beings, pure spirits, and God. The *perfectiones simplices* are utterly simple, as is being which is common to all things, but they are not identical with universal being. Universal being is the still undetermined what (*quid*) and is altogether imperfect; the *perfectiones simplices*, on the other hand, are determined *quale* and are altogether perfect.

Following St. Anselm of Canterbury, Scotus deals at length with the pure perfections and lays down an important rule about them. According to this rule, such perfections usually belong to those things for which it is better to have them than not to have them. This determination is of course ambiguous and calls for a clarifying restriction. How is it, first of all, not to be understood? The negation of the pure perfections may not be interpreted as a contradictory antithesis, as a non-having. Otherwise pure perfections would have to be generally ascribed to all possible subjects, from a stone up to a pure spirit. This would lead to great contradictions and is therefore rejected by both Anselm and Scotus. Something positive can certainly be finite, composite, and imperfect and yet belong to being, i.e., be in contradictory opposition to nothingness. But that is not the point at issue here. By the negation of pure perfection we rather mean every positive thing that is incompatible with a definite pure perfection, e.g., intuitive intellect or free will, and therefore cannot coexist with it. Consequently the positive thing that cannot coexist with a pure perfection already belongs to being, but is not pure being since it is affected by finiteness, partial negation, and composition. Over against pure perfection in the domain of being stands impure or mixed perfection.

[20] *Ord.* II (ed. Viv. XI, 180b): Creatio est productio totius creati in esse; cf. P. Minges, *J. Duns Scoti doctrina philosophica et theologica* (Ad Claras Aquas, Florentiae: 1930), II, 244-51, 259-66.

With regard to pure perfection we must further bear in mind that whoever is as a subject in possession of a pure perfection must also be capable of coming into possession of it. Thus a dog cannot possess wisdom and goodness, since these perfections are incompatible with his animal nature and destructive of it. Finally, one other thing is to be noted: pure perfections are not exclusive of one another but are compatible with one another.

Perfectiones simplices will play a large part in the fourth proof of the *univocatio transcendentalis*. They expand quidditative univocation of being to qualitative universality of being and permit an ontologically grounded determination of essence with reference to pure intelligence (as intuitive activity) and pure will (as self-determining freedom).[21]

4. Being as Basis of Cognition in *Ordo Adaequationis*

a. *Ordo adaequationis* and Preceding Orders

The *ordo adaequationis* terminates what the *ordo originis* and the *ordo perfectionis* prepared in the area of our human intellection. The *ordo originis* had already, with the help of the *resolutio*, opened the way to being. Being is an ultimate conceptual oneness which cannot be reduced any further. From being so conceived the descent can be made *per modum divisionis* to concrete essences.

In the *ordo perfectionis* we noted the scope of a possible intellection which spanned the range between the absolute spirit of God *(ens perfectissimum)* and corporeal matter. Of course, in our present intellection a limitation becomes apparent. We now cognize most perfectly whatever comes to us through the higher senses and makes a lasting impression on them. We also cognize God in this life, but only in a very imperfect way, i.e., in his most general notes or characteristics.

The *ordo adaequationis* takes up all these thoughts and formulates them in a still greater interconnection, passing from conceptual to judicial cognition. Here valuable service is rendered by certain logical types of judgment which prior to Scotus were employed only in the area of finite objects. What is meant are *praedicatio in quid* and *in quale* and *praedicatio per se primo* and *per se secundo modo*. Scotus employed them also to clarify the relation

---

21 Cf. *Quodl.* (ed. Viv. XXV, 211a); *Ord.* I (ed. Vat. III, 25-27); Anselm, *Monologion*, c. 15 (PL 158, 163); cf. W. Hoeres, *Der Wille als reine Vollkommenheit nach Duns Scotus* (München: 1962), 26 sqq.

of being to other transcendental structures. Much more will be said on this in the following sections.

For the moment we must occupy ourselves a little more with the term *adaequatio*. From a number of texts we can take various elements which clarify the meaning of *adaequatio*. Thus we read in *Ord.* I, d. 3, p. 1, q. 2, n. 70 that *adaequatio* has to do with an isolating abstraction *(praecisio)* and with what is first *(primum)* insofar as it is universal *(universale)*. The isolating abstraction is an intellectual act which denotes the positive side of abstracting, i.e., of throwing something into relief, and which prepares conceptual cognition. Through *praecisio* a special element is singled out from the structural content of an object in order to bring it within the grasp of our cognition. Abstraction is not only a process of disregarding but also one of singling out.

Hence we already stand in the presence of something else, of something that has content and is first inasmuch as it is a *commune* or *universale*. The universal admits of gradations; hence we can speak of a first, second, third universal. The first and basic universal is being. Being is obtained through analysis and precision and introduces the conceptual cognition of objects *(cognitio distincta)*.

Accordingly, the basis of our intellectual cognition is to be laid bare in the *ordo adaequationis*. But what then is the meaning of adequation if we are here concerned with the first universal which is common to all things? Adequation may not be taken here in an original quantitative sense as we find it in the corporeal-quantitative area; otherwise our intellectual cognition would be definitely fixed and could not transcend the corporeal-quantitative area. Adequation is here taken in a much wider sense and denotes the relation or proportion which unites the corporeal and the incorporeal with one another. Where, however, proportion obtains among beings, there is no need of having an equality or similarity in the *modus essendi*. In this case the broad connecting proportion suffices. The many cases of proportion are based, so to say, on the dissimilarity of the interrelated members.

That a relation can obtain despite the dissimilarity of the interrelated members is of importance for our present intellection. There need be no similarity in the *modus essendi* between our intellectual faculty which is spiritual and active, and the object of cognition. The relation of proportionality is altogether sufficient. With its aid we can cognize totally different structures, such as matter and form, part and whole, cause and effect, etc. All these structures have, despite their diversity, a relation to one another and are therefore cognizable by us. The ultimate basis of proportionality rests on being, and so it is precisely being that can serve as the adequate foundation of our intellection.

As a final word one may add that epistemological adequation of beings does not come to a halt at the point of conceptual cognition *(concipere)*, as in the *ordo originis*, but goes on to formulate cognition in statements *(praedicationes)* and sentences *(propositiones)*. The *adaequatio secundum praedicationem* differs from another *secundum virtutem*. Adequation with reference to a statement denotes that in some manner, whether essentially or qualitatively, we predicate being of all concrete structures of both the finite and the infinite order. The other adequation with reference to power *(virtus)* occurs only with God and his cognition. God has for adequate object his own essence, which he intuits; everything else he cognizes virtually in his essence.[22] Since various solutions were offered in the thirteenth century concerning the adequate foundation of our human intellection, we shall have to treat of them first. They will also clarify the position of Duns Scotus, who dealt with them very thoroughly.

b. Other Conceptions of the *Ordo adaequationis*

Among the doctrines separating Aristotelianism and Augustinianism in the thirteenth century belongs the epistemological-metaphysical question: on what basis does our human cognition rest? Aristotelians offer a solution which takes into account the material-spiritual constitution of human nature; Augustinians insert God in some way; others finally attempt a solution that is neither purely earthbound nor purely transcendental but something intermediate between the two.

The basic thesis of Aristotelianism states that the first object of our intellect is the essence of material things, since a cognitional faculty must assimilate itself to its object. Thomas Aquinas expresses it this way: our intellect, according to its being, is united with matter, but this is not so with regard to its activity, since it

---

[22] *Ord. I* (ed. Vat. III, 49): De tertia primitate habetur I Posteriorum in definitione 'universalis,' quia 'primo' ibi dicit praecisionem sive adaequationem; *Ord. I* (ed. Vat. III, 44): Non considerando illud a quo abstrahit; *Ord. II* (ed. Viv. XII, 517): Proportionalitas non semper includit similitudinem, sed multoties dissimilitudinem; *De An.* (ed. Viv. III, 612a): Adaequatio secundum praedicationem . . . adaequatio secundum virtutem. . .

does not employ the material or corporeal organs. Following the Neoplatonizing Avicenna, Thomas presents a still deeper and more comprehensive thesis when he declares being to be the *quasi notissimum* of our intellect and reduces all our concepts to it. In declaring this Thomas surely anticipates some of the points that are basic in the philosophy of Scotus, but as to how this thesis of being agrees with the other concerning the *quidditas* or *natura in materia existens,* neither Thomas nor his later interpreters achieved a uniform solution. This is of lesser importance to us here; what is of more importance is to know what reasons Scotus opposes to the Aristotelian conception.[23]

The objections are both philosophical and theological in nature. The weightiest philosophical reason may be summed up as saying that our intellect, being a spiritual and active faculty, has a natural desire for supersensible and truly metaphysical objects. But the way to these things is only open when being, which transcends the sensible and material, and unites the sensible world with that of the supersensible, is the foundation of our intellection. If metaphysics is to be really a *scientia transcendens* distinct from physics, the intellect must be a *potentia transcendens* and have being for its fundamental object or *objectum primum adaequatum*. It is being that transcends our sense experience and extends the horizon of our cognition from the finite to the infinite.[24]

Our intellect can make being as the first basis of our intellection clear to itself by reducing the possible content of our cognition to its foundation by means of a metaphysical abstraction or analysis. Scotus supplements this first thesis with a second. Summing up this thesis, he concedes that the situation is indeed quite different in our present existence. Here it is the essence of sense objects to which our intellect is adapted and by which it is determined. Hence we cognize only what is in some way contained in this prime determining object. The doctrine of our present condition and its consequences for cognition therefore does not have its basis in the ancient hylomorphism of body and spiritual soul; its root does not lie in the constitution of man's essence but in a concrete fact known

---

[23] St. Thomas Aquinas, *S. th.* I, q. 84, a. 7, c; *S. th.* I, q. 85, a. 1 c; *De ver.* q. 1, a. 1: Ens . . . quasi notissimum; cf. Scotus, *Ord.* I (ed. Vat. III, 69, 70); *Prim. lect.* (ed. Vat. XVI, 259 sq.); cf. P. Descoqs, *Praelectiones theologiae naturalis,* II (Paris: 1935), 144-146; H. Meyer, *Thomas v. Aquin, sein System und seine geistesgeschichtliche Stellung* (Paderborn: 1964), VIII, 412 sqq.

[24] Scotus, *Ord.* IV (ed. Viv. XX, 38a): Intellectio . . . cognitio transcendens omne genus sensationis; cf. E. Gilson, *Jean Duns Scot* (Paris: 1952), 11-115.

only to the man of faith: in a decision of God's will and in the lapse of our first parents. These are matters of faith, of which philosophy as such knows nothing. For us God's free will in its concrete decisions is philosophically unsearchable; accordingly, only the believing Christian can know original sin and its consequences. The object that determines our intellect is therefore *de facto* but not *de jure* the essence of the sensible thing. With the help of analysis and abstraction we can then transcend the *objectum motivum* and show the *ens commune* as the horizon of our intellection.

From the dialogue with the Aristotelians we learn that Scotus primarily wanted to show what our intellect as a spiritual faculty *(ex natura potentiae)* could do. The determining object in the area of sense has therefore no constitutive character, but goes back to a concrete historical fact, a fact known only to the believing Christian. For the Aristotelians, however, the *objectum movens* in the area of sense and materiality stands in the foreground of interest and determines the point of departure and the basis of our intellection. The Christian motif of our present status was, of course, also known to Thomas Aquinas. In the *Summa Theologiae* he at times speaks of the *status praesentis viae* and adds further that the intellect, after ending its conversion to corporeal being *(cessante conversione ad corpus),* turns to higher objects *(ad superiora convertitur).*[25]

While the Aristotelians laid the general cognitional foundation of our intellect too deep, others of the Augustinian school fell into the other extreme and demanded too much of the first adequate object of our intellection. Their thesis may be expressed in the words of Scotus: "Another opinion maintains that God is the first object of our intellection." This conception harks back to Augustine and certain Platonizing Aristotelian texts and was represented at the end of the thirteenth century especially by Henry of Ghent. The reasons advanced for it may be fittingly summed up as follows: In every genus—as a limited area—there is a first which is at once the cause of being and the ground of cognition, inasmuch as

[25] *Ord.* I (ed. Vat. III, 49, 82): Resolutio; *Ord.* I (ed. Vat. III, 87): Abstractio . . .; *Ord.* I (ed. Vat. III, 113): Pro statu isto . . . quiditas rei sensibilis; *Ord.* I (ed. Vat. III, 114): Sive ex mera voluntate Dei sive ex justitia puniente; *Ord.* I (ed. Vat. III, 117): Facilis abstractio; St. Thomas Aquinas, *S. th.* I, q. 87, a. 1 c: Secundum statum praesentis vitae; *S. th.* I, q. 89, a. 1 ad 3: Ad superiora convertitur; cf. R. L. de Munain, "La conoscibilidad de Dios en Escoto," in *Verdad y Vida,* 20 (1962), 613.

it pertains to this area. This thought, which is taken from the metaphysics of Aristotle, is now transferred to God, who is of all beings the first and the most perfect being. In other words, because God is the most perfect of all cognizable beings he is also the ground of cognition (*ratio cognoscendi*) of all created being. Hence this would mean that for our intellection God is the first adequate object of the intellect.

Scotus takes issue with both the maximum thesis of the Augustinians and with the minimal thesis of the Aristotelians. Over against the Augustinians he insists that the first natural object of a faculty must have a natural ordination to that faculty. Now such a natural ordination is not given between God and our human intellection. God does not move our intellect before all other objects so as to become the first determining cause of our cognition. One could, at most, admit that God, with respect to the most common attribute, is the first object of our cognition. This would then agree with the other thesis that God is cognized *in rationibus generalibus*. Being takes the first place among these *rationes generales*. But then the particular being of God is no longer the first object of our intellection, but rather that common being which lets all particular beings appear only later.

Add to this that God does not have the fundamental and common likeness *(adaequatio)* for our intellection; for knowledge of God is not a necessary requisite for knowledge of other objects. Such a *primitas adaequationis* rather refers to God alone and means that God intuits himself first, and actively cognizes in his essence all that is virtually contained in it *(adaequatio virtualitatis)*. But it does not follow from this at all that God is also the first adequate object for our intellect. The objects of our world determine our intellect by their own power, because they essentially have being in themselves. For this reason there is an essential difference between our cognition and that of God. For the divine intellect it is the divine essence that is the first object of intellection; for our intellect it is being which bridges the span to all things essentially cognizable.[26]

Scotus also rejects a third thesis, which lies between Aristotle and

---

[26] *Ord.* I (ed. Vat. III, 78): Deum esse primum objectum intellectus . . . Aristotle, *Metaph.* II, 1 (993b 24-31); *Ord.* I (ed. Vat. III, 38 sq.): Deus non cognoscitur naturaliter a viatore in particulari. . . . Sub ratione generalis attributi; *Ord.* I (ed. Vat. I, 102): Theologia in se . . .; *Ord.* I (ed. Vat. I, 135 sqq.): Theologia divina . . . theologia nostra. . .

Augustine, and which maintains that substance is the first adequate object of our intellect, because substance is the decisive ontological principle for all things in this world. Over against this he holds that this has no influence on our cognition, even if the accidents derive their being from the substance. The accidents as manifestations of things have a determining power of their own on our intellect because they, too, essentially have being in themselves. Being, it must be noted, is not only what is inmost in things, it also manifests itself in their external appearances, i.e., in their accidents. It is in these accidents that being is first apprehended by our intellect and it is through them we are led to the knowledge of their inner supporting ground—substance. Here, too, it again becomes apparent that there is no simple parallel between the order of our cognition and the order of being.

When we place the Scotistic solution of the first adequate object of our intellect in its historical-ideological context, we may say that its background is Platonic-Augustinian, in a broad sense, since the doctrine of being as the first adequate object of our intellect derives from Avicenna, whose metaphysics is of a Neo-Platonic character. The foreground is, to be sure, Aristotelian through the factual completion of the *objectum movens,* which is the essence of the material thing. Between the Aristotelian foreground and the Platonic background there is still an Augustinian connecting link taken from Christian revelation. The human intellect is now subject to the consequences of a free disposition on the part of God— a punishment for the original guilt of our first parents—and is therefore dependent in its cognition on the determination it receives from material things. All in all, the Scotistic doctrine attempts a synthesis of Platonic Augustinianism with Aristotelianism and in it the Platonic-Augustinian motifs hold a certain priority over the Aristotelian. The Platonic-Augustinian motifs form the background and the basis for the foreground and the superstructure which bears an Aristotelian character.[27]

c. *Ordo adaequationis* and Judgment

The *ordo adaequationis* seeks to disclose the foundation or the first adequate object of our intellection, which is being. The cognition that apprehends and determines being is conception. In the

[27] *Ord.* I (ed. Vat. III, 80); *Lect.* I (ed. Vat. XVI, 260 sq.); cf. T. Barth, "Scotus und die ontologische Grundlage unserer Verstandeserkenntnis," in *Franz. Stud.* 33 (1951), 348-84, spec. 356.

process of conception we pass through several stages, which begin with simple apprehension *(simplex intelligentia)* and develop through analysis and division into a definition. Through analysis we attain to altogether simple and irreducible concepts. The final irreducible concept in the order of essence is being as a pure *quid* and without any differentiation.

Being is not only conceivable but also suitable for a judgment, especially as an essential predicability. The essential predicability of being has a wide scope. It extends from the *ens increatum* to the ten categories and their essential parts. In another passage we read of still greater differentiation: all genera, species, individuals, essential parts (matter and form) and the *ens increatum* are essentially included in being. But the essential predicability of being has its limitations. It ends where the altogether simple differences and the properties of being are concerned; they are indeed intimately and inseparably related to being, but are nevertheless distinct from it, since although they determine being they are not essential being themselves.[28]

This stems from the absolute simplicity of being as well as from that of the simple differences and the properties of being. In all three cases we have an absolutely simple content before us: either the pure undifferentiated *quid* of being or something ultimate of the differentiating *quale* of the simple differences and the properties of being. Here the *quid* retains a certain priority over the *quale*, since it is the presupposition or the subject for the determining *quale*. This leads to a twofold priority of being, namely, to *primitas communitatis* and *primitas virtualitatis*. Both priorities belong to the much debated characteristics of Scotistic metaphysics and are established by means of various kinds of judgments. Thus Scotus continues in the *ordo adaequationis praedicationis* what he began in the *ordo originis* concerning things conceptually intelligible.[29]

---

[28] *Ord.* I (ed. Vat. III, 84): Ens increatum . . . decem genera . . . partes essentiales; *Ord.* I (ed. Vat. III, 85): Omnia genera et species et individua, et omnes partes essentiales generum, et ens increatum includunt ens quiditative; *Ord.* I (ed. Vat. III, 81-85): De differentiis ultimis. . . . De passionibus entis.

[29] *Ord.* I (ed. Vat. III, 54 sq.): Ens . . . habet conceptum simpliciter simplicem; *Ord.* I (ed. Vat. III, 82): Resolutio ad conceptum determinabilem et determinantem, ita quod resolutio stet ad conceptus simpliciter simplices; *Lect.* I (ed. Vat. XVI, 262); *Ord.* I (ed. Vat. III, 91): Quilibet talis conceptus (differentiarum et passionum) est simpliciter simplex; cf. A. B. Wolter, *The Transcendentals*, p. 101.

The following judgments and conceptual antitheses play an important part here: to be employed in the first place is *dici in quid* and *dici in quale,* which derives from Porphyry. Closely connected with it is the conceptual antithesis of the determinable and the determining concept. Finally we once again come upon the denomination which derives from Aristotle and was developed by Boethius. With the equipment of these logical species of concepts and judgments Scotus seeks to determine the relation of being to the simple differences.[30]

Add to this the Aristotelian difference between *subjectum* and *passio* and the predication applied to this relation—the *praedicatio per se primo* and *per se secundo.* With these logical aids the relation of being to its properties is clarified. Moreover, the *dici in quid* and *quale* plays a part.[31] In the following sections we shall deal with the very subtle problem of these fundamental metaphysical structures.

d. Relation of Being to the Differences and Properties of Being

We turn to the first problem and consider in the predicative order of adequation the relation of being to the differences of being. According to content the predications fall under two important heads—*praedicationes in quid* and *praedicationes in quale.* It is an old division, which was already developed by Porphyry in his *Introduction to the Categories* in the domain of the five finite predicables. Scotus takes them over from him and explains them in his commentary on the *Universalia Porphyrii.*

By *praedicari in quid* we understand that either the entire essence, i.e., the species, or at least the determinable part of essence, i.e., the genus, is predicated of something. And we speak of *praedicari in quale* when the predicate signifies a determination or qualification of the essence. The qualification is either essential, and then it signifies the specific difference or the *quale quid;* or it is not essential, and then it signifies the properties and accidents or the *quale accidentale.*

---

[30] Aristotle, *Categ.* I (1a 12-15); Boethius, *In Categ. Aristotelis* I (PL 64, 167-68); Scotus, *Un. Porph.* (ed. Viv. I, 155b; 322ab); *Ord.* I (ed. Vat. III, 81-83); *Collationes* (ed. Harris 373); A. B. Wolter, *The Transcendentals,* pp. 81, 96.

[31] Aristotle, *An. Post.* I, 4 (73a 37- b 5); *Metaph.* IV, 2 (1004b 10-18), VII, 5 (1031a 2-14); Scotus, *Ord.* I (ed. Vat. III, 83-85); cf. T. Barth, *De fundamento univocationis apud J. Duns Scotum* (Romae: 1939), 53 sqq. P. C. Vier, *Evidence and Its Function According to J. Duns Scotus* (St. Bonaventure, N. Y.: 1952), 40-85.

The *praedicari in quid* and *in quale* is still further supplemented and determined by an important addition. The *praedicari in quid* is a predication of the essence *per modum subsistentis;* in *praedicari in quale* the predication is an essential or non-essential qualification *per modum denominantis.* This leads us to the grammar and linguistics of that day. What is predicated *per modum subsistentis* is a substantive or a noun. Thus substance, coloration, spirit, and life are substantives, and when they occur as predicates in a proposition they form essential predications. They denote either the whole (specific) essence or a still determinable part of it.

Denominative words, on the other hand, are always derived from a substantive, as grammarian from grammar and philosopher from philosophy. So too all adjectives are derived words and qualify the subjects of which they are predicated. Thus substantial, accidental, red, colored, spiritual, and the like are always predicated *in quale.*[82]

In his later works, especially in his commentary on the *Sentences,* Scotus transfers the *praedicatio in quid* and *in quale* from the order of the five predicables to the order of the transcendentals; in other words, he goes beyond the finite ways of predication, the predicables, and opens the way to the infinite. Accordingly, being *(ens)* and reality *(res, realitas)* are predicated *in quid* and *per modum subjecti,* while the differences of being or modes, e.g., such as finite and infinite, potential and actual, necessary and contingent, substantial and accidental form qualifying or denominative predications.

Being is the first common but determinable element of our conceptual cognition. As such it is the first and fundamental structure of thing and concept and denotes the determinable what *(quid determinabile)* or the basis *(ratio subjecti)* without which no predication would be possible at all. Here, then, *quid* as *ratio subjecti* at once carries over to the essential realm of the determinable subject and so makes every further predication possible. Being is therefore for Scotus always viewed in connection with concrete being, in which it, as *ratio subjecti,* lays the foundation for all predicability. Hence being is for Scotus never separated from concrete being; nor is it something like the Platonic idea which has its essence in itself and can exist without earthly beings. Despite its absolute simplicity

---

[82] Boethius, *In Categ. Arist.* I (PL 64, 167-68); Scotus, *Un. Porph.* (ed. Viv. I, 155b, 332ab); *R.P.I.* (ed. Viv. XXII, 170b-71a); *Ord. I* (ed. Vat. IV, 195); cf. A. B. Wolter, *The Transcendentals,* p. 80.

and primal commonness, being has an inner reference to the concrete being of real things.[33]

Scotus takes being in the concrete sense as a noun, indeed, as a fundamental noun: as *ratio subjecti*. In this concrete sense being is essentially *(in quid)* predicated of finite concrete being and of the infinite being of God. But being does not mean the entire essence or the entire being, but only the first determinable and common element which is found in all concrete things and concepts, and which as *ratio subjecti* makes a judicial cognition possible. Being which, on the one hand, is altogether simple, common, and determinable, is on the other hand not separate from concrete being and is therefore the *ratio subjecti*. This cannot be stated so much in a positive way as in a negative way, since we here stand on the confines of possible predications. To be sure, being as the *ratio subjecti* is not yet the substance, but something which is essentially found in the accidents as well as in the substance, which leads us from the knowledge-determining accidents to the substance. It is for these reasons that Scotus will not have substance as the first adequate object of our intellect. It is rather being that is the basis of our intellection. Along the same line is also the important continuation of this thought that being is the *primum transcendens* and as such the presupposition for all further differentiation, to which also the disjunctive antithesis of accidentality and substantiality belongs. Hence one may safely say that the Scotistic being is the foundation of every concrete and possible predication; wherefore it is predicated *in quid* and as *ratio subjecti*. The following differentiations are also altogether simple and confer upon quidditative being something new, which scholastics call the *quale determinans*. The simple differentiations are broken down into primary differences, such as *infinitum* and *finitum* and *necessarium* and *contingens*, intermediary differences (some specific differences),

---

[33] *Ord.* I (ed. Vat. IV, 195): Ratio entis . . . ratio subjecti; *Ord.* I (ed. III, 107); Ens . . . primum subjectum metaphysicae; *Ord.* I (ed. Vat. IV, 206 sq.): Necessarium vel possibile, actus vel potentia, et huiusmodi . . . Franciscus de Marchia O.F.M. (s. XIV) *Sent.* I, d. 8, q. 1, a. 1; Cod. Vat. lat. 1096, f. 46va, 47 rb: Ens contrahibile est per rationes transcendentes extra rationem suam existentes. . . Unde hic sunt tres propositiones; prima: differentiae entis non sunt quiditative ens, et illa est vera; secunda: differentiae sunt non quiditative ens, et illa est simpliciter vera sicut prima; et tertia: differentiae entis sunt quiditative non ens et illa est duplex; nam unus sensus est: differentiae entis quiditative non ens, i.e. non quiditative aliquid, quod non est quiditative ens, et ille sensus est verus. Alius sensus: sunt quiditative non ens, i.e. quiditative negatio entis, et ille sensus est falsus.

and ultimate differences (of the individual kind). The qualitative differences therefore complement the quidditative common being and confer upon the concrete being its synthetic character.[34]

If we now ask further whence they derive this function, and why they pertain to being at all, a preliminary answer is given by the *denominatio*. The simple differences are derived being and as such have the function to determine common being and render it concrete. Of course, this leaves much still open and unsaid. We shall have to revert to this question when we deal with the *primitas communitatis* and the *primitas virtualitatis*.

We are now concerned with a further important relationship—the one that obtains between being and its properties or attributes. To these properties belong the one, the true, and the good. The logical aid is again judgment in two notable manifestations, namely, in the *praedicatio per se primo modo* and *per se secundo modo*. The distinction goes back to Aristotle and was employed by scholastics to give a further determination to the relation of subject and predicate.

According to scholastic usage the first mode of a *praedicatio per se* is had when the predicate constitutes a part of the essential structure of the subject. It is then that the subject contains the predicate essentially and necessarily. Hence the predicate can by analysis be derived from the subject and adds really nothing new to the subject, since it is always already contained in it.

The case is different with the second mode of a *praedicatio per se*. Here the predicate is an attribute or a property which adds something to the subject, and is therefore not already contained in it. Thus the sum of the angles of all Euclidian triangles is 180 degrees, but not all Euclidian triangles are right triangles. Some of them are acute triangles, some obtuse. Or, all human beings are endowed with rationality; but not all human beings are masculine; some are feminine. On the other hand, attributes or properties are always intrinsically ordained to a subject, since they cannot be without it. The predicate is necessarily predicated of a subject, without the latter containing the former essentially, since the

---

[34] *Ord.* I (ed. Vat. III, 82): Conceptus tantum determinabilis ... conceptus entis; *Ord.* I (ed. Vat. III, 80): Non ... primum objectum intellectus nostri substantia; *Ord.* I (ed. Vat. IV, 207): Cum primo transcendente, scilicet ente; *Quodl.* (ed. Viv. XXV, 140b-41a); *Collat.* (ed. Harris 373): Differentiae, simplices et primae et ultimae, dicunt formaliter quale... *Ord.* II (ed. Viv. XII, 134b): Aliqua (differentia specifica) habet conceptum simpliciter simplicem, quae scilicet sumitur ab ultima abstractione formae.

predicate is an addition to the subject. The subject contains the predicate not essentially but only virtually. Attributive predicates and their subjects are essentially related; nevertheless such predicates cannot be analytically derived from the subject, since they add something new to it.

A further significant point to be noted: although the attributes or properties determine a subject and add something to it, they have nevertheless an intrinsic relation to the subject. Attributes and properties cannot be without the subject. Hence the subject has a natural priority over all modifying and qualifying attributes or properties. The *quid* of the *ratio subjecti* has a priority over the *quale* of the attributes or properties. The relation of subject and synthetic properties (also called *passiones propriae*) which can be expressed by means of the *praedicatio per se secundo modo* is applied by Scotus to being and its immediate consequences. Being and unity, truth, and goodness stand in a necessary but synthetic relation to one another. For one thing, being and unity, truth, and goodness belong inseparably together. Where you find the one, you also find the other. More than this, unity, truth, and goodness are necessarily related to being. Being is their foundation or the subject without which they cannot be.[35]

On the other hand, unity, truth, and goodness cannot be simply derived from being. For being is absolutely simple and utterly irreducible. Hence they add something to being which being does not yet possess of itself. Being is for the concrete the real core or the fundamental subject. Unity gives to being its undividedness and distinctness from every other thing; truth gives it the capability to manifest itself to others; and goodness gives it its intrinsic perfection. Unity is of particular importance since it unfolds being in its many gradations. These begin with the *unum proportionale* or *analogum,* progress to the *unum univocum,* and differentiate themselves through the genera and species to reach the individual.

Thus being and unity, truth, and goodness belong together and yet are not identical. There is a definite order in this relationship, since the priority belongs to being as *ratio subjecti* to which unity, truth, and goodness are referred. Although being is formally distinct from the properties of unity, truth, and goodness, it never-

[35] Aristotle, *An. Post.* I, 4 (73a 37- b 5); *Metaph.* IV, 2 (1004b 10-17); VII, 5 (1031a 2-14); Scotus, *Ord.* I (ed. Vat. III, 83-85, 104-12); *Lect.* I (ed. Vat. XVI, 262-63, 277-81).

theless contains them virtually. Over against unity, truth, and goodness being holds the *primitas virtualitatis,* which is a likeness of the supreme orderer, God, who contains in himself all possible properties virtually and in an eminent degree.[36]

When we turn from here to modern philosophy, a comparison with Kant is indicated. One may ask whether in the *praedicationes per se secundo modo* we are not dealing with a synthesis a priori, which is still deeper and more primordial than that of Kant. Kant's synthesis a priori goes back to the activity of a superpersonal but still intramundane subject; this subject, being regulative, lays the foundation for mathematical and scientific cognition and so expands human knowledge.

Scotus' synthesis a priori goes back still further, inasmuch as it transcends the difference between human subject and human object and leaves all finiteness and limitation behind. Scotus finds this transcendental-ontological domain in every intellectual act, whether it be directed reflexively upon one's own thinking or directly upon the objective things of the world about us. This domain discloses itself as a community of being, unity, truth, and goodness. Being, unity, truth, and goodness not only stand in an analytical relation to one another, i.e., they are not only mentally distinct, but they also stand in a synthetic relation to one another, since they are *formaliter a parte rei* distinct from one another. They have different transcendental functions which cannot be derived from one another, even if they are never separated from one another.

To establish this synthesis a priori Scotus employs purely logical means, which absolutely transcend all sense experience. Preparation for this comes from resolution and division, which clarify the ultimate simple conceptual structures and so reveal the basic structures of the concrete things. Judgment can then build on it and clarify, with the help of the *praedicatio per se secundo modo,* the necessary but synthetic relation between being and its properties and differences. Behind this logically established and ontologically meaningful synthesis a priori there lies a metaphysical-theological principle

[36] *Ord.* IV (ed. Viv. XVI, 532a): Unum est indivisum in se, et ab alio divisum; *Metaph.* VII (ed. Viv. VII, 337ab): (Ratio) sui manifestativa; *R.P.* II (ed. Viv. XXIII, 170ab): (Bonum) perfectione essentiali intrinseca; *Ord.* I (ed. Vat. III, 85): Omnes passiones entis includuntur in ente et in suis inferioribus virtualiter; *Ord.* III (ed. Viv. XIV, 44a): Infinitum . . . habet in se quodcumque . . . virtualiter et eminenter. *Metaph.* V (ed. Viv. VII, 207 sqq.): Divisio unius in unum genere, specie, numero, et proportione.

of unity—God. God is the ultimate reason for the synthesis of being, unity, truth, and goodness and for the relation of identity and difference. His infinite being transcends not only all finite being, but is also the reason why such finite being can be at all. In his infinity is laid up all finite perfection *virtualiter et eminenter*.[36a]

e. The Double Priority of Being

The *ordo adaequationis* has disclosed being as the basis of our intellection. Thus, on the one hand, the relation of being and the concrete structures of being *(prima intelligibilia)* could be determined; on the other hand, it becomes apparent in what relation being stands to the simple differences and properties of being *(per se intelligibilia)*. The result is in both cases a different one and led Scotus to his well-known but highly controversial "double priority of being."

The concrete essential structures, i.e., all genera, species, individuals, the essential parts of the genera (matter and form) and the uncreated being of God, essentially contain being, since they are not absolutely simple essential structures, but have a concrete or contracted being. The altogether simple structures of the differences and properties of being do not essentially contain being, since they are altogether simple and determine or qualify being and its concretions. Nevertheless, if being here has a priority, its priority is different from the one over against the concrete essential structures. The priority here is not the *primitas communitatis* but the *primitas virtualitatis*.

The twofold priority is the result achieved with the help of analysis, synthesis, and definite forms of judgment. With the help of a more ascending or retrogressive analysis our intellect comes upon being and the simple differences and properties of being. The more deductive and synthetic division comprises the analysis and arrives at definitive concepts which contain the constitutive elements of the structures. The relation of being and its simple differences and properties is made still clearer through some forms of judgment. One could now surmise that Scotus meant this result

[36a] I. Kant, *Kritik der reinen Vernunft* B 10-25, 157 sq. Cf. J. B. Lotz in: *Kant und die Scholastik heute* (Pullach bei München, 1955), 75 sq.; Scotus, *Ord.* IV (ed. Viv. XX, 38a): Intellectio . . . cognitio transcendens totum genus sensationis; *Ord.* I (ed. Vat. II, 242): Bonum imperfectum reducitur ad . . . summum ens et ad summum bonum, quae includunt virtualiter illam perfectionem; *Quodl.* (ed. Viv. XXV, 212a); cf. T. Barth, "Scotus und die ontologische Grundlage unserer Verstandeserkenntnis," in *Franz. Studien*, 33 (1951), 380.

as something purely logical. This would be a grave misconception. Although he lets ultimate, utterly simple structures become visible, he does not regard them as purely logical conceptions but as ultimate metaphysical or—in modern language—as transcendental-ontological structures. More will be said on this head in the subsequent section. For the time being it may suffice to say that being has a priority over all other concrete structures which essentially contain being in themselves. This priority finds its expression in the common primacy of essential being in which all beings are grounded. Equivalent to it is the other formulation: being is the *ratio subjecti* for the *entia concreta*. The common primacy of essential being has a real character and constructs the reality in the several domains of the real world. Scotus goes still further in his *Quodlibet* and exposes the *communissimum*, which as a contradiction-free unity is basic for the *ens reale* as well as for the *ens rationis*.[37]

More must be said about the *primitas virtualitatis*. Virtuality is originally an ontological concept which is to determine the relation of cause and effect. That is to say, the active cause contains its effects virtually. Thus God contains in himself all creatures as ideas virtually and eminently, and through a creative act he then confers on them real being. So, too, substance virtually contains in itself all its accidents.[38]

The idea of containing something virtually is next taken into the order of cognition and thought. Thus the premises of a syllogism contain the conclusion virtually. Of course, when the known content is very simple, it contains a false proposition neither formally nor virtually nor proximately; it is then apprehended either totally or not at all. A science is said to contain its first object virtually. Every scientific *habitus* has a first object in which all truths are germinally or virtually contained. This is so perfectly only in the theology of God *(theologia in se)* which holds

---

[37] *Ord.* I (ed. Vat. III, 85): In ipso (ente) concurrit duplex primitas, scilicet communitatis et virtualitatis; *Ord.* I (ed. Vat. III, 85): Prima intelligibilia; *Lect.* I (ed. Vat. XVI, 263): De differentiis ultimis . . . de suis passionibus, quae . . . sunt per se intelligibilia; *Ord.* I (ed. Vat. III, 93): Primitas communitatis in 'quid' ad omnes conceptus non-simpliciter simplices, et primitas virtualitatis—in se vel in suis inferioribus—ad omnes conceptus simpliciter simplices; *Quodl.* (ed. Viv. XXV, 113b-14a).

[38] *Ord.* I (ed. Vat. III, 332): Continere virtualiter competit causae activae; *Ord.* III (ed. Viv. XIV, 44a): Virtualiter et eminenter; *Ord.* I (ed. Vat. IV, 207 sq.): Substantia . . . continet virtualiter omnia accidentia.

all theological truths virtually. We shall later revert to this thought. For the time being we can state that virtual inclusion supplements formal or essential inclusion. Through virtual inclusion different structural elements are so combined with one another that the difference still remains, but one of them has the priority without which the other elements could not be.[39]

Scotus also speaks of a virtual priority of being when he treats of being and its relation to properties *(passiones simplices)* and differences, especially the ultimate differences. Concerning the relation of being and its properties, to which unity, truth, and goodness belong, the statement is at first merely negative—that being is not essentially predicated of its properties. Being as pure "what" *(quid)* is simply different from the *quale* of the properties. Nevertheless they cannot be separated from one another, since both pertain to the structure of beings. How then are we to understand the positive relation of each to the other? The positive relation means that the properties of being are virtually included in being itself and in its inferiors. This formulation is very discreet and shows how Scotus always views being in relation to its concretions *(inferiora)* and not as self-sufficient after the manner of a Platonic idea.[40]

In dealing with the other relation of being and its differences, by which Scotus primarily means the ultimate and individual differences, he is still more cautious. Here again his statement is at first merely negative, namely, that being cannot be essentially predicated of its ultimate differences. Being as pure and not yet determined *quid* differs from the ultimate *quale* of the individual differences. The positive supplement says that all ultimate differences are essentially included in some essential structures, i.e., in genera, species, individuals, and essential parts of the genera, and in the uncreated being of God. This actually does not predicate anything positive concerning the relation of essential and ultimate differences. The connection is no longer directly determinable, but remains open and can be apprehended only in the concretions of being. The place

---

[39] *Ord.* Prol. (ed. Vat. I, 96): Propositiones . . . immediatae continent (virtualiter) conclusiones; *Ord.* I (ed. Vat. III, 91): Simpliciter simplex non includit virtualiter, proximo, nec formaliter propositionem falsam; *Ord.* Prol. (ed. Vat. I, 102); *R.P.I.* (ed. Viv. XXII, 500b-501a); cf. A. B. Wolter, *The Transcendentals*, p. 7 sq.

[40] *Ord.* I (ed. Vat. III, 85): Quidquid est primo passio entis, . . . non includit ens quiditative; *Ord.* I (ed. Vat. III, 85): Omnes passiones entis includuntur in ente et in suis inferioribus; *Ord.* I (ed. Vat. III, 41): Ens includit virtualiter verum et bonum in se; cf. *Ord.* I (ed. Vat. III, 105 sq.).

of the abstract consideration of being is taken by another which adheres to the concretion of actual reality. In this sense Scotus comes to a definitive synthesis, which we may represent in this way: being has a priority *(primitas)* of commonness over against all objects which are primarily cognizable by the intellect. This comprises the essential concepts of the genera, species, individuals, all essential parts of these things (namely, matter and form) and the uncreated being of God. Besides, being has also the priority *(primitas)* of virtuality. This priority has to do with all cognizable structures which are included in the things just referred to. To these belong the qualitative concepts of the ultimate differences and the properties of being, unity, truth, and goodness.[41]

Through this synthesis the relation of being, ultimate differences, and properties of being is drawn closer together, inasmuch as being has the *primitas virtualitatis* with reference to both. But here, being is not taken in its abstract quiddity, but rather as we find it in the concrete order of reality. It belongs also to the concrete things of the order of reality that they have an inner unity and that they can manifest themselves and possess an internal essential perfection: they receive their ultimate differentiation through their individuality *(haecceitas)*.

The transition from *ens abstractum* to *ens concretum* might derive from the purely logical handling of being, differences, and properties, all of which are simple structures. To make some progress we must turn to being in its concretions, where we shall see that being, differences, and properties of being belong together and that being has, besides the *primitas communitatis*, still another, namely, the *primitas virtualitatis*.

Behind the twofold priority of being for Scotus, the theistic and Christian philosopher, stands still something else which holds the unity and difference of reality together—God. With this we come to what we have mentioned several times. Behind the abstract

---

[41] *Ord.* I (ed. Vat. III, 81): Ens non . . . dictum in quid de omnibus per se intelligibilibus, quia non de differentiis ultimis, nec de passionibus propriis entis; *Ord.* I (ed. Vat. III, 85): Omnes autem differentiae ultimae includuntur in aliquibus istorum (i.e. in aliquibus generibus, speciebus, et individuis, et in partibus essentialibus generum, et in ente increato) essentialiter; cf. A. B. Wolter, *The Transcendentals*, p. 92. *Ord.* I (ed. Vat. III, 85): Et ita patet, quod ens habet primitatem communitatis ad prima intelligibilia, hoc est ad conceptus generum . . ., et habet primitatem virtualitatis ad omnia intelligibilia in primis intelligibilibus, hoc est ad conceptus qualitativos differentiarum ultimarum et passionum propriarum.

discussion of being, which Scotus intended to be definitely real-metaphysical, stands a theistic metaphysics which in the last analysis holds together severely logicalized being and its complementary structures—differences and properties of being.

For Scotus this means that God is the infinite being and as such has an immediate and perfect cognition not only of himself but also of all that is not himself, namely, of created being. Created being is virtually included in his self-knowledge. God possesses perfect knowledge of his creatures; their being is included in him not formally indeed but nevertheless virtually and eminently. *Infinitum habet in se eminenter et contentive omnem perfectionem limitatam*. Upon the divine cognition of the creatable but still ideal being follows the actual creation of finite being out of nothing. Through creation, which is effected by the divine will, finite being receives its total being, i.e., its real essence and its real existence. To the total created being belong real essence *(Sosein)* and real existence *(Dasein)* in an inseparable unity. Accordingly, through divine creation, the ideal-finite essence does not merely receive a real-finite existence. This would not be a true creation out of nothing. When God creates, he gives to his creatures their entire real and actual being. The ideal being of creatures is only the antecedent plan in his mind. A common likeness of this divine plan and of its general structures of commonness and difference is the analogy of being. This analogy is also maintained by Scotus when he discusses the categorical-intramundane relation of substance and accidents and the metaphysical-supermundane relation of God and the world. As is to be expected, he bases his analogy on a transcendental-ontological univocation, which calls for specific treatment.[42]

5. Transcendentality and Reality of Being

The investigation of being we have made so far must be supple-

[42] *Ord.* Prol. (ed. Vat. I, 211): (Deus) prius naturaliter volitione potest habere omnem notitiam sufficienter virtualiter inclusam in intellectione prima objecti; cf. *Ord.* Prol (I, 102, 135); *Ord.* III (ed. Viv. XIV, 44a): Infinitum non habet in se quodcumque formaliter, sed virtualiter et eminenter; *Ord.* I (ed. Vat. II, 226): Intellectus infinitus cognoscit intelligibile quodcumque perfectissime, quantum est intelligible in se; *Ord.* II (ed. Viv. XI, 180b): Creatio est productio totius creati in esse; cf. P. Minges, J. *Duns Scoti doctrina philosophica et theologica*, II, 107 sqq., 120 sqq., 259 sqq.; *Ord.* I (ed. Vat. III, 101): Accidens . . . attributionem habet essentialem ad substantiam; *Ord.* I (ed. Vat. III, 18): Non tantum in conceptu analogo conceptui creaturae concipitur Deus; *Ord.* I (ed. Vat. III, 24, 26; IV, 191 sq.).

mented in two ways before we can turn our attention to univocation and analogy. The supplementation pertains to the reality and transcendentality of being, which Scotus deals with primarily in *Ord.* I, d. 8, p. 1, q. 3. Here, too, the background is metaphysical-theological. The question concentrates on whether or not it is compatible with the simplicity of God that something of God and the creatural world be found in a common genus? Over against the positive thesis and the negative antithesis our philosopher places his mediating synthesis: it is indeed compatible with the simplicity of God that certain concepts be common to him and creatures; these concepts, of course, do not belong to a common genus, since this is finite and restrictive.[43]

In this connection being is further determined in its character as reality and transcendentality. We shall first treat of being as reality and refer to certain things incidentally touched on in *Ord.* I, d. 3, p. 1, q. 1-3. According to its conceptual structure, being is the basis for all conception *(primus conceptus distinctus)* which makes all definite cognition really possible. Its concept is utterly simple and as such signifies the undetermined "what" *(indeterminatum quid)* and the possible "that" *(potest esse)*. In judgment being is essentially predicated of all concrete things of the essential order and occupies as *ratio subjecti* the first and fundamental position. One could ask whether such a concept of being has anything to do with concrete reality. We shall attempt an answer according to Scotus' mind. In scholasticism logic and metaphysics are intimately related; Scotus even says that both philosophical disciplines cover the same area and differ only in their *modus considerationis*. Consequently, the inquiry into the being of God is an *inquisitio metaphysica*. Metaphysics, with the help and on the foundation of being, is to be basic for the other sciences. Because it has to go beyond the other sciences, it is a transcendent science.

Metaphysics has to do with real being which is attained by the first or direct intention of our intellection. Logic, on the other hand, has to do with the *ens rationis* which is attained in its pure conceptuality through the reflection *(intentio secunda et reflexa)* of

---

[43] Cf. *Ord.* I, d. 8, p. 1, q. 3 (ed. Vat. IV, 169): Tertio quaero utrum cum simplicitate divina stet quod Deus, vel aliquid formaliter dictum de Deo, sit in genere; *Ord.* I (ed. Vat. IV, 198): Teneo opinionem mediam, quod cum simplicitate Dei stat quod aliquis conceptus sit communis sibi et creaturae,- non tamen aliquis conceptus communis ut generis . . .; *Ord.* I (ed. Vat. IV, 205): Quidquid est alicuius generis . . . est limitatum necessario.

our intellection. In other words, the metaphysician considers being as it is essentially found in all beings and removes it from them through abstraction. The logician, on the other hand, takes being in its pure and ultimate conceptuality and employs it in predications of all *entia concreta*. These logical predications, however, rest on a previous *intentio prima* of our metaphysical cognition of being. Hence the concept of being that we predicate of God and the created world is, according to the *Prima Lectura*, a real concept.[44]

The *Ordinatio* brings us an added refinement and supplement inasmuch as it still further determines the real conceptuality of being. There a weighty objection confronts us which goes back to Henry of Ghent. The objection may be formulated as that God has nothing in common with a creature, not even a certain common concept. Scotus answers this objection in several stages. In the first place, he insists that God and creature have at least a common concept, and that in this common concept the original difference does not come to the fore. But the case is different with regard to their reality. Here they differ in their primordial being and therefore agree with one another in no reality. This answer may seem surprising at first sight and arouse the suspicion that Scotus had abandoned the reality of the concept of being between God and the world which he had asserted so clearly in the *Prima Lectura*.

Scotus does not retreat but continues to say that he will later revert to the subject and show how a common concept of God and world can obtain without agreement *in re vel in realitate*. The solution is as follows: being is related to its first differences, i.e., to the differences of finiteness and infiniteness, not as ordinary differences are related to their (finite) genus, but as internal modalities to a still perfectible reality. Being, it is true, can be apprehended without its internal modes, but it is then still something imperfect and altogether undetermined. Consequently, the common concept of being without its first differences or modes is an imperfect con-

---

[44] *Perih.* (ed. Viv. I, 554a): Nihil enim habet essentiam nisi quod aptum natum est existere; *Ord.* IV (ed. Viv. XVII, 7b); *Ord.* I (ed. Vat. IV, 224): . . . Indifferens . . , determinabilis (conceptus); *Ord.* I (ed. Vat. III, 102): 'Ens' vel 'quid' . . .; *Metaph.* VI (ed. Viv. VII, 346a): Modus alius considerationis . . .; *Ord.* I (ed. Vat. III, 26): Inquisitio metaphysica . . .; *Ord.* I (ed. Vat. III, 55): Certificare principia aliarum scientiarum . . .; *Ord.* I (ed. Vat. III, 73): Metaphysica . . . scientia transcendens; *Lect.* I (ed. Vat. XVI, 273): Conceptus entis communis Deo et creaturae sit conceptus realis . . .; cf. T. Barth, *De fundamento univocationis* . . . 41-51, spec. 50.

cept. The concept of being becomes a perfect and proper concept through its modalities. But in this second case the concept of being has relinquished the commonness of which we spoke above. In this sense, then, we must say that God and world agree in no reality. However, in another sense, i.e., in the first sense just mentioned, one can say that the common concept of God and world is a real concept. The reality of this concept rests on being as reality which is apprehended without a definite mode and is therefore an imperfect concept of that concrete thing. Of course, only our intellect can make so fine a distinction; nevertheless it is a distinction which has its foundation in the concrete thing *(distinctio in re)*. We have here the so-called modal distinction, which is not only purely mental, but also applies to something which exists outside our thought: *tamen est pro re extra*.

Consequently, for Scotus common being is that minimum of reality which binds all *concreta realia* together, and can therefore be abstractively considered (not separated) and apprehended by our intellect. In this sense concepts for which being is the ultimate basis are the natural signs of things.

In *Quodlibet* q. 3 this relation of *ens reale* and *ens rationis* is studied more closely. The general sense of being and reality extends to everything that is not contradictory, whether it be an *ens reale* or an *ens rationis*. This comprehensive meaning of being and reality may also be sufficiently derived from the common *modus loquendi* and seems to give the widest extension to that meaning. Hence Scotus also speaks of *res realis* and *res rationis* in order to give expression to this ultimate relational commonness. The ultimate metaphysical basis of this relation is again God, who as infinite being is altogether real and through his thinking produces the ideas or *entia rationis*.[45]

The other fundamental property of being is its transcendentality. We have already come upon this occasionally and must now sum-

[45] *Ord.* I (ed. Vat. IV, 172-225); *Ord.* I (ed. Vat. IV, 172): . . . Nec in aliquo conceptu communi; *Ord.* I (ed. Vat. IV, 190): . . . Non primo diversa in conceptibus . . . tamen primo diversa in realitate . . .; *Ord.* I (ed. Vat. IV, 222): . . . Realitas absque modo . . . conceptus imperfectus illius rei; . . . sub illo modo . . . conceptus perfectus illius rei; *Ord.* I (ed. Vat. IV, 221): Conceptus communis Deo et creaturae realis . . .; *Ord.* I (ed. Vat. IV, 222): Conceptus imperfectus illius rei; *Ord.* I (ed. Vat. IV, 223): Distinctio in re; *Ord.* I (ed. Vat. IV, 225): Tamen est pro re extra; *Ord.* IV (ed. Viv. XVII, 229c): Conceptus . . . signa rerum naturaliter . . .; *Quodl.* (ed. Viv. XXV, 115a); cf. A. B. Wolter, *The Transcendentals*, pp. 24-27; M. J. Grajewski, *The Formal Distinction of Duns Scotus* (Washington, 1944), pp. 39-66.

marize the matter already at hand and utilize it systematically with special regard to being. Metaphysics is a science that transcends the special sciences, such as physics, mathematics, and geometry. All these special sciences have a particular being for their object, but metaphysics treats of being as such and seeks to disclose its general structures and principles. Hence metaphysics is also called *scientia circa transcendentia,* a formulation which is very apposite and, as far as we know, non-existent before Scotus. The intellect as a cognitional faculty must perform transcending acts that go beyond the whole domain of sense experience. These acts attain their completion when, with the help of being and its modalities, they seek the origin of finite being and, transcending the finite, turn to the infinite. Scotus occupies himself extensively with this final transcendence when he deals with the proofs for the existence of God and with the ways we employ to know God. The means that permits and makes this transcendence possible is being. To being, therefore, belongs a priority over all other transcendental structures. Being is the *primum transcendens.*

We can now say what meaning Scotus attached to the term *transcendens.* Transcendent or transcendental is used by Scotus primarily in connection with being and only secondarily in connection with our cognition, which can advert to being and apprehend its transcendentality. Inasmuch as being transcends the particular entities of our world, it has no limitation and stands outside every finite genus *(extra omne genus).* Thus the horizon of being lies open and unlimited. Being is indifferent to finiteness and infiniteness. Likewise, what follows immediately and inseparably from being has a transcendental character. Unity, truth, and goodness appear everywhere together with being, even if they are, according to Scotus, formally distinct from being.

In like manner, all simple perfections which belong to God and to all spiritual beings are transcendental, e.g., memory, intellect, and free will. Some simple perfections transcend all finiteness radically and belong only to God. These, too, e.g., divine omniscience and omnipotence, are therefore to be classed with the transcendentals. Finally, Scotus also recognizes the *transcendentia disjuncta,* which present themselves as opposites and as such render all being concrete. To these opposites belong the modalities of finiteness and infiniteness, possibility and actuality, contingency and necessity, etc. By means of the transcendental keynote one could work out a complete metaphysics, which would not only possess a great internal compactness, but also great actual value for a meeting of ancient and modern metaphysics. Outlines of it are sketched by Scotus, but he did not live to elaborate it since death overtook him too early, and his outline thus remains a challenge for us today. To meet it would no doubt prove highly rewarding. Before we proceed, let us note that Scotus did not yet connect his transcendental philosophy with univocation. Although such a connection suggested itself, this was reserved for his disciples and followers. Such a connection is clearly expressed by Peter of Aquila († 1361) who distinguished transcendental from predicamental univocity.[46]

PART II

BEING, UNIVOCITY, AND ANALOGY

1. Univocity, Denomination, and Analogy

It depends on the determination of being whether we are dealing with univocation, equivocation, or analogy of being. All three terms have undergone in the course of history an interesting change in meaning, which we cannot fail to consider if we wish to understand each philosopher correctly. What is of primary importance in our context is the change of meaning undergone by the term "univocal" or the synonyms.

In antiquity it was especially Aristotle who dealt with synonymy. The synonym is for him a unity of term, concept, and being, and has its ontological basis in the essence (οὐσια) and its structural elements, genera, species, and specific differences. Thus univocity was precisely determined but also narrowly limited. The first to break through the narrow limits was Porphyry, who included also

---

[46] *Ord.* I (ed. Vat. III, 73): Metaphysica . . . scientia transcendens; *Metaph. Prol.* (ed. Viv. VII, 7a): Metaphysica . . . scientia circa transcendentia; *Ord.* IV (ed. Viv. XX, 38a): Intellectio . . . cognitio transcendens totum genus sensationis; *Ord.* I (ed. Vat. IV, 207): Cum primo transcendente, scilicet ente; *Ord.* I (ed. Vat. IV, 206): Transcendens est extra omne genus; *Ord.* I (ed. Vat. III, 26): Non concludit imperfectionem . . . nec limitationem; *Ord.* I (ed. Vat. IV, 206): Indifferens ad finitum et infinitum . . .; *Ord.* I (ed. Vat. IV, 206): Passiones simplices convertibiles,- sicut unum, verum, bonum . . . passiones opposita . . . sicut necesse esse vel possibile . . .; cf. A. B. Wolter, *The Transcendentals . . .*, 10-12; H. Knittermeyer, *Der Terminus 'transzendental' und seine historische Entwickelung bis Kant* (Marburg, 1920); cf. n. 49.

the properties in the domain of univocity. Building on him, Boethius numbered the last of the five predicables, accident, among the *univoca*. It remained so for a long time. No one dared to transgress the limits of the five predicables, all of which had a finite character of predicability in them. St. Thomas Aquinas still held that everything predicated of several things univocally belongs either to a genus, a species, a specific difference, an accident, or a property.

A further development is first found in the works of Duns Scotus. With the aid of the logic of his day he approached the problem very cautiously and offered various solutions. In his early logical writings, the *Quaestiones super Praedicamenta Aristotelis, super Universalia Porphyrii*, and *super Elenchos Aristotelis*, he still adheres to the traditional opinion. Accordingly, univocation is a strict equality of word, concept, and being, which is found only in the domain of finite "So-being"-structures (genera, species, specific differences, properties, and accidents). There, on account of the prevailing difference, he assigned analogy to equivocation. Analogy forms, in a logical respect, a special case of equivocation: the *aequivocum a consilio*. This is more than a purely accidental equivocation *(aequivocum a casu)*, since a real relation, indeed one of dependence, obtains between the subjects of this denomination. Since nevertheless a difference prevails, analogy belongs to equivocation and differs from univocation.

In *Quaestiones super Metaphysicam Aristotelis* and *Quaestiones de Anima Aristotelis* a new insight comes to the fore. Here the subtle teacher seeks to disclose the ultimate basis of cognition and being for the ten categories and for the relation of God and world. He finds a suitable means for this in his expanded form of univocation. The expansion is successful through the abstractive transcending beyond all finite determined being and through the precisive exposition of an open horizon, into which also the infinity of God can somehow be brought in. Thus we have an ultimate community of all entities, to which a metaphysical analogy can be connected. On the strength of the different intensity and perfection of the various modes of being, there arises on the basis of an ultimate univocation what is meant by the analogy of proportionality, and above all by the analogy of attribution. Extension of univocation into the region of the transcendentals is carried out with logical means and is treated very thoroughly in the various redactions of the *Commentary on the Sentences* and in the *Collationes*. The problem is touched on shortly in the *Theoremata* and answered in the sense of a universal univocation of being. The *Quodlibet*, possibly the last work of Scotus, leaves the question undecided as to whether the universality of being is one of analogy or one of univocation.

The final draft of the *Commentary on the Sentences*, the so-called *Ordinatio*, presents a fuller determination of univocation in a transcendental sense. Scotus does not yet employ the term "transcendental univocation." He only speaks of a *conceptus univocus*, *conceptus aliquis univocus (Ordinatio)*, and once of a *conceptus communis . . . univocus logice loquendo (De Anima)*. Only later, e.g., in the writings of Peter of Aquila (†1348), do we hear of a *univocatio transcendens*.

In the *Ordinatio* and in the *De Anima* the unity of the Scotistic univocation is brought into most intimate connection with the principle of contradiction. That is to say, such a unity results in a contradiction when it is affirmed and denied of the same subject at the same time. On the basis of this noncontradiction, unity also satisfies the conditions for a middle term in a syllogism. When it serves to unite the extremes, i.e., the subject and the predicate of a conclusion, the combination can be performed validly without risking a false conclusion. Accordingly all that is necessary for a univocal concept is an uncontradictory unity. By means of such a unity we can arrive at uncontradictory predications and conclusions. A definite and, above all, finite unity of being is no longer necessary. Hence there can be something like univocity also beyond the finite in the realm of transcendentality. In this considerably expanded sense Scotus applies univocity to being (1st proof of univocation), to the fundamental structure of our cognition (2nd and 3rd proofs of univocation), and to the simple perfections (4th proof of univocation).

Later Scotus modifies this purely formal concept of univocity by taking into consideration the different function of the quidditative being, the qualifying properties (unity, truth, and goodness), and the simple differences. If by the ultimate conceptual unity we understand the *ratio subjecti*, which is basic for all distinct apprehension and necessary predication, then univocation pertains only to being as fundamental "what." All qualifications would then be no more univocal, but would belong to denomination and equivocation. Thus in the realm of transcendentality univocity would be restricted to being, inasmuch as being signifies pure "what" and possible "that" *(Dass)*. Accordingly, univocity would stand over against denomination and equivocation.

However, univocation can be considered from yet another viewpoint, namely, one can look only at its formal or uncontradictory unity. In this case it is not merely the still undifferentiated being that is univocal, but also whatever is immediately determined and qualified by being, such as the coextensive properties of being (unity, truth, and goodness) and the simple differences of being in their domain. Being is then predicated *univoce in quid* and as *ratio subjecti*; the coextensive properties and the simple differences are predicated *univoce in quale* or denominatively. In the last analysis difference between quidditative and qualitative univocity derives from being itself and signifies its twofold priority, namely, the basic priority of the essential commonness *(ens ut ratio subjecti)* and the supplementing priority of virtuality, which differentiates and qualifies being in things *(ens ut quale)*. Thus the qualifying *denominativa* are removed from equivocation and mediate between quidditative transcendental univocation and pure equivocation. They are then a necessary supplement of the quidditative univocation and build the bridge to equivocation and analogy. In this sense one may say: "That is univocal whose conceptual content *(ratio)* is homogeneous, whether this conceptual content is the *ratio subjecti* or denominates a subject or is predicated of a subject *per accidens*."[47]

Before we proceed to the several arguments for Scotistic univocation, let us add something concerning analogy and its very complicated history. Plato derived analogy from mathematics, where it

[47] Cf. Aristotle, *Categ.* 1 (1a 6 sq.); Porphyry, *Isagoge sive quinque voces* (ed. A. Busse 16); Boethius, *In Categ. Arist.* I (PL 64, 166); St. Thomas Aquinas, *CG* I, 32; Scotus, *Praed.* (ed. Viv. I, 439-455); *Un. Porph.* (ed. Viv. I, 119-121, 348 sq., 356 sq., 383-85); *Elench.* (ed. Viv. II, 20-25); *Metaph.* IV (ed. Viv. VII, 152 sqq.); *An.* (ed. Viv. III, 612a-28b); *Coll.* (ed. Viv. V, 199b-204b); *Theor.* XIII (ed. Viv. V, 33); cf. Cod. Claustroneoburg. 307, f. 121rb: Conceptus communissimus . . . est entis . . . comparatio autem et connumerata in aliquo univocantur; *Quodl.* (ed. Viv. XXV, 114a): Sive illa communitas sit analogiae sive univocationis, de qua non curo modo; *Ord.* I (ed. Vat. III, 18): Univocum conceptum dico, qui ita est unus quod eius unitas sufficit ad contradictionem, affirmando et negando ipsum de eodem; sufficit etiam pro medio syllogistico, ut extrema unita in medio sic uno sine fallacia aequivocationis concludantur inter se uniri; *Ord.* I (ed. Vat. IV, 195): Univocum est cuius ratio est in se una, sive illa ratio sit ratio subjecti sive denominet subjectum. . . Cf. T. Barth, "Zum Problem der Eindeutigkeit," in *Philos. Jahrb.* 55 (1942), 300-21. Cf. n. 49.

signifies the equality of several mathematical proportions. Even if it cannot be taken over into philosophy in this strict form, it is nevertheless in some manner the way we must follow to go from our real world of sensibility to the supersensible world of ideality. What Plato began was continued in Neoplatonic teachings, which expanded the doctrine of the internal likeness of the relation to the doctrine of cause and effect. Precisely this expansion became the basis of the Christian doctrine on creation and analogy (analogy of attribution).

Aristotle, too, was acquainted with analogy, but dealt with it very cautiously. He was acquainted with analogy in the domain of mathematical proportions; in philosophy he employed analogy for the formation of metaphysical concepts (matter and form, possibility and actuality) and for the determination of the good. However he did not apply the concept of analogy to being itself. Being is for him predicated in many ways (πολλαχῶς) : between substance and accidents obtains the relation of "to-one" (πρὸς ἕν) and "from-one" (ἀφ ἑνός.)

What is important is that analogy, according to *Physics* VIII, 4, forms a kind of equivocation. According to this conception analogy does not stand between univocation and equivocation—as later many representatives of the golden age of scholasticism held—but is a kind of equivocation, namely, the *aequivocum a consilio*, as Boethius said in accord with Porphyry. This interpretation later played an important part in the thinking of Abelard, Duns Scotus, and Ockham.

With regard to Porphyry it must be said that he made a clear distinction between *aequivocatio a casu* and *aequivocatio a consilio*. He subdivided *aequivocatio a consilio* into likeness, analogy, and relation of "to one" (πρὸς ἕν) and "from one" (ἀφ ἑνός). What is new here is the insertion of the "to one" and the "from one" among the *aequivoca*, and, it must be noted, as two distinct kinds. Porphyry had already remarked that other philosophers conceived of the "to one" and "from one" relations as something midway between univocation and equivocation, as did Alexander Aphrodisias, Syrianus and Asclepius. The Porphyrian division was essentially taken over by the other commentators of Aristotle and still further refined.

Interesting variations are presented by Proclus and Asclepius with reference to being. According to Proclus, being which unites the supersensible with the sensible world is not equivocal (ὁμώνυμον) but univocal (ουνώνυμον). Nevertheless this does not exclude the other—that all being stems from a first monad and gravitates back to it. According to Asclepius it is just the reverse; being that belongs to all entities is not a univocal but an equivocal unity. This solution is an important anticipation of something that appears once more later on—even if in an altered form—in the golden age of scholasticism. Most of the golden age scholastics reject a univocation of being and accept an analogy of being, because in their conception univocation occurs only in the domain of definite finite structures. Duns Scotus, on the other hand, is of the opinion that a minimum of transcendental univocity of being is necessary, if the individual beings are to meet one another ontologically and epistemologically. Analogy is made possible only on the basis of a transcendental univocation. In his *Ordinatio* Scotus usually employs analogy in the sense of an analogy of attribution, where the element of difference predominates and that of commonness recedes into the background. Occasionally he also speaks of proportionality, namely, when he discusses the relation of cognitional faculty and cognitional object. But he remarks that the proportion usually has to do with dissimilar members of a relation. After this exposition of the semantics of univocation, denomination, equivocation, and analogy, we can turn to the chief reasons that have induced Scotus to speak also of a transcendental univocation.[48]

2. Univocation, Analogy and Their Relation to Being

Scotus employs univocation, which has been expanded into the transcendental area, to show that with regard to God and man there is not only an analogous but also a univocal concept. In fact, these transcendental-univocal structures are for him presupposed if

[48] Cf. J. Owens, *The Doctrine of Being in the Aristotelian Metaphysics*, (Toronto: 1951); G. L. Muskens, *De vocis analogiae significatione et usu apud Aristotelem* (Groningen, 1943); H. Lyttkens, *The Analogy between God and the World. An Investigation of Its Background and Interpretation of Its Use by Thomas of Aquino* (Upsala, 1952); H. Hirschberger, "Paronymie und Analogie bei Aristoteles," in *Philos. Jahrb.* 68 (1960), 192-203; T. Barth, "Das Problem der Vieldeutigkeit bei Aristoteles," in *Sophia* 10 (1942), 11-30; cf. Scotus, *Ord.* I (ed. Vat. III, 18-27; 94-103; IV, 191 sq.); *Ord.* I (ed. III, 74): (Potentia et objectum) sunt tamen proportionata, quia ista proportio requirit dissimilitudinem proportionatorum, sicut communiter est in proportione... M. C. Menges, *The Concept of Univocity Regarding the Predication of God and Creature According to W. Ockham* (St. Bonaventure, N. Y., 1952); C. L. Shircel, *The Univocity of the Concept of Being in the Philosophy of Duns Scotus* (Washington, 1942), 1-38.

we are to have a well-founded analogy at all. The comprehensive problem—as presented in the new edition of the *Ordinatio*—is developed in five arguments or proofs. The form of expression varies considerably. Sometimes the thoughts are well worked out and relatively easy to understand; sometimes they are merely indicated and are therefore obscure and difficult. This might suggest that Scotus struggled hard with this question and was constantly seeking new formulations for it. So far as these thoughts are of philosophic import, we shall here present the weightiest of them in such a way as to make them generally intelligible.

The first proof proceeds from the fact that in cognition we must distinguish certain from doubtful elements. This shows that we cannot be at the same time both certain and uncertain or in doubt about the same thing. The first thing we can know for certain about an object is that it is a being. Accordingly, our intellect is ordained for being and discovers that in every concrete entity there is an ultimate common structure. We always come upon this ultimate common structure, whether an entity is finite or infinite, created or uncreated, accidental or substantial. We can therefore say that the ultimate commonness of things or realities rests on a transcendental univocal basic construct of being. Thus understood, the univocity of being makes possible all our certain intellectual cognition, including the cognition of God.

The teaching of Scotus on *univocatio entis* is chiefly directed against his contemporary, Henry of Ghent, who was for many years *magister theologiae* in Paris. The Doctor Solemnis calls the conceptually apprehensible unity of being only an apparent one, since it rests merely on the common word "being," and in place of this apparent verbal unity he posits an original duality of being. The being of God and the being of the creature are totally different and have nothing in common. Accordingly, the analogy based on it lacks internal consistency, since it really possesses only a *communitas vocis*. Hence it stands in a remarkable proximity to a mere accidental equivocation *(aequivocatio a casu).*

To escape this difficulty, Scotus posits a univocation of being before the analogy of being, and in the *Quaestiones de Anima* calls it *univocatio logica*. A later Scotist, Peter of Aquila († 1361), calls it *univocatio transcendens*. The terminological formulation of Peter of Aquila is better and more comprehensive than that of Scotus, but corresponds fully to the real intention of the master.

We shall therefore retain this term; being as *primum transcendens* has a transcendental-univocal unity. The function of the transcendental-univocal unity of being is to keep the horizon of cognition open and at the same time to guarantee its ultimate foundation. By means of being, which is essentially in all things, a meeting of the subject and the object of cognition becomes possible, as well as a transition from the finite to the infinite. One may therefore say that being is primarily "that which is common to all things; being as being posits identity, not difference" (E. Coreth).[49]

The second proof continues the problem at hand and discloses the common difficulties experienced by both the representatives of analogy and by the representatives of a univocation with ensuing analogy, when they enter the transcendental region of being and wish to go from here to the infinite being of God. In this undertaking Scotus has to come to terms with the theory of innate transcendental ideas and of a special divine illumination *(illustratio specialis)*. This theory, as accepted by some representatives of thirteenth-century Augustinianism, is rejected by Scotus in a searching critique. All our ideas arise from the cooperation of the object given in the sensible image (the objective factor) and of the activity of our intellect (the subjective factor). In maintaining this, Scotus can appeal to an Augustinian principle according to which "our cognition comes from both the cognizing subject and the known object *(a cognoscente et cognito paritur notitia)*." Here the intellect, as the spiritual cause, has the higher rank and occupies the place of a *causa principalis,* because it confers upon the object its intelligible being in our consciousness.

The abstracting intellect is active in the formation of our metaphysical concepts; out of the finite concrete objects it isolates and abstracts the pure and still undifferentiated being. The still undifferentiated being bears an inner relation to the concrete being

---

[49] Henry of Ghent, *Summa Quaestionum*, a. 21, q. 2 (ed. Paris, 1518, ff. 124v-125v); Scotus, *Ord.* I (ed. Vat. III, 18-21); *Lect.* I (ed. Vat. XVI, 232 sq.); *Ord.* I (ed. Vat. IV, 207): Cum primo transcendente, scilicet ente. *An.* (ed. Viv. III, 618a): Conceptus communis . . . univocus logice loquendo. Petrus de Aquila, *Sent.* I, d. 3, q. 1, a. 3 (ed. Levanto, 1907, p. 76): Est quaedam univocatio transcendens et quaedam praedicamentalis et prima convenit enti. Petrus Thomae O.F.M. († 1350), Cod. Vat. Lat. 2190, f. 40v: Licet tamen enti dependenti et independenti non possit esse aliquod univocum praedicamentale, et potest tamen esse aliquod univocum transcendens. Cf. T. Barth, "De argumentis et univocationis entis natura apud Joannem Duns Scotum," in *Collectanea Franciscana* 14 (1944) 35, 45. E. Coreth, "Die Gestalt einer Metaphysik heute," in *Philos. Jahrb.* 70 (1963), 247.

and hence does not occur by itself alone and separate from concrete being, but it is the basis of all objectivity and is therefore rightly called the *ratio subjecti*. By means of being, the human intellect can perform what is called a metaphysical-transcendent act. Being, as the first transcendental basic structure, guarantees our intellect a transcendental activity which goes beyond the whole realm of sensibility and really penetrates into what is properly metaphysical. Nevertheless, it is apparent that transcendental being does not contain God, either formally or virtually, but only keeps the horizon open for us to go beyond the finite and turn to the infinite by a reductive conclusion.[50]

The third proof seeks to preserve univocation from misconceptions. By means of the transcendental univocation of being we do not arrive at a concept of God which contains in itself all the conceptual structures that necessarily belong to it. For that would mean that we had a concept of God corresponding to his proper structure *(conceptus proprius)*, from which we could derive all his particular characteristics. But this is by no means so. We have in this life no such concept of God from which we can infer everything that pertains necessarily to him. This is clear for the believing Christian from the mystery of the Blessed Trinity and other articles of faith, e.g., God's omnipotence and omniscience, which are necessarily connected with divine being.

What the transcendental univocal concepts accomplish is therefore something much more modest. They help us to cognize all things, God included, in their most common contours. This means, first of all, that God is a being and is thus within reach of our intellection. Further, certain common structures of the created world—e.g., the possibility of effectibility, of being directed to an end, and of being perfected—permit a reductive conclusion to a first necessary being which produces all other things and directs them to their ends and is altogether perfect and therefore infinite.[50a]

---

[50] C. L. Shircel, *The Univocity of the Concept of Being in the Philosophy of John Duns Scotus* (Washington, 1942), pp. 104-26; E. Gilson, *Jean Duns Scot* (Paris, 1952), 84-115.

[50a] Scotus, *Ord.* I (ed. Vat. III, 21-24); *Lect.* I (ed. Vat. XVI, 233-35); *Ord.* I (ed. Vat. III, 293 sqq.); Augustinus, *De Trin.* IX, 22 (PL 42, 970); Aegidius Romanus, *Sent.* I, d. 3, p. 2, princ. 3, q. 4 c (ed. Venet. 1521), f. 28 PQ. Cf. T. Barth, "De univocatione entis scotisticae intentione principali" . . . in *Antonianum* 28 (1953), 89-94; R. Messner, *Schauendes und begriffliches Denken bei Duns Scotus* (Freiburg, 1942), 5-18; E. Bettoni, *Il problema* . . . 256-70, 348-55; F. Prezioso, *La critica di Duns Scoto all' ontologismo di Enrico di Gand* (Padova, 1962), 62-158, 166-70.

Such a concept of God already predicates something that is true of him but it still remains general and therefore far from what God really contains in his concrete form and fullness. God's individual essence is for us not an *objectum naturale* but an *objectum voluntarium*. God can, but need not, manifest himself to us in his concrete totality and fullness. He can also conceal himself from us; what we cognize of him now remains in the realm of general concepts and is known by us through reasoning. Compatible with this is the further statement that we have certain concepts of God which belong to him alone and to no creature, our absolute transcendental concepts. Infinity as an internal mode of the divine being occupies first place among them. Compared with other concepts, divine infinity is for us the relatively most perfect and most simple concept, even if we have formed it by negation. Infinitude is the negation of all that is finite and limiting.[51]

While the first three proofs remain within the realm of transcendental being and at least always employ it as a possible mediation, the fourth proof proceeds a step further and introduces a new thought. Being is for Scotus something common, fundamental, and transcendent of what is limited, but it is not yet something perfect and complete. Even if it places no obstacles in the way of perfection and completeness, it achieves its proper completion and fullness only through its inner modalities, differences, and properties. Being reaches its ultimate perfection only when it becomes wholly conscious of itself—when it becomes a spirit that can know self and other things and make free decisions.

The pure perfections of the spirit are looked upon as of great importance by the philosophers of the Middle Ages. Anselm of Canterbury dealt with them specially in his *Monologium* c. 15 and developed their importance for all beings endowed with mind. The principle governing pure perfections says that possession of them is simply better than the non-possession. In connection with this, Scotus shows that we can form something like essential concepts *(rationes formales)* of intellect, will, memory, wisdom, goodness, justice, and the like. To reach such essential concepts, we perform, to use a modern expression, a sort of essential reduction. After the essential reduction there follows another reduction of a transcendental sort. Here those structures which transcend everything finite

[51] *Ord.* I (ed. Vat. III, 24-25); *Ord.* I (ed. Vat. II, 125-211); *Ord.* I (ed. Vat. III, 38-39); *Ord.* I (ed. Vat. III, 40-42).

and limiting show themselves in their ontological purity and perfection, e.g., productive memory, intuitive intellect, free decision for what is perfect, and generous goodness. These pure transcendental perfections are altogether simple and by means of an absolute intensification can be raised to an infinite perfection. This third stage of forming ideas becomes pertinent with regard to God. We could here speak of a theological reduction. We clearly see that transcendental reduction discloses those conceptually apprehensible structures which clear the way for a theological reduction. To put it more exactly, the intensity and tension which obtain between the finite and the infinite can build on the basis of transcendental-univocal structures. The intensive stress relationship between the finite and the infinite then passes through a final reduction into what we call the analogy between God and world.[52]

We shall be brief in presenting the fifth proof, the linguistic form of which offers considerable difficulties. Let us emphasize only one thought, which was already touched on in the second and third arguments. There we stated what *univocatio transcendentalis* can do and what it cannot do. It is its function to prepare the way for us to transcend all that is finite and gain a view of something altogether different. What is altogether different is the infinite being of God. The means to it is the conceptual abstraction or analysis *(resolutio)* in its ultimate possibility and radicality—as transcendental and theological reduction. Further means necessarily belonging to the theological reduction are intensification, negation, and reasoning. If we keep this in mind, we must say that Scotus' *univocatio entis* cannot lead to an intuitive knowledge of God. It rather lays the foundation for a mediate, i.e., an abstractive and discursive, knowledge of God. We must now rest content with a knowledge of God that is still very imperfect.[53]

When we reflect upon all this and finally ask once more whether Scotus intended to supplant the *analogia entis* with his *univocatio entis* we can answer: according to Scotus the univocation of being is not opposed to the analogy of being; it rather accompanies it and

---

[52] *Ord.* I (ed. Vat. III, 25-27); *Lect.* I (ed. Vat. XVI, 235-237); *Quodl.* (ed. Viv. XXVI, 196 sq.): Memoria perfecta in supposito conveniente est principium perfectum producendi Verbum; *Quodl.* (ed. Viv. XXV, 35b sq.): Nam haec est ratio memoriae perfectae: intellectus habens objectum intelligibile proportionatum actu sibi praesens. Cf. P. Minges, *J. Duns Scoti doctrina* . . . I, 203-207.

[53] *Ord.* I (ed. Vat. III, 27-29).

strives to make it really possible inasmuch as it brings the transcendental commonness and ultimate identity of being into sharp relief. This speculative venture was no easy undertaking for our philosopher. He well knew that his *univocatio entis* gave rise to many new questions. He would not evade them, but would encounter them with open eyes and would devote four long questions to them in his *Ordinatio*. Since he had to expound principally the *univocatio entis* as a new possibility basic to analogy, he had to linger over it, while he dealt rather briefly with the traditional analogy of being. This always happens when a new insight is proposed. Later he will have something to say about the *analogia entis* by placing it primarily over against the *univocatio entis* and showing in a positive way how the two are related to each other.[54]

This fact is not always noticed and as a result not a few have asserted the unfounded opinion that Scotus defended only the *univocatio entis* and rejected the *analogia entis*. However this is not the case. What he really wanted to do was to provide a logically clear and epistemologically certain foundation for the *analogia entis*. For this reason he devoted, by means of the prevailing logic, more time and space to the *univocatio entis* than to traditionally recognized *analogia entis*. A few texts may clarify what he thought of the relation of *univocatio transcendentalis* and *analogia attributionis*.

Analogia attributionis has an attributive or distributive function. For one thing, it is used to clarify the ontological relation of substance and accidents. Since being belongs originally *(primo)* to substance and through it is attributed to accidents *(secundo)*, there obtains a definite ontological order which cannot be reversed. With this diverse attribution of being something else can and must coexist which unites the various categories with one another and brings them together with its unifying commonness. This is done through transcendental univocation and the identity of being.

The same thought is expressed still more distinctly in another place, where we read: if the unity of attribution is not carried and supported by a unity of univocity and identity, it is weak and at least questionable. Wherever the relation of measure and measured or of surpassing and surpassed obtains, there must already be a minimum of univocal unity, if a relation of attribution is to come about at all. These texts should make it sufficiently clear that

[54] *Ord.* I (ed. Vat. III, 94, 95; 100-103); *Lect.* I (ed. Vat. XVI, 264-73).

Scotus had no intention of doing away with an *analogia entis*. He rather wanted to retain it and give it a solid basis. The means to this end was for him the transcendental univocity of being. For Duns Scotus, therefore, transcendental univocity and metaphysical analogy do not go against each other but with each other. What transcendental univocity started and established, is carried on and completed by analogy of being by means of the different intensity and modality of the first differences of being.[55]

Franziskaner Akademie, Sigmaringen

Translated from the German by Edwin Dorzweiler, O.F.M. Cap.

[55] *Ord.* I (ed. Vat. III, 102): 'Ens' . . . vel 'quid' . . . simpliciter dicitur de accidente . . . et de substantia, sed non aeque primo. Et non obstante ordine, potest bene esse univocatio. *Ord.* I (ed. Vat. IV, 191 sq.): In ratione entis, in qua est unitas attributionis, attributa habeant unitatem univocationis, quia numquam aliqua comparantur ut mensurata ad mensuram, vel excessa ad excedens, nisi in aliquo uno conveniant.

11

FRANCIS SUAREZ AND THE TEACHING OF JOHN DUNS SCOTUS ON *UNIVOCATIO ENTIS*

by

WALTER HOERES

There can be no doubt that Francis Suarez was very reluctant to reject the *univocatio entis* of the Doctor Subtilis, and that he therefore had to attempt a critical evaluation of the reasons Scotus advances for his thesis. But of themselves Suarez' considerations of the unity and analogy of the concept of being lead back to Scotus' view of the *univocatio entis*. Although Suarez would not admit it, his investigations largely appear not so much as a refutation of the Scotistic teaching as a defense of it. He subscribes to many arguments given by Scotus, and it is therefore strange that in the end he should repudiate the Scotistic doctrine. Thus both the hesitation with which he does so and the question whether one might nevertheless speak of a *univocatio entis* become intelligible. Obviously, the study of this formal rejection yet really broad acceptance of the Scotistic *univocatio entis*, discloses valuable information on the cogent character of the reasons the Subtle Doctor adduces for his position.

PART I

CONCEPT OF BEING AND *UNIVOCATIO ENTIS*

1. Unity and Precision of the Concept of Being

The second of the *Disputationes Metaphysicae* of Suarez[1] is for our context of decisive importance. Here he investigates the essential content of the concept of being. First, he inquires whether the conceptual act with which we apprehend being as such is a single

[1] Subsequently abbreviated: DM and cited according to the Venice edition of 1751.

act that can be extended to all things.² From this conceptual act, the *conceptus formalis,* Suarez distinguishes the traditional proper concept itself, the *conceptus objectivus,* "which is called the thing itself, as it is properly and immediately known and represented through the act of conception."³ Suarez now proves the strict and all-comprising unity of the *conceptus formalis* of being from its utter simplicity. We experience this simplicity, he says, when we hear the word being, for then our mind is not divided into several acts but is gathered into one act. This is so, he continues, because the word being is predicated of things with an identical meaning, since it does not designate several things in as much as they differ from one another but in as much as they agree in their likeness. Through other concepts we apprehend this or that being, but in the concept of being we abstract from all composition and determination. Hence it is that the concept of being is said to be not merely one, but absolutely simple—*simplicissimus.*⁴ With the oneness of the *conceptus formalis entis* is also necessarily given the unity of the proper concept of being, that of the *conceptus objectivus entis.* Even if Suarez begins with the act of conception as the better known element, he is fully aware that the act receives its structure from the object. Cajetan and others would indeed have rejected the thesis of the unity of the *conceptus formalis entis* precisely because it must be based on the unity of a thing or a concept. But they would have feared that the unity of the concept of being would necessarily lead to the thesis of the *univocatio entis,* and in order to avoid this conclusion, they also denied the unity of the *conceptus formalis.*⁵ According to Suarez, the latter has for its immediate object the objective concept of being, which predicates nothing explicitly of substance or accident and of God or creature but comprises all these objects after the manner of a unity.⁶ Accordingly, if the formal act with which I think of being as such is altogether simple, then such too must be the *conceptus objectivus.*⁷ That is, the conceptual content of being must for the very reason of its utter simplicity and indistinctness be distinct

---

² Sectio 1: "Utrum ens in quantum ens habeat in mente nostra unum conceptum formalem omnibus entibus communem."
³ l.c. n. 1.
⁴ l.c. n. 11.
⁵ l.c. n. 2.
⁶ DM 2, 2 n. 8; cf. also José M. Alejandro, S.J., *La gnoseologia del Doctor Eximio y la acusasion nominalista* (Comillas (Santander): 1948), p. 126.
⁷ l.c.

from every other content. Indeed from the utter simplicity of the *conceptus formalis entis* the Doctor Eximius had already established its distinction from all other acts,[8] and this train of thought recurs where he establishes the unity and simplicity of the *conceptus objectivus*.[9] It is primarily true of this concept that it differs from the other concepts precisely because of its simplicity.

It is not accidental that we here prescind for the time being from a further clarification of the content of the Suarezian concept of being, and proceed after the manner of Suarez himself, who expounds the oneness and simplicity of the concept of being before he determines its content. Thus our exposition will make it clear that with Suarez as with Scotus, the *univocatio entis* will necessarily result already from the unity of the concept of being alone.

From the simplicity and the indistinctness of the concept of being it follows first of all that it stands as a medium between the act by which being is cognized and the individual beings. That is, by the word and the signification of being I immediately designate neither substance nor accident, nor any other categories of being, but that objective conceptual content of being which I can then apply to individual things. Suarez illustrates this with the word *homo*, which immediately designates the essential content of man and only mediately Peter and Paul.[10]

This doctrine concerning the concept *ens* as medium forms the basis of the sharp contrast to the Thomistic school inspired by Cajetan. Cajetan denies that the concept of being represents the unity of a *ratio communis* applicable to all things in whatever different measure it may be. Rather, the abstract concept of being, according to Cajetan, extends itself immediately to all individual beings. Nevertheless it does not designate the bare aggregate of an *unum per accidens,* but throws into relief the proportional likeness of things in being.[11] But this likeness is not in that strict sense intelligible as a conceptual *oneness*, as is the Suarezian *conceptus objectivus entis* in its utter simplicity. Cajetan regards the abstraction of a simple *ratio entis* with omission of all differences as quite impossible, and thus for him, in direct opposition to Suarez, the

---

[8] DM 2, 1 n. 11: "quia hic conceptus in se est simplicissimus, sicut objective, ita etiam formaliter: ergo is se habet unam simplicem rationem formalem adaequatam: ergo secundum eam praescinditur ab aliis conceptibus formalibus."
[9] DM 2, 2 n. 10.
[10] l.c. n. 22.
[11] *De Nominum Analogia,* c. 6 ed. De Maria p. 265.

concept of being is an external comprehensive view of the multiplicity of things under the aspect of their proportional likeness: "The abstraction of being does not consist in this that the beingness *(entitas)* is thrown into relief to the neglect of substance and quantity; it consists rather in this, that substance and quantity are viewed as each of them is related to its own being. From this one can then infer the likeness of the proportion"[12] which is obviously expressed in the word "being."

We can forego a thorough exposition of Cajetan's teaching on being and analogy, which has been recently subjected, in the spirit and reasoning of Suarez, to an exhaustive and sharp critique by Father José Hellin, S.J.[13] What is important in our context is this: Cajetan's concept of being, as well as that of his numerous followers, extends immediately to all individual beings in so far as they are united with one another in their likeness of proportion, but it does not express a truly internal *ratio communis*. The Suarezian concept of being, on the contrary, is a medium abstracted in its utter simplicity from all things, but for that very reason it can be predicated of them *identice*.

2. The Univocal Application of the Concept of Being

This characterization of the concept of being as an absolutely simple concept and as a medium is of the greatest importance for the establishment of its univocal use. If the word being, as Suarez explains in DM 2, 2 n. 24, does not immediately mean the different things themselves but the content of the concept, which in its simplicity can be common to many things, then this word can be applied to all things "with a single and first imposition" *(ut ex unica et prima impositione illa omnia comprehendat)*. "And this is an indication that it does not designate all these things immediately but by means of that objective concept which is common to them all."[14] By this designation *ex unica et prima impositione* Suarez distinguishes here the relation of the concept of being to its inferiors from all those cases of "mere" proportionality or of only extrinsic attribution to an analogate, in which a name is primarily predicated only of that object which it actually means, and is then

---

[12] l.c. c. 5 De Maria p. 261.
[13] *La analogia del ser y el conocimiento de Dios en Suarez* (Madrid, 1947); cf. especially pp. 147-191.
[14] DM 2, 2 n. 24.

applied *per metaphoram aliquam* to other things. One is here always concerned with a double use of the name—the proper sense of it and the metaphorical. Suarez employs the well-known example of the concept of health, which *ex prima impositione* designates only health and is then applied to those things that are related to it. From this analogous application of the name, which is here predicated primarily of a proper subject and by dependence on it of other subjects, Suarez distinguishes equivocation in which a multiple use of the name occurs without such dependence of things on one another *(utraque impositio aeque prima)*. In such cases of extrinsic analogy and equivocation, several uses of the word are made. This is either because we do not employ one concept but several, or because there is only an extrinsic relation between things.[15]

This is not the case with the word *ens*. Here the word is predicated of one being as well as of another, since its conceptual content is altogether intrinsic and common to all things. However we may add that this is based on the fact that the concept of being as Suarez describes it, because of its simplicity, is predicated either totally or not at all, and therefore always in the proper sense of the word. Hence the equivalently proper application of the name to all its inferiors derives from that single, simple concept of being as medium by means of which the mind cognizes the individual beings as beings. With this doctrine of the *unica et prima impositio* of the concept of being on all its members, the thesis of its univocal application is necessarily given. However, we seem here to meet with a contradiction in as much as precisely in the passage where Suarez speaks of the equivalent *impositio* of the concept of being, he designates it expressly as analogous. The analogy that Suarez has here in mind has been aptly designed by the Suarezians as *analogia attributionis intrinsecae*. This is given when an essential form is intrinsically, properly, and completely realized in the subjects of the analogous term. Of course, it is realized in one subject absolutely, in the other only in relation to the first; otherwise for Suarez there would be no analogy at all. For him, this relation of *prius* and *posterius* is absolutely necessary to establish an analogy. The one subject carries the analogous form only in dependence on, and in virtue of, the relation to the primary subject, which possesses the form absolutely and without such a relation. But this does not exclude

---

[15] l.c.: "extrinseca habitudo vel proportio."

in the case of the *analogia attributionis intrinsecae* that the essential form be intrinsic in both subjects; therefore I can form a common concept of both (*unus conceptus formalis et objectivus*) which represents the common form.

Being is an example of this analogy for Suarez, inasmuch as being pertains to God and creatures and to substance and accidents. He distinguishes this analogy from that of extrinsic attribution, which is given when the essential form is intrinsic in one subject only and is predicated of the other on the basis of its extrinsic relation to the first, as the example of the concept of health, already mentioned, demonstrates. According to Suarez, here, as in the case of *analogia proportionalitatis*, we have an extrinsic analogy, where the essential form belongs to the one analogate only improperly, and this second analogate is defined as such through the first and in respect to it. Hence in this case there can be no question of the *unica et prima impositio* of the analogous term, nor is a common concept for both analogates possible, since the essential form which could be the basis of such a concept is intrinsic in only one of them.[16] Accordingly, only the intrinsic analogy of being would come into question. However, even this is excluded when Suarez maintains that the predication of being is equally original in all cases. Naturally, being belongs to creatures only in dependence on God. If the concept of being expressed this dependence already of itself, it could not be applied to God and creatures with an equally original *unica et prima impositione*. The fact that I can predicate being of all things proves that I need not refer to God when I affirm of a creature that it is a being; otherwise the predication of being could be applied to the latter only *secunda impositione*. But this is excluded since the *ratio entis* belongs also to the creature intrinsically and properly and can therefore be cognized in it and predicated of it without recourse to any other being.

That the concept of being in its simplicity does not express the dependence of creature on God and of accident on substance comes to light precisely in those passages where Suarez propounds his view in favor of the analogy of the concept of being between God and creature and between substance and accident. In DM 32, 2 n. 4 Suarez first cites an argument that seems to favor the analogous meaning of the concept of being with reference to substance and accident, but does not convince him, since accident would be de-

[16] DM 28, 3 n. 14; 32, 2 n. 14; Cf. also Hellin, *La analogia*. . . l.c. pp. 63-108.

fined through assistance and therefore could not agree with substance in the univocal concept of being. Suarez adds the critical remark that the concept of substance does indeed pertain to the definition of accident as accident, but does not pertain to it inasmuch as the accident is considered as being only.[17] A little later he inquires whether one could term the accident, despite its close dependence on the substance, a being at all, and he answers in the affirmative by stating: *Cum autem dicitur, accidens esse ens, non excluditur, quod sit entis ens, sed tantum non exprimitur.*[18] Hence the dependence of accident is neither denied in the concept of being, nor is it contained in it. It is therefore incomprehensible how Suarez, in affirming the analogy of the concept of being in substance and accident, suddenly derives this dependence. Still more informative are the passages where he intends to establish the analogy of the concept of being between God and creature. To point out that this analogy is truly intrinsic, he writes: "It is certain that the creature as a being is not defined through the creator or God's being, but through being as such *(esse ut sic)* and because it is outside nothing; for when the reference to God is added and we say by way of example that the creature is a being because it participates in the divine essence, we no longer designate the creature as a mere being but as a determinate being, i.e., as created being."[19] Suarez brings this up to show that being admits of no extrinsic analogy in which one analogate must be defined through the other. But he also proves here that analogy sets in only when I regard beings in their diversity and not as mere beings, i.e. when I look to *tale ens* and not to *ens qua tale*.

The contradiction in which Suarez involves himself when he clings to the analogy of the concept of being becomes especially obvious in his "Solution of the Question." Here he states that being is predicated of the creature with reference to God, and therefore analogically, and speaks of an *analogia seu attributio, quam creatura sub ratione entis potest habere ad Deum*, only to add the remark: "This is not to be understood in such wise as if the creature, viewed under the aspect of a completely abstract and general concept of being as such, bespeaks a relation to God. This is altogether impossible. . ., since under this aspect the creature is not viewed as a finite and limited thing; no, we completely abstract

[17] DM 32, 2 n.n 7
[18] l.c. n. 19.
[19] DM 28, 3 n. 15.

from all that, and view the creature only in a general way under the aspect of being outside nothing. [That proposition on analogy] is therefore to be so understood that in existing reality the creature participates in the nature of being only through an essential subordination to God. . . ."[20]

Without detriment to our later exposition of the reality-content of the univocal concept of being, we can insist against Suarez that in dealing with univocation or analogy we are not primarily concerned with reality in itself, but with the possibility of a concept of being that surpasses the real diversity of all actual things. What is in question is the possibility of forming a univocal concept of things that are diverse and relationally dependent upon one another. Suarez says so much himself in a very striking way when he essays a solution that apparently does away with the whole problem in as elegant a way, as when in the passage cited above, he distinguishes the "abstract" concept of being from the real being of things, and so evades the question concerning the analogy of the concept. That attempt at a solution says: If you take being inasmuch as it comprises the various contents of beings *(ut includit proprias rationes inferiorum)*, it is analogous, since it then also comprises the order of the individual things in relation to one another. But if you take being inasmuch as it does not comprise the diversity of its inferiors, then it is not analogous. But neither can it then be properly called univocal, since the univocal or the analogous is so called because of a reference to its inferiors. Suarez aptly observes with regard to such a solution that being, inasmuch as it includes its inferiors, is not the object of the present discussion. For as such it would no longer be mere being but either infinite or finite being, substance or accident, etc. But this diversity could not, he holds, be comprehended in that one concept of being, and thus the distinction would be of no help in solving the problem.[21] With that he admits that the real dependence of things finds no expression in the concept of being, but he also tells us here that the problem of univocation or analogy is precisely concerned with this abstract concept of being. To pose this problem he does not regard it necessary to actually relate a concept to its inferiors. The concept of man, then, would also be univocal if I did not relate it to individual human beings. Only this, says Suarez, pertains to a concept

[20] l.c. n. 16.
[21] l.c. n. 18.

that it *can* be related to its subjects and predicated of them *(comparatio aptitudinalis ad inferiora)*, and this possibility is enough to pose the question concerning univocation: "When we say that creatures, whether substance or accident, are beings, we do not predicate this being inasmuch as it actually comprises its inferiors, but only according to the common concept of being; and this concept must therefore be either univocal or analogous."[22]

3. The Apparent Analogy of the Concept of Being

Thus by his consistent distinction between the concept of being as *ens qua tale* and all further determination of things as *talia entia*, the Doctor Eximius repeatedly makes clear that the problem of the univocation of the concept is by no means solved by reference to reality. All the more urgent is the question whether, in spite of all that, he may not have a positive reason to retain the analogy of the concept of being.

The answer is that Suarez does see a difference between the unity of concept and its univocation. Unity does not suffice for univocation; in univocation the conceptual content has to be applied to all its inferiors in the same way *(aeque)*; the univocal concept denotes "a common essential content which is found in the inferiors in the same way."[23] That is, univocal concept is indifferent as to whether it is first actualized in this and then in that of its inferiors. It does not of itself demand that it be actualized in its inferiors in any definite order of dependence.[24] Hence, if I consider a univocal concept, I do not know in any way that it can be realized in one of its inferiors only in dependence on the other. What this means is conversely clear from the analogous concept of being which, in the strict sense, is indeed one concept but is not found in its inferiors in the same relation and in the same order. By this Suarez means not only, as in the passages cited above, that a conceptual content is found in actual things with a different distinctness, inasmuch as these things stand in an orderly relation to one another in virtue of the essence expressed in that concept, but rather he means that the concept of being even of itself, i.e., viewed in its content, calls for a different actualization according to the relation of before and after.[25] Even

[22] l.c. n. 19.
[23] DM 32, 2 n. 6.
[24] DM 28, 3 n. 17: "nam univocum ex se ita indifferens, ut aequaliter, et sine ullo ordine vel habitudine unius ad alterum ad inferiora descendat. . . ."
[25] l.c.

the very simple and abstract concept of being already demands of itself *(ex vi sua)* the order that it belong to the proper being in the first place and then, in dependence on it, to the other.

Again, Suarez is especially clear on this matter when he deals with the analogy of the concept of being in respect to the relation of substance and accident. "This analogy can consist in nothing else but in this, that the formal content of being *(ratio formalis entis)* does not descend *(descendit)* to substance and accident in a fully equal degree *(aequaliter)*, but in a certain order and in a relation which it (the *ratio*) demands of itself; that is, the *ratio formalis* is actualized in the substance absolutely and then in the accident with reference to the substance."[26] Hence the difference in rank and order of the actualization of being does not derive from the essence of substance and accident alone; the concept of being is of itself already directed to this order of precedence among its inferiors. Its unity and simplicity must not mislead us to the assumption that it is indifferent with regard to its inferiors. The unity of univocation is therefore still greater than mere unity of concept, since the univocal concept is equally indifferent to all its inferiors.[27]

Suarez elucidates this still more by distinguishing the concept of being from the generic concept. This too, he says, is given in the species in various degrees of perfection, and is therefore analogically actualized in the thing. But the different degrees of perfection pertain to the generic concept only because of the specific differences. Of itself, it abstracts completely from such unlikeness and therefore from every reference of one of its inferiors to the other, since it does not pertain to the one species because of its dependence on the other. The inverse, however, is true of being. If the conditions of the generic concept were like those of the concept of being, the unlikeness of their actualization would already have to appear in the *ratio generica*.[28]

Hence Suarez believes that he can also reject the arguments Duns Scotus advances for *univocatio entis* by conceding to him, on the one hand, the unity of the concept of being, while, on the other hand, insisting that this unity is still not identical with univocation.[29] However it is clear that this attempt to find a different rela-

---

[26] DM 32, 2 n. 14.
[27] l.c. n. 15.
[28] l.c. and DM 28, 3 n. 20.
[29] l.c. n. 18 and DM 32, 2 n. 15: "Et ita solvitur fundamentum Scoti. Recte enim probat, ens significare substantiam et accidens medio eodem conceptu

tion already in the concept of being must fail because of its simplicity. Without internal differentiation and structure in the concept of being itself it is impossible for the concept to give rise by itself alone—and that is the point in question—to a different *habitudo ad inferiora*. We have seen, according to Suarez, that the unity and simplicity of the concept of being establishes just the opposite of that different *habitudo,* namely, the *unica et prima impositio* for all of them.

It is therefore not surprising that the Doctor Eximius has again conceded indirectly that the unity and univocation of the concept of being are inseparable. It is also very significant in this connection that he rejects the Thomistic objections to the univocation of the concept of being between God and creature, which are based on the difference of being on both sides. These objections, he holds, would destroy the unity of the concept of being: "For it is incomprehensible that one could detect an essential difference in one concept as such: *nam intelligi non potest, quod in uno conceptu ut sic, sit varietas essentialis."* Against the Thomists he adduces here his distinction between being as such and beings in their variety.[30] However, not only in this passage but also in DM 32, 2 nn. 6 and 8, where he deals with the analogy between substance and accident, he regards the Thomistic reasons with open displeasure, since they militate against the unity of the concept of being. Hence it is also profoundly significant that he warns us not to abandon the unity of the concept of being in order to save its analogy. If one of the two has to be denied, let it be analogy that is uncertain, while the unity of the concept of being can be solidly established. Whatever has been said about the unity of the concept of being appears to be far clearer than what might be said in favor of the analogy of being.[31] Possibly out of regard for tradition he makes the simple concession that the reasons against univocation are serious and weighty;[32] and this may have been the motive why he finally decides against univocation. Even so, he definitely departs from the way taken by the Thomists.[33] On the other hand, he openly admits his sympathy for the doctrine of the univocation of being: "For those who admit a

---

formali et objectivo, negamus tamen id satis esse, ut sit univocum proprie, nisi sit etiam perfecte unum in habitudine et indifferentia ad inferiora."
[30] DM 28, 3 n. 9.
[31] DM 2, 2, n. 36.
[32] DM 28, 3 n. 9.
[33] DM l.c. n. 10.

common concept of being there can hardly be a dispute in this question *quoad rem* but only *quoad modum loquendi*. Without doubt being has a great similarity to univocal terms, since it is predicated absolutely and without addition of God and creature by means of one concept."[34] It is true, that in the same passage he states that if we consider the various modes in which being is found "in God and the others," it falls far short of univocation.[35] However, the whole question, according to Suarez' own admission, has nothing to do with these various modes.

4. The Concept of Being as the Univocal Measure of Beings

This characterization of Suarez' concept of being, from which its univocation necessarily flows, is the same as in Scotus. The concept of being is for Scotus a *conceptus simpliciter simplex* which cannot again be resolved into several concepts. As such, it is either cognized wholly and entirely or it is not cognized at all.[36] Thus it contains that internal unity in the highest degree which Scotus demands for univocal concepts and which renders univocal predication primarily possible: *Univocum conceptum dico, qui ita est unus quod eius unitas sufficit ad contradictionem, affirmando et negando ipsum de eodem* . . . .[37]

Scotus too, like Suarez, sees the univocal relation of being to its inferiors grounded in the inner unity of the concept of being, which together with its distinct medium-character follows from its simplicity. This inner unity of the concept of being is not only the presupposition of its univocal predication; it also makes it possible for the concept to serve as a middle term in a syllogism. For Scotus this is another weighty argument for univocal concepts.[38]

According to Scotus, being is a univocal medium in still another sense. It forms the *tertium comparationis* when we compare individual things with one another. If I wish to compare individual things with respect to the measure in which they participate in the nature of being and actualize the *ratio entis* more or less in themselves, then the measure of comparison must not itself participate again in the gradation of being which must first be established through it. The concept of being which represents the *tertium*

[34] l.c. n. 17.
[35] l.c.
[36] *Ord.* I d. 3 p. 1 q. 3 n. 148 (Ed. Vat. III, 92).
[37] *Ord.* I d. 3, p. 1 q. 1-2 n. 26 (Ed. Vat. III, 18).
[38] l.c.

comparationis must therefore be predicated no more and no less of this than of that being. Precisely because some things possess more of being than others, this "more of being" must be measured by means of being which is neutral to all these grades and hence applies to all of them univocally. Thus Scotus can say that "every comparison comes about through a univocal medium. . . . Hence when different things are compared in their being, in which one depends on the other and this one is more perfect than that, then this being must be in some way common to both extremes [of the comparison]."[39] It is precisely in this way that the cognition of the intrinsic *analogia entis* presupposes the possibility of a univocal concept of being.

Suarez has exactly the same understanding of the concept of being as a middle term in the syllogism and as a *tertium comparationis*. In the same passage DM II, 2 n. 25 he deduces from the unity of the concept of being the possibility of a comparison of the perfection in beings and of the function of the concept of being as a middle term in the syllogism. The mere unity of a designation or of a word does not suffice for this possibility. What is needed is the unity of the concept *(communis ratio)*. True, he says in another passage, where he deals expressly with the analogy of being between God and creatures, that *ens* is univocal only for the logician who can employ the concept of being as a middle term in a reasoning process *(ad usum dialecticum)*, but not in the domain of metaphysics.[40] What this restriction imports we shall only see in Part II.

While Scotus when comparing things looks manifestly in the first place to the measuring of their different grades of being, Suarez employs the word *comparatio* in a still more comprehensive sense. I can establish a comparative relationship between the concept of being and its inferiors in the same way as I can do that with the other concepts which I have abstracted from things. The very fact that I can apprehend the concept of being by itself enables me to discover substance and accident and all the other things as beings.

[39] *Ox.* I d. 8 q. 3 n. 12 (Vivès IX 591 a) Cf. also Parthenius Minges, O.F.M., "Beitrag zur Lehre des Scotus ueber den Seinsbegriff," *Philos. Jahrb. der Goerresgesellschaft*, 20 (1907), p. 311: "So muessen um so mehr im Wesen des Seins, in welchem Einheit der Attribution ist, die Attribute Einheit der Univokation haben, weil nie etwas Gemessenes im Verhaeltnis zum Mass verglichen wird, wenn nicht beide in irgend einem Punkt uebereinstimmen; denn jede Vergleichung findet nur zwischen dem Statt, was irgendwie univok ist."
[40] DM 28, 3 n. 20.

Only the enucleation of the simple *ratio entis* makes it possible for me to see how the things in their diversity nevertheless all realize their own entity. Thus in this way also the concept of being becomes a univocal term of comparison—not merely for the different grades of being but also for its various actualizations in general.[41] Accordingly, much as with Duns Scotus, being has all the functions of a univocal concept, even if Suarez once again emphasizes its analogy. But this is also the passage already cited, where he warns us not to abandon the unity of the concept of being in order to save its analogy.[42]

5. Proof for the *Univocatio Entis* from the Simplicity of the Concept of Being

Together with the treatment of the unity and simplicity of the concept of being, as we have presented it in the foregoing sections, Suarez also acknowledges exactly the same presuppositions and reasons from which Duns Scotus, in the first of his five proofs, deduces the *univocatio entis*. This is most strikingly apparent in the interpretation that Hellin gives of the passage cited DM 2, n. 34, concerning the comparison of being with the individual beings: if you consider being by itself, no diversity or manifoldness becomes visible in it. If we say that the creator is being, the creature is being, and substance and accident are beings, the conceptual content of the concept of being does not change in any of these statements. For if we do not come to know from other sources the manifoldness of the things of which we predicate the concept of being, we will not as yet know from this predication whether we are dealing with different things and the difference, if any, between them.[43]

With that Hellin hits exactly on the intention of the Doctor Eximius. For to prove that in the concept of being we are dealing with a *ratio* which in its simplicity differs from every other *ratio*, Suarez points out that after apprehending something as being, we can still doubt whether we have to do with substance or accident,

---

[41] DM 2, 2 n. 34. For the specific ability of the intellect to penetrate things precisely in their being-so-and-so "in der Erkenntnis des verschiedenen Soseins" and at the same time their entity, cf. also my book "Sein und Reflexion," vol. XI *Forschungen zur neueren Philosophie und ihrer Geschichte* (Wuerzberg: 1956), 10 ff.

[42] l.c. n. 36.

[43] *La analogia*. . ., l.c. p. 206; cf. also p. 253.

etc.⁴⁴ Suarez here follows faithfully and quite literally the train of thought taken by Scotus, who writes:

> Omnis intellectus, certus de uno conceptu et dubius de diversis, habet conceptum de quo est certus alium a conceptibus de quibus est dubius. . . . Sed intellectus viatoris potest esse certus de Deo quod sit ens, dubitando de ente finito vel infinito, creato vel increato; ergo conceptus entis de Deo est alius a conceptu isto vel illo, et ita neuter ex se et in utroque illorum includitur; igitur univocus.⁴⁵

Here it is patent that, just as with Suarez, the concept of being represents, precisely through its simplicity, a unity that differs from our other concepts of divine or creatural being. Like Suarez, Scotus proves from his own intellectual experience that even when we abstract from all differences in objects we still have an altogether simple thought content in our possession, namely, that of being as such. That Scotus really derives the unity and univocation of the concept of being from its simplicity follows particularly from the *probatio minoris* of his demonstration. Here he shows that the dispute of philosophers concerning the nature of the first being extends to all conceivable determinations of that being, but never to the question whether it is a being at all. And like Suarez, so also Scotus here proves expressly the patent distinction of the concept of being from all other concepts on the basis of its simplicity.

Timotheus Barth is therefore right in saying that the whole strength of this first Scotistic proof for the *univocatio entis* rests on the utter simplicity of the concept of being. As Barth explains, this simplicity is the highest possible degree of unity in a concept, since it admits only complete unity of meaning and understanding of the conceptual content, which is equivalent to univocation.⁴⁶

PART II

UNIVOCATIO ENTIS AND REALITY

1. The Content of the Concept of Being

In our book on Scotus we took sharp issue with the method of

⁴⁴ DM 2, 2, n. 17.
⁴⁵ *Ord.* I d. 3, p. 1 q. 1-2 n. 27 (Ed. Vat. III, 18).
⁴⁶ "De argumentis et univocationis entis natura apud Ioannem Duns Scotum," *Collectanea Franciscana* 14 (1941) 27, 28.

disposing of the problem of Scotistic univocation by simply saying that Scotus restricts univocation to the logical domain, while in the domain of reality he accepts analogy.[1] To be sure, Scotus, together with Aristotle, accepts only univocal or equivocal concepts in the logical domain. But a clear-cut division into domains does not do justice to the sharply defined realism of Scotus, according to which our concepts are mirrors of reality. Naturally also Scotus holds the analogy between real things, but he also maintains that the univocal concept "bears a relation to reality to the extent that reality can be apprehended through it."[2] The univocal concept has a foundation in reality, even if it is an imperfect one.[3] It designates being in God and creatures, but without the inner mode without which no real thing can exist. Only the mode of infinity or finiteness makes the concept of being a proper concept expressing the existing reality of God and creatures.[4] However, it does not follow from this that the concept which abstracts from modal determination does not possess any cognitional value or any relation to reality. Indeed it does no longer designate the inner mode of the divine or the creatural being and therefore neither this nor that as such, but it does still designate an aspect that can be found in both.[5] The concept of being is for Scotus a pure, still undetermined entity (*Sosein*) which certainly does not exclude the possibility of existence; in fact, it is ordained for existence.[6] But doubtless this being belongs, without prejudice to its further determination, to God and creatures. It is really unintelligible why one should incur the danger of pantheism and the mixture of divine and creatural being when one makes the statement that God and creature possess being in this sense. Whether such a danger exists depends

---

[1] Walter Hoeres, *Der Wille als reine Vollkommenheit nach Duns Scotus*, Vol. I of "Salzburger Studien zur Philosophie" (Muenchen: 1962), p. 55 ff.

[2] Michael Schmaus, *Zur Diskussion ueber das Problem der Univozitaet im Umkreis des Johannes Duns Scotus* (Muenchen: 1957), p. 8.

[3] Timotheus Barth, "De univocationis scotisticae intentione principali necnon valore critico," *Antonianum* 28 (1935) Fasc. 1-2, p. 78: "Univocationem . . . non esse unitatem mere conceptualem . . . sed potius conceptualem cum fundamento, licet imperfecto in re."

[4] For the Scotistic concept of mode cf. the following Section 2.

[5] Cf. the excellent formulation by Allan Wolter, O.F.M., in *The Transcendentals and Their Function in the Metaphysics of Duns Scotus*, The Franciscan Institute, St. Bonaventure, N. Y., 1946, p. 44.

[6] Cf. T. Barth, "Das weltliche Sein und seine inneren Gruende bei Thomas von Aquin und Johannes Duns Scotus," *Wissenschaft und Weisheit*, 21 (1958), p. 180.

surely altogether on what we understand by this being and how concretely or how broadly we take its concept.

It is not our task here to give a detailed development of the *univocatio entis*.[7] We would rather only point out that the distinction between logical univocation and metaphysical analogy does not settle the question before us, and that the Scotistic univocal concept of being has true cognitional value in the domain of reality. The same is also true of the Suarezian concept of being, the clarification of which is taken up in DM 2, 4. Being is for Suarez very much as it is for the Doctor Subtilis, that which has real essence and is directed toward real existence: *habens essentiam realem . . . veram et aptam ad realiter existendum*.[8] Suarez speaks of a real essence *(Sosein)* which as such involves no contradiction, but is intrinsically possible and is therefore fit to exist.[9] We can take the word being not only in this substantive sense *(in vi nominis)* but also as a participle, and then it designates something really existent. This is nothing else but being in the first-named sense as the subject of the real essence which is disposed for existence—only that this disposition has been actualized in existence.[10] Suarez has therefore no double concept of being; in both cases he deals with the same concept which appears more or less determined. Accordingly, being, *in vi nominis*, designates that which has a real essence; however we abstract from its actual existence without excluding or denying it. This being is therefore not identical with potential being *(ens in potentia)*, which signifies not only a precision from the act of existence but rather the negation and privation of it. Hence, being, *in vi nominis*, can be predicated equally well of actual things as of potential things, and can also be used when I do not think of actual existence at all. In this sense a statement, like "Man is a being," is an eternal verity. Being as a participle, however, designates the same thing only in a more determined manner, inasmuch as existence is now expressly included.[11] Being

---

[7] Cf. for this, besides the works of Gilson and those already mentioned, the full treatment by Cyril L. Shircel, O.F.M., *The Univocity of the Concept of Being in the Philosophy of John Duns Scotus* (Washington, D. C.: 1942).

[8] DM 2, 4 n. 5.

[9] Marius Schneider has recently shown that this concept of being as understood by Suarez leads in no way whatever to essentialism and rationalism, as many maintain it does. Cf. his "Der angebliche philophische Essentialismus des Suarez," *Wissenschaft und Weisheit*, 24 (1961/I) pp. 40-68.

[10] DM 2, 4 nn. 3, 4.

[11] l.c. nn. 9, 11, 12.

in this sense is therefore "magis contractum" over against *ens in vi nominis*. No matter how this contraction is to be understood, we can at least say of this *ens in vi nominis* that its concept is altogether simple and can therefore be predicated of all things univocally. We can say of everything, of God and creature, that it is a *habens essentiam realem*;[12] and so we establish not only the univocation of our statement but also its reality-content. Being in this sense is for Suarez synonymous with *res*—reality or real thing.[13]

Accordingly this concept of being is the "ratio communissima entis" Suarez was looking for.[14] Apropos to this *ratio* as *communissima* he can say: "ens in vi nominis sumptum commune est Deo et creaturis;"[15] and "habere essentiam realem convenit omni enti reali . . . etiamsi non existat,"[16] because this "habere essentiam realem" is simply synonymous with the "ens reale." That this concept of being is univocal follows from the fact that it is not predicated just in any way or a variety of ways, but always essentially and quidditatively, i.e., after the manner of an essence with reference to its inferiors.[17] Also being taken as a participle is for Suarez nothing else but a paraphrase and explication of the very simple concept of being, inasmuch as being is primarily looked upon as really existent.[18] But this concept of being is not altogether comprehensive, since it is common to actual things only and not to all things as is the *ens in vi nominis sumptum*, which is placed over against nothingness. Being can therefore still be divided into actual and possible being.[19] Consequently the concept of being taken as a participle is no longer altogether simple since it is a further determination of the common concept of being,[20] and can therefore no longer be expressed in completely simple terms.[21] But we come to know simplicity as the principal basis of univocation, wherefore the concept which is further determined by a mode, say, that of

[12] l.c. n. 9.
[13] DM 2, 4 n. 15.
[14] l.c. n. 13.
[15] l.c. n. 11.
[16] l.c. n. 14.
[17] l.c. n. 13.
[18] l.c. n. 4.
[19] l.c. n. 12.
[20] l.c. n. 9, 12.
[21] l.c. n. 12. Here Suarez is primarily concerned with *ens in potentia* and says of it that it is already expressed through *termini complexi*, but the context shows that this is also true of the *ens in actu*, i.e., of being taken as a participle, over against which the *ens in potentia* is here distinguished.

actual existence, is no longer univocal, as it is not for Scotus either; only the utterly simple concept of being is univocal. Besides, this further determination of being as an actually existent being is necessarily given only with the being of God, not with that of the creature; and for that reason, too, being as a participle cannot be absolutely predicated of all things in an essentially *in quid* and univocal manner.[22]

The concept of being *in vi nominis* is therefore the Suarezian univocal concept of being. It is not accidental that it has, as a *Sosein* (essence) ordained for reality, the same content and meaning that Scotus gives it, since actual reality is a further determination of it and deprives it of its complete simplicity and univocation. What was said of Scotus in our treatment of the concept of being is expressly insisted upon by Suarez: namely, the question of the range and applicability of the concept of being depends entirely on what meaning you ascribe to the term being. This is "multum pendens ex conceptione nostra;"[23] and universal conception shows that we can also form a concept of being which in its universality is exclusively reserved neither for God nor for creatures.[24]

2. The Origin of the Concept of Being

Suarez, it may be noted, displays a high degree of critical insight when he derives the meaning and value of such a concept of being from its origin. We have the possibility to form a concept which expresses the ratio wherein all things agree. This does not mean an agreement of things in their real particular being. But the human mind can consider things from the most diverse viewpoints, and apprehending them in its abstractive and comparative manner, it can detect greater or lesser likeness and agreement in them and arrest it in a concrete or abstract concept.[25] Now there is doubtless between all real things a real agreement (*convenientia realis*) and likeness under the aspect of being (*in ratione entis*). This is for Suarez so self-evident that he finds it improbable that Cajetan could have really denied it, and he also refers us to Thomas, according to whom the *analogia entis* does not prevent the *ratio entis* from belonging intrinsically to all analogates. That the real agreement in

[22] l.c. n. 13.
[23] DM 2, 1 n. 1.
[24] l.c. n. 6.
[25] DM 2, 3 n. 11.

the *ratio entis* is not so marked as it is between two substances as such or between things of the same genus and species, does not prevent it from being present at all and so making the precision of a concept possible.²⁶

Thus our mind obtains a concept of being which is indeed completely abstract, but only such a concept can be all-embracing. The concept of being therefore presupposes a real agreement of things; but this agreement places every being only as a real essence over against nothingness. And this is true of God and creatures, wherefore nothing will prevent this being from being predicable of God and creatures "secundum tantam abstractionem suam." "For who would say that being immediately designates God as God. . . . And the same question could be asked with regard to substance, accident and the other genera."²⁷ So we see that the concept of being is for Suarez just as it is for the Doctor Subtilis, an imperfect concept, since it rests on a very imperfect agreement and likeness of things.²⁸ Suarez expresses this especially in DM 2,3 n. 13 in a way very similar to that of Scotus: "Since all beings in reality possess that likeness and agreement in which the intellect conceives them in its cognition of being, and since the intellect conceives things as they are in themselves only inadequately, one must say that the concept of being so conceived does not comprise the definite mode of things. Hence, there is no question here about the essence of being as it is in itself, but only in so far as it appears in the denomination of the intellect (sub denominatione intellectus)." Consequently the concept of being truly designates reality, albeit inadequately, since it prescinds from all further determination of things. When Suarez himself occasionally tries to solve the question concerning the *univocatio* and *analogia entis* by simply saying that being is univocal in the logical realm and analogous in the metaphysical realm,²⁹ he wants to separate the two realms from each other and to deny

---

²⁶ DM 2, 2 n. 18: "Quod autem haec convenientia fortasse non sit tanta, quanta est inter substantias vel accidentia in propriis rationibus, ad rem praesentem non refert, nam ad summum concludit, unitatem conceptus entis non esse tantam, non vero quod non sit aliqua et sufficiens ad praecisionem conceptus objectivi secundum rationem." This does not contradict our exposition of the highest unity of the concept of being, which is based on its simplicity. For this passage has to do not with the internal unity of the concept of being in itself, but with the degree of agreement of things in the *ratio entis* as the foundation of the concept of being.
²⁷ DM 2, 1 n. 6.
²⁸ DM 2, 3 n. 16.
²⁹ DM 28, 3 and 20.

the real content of the univocal concept of being just as little as
Scotus did. The Doctor Eximius very fittingly says here that things
in their radical difference can also be the foundation for the unity
of the concept of being, because both—difference and unity—belong
to different orders. The former belongs to the order of reality,
while unity belongs to that of the intellect. But unity has, he adds,
its foundation in things themselves inasmuch as they agree with one
another, imperfectly, indeed, but nonetheless really. Thus both
difference of being and unity of the concept of being are based on
the same thing, as Suarez expressly assures us here, and so he rises
above, in our question, the separation of the logical domain from
that of reality.[30]

3. Contraction of the Concept of Being

Obviously, questions concerning the reality and origin of the
univocal concept of being can only be answered in connection with
the problem of its contraction. How is the abstract concept of being
further determined to the concept of a definite being, and what
difference corresponds *in rerum natura* to that of the two concepts?

Both Scotus and Suarez agree that being is not a generic concept. From this it would seem to follow necessarily that an abstraction of the concept of being in the sense of a precision from the
other determinations of an object is no more possible than is a
real contraction in which determinations are added to the concept
of being which are as little contained in it as are the specific differences in the genus. Now Suarez inclines to the opinion that Scotus
accepts a difference in the thing itself between its being and the differences which determine it further to this or that thing. The
conception is commonly ascribed to Scotus that being as "conceptus
objectivus entis" is in the thing itself distinct from the inferiors
and even from utterly simple essences.[31] Suarez wrote the entire
section 3 of the Disp. Met. 2: "Utrum ratio seu conceptus entis in
re ipsa et ante intellectum sit aliquo modo praecisus ab inferioribus" solely for the purpose of refuting this opinion. In the context,
it is true, he speaks of a distinction between being and its modes.
Consequently, he seems to be acquainted with the difference between *distinctio modalis* and *formalis,* between modes and formalities in the philosophy of Scotus, and he rightly seems to be of the

[30] DM 2, 3 n. 16.
[31] DM 2, 3 n. 6.

opinion that the Doctor Subtilis employs the former and not the latter in our case.[32] This is deduced from the refutation itself in which Suarez first advances the argument that being cannot be distinct from its *modus contractivus*, otherwise the *modus* would not participate in being and would so be nothing. However, he is not satisfied with this answer: being as a simple and altogether general concept could be distinguished from being as a simple but already further determined concept, with the result that the general concept would be included in this particular one, but not vice versa.[33]

Precisely this distinction between the utterly simple and therefore all-embracing and transcendental concept ("conceptus simpliciter simplex") and the merely simple concept is employed by the Doctor Subtilis in his treatment of being and the other pure perfections. Only the former and not the latter is univocal. The "conceptus simplex" over against the "simpliciter simplex" is further determined by the mode. The mode may be looked upon as a grade in which being or a pure perfection exists. Nothing can exist without being determined to such a grade in the range of being. Consequently, the concept which contains this grade within itself is indeed no longer as simple as the "conceptus simpliciter simplex," but it alone covers an actually present reality as such and can therefore be called a "conceptus perfectus."[34]

The modes that determine being in the first place are infiniteness and finiteness. The visualization of the mode as a grade makes it clear why the mode does not add a new content to the concept of

---

[32] Suarez, it is to be admitted, also hesitates in the question as to whether Scotus really cognized a distinctio formalis as a distinction in the thing itself, or whether he understands by it merely a distinctio fundamentalis in the sense of his distinctio rationis ratiocinatae or a mere distinctio virtualis; he notes that Scotus repeatedly speaks of a distinctio virtualis. Cf. DM 7, 1 n. 13. Here n. 15, he states in reference to our problem that the distinctio formalis is practically nothing else than his distinctio rationis ratiocinatae. For the concept of mode and for the difference between distinctio formalis and modalis in the writings of Scotus, cf. our work: *Der Wille als reine Vollkommenheit*. . . ., l.c. pp. 37-60, especially p. 37; Maurice Grajewski, O.F.M., *The Formal Distinction of Duns Scotus* (Washington, D. C.: 1944), pp. 81-87; Allan Wolter, O.F.M., *The Transcendentals*. . . ., l.c. pp. 24-27.

[33] DM 2, 3 n. 9: "ut simplicem conceptum communem a simplici conceptu particulari, ita ut communis in particulari includatur, quamvis non e contrario."

[34] Ox. I d. 8 q. 3 n. 27 (Vivès IX, 627 a): "quando intelligitur aliqua realitas cum modo intrinseco suo, ille conceptus non est ita simpliciter simplex, quin possit concipi illa realitas absque modo illo, sed tunc est conceptus imperfectus illius rei; potest etiam concipi sub illo modo, et tunc est conceptus perfectus illius rei."

being or to the concept of the pure perfection, and therefore imports no composition into it either. It also makes it clear that the modally undetermined concept of being still possesses real cognitional content, and that the modally determined concept remains a "conceptus simplex." For the grade adds nothing new to the thing, but only signifies the same thing in a definite intensity. Modal determination is therefore something altogether different from the contraction of a genus through its specific differences; for here new content is added.[35]

Suarez has therefore a certain recognition of the Scotistic distinction between mode and formality, since he takes it upon himself to reproach Scotus for making a distinction between being and mode. But he has failed to understand the Scotistic conception of mode as a *gradus perfectionis,* possibly because he employed the word *modus* in a different sense.[36] Hence it seems to him that the distinction between the common, completely simple concept and the further determined simple concept of being, which he adduces in favor of the Scotistic distinction between being and its further determination, does really not speak for Scotus but rather against him. For the further determined concept, too, is to be simple and therefore not again resolvable into several concepts.[37] Accordingly "simple" is quite certainly "simple," which, however, is not the case when we take mode as a grade of being which does not affect the simplicity of being. That Suarez does not think of this concept of mode is clear from DM 2, 3, where he takes for his example of "modus contractivus" not infiniteness and finiteness, although that would have suggested itself in the first place, but *perseita*s, which determines being as a substance.

Hence, as Scotus understands it, mode is on the one hand not a being, and therefore the concept of being can not be predicated of it *in quid*. On the other hand, it is something positive as a *gradus*

[35] Ox. I d. 8 q. 4 n. 17 (Vivès IX, 664 b): "infinitas enim non destruit formaliter rationem illius cui additur, quia in quocumque gradu intelligitur esse aliqua perfectio, qui tamen gradus est gradus illius perfectionis, non tollitur ratio formalis istius perfectionis propter istum gradum. . . ."

[36] Cf. DM 7, 1 n. 16 ff. Here in n. 19 he says that there must be modes, "quia cum creaturae sint imperfectae, ideoque vel dependentes, vel compositae, vel limitatae, vel mutabiles secundum varios status praesentiae unionis, aut terminationis, indigent his modis, quibus haec omnia in ipsis compleantur." Modes are therefore based on the finiteness of the creature, as, e.g., the actual inherence of the accident, the subsistence of nature, the presence in a place, etc. This concept of mode does not coincide with that of Scotus.

[37] DM 2, 3 n. 9.

perfectionis. Accordingly, the critical question of the Doctor Eximius: "Quomodo enim possunt constituere varias rerum essentias, et essentiale discrimen inter illas, si non essent reales modi et positivi? Si autem huiusmodi sunt, quomodo mente concipi potest, eas non includere intrinsece et essentialiter ens?"[38] does not do justice to the subtlety of the Scotistic concept of mode. The mode concept can not be disposed of with the disjunction of *ens aut non ens.*

The same seems to be also true of the "differentiae ultimae" of Scotus. These are the final differentiations of being which are not themselves beings. If they were, there would be a regressus in infinitum. But this would destroy every cognition; we must therefore arrive at concepts which are ultimate, no longer resolvable, and altogether simple, i.e., at the "conceptus simpliciter simplices" already mentioned. Such a concept is being, and so also is whatever determines being to be this or that being. Every cognition of a thing therefore arrives finally at a merely determinable and a merely determining moment. The concept of being is here naturally the final determinable element, and the "ultimate differences" are to be the final, irresolvable, and determining element of our cognition. Hence they can not themselves be *ens*; they rather determine *ens* to be this or that being.[39] This exposition of the ultimate differences is obscure and requires further explanation. Scotus counts among them whatever ultimately makes a being to be this individual or of this species, that is to say, the ultimate individual and specific differences. It is not our objective here to make a thorough examination of this doctrine. But so much may be said that Suarez proceeds against the finality of the *differentiae ultimae* with fundamentally the same simple argument by which he contends that the modes are either being or nothing at all.[40] Here, too, one can object to Suarez that being is further determined by the ultimate differences to be such and such a thing, and that it can therefore be predicated of them just as little as the subject of its quality. Mode as a grade of being is not being itself nor yet something else; the ultimate difference as a qualification of being is not itself being, and yet just as little distinct from it as any quality is distinct from its subject.

[38] DM 2, 5 n. 8.
[39] Ord. I d. 3 p. 1 q. nn. 131-133 (Ed. Vat. III, 81/82).
[40] DM 2, 5 n. 6 ff.

Between the modes and the ultimate differences there is indeed the difference that the former as grades of perfection cannot in themselves be represented. Just as the brightness of the light can not be conceived without the light, so neither can I conceive of a grade without that of which it is a grade.[41] Hence there is no *distinctio formalis* between being and mode, for every formally distinct content can be, according to Scotus, the object of a special and complete act of cognition.[42] But this is undoubtedly possible with the specific and other ultimate differences, wherefore a *distinctio formalis* between them and being is to be admitted. Hence, when Allan Wolter says that the mode is essentially an internal qualification of its subject and therefore always includes in its definition the being which it determines,[43] it is not equally true of the other ultimate differences, since the mode affects its subjects more intimately than these do. But both have this in common that they do not determine being as new adventitious entities, but only determine its entity further to this or that being. Thus being, according to Scotus, is not finally contracted by being but through its further unfolding which does not differ from it *qua ens* and for that very reason determines it intrinsically. This becomes especially apparent with respect to the mode.

Suarez seems at first sight to continue this doctrine concerning the contraction of being. His critique of Scotus only shows that he simply had no correct understanding of the mode-doctrine of Scotus. Hence he was confronted with the dilemma that being is contracted either through being or non-being. The first solution, however, would involve the regressus in infinitum, and the second is obviously impossible. Suarez is of the opinion that in both attempts at a solution the contraction of being is still always taken as a composition, such as that of generic and specific differences. As a matter of fact, contraction is to be so understood, that the concept of being be taken, in the one instance, in a more developed and determined manner *(expressius)* than in the other instance *(solum confuse)*. We can comprehend a thing either more sharply and explicitly as it is in its proper and concrete being or only in its general essential features in which it agrees with other things. All this can come about, Suarez holds, without a conceptual addition:

[41] Ox. I d. 8 q. 3 nn. 27-29 (Vivès IX, 626-628).
[42] *Ord.* I d. 2 p. 2 q. 1-4 n. 329 (Ed. Vat. II/351): "alia distinctio, maior, est in intellectu, concipiendo duobus actibus duo obiecta formalia. . . ."
[43] l.c. p. 25.

one and the same thing is cognized in only a more or less explicit manner, and therefore abides in both instances by a simple concept, more or less developed.[44]

The similarity with Scotus becomes more tangible when we consider the examples with which the Doctor Eximius clarifies this matter. The concept of a definite degree of heat would not really add to the concept of heat, by way of a composition, a mode distinct from the concept, but would represent the heat expressly as it is in the thing. So, too, according to the mind of Suarez, we must regard the determination of being to infinite being, for infiniteness is not added to it as a mode distinct from it, so that the mode is something else and therefore inferior to infinite being. The concept of infinite being is only the more explicit and more determined concept over against being taken simply; hence the latter also, over against the former, cannot be called the more simple but only the more abstract concept.[45] Scotus could have employed these formulations in exactly the same way. Nevertheless, there persists a difference in the doctrine on the contraction of the univocal concept of being; it derives from the different conception both thinkers have of cognition. Suarez merely says that the distinction between the abstract concept of being and the more determined concepts is not made as in the abstraction of the genus from the species in that the intellect omits a content in the one case and not in the other; no, both concepts are of themselves already distinct in cognition when they represent the same thing in either a general way or in a more determined and definite way.[46]

But in order to distinguish the simple from the more determined concept of being, Scotus would still demand a reason for it in the thing. He would insist that the more determined concept actually brings with it new moments which are not thought of in the simple concept, and that therefore the matter is not settled by a mere *confusio* and a comparison which represents only the common element in order to arrive from that concept to this one; what is needed is a genuine *praecisio*. This *praecisio*, however, must have its basis in the thing. That is, the distinction of the concepts calls for a difference in the thing; for it is a principle for Duns Scotus that we must coordinate the different acts of our comprehension with the

[44] DM 2, 6 n. 7.
[45] l.c.
[46] l.c. n. 10: "non est per separationem praecisivam unius gradus ab alio, sed solum per cognitionem praecisivam conceptus confusi a distincto et determinato."

different moments in things.⁴⁷ Suarez denies this principle: not only in regard to the concept of being but also in regard to the genus-species relationship he explains the difference in concepts by saying that they express things adequately or inadequately. Thus the difference in concepts still has its foundation in things, but in another and essentially more mediate way than with Duns Scotus.⁴⁸ At all events, Suarez has also this antithesis in mind when he attacks the opinion of Scotus that there is a difference in the thing between being and its further determinations, even if he did not realize the subtlety of this distinction.

When the Doctor Subtilis, in accordance with his idea of cognition, speaks of such a difference in the thing, he naturally does not mean that the being of the thing lies in some way beside its *modus contractivus* and becomes a definite being only through composition—a conception which he rejects as absurd, and this not only with reference to the simple essence of God. But what he means is that being as such, as an object of our cognition and not as a mere *conceptus mentis,* much less as a pure *flatus vocis,* is of itself indifferent with regard to the modes of infiniteness and finiteness. Neither do wisdom and the other pure perfections already contain in their pure essence that grade in which alone they can become real.⁴⁹ But as little as this grade is anything else than wisdom itself, so little does the mode, which "contracts" the in-itself-univocal and indifferent being to an analogous one, import a composition into it.

Hence we can take it as the conclusion of this section as well as of the entire Part II: Scotus and Suarez teach that the univocal and the already-further-determined analogous concepts of being mean the same simple reality, and therefore that being *a parte rei* is strictly one with whatever distinctness it may have. The assertion made by Manser that for Scotus "being as such and as it is in things is an actual absolute form which exists in God and creatures, substance and accident, and in all genera and species of

---

⁴⁷ Cf. Gilson, *Jean Duns Scot* (Paris: 1952), p. 498, who traces this Scotistic thesis back to Avicenna.

⁴⁸ Cf. my treatise: *Wesenheit und Individuum bei Suarez, Scholastik* 37 (1962/11), pp. 181-210.

⁴⁹ In our work on *Der Wille als reine Vollkommenheit. . . .* we insist on the enormous importance of this doctrine of being and the pure perfections, inasmuch as they are in themselves, i.e., *a parte rei,* indifferent with regard to modal determination. This doctrine, we stated, is of supreme importance for the whole philosophy of Scotus.

things as a primal and most common form,"[50] is therefore true of neither the one nor of the other; hence there is no basis for the statement that this concept of being has an eminently monistic tendency *(eminent monistischen Zug)*.[51] Both Scotus and Suarez employ the concept of the *gradus perfectionis* as well as the illustration of intensity to show that the further determination of being does not imply a composition, and that the acceptance of a primal simple and univocal concept of being does not call for such a consequence. The different conception of cognition has this result: unlike Suarez, Scotus is not content with the statement that the univocal concept of being is a more imperfect picture of reality than the more determined concept, but seeks for it an immediate foundation in the thing itself, which is also independent of cognition. Scotus can therefore base the *univocatio entis* more immediately in the thing than Suarez can. This does not alter the fact that in the system of each thinker not only the *analogia entis* but also the *univocatio entis* is a true expression of reality.

University of Salzburg

Translated from the German by Edwin Dorzweiler, O.F.M. Cap.

[50] Gallus Manser, O.P., *Das Wesen des Thomismus*, 2. Aufl. Freiburg (Schweiz) 1935, pp. 378/79. Cf. Hans Meyer, *Thomas von Aquin*, 2. Aufl. (Paderborn: 1961). This is a large-scale exposition of Thomism, which also really does justice to the philosophy of Duns Scotus, and which does not hesitate to supplement with Scotus some of the positions taken by St. Thomas.
[51] Manser, op. c. p. 380.

12

WILLIAM OF VAUROUILLON, O.F.M.
A FIFTEENTH-CENTURY SCOTIST

by

IGNATIUS BRADY

As we commemorate the birth of John Duns Scotus, it is perhaps quite proper to mark at the same time the five-hundredth anniversary of the death in 1463 of one of his most devoted followers, William of Vaurouillon, O.F.M. Not a profound thinker or metaphysician of the first rank, William was nonetheless considered in his own day to be among the better Scotists; and his own words reveal his admiration for the Subtle Doctor: Nunc ad te, amor meus, O Doctor Subtilis, Joannes dictus de Donis, se convertit lingua mea . . . Mirum unum comperio, quod tot subtilia scribens in errore non es comprehensus.[1] Perhaps the most outstanding Scotist of the fifteenth century,[2] he is at the same time a witness to a certain unity and continuity, despite vast differences, in the Franciscan school, and indeed in Scholasticism itself. In this, as much as in his Scotism,[3] lies his contribution to medieval thought.

I. LIFE (c. 1390/94—1463)[4]

A Breton, William was born about 1390/94 in the hamlet known today as Vauruellan. While Vaurouault has been proposed as his

---

[1] *In IV Sent.*, epilogus (ed. Venetiis 1496, fol. 316b).
[2] "Der bekannteste (berühmteste) Verteidiger des Scotismus im 15. Jahrhundert," acc. to B. Roth, *Franz von Mayronis O.F.M.* [Franziskanische Forschungen 3], Werl 1936, 6 (and 26); "Prae ceteris Scoti discipulis saec. XV, Guillelmus Vorillong particulari modo eminet," writes C. Balić, *Relatio a commissione scotistica exhibita*, Roma 1939, 88.
[3] Which, perhaps, the late Fr. Franz Pelster somewhat over-emphasized in his basic article: "Wilhelm von Vorillon, ein Skotist des 15. Jahrh.," *Franz. Studien*, 8 (1921), 48-66; see also E. Wegerich, "Bio-bibliographische Notizen über Franziskanerlehrer des 15. Jahrhunderts," *Franz. Studien*, 29 (1942), 193-197. The present article supplements, but does not supplant, these two studies.
[4] This paragraph is a summary of "William of Vaurouillon († 1463): a Biographical Essay," in *Miscellanea Melchor de Pobladura*, Vol. I (1964), 291-315.

birthplace, it has no resemblance to the various forms of his name.[5] Hence we consider Vauruellan more likely. His date of birth is unknown, save by deduction from the studies and teaching he must have undertaken before being assigned to Paris in 1427. William himself tells us he entered the Franciscan order *in iuvenili aetate*, and that he made all or most of his studies within the order.[6] Current legislation moreover demanded that before being chosen to read the Sentences at Paris, a Friar Minor was to have taught arts and philosophy for a number of years and to have spent at least one year in commenting on Peter Lombard in some Studium of the order.[7] Vaurouillon must thus have been about thirty-five years of age when appointed to Paris by the chapter of Vercelli (1427). Where he taught following his ordination to the priesthood is not apparent, though there is some slight probability that it may have been at Saint-Saturnin in Toulouse.[8] Because of some confusion at Paris, he did not begin as bachelor of the Sentences before the Fall of 1429; and for reasons unknown, though likely bearing on the capture and trial of St. Joan of Arc, he completed only the first three books and left Paris early in 1431. Only in September 1447 was he to return and complete the fourth book, and then receive his licentiate on January 29, 1448.

The intervening years saw him in Italy and Germany, at the council of Basel (September 1433), at Châteauroux (perhaps as guardian), and at Fougères in Brittany (1441-1442). Whether he taught meanwhile cannot be established, though the compilation of his *Repertorium* or *Vademecum* to the Sentences of Duns Scotus would rather point to a period of teaching or at least of peaceful research. There is likewise the barest indication in the fourth book

[5] The three most common (and surest) forms are: *de Valle Rouillonis*, Latin form used in two papal documents, by George le Maalot (a disciple), and in the one known manuscript of his Sentences; *Vaurouillon*, French form found in two documents of 1442; and *Vaurillon* (French) or *Vorillon* (Latin and non-French), a form apparently used by William himself. In addition, there are at least 18 variants!

[6] *In IV Sent.*, epilogus: "Ad te venio, O pauperum patriarcha Francisce, pater inclite, cuius ordo me de mundana conversatione in iuvenili aetate revocavit, nutrivit in moribus, in scientiis erudivit" (fol. 315d).

[7] See *Archivum Fran. Historicum*, 30 (1947), 349 (Constitutions of Benedict XII); and N. Glassberger, *Chronica*, in *Analecta Franciscana*, II, 276 (Chapter of Forlì, 1421).

[8] Another friar of Touraine, Peter Mazoti, was bachelor of the Sentences at Toulouse, 1419-1420. He was however to obtain the magisterium there. Cf. M. Bihl, "De Fr. Petro Mazoti O.F.M. baccalaureo theologiae Tolosano an. 1419-20," *AFH*, 23 (1930), 252-266.

of his Sentences that he may have taught at the University of Poiters. Upon receiving the license and doctorate (on April 1, 1448), William remained at Paris as Magister regens until the end of the scholastic year, but moved to Poitiers for the school year 1448-1449 (or perhaps, 1449-50), where he wrote his *Liber de anima*.

Thereafter, more likely in the summer of 1449 than of 1450, he was elected Minister Provincial of Touraine, a post he held until 1460 or 1461. Little is known of the years of his provincialate beyond a prolonged and even bloody battle over the possession of the convent of Châteauroux. The Observants had been in peaceful possession for some decades, but when they sought to withdraw from the jurisdiction of the provincial and subject themselves and the house to John Maubert, ultramontaine vicar of the Observance, William's predecessor in office, Peter Leger, had taken legal action at Paris against them. The suit was still undecided when William was elected provincial superior. The Observants in turn, through Count Guy II de Chauvigny, lord of Chateauroux, obtained a decision from Pope Nicholas V, 1453, giving the convent to them. Because the decree was rather uncanonically promulgated, William launched a counter-appeal and received a more favorable reply. But this with other papal documents (plus constant friction) precipitated a crisis in the summer of 1456, and a skirmish within both cloister and church. The provincial was attacked and unceremoniously ejected from the church. The affair dragged on until 1462, when Pope Pius II gave the convent to the Observants and forbade further interference from the Conventuals.

By this date, William was no longer superior, but was involved in two controversies that occupied the last two years of his life. Where and in what circumstances we know not, but in 1461 (or the Lent of 1462?) in a sermon to the people he declared that the words of Christ *Ecce filius tuus* were of such efficacy that they *could* have transformed Saint John into the natural son of our Lady. When this was reported to the Roman curia, William was summoned to answer charges of error and scandal. While thus in Rome in the course of 1462, he became involved in the violent controversy over the Precious Blood occasioned by the Easter sermon of St. James of the Marches.[9] The latter had said that the blood which Christ shed on the cross—the blood, that is, which stained the cross or fell to

---

[9] For a general account of the controversy, cf. M.D. Chenu, art. "Sang du Christ," in *Dict. de Théol. Cath.*, XIV, 1094-1097.

the ground—was no longer united to his divinity and was not reassumed at the Resurrection. The Dominican inquisitor, James of Brescia, declared such a teaching false and heretical and carried the affair to the Holy See. The two orders were soon so divided on the question that Pope Pius II called for a public dispute late in the same year. With Francis della Rovere, future General of the Order and later Pope Sixtus IV, and Francis of Rimini, Vaurouillon defended the Franciscan position. The memoirs of Pius II claim he gave a very poor performance incommensurate with his renown, perhaps because he was already an old man in poor health. He did not live long after the disputation, but died early in 1463, likely on January 22, and was buried in Aracoeli.

II. WRITINGS

A. *Commentary on the Sentences.*

William's reputation rests largely on his *Compendium* or commentary on the Sentences, which was published at least five times between 1489 and 1510. The *editio princeps* was printed at Lyons by John Trechsel in 1489, and was reprinted by him ten years later.[10] Two editions were made at Venice, one in 1496 (which we have used), the second in 1502,[11] and one at Basel in 1510. The last, prepared by the Observant friar Daniel Agricola,[12] seems to differ in slight details from those preceding it, as it includes an introduction by Agricola (fol. 2r), and one by the printer Adam Petri de Langendorf (fol. 2v), who informs the reader that the titles to the questions are from Friar Daniel.[13] The latter does not seem to have used any new manuscripts for the edition; he has, however, made some very minor changes, adding *sanctus* for Bonaventura (can-

---

[10] Incipit: Sacre pagine professoris eximii magistri Guillermi Vorrilong OFM: opus super quattuor libros sententiarum feliciter incipit.—Explicit: . . . opus super quatuor libros sent. feliciter consummatum est in inclita urbe lugdunensi die XXIIII. Augusti MCCCCLXXXIX.—Cf. W. A. Copinger, *Supplement to Hains Repertorium Bibliographicum*, II, 2 (London 1902), n. 6559 (copy in Newberry Library, Chicago). On the edition of 1499, *ibid.*, n. 6561.

[11] Cf. Copinger, *op. cit.*, II, 2, n. 6560, for ed. of 1496 (copy in Newberry Library, Chicago); a copy of the ed. of 1502 is found at St. Bonaventure, N. Y.

[12] On Agricola, cf. J. H. Sbaralea, *Suppl. et castigatio ad Scriptores trium ordinum S. Francisci*, ed. nova, Romae 1908, I, 233; and *Franz. Studien*, 14 (1927), 309-313; a copy of his edition, in Holy Name College, Washington.

[13] Thus, *In II Sent.*, d. 3, p. 1, is introduced by the title: Questio ista docet de compositione angelicalis nature ex forma et materia metaphisicali in qua opinionem Thome acriter impugnat, de quo Scotum vide hac distinctione q. 1 et aliis (fol. 131 A).

onized in 1482) and substituting *Bonaventura* for Vaurouillon's occasional use of *Johannes Bonaventurae* (which occurs also in the *Liber de anima*). I have not found any passage, however, where he changed *doctor devotus* to *doctor seraphicus*.

Only one manuscript of the commentary is known, that of Rennes, *Ville 41*. Those listed by Mons. F. Stegmüller are rather the original and copies of the course on the Sentences given by John Findling, O.F.M. at Ingolstadt 1512-1516, for which he used as basis the *Compendium* of Vaurouillon.[14] The Rennes codex, which I have not been able so far to examine, quite evidently lacks the exordium of the printed editions, the epilogue after the fourth book, and apparently the *collationes* before the individual books. In their place is a new introduction which likely explains or defends the text itself: Dixit mihi amicus: Scriptum tuum super Sententias aut corrige aut videas. Aut enim deffecisti scribendo aut homo inimicus superseminavit zizania aut lolium.[15] Whether the text of the commentary corresponds to the printed version of the *Compendium*, remains to be investigated.

A close examination of the commentary bears out the fact that the fourth book is separated from the first three by a number of years. The early books well merit the estimate given by Fr. Pelster, that the compendium is primarily a school book, with no great originality or newness, since its purpose is to explain and defend Scotus, briefly, clearly, summarily.[16] The author's main sources

[14] Cf. F. Stegmüller, *Repertorium commentariorum in Sententias Petri Lombardi*, I, Würzburg 1947, n. 304, p. 141.—Perhaps Findling commented on the third and fourth books only, since no manuscripts of books one and two are extant or at least known. On the third book: *Collecta circa tertium Sent. iuxta lecturam doctoris Guilhelmi Vorillon* (codex of Münich, *Clm 11695*); and *Collecta quaedam admodum utilia pro faciliori intellectu tertii scripti doctoris brevis Guilhelmi Vorillon* (ms. of Paderborn Friary, on which cf. R. Menth, "Eine bisher unbekannte Handschrift von P. Joh. Findling OFM," in *Franz. Studien*, 14 [1927], 346-349). The fourth book is found in three manuscripts: Münich, Universitätsbibl., cod. 8° 28, 8° 30, and 8° 34 (cf. M. Bihl, *Der Katalog des P. Joh. Findling vom Jahre 1533*, Ingolstadt 1921, 27-31).—In most of these manuscripts Vaurouillon is called *Doctor brevis*; the last listed (8° 34) contains a list of scholastic titles, fol. 169v-170, published by F. Ehrle, *Ehrentitel der scholastischen Lehrer des Mittelalters*, München 1919, 51-52, in which William is again termed *Doctor brevis*. On the other hand, Daniel Agricola calls him *Doctor acerrimus* (ed. cit., fol. 2r); he may have meant this as a simple adjective.

[15] Cf. [A. Vétault,] *Manuscrits de la Bibl. de Rennes*, in *Catal. gén. des mss des bibl. publiques de France*, Départments, tome XXIV, 29-30. At the end of this prologue the same hand has written: "Ponatur in principio lecture super sententias fratris Guillelmi de Valle Rouillonis."

[16] *Art. cit.*, 62.

throughout the first three books are the commentaries of Bonaventure, Thomas, and Duns Scotus; more use of Francis de Meyronnes is shown in Book I than in the second and third.[17] At the same time, Vaurouillon manifests a fairly wide knowledge of scholastic literature, ranging from the *Corpus dionysiacum* and the Victorines, Alexander of Hales and Albert the Great, to Giles of Rome, Henry of Ghent, Godfrey of Fontaines, together with a few scholastics after Scotus: Nicholas Boneti, Guiral Ot (Gerard Odonis), Nicholas of Lyra, etc. On the other hand, the fourth book is considerably longer than any of the earlier ones, largely because certain questions are made the vehicles of lengthy philosophical discussions; the subtleties missed, perhaps, in the other books are here supplied *per longum et latum*. From distinctions 32 and 42 (the incipits of which differ with different scholastics) we readily gather that William has expanded his main sources in the fourth book to include Richard of Mediavilla, who is constantly cited, Francis de Meyronnes, and Landulphus Caracciolo. More vehemently Scotistic than ever, Vaurouillon devotes more attention—thanks, no doubt, to his *Vademecum*—to the scholastics considered and opposed by the Subtle Doctor: Giles of Rome, Henry of Ghent, and Godfrey; and expands considerably his use of the early disciples of Scotus, de Meyronnes, Hugo de Novo Castro, Antonius Andrea, Landulph, with occasional mention of John of Rodington and John of Ripa, and a passing reference to Aufred Gontier. In addition, it is not unfair to say he makes a great display of erudition and of a wide range of reading; e.g., in his curious etymologies of many terms, his use of the *Summa* of Godfrey of Poitiers (long since forgotten by others), the *Summa* of Astensanus, Peter of Tarentaise, Roger Bacon, etc.

Yet without examining and comparing the commentaries of his contemporaries and teachers, e.g., Jacques Textor, Luke of Assisi, Gerard Fuleti, etc., none of which are known, it is well nigh impossible to say whether William's work is representative of the first part of the fifteenth century. The *Compendium* is full of curious knowledge, but is this a personal trait or does it reflect a tendency of that day? The fact that his commentary has survived in so many editions would rather indicate that it was regarded as outstanding. Certainly it is almost encyclopedic in its use of earlier scholastics,

---

[17] All pertinent texts will be found in B. Roth, *Franz von Mayronis O.F.M.*, pp. 87-91 and esp. 554-572.

and rich in historical references. Frequently William takes pains to give the incipit of a work and/or cites directly from it: a help in identifying anonymous writings. To some extent his work likewise reflects the theological situation of his day, even if he shies away from such a question as the relation of council to Pope: Etiam si haec opinio esset vera, Papa non teneretur confiteri, dato quod esset super concilium generale: hanc abyssum non introeo pro praesenti.[18]

The work as a whole, as Pelster has pointed out, labors under the bane, if not the curse, of ternaries: every question has three articles; the first considers three terms, often with a ternary of binaries or ternaries when there are six or nine meanings available; the body of the question, the second article, has three conclusions, often subdivided; and these in turn are followed by three difficulties which form the third article. As a result, Francis de Meyronnes, who delighted in groups of fours, receives constant criticism as straining the truth to make a quaternary: melius est habere bonum ternarium quam malum quaternarium.[19] The same fatal tendency is found throughout the *Liber de anima*.

B. *Repertorium* or *Vademecum*.

From Vaurouillon's own testimony we know that in the years before he returned to Paris he had composed "a tract on the opinions which are found in the [works of the] Subtle Doctor,"[20] or, as the title of the Padua edition (c. 1485) phrases it, "of the opinions presented anonymously by Scotus."[21] This edition, itself quite rare,

[18] *In IV Sent.*, d. 17, a. 2 (fol. 254c). He has some interesting points on the episcopacy as an order, *ibid.*, d. 25, a. 2, concl. 2 (fol. 266c).
[19] *In IV Sent.*, d. 14-16, a. 2, concl. 1. Cf. also *In I Sent.*, d. 28, a. 1: "Qui sic defendit Franciscum, vadat ad vicum straminis, et in 2° Perihermenias audiet istam conclusionem non valere . . . Unde dico quod debebat sibi sufficere unus bonus ternarius et non addere istum quartum modum, qui simpliciter est falsus, ut malum haberet quaternarium" (fol. 47b).—See other instances in B. Roth, *op. cit.*, 90-91.
[20] *In IV Sent.*, d. 11, a. 2: "Unde motus doctor solemnis dicit, Quodlibet 3, q. 6, 8, 15, 20, et in multis aliis locis quae notavi in tractatu quem composui de opinionibus quae sunt in Doctore Subtili" (fol. 247b).
[21] *Incipit repertorium magistri Guillermi Varrillonis quod alio nomine dicitur Vademecum vel collectarium non opinionis Scoti: sed opinionum in Scoto nullatenus signatarum.*—This is followed (fol. 60v-68r) by the *Vademecum* to the *Quodlibeta* (see below), and then under new pagination the decrees or condemnations of 1277 and 1240; finally, in an unnumbered section: *Formalitates modernorum de mente clar. doct. subt. Scoti . . . compilate per . . . mag. Ant. Sirecti prov. turonie O. Min.* This bears the date at the end: MCCCCLXXXIIII,

was preceded by one published at Paris about 1483, which seems almost unavailable.[22]

No manuscript is known of the complete *Vademecum*. There is, however, a slightly reduced form of the fourth book in a few manuscripts and in one edition of Scotus. Since it is called a *Summaria recapitulatio . . . sumpta ex collectario magistri Guillermi Varrillonis*,[23] it is quite evidently not the work of William himself. It reveals, however, the popularity of his handbook.

The published text proved immediately helpful to editors of Scotus, for it provided them with ready marginal references to the quidams and opinions discussed in the text. The first example of this seems to be the edition of the *Opus Oxoniense* revised and emended by the Franciscan Master Philip of Bagnocavallo, Venice, 1497, which plainly advertises: *additis annotationibus opinionum diversorum doctorum ac etiam textuum commentorum Aristotelis in marginibus*.[24] Master Philip could well have derived the citations of Aristotle from any of several editions of Aristotle-Averroes printed at Venice in the previous decade or more.[25] But the marginal annotations identifying the opinions examined by Scotus are taken literally from Vaurouillon.[26] Even when the *Vademecum*

---

die XVIII Jan. Printed at Padua by Matthaeus Cerdonis de Vindesgretz. Cf. W. A. Copinger, *Supplement*, II, 2, n. 6562 (copy in Walters Art Gallery, Baltimore).

[22] Publ. by Simon Doliatoris de Prussia. I have not found a copy of this.

[23] The fourth book appears as an appendix to the *Quaestiones in Libr. IV*, published at Paris 1473 by Gering-Crantz-Friburger. Cf. *Gesamtkatalog der Wiegendrucke*, VII, Leipzig 1938, n. 9083, col. 714, according to which the text presented is a shortened form of the Vademecum. Manuscripts: *Vat. Ottobon. 476*, fol. 209a-226a; *Marseilles 254*, fol. 348d-388v; and (incomplete) Cambridge, *Peterhouse 16*, fol. 149r-150r.

[24] Cf. *Gesamtkatalog*, VII, n. 9077, col. 709; I have access only to the second volume (Libri III-IV) of this edition. As far as I can ascertain, no edition of Scotus before 1497 carries such notes (cf. *Gesamtkatalog*, VII, nn. 9073-76, col. 702-709). On Phillip Porcacci, or de Porcatiis, de Bagnocavallo († 1511), cf. Sbaralea, *Supplementum* II, 383b-384a; and C. Piana, *Ricerche su le Università di Bologna e di Parma nel secolo XV*, Quaracchi 1963, 182-183 and index.

[25] Cf. *Gesamtkatalog*, II, 1926, nn. 2337-41, col. 563-574.

[26] A few passages should suffice to illustrate. Thus the *Vademecum* for III, d. 1, q. 1: "Circa primam distinctionem tertii apud doctorem subtilem sunt quinque questiones. Prima utrum possible fuerit naturam humanam uniri Deo in unitate persone. Et probato secundo articulo, scilicet possibilitate talis unionis ex parte persone que assumit, secundum mentem propriam, tangitur probatio fratris guill'i var. libro 3 q. 1 . . . Quo ad tertium articulum . . . Primo ponitur probatio eiusdem fr. Guill. Var., tertio ibidem . . . Tunc descendo ad argumenta quomodo potest respectus terminare dependentiam. Dicit henricus, quodl. 13, q. 15." These references are reproduced to the letter in the edition

unwittingly oversteps the bounds of historical accuracy, the Venetian editor follows. Thus William cites at least once the *Ethics* of Guiral Ot among the sources of Scotus, whereas its author was at Paris only years after the Subtle Doctor.[27] Such mistakes were perpetuated save when the sharp eye of an editor caught some unhistorical citation.[28]

C. The *Liber de anima*.

The last work, apparently, that Vaurouillon wrote before becoming provincial of Touraine, is his rather encyclopedic treatise on the soul.[29] It is very definitely written after his Sentences, on which it draws heavily on occasion; and quite certainly not at Paris.[30] Of the two manuscripts known, one was copied at Poitiers by his disciple George le Maalot while William was still provincial. Hence we conclude that the work was written (and given as a course) at the university of Poitiers in the scholastic year 1448-1449.

In his colophon, le Maalot calls the work an *apparatus trium librorum de anima,* implying apparently that it is a kind of commentary on the *De anima* of Aristotle. While this is a correct estimation, since the piece does follow Aristotle's general line of thought, Vaurouillon himself seems to have looked upon it as a modernization and expansion of the *Summa de anima* of John of La Rochelle, also of the Province of Touraine. Using Rupella's

---

of 1497, tom. II, fol. 2c, and 3d.—At the same time, Philip has occasionally added a fresh reference; e.g., in III, d. 3, q. 1, to Vaurouillon's citation (fol. 31r) of *Tho. I-II, q. 81, a. 2,* our editor joins *et in 3. Scripto d. 3* (fol. 9d).

[27] On Book III, d. 38, William writes: "In dist. 38 queritur utrum omne mendacium sit peccatum. Conclusio certa quod sic; sed ratio queritur. Dicit ut videtur: si spiritualis limitetur ad Deum. Fr. Petrus de Tharentasia in presenti dist., q. 4 . . . Dicit Tho. 2-2, q. 110, a. 3 . . . Dicit tertio Bonav. in presenti dist., q. 2, et girardus odonis, 1 Ethycorum" (fol. 35r). These citations reappear in Philip's edition, II, fol. 64b. We may note that Ot does treat lying in a rather incidental way in Book I, q. 15: Utrum veritas sit preferenda amicitie (*Sententia et Expositio cum questionibus Geraldi Odonis super libros Ethicorum Aristotelis cum textu eiusdem,* Venetiis 1500, fol. 10b-11a). This is likely what William has in mind; but it is not a source of Scotus!

[28] For an example, cf. *Medieval Studies,* XI (1949), p. 252, note 22.

[29] Edition by I. Brady, "The *Liber de anima* of William of Vaurouillon O.F.M.," in *Medieval Studies,* X (1948), 225-297 (for Books I-II); and XI (1949), 247-307 (Book III).

[30] In Book II, c 10, William refers to his Fourth Book of the Sentences: "De quo dixi super quartum" (*Med. Stud.,* X, 287). Several times mention is made of Paris and its customs; e.g., I, prologue: "Hic doctorum ternarius triplex flos censetur Parius" (*Med. Stud.,* X, p. 232); II, 13: "Secunda opinio est Henrici de Gandavo, quem doctores Parisius Doctorem Solemnem nominant" (*ibid.,* 294).

material at great length, Vaurouillon expands it by additions from the *Summa fratris Alexandri,* Bonaventure, Duns Scotus, a tract he attributes to St. Thomas, and his own Sentences.[31]

In form, he follows Aristotle, at least in Book I, where he examines "the opinions of the ancient philosophers on the soul," to lead up to the doctrine of Aristotle, *quae vera est* (II, 1). The second book resembles more closely the plan of Rupella's *Summa,* since it considers the definitions offered by Christian tradition, and then successively the causes and attributes of the soul, its dignity as image of God, its union with the body, its immortality and passibility apart from such a union. Very much the same order as in the *Summa's* second tract, on the soul and its powers, is followed in the third book. Taking his cue from Rupella but his doctrine from Scotus, William opens the last book with the question of the relation of the powers to the essence. Only in treating the inner senses and the intellect does he add much that is new, and rather complicated the work of the editor by the use of unusual sources. The chapters on the interior senses rely greatly on a tract or two tracts he ascribes to St. Thomas: *De sensu communi,* and another *De potentiis animae interioribus,* both in actuality the work of a disciple of St. Albert the Great.[32] In the final chapters William expands at length on Rupella's sparse remarks on the intellect, by considering the "division of the intellect according to the philosophers" (that is, the Aristotelian tradition through the Arabians) and then according to the theologians, especially Bonaventure and Scotus. In conclusion he adds new material on the spiritual senses and on the synderesis and conscience.

The work, which does not perhaps present an altogether cohe-

---

[31] His ideal, as proposed in the Prologue, is to achieve "aliqualem animae humanae notitiam iuxta vires modicas . . . tres Minores velut stellas tres praefulgidas imitatus, fratrem Alexandrum de Hales . . . fratrem Joannem Bonaventurae, qui exstat Doctor Devotus seu Seraphicus, et fratrem Joannem de Rupella" (*ibid.,* 232).—The *seu Seraphicus* may strike us, since in his Sentences William never varies from the title *Doctor Devotus.* We may suspect that *Seraphicus,* used by John Gerson already in 1426, was not yet known at Paris in William's day.

[32] See Book III, ch. 10 and 11 *(Med. Studies,* XI, pp. 271, 272). These tracts, which belong neither to St. Thomas nor (as I once imagined) to St. Albert, have since been published: I. Brady, "Two Sources of the *Summa de homine* of Saint Albert the Great," *Rech. de théol. anc. et méd.,* XX (1953), 222-271; with additional note, "Source or Extract," *ibid.,* XXV (1958), 142-143. As a result, the discussion in *Med. Stud.,* XI (1949), 248-250, is quite beside the point, as is also much in the introduction in *RTAM,* 1953, 228-234.

sive doctrine, remained quite unknown and without influence. It is nonetheless important in its witness to the feeling of a certain unity within the Franciscan school, another proof that the Scotistic group was not as rigid and narrow as it is sometimes pictured.

III. UNAUTHENTIC WORKS

A. *Collectarium super Quodlibeta Scoti.*

In the Padua edition, the *Vademecum* is followed by a similar work on the quodlibetal questions of Scotus (fol. 60v-68r), with the simple incipit: *Circa quodlibeta sunt 21 quaestiones.* Quite evidently, this short work is intended to accomplish for the *Quodlibeta* what the *Vademecum* had done for the *Opus Oxoniense.* But in contents it is much poorer; e.g., the short tract on the first question is hardly more than a summary, with no reference to opinions. Other questions are somewhat more detailed.[33]

This cannot be considered the work of Vaurouillon, since the text itself twice cites the *Vademecum* as the work of Magister Guillelmus: In decima quaestione qua quaeritur utrum Deus posset species in eucharistia convertere in aliquid praeexsistens[34] . . . In tertio articulo ponuntur tres opiniones. Prima in principio quae est Henrici de Gadavo [sic] quodli. 9, q. 9, et quodli. xi, q. 4, et Quodli. 2, q. 10, ut patet in Collectorio magistri Guill'mi super quartum dist. xi q. 4[35] . . . Tertia opinio . . . est opinio Varronis in quarti dist. xi, cui concordat fr. Joh. Paris., ut patet in quarto Scoti in dist. praeallegata, q. 3, quam Magister Guillelmus recitat et ad lucem reducit, ut patet in loco dicto (fol. 64v-65r).

The colophon indicates this new *Vademecum* was brought from Paris to Padua by Petrus de Cruce, magister regens at the Studium of San Antonio,[36] who may be the author. It seems unlikely, how-

---

[33] Thus Quaest. 2: ". . . quatuor rationes impugnate que sunt Thome prima parte Summe, q. 7, a. 1°, et 2° Scripti dist. 3, q. 4, et Egidii de Roma quodlibeto 2° q. 7, deinde ibi . . . Ista ratio est Henrici de Gandavo quodlibeto 6° q. 1" (fol. 61r).

[34] Cf. Duns Scotus, *Opera omnia*, ed. Vivès, Paris 1895, tom. XXV, 401.

[35] Cf. *Vademecum:* "Quarta questio . . . In principio ponitur opinio Gandensis quodlibeto 9, q. 9, et quodlibeto xi, q. 4, et quodlibeto 12, q. 10" (fol. 43v).

[36] "Explicit collectarium super quodlibeta Scoti . . . delatum ab urbe Parisii per mag. Petrum de Cruce regentem in conventu S. Antonii Padue et ad ipsius petitionem ut omnibus proficeret: impressum per magistrum Mattheum Cerdonis de Vindesgretz" (fol. 68r).—Master Peter is mentioned briefly by Luke Wadding, *Scriptores Ord. Minorum*, Romae 1906, 187a; and is given lengthy treatment by I. H. Sbaralea, *Supplementum*, II, Romae 1921, 337-338. This Colophon, missed

ever, that he would publish it anonymously. The work is not found, apparently, in the earlier edition of the *Vademecum* of Vaurouillon (Paris, c. 1483); nor does the latter mention it. Hence we are justified in considering it unauthentic.[37]

B. *Decisiones Regulares.*

In treating *Guilelmus Forleo,* whom he erroneously distinguished from William Vorilongus, Wadding ascribes to the former a work on the Franciscan order: *Decisiones regulares, praesertim circa vitam et Regulam Minorum,* which was published (he claims) at Paris *apud Joan. Parvum* in 1471. Though his note on Forleo is drawn largely from Trithemius, the latter is silent on anything resembling such a work.[38] Whence Wadding derived his notice is difficult to say. However, since Jean Petit did not begin to print before 1492, while no *Decisiones regulares* exists among books printed by him,[39] we may well doubt its existence.

C. The Sermon *Necdum.*

Several years ago, in furnishing me information on the manuscripts of the *Liber de anima,* Father Ephrem Longpré, famed Franciscan scholar, suggested that the sermon on the Immaculate Conception known as *Necdum erant abyssi* might well be the work of Vaurouillon. Before the text was available for study in a modern edition[40] I was inclined to agree with him on the basis of a rather meager knowledge of its contents.[41] Certainly the work is con-

---

by Sbaralea (who did know the Vademecum in this edition), adds a further date to his life. He was instrumental in publishing other works besides one of his own.

[37] Fr. Pelster, who thought perhaps it was the work of a disciple, is rather overcautious; cf. his "Wilhelm von Vorillon," in *Franz. Studien,* 8 (1921), 59.

[38] *Scriptores Minorum,* ed. 1650, p. 152b; ed. 1906, p. 104b. Trithemius's work, the first edition of which was published at Mainz 1494, was reprinted at Paris by John Parvus in 1512: *De Scriptoribus ecclesiasticis disertissimi viri Johannis de Trittenhem Abbatis Spanhemensis* . . . Parisiis, Remboldt et Joan. Parvus. William Forleon is considered fol. 180r, with mention of Stephen Brulefer as his disciple.

[39] See K. Burger, *The Printers and Publishers of the XV Century.* With lists of their Works. Index to the Supplement [of Copinger] to Hain's Repertorium Bibliographicum, etc., Berlin 1926, 531-532.

[40] Ed. A. Emmen et C. Piana, *Franciscus de Arimino, O.F.M. Sermo ad Clerum de Conceptione B.V.M.,* in *Tractatus Quatuor de Imm. Conceptione B.M.V.* [Bibl. Fran. Scholastica XVI] Quaracchi 1954, 335-391.

[41] A background study is provided by A. Emmen, "Historia opusculi mediaevalis 'Necdum erant abyssi' olim S. Bernardino adscripti," in *Collectanea Franciscana,* XIV (1944), 148-187.

temporary with Vaurouillon (c. 1424-1435), and contains material and authorities in common with his Sentences, but these are, for the most part, commonplaces of the period and the Scotist school of Paris.

A closer study of the text, however, both in itself and in comparison with the *Compendium* of our scholastic rather peremptorily excludes him as author of the sermon. Thus, William's penchant for ternaries hardly squares with the unvarying use of "sevens" on the part of the author of *Necdum*: seven proofs from the absolute power of God, seven from the *potentia ordinata,* seven reasons for the fitness of the Immaculate Conception, seven conclusions on original sin, seven saints (mostly spurious), seven Franciscan doctors, seven authorities, seven miracles, etc. Besides, we can point to several doctrinal divergencies; e.g., a slightly different explanation of the *potentia ordinata,* since the author of *Necdum* emphasizes divine wisdom, William the divine will.[42] Again, a very clear contrast is found in the definition of a miracle: both cite practically the same definition, but *Necdum* ascribes it to Master Jacques Textor, O.F.M., whereas William much more correctly traces it to St. Augustine.[43] One would hardly cite a Parisian master if Augustine were known as the source. Two other differences may suffice to reinforce our conclusion. For the preacher, original sin is not an *infectio morbida formaliter,* but rather the *carentia originalis iustitiae;* for the scholastic, it is not a *qualitas morbida,* but a *privatio*.[44] Lastly, the sermon speaks of a threefold sanctification only of our Lady: in the instant of her conception, at the Annunciation, and at Pentecost; whereas William sees a triple sanctification *in utero* and another threefold sanctification *extra uterum*.[45]

---

[42] *Necdum,* pars I: "Secunda [potentia], scilicet ordinata, est eadem potentia omnium possibilium, quae non includunt contradictionem, confirmata legibus a sapientia divina institutis" (*ed. cit.,* p. 353). By contrast, William writes, *In I Sent.,* d. 44, a. 1: "Potentia ordinata dicitur quae leges sequitur a divina voluntate positas" (fol. 73b).

[43] *Necdum,* pars tertia, § 7: "Sed primo videamus quid est miraculum. Dico quod sec. mag. Iacobum Textoris . . ." (p. 386-387).—Vaurouillon, *In II Sent.,* d. 7, a. 1: "Miraculum sec. beatum Augustinum in libro De utilitate credendi est aliquid arduum et insolitum supra spem et facultatem admirantis" (fol. 103b; cf. S. Aug., *De util. cred.,* c. 16, n. 34, in PL 42, 90; CSEL 25, 43).

[44] *Necdum,* p. 2, § 2, pp. 361-362; William, *In II Sent.,* d. 30, a. 2: "Secunda conclusio est de culpe originalis quidditate, et est hec: privatio culpe originalis formale sic censetur ut concupiscentia materiale dicatur . . . Ex quo patet quod peccatum originale non est qualitas morbida" (fol. 142a).

[45] *Necdum,* p. 2, § 4, pp. 379-380; and by contrast, William, *In III Sent.,* d. 3, p. 1, a. 2: "Unde imaginor in utero Mariam fuisse sanctificatam primo in

Whoever may be the author of *Necdum*—the editors with fairly convincing proof attribute it to Francis of Rimini[46]—he is not William of Vaurouillon.

D. Other Works.

With Trithemius, Wadding states that William wrote *Opuscula doctissima in sacram Scripturam, Quaestiones variae, et alia complura*. Among the last, perhaps, may be reckoned the *Liber de anima* discovered and identified only in the last fifteen years. It is possible that further research may reveal the existence of works on Scripture or some disputed questions. Yet this seems unlikely, given the known facts of William's life.

IV. WILLIAM AS A SCHOLASTIC

A. His Scotism.

The *Vademecum* is a standing proof of Vaurouillon's desire to understand the text as well as the doctrine of Duns Scotus, by discovering the authors of the opinions cited by the Subtle Doctor. Both it and the *Compendium*, especially on the fourth book of Lombard, bear witness also that he was conscious of the textual problems involved in studying *doctor noster*. The latter's *opus principale* is usually called his *Ordinarium*,[47] and sometimes *Opus Anglicanum*.[48] Questions that Scotus did not treat in England are

---

carne ante anime infusionem a corruptione, scil. vitiosa; secundo in anime infusione ne peccatum contraheret originale, in quo signo et gratia ei collata est; tertio in alicuius virtutis usu et executione . . . Extra uterum etiam ter fuit sanctificata: primo in conceptione Verbi . . .; secundo in Sancti Spiritus missione super ipsam et apostolos; tertia in sua gloriosissima assumptione" (fol. 168c).

[46] The most important proof is a parallel account of the *Mariale* falsely attributed to Alexander of Hales, in both the sermon (*ed. cit.*, 368-369) and Francis's tract *De sanguine Christi* (*ibid.*, 349). Yet no manuscript attributes it to Francis of Rimini, whereas two codices carry the name of *Mag. Antonius de Populo OFM* (*ibid.*, 346-347). It might therefore be profitable to see if a certain Antonius de Arezzo, licensed at Paris under Jacques Textor, 3 March 1424, and master 28 June (CUP n. 2234; tom. IV, 428), may not well be the author; or even Fr. Antonius de Bitonto († 1465), who certainly knew and used the sermon. Cf. C. Piana, "Antonio de Bitonto OFM. Praedicator et Scriptor saec. XV," in *Fran. Studies*, 13 (1953), n. 2-3, p. 187. The sermon is found in a Padua manuscript which contains other sermons of the same preacher (*ibid.*, 190).

[47] E.g., *In I Sent.*, d. 32, a. 2; d. 33, a. 3; d. 38, a. 2, etc. *Ordinatio* does not seem to be used.

[48] *Vademecum*, fol. 1r; *In IV Sent.*, d. 7, a. 1; d. 29, a. 1; *De anima*, I, 2; II, 2; II, 8; etc.

sometimes incorporated into the *Ordinarium* from his *Reportata Parisiensia*.⁴⁹ The Paris commentary is sometimes quoted for itself, sometimes in contrast with the *Ordinarium*.⁵⁰ Of the other works of Scotus, Williams once cites the incipit of the *De primo principio*, together with a book on logic which begins: *O Deus qui es terminus sine termino*.⁵¹ He makes one slight reference to the *Quaestiones de anima;* but the work has no place later in his own *Liber de anima*.⁵² Again, the *Quodlibeta* is used, but rather infrequently. William, finally, is somewhat acquainted with the problem of the *Ordinatio*, I, d. 26, discussed by the Scotist Commission in the latest volume of the Vatican edition.⁵³ In the *Liber Scoti,* that is, the *Ordinatio,* the distinction is rather brief, while in later arrangements of the *Opus Oxoniense* much was introduced from the concluding question of Distinction 1 of Book III. Vaurouillon has at least seen different versions of Book I, d. 26, since he remarks that the question of what constitutes a Divine Person is very long, at least when it is given in its entirety, for some books give a shorter form.⁵⁴

Doctrinally, he makes a deliberate effort to follow Duns Scotus carefully and faithfully. When he comes upon some question the

---

⁴⁹ *Vademecum:* ". . . in secundo suo super Sententias quem non integravit in Anglia ex parisiensibus reportatis a XV distinctione usque ad XXVI exclusive insertum est" (fol. 1r). This is repeated with variations in *In IV Sent.,* d. 29, a. 1: ". . . In opere enim anglicano super illis distinctionibus nil scripsit quod habeatur citra mare; sed communiter ponitur modo in libris et conflatur unus secundus ex Anglia et Francia, licet Scotus neuter fuit" (fol. 273c).

⁵⁰ As in *In I Sent.,* d. 33, a. 3 (fol. 57a).

⁵¹ Principium to Book II of the Sentences (fol. 84b). The Logic defies identification.

⁵² *In II Sent.,* d. 3, a. 2: "Idem dicit Doctor Subtilis in Questionibus de anima, ubi illam materiam metaphysicam in anima ponit ex qua a simili arguitur in angelis" (fol. 91c).—The *Liber de anima* refers back to the Sentences for further development: "Ens finitum est, de quo super secundum Sententiarum, dist. 3, dixi! Illic quaere; ibi invenies!" (II, 5; p. 272).

⁵³ *I. Duns Scoti: Ordinatio, Lib. I a Dist. 26 ad 48* [Opera omnia VI], Vatican Press 1963, pp. 1*-26*.

⁵⁴ *Vademecum:* "Circa dist. 26 querit doctor: utrum persone divine constituantur in esse personali per relationes originis . . . Et de ista questione est notandum quod est multum longa dum est completa, utputa 7 vel 8 foliorum; quod pro tanto dico quia in diversis libris diversimode habetur" (fol. 14r).—In his *In I Sent.,* d. 26, a. 2, he claims that it was John of Ripa and not Bonaventure who held the Persons were constituted *per absoluta;* and that Scotus was somewhat of this opinion: "Ex quo infero opinionem magistri Joh. de Rippa esse falsam, qui posuit personas per absoluta constitui . . . Qua propter doctor subtilis magis ad hoc quodammodo declinare videtur; doctor devotus, doctor sanctus [Thomas], et ceteri de communi tenent oppositum" (fol. 44d).

Subtle Doctor had not explored at length, he has recourse to the early Scotist school in hopes of finding a solution: Landulph, Hugo, Meyronnes, or again Nicholas Boneti, etc. They are not always considered as representative of Scotus's true position, and accordingly are often criticized for their interpretation.[55] On the other hand, William frankly admits that there are three doctrines in which "this dwarf does not follow so great a giant, perhaps because I do not understand him."[56] None are points of outstanding importance. "In the second book," he continues, "in the question of the place of Paradise, I took my stand with Alexander of Hales, St. Thomas of Aquino, the Doctor Devotus, Albert the Great, and our Touraine Friar Nicholas Boneti, against him."[57] Again, in the fourth book, he holds against Scotus that one can be punished with death for a simple theft, choosing instead to follow the English doctor John of Rodington.[58] Lastly, on the question of slavery or servitude, he refuses to accept the statement of Scotus that there is no approbation to be found in Scripture for voluntary slavery.[59] This, retorts Vaurouillon, is not too well phrased: *hoc est minus caute dictum*, since one can cite Exodus 21: 5, 6. For this reason I choose to disagree with him.[60]

While the fundamental positions of Scotus[61] are thus to be found in the writings and thought of our scholastic, not all are developed at length; William strives rather to compress them into short clear statements and proofs. At the same time, we may note that like many of the earlier disciples of the Subtle Doctor he does not make

[55] Thus in the controversy (which bears further study) on the being things possess in the divine ideas, he denies that Scotus attributes to them any *esse essentiae;* if such existence is predicated of them, this is the opinion either of Henry of Ghent, Francis de Meyronnes, or Nicholas Boneti, but not that of Scotus (*In I Sent.*, d. 36, a. 2, fol. 62c).

[56] *In IV Sent.*, d. 26, a. 2 (fol. 268b).

[57] Cf. *In II Sent.*, d. 17, a. 2: "Et licet hic doctor subtilis dicat valde subtiliter . . . fateor hoc in loco eum non capio" (fol. 120d-121a).

[58] *In IV Sent.*, d. 14-16, a. 2: "Sed nunquid potest quis occidi pro furto simplici? . . . Dicit hic doctor quod non. Cui obviat frater Joh. de Rodinthon. Non enim est verisimile totam humanam politeiam in isto errare . . . Cui secundo Johanni assentior, et primum Joh. in hoc passu secundo dimitto" (fol. 253b).

[59] Cf. Duns Scotus, *In IV Sent.*, d. 26, q. unica, n. 10: "Unde potest quis se vendere in servum, licet de hoc non inveniatur specialis approbatio divina in scriptura . . ." (tom. XIX, 161b).

[60] *In IV Sent.*, d. 26, a. 2 (fol. 268b-c).

[61] Cf. C. Balić, art. Duns Scoto, in *Enciclopedia cattolica*, IV, 1982-1990; E. Gilson, *Jean Duns Scotus. Introduction à ses positions fondamentales* (Paris 1952); E. Bettoni, *Duns Scotus: the Basic Principles of his Philosophy* (Washington 1961).

use of the formidable Scotist proof for the existence of God; nor does he seem to dwell at any length on the problem of the knowledge of the singular, the value of the proofs for the immortality of the soul,[62] the role of hecceity in individuation, etc.

B. Vaurouillon and Scholasticism.

There are indeed certain aspects of Vaurouillon's thought, or perhaps of his approach to scholasticism, that give us reason to doubt if he should be called a rigid Scotist—if there is such a species; or ask if perhaps we should not revise our image of the Scotistic School. William, for example, in choosing to be a follower of John Duns Scotus does not see the need to break with the earlier Franciscan school[63] or, indeed, with the whole tradition of Scholasticism. His *principia* and *epilogus* abound in rhetoric and eloquence, no doubt; but they also reveal a genuine respect for and appreciation of the great scholastics, whether Dominican, Augustinian, Franciscan, or seculars like Henry of Ghent and Godfrey of Fontaines. The text itself of the Commentary bears out the justice of his peroration to the fourth book: *Hoc igitur doctorum ternario* [Thomas, Bonaventure, Scotus] *solidatus hoc anno, merito redarguendum me dicerem nisi eis aliquas expressissem gratias* (fol. 316c). It is true he feels constrained to beg pardon of St. Thomas because he has not always agreed with him; but he readily acknowledges his great dependence on him.[64] He continues in the same vein to proclaim his adherence to Bonaventure, the Doctor

---

[62] In the Sentences, II, d. 19, a. 2, he makes use of Bonaventure's proofs, but says nothing of their value (fol. 124d-125a); when he repeats these, with variations, in the *Liber de anima*, II, 12, he is content to qualify them as persuasions (*Med. Studies*, X, 290).

[63] Long before the *Liber de anima* had been identified as Vaurouillon's, Professor Gilson had made this point against certain statements of Cardinal Ehrle, through use of one of the manuscripts of the work. Cf. his review of F. Ehrle, *Der Sentenzenkommentar Peters von Candia*, in *Rev. d'histoire franciscaine*, III (1922), 128-133.

[64] *Epilogus* to the fourth book: "Parce mihi, parce doctor sancte, si hoc in anno aliquibus in passibus tue obviavi sententie; non quidem hoc feci contradicens, sed veritatem inquirens . . . Fateor hoc humile ut debeo: penna et lingua hoc in anno meis in factis aruisset nisi sanctiora dicta tua affuissent iuvamini. O decor philosophie, o fastigium theologie, o religionis venustas!" (fol. 316a-b).— We should add that for the most part William cites the *Scriptum* on the Sentences; the *Contra Gentiles* is used but once; the *Summa theologiae*, not more than a dozen times, and mostly in the fourth book, following the *Vademecum*. See also the unusual manner of citing the *Summa* (I, q. 400) in the *Liber de anima*, III, 19 (*Med. Studies*, XI, 302 and 306).

Devotus. Of the great scholastics, only William Ockham does not occupy an influential position. He is indeed the *flos modernorum,* the *venerabilis inceptor;* yet his Sentences are cited but once, and his other works but seldom.[65]

What may be surprising is the considerable use made of the *Summa* of Alexander of Hales, all four parts of which are cited in the Sentences and which is made one of the principal sources of the *Liber de anima.* Perhaps we need to know more of the use made of that Summa in the later Middle Ages. Roger Bacon had slightingly remarked: *Nemo facit eam de cetero scribi; immo exemplar apud Fratres putrescit.*[66] This is not borne out however by the number of manuscripts still extant of the thirteenth and fourteenth centuries, nor by legislation within the order. In 1331 the Chapter of Perpignan, or rather Guiral Ot, bade the lectors use the Summa: *ibi enim uberrimus theologicarum inquisitionum fluvius invenitur.*[67] Closer to William's day, Leonard Rossi (de Rubeis) de Giffoni, Minister General in 1373, was to decree at the chapter of Toledo that lectors who did not quote Alexander of Hales in their scholastic works and sermons were unfit for scholastic promotions.[68] Alexander was thus by no means forgotten as the founder and first master of the Franciscan school at Paris, *harum scholarum primus doctor,* the divine Alexander.[69] Yet without knowing it, William

---

[65] *In IV Sent.,* d. 11, a. 2: "Fr. Guill. de Okan . . . in quarto in materia eucharistie" (fol. 246b; perhaps a hearsay reference).—*In I Sent.,* d. 3, arg. 2, an argument suggested by Ockham against univocity (fol. 10c); I, d. 12, p. 2, a. 1, an explanation of *signum* (fol. 29d); I, d. 32, a. 1: "forma . . . quasi foris manens, licet frater Guilh. Ockhan Super predicamenta in suo commento dicat quod idem sunt forma et figura; sed de hoc Guilh. modicum est hic curandum" (fol. 54c); I, d. 45, a. 2: "Hic dicit Guil. Ockan in suo Centilogio quod posset quis meritorie odire Deum" (fol. 76d); *In II Sent.,* d. 1, ad 1: "Et ad regulam philosophi respondit egregie frater guilelmus okan in logica aurea" (fol. 88b).

[66] *Opus minus,* ed. J. S. Brewer, in *Fr. R. Bacon Opera hactenus inedita,* London 1859, 327.

[67] See *AFH,* 2 (1909), 415. The Constitutions here promulgated were not destined to have a warm reception or lasting influence in the Order; cf. E. Wagner, *Historia Cons. Gen. O.F.M.,* Romae 1954, 54-55.

[68] Cf. *AFH,* 15 (1922), 346. Father G. Abate claims this refers to Alexander of Alessandria († 1314), in *Miscellanea Franciscana,* 29 (1929), 164b, note 2. The text he edits (p. 172b) does indeed read (or he reads) Alexandria; yet the papal bull approving the doctrine of a Master Alexander manifestly is that of Alexander IV, 1255, calling for the completion of the *Summa fratris Alexandri.*

[69] *In I Sent.,* d. 31, a. 1 (fol. 52c); *In II Sent.,* d. 3, a. 2 (fol. 91c); III, d. 3, p. 1, a. 2, on his supposed *Mariale* (fol. 168b).—In passing, we may wonder whether the ideals of John Gerson had evoked a renewed interest in Alexander and Bonaventure among the friars at Paris.

discovers too the problem of the authorship of the Summa, because it sometimes contains a manifest contradiction in its parallel questions.[70]

Lastly, though seemingly far removed in time from Stephen Tempier and the condemnation of 1277, Vaurouillon reveals that its effects are still felt at the University of Paris.[71] For many, he candidly admits, it has little force, though his own reverence for the university will not allow him to call the document outmoded or no longer in effect.[72]

In this appreciation of a certain inner unity of the Franciscan school and of scholasticism as a whole, William does not stand alone in the fifteenth century. Much the same outlook and the same use of sources is to be found among his contemporaries of the German provinces, especially at the school of Erfurt: Matthias Doering, John Bremer, Henry of Werl, Kilian Stetzing and others, who were themselves influenced by the traditions at Paris.[73] Scotists to a great extent, with Vaurouillon they knew and loved and used the legacy bequeathed them by all the great scholastics. Once

---

[70] *In IV Sent.*, d. 21, a. 2 (fol. 262a). I suspect, however, that William opens up a problem here I am not able to solve at present. Both here and later, in dist. 31, he cites a "literal exposition" of Alexander on the Sentences, and indeed used the word *glossa*. Thus: "Ex quo patet defectus fratris Alexandri de Halis in expositione litterali presentis distinctionis" (d. 21, fol. 261a); and: "Dicit fr. Alexander de Halis super magistrum in glossa in presenti distinctione . . ." (d. 31, fol. 279b). Yet whatever text William has before him, it is not the *Glossa in Librum Quartum* published at Quaracchi 1957; nor is it, since the second reference is to a question on marriage, simply the fourth part of the *Summa fratris Alex.*, which stops with the sacrament of penance.

[71] Cf. *In I Sent.*, collatio 2 (fol. 3c); *In II Sent.*, d. 3, p. 2, a. 2, on angels and species (fol. 93c); d. 5, a. 2 (fol. 100 b); d. 19, a. 2, cited against Bonaventure! (fol. 125a); *In IV Sent.*, d. 49, a. 2 (fol. 311b); *Liber de anima*, III, 1 (*Med. Studies*, XI, 253).

[72] *In II Sent.*, d. 2, a. 2: "Ex quo patet grandis valde defectus sancti Thome in primo Scripti, dist. xxxvii, p. 2, q. 1 et 2, dicentis angelos solum esse in loco per operationem. Oppositum patet ex conclusione. Et confirmatur quia videtur articulus damnatus Parisius ab episcopo parisiensi quod angeli solum sint in loco per operationem, et excommunicatus. Sed aliqui dicunt quod ista excommunicatio non transit pontes: hii valde imprudenter contra tantam universitatem os suum aperiunt, inquientes quod posse huius universitatis solum pontes huius attingat civitatis. Secundi dicunt quod non transit dyocesim. Tertii dicunt quod non transit mare; et ita non vadit in Angliam. Contra hos . . . Et quicquid sit, ex quo in famosissima totius mundi universitate a viris famosissimis damnata est non est revocanda in dubium" (fol. 90a).

[73] Cf. L. Meier, "De schola Franciscana Erfordiensi saeculi XV," *Antonianum*, V (1930), 57-84; his *Die Barfüsserschule zu Erfurt* [BGPTMA, XXXVIII, Heft 2], Münster, 1958.

again perhaps we should look for the things that unite rather than for the differences that make for separation and division into opposing schools.

ADDENDUM

Since writing this article, I have had the opportunity, through the kindness of the Institut de Recherche et d'Histoire des Textes of the Centre National de la Recherche Scientifique (Paris), to examine the codex of Rennes *Ville 41* mentioned in note 15. The first folios contain what William calls a *declaratio* or *retractatio* on his Commentary on the Sentences. In the course of a long discussion (fol. 2c-3a) on Book II, distinction 10, he defends his assertion that there are *plures angeli assistentes quam ministrantes,* and concludes: *De hoc dixi super Apocalypsim, lectione 45 in secunda parte principali, et lectione 55 in secundo principali.* Trithemius and Wadding (cf. note 38) are therefore correct in ascribing commentaries on Scripture to William. The text remains to be identified.

Collegio S. Bonaventura

Quaracchi, Florence

13

DUNS SCOTUS, NOMINALISM, AND THE COUNCIL OF TRENT

by

HEIKO AUGUSTINUS OBERMAN

In the *Collectio Judiciorum de Novis Erroribus,* published by the Parisian Doctor Carolus du Plessis d'Argentré, we find under the year 1315 a ten point "summary" of the thought of Johannes Duns Scotus. If its entry in a book "de Novis Erroribus" would still leave room for doubt, the heading chosen by d'Argentré for this section makes it unambiguously clear that key points in the doctrine of the great Franciscan theologian are regarded as deviating from Catholic truth: *Johannis Duns Scoti, O.F.M., temerariae opiniones, quas Doctorum Theologorum multitudo improbat.*[1]

Though perhaps an unusual way to open an article dedicated to the memory of the Doctor Subtilis, a description of these *temerariae opiniones* affords us in the first place the opportunity to point to a central fact; only since the turn of this century, due to a renewed, detailed, and empathetic analysis of the sources by both Roman Catholic and Protestant scholars,[2] is the cloud of suspicion so long obscuring the true stature of Duns Scotus now being increasingly removed, exactly with regard to those points called into question by du Plessis d'Argentré.

[1] *Collectio Judiciorum,* I, Paris, 1724, col. 285-290.
[2] We limit our reference to two works published at the beginning of this century and two representing more recent scholarship: Reinhold Seeberg, *Die Theologie des Johannes Duns Scotus: Eine dogmengeschichtliche Untersuchung,* Leipzig, 1900; Parthenius Minges, *Die Gnadenlehre des Johannes Duns Skotus auf ihren angeblichen Pelagianismus geprüft,* Münster i.W., 1906; Werner Dettloff, *Die Lehre von der Acceptatio Divina bei Johannes Duns Scotus mit besondere Berückischtigung der Rechtfertigungslehre,* Werl. Westf., 1954: Wolfhart Pannenberg, *Die Prädestinationslehre des Duns Skotus im Zusammenhang der Scholastischen Lehrentwicklung,* Göttingen, 1954. A reliable basis for future studies is now being provided in the critical edition, *Opera Omnia . . . praeside P. Carolo Balić,* I—, Civ. Vat., 1950-. See further the excellent extensive bibliography by Odulf Schäfer, *Bibliographische Einführungen in das Studium der Philosophie,* XXII, *Johannes Duns Scotus,* Bern, 1953.

311

In the second place, we are here provided with a natural context within which decisive differences between the Scotist and Nominalist Schools of thought can be indicated, differences which will have to be borne in mind if one wants to understand the complexity and importance of the Franciscan contribution to the final decisions of the Council of Trent.

I. *Johannis Duns Scoti: temerariae opiniones*

1. It cannot surprise us that as the first of the "rash opinions rejected by most doctors of theology," the famous formal distinction is singled out for attack: "Scotus docet divinas virtutes et a se invicem et ab essentia Dei distingui ex natura rei, formali distinctione." After a few well chosen quotations[3] the conclusion follows: "Sed haec dicta Scoti effatis divinae Scripturae contraria sunt," followed by the *ad hominem* attack: "Captiosis autem ratiunculis Dialecticae abutitur Scotus in locis ante citatis." The formal distinction is said to imply exactly the same heretical position as that held by Gilbertus Porretanus, condemned by the Council of Reims (1148). It furthermore provides for the "instances theory" by which four stages are distinguished in the eternal counsel of God. To this crucial issue we shall return after a survey of the other nine points.

2. Scotus claims that *de potentia absoluta* God could have accepted human nature without the habit of grace *in puris naturalibus*.[4] Since d'Argentré does not permit the distinction between *potentia absoluta* and *potentia ordinata* his conclusion is: "Haec opinio Scoti pugnat cum divinis oraculis et errori Pelagii admodum favet . . . Quis enim, nisi Pelagianus, dicere audeat absolute fieri posse, ut noster animus natura sua Deum videat ita ut naturale donum sit aeterna vita, quae in aperta visione Dei posita sit?"[5]

3. Scotus claims that the necessity of infused faith cannot be established,[6] since man does not absolutely need the supernatural habit of faith to believe firmly in the articles of faith. Acquired faith suffices for such an act, since man by nature believes that God

---

[3] I *Sent.* d 8 q 4 n 4; n 14; n 21; I *Sent.* d 2 q 7 n 41; n 42. All references are to the *Opus Oxoniense. Collectio*, col. 285.2.

[4] I *Sent.* 17 q 3 n 21; n 29. *Collectio*, col. 286.2.

[5] Adam Woodham, John of Ripa, and John of Mercuria (Mirecourt) are grouped together as followers of Scotus by adhering to "these absurd Scotist teachings." *Ibid.*

[6] III *Sent.* d 23 q 1 n 4.

is true and since he has no reason to doubt the officially approved tradition of the Church, including Holy Scripture.[7] This opinion of Scotus is apparently so clearly contrary to orthodox truth that d'Argentré does not feel that an explicit censure is called for.

4. Scotus introduces a "new doctrine" when he argues that sanctifying grace does not necessarily delete the guilt and stain of sin.[8] With a few biblical references—Rom. 3:24: "Justificati gratis per gratiam ipsius"; I Cor. 6,11: "sed abluti estis, sed sanctificati estis, sed justificati estis," etc.—it is shown that Scotus' teaching runs contrary to the testimony of Holy Scripture: "Hac de re Sanctus Thomas recte disserit."[9]

5. Intimately connected with this point is the next accusation: Scotus holds that guilt can be forgiven without the infusion of grace since God can *de potentia absoluta* create a man without guilt and without grace *in puris naturalibus*. He can, therefore, also after the fall restore man by forgiving his guilt without the infusion of grace.[10] This thesis of Scotus and his followers contradicts the divine Scriptures. The conclusion is again: "doctrina Scoti erroribus Pelagii favet."[11]

6. The attack turns now to the doctrine of acceptation as such. Against the clear witness of Holy Scripture and the common teaching in the Schools, Scotus holds that no degree of love is sufficient for the justification of man:[12] "in scholis Theologorum multitudo cum S. Thoma docet. Quam sententiam ex divinis oraculis et sanctis Patribus accepimus."[13]

7. Scotus is said to argue that the character received in the Sacrament of Baptism is not an inherent imprint on man's soul but an extrinsic relation between the baptised and God.[14] This is ob-

---

[7] "Quia homo non dubitat de veracitate Dei, quia hoc cuilibet naturaliter inseritur, scilicet Deum esse veracem; nec dubitatur de approbatione Ecclesiae, quae approbat dicta et scripta virorum praecedentium. Ideo non dubitatur de his quae in Scriptura revelantur, sed, fide acquisita ex auditu, firmiter eis adhaeret . . ." *Ibid.*, n 5. *Collectio*, col. 287.1.

[8] ". . . culpa et gratia non sunt formaliter opposita, nec formaliter oppugnantia." II *Sent.* d 16 q 2 n 4.

[9] *ST* I. II. 113. art. 6. *Collectio*, col. 287.2.
[10] II *Sent.* 16 q 2 n 4.
[11] *Collectio*, col. 287.2.
[12] III *Sent.* d 27 q 1.
[13] *Collectio*, col. 288.2.
[14] IV *Sent.* d 6 q 9 n 4.

viously contrary to Scripture as documented e.g. by II Cor. 1,22: 'Et qui unxit nos Deus, et qui signavit nos?'[15]

8. Scotus undermines the Catholic doctrine of creation by claiming that *by nature* man loves himself more than God.[16] When man was created God called him good; but to love oneself more than God is not good. Furthermore, when Deuteronomy 6,4 commands "You shall love the Lord your God with all your heart," it formulates a natural law. This eighth point is the shortest and least documented of all.[17]

9. Scotus is unbiblical and deviates from St. Augustine in his claim that some voluntary acts can be so neutral that they are neither good nor bad.[18] The critique of this point is not very revealing insofar as neither the historical[19] nor the systematic context of Scotus' discussion is taken into account.[20]

10. More significant, we feel, is the related charge that Scotus separates the wisdom and justice of God by separating the eternal law of God from the natural law as expressed in the second table of the Decalogue. Followed by Gabriel Biel and Jacob Almain, he holds that "res prohibitas in secunda tabula Decalogi (nec excepto mendacio) per se malos non esse. Item Gabriel censet et Almain."[21]

When one surveys this presentation of these *temerariae opiniones,* one realizes that the thought of Duns Scotus is not only measured on all ten points by the standard of adherence and subservience to the conclusions of Thomas Aquinas, but also that the critique tends to move from Scotus to his *sequaces* with which such Nominalists as Woodham and Biel are counted. It should furthermore be granted that almost every one of the Scotist theses presented here has found its way into the world of Nominalistic thought, to

---

[15] *Collectio,* col. 288.2. Cf. however the context as presented by Parthenius Minges, *Ioannes Duns Scoti Doctrina Philosophica et Theologica,* II, *Theologica Specialis,* Ad Claras Aquas, 1930, p. 555.

[16] *Collectio,* col. 289.1.

[17] In the *Opus. Ox.* we find exactly the opposite: "Diligere Deum super omnia est actus conformis rationi naturali rectae . . . Illud praeceptum 'Diliges Dominum Deum tuum' est de lege naturae et ita naturaliter notum est hunc actum esse rectum." III *Sent.* d 27 n 2.

[18] *Collectio,* col. 289.1; d'Argentré documents his charge with a quote which occurs in II *Sent.* d 41 q 1 n 3.

[19] See for this the question raised by St. Thomas, "utrum aliquis actus sit indifferens secundum individuum" in *ST* I. II. q. 18 art. 9.

[20] See Minges, *op. cit.* I, pp. 400-403.

[21] *Collectio,* col. 289. 2-290.1: III *Sent.* d 39 n 3; For a discussion of this issue see my *Harvest of Medieval Theology,* Cambridge, Mass., 1963, pp. 105-111.

the point that some of them as e.g. the doctrine of acceptation and its corollaries (2-6), as well as the new understanding of the relation of eternal and natural law (10), have long been regarded as characteristically Nominalistic.

Before we can turn to an analysis of the Tridentine discussions of the doctrine of justification and the proper interpretation of such terms as *meritum de congruo, meritum de condigno, mereri,* and *promereri,* it is essential to emphasize the significance of the difference between Duns Scotus on the one side and Occam *cum suis* on the other side, with regard to the first point on the list of du Plessis d'Argentré. The formal distinction, posited there, forms the basis of Scotus' doctrine of predestination *ante praevisa merita,* since it allows for a formal distinction between four instances or stages in God's planning, his eternal counsel, applied to Peter and Judas as the traditional symbols of the elect and the reprobate. In the first two instances God is solely concerned with Peter: First, God predestines Peter to eternal glory; Second, He wants to give Peter the means to this end, grace. In the third instance Judas appears for the first time as an object for God's will: God permits Peter and Judas to belong to the mass of perdition. Finally, Peter is saved and Judas rejected, according to justice, since Judas persevered in sin.

Along with the formal distinction, Occam and his followers reject the four "instances theory" and therefore the doctrine of predestination *ante praevisa merita.*[22] The weighty consequence is

---

[22] Occam: ". . . non videtur bene dictum quod deus velit prius finem quam illud quod est ad finem; quia non est ibi talis prioritas actuum, nec sunt ibi talia instantia . . ." I *Sent.* d 41 q 1 F; Biel: ". . . falsum est quod prius vult finem et post ordinata in finem quia non est nisi unus actus divine voluntatis . . . quia ordo presupponit distinctionem ordinatorum . . . Nec tamen aliquod horum deus prius vult altero, sed quecunque vult, similiter et ab eterno vult." II *Sent.* d 20 q 1 art. 1 nota 3; cf. I *Sent.* d 41 q 1 art. 3 dub. 2. In the *Collectio Judiciorum,* col. 40, a number of statements by Gerson against the formal distinction are collected; on col. 286 Gerson is cited to support d'Argentré's exhortation to return not only to St. Bonaventure but also to St. Thomas. Cf. Gerson, *Opera Omnia,* ed. L. E. du Pin, I, Antwerpen, 1706, 91 D. Gerson's attack on the scholastic theology of his time should not be interpreted as an attack on Nominalism but rather seen as motivated by a Nominalistic ideal: to restore unity within the realm of theology: ". . . studeo eos quos Scotistas appellamus ad concordiam cum aliis doctoribus adducere . . ." *Opera* I, 101 C. As can be documented by Gerson's actual teaching *re* predestination and justification, it is more likely that he criticized the formal distinction from a Nominalistic rather than from a Thomistic vantage point. With regard to these central doctrines, we find no evidence for the development from Nominalist to Thomist as presented by André Combes in relation to mysticism.

that the school of Occam does not merely reject the first of the ten *temerariae opiniones,* but that all the other articles which deal with justification (when taken in the narrow sense: 2-6) in which they seemed to agree with the Doctor Subtilis, are placed in a radically different context.

This decisive change can perhaps best be described by recalling the great advances in Scotus scholarship in this century. What had long been regarded as Pelagianism or semi-Pelagianism proved to be the freedom of man due to the elasticity of his lifeline which is at both ends, at the beginning by predestination *ante praevisa merita,* at the end by the *acceptatio divina,* firmly fastened in God's eternal counsel. Occam and his School, while rejecting Scotus' doctrine of predestination,[23] retained the latter's concern for the dignity of man and the sinner's responsibility for his own damnation. Whereas the same terminology is employed with regard to such issues as the habit of grace, merits *de congruo* and *de condigno* and more generally use is made of the paired terms *potentia absoluta* and *potentia ordinata,* the doctrine of predestination *post praevisa merita* changes the relation between the sovereign God and his *viator.* The *viator* still does not have a claim to the habit of grace or final acceptation, but he now has to take the decisive responsibility for reaching either the beatific vision or eternal damnation according to his use of the *facere quod in se est.*[24]

When we now turn to the *acta* of the Council of Trent, we are forewarned that many so-called Scotistic statements with regard to the doctrine of justification may actually have come from Council fathers deeply influenced by Nominalistic thought. Due to the fact that the doctrine of predestination was *de facto* dissociated from the doctrine of justification in the debates, and relatively only lightly touched upon and ultimately relegated to a separate chapter, the basis for distinguishing Scotistic and Nominalistic "interventiones" on this issue is *terra infirma.* For this reason we shall often have to refer to the joint impact of Scotistic and Nominalistic thought in terms of the "Franciscan contribution" to the Tridentine deliberations. But when finally at the end of this article we hope

---

See his *Essai sur la critique de Ruysbroeck par Gerson.* III. 1 (Paris, 1959), p. 316f.

[23] Cf. my *Harvest of Medieval Theology,* p. 185-217.

[24] For documentation see *Harvest of Medieval Theology,* p. 208, note 58 and p. 209, note 60. For the opposite conclusion, see Paul Vignaux, *Justification et Prédestination,* Paris, 1934, p. 138f.

to have established that the "Franciscan contribution" has been far more penetrating than it usually has been given credit for, we are alerted to the importance of distinguishing between three rather than just two theological contexts for the Tridentine decree of justification: Scotism, Nominalism, and Thomism.

II. *Partim-Partim*

In recent years the Council of Trent has attracted a considerable amount of attention in popular books and learned journals alike. This concerns, however, not so much the doctrine of justification, in the sixteenth century the *articulus stantis et cadentis ecclesiae*,[24a] but rather the Tridentine decree on Scripture and the *sine scripto traditiones*. The phrase 'partim-partim' has acquired a new, almost symbolic, significance since its change into *et* in the final decree has been interpreted to indicate that the Fathers of Trent did not regard the time ripe for a definition of the relation of Scripture and Tradition.[25] It is argued that whereas what pertains to faith would be *totum in Scriptura, et iterum totum in Traditione*, the 'partim-partim' only applies to morals and observances.[26] A further study of the late medieval setting of the conciliar discussions might well be decisive in determining the historical intention of the Council fathers without thus necessarily settling the problem of theological interpretation.[27]

A similar issue and identical task awaits us with respect to the Tridentine decree on justification. Andreas de Vega († 1549), the Spanish Franciscan, significant author and influential participant in the Council,[28] reminds us that the doctrine of justification as

[24a] Hubert Jedin regards this same article as the pivot of Tridentine teaching. Cf. "Das vierhundertjährige Jubiläum der Eröffnung des Konzils von Trient und sein wissenschaftlicher Ertrag," in *Das Weltkonzil von Trient. Sein Werden und Wirken*, ed. Georg Schreiber [henceforth abbreviated as WT] I, Freiburg 1951, pp. 11-31; p. 23.

[25] J. R. Geiselmann, "Das Missverständnis über das Verhältnis von Schrift und Tradition und seine Überwindung in der katholischen Theologie," in *Una Sancta* II (1956), p. 139.

[26] Geiselmann, *Die heilige Schrift und die Tradition, Quaestiones disputatae*, Freiberg 1962, p. 284.

[27] Cf. the presentation of the fifteenth-century discussion in my *Harvest of Medieval Theology*, pp. 371-412. On the problem of interpretation in connection with the different hermeneutics of Protestant and Roman Catholic historians see "Quo Vadis, Petre?" *Scottish Journal of Theology*, 16 (1963), pp. 252ff.

[28] Cf. B. Oromi, "Fr. Andreas de Vega O.F.M., theologus Concilii Tridentini," *Archivum Franc. Historicum*, 36 (1943), pp. 3-31.

discussed and defined by the Council fathers might also be understood in terms of the relation of 'partim-partim' and 'et.'[29]

So far as the relation of Scripture and Tradition is concerned, there can be little doubt how Vega interpreted the conciliar decree of which he had witnessed the makings. For him the 'sine scripto traditiones' are not the interpretations of Scripture nor observances in contrast to doctrines.[30] The unwritten traditions, which derived either directly from Christ or from the Apostles inspired by the Spirit, have explicitly doctrinal significance by containing such dogmata as the virginity of the Mother of God *post partum*, the dogma of the veneration of images and relics of the Saints, and of the total of seven sacraments, etc.[31] Though we have not found him to use the expression, it is clear that Vega interpreted 'et' in the sense of 'partim-partim'; in view of Vega's intimate involvement in the proceedings at the Council this conclusion should have significance for our interpretation of the Council's mind.

We shall return to Vega in reference to the second 'partim-partim' issue—the one taken up at the sixth session. This issue is at stake in the question, whether God is committed to give those who do their natural best—'facientibus quod in se est'—first grace so that a *meritum de congruo* is constituted which is not a merit

---

[29] "Et ea tum raritas vel difficultas [facere bona opera sine gratia] partim proficiscitur ex parte nostra, partim ex parte Dei aut aliorum qui nos possent allicere et adiuvare ad operandum et non faciunt." *De iustificatione doctrina universa, Libris XV, absolute tradita et contra omnes omnium errores iuxta germanam sententiam Orthodoxae veritatis et sacri concilii Tridentini praeclare defensa*. Coloniae 1572. First ed. Venetiis 1548. XIII. 13. fol. 523.

[30] The interpretation of *traditiones* as *facienda* instead of *credenda* is suggested by Father Maurice Bevenot in "Traditiones in the Council of Trent," *The Heythrop Journal*, IV (1963), pp. 333-347: ". . . in the discussions themselves 'traditiones' referred always primarily to the various rites, observances, and practices of the Church and only indirectly to the fact that some of them (e.g., the sacraments) involved the faith too," *Ibid.* pp. 341-342. Michael Hurley comes to the same conclusion in his interesting article "A Pre-Tridentine Theology of Tradition. Thomas Netter of Walden († 1430)," *The Heythrop Journal*, IV (1963), pp. 348-366; cf. p. 364.

[31] In an argument against John Calvin's holding the *verbum Dei* as the *optima interpres scripturarum:* "Sed te ista fugiunt, quia contemnis definita a Patribus in hoc concilio sessione 4 et fidem adeo vis pendere ab scripturis, ut nec illas traditiones quae sine scripto a christi ore vel ab Apostolis, Spiritu Sancto dictante, quasi per manus tradite ad nos usque pervenerunt, ad fidei doctrinam spectare credas. . . Et huiusmodi sunt dogmata quae certa et indubitata tenet tota Ecclesia. Qualia sunt: Deiparam virginem fuisse perpetuo virginem, imagines et reliquias sanctorum esse reverendas, septem esse Ecclesiae sacramenta et multa alia huiusmodi. . . Nunquid apud aliquem minoris est authoritatis verbum alterius quam scriptura ipsius?" *De iustificatione* XV. 6. fol. 686.

in the strict sense of the word, as is the *meritum de condigno,* but relates to that effort for which man is responsible before or while he is taken into the economy of grace.

III. *Meritum de congruo*

In his important studies in early scholastic thought, Arthur Landgraf has shown that with respect to the relation of preparation and justification, a number of different solutions were advanced.[32] He points out that whereas some of them have a Pelagian ring for modern ears, nevertheless no one in that era posited an inner connection between nature and grace. Whenever such a connection is upheld, it is understood to depend on the merciful and faithful will of God; and whenever merits are admitted to precede grace, these merits are not understood to be merits in the full sense of the word but rather *merita interpretativa* or *de congruo*.[33]

There are also those who hold that no human merits whatsoever, even those that result from grace, are merits in a strict and full sense of the word. In a Lombardian commentary on St. Paul, we find that interesting combination of Romans 8:18 and Hebrews 13:16 which would be repeated time and again in the succeeding period. St. Paul's statement that there is no condignity between our sufferings of the present and the glory to come is interpreted to mean that man can not *promereri* his future glory in the full sense of the word.[34] The same point is made when, in a collection of

---

[32] *Dogmengeschichte der Frühscholastik I. Die Gnadenlehre.* Band I, Regensburg 1952, pp. 238-302.

[33] "Ausdrücklich sei noch enimal festgestellt, dass wir nirgends einen inneren Konnex zwischen Natur und Gnade angedeutet fanden. Wenn beide einmal mit Notwendigkeit verknüpft erscheinen, dann ist als Band der freie, erbarmende und getreue Wille Gottes eingefügt. Wo von einem Verdienst für die Gnade die Rede ist, baut entweder das Verdienst schon auf der Gnade selber auf, oder aber es handelt sich um ein Verdienst im uneigentlichen Sinn, wo Werk und Gnade wiederum nur aüsserlich durch Gottes Willen verknüpft werden." Landgraf, *op. cit.,* p. 302.

[34] "Caritas, qua quis sustine passiones, digna est future glorie. Ergo et ipse passiones, cum eiusdem sint meriti. Unde apostolus in epistola ad Corinthios: id quod in presenti est momentaneum et leve tribulationis nostre, supra modum in sublimitatem glorie eternum pondus operatur in nobis. Sic ergo accipe: non sunt condigne passiones ad futuram gloriam, scilicet ad tantam gloriam promerendam, quanta nobis dabitur. Semper enim plus dat de corona et minus de pena, quam homo mereatur. Vel potest dici, quod non sunt condigne quantum ad se, nisi ex Dei institutione, sicut se imperator statueret, ut qui citius campus percurreret, Xcem marcas acciperet. Et vere posset dici, quod cursus ille non esset dignus ad promerendas X marcas, utique ex se, tamen ex institutione imperatoris.

Questiones which suggest Gilbertian influence, it is said that: "except for Christ, no one's merit suffices to earn (*promereri*) life eternal."[85]

How much influence the condemnation of this thesis at the Council of Reims (1148)[86] has exterted is difficult to establish. At the transition to high scholasticism, the question of the possibility of true merit has clearly shifted from life eternal to first grace. A considerable section of theological opinion in the thirteenth[87] and fourteenth centuries,[88] especially among the Franciscans, taught that one cannot earn first grace in a strict sense of the word, but that nevertheless God gives his grace to those who do what is in their power. The most sympathetic evaluation of this thesis is that it expresses a deep pastoral concern.[39] Between God's bestowal of grace and sinful man's best deeds there is no relation of condignity, but only one of congruity, resting in God's goodness. Grace is no reward but rather a gift on which man may count, since God has committed himself to give his grace "facientibus quod in se est."

Passionately Johannes Auer has defended the graciousness of God as the moving power behind the *meritum de congruo* against the critique of Adolf von Harnack who found here conclusive evidence for the total disintegration of the Augustinian concept of grace.[40] According to Auer, this critique is completely uncalled for; in the first place, man's activity is set in the context of grace and, in the

---

Vel non sunt condigne, id est si districte ageretur, nullo modo ei comparari possent. Tribulatio namque est cum fine, merces erit sine fine, et multo maior erit ibi gloria quam hic labor." Cod. Bamberg. Bibl. 132, fol. 2v; quoted by Landgraf, *op. cit.*, p. 269, n. 4.

[35] "Nullius enim meritum sufficit ad vitam eternam promerendam, nisi solius Christi . . ." *Questiones*, col. British Museum, Harley, lat. 1762, fol. 144v; quoted by Landgraf, *op. cit.*, p. 272.

[36] The condemned *sententia* is quoted by Otto of Freising as: "quod naturam humanam attenuando nullum mereri diceret praeter Christum," *Monumenta Germaniae Historica*. Script. XX (1868), p. 379. Since late medieval Nominalism is often said to show Pelagian tendencies, it is interesting to note that the Gilbertian heresy is regarded by Joh. Auer as "verbunden mit einer nominalistischen, rationalistischen Philosophie"! *Die Entwicklung der Gnadenlehre in der Hochscholastik*. II, *Das Wirken der Gnade*, Freiburg, 1951, p. 60.

[37] Landgraf, *op. cit.*, pp. 378ff.

[38] Auer, *op. cit.*, pp. 84ff.

[39] "Es war das religiöse und vielleicht seelsorgliche Bedürfnis, aus der Güte Gottes die Möglichkeit einer wirksamen Vorbereitung auf die Gnade zu erweisen." Auer, *op. cit.*, p. 85.

[40] Harnack, *Lehrbuch der Dogmengeschichte*, III⁵, Tübingen 1932, p. 636; 650ff.

second place, actual or prevenient grace has to incite man before he is able to dispose himself properly.[41]

Neither Harnack's attack nor Auer's defense takes account of the variety of ways in which the *merit de congruo* functioned. One is inclined to answer Harnack that the *meritum de congruo* is by all and always seen within the context of grace. The rule that God does not deny his grace to those who do their very best is a rule of grace. Turning now to Auer's second argument, it should be pointed out that it is by no means as clear as he suggests that this preparation for the reception of first grace is necessarily due to the influx of actual grace. In the case of the mature Aquinas there can indeed be little doubt, since for him the merit *de congruo* does not precede justification in time but is the meritorious action considered as the result of the action of free will, whereas the merit *de condigno* is that *same* action considered as proceeding from grace.[42]

The English Archbishop of Canterbury, Thomas Bradwardine († 1349), on the other hand, feels that the merit *de congruo*, as a merit preceding the gift of grace, is "propagated very much in our days, and many are blindly rushing into Pelagianism."[43] Gregory of Rimini († 1358) likewise opposes the opinion of some "modern doctors" that one can earn first grace *de congruo*.[44]

---

[41] "Dass diese Lehre nichts mit den von Harnack aus tiefem innerem Unverständnis für die Hochscholastik geborenen Vorwürfen eines Neosemipelagianismus zu tun hat, ist ganz selbstverständlich, wenn man das ganz auf Gottes Barmherzigkeit gebaute interpretative Verdienst (das mit Harnacks menschlichbürgerlichem Verdienstbegriff nichts zu tun hat) und die ganz in Gottes Gnade gesetzte Betätigung des Menschen überhaupt und die eigens vorausgesetzten aktuellen göttlichen Anregungen für diese Bereitung des Menschen für Gott ins Auge fasst. Im Gegenteil ist durch diese Lehre vielmehr die Heiligkeit und Liebe Gottes, die in so erhabener und zarter Weise um den Menschen wirbt, und der tiefe Ernst, der in diesem Anruff Gottes an den freien Menschen liegt, wie auch das Unaussprechliche des menschlichen Suchens und des Sich-begegnens, in seiner Zartheit wie in seiner ernsten Verpflichtung gesehen, über allen Vergleich wirklichkeitstreuer und erhabener und religiös tiefer und frömmer, als es je ein aus verantwortungsloser Selbstpreisgabe oder verzweifelter Selbstbehauptung geborener Fiduzialglaube darstellen könnte." *Op. cit.*, pp. 86-87.

[42] ". . . opus meritorium hominis dupliciter considerari potest: uno modo, secundum quod procedit ex libero arbitrio; alio modo, secundum quod procedit ex gratia Spiritus Sancti." *ST* I. II. q 114. art. 3. c.a. The footnote in the Marietti edition, Romae 1952, p. 567, n. 2 reads the young Thomas into this text when it states that a merit *de congruo* "non praesupponit statum gratiae, sed dispositionem quandam ad gratiam vel orationem ut est in peccatore." Cf. Aquinas as "sententiarius," II *Sent.* d 28 q 1 art. 40.

[43] ". . . dicunt enim homines ex solis propriis viribus gratiam Dei mereri de congruo, non autem de condigno." *De Causa Dei Contra Pelagium*, I. 39. 325ff.

[44] ". . . nemo potest mereri primam gratiam de condigno; nec etiam de congruo

John Wyclif develops a theology of merits in the same line, but with a fresh radicality which reminds one of the twelfth century Gilbertian school. He does not reject the merit *de congruo:* on the contrary, this is the only kind of merit he admits. In his opinion one earns merit *de congruo* when God rewards *de pura gracia* those works which issue from his prevenient grace; *de condigno* one would earn merit when God rewards *de pura iustitia* those works which are completely man's own, in which God therefore does not *graciose* cooperate. This unusual definition of the merit *de condigno* forces Wyclif to reject merits *de condigno* altogether, since God always cooperates *graciose*: all merits are rewards *de pura gracia* and therefore always *de congruo*.[45]

In the pre-Wyclif tradition, the merit *de condigno* is also based on *iustitia;* but this *debitum iustitiae* is never understood as *pure* justice. Hus, who quotes Wyclif's definition of merit, tries to reconcile the two positions by pointing out that *pura iustitia* presupposes indeed an equality between work and reward, but that this equality can be taken either as an *equalitas quantitatis* or as an *equalitas proportionis*. One is right in rejecting the merit *de condigno* when condignity is understood in a quantitative sense; but it is quite defensible when understood only to indicate a proportionate equality.[46] It is nevertheless clear that Hus prefers Wyclif's rejection of the merit *de condigno* in favor of the merit *de congruo*.[47]

This position of the "late medieval Gilbertian school" remained

---

contra aliquorum sententiam modernorum." II *Sent.* d 26, 27, 28 q 1 art 1; fol. 93 Q.

[45] "Et est duplex meritum, scilicet de congruo et de condigno: de congruo quando aliquis meretur de pura gracia premiantis, ut puta, quando premians prevenit cooperando omne meritum merentis . . .; de condigno autem dicitur quis mereri, quando meretur de pura iusticia ab alico premiante, quod fuit quando premians non graciose coagit cum illo . . ." *De Sciencia Dei*, fol 61va-vb; quoted by J. A. Robson, *Wyclif and the Oxford Schools*, Cambridge 1961, p. 209, n. 1. We are unable to agree with Mr. Robson when he claims that Wyclif "makes the customary distinction between congruous and condign merit." Cf. his interpretation of this quotation, *op. cit.*, pp. 208f.

[46] "Qui ergo dicunt, quod non potest homo mereri vitam aeternam de condigno, attendunt equalitatem quantitatis; qui autem dicunt, quod homo potest mereri de condigno atendunt equalitatem proporcionis." II *Sent.* d 27 q 5; *Opera omnia*, II, ed. V. Flajshans, Prague 1905, p. 307. Cf. Thomas, III *Sent.* d 18 q 1 art. 2 C.

[47] ". . . non potest pura creatura de condigno mereri vitam eternam." *Ibid.*, p. 308. ". . . impossibile est creaturam mereri a Deo . . . nisi a Deo mereatur illud premium de congruo, non de condigno." *Ibid.*, p. 309.

the exception; a very different interpretation of the merit *de congruo* prevailed in the fifteenth century. In Scotistic and Nominalistic circles the merit *de congruo* refers to God's gracious acceptation of the sinner's *facere quod in se est,* which is not a merit in the strict sense of the word since it does not establish a *debitum iustitiae*.[48] So can the Dominican Durandus de St. Pourçain († 1334) regard the *meritum de congruo* as a *meritum ante gratiam*.[49] A detailed analysis of the thought of William of Occam († 1349), Robert Holcot († 1349), and Gabriel Biel († 1495) has led us to the conclusion that this gracious condescension of God is understood as a commitment by which God in eternity obligated himself to impart to man's action a dignity which it would not have in itself. The golden rule of grace, "facientibus quod in se est Deus non denegat gratiam," can be designated by the symbol "partim-partim" insofar as it implies that if man goes halfway, God will meet him with the gift of grace. Without this gift of grace man is helpless; but it is just as true that without the full use of man's powers, the offer of grace is useless.[50] It is by no means always clear that this merit *de congruo* requires the prevenience of actual grace (*gratia gratis data*) or that this grace when posited is more than an exterior acquaintance with the law of God instead of an interior liberating power.[51]

Though the fifth chapter of the Tridentine decree on justification has retained the "partim-partim" structure,[52] it is more firmly embedded in the doctrine of the prevenience of grace than had been the case in large sections of late medieval thought.[53] But neither for the disciples of Bonaventure nor for those of Biel did this formulation necessarily imply a correction of their views. For the first in his *Breviloquium* had stated that nobody could sufficiently do what is in him to prepare himself for salvation without actual

[48] Cf. Auer, *op. cit.,* pp. 81ff.
[49] II *Sent.* d 27 q 2; ed. Lugduni, 1562.
[50] Cf. my "Facientibus quod in se est Deus non denegat gratiam. Robert Holcot, O.P. and the Beginnings of Luther's Theology." *Harvard Theological Review,* 55 (1962), pp. 317-342.
[51] Cf. *The Harvest of Medieval Theology,* pp. 132ff.
[52] ". . . neque homo ipse nihil omnino agat, inspirationem illam recipiens, quippe qui illam et abicere potest, neque tamen sine gratia Dei movere se ad iustitiam coram illo libera sua voluntate possit." *Denz.* 797. *Concilium Tridentinum,* ed. Goerresiana, Friburgi Br. [henceforth cited as *CT*], V. 793.
[53] ". . . ipsius iustificationis exordium in adultis a Dei per Christum Iesum praeveniente gratia sumendum esse"; ". . . Dei nos gratia praeveniri confitemur." *Denz.* 797. *CT* V. 792, 793.

grace.[54] The second had taught in his popular commentary on the Mass, *Canonis Misse Expositio*, that the possibility of *facere quod in se est* was a gift of grace; for that very reason this disposition for sanctifying grace could not be regarded as constituting a merit *de condigno*, but rather a merit *de congruo*.[55]

Silvester Prierias, O.P. († 1523), friend of Cardinal Caietanus († 1534) and from 1515, as *Magister Sacri Palatii* in Rome, the advisor of Pope Leo X in the process against Reuchlin and Luther,[56] provides us with a clear example of the way in which a theologian of unquestioned orthodoxy can combine the *facere quod in se est*, as usually understood in the late middle ages, with the Tridentine emphasis on the prevenience of grace.[57] In his often reprinted *Aurea Rosa* of 1503,[58] he points out that without the aid of grace the sinner is able of his own free will to desire the gift of grace which God grants either instantaneously or over a period of time.[59] Moreover God will *never* grant his grace *unless* it is preceded by such a desire on the part of the sinner to receive it.[60] Since humility belongs to the *facere quod in se est*,[61] self-humiliation in

---

[54] ". . . et sine hac [gratia gratis data] nullus sufficienter facit quod in se est, ut se praeparat ad salutem." *Brevil*. 5.2.

[55] ". . . faciendo quod in se est non meretur primam gratiam que est gratia iustificians peccatorem de condigno, licet mereatur de congruo . . . nullum enim donum gratie gratis date commensurabile est gratie gratum facienti." *Sacri Canonis Misse Expositio*, Basel 1510, Lect. 59 T. Edition Oberman-Courtenay, Wiesbaden 1965, p. 447.

[56] Cf. F. Laus s.v. *Prierias* in *RGG* V³, Tübingen 1961, col. 568; more extensive, Th. Kolde, s.v. *Prierias* in *RE* XVI, Leipzig 1905, cols. 30-32. A new study of Prierias' theological position is urgently needed.

[57] ". . . vocatione, qua nullis eorum existentibus meritis vocantur . . ." *Denz*. 797. *CT* V. 792.

[58] *Aurea Rosa, R.P.F. Silvestri de Prierio Pedemontani Sacri ordinis Praedicatorum de Observantia, videlicet clarissima expositio super Euangelia totius anni, de Tempore et de Sanctis, tam secundum Ordinem Praedicatorum quam secundum Curiam, continens flores et rosas expositionum sanctorum Doctorum antiquorum.* We have used the edition published in Venice in 1582.

[59] ". . . istud desiderium habendi donum Dei quod ex nostra libertate stante Dei generali influentia procedit, aliquando Deus statim mentibus infundit, vel ad illud movet, ut in Paulo. Aliquando paulatim nos ad illud provocat." *Aurea Rosa, Tractatus secundus*, Feria 6. post Domin. 3, in Quadrag., fol. 136 br.

[60] "Sed dicendum est, quod nunquam Deus homini suam gratiam infundit secundum modum consuetum iustificandi, nisi illam desideret habere, quod est petere donum Dei . . ." *Ibid*. This 'modum consuetum' allows for the exceptional cases of John the Baptist, the Virgin Mary, and St. Paul.

[61] The testimony of the Spirit is sufficiently clear *ad convertendos dispositos ad viam suae salutis*: ". . . Deus et natura non deficiunt in necessariis . . . unde cuilibet facienti, quod in se erat, istud testimonium erat sufficiens . . . unde

the form of awareness of one's own sins is the basis for the infusion of grace, which in turn leads to eternal glory.[62]

Whereas we have found no evidence that Prierias would be willing to admit that the sinner can earn first grace or that God's vocation is a *reward* for good works preceding justification, this influential Inquisitor states unambiguously that God can nevertheless be relied on to respond with the *gift* of grace to the sinner's best efforts. And this is exactly what both Scotistic and Nominalistic schoolmen intended to express when they employed the term *meritum de congruo*.

IV. The Present State of Scholarship

When we for the purposes of this article limit our investigation to that aspect of the justification of the sinner which deals with his preparation for the reception of sanctifying grace—usually called *gratia gratum faciens* or habitual grace—we note that presently there exists an interconfessional consensus that Trent opted for the Thomistic doctrine on this point. The Protestant church historian and influential Tübingen professor, Hanns Rückert, decsribes in a still authoritative study of Trent's doctrine of justification the development of the debate of the Council fathers on the problem of the disposition of the sinner. Whereas representatives of Nominalistic thought do not function in Rückert's account, he comes to the conclusion that the debates led to a clear victory of the Thomists over the Scotists. This victory is, in Rückert's opinion, clearly expressed in Trent's rejection of the meritorious nature of the disposition for justification. The Franciscan party after first having defended the *meritum de congruo* as God's liberal award for men's best efforts without the aid of sanctifying grace, finally had

---

bene ibi [Matt. 11:25, Lk. 10:21] 'parvulis,' id est humilibus et non superbis." *Aurea Rosa, Tractatus tertius*, Q. 44, fol. 323 a^r.

[62] "Et qui se humiliat per peccatorum cognitionem et praesentiam, exaltabitur in praesenti per gratiam et in futuro per gloriam." *Aurea Rosa, Tractatus secundus*, Dominica 11. post Trinitatem, fol. 263 b^v. Luther must have had this position in mind when he affirms in his 1521 defense of the articles condemned by Pope Leo X that contrition has to precede awareness of sins as the tree precedes the fruits. With a jibe which might well be an allusion to Geiler of Keisersberg's *Ship of Fools* he adds that in the country of the Pope everything is topsy-turvy, since there the trees grow on the apples: "gleichwie sie auch auf den Ohren gehen" *WA* 7. 361. Cf. the Woodcut in the Strassburg 1510 edition of the *Navicula sive speculum fatuorum . . . a Jac. Othero collecta*, where the artist (Hans Burgmaier? Cf. Brunet, II. 1576) shows a fool walking on his head.

to yield to the Thomistic drive to have this concept stricken out of the final decree.[63]

In his impressive study on the relation of the Roman Catholic doctrine of justification to that of Karl Barth, Hans Küng argues that both can be characterized by *sola gratia* and by *sola fide*. He concludes by saying: "Man is therefore justified by God's grace alone. Man does not produce anything . . . he does not work, he believes."[64]

The key prooftext for Hans Küng seems to leave little doubt that this interpretation is completely justified and that Trent indeed rejected the doctrine of the *facere quod in se est* as the basis for a *meritum de congruo:*

> "none of the acts which precede justification, whether faith or works, merits the grace of justification"[65]

In the following, however, we want to show that the interpretation and translation of this passage is not so clear as generally assumed. The Latin verb used here and above translated as "to merit" is *promereri* and not *mereri*. On the strength of evidence drawn from late medieval sources and from the debates at the Council itself, we would rather suggest that *promereri* is to be distinguished from *mereri* and is to be translated as "to merit truly," "completely" or "fully." We would further suggest that whereas *mereri* is associated with the *meritum de congruo, promereri* re-

---

[63] "In der Folgezeit ist dann die franziskanische Partei nicht mehr stark genug um die Wiederaufrichtung des meritum de congruo durchzusetzen." *Die Rechtfertigungslehre auf dem Tridentinische Konzil*, Bonn 1925, p. 185. Cf. Adolf von Harnack: "Das Decret über die Rechtfertigung, obgleich ein Kunstprodukt, ist in vieler Hinsicht vortrefflich gearbeitet; ja man kann zweifeln, ob die Reformation sich entwickelt hätte wenn dieses Decret auf dem Lateranconcil am Anfang des Jahrhunderts erlassen worden und wirklich in Fleisch und Blut der Kirche übergegangen wäre." *DG* III5, Tübingen 1932, p. 711.

[64] "Gerechtfertigt wird der Mensch also durch Gottes Gnade allein. Der Mensch leistet nichts . . . er werkt nicht, er glaubt . . ." *Rechtfertigung Die Lehre Karl Barths und eine Katholische Besinnung*, Einsiedeln 1957, p. 246; cf. p. 245 and p. 259. Cf. also Joseph Hefner: ". . . das menschliche Tun steht nur in einem konsekutiven, nicht aber in einem kausalen Verhältnis zur Rechtfertigung und so bleibt einerseits die Würde des Menschen als sittlicher Persönlichkeit, wie anderseits die Freiheit Gottes im Werke der Rechfertigung unversehrt bestehen." *Die Entstehungsgeschichte des Trienter Rechtfertigungsdekretes*, Paderborn 1909, p. 206.

[65] ". . . nihil eorum, quae iustificationem praecedunt, sive fides, sive opera, ipsam iustificationis gratiam promereretur." Concilium Tridentinum, Sessio VI, Caput 8; *CT* V, 794.

fers to the *meritum de condigno,* i.e., full merit, which by definition can only be produced in a state of grace, *after* the reception of the *gratia gratum faciens.*[66]

If this is the case, the key prooftext in the Tridentine decree cited above has to be translated as:

". . . none of the acts which precede justification, whether faith or works, *fully* merits the grace of justification."

It is usually said that the Council of Trent in its definition of the truly Catholic doctrine of justification opted for the *via media,* steering away from both the Scylla of Lutheranism and the Charybdis of Nominalistic Pelagianism. If our interpretation is *e mente auctorum,* a true presentation of the mind of the Fathers of Trent, the nominalistic doctrine of justification has substantially contributed to the final formulation of the decree, and the Scotistic interest in the *meritum de congruo* has been fully validated, taken into account and safeguarded.

V. *Andreas de Vega, O.F.M., and the Pre-Conciliar Period*

One of the most influential *periti* in the first stage of the Council of Trent is doubtlessly the Spanish Observant Franciscan Andreas de Vega (1498-1549). Realizing the central importance of the doctrine of justification in Reformation thought, he had the foresight to publish his *Opusculum de iustificatione, gratia et meritis* in time to have it in the hands of the Council fathers before this subject matter was broached.[67] Vega is probably the co-author of the orig-

[66] Without giving an analysis of the history of *promereri,* J. Rivière seems to support this interpretation: "Ainsi, tout en évitant le terme technique *mérite de congruo,* qui soulevait des contestations, le concile en consacre manifestement l'idée." Mérite (au Concile de Trente), *DThC* X.1. col. 754. Cf. Eduard Stakemeier: "Damit war die Möglichkeit eines Billigkeitsverdienstes ausdrücklich ausgesprochen worden." *Glaube und Rechtfertigung.* Freiburg i. B. 1937, p. 120. Dr. Stakemeier nevertheless regards the decree as documenting a Thomistic victory. *Ibid.* In his interesting article "Trienter Lehrentscheidungen und Reformatorische Anliegen" he goes on to say: "Die Hauptanliegen der Protestanten sind in diesem Dekret erfüllt," *WT* I, p. 98. W. F. Dankbaar contends that Küng e.a. have overlooked that the *sola fide* and *sola gratia* aspect of the Tridentine decree applies only to the "first status" of justification: "This 'sola' applies only to the preparation, but is insufficient for justification itself" [my transl., H.A.O.]; "Calvijns cordeel over het Concilie van Trente, bepaaldelijk inzake het Rechtvaardigingsdecreet," in *NAK* 45 (1962), pp. 78-112; p. 102.

[67] *Opusculum de iustificatione, gratia et meritis, autore F. Andrea Vega ordinis minorum regularis observantiae, ex alma provincia sancti Iacobi, Sacrae theologiae magistro Salmaticensi,* Venetiis 1546. The introduction is signed "Tridenti calendis Ianuarii anno Salutis 1546."

inal draft for the decree on justification dated some seven months later, which formed the basis of the first discussions.[68] And again after the Fathers have had time for discussion and critique, it is Vega who writes a draft incorporating some of the more important observations made.

It is interesting to note that Vega, too, feels that the Council has to find the *media via,* but this time defining the Scylla and the Charybdis in terms different from the ones current in present-day Tridentine studies. According to Vega there are three schools of thought which constitute at the same time the three possible options as regards the problem of disposition. These are the Pelagians, the Thomists, and the followers of Gabriel Biel.

The *Pelagiani* are a dated school virulent around the time of St. Augustine, though, according to Thomas Bradwardine, this school later came to life again in Great Britain.[69] This school holds that justification is based on merits.[70]

[68] The so-called *propositum a deputatis* or *prima forma* is dated July 24, 1546. See *CT* V, 384-391. According to the editors, St. Ehles and V. Schweitzer, from Vega's hand in view of the striking similarities with a draft published in *CT* XIII, 637-643, which Cardinal Cervini certifies as a work of Vega. Cf. *CT* XII, 637, n. 2. More recently Valens Heynck, O.F.M., has argued that *CT* XII, 637 ff. is only "eine nachträgliche Bearbeitung der 'prima forma' auf Grund der annotationes der Theologen und vielleicht auch der Zensuren der Väter." See his "Der Anteil des Konzilstheologen Andreas de Vega O.F.M. an dem ersten amtlichen Entwurf des Trienter Rechtfertigungsdekretes," *FS* 33 (1951) p. 59. His main argument for the dissimilarity between the *prima forma* and Vega's draft hinges, however, on the interpretation of *promereri,* which Heynck sharply distinguishes from *vere mereri:* "In der amtlichen Vorlage wird schlechthin ein 'promereri' der heiligmachende Gnade durch die der Rechtfertigung vorausgehenden guten Werke zurückgewiesen; bei Vega bezeichnenderweise nur ein *'vere et proprie mereri,'* so dass dadurch ein meritum de congruo, das unser Theologe mit der ganzen mittelalterlichen Franziskanerschule für zulässig hält ... nicht ausgeschlossen ist." *Ibid.* p. 57; cf. p. 75. If we are right in translating *promereri* with 'to merit fully,' at least one of Heynck's more convincing arguments falls away. More important is that Vega himself can use *mereri* as a parallel expression for *promereri* in his *Opusculum* which antedates the *prima forma!* "Igitur *vere* potest quicunque peccator suam iustificationem mereri. Ea enim *promereri* possumus quae assequi per nostra opera possumus." *Opusculum,* Q VI, fol. 184. Though the authorship of the *prima forma* will always remain open to debate without further discoveries of sources, it seems of one piece with both the later *CT* XII, 637ff. draft and the earlier *Opusculum.* Luchesius Spätling is therefore too apodictic: "Vegas Autorschaft . . . steht unzweifelhaft fest," in "Der Anteil der Franziskaner am Konzil von Trient," *WT,* II, p. 517.

[69] "Revixit et postea in Scotia teste magistro Thoma Bradabaerdino decano Londoviarum, in Summa contra Pelagianos." *Opusculum,* Q VI, fol. 147.

[70] ". . . iustificatio ex meritis." *Ib.,* fol. 146.

The second school is that of St. Thomas, which holds that no merits whatsoever precede the grace of justification.[71] To this school should be counted Nicolaus of Lyra († 1340), Thomas Netter († 1430), and that great defender of St. Augustine, Gregory of Rimini († 1358). Here both kinds of merit, *de condigno* and *de congruo*, are denied to the sinner.[72]

The third school can be identified by the names of the more recent theologians: Biel, Maior († 1550) and Almain († 1516). This is by no means, however, a new school since already at the time of Duns Scotus theirs was the *opinio communis* in the universities.[73]

This last school now is the *via media,* since it holds with the Thomists that man cannot acquire first justification by merits *de condigno* while it grants the Pelagians that the sinner can be justified on grounds of merits *de congruo*.[74]

In this venerable school, the *via media* of Gabriel Biel *cum suis,* Vega himself stands. He does not deny that one can merit first grace to a certain extent; what he denies is that one can merit this grace in an absolute sense of the word.[75] Merits *de congruo* have no claim on God's justice since they are committed in a state of sin. Nevertheless sinners still can perform acts of such moral qual-

[71] ". . . nulla prorsus merita antecedere gratiam iustificationis." *Ib.,* fol. 146.

[72] ". . . nullum esse in peccatore meritum suae iustificationis neque ex congruo, neque ex condigno. Et eadem sententiam tenent noster Nicolaus Lyranus super Ioannis primum, Thomas Waldensis in libro de sacramentalibus, et valens ille Gregorius Ariminensis, maximus et studiosissimus divi Augustini propugnator in II d. 26." *Ib.,* fol. 148.

[73] ". . . theologi recentiores Gabriel, Maioris, Almaynus et similes; et ante illos, ne adeo nova existemetur, videtur iam tempore doctoris subtilis fuisse haec opinio communis in scholis." *Ib.,* fol. 148.

[74] ". . . mediam quandam secuti sunt viam, concedentes cum posterioribus peccatores non iustificari ex meritis de condigno, sed interim dantes hoc prioribus quod tamen iustificentur ex meritis de congruo." *Ib.,* fol. 146. This surprising willingness to associate with the 'Pelagiani' even to a limited extent, a school of thought in which he obviously feels to stand himself, is due to the fact that so far as we can see for the first time a more historical and less 'dogmatic' picture of Pelagius' thought is given. Vega already saw that Augustine's presentation of Pelagianism, which had become the current medieval caricature, proves to be less than reliable if tested by Pelagius' actual statements: "Et quamvis ex nonnullis verbis divi Augustini contra Pelagianos . . . aliquis colligere possit sic dixisse eos sufficere posse nobis liberum arbitrium ut sine gratia vel meritis Christi possimus remissionem peccatorum impetrare et beatitudinem consequi, tamen . . . adduci non possum ut credam Pelagium sic sensisse." *Opusculum,* Q VI, fol. 154.

[75] ". . . absolute non possumus primam gratiam mereri." *Ib.,* fol. 171.

ity that it is fitting for God to accept them in his goodness as "half" merits.[76]

One can point to several weaknesses in Vega's historical presentation. One might argue that he is too optimistic in seeing "Pelagianism" contained to Great Britain; furthermore, he does not differentiate here between the positions of Thomas and Gregory.[77] The greatest flaw is perhaps one that contaminates even contemporary research: the crucial difference between the Scotistic and the Nominalistic support of the merit *de congruo* is overlooked. As we pointed out, Duns Scotus can allow for a great amount of freedom in man, even in man as a sinner, because the doctrine of justification is surrounded by the two clear and explicit doctrines of predestination and acceptation which safeguard God's sovereignty and eternal prevenience. The *homo peccator* can therefore do what is in him and thus produce merits *de congruo*, but he is never able to move himself into the operational sphere of God's predestination.[78] Since the Nominalistic theologian rejects Scotus' doctrine of predestination, while retaining the inner structure of Scotus' doctrine of justification, he has removed a central part of the outer safeguard or protecting wall. While he can make statements identical with the Scotists on such an issue as the merit *de congruo*, they are transferred into a new context in which divine acceptation alone has to perform the function which for Duns Scotus was performed by predestination and acceptation together.

Dominicus Soto (1495-1560),[79] the great Dominican *peritus*, learned opponent of Vega and specialist on this issue for the Thomistic party at the Council, is quick to point out this weakness and repeatedly claims Duns Scotus for his own position.

---

[76] "Alia vero sunt merita ex congruo quae in peccatoribus reperiuntur quae nullo praemio digna sunt quia fiunt ab hominibus Deo ingratis et exosis, sed tamen eiusmodi ex se sunt, ut congruum sit et divinam bonitatem condeceat ea ex liberalitate et benignitate sua acceptare, ut trahat peccatores ad suam gratiam. Et huiusmodi merita sic merita sunt ut tamen non necesse sit ea dicere merita absolute sed tantum merita ex congruo. Atque ideo quamvis fideles peccatores dicamus posse mereri ex congruo suam iustificationem, non est opus concedere absolute eos posse mereri suam iustificationem." *Opusculum*, Q VIII, fol. 211.

[77] Since Vega elsewhere proves to be very well aware of the differences between Thomas and Gregory—cf. Q V, fol. 133—he apparently generalizes for cataloguing purposes.

[78] See my *Harvest of Medieval Theology*, p. 212ff.

[79] On his life and works see the article by V. Beltram de Heredia in *DThC* XIV 2, col. 2423-2431. Most careful Friedrich Stegmüller, "Zur Gnadenlehre des Spanischen Konzilstheologen Domingo de Soto," in *WT*, I, pp. 169f.

For Soto all those who defend the merit *de congruo* are obviously Pelagians since the relation between predestination and justification is so intimate that the claim to earn one's justification *de congruo* at once implies the claim to earn one's predestination *de congruo*. Thus he could drive a wedge between the Scotist and the Nominalist positions.[80]

In his presentation of the *via media* of Gabriel Biel, however, Vega has been accurate. It is in this school that we shall have to look for the beginnings of the distinction between *mereri* and *promereri* or *vere mereri* when we turn to the history of the word *promereri* at the Council itself.

VI. *Some Notes on the Preconciliar History of* PROMERERI

A definitive history of the use of *promereri* by the Church fathers and medieval theologians must of course be a communal effort; only through team work can definite results be expected. The general presupposition has hitherto obviously been that *promereri* is nothing more than an embellished or rhetorical *mereri*. Only after we have been alerted to the possible importance of the distinction between *promereri* and *mereri* might we expect to collect extensive evidence. In every *Index verborum* to editions of Western theological texts which we have consulted, we have found the entry *promereri* wanting. A. Souter alerts us, however, to the fact that a disciple of Pelagius uses the verb three times to clarify the intention of his master.[81]

In an important article on the concept of merit in the writings of some early Latin Fathers, J. N. Bakhuizen van den Brink comes to the conclusion that 'merit' does not entail a claim on God's justice or an obligation on his part to reward. Throughout, the context suggests the minimal interpretation, so that e.g. ". . . re-

[80] "Qui diceret quod iustificamur ex huiusmodi operibus quomodocumque seu tempore seu natura praecedentibus gratiam, publicus esset Pelagianus . . . non consideraverunt unam eademque esse rationem et praedestinationis et iustificationis . . . quapropter illi qui defendunt meritum de congruo antecedens gratiae, sequenter opinantur praedestinationis, puta de congruo . . ." *In epistolam divi Pauli ad Romanos Commentarii*, Antwerpiae 1550, fol. 270.

[81] See the Commentary on Rom. 9:2; II Cor. 5:9 and I Thes. 5:23. *Pelagius's Expositions of Thirteen Epistles of St. Paul: Pseudo Jerome interpolations.* Ed. A. Souter, Cambridge, Eng. 1931, p. 17, 46, 62. Cf. also Pelagius himself, commenting on Rom. 9:15: "Hoc recto sensu ita intelligitur: illius miserebor quem ita praescivi posse misericordiam promereri, ut iam tunc illius sim misertus," A. Souter, *Pelagius's Expositions of Thirteen Epistles of St. Paul: Text and Apparatus criticus*. Cambridge 1926, p. 75f.

missionem mereri is just 'to receive forgiveness'."[82] It is striking to note that the definition of the *meritum de congruo* in late medieval theology[83] describes precisely what in early Latin Fathers was meant by the concept of merit as such: "What both Tertullian and Cyprian had meant is nicely formulated by St. Augustine (*Sermo* 111.4.4): 'non debendo enim sed promittendo debitorem se Deus facit';"[84] "There is so little quality of merit in all this . . . it is only the will of God . . . ."[85] The controversy between Augustine and Pelagius, however, meant the end of an era, according to Bakhuizen van den Brink; it terminated "the ingenuous use of *mereri* and *meritum*."[86]

Certainly by the time of the early Scholastics this simple use of *mereri* has given way to explicit considerations of God's obligations to those who do their very best before and after the reception of grace.[87] Due to the reception of Aristotle in the West, the problem of the relation of the natural to the supernatural, and of *materia* to *forma*, was posed in a new fashion. The most important scholastic distinction of grace as *gratia gratis data* or actual grace and *gratia gratum faciens* or habitual grace come to be paralleled by the distinction of *meritum de congruo* before the reception of habitual grace and *meritum de condigno* after the reception of habitual grace. It is therefore by no means surprising that different verbs should indicate the difference between acquiring merits *de congruo* and acquiring merits *de condigno*. Surprising is rather that it is so hard to establish that when *promereri* occurs it is consciously and intentionally chosen in contradistinction to *mereri*.

Thanks to Isidore of Seville († 636), we know that in the theological terminology antedating the seventh century, on the eve of early Scholasticism, *promereri* is understood in contrast to *mereri*. Whereas *mereri* is an ambiguous verb which can mean to merit

---

[82] "Mereo(r) and *meritum* in some Latin Fathers," *Studia Patristica*, Vol. III. Part I, ed. F. L. Cross (Berlin 1961), pp. 333-340; p. 336. Cf. p 335: ". . . *mereri* loses its strict notion of merit in proportion to the notion of grace which is inherent in its object."

[83] *Harvest of Medieval Theology*, p. 170ff.

[84] *Art. cit.*, p. 334.

[85] *Ib.*, p. 337.

[86] *Ib.*, p. 338.

[87] A. M. Landgraf, *Dogmengeschichte der Frühscholastik*, I. 1, Regensburg 1952, p. 260, n. 58; p. 269; p. 272; p. 280, n. 3.

punishment as well as to earn a reward, *promereri* can only have the positive connotation of earning a reward.[88]

This distinction may well have been in the mind of many theologians who in the following centuries made use of the verb *promereri*. As late as the beginning of the fifteenth century we find *promereri* used by John Hus in contrast to *demereri*.[89] The same author can say however that only Christ can in a fundamental way *promereri*,[90] and since he clearly admits man's ability to *mereri*, one is inclined to translate Hus' observation to mean that 'only Christ can merit in the full sense of the word.'

As we shall see, this development of a new contrast between *mereri* and *promereri*—different from the one known to Isidore— has become explicit by the time of the Council of Trent. In present day Mariology the term *promereri* can serve to define the association of the Virgin Mary in the Redemption through Christ and thus to further the *Corredemptrix* doctrine. Though there is no indication that the Mariologists involved are aware of the long prehistory of the words, the association of the Virgin Mary in the work of Christ is expressed by using the verb *promereri* for their joint work of redemption whereas the terms *"de condigno"* and *"de congruo"* indicate the different modes of participation in it.[91]

Between Isidore and Hus, however, evidence of a consciously intended distinction between *promereri* and *mereri* is exceedingly sparse. The medieval history of *promereri* is therefore so hard to trace because the burden of proof is on the one who claims that it

---

[88] *Differentiae sive de proprietate sermonum. I, De differentiis verborum;* I. 361: "' meruit' commune est ad poenam et ad praemium, 'promeruit' tantum ad praemium." *Thesaurus linguae Latinae*, vol. VIII, Lipsiae 1952, p. 802. Whereas the positive connotation of *promereri* is clear and consistent, the ambiguity of the use of *mereri* appears from a reference drawn from Don. Ter. Hec. 487: "mereri bona dicimus, commereri mala," *Ibid. Commereri*, then, is synonymous with *demereri*.

[89] ". . . sicut in nulla materia quis compendiosius promeretur, sic nullibi facilius aut periculosius demeretur." III *Sent*. Inceptio. *Opera Omnia* II, ed. Wenzel Flajshans, Marie Kominkova, Prag 1905, p. 373, line 13.

[90] ". . . solum christus est homo fundamentaliter promerens." *Sent*. IV d 45 q 4; *ed. cit*. p. 715, l. 18/19; cf. *ibid*., p. 607: "Solus ille potuit capitaliter promereri." Cf. *De Ecclesia*, ed. Harrison Thomson, Cambr. 1956, p. 8, p. 82.

[91] Cf. Pius X, *Ad diem illum*, Febr. 2, 1904, *AAS* 36 (1903-1904), p. 454: ". . . a Christo ascita in humanae salutis opus de congruo, ut aiunt, promeret nobis quae Christus de condigno promeruit." See René Laurentin, *La Question Mariale*, Paris, 1963, p. 164. Cf. for the present state of the debate Guilelmus Baraúna, O.F.M., *De Natura Corredemptionis Marianae in Theologia Hodierna (1921-1958)*, Romae 1960, esp. p. 173ff.

means more than a "poetic" *mereri*. In early scholastic literature we find the verb *promereri* often enough used in the sense of *mereri de condigno*, but seldom explicitly contrasted with *mereri* in the sense of initial merit by the sinner who does his very best.[92] In both the treatise "On grace and free will" of Bernard of Clairvaux and Abelard's "Commentary on Romans" is the prefix *pro* employed; but in either case can its use very well have no more profound meaning than the wish of the author to vary the key terms of his argument.[93]

With the high scholastic Franciscan doctors such as Alexander of Hales and Bonaventure, the terms *meritum de condigno* and *meritum de congruo* are so prominent that we are inclined to suggest that for this reason no need is felt to apply consistently the parallel distinction between the verbs *promereri* and *mereri*. When Thomas Aquinas sometimes uses the verb *promereri*, there is nothing to prove that he intended to avoid *mereri*,[94] the very structure of his mature doctrine of justification makes this highly unlikely. And when the great fourteenth century protagonist of St. Augustine *contra Pelagianos*, the Archbishop of Canterbury Thomas Bradwardine, insists that no one can *promereri* first grace, there is little reason to suspect that he wants there to safeguard the possibility of meriting *(mereri)* first grace in any sense![95] Elsewhere, however,

[92] The most notable exception here is Roland of Cremona: "Ad ultimum dicimus, quod nullo potest promereri gratiam ex condigno. Tamen dicitur, quod aliquis ex quadam congruitate potest mereri gratiam, quia si homo facit quod suum est, congruum est, ut Deus faciat, quod suum est," Summa, Coll. Paris MLat. 795 fol. 101; Landgraf, *op. cit.*, p. 279.

[93] Bernard: "Dei sunt proculdubio munera, tam nostra opera, quam eius praemia; et qui se fecit debitorem in illis, fecit et nos promeritores ex his." *Tractatus de gratia et libero arbitrio*, cap. 13. 43; *PL*. 182, 1026; 1029/1030. Abaelard: "Estne tanta illa haereditas, ut pro ea promerenda patiendum sit usque ad mortem sicut Christus passus est? Respondet . . . Sola quippe charitas, quae nunquam excidit, vitam promeretur aeternam . . ." *Expositio in epistolam Pauli ad Romanos*, cap. 9.15; *PL* 178. 903.

[94] One could of course regard 'advocari' in *Summa contra Gentiles* III. 159, as a synonym for 'mereri': ". . . licet aliquis per motum liberi arbitrii divinam gratiam nec promereri nec advocari possit, potest tamen seipsum impedire ne eam recipeat . . ." *ST* I. II. q 112 art. 3 corp. art.

[95] Cf. my *Archbishop Thomas Bradwardine, A fourteenth century Augustinian*, Utrecht, 1958, p. 158. The same argument applies *a fortiori* to John Calvin: "Et accessus quidem nomine initium salutis a Christo esse docens, praeparationis excludit, quibus stulti homines Dei misericordiam se antevertere putant: ac si diceret, Christum nihil promeritis obviam venire manumque porrigere," J. Calvinus, *Commentarius in Epistolam Pauli ad Romanos*, cap. 5:2; *CR* 77 (Opera Calvini 49). Brunswigae 1892, col. 89. Cf. "Operantem vocat [Paulus] non quisquis bonis operibus addictus est, quod studium vigere debet in omnibus

Bradwardine, in speaking not merely about the *Pelagiani moderni*, but now about an even more modern *(recentissimus)* error, points to the latest 'trick' which consists in distinguishing between *promereri* and *impetrare*.[96]

Thus far our investigation has yielded no proof that in high scholasticism *promereri* is intentionally distinguished from *mereri*. Summarily stated one might say that the Thomistic school of thought would be in principle opposed to developing the doctrine of the *facere quod in se est*,[97] whereas the Franciscan theologians can say all they want by employing the distinction between *meritum de congruo* and *meritum de condigno*.

It is with the English Dominican and opponent of Thomas Bradwardine, Robert Holcot († 1349), that we find the first real evidence that early scholastic tendencies are reviving. In what seems to be a personal dialogue with Bradwardine the Nominalist Holcot states that of course no one can fully earn *(promereri)* sanctifying grace. But, he continues, this does not mean that the sinner would be unable to merit at all. He can indeed prepare himself *de congruo* for the infusion of grace.[98] A similar statement can be found with the Parisian Chancellor John Gerson († 1429), who had little sympathy for Bradwardine. In his treatise on prayer Gerson denies that one who is not in a state of grace can merit *de condigno*, since *promereri* is only possible for one moved by charity.[99]

Dei filiis, sed qui suis meritis aliquid promeretur." Cf. "Si quis sit qui promereatur aliquid opere suo, res promerita non imputatur illi gratis, sed ut debita redditur." *Ibid.*, cap. 4:4; *ed. cit.*, col. 70. Erasmus uses *promereri* in reference to Scotus. LB (Leiden edition) X. 1327 DE. cf. LB X. 1457B; X. 1487A.

[96] Compare with: "Nullum posse primam gratiam promereri," *De Causa Dei*, II. 31. 606 E, Bradwardine's earlier statement: "Ex his autem clare convincitur error quidam recentissimus Pelagianorum fingentium quod licet homo nullo modo neque de condigno neque de congruo valeat gratiam promereri, potest tamen ipsam propriis tantum viribus impetrare." I. 39. 363 E.

[97] Cf. the development of Aquinas on this point: *Harvest of Medieval Theology*, p. 142f.

[98] ". . . primam gratiam nullus potest promereri. Nam cum omne meritum sit ex gratia, si prima gratia caderet sub merito, primam gratiam precederet gratia. Et ideo deus sponte dat homini primam gratiam, homini, inquam, se ad gratiam disponenti dispositione naturali et non prebenti obicem gratie per malum usum liberi arbitrii. Licet autem ante primam gratiam requiratur dispositio conveniens, illa tamen non meretur gratiam merito condigni sed congrui tantum." *Super Libros Sapientiae*, Hagenau 1494, Lect. 116 A/B.

[99] "Porro si sit petitio per modum meritorie actionis, tunc nullus impetrat de condigno qui caret charitate; qui vero charitatem habet, eo, ceteris paribus, est efficacior oratio sua pro seipso quoad praemium essentiale beatificum promerendum quo fervor charitatis et conatus fuerit maior." "De Oratione et eius

But in the school of Gabriel Biel we have as yet been unable to find *promereri* used in the technical sense of the word.[100] Biel's younger friend and theological ally, the influential Strassburg preacher John Geiler of Kaisersburg († 1510), emphasizes the necessity of preparation for grace and insists that it is to be believed with certain faith that God will turn to any man who turns to him.[101] Whereas he is willing to admit this preparation as a *merit de congruo* he denies the possibility of *promereri*.[102]

At the end of this summary of medieval data, we may conclude that the distinction between *promereri* and *mereri* to differentiate between meriting in the full sense in a state of grace after the reception of justifying grace, and meriting *de congruo* in a state of sin, according to the evidence now before us, cannot be said to have consistent school support. Whereas we had not expected to encounter this distinction in the works of the Thomist school, we have not found it generally used in the Franciscan tradition, either in its Scotistic or Nominalistic varieties, where it would seem to be useful.

At the same time we may state that the distinction as we shall encounter it in the *acta* of the Council of Trent is not without precedent in the preceding medieval tradition. Only at a time when the expression *meritum de congruo* came under the double attack of Luther[103] and a reviving Thomism did it become im-

---

Valore," *Opera Omnia*, Antwerpen 1706, ed. E. du Pin, III. 251 B. At the same time Gerson can repeatedly stress that God has committed himself to infuse his grace in those who do their very best. Cf. *Opera* III. 7 D; III. 123 C. Cf. III. 86 C: "nulli facienti quod est in se, hoc est bene utenti donis dei iam habitis, deest Deus in necessariis ad salutem sive sint illa credenda sive operanda."

100 At one place *promereri* is clearly related to meriting final acceptation rather than first grace: ". . . petitur bonum spiritualis gratie quo in via ad promerendam celestem gloriam preparamur. Preparamur autem ad hanc promerendam per gratiam . . ." *Expositio Canonis Misse*, Lect. 68 A. Cf. however, IV *Sent.* d 16. q 2. art. 3, dub. 4: ". . . opera bona moraliter et per consequens de genere, nihil merentur de condigno, neque premium eternum, neque temporale. Cuius ratio: quia inimicus nihil meretur de condigno (quod proprie est meritum) . . ."

101 See the 1963 Harvard Ph.D. thesis, soon to be published, by E. J. Dempsey, *The Doctrine of Justification in the Preaching of Doctor John Geiler of Keisersberg*.

102 "Unde manifestissime probatur ne a domino quidem viam perfectionis quampiam promereri [potest]. . .", "De vita veri christiani," in *Sermones et varii tractatus*, fol. 95r2.

103 Conclusio 30: "Ex parte autem hominis nihil nisi indispositio, immo rebellio gratiae gratiam praecedit." "Contra scholasticam theologiam," *WA* I. 225. See further the important study by Leif Grane, *Contra Gabrielem. Luthers*

portant for theologians to look for a different terminology to safeguard human responsibility and initiative in the first stage of the road towards justification and final acceptance.

VII. PROMERERI *at the Council of Trent.*

Three times the verb *promereri* occurs in Trent's final decree on justification: once in connection with the disposition of the sinner[104] and twice in the statements dealing with man's ability in a state of grace to merit a growth of grace and eternal rewards.[105] It cannot surprise us that the *acta* only provide us with background information with regard to its first use. After all, Nominalists, Scotists, and Thomists had no difficulty in agreeing that man once justified can perform God-pleasing acts by which he is able in the fullest sense of the word to merit *de condigno:* he can therefore *promereri.*

A more elaborate documentation for the intention of the Council fathers we may expect to find in the discussion of the possibility of merit before the reception of the grace of justification.

The original proposal of July 1546 employs the verb *promereri* in a statement cast in the form of an anathema: Anathema on anyone saying that one can *promereri* the grace of justification with preceding works. It is immediately made clear that this only applies to *merita de condigno* and does not exclude *merita de congruo*: no such preceding works can entail a claim on God's justice.[106] Added to this anathema we find the explanatory comment: "In this justification the merits of man have to be silent, so that the *sola gratia* of Christ may reign."[107]

It may well have been this reference to *sola gratia* which led John Calvus of Corsica, the General of the Conventual Franciscans, to ask three weeks later, on August 17, for an explicit mention of the *meritum de congruo*. The original manuscript adds the observation that the decree actually does mention this merit. Though

---

Auseinandersetzung mit Gabriel Biel in der Disputatio contra scholasticam Theologian 1517, Gyldendal 1962; esp. p. 336f; p. 372.

[104] *Denz.* 801. *CT* v. 794.

[105] *Denz.* 809; 812. *CT* v. 797; *ibid.*

[106] "Si quis dixerit quod suis operibus hanc iustificationis gratiam praecedentibus eam infidelis valeat promereri, cum in illis, quantumlibet bonitate praepolleant, nihil sit iustitiae vel debiti, ut inquit et probat div. Paulus: anathema sit." *CT* V. 387.

[107] "In hac enim iustificatione merita hominis tacere debent, ut sola Christi gratia regnet." *CT* V. 387.

this last clause is later deleted, it allows for only one interpretation, namely that its author understood *promereri* to apply solely to *merita de condigno*.[108] That same day the bishop of the Canary Islands makes a similar request.[109]

Andreas de Vega, in an effort to incorporate the suggestions made, replaces *promereri* with the words *vere et proprie mereri*, its equivalent, as we believe, but less subject to misinterpretation. The words *nihil iustitiae vel debiti*, in an exact parallel, are replaced by the synonymous but more current phrase *nihil illis ex iustitia debetur*.[110] Whereas the future Cardinal Seripando († 1563) states in his draft of August 19, that merits as such are to be excluded before justification,[111] the so-called September draft significantly changes his phrasing so that only merits in the full sense of the word are exluded.[112]

Though it has been suggested that during the Sixth Session of the Council of Trent the Franciscan influence decreased with the progress of time, we find rather evidence for the contrary. In the beginning the representatives of the Franciscan mode of thought are far more defensive than proves to be the case later on. On October 7, 1546, the General of the Conventual Franciscans states in

---

[108] "Gener. min. convert. cuperet fieri mentionem de meritis de congruo" [*Del:* 'quae tamen in decreto fit']. *CT* V. 410.

[109] "In 9 canone placent omnia; si tamen aliqua fieret mentio de merito congrui, cum non ponat ius sed aequitatem, non esset inconveniens" *CT* V. 414.

[110] "Si quis dixerit quod infidelis suis operibus suam possit iustificationem vere et proprie mereri, anathema sit. Iustificamur enim gratis per gratiam Christi Iesu . . . Quantumlibet enim bonitate praecellunt opera praecedentia iustificationem nihil illis ex iustitia debetur; donatur namque magis quam comparatur; tribuitur, non retribuitur . . ." *CT* XII. 639.

[111] ". . . et ea quoque, quae ante eam ipsam iustificationis gratiam cum fide aliqua fiunt, tamquam merita excludantur" *CT* V. 829. Though he is willing to admit formal differences, it is a denial of the importance of this issue when Luchesius Spätling states that Seripando's proposal "sich hinsichtlich der Lehre im Wesentlichen mit dem von A. de Vega deckte (ausgenommen die Frage der doppelten Gerechtigkeit) . . .," *art. cit.*, p. 517. The same thesis underlies the dissertation of Bonaventura Oromi, *Los Franciscanos Españoles en el Concilio de Trento*, Madrid 1947, esp. p. 97ff.

[112] ". . . et ea quoque quae post illuminationem Spiritus Sancti ante iustificationis gratiam cum fide aliqua fiunt, tamquam proprie merita excludantur" *CT* V. 423. In the November draft (Nov. 5) this sentence reads: ". . . ea quoque quae post illuminationem Spiritus Sancti tamquam ad iustificationem necessaria et disponentia, cum fide aliqua fiunt tamquam merita, quibus gratia debeatur, ab ipsa iustificatione excludantur" *CT* V. 636. Ten Council fathers prefer *proprie merita* rather than *merita quibus gratia debeatur*. *CT* V. 681. The Dec. 10 proposal concedes to the Franciscan party even more than they asked: ". . . tamquam proprie merita, quibus gratia debeatur . . ." *CT* V. 696.

another intervention on the *meritum de congruo* that he stands over against "multi" or "nonnulli ex patribus" since they deny that justification follows the disposition with necessity, i.e. *de potentia ordinata*. This is the same interpretation of the *meritum de congruo*—a commitment of God to those who do their very best in preparation for justification—which we find with Gabriel Biel[113] and more generally with late medieval Nominalism.[114] The November draft mirrors the Franciscan concern even more clearly than did the September draft.

Since it is not our intention to follow the debates in all details, we turn now to the prelude to what we regard as the decisive discussion. Two days before Christmas 1546, Minoriensis and Bituntinus formulate the attack on the Nominalist-Scotist defense of the *meritum de congruo*. They suggest that the verb *mereri* should be employed, which in fact means a return to Seripando's suggestion that all merits are to be excluded.[115] This raises strong protests. Castellimaris wants at least the word *proprie* inserted[116] and the General of the Conventual Franciscans and the General of the Augustinians ask explicitly for a safeguard of the *merit de congruo*.[117]

[113] Cf. ". . . peccator disponens se ad gratiam faciendo quod in se est, meretur gratiam primam qua iusticatur de congruo . . ." IV *Sent.* d 16 q 2 art. 3 dub 4. For the status of Biel as *doctor catholicus* at Trent, see E. Stakemeier, "Die theologischen Schulen auf dem Trienter Konzil," *Theologische Quartalschrift.* 117 (1936), p. 343ff.

[114] "Nonnulli etiam ex patribus dixerunt dispositionem seu preparationem iustificationem ipsam non consequi; ego oppositum sentio inquiens, praeparationem ipsam ac dispositionem de necessitate sequi iustificationem, si particula ista 'regulariter' et 'de potentia ordinata' intelligatur et necessitas ista est immutabilitatis et infallibilitatis, ut disponentibus, praeparantibus se et facientibus quantum in se est Deus det gratiam, et est sententia Alexandri de Ales in 3. parte Summae q 69, art. 3 [vide: q. 64] cum quo est di. Thomas, Bonaventura, Ricardus et Scotus millies in eorum scriptis.

Multi sensurarunt particulam illam 'tanquam proprie merita excludantur' quos ego satis admiror, cum omnes theologi (excepto Gregorio Ariminensi ex ordine Eremitarum) ponant ista merita impropria, secundum quid, interpretativa, sive (ut uno verbo dicam) merita de congruo, distincta a meritis propriis, veris, gratuitis et de condigno. Ante ergo iustificationem nemo negat ex theologis, ut dixi, bona ista et merita impropria, licet quicumque excludat ea tanquam merita propria." *CT* V. 480. A few lines later, l. 49, Biel is referred to.

[115] ". . . gratis autem iustificari dicamur, quia nihil eorum quae iustificationem praecedet, vel fides vel opera, iustificationis gratiam merentur." *CT* V. 737; cf. *CT* V. 829.

[116] "Magis placent verba decreti; sed si poneretur 'proprie,' placeret." *CT* V. 737. Cf. also Armacanus: ". . . et posset loco 'excluduntur' dici 'proprie merentur'." *CT* V. 737.

[117] "Placet si non destruitur meritum de congruo." *CT* V. 737.

On January 8, 1547, Cervini, the presiding Cardinal-legate, asks whether it is necessary to add to *promereri* the phrase "secundum debitum iustitiae" which would make it explicit that only *merita de condigno* are rejected before justification.[118]

On that same day the weighty consensus is reached that the clause "secundum debitum iustitiae" does not need to be added, since it is sufficiently understood that *promereri* envisages only the merits *de condigno* so that the *merits de congruo* can be upheld.[119] In the final form of the decree, this decision is then implemented.[120]

Certain unclarities remain to be solved. We have no record for the debates on Chapter 16, *De fructu iustificationis,* and on its parallel in canon 32. Here both expressions occur: *vere promereri*[121] and *vere mereri*;[122] but it should be noted that here the Council is not directing itself to the Pelagian threat but rather to the Lutheran challenge of merits as such: on this point the Council could take a common stand.

The first three canons condemn a type of Pelagianism never taught by the Franciscan School, whether Nominalist or Scotist. Actually it condemns a Pelagianism never taught by *any* of the medieval doctors, including Pelagius himself. No Nominalist or Scotist ever taught that man could be justified before God without grace,[123] or that man could *promereri* life eternal.[124] And none even of the more Pelagianising Nominalists held that without prevenient grace one could fulfill the law *sicut oportet,* i.e., to use their terminology "in accordance with the intention of the Lawgiver, God" *(secundum intentionem praecipientis).* In short, the teachings condemned are those which the Franciscan Vega characterizes as Pelagian, not those which the Dominican Soto qualifies as such.

---

[118] ". . . an ibi 'iustificatione gratiam promerentur' sit addendum 'secundum debitum iustitiae' propter meritum de congruo." *CT* V. 764.

[119] "Et conclusum quod nihil additur, cum satis intelligatur meritum de congruo, ibi 'promerentur' scl. de condigno." *CT* V. 764. The further explanation added in a footnote refers to the discussion of Dec. 22, 1546: 'Id est: 'Cum satis intelligatur non destrui meritum de congruo,' prout innuerant die 22. decembris generalis Convent, et S. Augustini." *Ibid.,* n. 3.

[120] ". . . ipsam iustificationis gratiam promeretur." *CT* V. 794; Denz. 801.

[121] Denz. 809. *CT* V. 797.

[122] Denz. 842. *CT* V. 799.

[123] Can. 1, Denz. 811, *CT* V. 797.

[124] And all the less merely 'facilius': can. 2; Denz. 812. *CT* V. 797. The words 'sicut oportet' are overlooked by Reinhold Seeberg when he concludes that the Nominalistic position is condemned in canon 3. See his *Dogmengeschichte* IV4. 2, Basel 1954, p. 775, n. 2.

To summarize this section we may conclude:

1. It is the intention of the Council to exclude before the reception of justifying grace only the *merita de condigno*.

2. The verb *promereri* is intentionally differentiated from the verb *mereri* in such a fashion that the first is related only to *merita de condigno*, the latter to *merita de congruo*.

3. The Franciscan party, at the beginning of the debate on the defensive, has gained sufficiently in power to succeed in its stand for the *meritum de congruo*.

VIII. *Soto, O.P., and Vega, O.F.M.: Early Interpreters of the Decree*

When we now by way of final postscript return to two early interpreters of the decree, chosen as leaders in opposing camps, we do this to have a final check on our conclusions. Was the use of *promereri* understood by its interpreters *e mente auctorum*?

In his *De natura et gratia libri tres* of 1547, Dominicus Soto attacks the *meritum de congruo* head on. According to him there is no *facere quod in se est* possible without prevenient grace. He stretches the literal interpretation of the phrase when he argues that man can never do what is in him unless it be a response to the inspiration of God: ". . . before justification through the infusion of sanctifying grace, there is no merit whatsoever in human works, neither *de condigno*, nor *de congruo*."[125]

It is clear that for the Dominican Soto the verb *promereri* is equivalent with *mereri*. It should be observed, however, that in the first place Soto likes to interpret in a Thomist sense even Tridentine formulations which are now generally held to avoid a decision favoring one school or another.[126] In the second place Soto regards

---

[125] ". . . nimirum quod facere hominem quod in se est non intelligitur ante auxilium Dei, sed potius praeveniente Deo. Tunc enim homo facit quod in se est quando Deo inspiranti respondet cooperans et tunc certissima lege consequitur gratiam . . . ante iustificationem quae fit per gratiam gratum facientem, nihil humanis operibus insit meriti, sive condigni sive congrui." First ed. Venetiis 1547. The ed. used here is the second ed., Antwerpiae 1550, fol. 96. Friedrich Stegmüller discusses the accusation of semi-pelagianism by Soto's contemporary and fellow-Dominican Pedro de Soto who based his criticism on *De natura et gratia*. We believe with Stegmüller that this accusation is not justified. Cf. *art. cit.*, p. 170, 193.

[126] "Igitur sapienter sancta nostra Synodus Tridentina sessione 5, can. 2 pronuntiavit Adam accepisse sanctitatem (id est gratiam) et iustitiam" *De natura et gratia*, fol. 16. Cf. Denz. 789.

the merit *de congruo* as a *causa praedestinationis*, a conclusion which Scotists and Nominalists, albeit in different fashions, had studiously avoided. With this presupposition in mind, Soto could argue in his 1550 *Commentary on Romans* that the merit *de congruo* could no longer be upheld by a Catholic, since in its decree on justification the Council of Trent had confirmed the decision of the Council of Orange (529), that no merits can precede the gift of faith active in love.[127]

For Soto good works preceding justification are not completely excluded but rather to be regarded as *effects* of predestination, and therefore never as *causes* of predestination.[128] Soto's completely different point of departure from e.g., the positions of Gabriel Biel, or of the General of the Conventual Franciscans—cf. his speech on Oct. 7—, or of Andreas de Vega, strikes one with new force, when one reads that the sinner can indeed fulfill the law *quoad substantiam*, but that this legal obedience has no significance whatsoever *coram Deo* and gets all its possible reward in praise of fellow human beings.[129] In this framework no place can be left for the merit *de congruo*, and *promereri* is by necessity identified with *mereri*.

Lastly we turn to a work of Andreas de Vega which he wrote immediately after the termination of the debates on justification at Trent.[130] We have discussed his preconciliar *Opusculum* and noted his participation in the conciliar discussions. This third study *De iustificatione* of 1547 is important for us because it claims to be an objective exposition of the matter as defined by Trent.[131] In the introduction to the Cologne 1572 edition, Petrus Canisius high-

---

[127] ". . . in Concilio Arausicano cap. 25: "Ipse Deus nobis nullis praecedentibus bonis meritis et fidem et amorem sui inspirat. Cui nunc decreto Concilium Tridentinum subscripsit." *In Epistolam divi Pauli ad Romanos Commentarii*, Antwerpiae 1550, fol. 270. Cf. *Denz.* 198.

[128] "Sed est praeterea argumentum efficax quod cum opera illa quatenus praeparatoria sunt ad gratiam effectus sint praedestinationis quia fiunt per auxilium speciale Dei moventis nos in praedestinationis finem, nequent vel esse vel dici causa ipsius." *Ibid.*, fol. 271.

[129] ". . . si faciunt [gentes] mandata quoad substantiam operum reportabunt humana laudem, si vero per Dei auxilium quoad intentionem praecipientis, reportabunt mercedem a Deo . . . possit naturaliter homo legem implere quantum ad substantiam operum quae sint naturaliter bona, non tamen quantum ad intentionem praecipientis, ut sint coram Deo meritoria." *Ibid.*, fol. 85.

[130] *De iustificatione doctrina universa. Libris XV absolute tradita et contra omnes omnium errores iuxtra germanam sententiam Orthodoxae veritatis et sacri concilii Tridentini praeclare defensa*, Coloniae 1572. First ed. Venetiis 1547.

[131] Cf. *Praefatio ad Lectorem.*

lights Vega's authority as an eye-witness, as one who is able to interpret the Council from within.[132]

Vega lays the groundwork for his interpretation by pointing out that according to the majority opinion in the theological faculties, sinners are able to earn their justification *de congruo*.[133] It seems to him impossible to conceive how a Catholic can really doubt that all kinds of dispositions are in their own way causes of justfication, regardless of whether they are prompted by prevenient grace or not.[134]

When he then turns to the crucial *promereri* clause he points out that this is to be understood as excluding only a *debitum iustitiae* and therefore only the merits *de condigno*.[135] As he had said two years before in his *Opusculum*, the fact that we cannot fully earn our justification means that we can not earn it in an absolute sense of the word. This now is asserted in the Tridentine *promereri*.[136] "It is therefore completely clear that there is nothing in the edict of our Council that contradicts the opinion of those who assert the merit *de congruo*."[137]

Though there can therefore be no question as to Vega's interpre-

[132] "Eoque charior in hoc opere Vega esse debet qui Tridenti doctissimos theologos et sapientissimos patres tunc disserentes audivit cum de iustificatione multis est mensibus acerrime disputatum, ipse que cum disputatibus aliis sua sensa studiosissime contulit." *Ibid.*, Praefatio, B 5.

[133] "Porro haec sententia quod peccatores mereri possint ex congruo suam iustificationem communior nunc est in scholis theologorum." *De iustificatione*, VIII. 8. fol. 188.

[134] ". . . non video posse a quoquam catholico verti in dubium quin causae sint suo modo nostrae iustificationis omnes dispositiones per quas venimus in Dei gratiam, sive illae sint ex solis viribus nostris naturalibus, sive etiam ex auxilio Dei speciali." *Ibid.*, VIII. 9. fol. 192.

[135] "Et ita hic Patres asseverant neque fidem neque aliqua opera bona praecedentia iustificationem promereri ipsam iustificationis gratiam. Nullus enim peccator iustificatur ex debito, nullus ex rigore iustitiae, nullus ex condignitate suorum operum, sed omnes qui iustificantur gratis a deo iustificantur et ex gratia et misericordia et absque meritis et condignitate suorum operum. Et nisi ita accepisset sancta Synodus verbum 'promereri' non recte exposuisset verbum 'gratis'." *Ibid.*, VIII. 10. fol. 192.

[136] "Sed quando Patres hoc loco tam diserte tradiderunt neque fidem neque alia opera praecedentia iustificationem promereri iustificationis gratiam, decet profecto filios Ecclesiae sic temperare sua verba ut nunquam sine additione aliqua commoda et idonea dicant vel scribant peccatores bonis suis dispositionibus gratiam promereri . . . Et sicut gratia iustificationis absolute neque dicitur neque potest dici merces nostrarum dispositionum, ita videntur neque illae vocandae esse absolute merita." *Ibid.*, VIII. 15. fol. 203. Cf. VI. 41, fol. 129.

[137] "Manifesta igitur luce constat nihil repugnare opinonem asserentium meritum ex congruo verbis nostri Concilii." *Ibid.*, VIII. 10. fol. 194.

tation of *promereri,* two observations are in order. In the first place, the claim to objective explication of the decree from within cannot be documented from the argument reported above. We are surprised to find no mention of the decision of the Council fathers to regard *promereri* as solely related to merits *de condigno.* The basis of Vega's argument is rather that the majority opinion at his time requires this conclusion and that it is based on Scripture: "And if the Holy Synod would not have thus taken the word 'promereri,' it would not have rightly exegeted the word 'gratis.' "[138]

It is therefore more a theological argument *per analogiam fidei* than an historical analysis. In the second place we should note that Vega does not claim that the *meritum de congruo* is taught by the Council, but rather that such teaching does not run counter to the decree. With the records before us we are in the fortunate position to know that Vega's theological argument is, as we have seen, also historically sound.

We may therefore conclude not only that the Tridentine decree admits of such an interpretation which *allows for* the *meritum de congruo* in the same fashion in which the phrase "in qua constitutus fuerat"[139] admits of a Thomistic and a Scotistic interpretation of the decree on original sin. We may go a step further by concluding also that notwithstanding the Thomistic efforts, suggestions, and protests, it has been the decision of the Tridentine Fathers to safeguard the merit *de congruo* as a merit based on God's goodness and liberality rather than on God's justice.

Therefore we must point out that the fashionable presentation of the Tridentine decree on justification as the *via media* between the extremes of Pelagian Nominalism and Lutheran Augustinianism stands corrected. The Scotist-Nominalistic tradition is not only not touched by the *anathemata* in the *canones,* but had also a far more substantial part in the final formulations of the Council than hitherto has been supposed.

Harvard University,
The Divinity School

[138] *Ibid.,* VIII. 10. fol. 192.
[139] *Denz.* 788.

14

THE CONTEMPORARY SIGNIFICANCE OF DUNS SCOTUS' PHILOSOPHY

by

BÉRAUD DE SAINT-MAURICE

The actuality of Duns Scotus' philosophy is based on no scanty evidence. That psychological approach of existential import, leading to the supreme importance of love which characterizes Duns Scotus' philosophy, suffices to accredit it to present-day thought. This may seem very strange to some readers. How can a philosophy of the Middle Ages, which has been in discredit since the eighteenth century because misinterpreted and degraded by determined opponents, be of any actual importance? "There is perhaps no figure in the history of Western thought, except possibly Ockham, whose views are so consistently misrepresented as those of Duns Scotus," writes George Lindbeck.[1] Furthermore, Duns Scotus belongs to the apex of the Middle Ages; he shows himself strong in scholastic methods, uses scholastic vocabulary, and takes up the immediate concerns of his time. Notwithstanding this, Duns Scotus' philosophy, because it contains answers to certain problems of the present generation, can dispel like a rising sun the mists that shroud so many contemporary philosophies, and also give support to various valid doctrines that they advance.

Scotus' *Weltanschauung* has a broad and daring outlook on the progressive knowledge of truth. He rejects any kind of dogmatism in philosophy, and for that matter in theology also, except accepted doctrine. His turn of mind and the critical eye with which he probes the subjects he treats, his scientific approach to his topics, and his wish to get to the bottom of things, unsatisfied with mere logic but in search of objective truth only, can be epitomized in his own dictum: "In processu generationis humanae, semper crevit notitia veritatis."[2]

[1] George Lindbeck, "A Great Scotist Study," *The Review of Metaphysics* (March, 1954), 423.
[2] *Op. Oxon.*, IV d. 1 q. 3 n. 8; XVI 186.

Scotus' theses on the divisibility of matter *in potentia et in fieri*, the forms of corporeity, the active part of woman in conception, scientific induction, and self motion,[3] to mention but these few, are accepted by contemporary science. As an American philosopher, Charles Sanders Peirce, has written: "The logic and metaphysics of Duns Scotus adapted to modern culture would go far toward supplying the philosophy which is best to harmonize with physical science."[4] Moreover, his teaching that primary matter is *per se* in act and craving for all forms, implies a principle of evolution susceptible of arousing the interest of modern evolutionists. Again, in accord with contemporary thought, Duns Scotus rejects interference by philosophy with physical science. In his judgment the physical sciences have their own laws and standards, with which philosophy must not interfere except when called to do so in order to explain the higher reasons or ultimate causality of certain phenomena or of certain experiments. "Principia omnium aliarum scientiarum possunt concipi, et termini illorum, ante principia metaphysicae."[5]

This attitude proves wise, and in contrast to it we need only recall the severe criticisms made by physical scientists of certain other systems of philosophy. Thus Sir Edmund Whittaker, professor of mathematics at Edinburgh University, writes:

> In criticizing the metaphysician's line of argument, the man of science points out in the first place that most of the speculative philosophical systems of the past—notably Thomism, Kantianism and Hegelianism—when applied to natural philosophy, lead to conclusions that are demonstrably false. As a matter of history, each of these systems did much harm in obstructing the progress of true knowledge. The Thomists rejected every doctrine characteristic of modern science—the earth's rotation, the Newtonian dynamics and the atomic theory—while the Kantians succeeded in vetoing non-Euclidian geometry for nearly half a century and the Hegelians long prevented the acceptance of Ohm's law. Hegel himself gave a proof that the number of planets could not exceed seven in his *Dissertatio*

References to Duns Scotus' works are from the Vivès edition (Paris, 1891-1895), except those from the first book of the *Ordinatio*, which are taken from the Balić edition (Rome, 1950-   ).

[3] Cf. Roy R. Effler, *John Duns Scotus and the Principle "omne quod movetur ab alio movetur"* (St. Bonaventure, N.Y.: Franciscan Institute, 1962).

[4] Charles K. McKeon, "Peirce's Scotistic Realism," *Studies in the Philosophy of Charles Sanders Peirce*, ed. by Philip P. Weiner and Frederic H. Young (Cambridge, Mass.: Harvard University Press, 1952), p. 238.

[5] *Ord.*, I d. 3 p. 1 q. 1-2 n. 77; III 53.

philosophica de orbitis planetarum, which by an uncommon piece of bad luck, was published almost simultaneously with the astronomer Piazzi's discovery of an eighth planet. It is not to be wondered at that even the mild-mannered James Clerk Maxwell once referred in public to 'the den of the metaphysician, abhorred by every man of science.' Professor Born takes much the same attitude: 'Metaphysical systematization,' he says, 'means formulization and petrification.'[6]

We need not comment upon this statement; it is evident that a wrong has been done to philosophy through such incursions into scientific areas, and it is also evident how wise Duns Scotus was to avoid this. As a great Scotist authority, the late Philotheus Boehner, has written: "Scotus is one of the giants on whose shoulders we stand like dwarfs; like the other giants of the past, Scotus helps us not only to see what he saw, but he lets us stand on his shoulders to obtain a still broader and clearer vision."[7]

Significant of a Duns Scotus revival is the new critical edition of Duns Scotus' *Ordinatio,* which, as Fernand Guimet points out, "testifies to a renewed interest in the Subtle Doctor's thought."[8] Professor Gilson praises it and states that with it "a new era has begun for the study of Duns Scotus."[9] Needless to say, this achievement had been well prepared by such pioneers as de Basly, Minges, Bertoni, Seiller, Müller, and Boehner. After 1927, the Commission for the critical edition of Scotus' works was headed by Ephrem Longpré, until Carlo Balić, President of the Pontifical International Marian Academy in Rome, and his collaborators took charge. Besides this great enterprise, Allan B. Wolter, of the School of Philosophy at The Catholic University of America, has edited a volume of Duns Scotus' metaphysics, containing the Latin text and a facing English translation with notes and references. To these may be added noteworthy works on Scotus by such distinguished authors as Gilson, Bettoni, Barth, Oromí, Alluntis, Copleston, Bonansea, Shircel, Grajewski, de Gandillac, Vignaux, Stella, and Merton, and in 1963 Luchesio Giasson's Louvain doctoral dissertation, *Genre,*

---

[6] Quoted by Allan B. Wolter in *Select Problems in the Philosophy of Nature* (St. Bonaventure, N.Y.: Franciscan Institute, 1952), pp. 83-84.

[7] Béraud de Saint-Maurice, *John Duns Scotus, a Teacher for our Times,* translated by Columban Duffy (St. Bonaventure, N.Y.: Franciscan Institute, 1955), pp. vi-vii.

[8] Fernand Guimet, "Actualité de Duns Scot," *Recherches de Philosophie,* Vol. II: *Aspects de la dialectique* (Paris: Desclée de Brouwer, 1956), p. 315.

[9] *Bulletin thomiste,* VII (1947-1953), 115.

espèce et différence spécifique dans la philosophie de Jean Duns Scot.

Yet no matter how indicative of actual value this renewed interest in the Subtle Doctor's works may be, it is not to be interpreted as an antiquarian concern for a specimen of medieval thought. This renewed interest has a much deeper meaning. As a matter of fact, it tells of the appreciation that various philosophers today seem to have of Duns Scotus' ability to help solve contemporary problems.

The Psychological Approach

From the Renaissance to the atomic age, philosophers have focused their interest on man. Noematics has thus become highly accredited in today's philosophical fields. A brief survey of Scotus' psychological approach will show how he answers this present need for knowledge of the concrete existential in man. Duns Scotus weighs to the full the serious positive consequences intuitive intellective knowledge would bring to a Christian philosophy of love. He senses that without it we are doomed to the blind alley that is skepticism: "Cognitio quae dicitur intuitiva potest esse intellectiva, alioquin intellectus non esset certus de aliqua existentia alicujus objecti."[10] Kantianism, which rejects intellective intuition and thereby sweeps away all transcendental truths, because of our spatio-temporal condition, finds a most serious opponent in Duns Scotus.

Scotus also senses that love is of singular objects, not of the universal. Moreover, since there can be no love for that which is unknown, the singular object of love must be and is intelligible, despite the denials of Aristotle and his school. "Impossible est abstrahere universalia a singulari non cognito singulari, aliter enim abstraheret ignorando a quo abstraheret; igitur."[11] Scotus, therefore, reasons as follows: God is the singular *par excellence;* finite beings are finite singulars; hence the singular is intelligible and highly so. Our senses perceive the material singular; but our intellect, which is far superior to the senses, evidently has a broader capacity for knowledge; therefore it can and does know not only the material but also the immaterial singular. "Dicendum ergo, quod singulare est a nobis intelligibile secundum se, quia intelligibilitas

---

[10] *Op. Oxon.*, IV d. 45 q. 2 n. 12; XX 305.
[11] *De Anima*, q. 22 n. 3; III 629.

sequitur entitatem; secundo dico quod singulare est a nobis intelligibile pro statu isto."[12]

The question now arises: How is this done? It is done, says Duns Scotus, on the level of simple apprehension, where we have intuitive intellective and abstractive knowledge,[13] which latter, it must be remembered, is not equivalent to Thomistic abstraction. It never strips the singular object of its individual notes in order to seize the universal quiddity, which alone, according to Thomists, is intelligible. Abstractive knowledge for Scotus—still on the level of simple apprehension—is indifferent to existence or nonexistence, to the presence or absence of the singular object; it merely prescinds from these existential aspects and therefore never despoils the singular of its wealth. It acts something like an X-ray penetrating the flesh to reveal the bone structure alone. Charles Sanders Peirce's mode of abstraction is not unlike that of Scotus, and Peirce defines it as "the act of supposing some one element of a percept upon which the thought dwells *without paying any regard to other elements.*"[14]

Whether it is knowledge of the singular material or of the singular immaterial, intuitive intellective knowledge is a direct, immediate, simple awareness of things, events, or states of mind; it is an apperception or contact, and therefore requires no species, of a real singular as existing and as present *hic et nunc.* "Potest aliqua esse cognitio objecti secundum quod existens et secundum quod praesens in aliqua existentia actuali . . . eo modo quo dicimur intueri rem, sicut est in se."[15]

Because of this basic cognition we are able to form existential judgments such as, "I am awake," "I see Michael," "I am thinking," and so forth. But of course, *pro statu isto,* I cannot know Michael's singularity as such, *sub ratione propria singularis,* because its numerical unity is a uniqueness that shields the singular from all others and even from itself.

I know intuitively, when I directly apprehend the boy Michael seated at this desk in front of me. This means that I apperceive

[12] *Ibid.,* nn. 4-5, III 629-630.
[13] Cf. Sebastian J. Day, *Intuitive Cognition, a Key to the Significance of the Later Scholastics* (St. Bonaventure, N.Y.: Franciscan Institute, 1947).
[14] Thomas A. Goudge, "Peirce's Theory of Abstraction," *Studies in the Philosophy of Charles Sanders Peirce,* ed. by Philip P. Wiener and Frederic H. Young, p. 122.
[15] *Op. Oxon.,* II d. 3 q. 9 n. 6; XII 212.

Michael's *species specialissima,* that is to say, Michael's nature. Therefore, it is not the universal man that I intuitively know, but *this man Michael* in whom quiddity and singular coalesce, so to speak. In a word, I apprehend Michael together with his individual notes as this single human being, objectively here and now actually present.

Giasson remarks: "Parce qu'une nature existante est nécessairement singulière, en la connaissant dans son existence actuelle, nous saisissons quodam modo qu'elle y est singularisée sans proprement connaître ce qui la singularise." He rightly sees a link between sensation and intellectual intuition. Since sensation is already an active intuitive knowledge, if we have an intellectual intuition of the extra mental real, as Giasson says, it is precisely inasmuch as we have an intellectual consciousness of our sensations and through these of the objects to which they attain. The quiddities or natures of which our intelligence knows intuitively the existence are therefore the quiddities or natures of the accidents.[16]

Mentalist idealists deny this objective reality. To them, Michael is a mere product of my intellect, a subjective thought-object. Take away what appears to me and what is left? Absolutely nothing. One might reply, "If I leave the room where I saw Michael, what about him still sitting there for somebody else to see?" Evading the question, idealists proclaim that there is no such thing as material substance: no substratum to things, but only states of consciousness and impressions. The laws of association of ideas explain every phenomenon and also every asserted cause.[17] William James humorously observes: "Mental fire will never burn real logs, nor

---

[16] Luchesio Giasson, "Genre, espèce et différence spécifique dans la philosphie de Jean Duns Scot" (Unpublished Ph. D. dissertation, Institute of Philosophy, Catholic University of Louvain, 1963), pp. 122-123.

Such is also Wolter's opinion, who in a letter to the author (April 26, 1961) wrote: "I have always (up to now) understood it (the singular entity) of the most special species falling under some *accidental* category (e..g quality) for the following reasons: Substance, according to the scholastics, is not something that can be sensed *per se*. Both proper and common sensibles are *accidental* aspects of objects. Furthermore, Scotus expressly says that we do not have any immediate intellectual knowledge of any substance in this life, but we must reason to, or infer the existence of substance. Hence our first intellectual knowledge obviously is not of something substantial. What is more, the example given by Scotus of a most special species is that of an *accident:* 'In the order of confused knowledge, a color is first known under the aspect of "whiteness" before it is known under the aspect of color.'" (*Ord.,* I d. 3 p. 1 q. 1-2).

[17] Cf. André Cresson et Gilles Deleuze, *David Hume* (Paris: Presses Universitaires de France, 1954), pp. 30ff.

mental water extinguish real fire; no mental knife, however sharp it may be, will ever cut real wood; on the contrary, in the case of 'real' objects, consequences always follow."[18] For that matter, Duns Scotus himself might have added: Mental persons can neither love nor be loved.

The only possible concession to be made to mentalist idealists is that kind of experience pertaining to romanticism, according to which, for instance, to a poet in a dejected state of mind a flowing river appears to be a melancholy emblem of the futility and uselessness of life and things, suggestive of the Coheleth's complaint: "I have seen all things that are done under the sun, and behold all is vanity and vexation of spirit."[19] On the contrary, to a carefree picnicker the same river looks bright, buoyant, and the very image of youth. Yet the river objectively remains the same in both cases as it really flows along, unconscious of the different mental effects it produces in different minds.

Among the conclusions drawn by Duns Scotus, there is one which reveals a psychological insight very much in keeping with his philosophy of love. He writes: "Incognita non possumus diligere, sed per prius diligimus singulare quam universale."[20] This is profoundly true; for although I may love truth, justice, fair play, and the like, it is because they are indirectly at least connected with a person or persons. They are embodied in so and so. Furthermore, as we have written elsewhere, "The singular is empowered to become 'presence' as well as objectivation; in balance, therefore, with the 'thou' and the 'he.' On the contrary, the universal expresses nothing else than the *quod quid est,* or that which is common in things. . . . Now to consequences: for if it is true that I pledge myself only in regard to a person, it is equally true that this concept, 'man,' will not pledge me to 'Michael.' It merely furnishes casual registration references, allowing me to classify this object in the category of reasonable animals. Some amount of intellectual curiosity may accompany this act, but hardly any real existential concern for the same."[21]

---

[18] William James, *Essays in Radical Empiricism* (New York: Longmans Green, 1912), pp. 127-128. Cf. Gérard Deledalle, *Historie de la philosophie américaine,* ch. VIII (Paris; Presses Universitaires de France, 1954).
[19] *Ecclesiastes,* 1, 14.
[20] *De Anima,* q. 22 n. 5; III 630.
[21] Béraud de Saint-Maurice, "Existential import in the Philosophy of Duns Scotus," *Franciscan Studies,* IX (September, 1949), p. 296.

Bergson's theory of intuition adds to Scotus' scientific description something of St. Bonaventure's *penetrans acumen* of love, since to it are attached some elements of penetrating sympathy, allowing coincidence with the inexpressible singularity of the known object. Duns Scotus, however, treats intuition as the basic process of knowledge in order that love may not be frustrated in attaining its object, the individual singular concretely existing.

Intuitive knowledge can also be with regard to the past, provided the object or the event has been previously known intuitively. For example, I recall to mind Michael sitting at this desk sometime ago, or one of my past emotions of love, fear, or joy in such and such circumstances. This is to revive the intuitive knowledge of that person, event, or emotions as it was when actual and present. The English past progressive tense in grammar is suggestive of this: if I say, for instance, "I was watching TV at 10 o'clock last evening," I mean much more than just mentioning this fact in the preterit: I watched. I actually recall it as it was happening then.

Duns Scotus also refers to an intuitive knowledge of the future, which, Wolter says, is "a simple awareness of a situation that will occur in the future, i.e., an awareness of this situation, not abstractly as indifferent to existence or nonexistence, or as something merely possible, but together with the notes of (future) existence."[22] Scotus calls it *opinio de futuro,* which Wolter equates to a sort of natural precognition or a premonition.[23]

By the sure criterion of perfect intuitive cognition we may evaluate our dreams and know with evident certitude that we are awake when we really are awake. Our intellect passes an infallible judgment on the phantasy, and we know that our dreams in sleep were produced without the control of our judgment and will. Bergson has the strange notion that to be awake and to will are one and the same thing: "Veiller et vouloir sont une seule et même chose."[24] For him the dream represents the entire mental life minus the effort of concentration: "Le rêve est la vie mentale tout entière, moins l'effort de concentration."[25] We still perceive, we still remember, we keep on reasoning, all these can abound in the dreamer's

[22] Letter to the author, April 26, 1961.
[23] *Ibid.*
[24] Henri Bergson, *Mécanisme du rêve* (Conférence à l'Institut Général Psychologique, 26 mars 1901), quoted in André Cresson, *Bergson* (Paris: Presses Universitaires de France, 1961), p. 155.
[25] *Ibid.*

slumbering mind, for in things of the spirit abundance does not signify effort. The only thing that requires effort is precision in adjustment.[26] This Bergsonian notion of wakefulness and dreaming recalls Duns Scotus' concession to the will's control over the intellect, which depends on the will for its degree of concentration: "Voluntas potest intellectui imperare."[27] Here Bergson seems indeed to give implicit acknowledgment to Duns Scotus' thesis.

This empiristic approach, which brings Duns Scotus' philosophy "sensibly closer to the great trends of modern psychology," as Longpré says,[28] and safeguards both the possibility and the reality of the subject and object of love as well as love itself, is notably different from the Aristotelian approach. According to the latter school, so called simple apprehension is an act by which the intellect through a stripping abstraction perceives a quiddity, i.e., a universal from the material singular, without forming any judgment upon it, as if this meant simple apprehension. But who does not see that this is deceptive? What account can be given for that crucial illicit passage from sense data to the intellective order? In more explicit words, how can the intellect form any concept from the singular it never does and can never apprehend? According to Duns Scotus: "Impossible est abstrahere universalia a singulari, non cognito singulari; aliter enim abstraheret ignorando a quo abstraheret; igitur."[29] Such abstraction can only yield a universal concept, such as that of man, horse, or wood in general, and is therefore not a simple apprehension at all but a mere conceptual act of knowledge on the level of the universal order. From this it is easy to point out which basic act of knowledge is lacking in Aristotelian simple apprehension.

Duns Scotus grants that the universal is proper to intellection but adds that since intellect is superior to sense, it also knows the singular since this is superior to the universal. Concept, judgment, and inference must therefore be guaranteed by real, empiristic, existential awareness of the individual singular object as to its existence and presence *hic et nunc*.

Long before Descartes, Duns Scotus had sensed introspection as the initial shock of our existential experience for the basic evidence

[26] *Ibid.*
[27] *Op. Oxon.*, II d. 7 q. unica n. 23; XII 402.
[28] Ephrem Longpré, "The Psychology of Duns Scotus and its Modernity," *The Franciscan Educational Conference*, XIII (1931), 21.
[29] *De Anima*, q. 22 n. 23; III 629.

without which no real certitude whatsoever is possible for man: "Intellectus potest percipere actum meum intuitive . . . quodam sensu, id est perceptione interiori experimur."[30] Otherwise, he adds, we should never be certain of the existence of anything: "Alioquin intellectus non esset certus de aliqua existentia alicujus objecti."[31] Not only am I conscious of my intellective acts, when, on the level of simple apprehension, I am aware that I am thinking; but by a reflexive and therefore immaterial act of double consciousness I am aware that I am conscious of being aware. I am also immediately and directly aware of the acts of my emotions and of my free will. I not only feel and know these, but I am equally conscious of being aware of my feeling them and of my freely willing or not willing them. This "internal experience" according to Duns Scotus, as Longpré says, "is a witness in favor of the existence of human liberty."[32] "Experitur enim qui vult se posse non velle sive nolle, juxta quod de libertate voluntatis alibi diffusius habetur."[33] We may add that it is a witness of love also, since it is indissolubly one with it.

Duns Scotus' introspection, let us note, is not an emptying of all real objects with a view to obtain knowledge through knowledge in the manner of a conclusion arrived at through reasoning, as the Cartesian "cogito" is, but a first intuition evidence.[34] Precisely because it is such, insurance against idealism of the mentalist type is thereby implicitly given. We are generally inclined to think that Descartes was an innovator when he asserted his "Cogito ergo sum." The fact is that this foremost problem of philosophy goes back to Socrates and after him to St. Augustine's "Si fallor, sum." However, since the Cartesian *cogito* reaches directly nothing but the mind, we cannot be surprised at the mentalist turn to be found in Descartes' works. For instance: . . . "Je dois être persuadé que ma pensée existe, à cause qu'il peut se faire que je pense toucher la terre encore qu'il n'y ait peut-être aucune terre au monde, et qu'il n'est pas possible que moi, c'est-à-dire mon âme ne soit rien pendant qu'elle a cette pensée: nous pouvons conclure de même de toutes les autres choses qui nous viennent en la pensée, à savoir que nous qui les

---

[30] *Op. Oxon.*, IV d. 43 q. 2 n. 10-11; XX 40.
[31] *Op. Oxon.*, IV d. 45 q. 2 n. 12; XX 305.
[32] Longpré "The Psychology of Duns Scotus and its Modernity," p. 27.
[33] *Metaph.*, IX q. 15 n. 5; VII 609.
[34] Séraphin Belmont, "Essai sur la théorie de la connaissance d'après Jean Duns Scot," *La France Franciscaine*, XVII (avril-septembre, 1935), p. 208.

pensons, existons, encore qu'elles soient peut-être fausses ou qu'elles n'aient aucune existence."[35]

On the other hand, the solidity of Duns Scotus' first intuitive evidence is an existential act of self-investment making me conscious of the threefold process of my immaterial, reflexive soul. The "I" apperceives its act toward the "me" in "myself"; the "me" is real intrinsic object and objective reality of the "I," terminating in this reflexive act in which the "I" and the "me" identify. Hence, "I," "me," "myself" are the three introspective terms expressing the acts of a substance—subject, object to itself, the *ego*, by which I am *imago Dei*, as St. Bonaventure would say. This apperception mirrors the sparks of my intelligence and will, making me discover that since I know and will myself, I am love. Since love is of a person to a person, I am. It is impossible to escape this fundamental immaterial substratum of mine from which the "I," "me," "myself" operate, as idealists are prone to do. As Wolter pertinently remarks: "The *ego* of my experience is one numerically. It is always this 'I' which I call myself. Thus from the purely empirical or phenomenological analysis my *ego* or self appears as a principle of constancy and continuity, a numerically identical factor that endures from one experience to another. Objects and acts undergo change or flux, but my self, my *ego* remains."[36]

Duns Scotus does not imply that by introspection man can know the soul's nature or essence. The reason for such impossibility *pro statu isto* is the soul's ineffable uniqueness. Scotus therefore would not subscribe to Husserl's *Wesensschau* theory. In fact, he categorically denies such an apperception for the spatio-temporal: "Non cognoscitur anima a nobis nec natura nostra pro statu isto nisi sub ratione aliqua generali a sensibilibus abstrahibili."[37] Yet, because the soul's faculties are really identical with the soul and distinct from it by formal distinction *a parte rei* only, its acts being known *in actu secundo*, somehow the soul itself is known through its faculties *in actu primo*, since these acts spring from these faculties really identical to the soul. Curiously enough, Avicenna, having approached this problem when anticipating the Cartesian postulate to be, had come to the same conclusion as Duns Scotus was to up-

---

[35] Descartes, *Les Principes de la Philosophie*, 1ère partie, n. 10.
[36] Allan B. Wolter, *Select Problems in the Philosophy of Nature*, p. 130.
[37] *Ord.*, Prol. p. 1 q. unica n. 28; I 17.

hold. It is, he holds, not the essence but the acts of the soul that we attain to, and by way of consequence we become certain of the self as agent of the soul itself.[88]

Scotus' introspection does away with the wrong notion that consciousness is mere becoming, void of substance. It proves that any becoming whatsoever can only be the becoming of something or of someone, and is intelligible in so far only as it stands for the mode of a subject which remains the self same, despite its becoming.

The senses, of course, are subject to deception, and a deranged mind may suffer hallucinations; there is also the possibility of judging erroneously; nevertheless, says Scotus, of one thing I have absolute certitude: I see this stick held half way in water as broken, while to my touch it feels straight. Even when suffering from an hallucination, I am positive that I see or hear something although it is not actually there. When I judge the man in the distance to be a rock, this is not to be imputed to my consciousness of actually seeing, but only to the distance or dark that causes my judgment to err. To illustrate the unshakable evidence of introspection Duns Scotus suggests the sight of a man floating in space with scattered limbs having no relation to the body as a whole, and this to the extent that he could perceive nothing through his bodily members. Notwithstanding such impediments, this man would still hold to a firm certitude of his own existence, prior to the judgment "I exist." "Were this basic evidence lacking to us," says Bettoni, "the whole edifice of human knowledge could rightly be called fiction."[39]

For this reason, when the apriori Thomistic theory, according to which only the abstracted essence of the soul's faculties is known, deduces from this the nature of the acts of those faculties, it not only "puts the cart before the horse,"[40] but also precludes all issues leading to basic evidential certitude and thence proves its inability to refute idealism.

Let us give an example. The skeptic uses words; to posit the name of a thing, such as house, cat, or box, conveys the meaning of the thing signified by the term and obliges one to acknowledge im-

---

[38] Cf. Alexandre Labzine, "Avicenne," *Dictionnaire Biographique des Auteurs*, Vol. I: *A/J* (Paris: Laffont-Bompiani, 1957), p. 90c.

[39] Efrem Bettoni, *Duns Scotus, the Basic Principles of His Philosophy*, translated and edited by Bernardine Bonansea (Washington, D.C.: The Catholic University of America Press, 1961), p. 129.

[40] Sebastian J. Day, *Intuitive Cognition, a Key to the Significance of the Later Scholastics*, p. 130.

plicitly and with certitude the value of the first principle of contradiction. Ingenious as is this criterion, it is nevertheless illicit since it proceeds from mere sense data, leaping on to the level of the conceptual order, and offering therefore no guarantee to the evidence of reality, since it lacks the existential experiential grounding of introspection which alone can give evidence of the real against mentalist ideologies. Consequently, as Vier says, "if you reject introspective evidence, you must logically reject all self-evident propositions."[41] Why is this so? It is because, as we have pointed out in a previous work, "I cannot have certainty unless there is a nexus between the extrinsic world and my intrinsic self. Hence to deny or to ignore the certitude of introspection is to postulate universal doubt."[42] What evidence can the words just mentioned bring to the skeptic, since according to this Aristotelian conceptual theory he cannot directly apprehend his own acts of knowing and willing nor things extrinsic to himself?

Duns Scotus passes a peremptory judgment on one who refuses to acknowledge the evidence of self-apperception: "Et ideo si quis istos [actus cognitionis non sensitivae] neget, dicendum est eum non esse hominem, quia non habet illam visionem interiorem quam alii experiuntur se habere."[43] Whoever denies this evidence experienced by all men is not worthy to be called a man. At best he is a "protervus," as Scotus would say. To rest on solid, basic evidence, which alone can yield certitude and insure the findings of metaphysics, one must go back to Duns Scotus whose merit it is to have been the first scholastic to propound the doctrine of existential introspection.

Eminent contemporary philosophers have praised Duns Scotus for this phenomenological survey, and have said that in it lies the initial movement of modern and contemporary psychology. "In der Seelenauffassung des Duns Skotus liegt, wie schon Siebeck betont hat . . . der erste Beginn zur Psychologie der Renaissance und der ganzen Neuzeit."[44] The value and scope of this initial psychological approach cannot be overestimated; without it the entire order of

---

[41] Peter C. Vier, *Evidence and its Function According to John Duns Scotus* (St. Bonaventure, N. Y.: Franciscan Institute, 1951), p. 132.

[42] Béraud de Saint-Maurice, "Existential Import in the Philosophy of Duns Scotus," *Franciscan Studies*, IX (September, 1949), pp. 297, 299.

[43] *Op. Oxon.*, IV d. 43 q. 2 n. 11; XX 40.

[44] Quoted in Longpré, "The Psychology of Duns Scotus and its Modernity," *The Franciscan Educational Conference*, XIII (1931), 21, n. 15.

things and the whole universe vanish away as a mere figment of the mind. What then becomes of love?

The Making of the Person

Since love is from person to person, Duns Scotus is very intent on giving us the right notions of the person's constituents. The initial philosophical step to real individuation of the concrete being is real identity of essence and existence: "Numquam esse essentiae separatur realiter ab esse existentiae."[45] Minges does not exaggerate in saying that this Scotistic thesis is "maximi momenti," because it is basic concreteness.

There is much discussion nowadays of opposing existentialism to essentialism within neo-scholastic spheres. In the Middle Ages this question does not appear. What does appear is Platonism to some degree together with opposition to it. Duns Scotus takes a decided position against Platonism; for him the existing individual alone is in full measure real: "Individuum est verissime ens et unum."[46] It is indeed the only perfect existing being: "Nonnisi individuum seu singulare ens verum, ens verissimum, maxime ens est."[47]

On the other hand, essence, in so far as it does not identify with the existing individual, is merely an "ens cognitum" having a diminished existence, "in cognitione" only, "ut cognitum," in contrast to real individual being which exists absolutely. "Objectum in cognitione habet esse diminutum, substantia autem ut in se habet esse simpliciter et perfectum."[48]

Duns Scotus could not show more plainly his dissent from Platonism on this important question: "Ipse [Plato] enim posuit ideas quidditates rerum per se quidem existentes, secundum Aristotelem, et male; secundum Augustinum in mente divina, et bene."[49] He is deeply conscious that not only the concreteness of his philosophy but also his whole Trinitarian theology and his Christology are at stake here. By sweeping away Platonic essences, Duns Scotus achieves the first step towards individuation. No essence of man preexists the existence of man, nor is essence really distinct from

---

[45] Cf. *Op. Oxon.*, II d. 1 q. 2 n. 7; XI 63.
[46] *Metaph.*, VII q. 13 n. 17; VII 417.
[47] Parthenius Minges, *Joannis Duns Scoti doctrina philosophica et theologica*, Vol. I (Quaracchi: Ex Typographia Collegii S. Bonaventurae, 1930), p. 15.
[48] *Op. Oxon.*, IV d. 13 q. 1 n. 39; XVII 693.
[49] *Op. Oxon.*, I, d. 35 q. unica n. 12; X 554.

existence *in concreto*. The individual is as truly distinguished by its existence as by its essence, since existence is identified with essence.

As a consequence, the problem that divides existentialists from essentialists is no problem at all for Scotus. He would not agree with the essentialists, who claim that essence enjoys priority over existence; he would not agree with the existentialists, who assert that existence enjoys priority over essence. Not unlike the judge in La Fontaine's "L'Huître et les plaideurs," he hands a shell to each and swallows the oyster whole.

In the wake of this, what are we to think of the existential value assigned to the *jugement d'existence, ad mentem Scoti?* Can we truly say that it concerns the real because to judge is to assert and to assert is to posit an existence? Scotus would answer no, since judgment belongs to the conceptual order only, which lies on the level of an abstraction not previously guaranteed by the basis provided by intellective intuitive knowledge. Consequently, this so-called *jugement d'existence* is not existential but merely conceptual.

There is not the least doubt that the existentialists have understood the value of concrete existence in life. Furthermore, since this philosophical trend came about as a nauseous disgust over speculative reason, due to Hegelian absolute rationalism, it showed stern interest in existence, choosing it in preference to its concept, and expressed by the proverb: A live dog is worth more than a dead lion. Unfortunately, the existentialists, though in terms of phenomenology, have sacrificed some amount of concreteness to the arbitrary, in making a deliberate dichotomy between thinking and existing. They speculate abstractly upon both, using philosophy against philosophy, as Aristotle would say. They forget that total man cannot and does not exist without due respect to the fruits of his mind. Anguish and free choice cannot be prescinded from thinking and reasoning in real concrete life. Joy and ecstatic happiness cannot be overlooked as experiential existing to the sole benefit of nausea and the rest. To think, to reason, to will, to choose, to suffer distress, and to love are ways by which man exists, so that one cannot be arbitrarily considered at the expense of the others.

Unlike Kant's categories, which are mere laws of the mind and therefore considered nonexistential by Scotists as well as by existentialists, Kierkegaard's categories are concrete and individual. One of them, the category *unique*, according to which every individual is precisely himself and no one else and no other, brings us to Duns

Scotus' second and third steps towards the making of the person: the common nature and haecceity. The *natura communis* has often been interpreted as an instance of exaggerated realism by philosophers who accuse Scotus of having sacrificed to Platonism on this point. If we correctly understand Scotus, the reproach is undeserved. In reference to the individual the common nature is that which is singular in each individual of a similar group, each singular thing having its own common nature which is singularized by the individual difference. Scotus explains: "Si loquamur realiter, humanitas quae est in Socrate, non est humanitas quae est in Platone, et est realis differentia ex differentiis individualibus unitive contentis, inseparabilibus hinc inde";[50] "talis existentia est magis singularis quam universalis, quia non est universalis nisi in singulari."[51] The fact that the common human nature found in Socrates is not the common human nature found in Plato proves it to be singularized; at the same time, owing to its less than numerical unity, it can be made an intentional universal concept, because of its similarity; there are as it were many individual *similar* patterns. Therefore, Socrates is this man (common nature singularized, expressed by "this"), and he is also a man (common nature universalized, expressed by "a"), since Socrates being this man is also a man. Were this common nature denied its minor unity, which exists prior to the intellective act, it would be impossible for us to explain why we cannot derive a specific concept from Socrates and a stone as well as from Socrates and Plato. All science thereby would vanish into nothingness. Hence we can rightly credit great actual value to this thesis advanced by Duns Scotus.

As to the indifference of the common nature, it must be attributed to the paradox of the one and the multiple proper to finite beings. According to this, the nature, because it is in Socrates as well as in Plato, proves to be multiple and yet it is one as to its similarity in both. This common nature is *real* since we find it singularized in individuals, and universal when objectivized; thus it is indifferent, because effectible and objectivable. But let us remember that such indifference is arrived at through Scotistic abstractive knowledge, which, as has been said, causes no detraction whatsoever from the abundant wealth of the existing singular, but

[50] *Metaph.*, VII q. 13 n. 21; VII 421.
[51] *Ibid.*, n. 23; VII 424.

merely attains the object without considering it as present and existing.

This doctrine of the *natura communis* and its *unitas minor quam numeralis* reveals a deep and mysterious truth. It tells of the radical contingency of the universe. The common nature is our "faille de néant" that discloses us as finite, not infinite, beings. God alone, Scotus tells us, is his own singular nature: "Natura communis non est per se ipsam haec seu individualis. Solummodo in Deo est Natura seu deitas per se haec."[52]

Can Scotus' doctrine of the common nature be compared to Charles Sanders Peirce's categories of firstness, secondness, and thirdness? It is notable that Peirce was influenced by Duns Scotus to some extent on this matter, and there is no doubt as to his great admiration for the Subtle Doctor, whom he calls "a vast logical genius" and states that he himself is a "Scotistic realist." If correct, Peirce's firstness, secondness, and thirdness would correspond to Scotus' three universals: Firstness, to the physical universal *in re*; Secondness, to the metaphysical universal *in mente;* and Thirdness, to absolute nature considered in its indifference to universality or to singularity. Still we are not sure that Peirce's thirdness can be said to be equivalent to Scotus' indifference of the common nature. It appears to us rather as a form of exaggerated realism. In Peirce's own words, "I am myself a scholastic realist of a somewhat extreme stripe."[53]

The third step towards making the person is haecceity: the principle of individuation which Scotus defines as the *ultima realitas entis*. This principle contracts the common nature to individual numerical unity as *thisness*. The contraction proceeds to this matter, form, composite which make the individual.

> Principium individuationis verum est haecceitas, id est quaedam differentia vel proprietas, quae huic rei non alii rei, nonnisi Socrati non Platoni, competit vel competere potest. Socratitas est principium quare Socrates est individuum. Ulterior ratio non est quaerenda quia haec differentia vel proprietas est ultima realitas entis.[54]

[52] *Op. Oxon.*, II d. 3 q. 1 n. 9; XII 55. As stated by Minges, *op. cit.*, I, p. 69.
[53] Charles K. McKeon, "Peirce's Scotistic Realism," *Studies in the Philosophy of Charles Sanders Peirce*, edited by Philip P. Wiener and Frederic H. Young, p. 238.
[54] P. Minges, *Joannis Duns Scoti doctrina philosophica et theologica*, Vol. I, p. 65.

The common nature is inseparable from haecceity which contracts it; both are modes of one and the same individual. Neither indeterminate matter nor accident, such as quantity or quality, can serve as the principle of individuation, because nothing indeterminate, such as matter, nor an accident, such as quantity or quality, can be the principle of substantial determination. Scotus' haecceity principle, it is clear, is *toto coelo* different from Peirce's principle. The former is substantial, the latter, although nominally Scotistic, is relational and therefore accidental, thereby destroying Scotus' careful avoidance of individuation *per accidens*. Scotus' principle of individuation shows itself to be a dignifying of the singular individual, and especially of man. It testifies that matter, the lowest element of the composite, is not and cannot be the cause of real things, especially of man. It testifies that individuals are not an Averroistic series made like paper dolls out of one and the same stuff, but are each a unique *thisness* standing apart and high in perfection.

The fourth and final step leads from the individual to the person. Metaphysically speaking, the person adds absolutely nothing to the individual man, except the fact of being *sui juris*, the self-possessor of self in one's ultimate solitude. "Ad personitatem requiritur ultima solitudo sive negatio dependentiae actualis et aptitudinalis ad personam alterius naturae."[55] Psychologically speaking, the individual man is called a personality; metaphysically speaking, a person. We may compare the individual as such to a photographic negative and the person as such to the positive picture. The same elements appear in both film and picture, and so also the same elements belong to the individual and to the person. But the negative film is susceptible of a further touch, just as the individual is open to an hypostasis, whereas the positive picture cannot be further altered, and the person is not open to anything more since it is sealed within its ultimate solitude.

The Supreme Importance of Love

Duns Scotus' philosophy is a philosophy of love. Because of this, it answers a craving of the present generation which is so greatly concerned with love in liberty of action. For Duns Scotus, Gemelli writes, "all that is real is love: will-power, action, science, grace, beatific vision and even thought itself, in as much as it is dependent

---

[55] *Op. Oxon.*, III d. 1 q. 1 n. 17; XIV 45.

upon the will";[56] and Longpré points out that "a great and powerful synthesis completely ruled by the idea of love shows up in bold relief in the theological and philosophical work of the Blessed Duns Scotus."[57]

Love might even be said to characterize our atomic age, were it not for the fact that often its true meaning has, partly through Freudian influences, been degraded into mere sex. Since love has in a large measure been overrun by sexual passion, there has been widespread theory and practice blurring its very notion and leaving "no room for Agape which lives not by making claims but by giving."[58] Again, it would seem impossible to have a philosophy of love when rationalism and atheism prevail. When man has repeated Prometheus' theft of the divine fire and determined to become god himself, atheistic philosophy yields a solipsism contrary to the communion of love. At the same time, there has been a great practical reawakening to real love, with its scorn for sham and its yearning for true otherness. Moreover, scientific progress has expanded our horizons beyond our own petty interests. Communications having increased to dimensions and frequency heretofore unimagined, societies have been drawn closer together in every sphere of life. Most striking still is the religious ecumenism that aims at union in the one fold prayed for and prophesied by Christ. Teilhard de Chardin has foretold this planetisation as "the sublime call of that which goes by the name of love."[59]

Duns Scotus' main concern is focused on the nature and the primacy of love. He proves love to be essentially free to say yes or no to anything, thus disengaging it from natural appetite and the passions, and thus also disengaging it from the determination of the intellect. Kierkegaard's theory of choice, which asserts that liberty is the deepest characteristic of human beings, savors of Duns Scotus' own appreciation and doctrine on this matter. Whereas natural appetite is *per se* necessitated by its object, since it is a natural inclination towards one's own good and perfection and hence a capacity to receive, love, on the contrary, is a will free to give. "Voluntas est libera per essentiam; est appetitus cum ratione

---

[56] Agostino Gemelli, *Le message de saint François au monde moderne*, traduit de l'italien par Ph. Mazoyer (Paris: Lethielleux, 1948), p. 58.
[57] Ephrem Longpré, *La Philosophie du Bienheureux Jean Duns Scot* (Paris: Société et librairie S. François d'Assise, 1924), p. 160.
[58] *Time*, January 24th, 1964, p. 59.
[59] Claude Cuénot, *Teilhard de Chardin* (Paris: Ed. du Seuil, 1963), p. 48.

liber, propter amatum." For this reason, since it is better to give than to receive, its *ratio formalis* is far nobler than that of natural appetite; it is free otherness. "Ratio autem formalior voluntatis est magis libertas quam ratio appetitus."[60]

The immense service Duns Scotus' philosophy renders by shedding light on real and false, on perfect and imperfect love, cannot be overestimated. It offers the best solution to such human problems as domestic, racial, and religious. For were love rightly understood, the married couple could choose to undergo the transformation that leads to oblative love; the racial strifes resolve in brotherhood; and the different creeds unite in deeds of charity.

Love, according to Scotus, can be more or less perfect. Imperfect love is primarily self-seeking: "Amor concupiscentiae vel commodi, utilis." It is imperfect because it seeks the beloved in view of some advantage or pleasure: "Qui est propter aliud ut est bonum mihi."[61] Who does not see that imperfect love is impeded in its freedom by these selfish motives? If carried to an extreme it turns up a sterile narcissism.

Real love is unselfish, for it is heterocentric: *Propter amatum ut est in se bonum*. Being free, it is generous, and it is generous because it is perfect; that is to say, the more perfect the person and his love, the more liberal will he prove to be because love is essentially, formally, and effectively communicative. Hence, since God is infinite and absolute perfection, he is also absolute liberality, both intrinsically and extrinsically.

Duns Scotus states his own canon of liberality-love in glowing words: Every agent acts according to his degree of perfection; an absolutely perfect agent overflows with absolutely perfect liberality. On the contrary, one who acts for self-interest does not love with liberality but out of a certain amount of egotism. Man proves himself to be liberal when he does not expect a reward and gives all that he has *propter amatum*.

Liberality is, of course, found in nature—the sun, for instance, is prodigal of its light and warmth to plants, animals, and men. But its liberality is neither conscious nor free; it is blindly necessitated as all of nature is. When St. Francis of Assisi sang his Canticle of the Sun, he directed his praise not to the sun as such, but to God, its maker, through the sun, his creature.

[60] *Op. Oxon.*, II d. 25 q. unica n. 16; XIII 210.
[61] *Ibid.*, d. 21 q. 2 n. 2; XIII 139.

Pragmatic philosophy, it is clear, mars such love by promoting practical interest as a system, thus thwarting the end which love pursues: the good and the happiness of the beloved for the beloved. The very principle of pragmatism, "We should consider the practical effects we think could be produced by an object, and nothing more," is alien to disinterested otherness. A dramatic instance of this is found in Dürrenmatt's *Der Besuch der Alten Dame,* where the people of Güllen casually sacrifice Ill to the aged, cold, and vindictive woman of wealth, Claire Zachanassian, in order to assure the prosperity of their poverty stricken town.[62]

How far Sartre and his disciples are from the concept of love held by Duns Scotus, may be seen by comparing the Sartrian to the Scotist views of liberty and otherness. Sartre exalts a loveless and despairing liberty. In *Les Mouches* Electre is heard to say: "Libre? moi je ne me sens pas libre. Peux-tu faire que tout ceci n'ait pas été?" We are here confronted by Sartre's paradox of a liberty irretrievably fastened to a fatal choice, running to absurdism. Liberty, he says, is "la réalité humaine secrétant son néant,"[63] while love awakens a sense of shame because the other robs me of my own world by getting to know me, since to know is not to exist: *cogito non ergo sum.* Shame is also felt by the other because I also rob him of his own world, and this condition is hell for both: "l'enfer c'est les autres!" Hence the absurd trickery of a "love" that leaves place for nothing except "erotic masochism."[64]

How different a language to express a different thing Scotus uses, as we have seen. The *amor complacentiae* rejoices in the beloved and wills his good fortune, his improvement, his perfection, and his happiness even at one's own expense. The lover wants the beloved to attain to complete autonomy. Scotus also calls this love *amor amicitiae,* because it is ecstatic otherness, and *amor fruitionis,* because utter satisfaction in perfect peace and untold happiness results from union with the beloved.

It is easy to perceive the primacy that love holds over intelligence, since the intellect draws its object to itself and molds it to its own size, so to speak, whereas love goes to its object and, without restraint nor loss, attains it as it is in itself. "Love," says Prentice,

---

[62] Cf. Friedrich Dürrenmatt, *Der Besuch der Alten Dame,* ed. by Paul Kurt Ackermann (Cambridge, Mass.: Boston University, The Riverside Press, 1957).
[63] Roger Verneaux, *Leçons sur l'existentialisme et ses formes principales* (Paris: Pierre Téqui, s.d.), p. 125.
[64] *Ibid.,* pp. 129-137.

"far outruns knowledge." As St. Bonaventure is quoted to have said, "Ubi deficit intellectus, ibi proficit affectus." By raising knowledge to its own level, love works a mysterious symbiosis, so that the real individual person is known in his individuality.[65] Furthermore, the will can and does lord it over the intellect by diverting attention or intensifying concentration, and by bearing responsibility for good or bad. It is the will, it is love, that shows our highest resemblance to God,[66] for love is nothing less than man's relative aseity.

In one of his poems Thomas Merton appraises Duns Scotus' philosophy as being more flame than adjusted form, more life than universal concepts, and because of this, ready to set people aflame.[67] But it is most important never to overlook the strong articulations of that flame: the psychological approach through intuition and consciousness, together with the making of the real concrete individual and the person, leading to the all-importance of love. Only then does Duns Scotus' philosophy appear as it really is, perfectly coherent, and only then also does it prove its actuality for a world in which consciousness and love predominate. Then also, as through a veil, can be discovered the pattern that inspires his whole philosophy: the triune God, who is love, and Christ the alpha and omega of all creation.

This interior vision that guided Scotus in his philosophy explains why he has no difficulty in adjusting it to theological truth, never having to use the trick of a double truth to make ends meet. Thus intellective intuitive knowledge dispenses with accidental additions to man's substantial happiness in the hereafter. Thus also real identity of essence and existence keeps in perfect accord with biblical concreteness. Common nature as a guarantee to metaphysics allows knowledge of the existence of God. Haecceity and person assure Christ's complete integrity as perfect man and as the

---

[65] Robert P. Prentice, *The Psychology of Love according to St. Bonaventure* (St. Bonaventure, N.Y.: Franciscan Institute, 1951), pp. 105-106.

[66] "Ideo voluntas est potentia, principalior in imagine, in cujus figuratione consistit principaliter tota figuratio animae vel imaginis ad Trinitatem." *Op. Oxon.*, IV d. 6 q. 11 n. 4; XVI 651.

[67] "But flame
Fits ill within a form, as life fits ill
Within a universal. While he lived,—
And that was not for long,—he fired men
Until their minds flamed too, and lived."
This text is part of a poem *Resurrection at Quaracchi* published by Thomas Merton in *Commonweal* (1947).

divine Second Person. The supreme importance of love also responds to what Christianism is, namely, charity. The Trinity is essential love; the incarnation is God's plan of love, and the redemption Christ's free-liberality-love in the choice. Love again shall be man's ineffable bliss for all eternity: *visio* being raised to ecstatic *fruitio*.

It is worth noting that Duns Scotus' philosophy, based as it is upon the rock foundation of evident certitude which intellective intuition alone can assure, restores the scientific value of philosophy discredited by idealists and skeptics. To a world where desperate problems wait for the right solution, it opens a way to further research and criticism, ready to build the bridge between metaphysics and science that dogmatism has disrupted. Finally, man's dignity of freedom and love, in contrast to the Sartrian derelict, is exalted in proportion to its true grandeur. The contemporary significance of Duns Scotus' philosophy cannot be denied, for by teaching us to think straight in order to love rightly, it stands as a beacon to enlighten the world and glows as a flame to enkindle it.

Trois-Rivières, Québec, Canada

15

THE NATURE AND VALUE OF A CRITICAL EDITION OF THE COMPLETE WORKS OF JOHN DUNS SCOTUS

by

CHARLES BALIĆ

On September 8, 1950, during the International Scholastic Congress held in Rome in connection with the Holy Year under the presidency of Cardinal Aloisi Masella and with the participation of many civil and ecclesiastical notables—bishops, ambassadors, generals of orders, and rectors of universities, including Prof. Gilson and Father Perantoni, the General of the Friars Minor—there were publicly displayed the first two volumes of an edition of the complete works of John Duns Scotus.[1] Since that time a new volume has appeared every other year, so that seven volumes have now been published. Of these, the first six contain the whole first book of the *Ordinatio* (the so-called *Opus Oxoniense*), and vol. 16 the first part of the *Prima Lectura*, edited now for the first time. Volume 18, containing the last part of the *Prima Lectura*, is in press, and volume 7, the first part of book 2 of the *Ordinatio*, is in preparation. We shall briefly comment here on the nature and value of this edition,[2] which has been greeted as "one of our century's greatest achievements in the field of textual criticism."[3]

I. THE STRICTLY SCIENTIFIC NATURE OF THE EDITION

In the first volume of the series entitled "The Scheme of a Critical Edition of the Complete Works of John Duns Scotus," published in

[1] Cf. *Revue philosophique de Louvain*, 48 (1950), 528-32.

[2] Cf. *Ratio criticae editionis Operum omnium I. Duns Scoti*, I (Rome, 1939), II (Rome, 1941), III (Rome, 1951); *De Ordinatione I. Duns Scoti, disquisitio historico-critica*, in *Ioannis Duns Scoti Opera omnia*, I (Vatican City, 1950), 1*-329*.

[3] Cf. *Revista española de teologia*, 15 (1955), 698: "una de las más imponentes realizaciones de nuestro siglo en el campo de la crítica textual."

1939, the task involved in preparing a critical edition was thus defined: "The function of a critical editor is to find his documents by thorough search, distinguishing accurately between the genuine and the spurious, and to note with care any variant readings and so work out a positive and negative apparatus. He should, moreover, consider all the divergences and variations and the wording, investigating the origin and mutual dependence of the codices and elaborating laws, norms, and patterns according to which he will eventually discover the original text. Finally, he should reduce all his material to a methodical order."[4]

These directions were adhered to faithfully and put into practice by the Scotistic Commission, set up in Rome in 1938 and consisting of twelve internal and twenty-one external members. To the external members fell the task of investigating the catalogues of the various codices, carefully and methodically examining every library, large or small, and procuring the required photographic reproductions of codices. The internal members were to evaluate the rules of textual criticism (verbal, internal, and external), to discover the true reading of Scotus, and to provide right connections, a critical apparatus, and similar things.

To form an accurate judgment of the scientific value of this edition we must bear in mind that it embodies not only the Scotistic Commission's work since 1938 but also the labor of almost a century. Preparation was begun towards the end of the last century, at the outset of the adaptation of the historico-critical method to scholasticism. Thus, for example, Fidelis of Fanna, Ehrle, Duhem, and Grabmann, and later Pelster, Pelzer, and Delorme, aroused doubts about the authenticity of one or another of Scotus' works by drawing attention to the manuscript codices. I personally commenced in 1924 an inspection of all the European libraries, so that already in 1927, in a work entitled "Les commentaires de Jean Duns Scot sur les quatre livres des Sentences," published at Louvain as the first volume of the collection, *Bibliothèque de la Revue d'histoire ecclésiastique*, I described approximately a hundred codices, later commenting on them in greater detail and publishing an exemplar, as it were, for a new edition in "Joannis Duns Scoti Theologiae Marianae Elementa." Then, in 1927, there was set up at Quaracchi the "Sectio Scotistica" which, led by Father Longpré,

[4] *Ratio criticae editionis*, I, 65.

toiled until 1938 investigating and photographing the codices of Scotus, as well as restoring the text of the *Metaphysica*.

The Scotist Commission, heir to all this busy activity, separated the genuine works of Scotus from the spurious, adding to the edited works those yet unedited, and considered once more the criteria used for restoring a genuine text by the editors of St. Thomas and St. Bonaventure, and those of the critical edition of the Vulgate and other works of Christian antiquity. Thus the Commission determined its own method as regards principles for arriving at a true text or drawing up a critical apparatus and indicating the sources and various traditions.

Since Duns Scotus is the Subtle Doctor not merely for theologians and philosophers but also for editors, it was necessary to find and to adjust to this edition an almost unique method of procedure. Thus, for example, a prolonged study of not one but more than three hundred codices and over thirty editions of the *Ordinatio* showed that neither the rule of the "majority" or antiquity of codices, nor the rule of the soundness of a text, nor the famous rule, "The shorter reading the more likely," could be employed to find the true text of Scotus. Since Scotus did not finish his works, particularly the central and basic work, the *Ordinatio*, which was completed by his disciples, each following his own way, it is no wonder that there are great discrepancies in his writings and that questions were asked shortly after his death as to which of the greatly varying codices contained Scotus' own reading. Moreover, since we possess no autograph copy, no apograph or exact copy of an autograph manuscript, it was necessary after much thought, discussion and labor to work out some reliable principle on the basis of which we could decide on the genuine text. We have been successful in our endeavor, because a few years after Scotus' death his *Ordinatio* was widely disseminated and disagreement arose among his disciples and adversaries as to which had been the true reading of the great teacher. Thus a commission was set up, which declared that a certain copy of the *Ordinatio*, already in circulation, was the actual writing of Scotus.[5] This medieval edition, the only one of its kind, is in codex 137 in the municipal library of Assisi (codex A),[6] and in it we find carefully indicated which texts are not in Scotus' own

---

[5] Cf. C. Balić, "Die kritische Textausgabe der Werke des Johannes Duns Scotus," *Archiv für Geschichte der Philosophie*, 43 (1961), 303-317.

[6] Cf. *Disquisitio historico-critica*, 12*-28*; 259*-70*.

book, those for which he left space, meaning to fill them in later, as well as places where a later teacher has written, "Not by Scotus," or places that Scotus had crossed out.[7]

Yet since codex A does not present an original and exact transcript of the correlated exemplar, and because the scribe was frequently led into error by the multitude of corrections, or missed some of them, this codex had to be checked against the whole one hundred codices of the first book of the *Ordinatio,* the reasons for the mistakes discovered, and the original reading investigated.

So a very reliable basis for an edition was found in codex A. A format in minor 4° was then chosen and the text supplied with four apparatuses. One of these contains Scotus' own notes and interpolations, another the variant readings in the codices, the third the explicit allegations of Scotus himself, and the last the implicit allegations with tables of parallel passages and many illustrations. The beautifully finished edition was produced by the Vatican Polyglot Press, and was greeted by universal applause and unreserved approval. In the words of eminent textual critics, the Vatican edition of Scotus' works "représent à peu près le maximum de la perfection réalisable en ce domaine" (Masai), permitting "de suivre les démarches de la pensée authentique de Duns Scot" (Pelzer), since we have in it "le vrai Duns Scot" (Dumont). Among other critics who judged favorably of the scientific nature of the edition, it is worth mentioning Gilson,[8] Geyer,[9] Pelster,[10] and Van Steenberghen.[11] The critics thanked the editors for "das Meisterwerk textkritischer Arbeit" (Müller), and suggested that "La Commissione preposta all'edizione delle opere di Duns Scoto . . . dovrebbe essere presa ormai a modello di ogni futura edizione critica" (Nardi).[12]

---

[7] *Ibidem;* Balić, "Die kritische Textausgabe," 306-310.

[8] "Scientifiquement parlant, la nouvelle édition est aussi proche de la perfection qu'une oeuvre humaine peut l'être," *Bulletin Thomiste,* 8 (1947-1953), 115.

[9] "Die Edition selbst ist mit einer technisch fast unüberbietbaren Akribie gemacht," *Franziskanische Studien,* 33 (1951), 301.

[10] "Sie [Editionstechnik] kann mutatis mutandis . . . als Vorbild dienen füı andere mittelalterliche Textausgaben," *Archivum franciscanum historicum,* 44 (1951), 5.

[11] ". . . on se trouve en présence d'une oeuvre qui impose le respect par les plus hautes qualités scientifiques," *Revue philosophique de Louvain,* 50 (1952), 611-12.

[12] Cf. B. Hechich, "La edición crítica de las obras de Duns Escoto en el juicio de los doctos," *El Ensayo,* 37 (1953), 88-92, where references to the critics above mentioned are contained.

II. IMPORTANCE, NECESSITY, AND UTILITY OF THE CRITICAL EDITION

If we bear in mind that the later editions of Scotus' main work, the *Ordinatio* or *Opus Oxoniense*, differ among themselves to such an extent that in one edition there are whole passages missing from another, that in one edition one-hundred pages are called "an addition," while another mentions no such "addition," and that Cavellus, in the edition appropriated by Wadding, admits he has omitted unintelligible additions which contain unsound teaching[13] or make no sense, we see immediately the importance, necessity, and utility of the edition now being prepared by the Scotistic Commission.

Certainly, to expect the Vatican edition of Scotus to transform Scotism into Thomism is just as vain as to pretend that the Leonine edition of St. Thomas transformed Thomism into Scotism. Once this is admitted, it is still true, as Gilson has pointed out, that "l'image future de Duns Scot, sera, de toute manière, infiniment plus sûre, car il ne faut pas oublier que, nous apportant pour la première fois un texte critiquement controlé, tout ce que l'édition nouvelle conserve de l'ancienne est, en fait, nouveau. . ."[14] Indeed, all the old elements in the *Ordinatio* which criticism upholds as genuine may be thought of as something new, for in addition to many other reasons, now for the first time the text is critically confirmed. To study fruitfully and in a fitting manner the works of so great a teacher, one must be morally certain that he possesses an authentic text. However, in the course of centuries, and particularly in the last decades, so many doubts and suspicions about Scotus' text have accumulated that most scholars have given up all hopes of discovering what he himself wrote. This situation has in turn led to the perpetuation of old errors and false opinions about the Subtle Doctor. Even Scotus' faithful disciples, using Vivès' printing of the only complete edition, viz., Wadding's of 1639, encountered so many "additions" that they were forced several times to admit frankly, "Note that this passage is found in an addition. Perhaps it is not genuine."[15]

---

[13] "Delevimus . . . additiones multas, quarum nonnullae videbantur inintelligibiles, aliae malam doctrinam continebant." Cf. *I. Duns Scoti Opera omnia*, Vivès edition, VIII, 4; Balić, "Die kritische Textausgabe," p. 313.

[14] E. Gilson, "Duns Scot à la lumière des recherches historico-critiques," in *Scholastica ratione historico-critica instauranda* (Rome, 1951), p. 516.

[15] P. Minges, *Ioannis Duns Scoti doctrina philosophica et theologica*, I (Quaracchi, 1930), 564, n. 6.

In our edition, the texts which in Wadding are called "additions" and are printed in italics, are divided into *three classes,* so that the authentic additions by Scotus, his erasures, and the passages interpolated by his disciples are shown separately, each under its own heading. Furthermore, many "added texts" in Wadding's edition are not in fact additions, while many others, printed without any note, should be placed among the texts added by either Scotus or his disciples. In the apparatus of sources are indicated authors to whom Scotus paid constant attention, such contemporaries as Henry of Ghent, Godfrey of Fontaines, and Giles of Rome, but there is hardly mention of Thomas Aquinas. This shows how wrong are those who until now have continued to regard Aquinas as Scotus' rival, as though the Subtle Doctor had wished to overthrow every single opinion advanced by St. Thomas.

Again, since Scotus does not follow the classical form of setting down the question, it is often difficult, because of the many opposing viewpoints, to know whether Scotus or his opponent is speaking. This difficulty is increased by the fact that Scotus often refers back to what he had already said in relation to the question at issue. Hence in the critical edition the reader is led, as it were, by the hand (in apparatus T.) to find the places to which Scotus refers, parallel passages, and other useful references.

Nor should we fail to mention that in the ample apparatus of variant readings one can perceive that the love Scotus' disciples felt for their master led them to change the text by omissions, additions, and alterations in the belief that had Scotus given his work the final touches he would himself have made those corrections.

Lastly, since great interest is shown today in the development of an author's teaching, it is worth noting that whereas the text of the *Ordinatio* or *Opus Oxoniense* was always thought to be the beginning of Scotistic teaching, it is now proved in the Vatican edition that it represents the terminus and fruit of the various lectures Scotus held at Cambridge, Oxford, and Paris. Many of these "lecture notes," hitherto unknown or thought spurious, allow us to plot the formative progress and working out of Scotus' teaching, and to determine by direct dialogue with him what was really his position.

We shall now cite a few examples to show that by publishing for the first time many texts written by Scotus "outside the works," the critical edition can lead to a more accurate understanding of

Scotus' thought and correct certain views on his fundamental philosophical and theological position.

III. SOME ILLUSTRATIONS OF THE VALUE OF THE CRITICAL EDITION

As regards the natural cognition of the primary object of the intellect, it appears from a collation of the edited and inedited texts that there are two series of texts: those showing that we cannot know the adequate object of our intellect without revelation, and those in which Scotus tries to prove by natural reason alone that the natural object of our intellect is not the quiddity of sensible being. To discover Scotus' exact position here, we can use a note which is now published for the first time. In it, after refuting the opinions of Aristotle and St. Thomas concerning the primary object of the intellect, Scotus shows in concise terms where he agrees and where he disagrees with the Greek thinker and the great Aquinas.[16]

Scotus first notes where he agrees with Aristotle, then where he disagrees, and how it is impossible for a theologian to hold the nature of the material world as the primary object of our intellect. This is because the intellect, existing naturally as the same power, knows *per se* the nature of immaterial substance, as is obvious from our belief about the soul in glory. However, a power cannot remain the same and be reduced to act in regard to something that is not contained in its primary object. He asserts this reasoning to hold also "against Thomas," and then he asks, "Is it natural reason that shows this?"[17] He replies that if so, Aristotle is contradicted far more gravely; if not, then it corresponds to the threefold argument already used against the proposition that "our intellect can understand nothing that cannot be abstracted from the phantasm, and this not merely on account of some state or other but from the very nature of its power."[18]

If we consider, on the one hand, that this note is found in none of the thirty-three extant editions of the *Ordinatio* nor in ninety codices, and was published for the first time by the Scotist Commis-

---

[16] *Ordinatio*, I, dist. 3, pars 1, q. 3; Vat. ed., Vol. III, nn. 123-124, pp. 76-77.
[17] *Ibid.*, n. 124, p. 76.
[18] *Ibid.*, nn. 116-118, pp. 72-73.

sion in 1939 and critically edited in 1950;[19] if we consider, on the other hand, that in the note, which represents Scotistic teaching at its most developed stage, Scotus gives no answer, either yes or no, to the point at issue in Aristotle, then it becomes obvious that we should not attach great importance to those texts which conclude that being as such can or cannot be the adequate object of the intellect. Nor should we fail to mention that careful consideration of this additional text, hitherto unknown, seems to narrow somewhat the divergence between St. Thomas, as philosopher, and Scotus.

What of the univocity of being? In every previous edition the definition of univocity which occurs in Bk. 1, dist. 3, is prefaced by the words, "not asserting so, since this does not conform to accepted opinion."[20] In the Vatican edition these words are listed among the spurious passages! If we wish to review the various stages through which Scotus progressed to his final conclusion, we must admit that it would be impossible to pass any judgment on such a matter without a critical edition. It is sufficient to recall that in the *Metaphysica*, Bk. IV,[21] according to Wadding's edition and many codices, there seems to be a denial of univocity, while in the *Lectura Oxoniensis* we read: "The concept of being shared by God and created being is a real concept." Also, from an additional passage in Scotus' hand, for which we look in vain in previous editions and many codices, it seems that Scotus intended to deal once more with questions as the univocity of being and the primary object of the intellect. In fact, after saying that he wishes to inquire whether "any real concept can be univocally common to everything that is *per se* intelligible,"[22] he explains away the arguments of the negative opinion, then he adds: "After solving this question, we find either no primary object of the intellect, or the primary object must be taken in two different ways, since a single primacy, namely

---

[19] Cf. C. Balić, "Circa positiones fundamentales I. Duns Scoti," *Antonianum*, 28 (1953), 268-78.

[20] *Ordinatio*, I, dist. 3, pars 1, q. 1-2; Vat. ed., Vol. III, n. 26, p. 18.

[21] Duns Scotus, *Metaph.* IV, q. 1, n. 12, Vivès edition, VII, 153a. Cf. E. Gilson, "Avicenne et le point de départ de Duns Scot," *Archives d'histoire doctrinale et littéraire du Moyen Âge*, 2 (1927), 106; A. B. Wolter, *The Transcendentals and Their Function in the Metaphysics of Duns Scotus* (Washington, D.C., 1946), pp. 46-48; T. Barth, "De argumentis et univocationis entis natura apud Ioannem Duns Scotum," *Collectanea franciscana*, 14 (1944), 24, and n. 21.

[22] *Ordinatio*, I, dist. 3, pars 1, q. 1-2; Vat. ed., Vol. III, n. 24, pp. 15-17. See also Balić, "Circa positiones fundamentales," pp. 278-85.

of virtuality to all things, or of community, can be found nowhere. Therefore, in being there coincides a double primacy."[23]

To put the case briefly, even though after our critical edition it will still be true that Scotus taught the univocity of being, nevertheless the critical edition is seen to be an indispensable instrument for treating of the precise meaning of each element of Scotus' doctrine of univocity and his arguments for it, as well as for discussing the basis of that doctrine with a view to presenting Scotus' genuine teaching from the first beginning of his scientific activity up to his death.[24]

For a proper appreciation of the critical edition, it is useful to call to mind one or another of the questions about which Scotus' disciples and opponents say he spoke differently at Oxford and at Paris. Thus, for example, William of Alnwick states that regarding the relationship of intellect and will in the act of volition Scotus taught at Paris that the will is the sole effective cause of volition, while the object known is merely a necessary condition for it.[25] At Oxford, however, Scotus would have changed his mind, teaching that the object known is a partial effective cause of the act of volition: "being, with the will, the effective cause of volition." In 1931 I published for the first time a pertinent question reflecting Scotus' teaching at Oxford. It thus became obvious that at Oxford the Subtle Doctor came nearer to traditional intellectualism than when lecturing at Paris, so that William of Alnwick could well say that Scotus spoke differently at Paris and at Oxford.[26]

Concerning the constitution of the divine persons, we have the testimony of a most determined Scotus opponent, Thomas of Sutton, that the Subtle Doctor proposed as probable the opinion *de absolutis*, "of which he was forced to make a public retractation when he taught it at Oxford."[27] A disciple of Scotus, William of Nottingham, testified explicity that his master taught at Paris the doctrine of the constituent relationships among the divine persons after abandoning his earlier opinion, which, according to William, he never stated publicly. At present, then, bearing in mind the

---

[23] *Ordinatio*, I, dist. 3, pars I, q. 1-2; Vat. ed., Vol. III, n. 24, p. 16.
[24] Balić, "Circa positiones fundamentales," p. 285.
[25] Cf. C. Balić, *Les commentaires de Jean Duns Scot sur les quatre livres des Sentences*, Bibliothèque de la Revue d'histoire ecclésiastique, fasc. 1 (Louvain, 1927), pp. 264-301.
[26] C. Balić, "Une question inédite de J. Duns Scot sur la volonté," *Recherches de théologie ancienne et médiévale*, 3 (1931), 202-204.
[27] Balić, *Les commentaires*, p. 69.

four literary forms in which the *Ordinatio* gives Scotus' doctrine of the constitution of the divine persons, as well as various inedited *Reportationes*, we arrive at the following conclusion.

It is certain from the *Lectura Oxoniensis*, of which the first part appears in vol. 16 of the Vatican edition and the second is in press, that as a young man Scotus taught that the opinion according to which the divine persons are constituted by absolute properties is compatible with faith, the Church's doctrine, and sound reason. So he declared it more probable than the commonly accepted opinion. Yet later he inclined more and more towards the commonly accepted opinion, so that when he commented on Bk. 3 of the *Sentences* he thought that the opinion *de relativis*, earlier considered the less likely because of the greater difficulty to find supporting arguments for it, was more probable, though the other was not absolutely groundless or against faith.[28]

More specifically, Duns Scotus never denied that the divine persons are constituted by something relative, but he tried from the start to find whether it was enough to say that the persons are constituted and distinguished only by relationships (i.e., the Father by fatherhood, the Son by sonhood, and the Holy Spirit by passive expiration), and whether the relative principle is the prime constituent properly and strictly so-called.

We could go on and offer many other examples of the practical value of Scotus' critical edition, but this would be beyond the limits of this paper. If a new image of Scotus emerges from the critical edition of his genuine works such as the *Ordinatio*, what shall we say of those works—they are fully half of Wadding's edition—which will no longer be counted among Scotus' writings, because they are proved to be spurious? It suffices to recall the *De rerum principio*, wrongly attributed to Scotus, where on account of the sentence, "I am returning to the position of Avicebron" (qq. 7-8), many authors have concluded that Scotus really wished to return to Avicebron and embrace all his errors. For, as St. Thomas had seen, Avicebron has the seeds of monism, pantheism, a false idea of the material universe, of the hylomorphic composition of simple substances, etc. Hence Gilson could rightly say:

> "On ne dira jamais assez quel ravage a causé la fausse attribution du 'De rerum principio' à Duns Scotus . . . Ravages his-

[28] Cf. "Adnotationes ad distinctiones vigesiman sextam et trigesimam nonam," in *Ioannis Duns Scoti Opera omnia*, VI (Vatican City, 1963), 1*-26*.

toriques, lorsque Bernard Landry imagina une évolution doctrinale de Duns Scot à partir de ce traité . . . Ravages doctrinaux, car c'est sur la foi de ce traité que non seulement des historiens, comme Plusanski ou C. S. Harris, mais même des théologiens scotistes, comme le P. Déodat M. de Basly ou le P. Parthenius Minges, introduisent dans la pensée de Duns Scot des doctrines sur l'intuition de l'âme par elle-même ou sur l'hylemorphisme des substances spirituelles qui lui sont complètement étrangères."[29]

In his letter to Pope Alexander VIII at the beginning of his *Promptuarium Scoticum*, Charles de Varesio deplores the fact that "one author blames Scotus for being wrapped in darkness, another for being tied up by truth; one for disorganized writing and another for the excessive boldness of his investigations. He is called rash by one, defamed by another as inarticulate, and judged lacking."[30] Nor is it only his opponents who act thus. Scotus' disciples deplore his literary shortcomings, obscurity, and prolixity. The critical edition now explains for us the origin of Scotus' defects and obscurity.

St. Jerome, as is well known, laid down the principle that obscurity can have three causes: the vastness of the subject, the inability of the teacher, or the obtuseness of the listener.[31] Without doubt Scotus, known to his contemporaries as *subtilissimus*, devoted his attention to lofty and most important questions, so that it was rightly said that his teaching "was above the common grasp."[32] However it is also true that many people do not understand him, as Cavellus had already pointed out, because they have no adequate training and do not know the principles and terminology of his philosophy.[33] Can Scotus be called obscure because he lacks literary polish? Many have said so; but the critical edition shows that this is not the case. Rather it proves that Scotus' disciples, with the best of will naturally, completed the unfinished work of their master with so many additions, omissions, and alterations that they made of him a deformed little Scotus. Thus they are responsible for the obscurity and confusion of the *Ordinatio*.

This most subtle of teachers can never be easy to understand.

---

[29] Gilson, "Duns Scot à la lumière des recherches historico-critiques," pp. 506-507.
[30] C. de Varesio, *Promptuarium Scoticum*, I (Venice, 1960), "Beatissime Pater."
[31] S. Hieronymi, *Commentariorum in Ezechielem prophetam libri quatuordecim*, lib. XIII, "Proemium" (PL 25, 406).
[32] G. Vorrilong, *IV Sent.*, "Epilogus" (Venice, 1502), fol. 302.
[33] H. Cavellus, *Apologia pro Ioanne Duns Scoto*, chap. 3 (Antwerp, 1620).

But when his work is exactly restored to its original state, provided with adequate punctuation, the sources tabled, with a history of the variant readings and examples in an apparatus, then we see why Scotus is sometimes lacking, confused, or disordered. We also see why it is hardly fair to speak of the chaos of the Subtle Doctor, like the commentator who exclaimed, "You will travel very slowly over this chaos of Scotus!"

Commissio Scotistica

Rome

NOTES ON CONTRIBUTORS

Felix Alluntis, O.F.M., is Professor in the School of Philosophy, The Catholic University of America. He has translated and edited Scotus' *De primo principio* for the BAC (1960), has completed a Spanish translation of Scotus' *Quaestiones quodlibetales*, and published extensively in Spanish and English philosophical journals.

Charles Balić, O.F.M., is Professor at the Athenaeum Pontificium Antonianum and the Pontifical University of the Lateran in Rome, President of the Commissio Scotistica for the critical edition of Duns Scotus' works, and author of many authoritative Scotistic studies. He is also President of the Pontifical International Marian Academy and Consultant of the Holy Office.

Timotheus A. Barth, O.F.M., has served as Professor of Metaphysics and Medieval Philosophy in the following Franciscan colleges: Fulda (1938-1947), Sigmaringen (1947-1965), Hellin, Spain (1955-1956), and Antonianum, Rome (1959), and as a member of the Commissio Scotistica (1939-1942). He is associate editor of *Zeitschriften von Wissenschaft und Weisheit* and *Franziskanischen Studien* and is on the staff of *Philosophischen Jarhbuchs der Görres-Gesellschaft*.

Béraud de Saint-Maurice, a Canadian scholar, resident in Trois-Rivières, Québec, is the author of *Jean Duns Scot: un docteur des temps nouveaux* (Paris, Rennes: 1953), which has had an excellent critical reception.

Efrem Bettoni, O.F.M., is Professor of Philosophy at the Sacred Heart University, Milan and the author of many Franciscan studies, including *Vent'anni di studi scotisti, 1920-1940* (Milan: 1943), *Duns Scoto* (Brescia: 1946), *Il problema della conoscibilità di Dio nella scuola francescana* (Padua: 1950), and *Le dottrine filosofiche di Pier di Giovanni Olivi* (Milan: 1959).

Bernardine M. Bonansea, O.F.M., is Professor in the School of Philosophy, The Catholic University of America, and the author of many articles on medieval and renaissance thought. He is the translator and editor of the Bettoni work on Scotus under the title *Duns Scotus: the Basic Principles of His Philosophy* (Washington: 1961) and has completed a comprehensive study of Campanella's philosophy.

Ignatius C. Brady, O.F.M., is President of the Theological Commission at the Collegio di San Bonaventura, Quaracchi. Formerly Associate Professor of Philosophy at The Catholic University of America, he is the author of *History of Ancient Philosophy* (Milwaukee: 1959) and many articles on medieval thought and is Consultant for Medieval Philosophy for the new edition of the *Catholic Encyclopedia*.

Notes on Contributors

Geoffrey Bridges, O.F.M., is Professor of Philosophy at San Luis Rey College, California, and the author of *Identity and Distinction in Petrus Thomae* (St. Bonaventure, N.Y.: 1959).

J. R. Cresswell, Professor of Philosophy at West Virginia University, received his doctorate at Cornell University. He has specialized on medieval and Arabic philosophy, has been President of the Southern Society for Philosophy and Religion, and has served as a Lieutenant Colonel in Military Intelligence and as a Foreign Reserve Officer.

Roy Effler, O.F.M., is Professor of Philosophy at Duns Scotus College, Southfield, Michigan, and is the author of *John Duns Scotus and the Principle "Omne Quod Movetur Ab Alio Movetur"* (St. Bonaventure, N.Y.: 1962).

Walter Hoeres is Professor at the University of Salzburg and also at the Pädagogischen Hochschule, Freiburg. He has published two books—*Sein und Reflexion* (Würzburg: 1956) and *Der Wille als reine Vollkommenheit nach Duns Scotus* (München: 1962)—and articles on Olivi, Scotus, the Thomistic school, Suarez, and Husserl.

Heiko Augustinus Oberman is Winn Professor of Ecclesiastical History at the Divinity School, Harvard University. He is the author of *Archbishop Thomas Bradwardine* (Utrecht: 1957) and *The Harvest of Medieval Theology. Gabriel Biel and Late Medieval Nominalism* (Cambridge, Mass.: 1963), and has been a Protestant observer at the Second Vatican Council.

John K. Ryan is Elizabeth Breckinridge Caldwell Professor of Philosophy and Dean of the School of Philosophy, The Catholic University of America. He is the author of *The Reputation of St. Thomas Aquinas among English Protestant Thinkers of the Seventeenth Century* (Washington: 1948), translator and editor of St. Augustine's *Confessions* (Garden City: 1960) and St. Francis de Sales' *On the Love of God* (Garden City: 1963), and has contributed to *The New Scholasticism*, *The Modern Schoolman*, and other journals. He is editor of the philosophical works in "The College Readings Series" (Westminster, Md., 1958–) and Catholic Advisory Editor of *The Encyclopedia Americana*.

S. Y. Watson, S.J., has graduate degrees from St. Louis University (S.T.L.) and the Gregorian University (Ph.L.) and is a member of the faculty of Assumption Hall, the Jesuit House of Studies, Spring Hill College, Mobile Alabama. He is the author of "Univocity and Analogy in the Philosophy of Duns Scotus."

Allan B. Wolter, O.F.M., is Professor in the School of Philosophy, The Catholic University of America, and has been Visiting Professor of Medieval Philosophy at Princeton University. Among his publications are *The Transcendentals and Their Function in the Metaphysics of Duns Scotus* (Washington: 1946), *Duns Scotus: Philosophical Writings* (Edinburgh: 1962), "Duns Scotus on the Nature of Man's Knowledge of God," "The Theologism of Duns Scotus," and "The Realism of Scotus."

INDEX

Albert the Great, St., 30, 118, 120, 175, 192, 296, 306
Alexander VIII, Pope, 378
Alexander of Aphrodisias, 254
Alexander of Hales, 1, 15, 192, 296, 306, 308
Alluntis, F., 347
Almain, J., 314, 329
Anselm, St., 93, 165-68, 191, 226, 259
Anthony Andrea, 21, 23, 296
Aristotle, 29, 34, 35, 50, 91, 95, 104, 115, 117, 124, 129, 133, 147, 162, 168, 174, 188, 192, 197, 198, 204, 205, 207, 219, 232, 250, 254, 298, 299, 359, 375
Asclepius, 254, 255
Astensanus, 296
Auer, J., 320
Augustine, St., 29, 34, 90, 92, 114, 231, 303, 332
Averroes, 171
Avicebron, 397
Avicenna, 194, 230, 233

Bacon, R., 15, 192, 296, 308
Bakhuizen van den Brink, J.N., 331, 332
Balić, C., 105, 347
Bartholomew of Pisa, 18, 21
Barth, K., 326
Barth, T., 277, 347
Basly, D. de, 347
Bergson, H., 352
Bernard of Auvergne, 32
Bernard of Clairvaux, 334
Bertoni, A., 347
Bettoni, E., 169, 347, 356
Biel, G., 314, 323, 329, 331, 336, 339, 342
Bituntinus, 339
Boehner, P., 347
Boethius, 51, 235, 254
Bonansea, B. M., 347
Bonaventure, St., 2, 15, 30, 34, 36, 51, 94, 118, 120, 192-96, 209, 294-96, 300, 307, 323, 334, 352, 366, 370
Boneti, N., 296, 306
Boniface VII, Pope, 12
Bowmaker, R., 5
Bradwardine, T., 321, 334, 335
Bremer, J., 309
Brockie, M., 6

Cajetan, Cardinal, 48, 51, 264, 266, 281
Callebaut, A., 7
Calvus, J., 337
Canisius, St. Peter, 342
Caracciolo, L., 296
Castellimaris, 339
Cavellus, 376
Cervini, 340
Chauvigny, Guy de, 293
Christ, Jesus, 333, 366
Clapwel, R., 32
Clement III, Pope, 4
Coheleth, 351
Copleston, F., 347
Coreth, E., 257
Cyprian, St., 332

Daniel Agricola, 294
Della Rovere, Francis, 294
Delorme, F. M., 369
Descartes, R., 83, 353
Descoqs, P., 173, 192
Doering, M., 309
Duhem, P., 369
Duns, Elias, 6, 7
Duns, Ninian, 7
Duns Scotus, John, analogy in, 210-262; Aristotelianism in, 29-44; Augustinianism in, 37-44; birth, parentage, and career, 1-14; contemporary thinkers and, 345-67; critical edition of works of, 368-379; extrinsicism, 75-82; formal distinction of, 45-60; God, natural knowledge of, 45-60; nature of, 157-170; proofs for, 133-170; immortality of soul, 191-209; individual, doctrine of, 122-132; intellect, theory of, 83-121; nature, common, 122-132; nominalism, 311, 344; originality of, 29-44; realism, 61-82; Suarez and, 263-290; univocity, 263-290; will, theory of, 83-121
du Plessis d'Argentré, C., 311
Durandus de St. Pourçain, 323
Dürrenmatt, F., 365

Ehrle, Cardinal, 8, 369

Ferkić, M., 19, 20
Fidelis of Fanna, 369

382

Index

Findling, J., 295
Forleo, G., 302
Francis of Assisi, St., 364
Francis of Rimini, 294
Fuleti, G., 296

Gandillac, M. de, 347
Geiler, J., 336
Gemelli, A., 363
Gerson, J., 335
Geyer, B., 371
Giasson, L., 347
Giffoni, Leonard Rossi de, 308
Giles of Legnaco, 12
Giles of Lessines, 32
Giles of Rome, 32, 193, 296, 373
Gilson, E., 122, 149, 150, 347, 368, 371, 372, 377
God, 134-39, 184-87
Godfrey of Fontaines, 13, 24, 100, 177, 296, 307, 373
Godfrey of Poitiers, 296
Gonsalvus of Spain, 11, 13, 21, 31
Grabmann, M., 369
Grajewski, M., 347
Gregory of Rimini, 321, 329
Guimet, F., 347

Hannibal of the Annibaldi, 32
Harnack, A. von, 320, 321
Hellin, J., 266, 276
Henry of Ghent, 32, 38, 85, 90, 109, 174, 179, 193, 257, 296, 307, 373
Henry of Werl, 309
Hervaeus Natalis (of Nedellec), 24, 32
Hickey, A., 113
Holcot, R., 323, 335
Hugo de Novocastro, 296, 306
Hus, J., 333
Husserl, E., 355

Innocent III, Pope, 4
Isidore of Seville, 3, 333

James, W., 351
James of Brescia, 294
James of Carceto, 11
Joan of Arc, St., 292
John Damascene, St., 103
John of Baconthorpe, 23
John of Reading, 23
John of Ripa, 296
John of Rochelle, 196
John of Rodington, 296, 306

Kant, I., 130, 359
Kierkegaard, S., 359, 363
Küng, H., 326

La Fontaine, 359
Langendorf, Adam Petri de, 294
Leger, P., 293
le Maalot, G., 299
Leo X, Pope, 324
Lindbeck, G., 345
Longpré, E., 2, 4, 302, 347, 354, 369
Luke of Assisi, 296
Lychetus, 104

Maior, 329
Manser, G., 289, 290
Maritain, J., 206
Marston, R., 35
Mary, Virgin, 324, 333
Masai, 371
Matthew of Acquasparta, 31, 35
Maubert, J., 293
Mayron (de Meyroones), F., 23, 297, 306
Merton, T., 347, 366
Minges, P., 347
Minoriensis, 339
Müller, 347, 371

Nardis, 371
Netter, T., 329
Nicholas of Lyra, 296
Nicholas V, Pope, 293

Ockham, William of, 46, 52, 194, 308, 315, 316, 323, 345
Olivi, J., 32, 196
Oromí, M., 347
Ot, Guiral, 296, 299, 308
Owens, J., 168

Paul, St., 60, 114
Peckham, J., 30, 31
Peirce, C. S., 346, 349, 361, 362
Pelagius, 312
Pelster, F., 295, 297, 369, 371
Pelzer, A., 369, 371
Peter Lombard, 11, 19, 24, 47, 97, 135, 304
Peter of Aquila, 250, 252, 256
Peter of Godino, 24
Peter of Tarentaise, 296
Petit, J., 302
Petrus de Cruce, 301

Philip of Bagnocavallo, 298
Philip of Bridlington, 24
Philip the Fair, 4, 11, 12
Pius II, Pope, 293, 294
Plato, 122, 128, 253, 254, 361
Pluzanski, E., 186
Porphyry, 235, 254
Prierias, S., 324, 325

Quidort, J., 32

Richard of Middleton, 24, 118, 296
Rigaud, E. de, 196
Rückert, H., 325
Rupella, John of, 299
Russell, B., 59

Sartre, J. P., 365
Seiller, 347
Seripando, 339
Shircel, C., 347
Siger de Brabant, 29
Sixtus IV, Pope, 294
Socrates, 351
Soto, D., 330, 331, 341
Stegmüller, F., 295
Stella, P., 347
Stetzing, K., 309
Suarez, F., 46, 51, 118, 262-89
Syrianus, 254

Teilhard de Chardin, P., 363
Tempier, S., 30, 31, 192, 193, 309

Tertullian, 332
Textor, J., 296, 303
Thomas Aquinas, St., 15, 24, 31, 33-35, 38, 42, 45, 50, 51, 70-74, 83, 85, 90, 92, 96, 97, 100-02, 112-14, 118-20, 133, 168, 169, 172, 175, 179, 195, 198-201, 207, 230, 231, 300, 306, 313, 314, 334, 370-75
Trechsel, J., 294
Trithemius, 304, 310
Trivet, N., 12

Vanni Rovighi, S., 200
Van Steenberghen, F., 371
Varesio, C. de, 378
Vaurouillon, William of, 291-309 *passim*
Vega, A. de, 317, 318, 327-42, 344
Veuthey, L., 30, 37, 39
Vignaux, P., 347
Vitalis du Four, 31

Wadding, L., 1, 2, 19, 302, 304, 310, 372-77
Walter of Bruges, 31
Whittaker, E., 346
William de la Mare, 31, 174
William of Alnwick, 105-07, 376
William of Nottingham, 376
William of Ware, 11
Wittgenstein, L., 59
Wolter, A., 168, 287, 347
Woodham, A., 314

John Duns Scotus, 1265-1965, is the third and perhaps the most important volume in *Studies in Philosophy and the History of Philosophy*, a series that is gaining wide recognition for the seriousness of its purposes and the genuine scholarship of its contributions. The Scotus volume has been made possible through the generous and effective collaboration of leading Scotists in Europe, the United States, and Canada. Within its nearly 400 pages it condenses the results of long and painstaking research in the field of Scotistic studies carried out by men of varying academic backgrounds and different religious affiliations. Because of the high quality of its contents the present volume must be rated among the most valuable and authoritative sources of information on Scotus' thought and personality. It is a work that no student of medieval philosophy can afford to neglect.

Reviews of the previous volumes in this outstanding series:

"The very variety of the studies contained in this volume will afford interest to the many readers to whom it is offered; each reader will find among the various studies in philosophy and the history of philosophy at least one which will be of special interest to him."

A. Kořinek in *Gregorianum*

"This symposium, *Studies in Philosophy and the History of Philosophy*, ... is a scholarly work of the first magnitude. ... so rich in food for thought that it is (to adapt the words of Francis Bacon) not 'to be tasted' or 'to be read in part,' nor is it 'to be swallowed' or 'to be read cursorily'; rather it is among those few books that are 'to be chewed and digested,' that is, 'to be read wholly and with diligence and attention.'"

Patrick J. Aspell in *American Ecclesiastical Review*

"One may get an idea of the range and character of this book (Vol. 1) by merely glancing at the titles of the essays. ... Those interested in the history of philosophy will find this work extremely valuable and will rejoice at the thought that other volumes of similar quality are to follow."

Henri Saint-Denis in *Revue de l'Universite d'Ottawa*

"The second volume of the *Studies in Philosophy and the History of Philosophy*, edited by the Dean of the School of Philosophy at The Catholic University of America, contains nine extensive essays which are as original as they are provocative."

Paul K. K. Tong in *American Ecclesiastical Review*

"Cette nouvelle collection, non périodique, apporte assurément une des meilleures contributions venues d'Amérique en doctrine et histoire de la Philosophie."

A. Solignac in *Archives de philosophie*

About the two previous volumes in the series *Studies in Philosophy and the History of Philosophy:*

Volume 1—Contents: The Ideological Argument for God's Existence, by Bernardine M. Bonansea, O.F.M.; Gabriel Marcel and Proof for the Existence of God, by Sister M. Aloysius Schaldenbrand, S.S.J.; Berkeley and the Proofs for the Existence of God, by Sister Angelita Myerscough, Ad.PP.S.; A Philosophical Critique of Certain Psychiatric Theories of the Origin of Psychosis, by Marius G. Schneider, O.F.M.; Ulrich of Strasbourg and the Aristotelian Causes, by Mother Carol Putnam, R.S.C.J.; De Magistro: The Concept of Teaching According to St. Thomas Aquinas, by Robert S. Sokolowski; Philosophy and Theology in a Discourse by St. Thomas Aquinas on the Incarnation and Christ the King, by John K. Ryan; The Authenticity of a Homily Attributed to St. Thomas Aquinas, by John K. Ryan. $5.00

Volume 2—Contents: A Protreptic: What is Philosophy?, by Thomas Prufer; The Concept of Personality in Greek and Christian Thought, by C. J. de Vogel; Philosophy, Education, and the Controversy on St. Augustine's Conversion, by Eugene Kevane; St. Thomas Aquinas and the Doctrine of Essence, by Gilbert B. Arbuckle; The Question of the Validity of the Tertia Via, by Thomas G. Pater; The Metaphysical Crisis in Physical Theory, by Leo A. Foley, S.M.; Private Property and Natural Law, by Felix Alluntis, O.F.M.; The Political Thought of Tommaso Campanella, by Bernardine M. Bonansea, O.F.M.; Two Instances of the Tripartite Method in Machiavelli, by John K. Ryan. $5.95

www.ingramcontent.com/pod-product-compliance
Lightning Source LLC
Chambersburg PA
CBHW031403290426
44110CB00011B/242